MGMT 455

Purdue University

Third Edition

David P. Twomey | Marianne M. Jennings

Australia • Brazil • Japan • Korea • Mexico • Singapore • Spain • United Kingdom • United States

MGMT 455, Purdue University, Third Edition

Anderson's Business Law and the Legal Environment, Comprehensive Volume, 23rd Edition
David P. Twomey | Marianne M. Jennings

ISBN: 978-1-337-05425-6

Printed in Mexico

Cengage Learning
20 Channel Center Street
Boston, MA 02210
USA

Cengage Learning is a leading provider of customized learning solutions with office locations around the globe, including Singapore, the United Kingdom, Australia, Mexico, Brazil, and Japan. Locate your local office at: **www.international.cengage.com/region.**

Cengage Learning products are represented in Canada by Nelson Education, Ltd.

For your lifelong learning solutions, visit **www.cengage.com/custom.**

Visit our corporate website at **www.cengage.com.**

Brief Contents

Contents

PART 1

The Legal and Social Environment of Business

PART 6

Agency and Employment

PART 7

Business Organizations

PART 8

Real Property and Estates

PART 1

The Legal and Social Environment of Business

CHAPTER 1

The Nature and Sources of Law

Learning Outcomes <<<

After studying this chapter, you should be able to

LO.1 Discuss the nature of law and legal rights

LO.2 List the sources of law

LO.3 Describe the classifications of law

1-1 Nature of Law and Legal Rights

Why have law? If you have ever been stuck in a traffic jam or jostled in a crowd leaving a stadium, you have observed the need for order to keep those involved moving in an efficient and safe manner. The issues with bloggers' use of others' materials and continuing downloading of music and films without compensation to copyright holders illustrate the need for rules and order in this era of new technology. When our interactions are not orderly, whether at our concerts or through our e-mail, all of us and our rights are affected. The order or pattern of rules that society uses to govern the conduct of individuals and their relationships is called **law.** Law keeps society running smoothly and efficiently.

law–the order or pattern of rules that society establishes to govern the conduct of individuals and the relationships among them.

Law consists of the body of principles that govern conduct and that can be enforced in courts or by administrative agencies. The law could also be described as a collection or bundle of rights.

1-1a Legal Rights

right–legal capacity to require another person to perform or refrain from an action.

duty–an obligation of law imposed on a person to perform or refrain from performing a certain act.

A **right** is a legal capacity to require another person to perform or refrain from performing an act. Our rights flow from the U.S. Constitution, state constitutions, federal and state statutes, and ordinances at the local levels, including cities, counties, and boroughs. Within these sources of rights are also duties. A **duty** is an obligation of law imposed on a person to perform or refrain from performing a certain act.

Duties and rights coexist. No right exists in one person without a corresponding duty resting on some other person or persons. For example, if the terms of a lease provide that the premises will remain in a condition of good repair so that the tenant can live there comfortably, the landlord has a corresponding duty to provide a dwelling that has hot and cold running water.

1-1b Individual Rights

The U.S. Constitution gives individuals certain rights. Those rights include the right to freedom of speech, the right to due process or the right to have a hearing before any freedom is taken away, and the right to vote. There are also duties that accompany individual rights, such as the duty to speak in a way that does not cause harm to others. For example, individuals are free to express their opinions about the government or its officials, but they would not be permitted to yell "Fire!" in a crowded theater and cause unnecessary harm to others. The rights given in the U.S. Constitution are rights that cannot be taken away or violated by any statutes, ordinances, or court decisions. These rights provide a framework for the structure of government and other laws.

1-1c The Right of Privacy

right of privacy–the right to be free from unreasonable intrusion by others.

One very important individual legal right is the right of privacy, which has two components. The first is the right to be secure against unreasonable searches and seizures by the government. The Fourth Amendment of the U.S. Constitution guarantees this portion of the **right of privacy.** A police officer, for example, may not search your home unless the officer has a reasonable suspicion (which is generally established through a warrant) that your home contains evidence of a crime, such as illegal drugs. If your home or business is searched unlawfully, any items obtained during that unlawful search could be excluded as evidence in a criminal trial because of the Fourth Amendment's exclusionary rule. **For Example,** in *Riley v. California*, 134 S. Ct. 2473 (2014), David Riley was stopped by a police officer for driving with expired registration tags. The officer discovered that Mr. Riley's license had been suspended, so his car was impounded and searched. Officers also found Mr. Riley's smart phone and, in going through the phone, found pictures and information related to a gang shooting, and Mr. Riley was then charged with that earlier shooting. However, the court held that evidence from the smart phone could not be used at trial because there was no warrant and Mr. Riley had a right of privacy in the data on that phone.[1]

A second aspect of the right of privacy protects individuals against intrusions by others. Your private life is not subject to public scrutiny when you are a private citizen. This right is provided in many state constitutions and exists through interpretation at the federal level through the landmark case of *Roe v. Wade*,[2] in which the U.S. Supreme Court established a right of privacy that gives women the right to choose whether to have an abortion.

These two components of the right to privacy have many interpretations. These interpretations are often found in statutes that afford privacy rights with respect to certain types of conduct. **For Example,** a federal statute provides a right of privacy to bank customers that prevents their banks from giving out information about their accounts except to law enforcement agencies conducting investigations. Some laws protect the rights of students. **For Example,** the Family Educational Rights and Privacy Act of 1974 (FERPA, also known as the *Buckley Amendment*) prevents colleges and universities from disclosing students' grades to third parties without the students' permission. From your credit information to your Social Security number, you have great privacy protections.

1-1d Privacy and Technology

Technology creates new situations that may require the application of new rules of law. Technology has changed the way we interact with each other, and new rules of law have developed to protect our rights. Today, business is conducted by computers, wire transfers of funds, e-mail, electronic data interchange (EDI) order placements, and the Internet. We still expect that our communication is private. However, technology also affords others the ability to eavesdrop on conversations and intercept electronic messages. The law has stepped in to reestablish that the right of privacy still exists even in these technologically nonprivate circumstances. Some laws now make it a crime and a breach of privacy to engage in such interceptions of communications.[3]

CASE SUMMARY

If You Shout It Out the Window or on Facebook, Is It Private?

FACTS: Gina L. Fawcett (plaintiff) and her then-minor son, John, sued Sea High School and the parents of Nicholas Altieri (defendants) to recover damages for John's eye injury that he sustained in an altercation with Nicholas during a tennis match with St. Joseph High School. The defendants made a discovery request for access to John's social media accounts, including Facebook, MySpace, Friendster, Flickr, and others. Ms. Fawcett moved for a protective order to prevent discovery of the information on these sites because John's sites were not publicly available.

DECISION: The court held that a variety of factors must be considered before granting broad access to social media accounts, including privacy settings by the holder of the

[1] Police officers do not need a warrant in order to use the content of an incoming text message on a suspect's phone that is received while they are questioning the suspect because the sender does not have a right of privacy in the suspect's smart phone's content. *State v. Varle*, 337 P.3d 904 (Or. App. 2014).
[2] 410 U.S. 113 (1973).
[3] *Luangkhot v. State*, 722 S.E.2d 193 (Ga. App. 2012).

If You Shout It Out the Window or on Facebook, Is It Private? continued

account, relevancy of the information to the litigation, and protections afforded by the various social media sites. The court's decision provides the guidelines for determining whether the litigants in cases will be able to have discovery access to each other's social media sites. The parties will have to do depositions and then renew the request once more factual information is available for the analysis of the request for access. [***Fawcett v. Altieri*, 960 N.Y.S.2d 592 (2013)**]

ETHICS & THE LAW

Maybe a Little Too "LinkedIn"

LinkedIn, the popular professional connection service, has a tool called "Reference Search." A premium service, employers and recruiters are using the tool to cull their connections to see who knows job applicants in order to get background on them. Employers are checking with references that the applicants did not list, references that may not have all good things to say about them. The service provides employers with the list of LinkedIn contacts that they have who worked at the same companies as the applicants and at the same time.*

Applicants are worried that employers are basing employment decisions on the information that they receive, information that may not be true or verified or verifiable. The applicants do not always know that the employer is checking with other sources or which ones and do not have the opportunity to respond to negative information.

Discuss the ethical issues in the use of this LinkedIn service by employers.

*Natasha Singer, "Funny, They Don't Look Like My References," *New York Times Magazine*, November 10, 2014, p. BU4.

E-COMMERCE & CYBERLAW

A University's Access to Your Computer

Scott Kennedy, a computer system administrator for Qualcomm Corporation in San Diego, California, discovered that somebody had obtained unauthorized access (or "hacked into," in popular parlance) the company's computer network. Kennedy contacted the Federal Bureau of Investigation (FBI). Working together, Kennedy and the FBI were able to trace the intrusion to a computer on the University of Wisconsin at Madison network. They contacted Jeffrey Savoy, the University of Wisconsin computer network investigator, who found evidence that someone using a computer on the university network was in fact hacking into the Qualcomm system and that the user had gained unauthorized access to the university's system as well. Savoy traced the source of intrusion to a computer located in university housing, the room of Jerome Heckenkamp, a computer science graduate student at the university. Savoy knew that Heckenkamp had been terminated from his job at the university computer help desk two years earlier for similar unauthorized activity.

While Heckenkamp was online and logged into the university's system, Savoy, along with detectives, went to Heckenkamp's room. The door was ajar, and nobody was in the room. Savoy entered the room and disconnected the network cord that attached the computer to the network. In order to be sure that the computer he had disconnected from the network was the computer that had gained unauthorized access to the university server, Savoy wanted to run some commands on the computer. Detectives located Heckenkamp, explained the situation, and asked for Heckenkamp's password, which Heckenkamp voluntarily provided. Savoy then ran tests on the computer and copied the hard drive without a warrant. When Heckenkamp was charged with several federal computer crimes, he challenged the university's access to his account and Savoy's steps that night, including the copy of the hard drive, as a breach of his privacy.

Was Heckenkamp correct? Was his privacy breached?

[***U.S. v. Heckenkamp*, 482 F.3d 1142 (9th Cir. 2007)**]

1-2 Sources of Law

Several layers of law are enacted at different levels of government to provide the framework for business and personal rights and duties. At the base of this framework of laws is constitutional law.

1-2a Constitutional Law

constitution–a body of principles that establishes the structure of a government and the relationship of the government to the people who are governed.

Constitutional law is the branch of law that is based on the constitution for a particular level of government. A **constitution** is a body of principles that establishes the structure of a government and the relationship of that government to the people who are governed. A constitution is generally a combination of the written document and the practices and customs that develop with the passage of time and the emergence of new problems. In each state, two constitutions are in force: the state constitution and the federal Constitution.

1-2b Statutory Law

statutory law–legislative acts declaring, commanding, or prohibiting something.

Statutory law includes legislative acts. Both Congress and the state legislatures enact statutory law. Examples of congressional legislative enactments include the Securities Act of 1933 (Chapter 45), the Sherman Antitrust Act (Chapter 5), the bankruptcy laws (Chapter 34), and consumer credit protection provisions (Chapter 32). At the state level, statutes govern the creation of corporations, probate of wills, and the transfer of title to property. In addition to the state legislatures and the U.S. Congress, all cities, counties, and other governmental subdivisions have some power to adopt ordinances within their sphere of operation. Examples of the types of laws found at this level of government include traffic laws, zoning laws, and pet and bicycle licensing laws.

1-2c Administrative Law

administrative regulations–rules made by state and federal administrative agencies.

Administrative regulations are rules promulgated by state and federal administrative agencies, such as the Securities and Exchange Commission (SEC) and the Environmental Protection Agency (EPA). For example, the restrictions on carbon emissions by businesses have all been promulgated by the EPA. These regulations generally have the force of statutes.

1-2d Private Law

private law–the rules and regulations parties agree to as part of their contractual relationships.

Even individuals and businesses create their own laws, or **private law.** Private law consists of the rules and regulations parties agree to as part of their contractual relationships. **For Example,** landlords develop rules for tenants on everything from parking to laundry room use. Employers develop rules for employees on everything from proper computer use to posting pictures and information on bulletin boards located within the company walls. Homeowner associations have rules on everything from your landscaping to the color of your house paint.

1-2e Case Law, Statutory Interpretation, and Precedent

case law–law that includes principles that are expressed for the first time in court decisions.

Law also includes principles that are expressed for the first time in court decisions. This form of law is called **case law.** Case law plays three very important roles. The first is one of clarifying the meaning of statutes, or providing statutory interpretation. **For Example,** in *King v. Burwell*, the U.S. Supreme Court interpreted the phrase, "an Exchange established by the State" in the Affordable Care Act to determine whether tax credits were available to insurance exchanges operated by the federal government and not the states. The court held that "State," meant either the federal government or any of the states so that all exchanges qualified for the tax credits.[4] The second role that courts play is in creating precedent. When a court decides a new question or problem, its decision becomes a **precedent,** which stands as the law in future cases that involve that particular problem.

precedent–a decision of a court that stands as the law for a particular problem in the future.

Using precedent and following decisions is also known as the doctrine of ***stare decisis.*** However, the rule of *stare decisis* is not cast in stone. Judges have some flexibility. When a court finds an earlier decision to be incorrect, it overrules that decision. For example, in *National Federation of Independent Business v. Sebelius,* 132 S.Ct. 2566 (2012) the U.S. Supreme Court held that the Affordable Care Act (Obama Care) was constitutional. However, in 2014, the Court held, based on new issues raised, that a portion of the act violated the First Amendment because it mandated health care coverage of certain types of birth controls that were in violation of the religious beliefs of the owners of a corporation. *Burwell v. Hobby Lobby Stores, Inc.*, 134 S. Ct. 2751 (2014).

stare decisis–"let the decision stand"; the principle that the decision of a court should serve as a guide or precedent and control the decision of a similar case in the future.

The third role courts play is in developing a body of law that is not statutory but addresses long-standing issues. Court decisions do not always deal with new problems or make new rules. In many cases, courts apply rules as they have been for many years, even centuries. These time-honored rules of the community are called the **common law.** **For Example,** most of law that we still follow today in determining real property rights developed in England, beginning in 1066. Statutes sometimes repeal or redeclare the common law rules. Many statutes depend on the common law for definitions of the terms in the statutes.

common law–the body of unwritten principles originally based upon the usages and customs of the community that were recognized and enforced by the courts.

1-2f Other Forms of Law: Treaties and Executive Orders

Law also includes treaties made by the United States and proclamations and executive orders of the president of the United States or of other public officials. President Obama's executive order altering immigration policy is the subject of a constitutional challenge to the scope of executive orders.

1-2g Uniform State Laws

To facilitate the national nature of business and transactions, the National Conference of Commissioners on Uniform State Laws (NCCUSL), composed of representatives from every state, has drafted statutes on various subjects for adoption by the states. The best example of such laws is the Uniform Commercial Code (UCC).[5] (See Chapters 22–30, Chapter 33.) The UCC regulates the sale and lease of goods; commercial paper, such as checks; fund transfers; secured transactions in personal property; banking; and letters of credit. Having the same principles of law on contracts for the sale of goods and other commercial transactions in most of the 50 states makes doing business easier and less expensive. Other examples of uniform laws across the states include the Model Business Corporation Act (Chapter 43), the Uniform Partnership Act (Chapter 41), and the Uniform Residential Landlord Tenant Act (Chapter 50). The Uniform Computer Information Transactions Act (UCITA) as well as the Uniform Electronic Transactions Act

[4] *King v. Burwell,* 135 S.Ct. 2480 (2015).

[5] The UCC has been adopted in every state, except that Louisiana has not adopted Article 2, Sales. Guam, the Virgin Islands, and the District of Columbia have also adopted the UCC. The United Nations Convention on Contracts for the International Sale of Goods (CISG) has been adopted as the means for achieving uniformity in sale-of-goods contracts on an international level. Provisions of CISG were strongly influenced by Article 2 of the UCC.

(UETA) are two uniform laws that have taken contract law from the traditional paper era to the paperless computer age.

1-3 Classifications of Law

1-3a Substantive Law vs. Procedural Law

substantive law–the law that defines rights and liabilities.

procedural law–the law that must be followed in enforcing rights and liabilities.

Substantive law creates, defines, and regulates rights and liabilities. The law that determines when a contract is formed is substantive law. **Procedural law** specifies the steps that must be followed in enforcing those rights and liabilities. For example, once that contract is formed, you have rights to enforce that contract, and the steps you take through the court system to recover your damages for a breach of contract are procedural laws. The laws that prohibit computer theft are substantive laws. The prosecution of someone for computer theft follows procedural law.

1-3b Criminal Law vs. Civil Law

criminal laws–the laws that define wrongs against society.

civil laws–the laws that define the rights of one person against another.

Criminal laws define wrongs against society. **Civil laws** define the rights of one person against another. Criminal law violations carry fines and imprisonment as penalties. Civil laws carry damage remedies for the wronged individual.

For Example, if you run a red light, you have committed a crime and you will be punished with a fine and points on your license. If you run a red light and strike a pedestrian, you will also have committed a civil wrong of injury to another through your

SPORTS & ENTERTAINMENT LAW

When Players Break the Law and Owners Are Offensive

During 2014, professional sports had three events that resulted in a public engaged in the business decisions of the teams and their leagues. Baltimore Ravens player Ray Rice was accused of striking his fiancé (who would shortly become his wife) in an elevator. Local authorities declined to prosecute because his wife refused to cooperate with the investigation or the prosecution. Nonetheless, Roger Goodell, the NFL commissioner, suspended Mr. Rice from play indefinitely. Public opinion swung both ways, and Mr. Rice eventually won his appeal on the suspension and was reinstated. However, he lost his endorsement contracts with various companies, including Nike.

In the NBA, Donald Sterling was forced by the league to sell the LA Clippers franchise after an audio tape emerged of him making racist comments to his girlfriend. Steve Ballmer, the former CEO of Microsoft, bought the team for $2 billion. The team owners in the NBA made the decision by a vote to require Sterling to sell the team, a provision permitted under the bylaws of the corporation.

Back in the NFL, Adrian Peterson of the Minnesota Vikings was arrested for child abuse. Mr. Peterson entered a no-contest plea to the charges, which were based on his using a branch to hit his four-year-old son. The court's determination of guilt was postponed for two years as Mr. Peterson serves 80 hours of community service and pays a $4,000 fine. Under its bylaws, the NFL imposed a temporary suspension, and Mr. Peterson and the NFL are locked in a court and arbitration dispute over the suspension.

The three cases have these topics in common:

Private conduct affected business ownership and employment.

There were private bylaws involved that permitted league action against team owners and players.

There were also civil and criminal laws involved that required prosecution in two of the cases.

The law at various levels, including the authority of the leagues to do what they did, was at the center of these very public controversies.

carelessness. Civil laws provide that in addition to taking care of your wrong to society, you must take care of your wrong to the pedestrian and pay damages for the cost of her injuries (see Chapter 8 for more information about recovery of damages for accidents such as this).

1-3c Law vs. Equity

equity–the body of principles that originally developed because of the inadequacy of the rules then applied by the common law courts of England.

Equity is a body of law that provides justice when the law does not offer an adequate remedy or the application of the law would be terribly unfair. Equity courts developed in England as a means of getting to the heart of a dispute and seeing that justice was done. **For Example,** Christian Louboutin shoes have a distinctive red bottom that is their trademark. Yves Saint Laurent began producing its shoes with a red bottom. Common and statutory law provide for Louboutin to collect damages—the amount the company lost in sales through the copycat efforts of Yves Saint Laurent. However, if the Yves Saint Laurent shoes continue in production, Louboutin is never adequately compensated. Equity provides for an injunction, a court order to stop Yves Saint Laurent from making the red-soled shoes.[6]

At one time, the United States had separate law courts and equity courts, but today these courts have been combined so that one court applies principles of both law and equity. A party may ask for both legal and equitable remedies in a single court.[7] **For Example,** suppose a homeowner contracts to sell his home to a buyer. If the homeowner then refuses to go through with the contract, the buyer has the legal remedy of recovering damages. The rules of equity go further and could require the owner to convey title to the house, an equitable remedy known as *specific performance*. Equitable remedies may also be available in certain contract breaches (see Chapters 2, 11, and 19).

Make the Connection

Summary

Law provides rights and imposes duties. One such right is the right of privacy, which affords protection against unreasonable searches of our property and intrusion into or disclosure of our private affairs.

Law consists of the pattern of rules established by society to govern conduct and relationships. These rules can be expressed as constitutional provisions, statutes, administrative regulations, and case decisions. Law can be classified as substantive or procedural, and it can be described in terms of civil or criminal law. Law provides remedies in equity in addition to damages.

The sources of law include constitutions, federal and state statutes, administrative regulations, ordinances, and uniform laws generally codified by the states in their statutes. The courts are also a source of law through their adherence to case precedent under the doctrine of *stare decisis* and through their development of time-honored principles called the common law.

[6] *Christian Louboutin S.A. v. Yves Saint Laurent America, Inc.*, 778 F. Supp. 2d 445 (S.D.N.Y. 2011). The court eventually held that other companies could not copy the distinctive red sole. They could have colored soles but not the Louboutin trademark red sole.

[7] For example, when Jennifer Lopez and Marc Anthony were married, they filed suit against the manufacturer of a British company that produces baby carriages for using their images on its Web site and in ads without permission; they asked for $5 million in damages as well as an injunction to stop use of their photos and likenesses in the company's ads. *Lopez v. Silver Cross*, 2009 WL 481386 (C.D. Cal.). The case was settled prior to the dissolution of the Lopez and Anthony marriage. Silver Cross no longer uses the images of Lopez and Anthony in its ads.

Learning Outcomes

After studying this chapter, you should be able to clearly explain:

1-1 Nature of Law and Legal Rights

LO.1 Discuss the nature of law and legal rights

See Ethics & the Law for a discussion on the use of LinkedIn for finding more honest references about potential employees, page 6.

See E-Commerce & Cyberlaw for a discussion of a university student's privacy rights in using the university's server, page 6.

1-2 Sources of Law

LO.2 List the sources of law

See the *For Example* discussion of landlords developing rules for tenants on everything from parking to laundry room use, page 7.

See the list and explanation of uniform laws, page 8.

See the Sports & Entertainment Law discussion of leagues taking action against players for their private conduct, page 9.

1-3 Classifications of Law

LO.3 Describe the classifications of law

See the discussion of law, equity, procedural, substantive, criminal, and civil, pages 9–10.

See the Christian Louboutin example on its red-bottomed shoe being copied and footnote 8 with the discussion of the Jennifer Lopez/Marc Anthony suit.

Explain uniform state laws, page 10.

Key Terms

administrative regulations
case law
civil law
common law
constitution
criminal law
duty
equity
law
precedent
private law
procedural law
right
right of privacy
stare decisis
statutory law
substantive law

Questions and Case Problems

1. The Family Educational Rights and Privacy Act (FERPA) protects students' rights to keep their academic records private. What duties are imposed and upon whom because of this protection of rights? Discuss the relationship between rights and duties.
2. List the sources of law.
3. What is the difference between common law and statutory law?
4. Classify the following laws as substantive or procedural:
   a. A law that requires public schools to hold a hearing before a student is expelled.
   b. A law that establishes a maximum interest rate for credit transactions of 24 percent.
   c. A law that provides employee leave for the birth or adoption of a child for up to 12 weeks.
   d. A law that requires the county assessor to send four notices of taxes due and owing before a lien can be filed (attached) to the property.
5. What do uniform laws accomplish? Why do states adopt them? Give an example of a uniform law.
6. Cindy Nathan is a student at West University. While she was at her 9:00 A.M. anthropology class, campus security entered her dorm room and searched all areas, including her closet and drawers. When Cindy returned to her room and discovered what had happened, she complained to the dorm's senior resident. The senior resident said that this was the university's property and that Cindy had no right of privacy. Do you agree with the senior resident's statement? Is there a right of privacy in a dorm room?
7. Professor Lucas Phelps sent the following e-mail to Professor Marlin Jones: "I recently read the opinion piece you wrote for the *Sacramento Bee* on affirmative action. Your opinion is incorrect, your reasoning and analysis are poor, and I am embarrassed that you are a member of the faculty here at Cal State Yolinda." Professor Jones forwarded the note from Professor Phelps to the provost of the university and asked that

Professor Phelps be disciplined for using the university e-mail system for harassment purposes. Professor Phelps objected when the provost contacted him: "He had no right to forward that e-mail to you. That was private correspondence. And you have no right of access to my e-mail. I have privacy rights." Do you agree with Professor Phelps? Was there a breach of privacy?

8. Under what circumstances would a court disregard precedent?
9. What is the difference between a statute and an administrative regulation?
10. The Eminem ad for Chrysler that ran during the Super Bowl in February 2011 was rated as one of the best ads for the game. In May 2011, Audi ran an ad at a German auto show that had the "feel" of the Eminem Chrysler "Lose Yourself" ad. Subsequently, the German auto show ad made its way onto the Internet.

    The German ad caught the attention of Eminem and 8 Mile, Eminem's publishing company. They notified Audi that the ad constituted an unauthorized use of their intellectual property. Explain what rights Eminem and 8 Mile have and how the courts can help.
11. Give examples of areas covered by federal laws. Give examples of areas covered by city ordinances. What are the limitations on these two sources of laws? What could the laws at these two levels not do?
12. What is the principle of *stare decisis*?
13. Explain how Twitter, Facebook, and LinkedIn have resulted in the development of new laws and precedent.
14. During the 2001 baseball season, San Francisco Giants player Barry Bonds hit 73 home runs, a new record that broke the one set by Mark McGwire in 2000 (72 home runs). When Mr. Bonds hit his record-breaking home run, the ball went into the so-called cheap seats. Alex Popov was sitting in those seats and had brought along his baseball glove for purposes of catching any hits that might come into the stands.

    Everyone sitting in the area agreed that Mr. Popov's glove touched Bonds's home-run ball. Videotape also shows Mr. Popov's glove on the ball. However, the ball dropped and, following a melee among the cheap-seat fans, Patrick Hayashi ended up with Bonds's home-run ball.

    Mr. Popov filed suit for the ball, claiming it as his property. Such baseballs can be very valuable. The baseball from Mr. McGwire's record-breaking home run in 2000 sold for $3 million. List those areas of law that will apply as the case is tried and the owner of the baseball is determined.
15. Janice Dempsey has just started her own tax preparation firm. She has leased office space in a building, and she is incorporating her business as a Subchapter S corporation under the Internal Revenue Code. She has purchased desks, chairs, computers, and copiers from Staples through a line of credit they have established for her. Janice is a CPA in the state of Arizona and her license fees and continuing education hours are due within 90 days. Janice will begin with only a clerical person as an employee to serve as receptionist and bookkeeper. List all of the areas of the law that affect Janice in her new business.

CHAPTER 2

The Court System and Dispute Resolution

Learning Outcomes <<<

After studying this chapter, you should be able to

LO.1 Explain the federal and state court systems

LO.2 Describe court procedures

LO.3 List the forms of alternative dispute resolution and distinguish among them

2-1 The Court System

court–a tribunal established by government to hear and decide matters properly brought to it.

jurisdiction–the power of a court to hear and determine a given class of cases; the power to act over a particular defendant.

subject matter jurisdiction–judicial authority to hear a particular type of case.

original jurisdiction–the authority to hear a controversy when it is first brought to court.

general jurisdiction–the power to hear and decide most controversies involving legal rights and duties.

limited (special) jurisdiction–the authority to hear only particular kinds of cases.

appellate jurisdiction–the power of a court to hear and decide a given class of cases on appeal from another court or administrative agency.

appeal–taking a case to a reviewing court to determine whether the judgment of the lower court or administrative agency was correct. (Parties—appellant, appellee)

Despite carefully negotiated and well-written contracts and high safety standards in the workplace or in product design and production, businesses can end up in a lawsuit. **For Example,** you could hire the brightest and most expensive lawyer in town to prepare a contract with another party and believe the final agreement is "bulletproof." However, even a bulletproof contract does not guarantee performance by the other party, and you may have to file a suit to collect your damages.

Business disputes can be resolved in court or through alternative dispute resolution. This chapter covers the structure of the court system and the litigation process as well as the forms of alternative dispute resolution.

A **court** is a tribunal established by government to hear evidence, decide cases brought before it, and provide remedies when a wrong has been committed. As discussed in Chapter 1, sometimes courts prevent wrongs by issuing the equitable remedy of an injunction. **For Example,** in March 2012, a federal court issued an injunction against Cardinal Health because it was shipping too much oxycodone to its pharmacies in Florida, and the FDA had discovered that the prescriptions were fraudulent. The FDA needed to stop the flow of the drug while it pulled the prescriptions.[1]

2-1a The Types of Courts

Each type of court has the authority to decide certain types or classes of cases. The authority of courts to hear cases is called **jurisdiction.** One form of jurisdiction, **subject matter jurisdiction,** covers the type of cases the court has the authority to hear. Courts that have the authority to hear the original proceedings in a case (the trial court) are called courts of **original jurisdiction. For Example,** in a court of original jurisdiction witnesses testify, documents are admitted into evidence, and the jury, in the case of a jury trial, hears all the evidence and then makes a decision.

Other types of subject matter jurisdiction give courts the authority over particular legal topic areas. A court with **general jurisdiction** has broad authority to hear general civil and criminal cases. When a general jurisdiction trial court hears criminal cases, it serves as the trial court for those charged with crimes. General trial courts also have the authority to hear civil disputes, such as breach of contract cases and personal injury lawsuits.

A court with **limited or special jurisdiction** has the authority to hear only particular kinds of cases. **For Example,** many states have courts that can hear only disputes in which the damages are $10,000 or less. Other examples of limited or special jurisdiction courts are juvenile courts, probate courts, and domestic relations courts. States vary in the names they give these courts, but these courts of special or limited jurisdiction have very narrow authority for the types of cases they hear. In the federal court system, limited or special jurisdiction courts include bankruptcy courts and the U.S. Tax Court.

A court with **appellate jurisdiction** reviews the work of a lower court. **For Example,** a trial court may issue a judgment that a defendant in a breach of contract suit should pay $500,000 in damages. That defendant could appeal the decision to an appellate court and seek review of the decision itself or even the amount of the damages.[2] An **appeal** is a

[1] *Holiday CVS, LLC. v. Holder,* 839 F. Supp. 2d 145 (D.D.C. 2012).

[2] A case that is sent back for a redetermination of damages is remanded for what is known as *remitur.* For example, an appeal of Oracle's $1.3 billion verdict against SAP was sent back for another determination of damages, with the judge indicating $272 million was in the right range. *Oracle USA, Inc. v. SAP AG,* 2012 WL 29095 (N.D. Cal.).

reversible error–an error or defect in court proceedings of so serious a nature that on appeal the appellate court will set aside the proceedings of the lower court.

review of the trial and decision of the lower court. An appellate court does not hear witnesses or take testimony. An appellate court, usually a panel of three judges, simply reviews the transcript and evidence from the lower court and determines whether there has been **reversible error.** A reversible error is a mistake in applying the law or a mistake in admitting evidence that affected the outcome of the case. An appellate court can **affirm** or **reverse** a lower court decision or **remand** that decision for another trial or additional hearings.

CASE SUMMARY

Horseback Riding Videos and Judging Hairy Chest Contests—Good Evidence?

FACTS: Mary Kay Stanford (Stanford) was driving a truck for V.F. in late evening of February 7, 2006, when she began to feel nauseous. She pulled into a truck scale house to rest for the evening. She parked the truck, and as she attempted to climb into the sleeper compartment, she tripped over a cooler. Stanford fell into the sleeper compartment and hit her head on the bed rail; the fall knocked her unconscious. Stanford's husband, William Stanford, who was riding with her, attempted to revive her. After she regained consciousness, William offered to take her to the emergency room. Stanford declined and decided to stay in the sleeper compartment and rest until morning. Stanford contacted V.F. dispatch and made the notifications to the company about her injury. The company arranged for the two to return home.

On February 8, 2006, Mary Kay went to Dr. Allie Prater whose notes reflect that Stanford's chief complaints were blackouts, syncope, and slurred speech. Stanford told Dr. Prater that her symptoms had begun one week prior to her visit. Dr. Prater's notes do not mention Stanford's fall in the truck or that she was knocked unconscious. Dr. Prater diagnosed Stanford with benign essential hypertension and ordered blood tests, an ultrasound, and a brain MRI.

Dr. Prater referred Mary Kay to Dr. Glenn Crosby, a neurosurgeon. Before seeing Dr. Crosby, Stanford went to Dr. Johnny Mitias, an orthopedic surgeon, on March 15, 2006. There was no mention of her fall in Dr. Mitias's notes. In fact, he noted that "[t]here was no injury that started this." Dr. Mitias diagnosed Stanford with right sciatica and ordered physical therapy.

Dr. Crosby recommended and performed spinal surgeries on August 8, 2006. After surgery, Stanford began complaining of pain in her left buttock and down her left leg. Dr. Crosby ordered a lumbar MRI, which revealed a large rupture of the lumbar spine at L4. On November 28, 2006, Dr. Crosby performed a diskectomy at the L4 level.

Dr. Crosby's notes indicate that Stanford "had a fall this past year" that may have aggravated her back. However, Dr. Crosby's notes do not mention that Stanford suffered a fall at work until her follow-up visit with Dr. Crosby on May 30, 2008. Dr. Crosby testified that prior to that visit, Stanford had not disclosed any history of an accident at work. However, he testified that the problems with her neck and back were probably related to her work injury.

A hearing was held before an administrative judge (AJ), who denied Stanford's claim for workers' compensation benefits. There was evidence submitted at the hearing that Stanford had taken a cruise despite her medical issues. In addition, there was video of her riding horses during the time of her treatment. There were also videos of Stanford at parties and bars. In one video she appeared to be having a great time as a judge in a "hairy chest contest." Stanford appealed the AJ's decision to the Commission, which affirmed the AJ's decision. Stanford appealed the Commission's decision to the Circuit Court of Union County, and the circuit court affirmed the Commission's decision denying benefits. Stanford then appealed.

DECISION: The court affirmed the denial of workers' compensation benefits because the evidence indicated clearly that Stanford did not tell the doctors about her work injury. The testimony about the cruise and the videos of horseback riding were damaging to Stanford's case, but they did not indicate bias particularly because the AJ had allowed evidence from Stanford's husband, friends, and relatives about her condition. Because evidence is damaging to one party does not mean that it should not be admitted. **[*Stanford v. V.F. Jeanswear, LP*, 84 So. 3d 825 (Miss. App. 2012)]**

affirm–action taken by an appellate court that approves the decision of the court below.

reverse–the term used when the appellate court sets aside the verdict or judgment of a lower court.

remand–term used when an appellate court sends a case back to trial court for additional hearings or a new trial.

federal district court–a general trial court of the federal system.

2-1b The Federal Court System

The federal court system consists of three levels of courts. Figure 2-1 illustrates federal court structure.

Federal District Courts

The **federal district courts** are the general trial courts of the federal system. They are courts of original jurisdiction that hear both civil and criminal matters. Criminal cases in federal district courts are those in which the defendant is charged with a violation of federal law (the U.S. Code). In addition to the criminal cases, the types of civil cases that can be brought in federal district courts include (1) civil suits in which the United States is a party, (2) cases between citizens of different states that involve damages of $75,000 or more, and (3) cases that arise under the U.S. Constitution or federal laws and treaties.

Federal district courts are organized within each of the states. There are 94 federal districts (each state has at least one federal district and there are 89 federal districts in the United States with the remaining courts found in Puerto Rico, Guam, etc.). Judges and courtrooms are assigned according to the caseload in that geographic area of the state.[3] Some states, such as New York and California, have several federal districts because

FIGURE 2-1 The Federal Court System

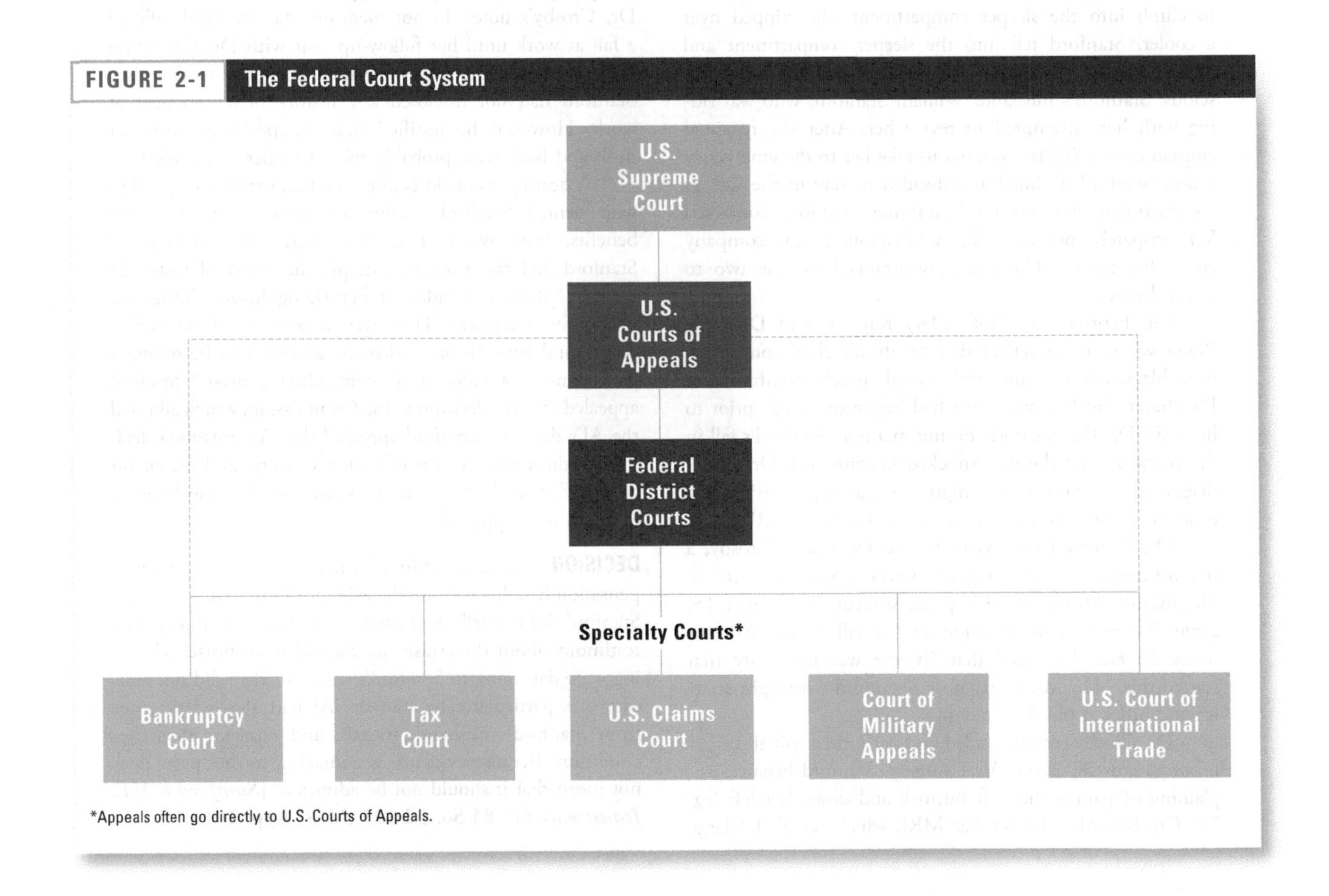

[3] For complete information about the courts and the number of judgeships, go to 28 U.S.C. §§81-144 and 28 U.S.C. §133.

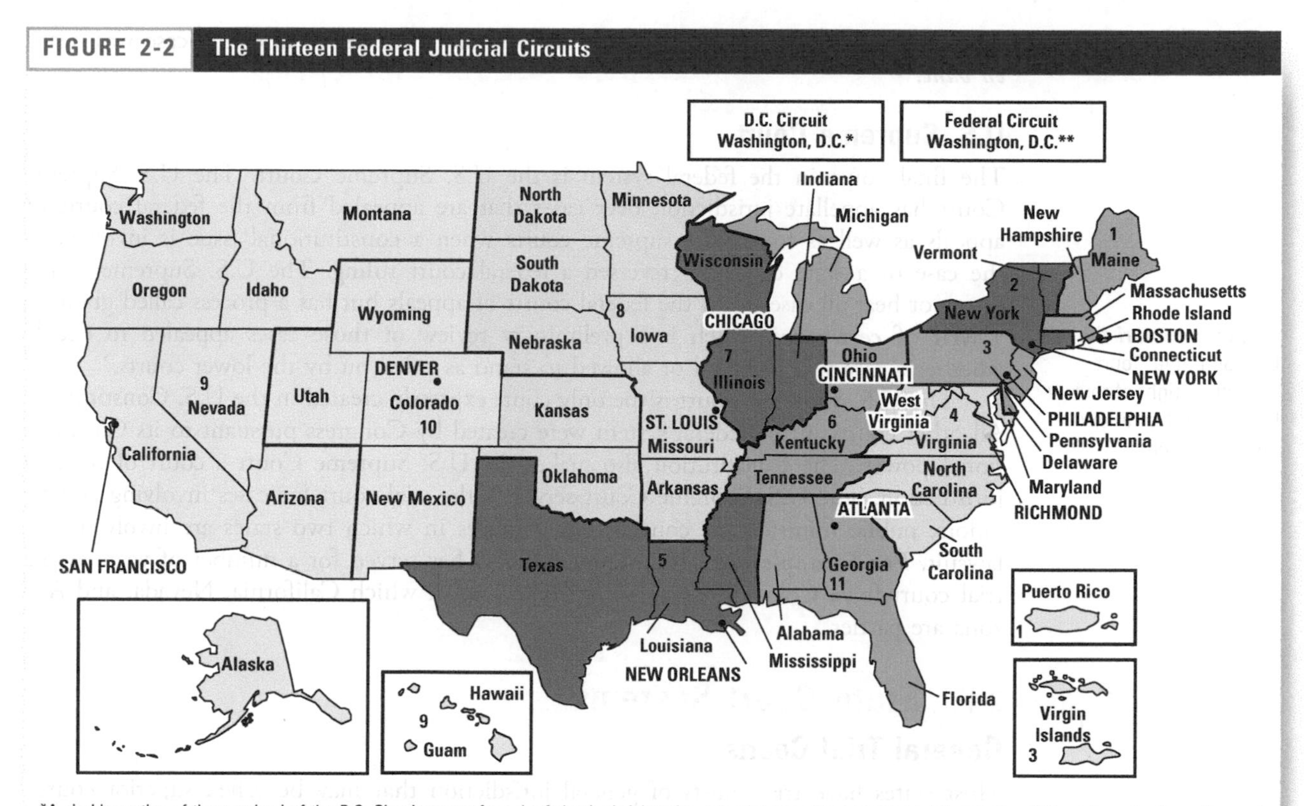

FIGURE 2-2 The Thirteen Federal Judicial Circuits

*A sizable portion of the caseload of the D.C. Circuit comes from the federal administrative agencies and offices located in Washington, D.C., such as the Securities and Exchange Commission, the National Labor Relations Board, the Federal Trade Commission, the Secretary of the Treasury, and the Labor Department, as well as appeals from the U.S. District Court of the District of Columbia.

**Rather than being defined by geography like the regional courts of appeals, the Federal Circuit is defined by subject matter, having jurisdiction over such matters as patent infringement cases, appeals from the Court of Federal Claims and the Court of International Trade, and appeals from administrative rulings regarding subject matter such as unfair import practices and tariff schedule disputes.

of the population base and the resulting caseload. Figure 2-2 shows the geographic structure of the federal court system, including the appellate circuits.

The federal system has additional trial courts with limited jurisdiction, differing from the general jurisdiction of the federal district courts. These courts include, for example, the federal bankruptcy courts, Indian tribal courts, Tax Court, Court of Federal Claims, Court of Veterans Appeals, and the Court of International Trade.

U.S. Courts of Appeals

en banc–the term used when the full panel of judges on the appellate court hears a case.

The final decision in a federal district court can be appealed to a court with appellate jurisdiction. In the federal court system, the federal districts are grouped together geographically into 12 judicial circuits, including one for the District of Columbia. Additionally, a thirteenth federal circuit, called the *Federal Circuit,* hears certain types of appeals from all of the circuits, including specialty cases such as patent appeals. Each circuit has an appellate court called the U.S. Court of Appeals, and the judges for these courts review the decisions of the federal district courts. Generally, a panel of three judges reviews the cases. However, some decisions, called ***en banc*** decisions, are made by the circuit's full panel of judges. **For Example,** in 2003, the Ninth Circuit heard an appeal on a father's right to challenge the requirement that his daughter recite the Pledge of Allegiance in the public school she attended. The contentious case had so many issues that the Ninth

Circuit issued three opinions and the third opinion was issued after the case was heard *en banc*.[4]

U.S. Supreme Court

The final court in the federal system is the U.S. Supreme Court. The U.S. Supreme Court has appellate jurisdiction over cases that are appealed from the federal courts of appeals as well as from state supreme courts when a constitutional issue is involved in the case or a state court has reversed a federal court ruling. The U.S. Supreme Court does not hear all cases from the federal courts of appeals but has a process called granting a **writ of *certiorari*,** which is a preliminary review of those cases appealed to decide whether a case will be heard or allowed to stand as ruled on by the lower courts.[5]

writ of *certiorari*–the U.S. Supreme Court granting a right of review by the court of a lower court decision.

The U.S. Supreme Court is the only court expressly created in the U.S. Constitution. All other courts in the federal system were created by Congress pursuant to its Constitutional power. The Constitution also makes the U.S. Supreme Court a court of original jurisdiction. The U.S. Supreme Court serves as the trial court for cases involving ambassadors, public ministers, or consuls and for cases in which two states are involved in a lawsuit. **For Example,** the U.S. Supreme Court has served for a number of years as the trial court for a Colorado River water rights case in which California, Nevada, and Arizona are parties.

2-1c State Court Systems

General Trial Courts

Most states have trial courts of general jurisdiction that may be called superior courts, circuit courts, district courts, or county courts. These courts of general and original jurisdiction usually hear both criminal and civil cases. Cases that do not meet the jurisdictional requirements for the federal district courts would be tried in these courts. Figure 2-3 illustrates a sample state court system.

Specialty Courts

Most states also have courts with limited jurisdiction, sometimes referred to as *specialty courts*. **For Example,** most states have juvenile courts, or courts with limited jurisdiction over criminal matters that involve defendants who are under the age of 18. Other specialty courts or lesser courts in state systems are probate and family law courts.

City, Municipal, and Justice Courts

Cities and counties may also have lesser courts with limited jurisdiction, which may be referred to as *municipal courts* or *justice courts*. These courts generally handle civil matters in which the claim made in the suit is an amount below a certain level, such as $5,000 or

[4] *Newdow v. U.S. Congress*, 292 F.3d 597 (9th Cir. 2002) *(Newdow I)*; *Newdow v. U.S. Congress*, 313 F.3d 500, 502 (9th Cir. 2002) *(Newdow II)*; and *Newdow v. U.S. Congress*, 328 F.3d 466, 468 (9th Cir. 2003) *(Newdow III)*. The U.S. Supreme Court eventually heard the case. *Elkgrove Unified School District v. Newdow*, 542 U.S. 1 (2004). Another *en banc* hearing occurred at the Ninth Circuit over the issues in the California gubernatorial recall election. The three-judge panel held that the voting methods in California violated the rights of voters and therefore placed a stay on the election. However, the Ninth Circuit then heard the case *en banc* and reversed the decision of the original three-judge panel.

[5] For example, the Supreme Court refused to grant *certiorari* in a Fifth Circuit case on law school admissions at the University of Texas. However, it granted *certiorari* in a later case involving law school admissions at the University of Michigan. *Gratz v. Bollinger*, 539 U.S. 244 (2003). A case challenging undergraduate admissions at the University of Texas (*Fisher v. University of Texas*) was heard by the U.S. Supreme Court (133 S. Ct. 2411 (2013)) and remanded, but the appellate court refused to remand the case for trial on a strict scrutiny basis. That decision of the federal court of appeals is on appeal again with *certiorari* granted. *Fisher v. University of Texas at Austin*, 2015 WL 629286.

FIGURE 2-3 Sample State Court System

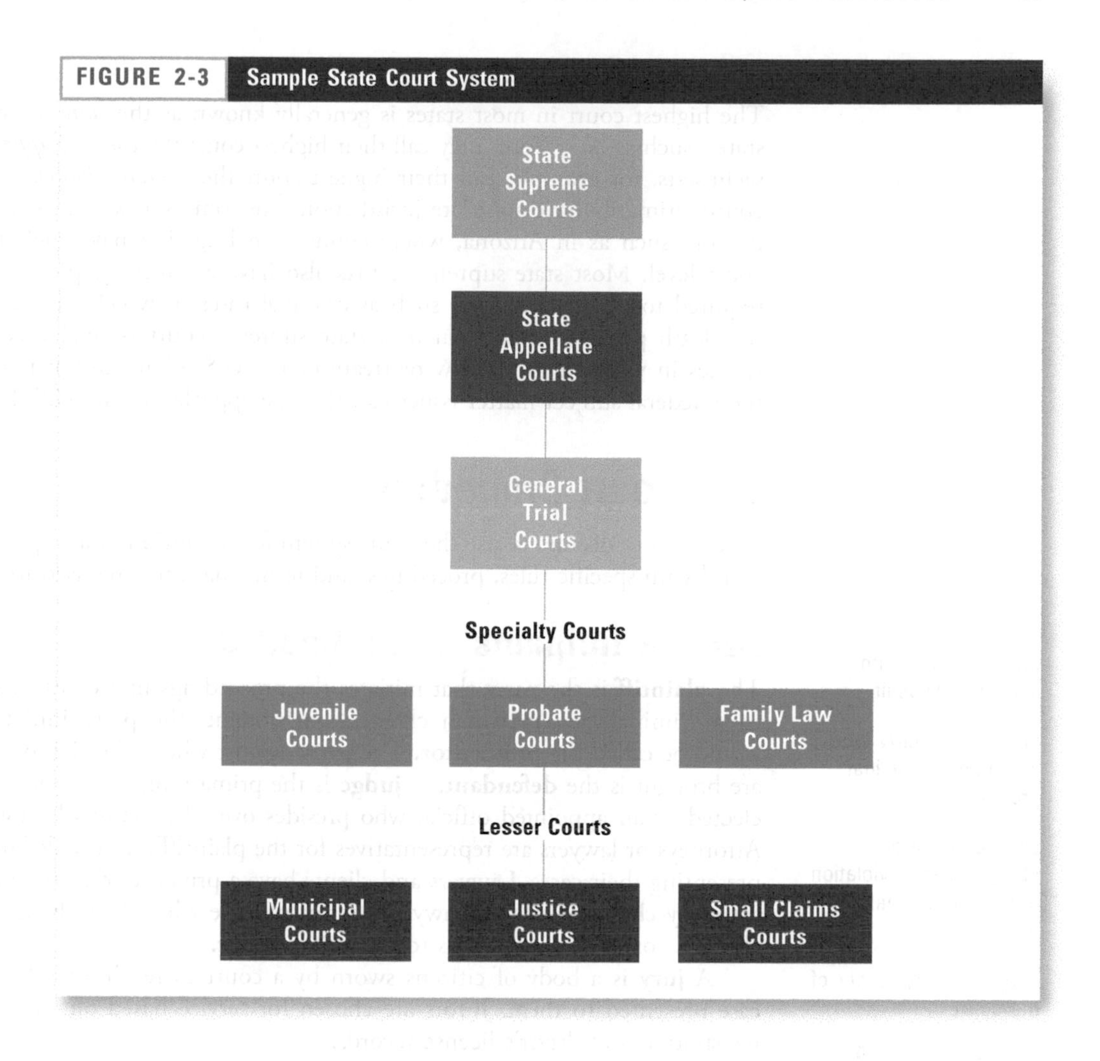

$10,000. These courts may also handle misdemeanor types of offenses, such as traffic violations or violations of noise ordinances, and the trials for them.

Small Claims Courts

small claims courts–courts that resolve disputes between parties when those disputes do not exceed a minimal level; no lawyers are permitted; the parties represent themselves.

Most states also have **small claims courts** at the county or city level. These are courts of limited jurisdiction where parties with small amounts in dispute may come to have a third party, such as a justice of the peace or city judge, review their disputes and determine how they should be resolved. A true small claims court is one in which the parties are not permitted to be represented by counsel. Rather, the parties present their cases to the judge in an informal manner without the strict procedural rules that apply in courts of general jurisdiction. Small claims courts provide a faster and inexpensive means for resolving a dispute that does not involve a large amount of claimed damages.

State Appellate Courts

Most states also have intermediate-level courts similar to the federal courts of appeals. They are courts with appellate jurisdiction that review the decisions of lower courts in that state. Decisions of the general trial courts in a state would be appealed to these courts.

State Supreme Courts

The highest court in most states is generally known as the *state supreme court*, but a few states, such as New York, may call their highest court the *court of appeals*; Maine and Massachusetts, for example, call their highest court the *supreme judicial court*. State supreme courts primarily have appellate jurisdiction, but some states' courts do have original jurisdiction, such as in Arizona, where counties in litigation have their trial at the supreme court level. Most state supreme courts also have a screening process for cases. They are required to hear some cases, such as criminal cases in which the defendant has received the death penalty. A decision of a state supreme court is final except in those circumstances in which a federal law or treaty or the U.S. Constitution is involved. Cases with these federal subject matter issues can then be appealed to the U.S. Supreme Court.

2-2 Court Procedure

Once a party decides to use the court system for resolution of a dispute, that party enters a world with specific rules, procedures, and terms that must be used to have a case proceed.

2-2a Participants in the Court System

plaintiff–party who initiates a lawsuit.

prosecutor–party who originates a criminal proceeding.

defendant–party charged with a violation of civil or criminal law in a proceeding.

judge–primary officer of the court.

attorney-client privilege–right of individual to have discussions with his/her attorney kept private and confidential.

jury–a body of citizens sworn by a court to determine by verdict the issues of fact submitted to them.

The **plaintiff** is the party that initiates the proceedings in a court of original jurisdiction. In a criminal case in which charges are brought, the party initiating the proceedings would be called the **prosecutor.** The party against whom the civil or criminal proceedings are brought is the **defendant.** A **judge** is the primary officer of the court and is either an elected or an appointed official who presides over the matters brought before the court. Attorneys or lawyers are representatives for the plaintiff and the defendant for purposes of presenting their cases. Lawyers and clients have a privilege of confidentiality known as the **attorney-client privilege.** Lawyers cannot disclose what their clients tell them unless the client is committing, or plans to commit, a crime.

A **jury** is a body of citizens sworn by a court to reach a verdict on the basis of the case presented to them. Jurors are chosen for service based on lists compiled from voter registration and driver's license records.

2-2b Which Law Applies—Conflicts of Law

When a lawsuit is brought, there is not just the question of where a case will be tried but also of what law will be applied in determining the rights of the parties. The principle that determines when a court applies the law of its own state—the law of the forum—or some foreign law is called *conflict of laws*. Because there are 50 state court systems and a federal court system, as well as a high degree of interstate activity, conflicts of law questions arise frequently.

Some general rules apply. For example, the law of the state in which the court is located governs the case on procedural issues and rules of evidence. In contract litigation, the court applies the law of the state in which the contract was made for determining issues of formation. Performance disputes and damages for nonperformance are generally governed by the law of the state where the contract is to be performed. International contracts follow similar rules. **For Example,** a California court will apply Swiss law to a contract made in Switzerland that is to be performed in that country.

However, it is becoming more common for the parties to specify their choice of law in their contract.[6] In the absence of a law-selecting provision in the contract, there is a

[6] For example, when tourists from other countries engage in activities there, they sign a combination waiver and contract that provides in the event of an injury that they agree to be governed by the laws of that country in terms of recovery and not those of the United States. *E & H Cruises, Ltd. v. Baker*, 88 So. 3d 291 (Fla. App. 2012).

growing acceptance of the rule that a contract should be governed by the law of the state that has the most significant contacts with the transaction.

For Example, assume the buyer's place of business and the seller's plant are located in Nebraska, and the buyer is purchasing goods from the seller to resell to Nebraska customers. Many courts will hold that this is a contract governed by the law of Nebraska. In determining which state has the most significant contacts, the court considers the place of contracting, negotiating, and performing; the location of the subject matter of the contract; and the domicile (residence), states of incorporation, and principal place of business of the parties.

2-2c Initial Steps in a Lawsuit

The following steps in a lawsuit generally apply in cases brought in courts of original jurisdiction. Not every step applies in every case, but understanding litigation steps and terms is important for businesspeople.

Commencement of a Lawsuit

A lawsuit begins with the filing of a **complaint.** The complaint generally contains a description of the wrongful conduct and a request for damages, such as a monetary amount. **For Example,** a plaintiff in a contract suit would describe the contract, when it was entered into, and when the defendant stopped performance on the contract. A copy of the contract would be attached to the complaint.

Service of Process

Once the plaintiff has filed the complaint with the proper court, the plaintiff has the responsibility of notifying the defendant that the lawsuit has been filed. The defendant must be served with **process.** Process, often called a *writ, notice,* or *summons,* is delivered to the defendant and includes a copy of the complaint and notification that the defendant must appear and respond to the allegations in the complaint.

The Defendant's Response and the Pleadings

After the defendant is served with process in the case, the defendant is required to respond to or **answer** the complaint within the time provided under the court's rules. In answering the plaintiff's complaint, the defendant has several options. For example, the defendant could make a **motion to dismiss,** which is a request to the court to dismiss the lawsuit on the grounds that, even if everything the plaintiff said in the complaint were true, there is still no right of recovery. A motion to dismiss is also called a **demurrer.**

A defendant could also respond and deny the allegations. **For Example,** in a contract lawsuit, the defendant-seller could say he did not breach the contract but stopped shipment of the goods because the plaintiff-buyer did not pay for the goods in advance as the contract required. A defendant could also **counterclaim** in the answer, which is asking the court for damages as a result of the underlying dispute. The defendant-seller in the contract lawsuit might ask for damages in the counterclaim for the plaintiff-buyer's failure to pay as the contract required.

All documents filed in this initial phase of the case are referred to as the **pleadings.** The pleadings are a statement of the case and the basis for recovery if all the facts alleged can be proved.

Discovery

The Federal Rules of Civil Procedure and similar rules in all states permit one party to obtain from the adverse party information about all witnesses, documents, and any other items relevant to the case. **Discovery** requires each side to name its potential witnesses

complaint–the initial pleading filed by the plaintiff in many actions, which in many states may be served as original process to acquire jurisdiction over the defendant.

process–paperwork served personally on a defendant in a civil case.

answer–what a defendant must file to admit or deny facts asserted by the plaintiff.

motion to dismiss–a pleading that may be filed to attack the adverse party's pleading as not stating a cause of action or a defense.

demurrer–a pleading to dismiss the adverse party's pleading for not stating a cause of action or a defense.

counterclaim–a claim that the defendant in an action may make against the plaintiff.

pleadings–the papers filed by the parties in an action in order to set forth the facts and frame the issues to be tried, although, under some systems, the pleadings merely give notice or a general indication of the nature of the issues.

discovery–procedures for ascertaining facts prior to the time of trial in order to eliminate the element of surprise in litigation.

and to provide each side the chance to question those witnesses in advance of the trial. Each party also has the opportunity to examine, inspect, and photograph books, records, buildings, and machines. Even examining the physical or mental condition of a party is part of discovery when it has relevance in the case. The scope of discovery is extremely broad because the rules permit any questions that are likely to lead to admissible evidence.

deposition–the testimony of a witness taken out of court before a person authorized to administer oaths.

Deposition. A **deposition** is the testimony of a witness taken under oath outside the courtroom; it is transcribed by a court reporter. Each party is permitted to question the witness. If a party or a witness gives testimony at the trial that is inconsistent with her deposition testimony, the prior inconsistent testimony can be used to **impeach** the witness's credibility at trial.

impeach–using prior inconsistent evidence to challenge the credibility of a witness.

Depositions can be taken either for discovery purposes or to preserve the testimony of a witness who will not be available during the trial. Some states now permit depositions to be videotaped. A videotape is a more effective way of presenting deposition testimony than reading that testimony at trial from a reporter's transcript because jurors can see the witness and the witness's demeanor and hear the words as they were spoken, complete with inflection.

interrogatories–written questions used as a discovery tool that must be answered under oath.

request for production of documents–discovery tool for uncovering paper evidence in a case.

Other Forms of Discovery. Other forms of discovery include medical exams, particularly in cases in which the plaintiff is claiming damages for physical injuries. Written **interrogatories** (questions) and written **requests for production of documents** are discovery requests that can be very time consuming to the answering party and often lead to pretrial legal disputes between the parties and their attorneys as a result of the legal expenses involved.

Motion for Summary Judgment

motion for summary judgment–request that the court decide a case on basis of law only because there are no material issues disputed by the parties.

If a case has no material facts in dispute, either party can file a **motion for summary judgment.** Using affidavits or deposition testimony obtained in discovery, the court can find that there are no factual issues and decide the case as a matter of law. **For Example,** suppose that the parties can agree that they entered into a life insurance contract but dispute whether the policy applies when there is a suicide. The facts are not in dispute; the law on payment of insurance proceeds in the event of a suicide is the issue. Such a case is one that is appropriate for summary judgment.

Designation of Expert Witnesses

In some cases, such as those involving product safety, the parties may want to designate an expert witness. An **expert witness** is a witness who has some special expertise, such as an economist who gives expert opinion on the value of future lost income or a scientist who testifies about the safety of a prescription drug. There are rules for naming expert witnesses as well as for admitting into evidence any studies or documents of the expert.[7] The purpose of these rules is to avoid the problem of what has been called *junk science*, or the admission of experts' testimony and research that has not been properly conducted or reviewed by peers.

expert witness–one who has acquired special knowledge in a particular field as through practical experience or study, or both, whose opinion is admissible as an aid to the trier of fact.

2-2d The Trial

Selecting a Jury

***voir dire* examination**–the preliminary examination of a juror or a witness to ascertain fitness to act as such.

Jurors drawn for service are questioned by the judge and lawyers to determine whether they are biased or have any preformed judgments about the parties in the case. Jury selection is called ***voir dire* examination. For Example,** in the trial of Martha Stewart, the multimedia home and garden diva, it took a great deal of time for the lawyers to question

[7] *Daubert v. Merrell Dow Pharmaceuticals, Inc.*, 509 U.S. 579 (1993).

E-COMMERCE & CYBERLAW

Google's Impact on Trials

The courts continue to struggle with the effects of the Internet on the jury selection process as well as with the jurors themselves in accessing social media sites while serving on a jury. There have been 134 cases in the past three years that involved issues with Google and jurors. In *McGaha v. Com.*, 414 S.W.3d 1 (Ky. 2013), the court held that a juror's failure to disclose being a friend of the defendant's wife on Facebook is not a presumed reason for disqualification of that juror on the basis of bias or lack of impartiality. In *People v. Levack*, 2014 WL 2118088 (Mich. App.), the jurors used Google Maps to determine whether there was a shortcut to the victim's home, as claimed in the testimony. The jurors did not consider the Google information in their deliberations and the court found that a new trial was not necessary.

The key points of these cases are that prospective jurors should disclose online connections with any of the parties in a case and that jurors should not consider any information that was not provided through the trial process. The courts follow these basic principles when evaluating whether a mistrial is necessary when the Internet has affected jurors or prospective jurors. In fact, judges often include an instruction similar to this one in turning the case over to a jury:

> *Do not visit or view any place discussed in this case, and do not use any internet maps or Google Earth or any other program or device to search for or view any place discussed in the testimony.**

******State v. Feliciano***, 2014 WL 1577768 (N.J. Sup.).**

opening statements–statements by opposing attorneys that tell the jury what their cases will prove.

admissibility–the quality of the evidence in a case that allows it to be presented to the jury.

direct examination–examination of a witness by his or her attorney.

cross-examination–the examination made of a witness by the attorney for the adverse party.

redirect examination–questioning after cross-examination, in which the attorney for the witness testifying may ask the same witness other questions to overcome effects of the cross-examination.

recross-examination–an examination by the other side's attorney that follows the redirect examination.

the potential jurors about their prior knowledge concerning the case, which had received nationwide attention and much media coverage. Lawyers have the opportunity to remove jurors who know parties in the case or who indicate they have already formed opinions about guilt or innocence. The attorneys question the potential jurors to determine if a juror should be *challenged for cause* (e.g., when the prospective juror states he is employed by the plaintiff's company). Challenges for cause are unlimited, but each side can also exercise six to eight peremptory challenges.[8] A peremptory challenge is a challenge that is used to strike (remove) a juror for any reason except on racial grounds.[9]

Opening Statements

After the jury is chosen, the attorneys for each of the parties make their **opening statements** to the jury. An opening statement, as one lawyer has explained, makes a puzzle frame for the case so jurors can follow the witnesses and place the pieces of the case—the various forms of evidence—within the frame.

The Presentation of Evidence

Following the opening statements, the plaintiff presents his case with witnesses and other evidence. A judge rules on the **admissibility** of evidence. Evidence can consist of documents, testimony, expert testimony, medical information from exams, and even physical evidence.

In the case of testimony, the attorney for the plaintiff conducts **direct examination** of his witnesses during his case, and the defense attorney conducts **cross-examination** of the plaintiff's witnesses. The plaintiff's attorney can then ask questions again of his witnesses in what is called **redirect examination.** Finally, the defense attorney may question the plaintiff's witnesses again in **recross-examination.** The defendant presents her case after the plaintiff's case concludes. During the defendant's case, the lawyer for the

[8] The number of peremptory challenges varies from state to state and may also vary within a particular state depending on the type of case. For example, in Arizona, peremptory challenges are unlimited in capital cases.

[9] *Felkner v. Jackson*, 562 U.S. 594 (2011).

THINKING THINGS THROUGH

Why Do We Require Sworn Testimony?

There is a difference between what people say in conversation (and even what company executives say in speeches and reports) and what they are willing to say under oath. Speaking under oath often means that different information and recollections emerge. The oath is symbolic and carries the penalty of criminal prosecution for perjury if the testimony given is false.

The *Wall Street Journal* has reported that the testimony of executives in the Microsoft antitrust trial and their statements regarding their business relationships outside the courtroom are quite different. For example, the following quotations indicate some discrepancies. Eric Benhamou, the chief executive officer (CEO) of Palm, Inc., said:

> *We believe that the handheld opportunity remains wide open .... Unlike the PC industry, there is no monopoly of silicon, there is no monopoly of software.*

However, at the Microsoft trial, another officer of Palm, Michael Mace, offered the following testimony:

> *We believe that there is a very substantial risk that Microsoft could manipulate its products and its standards in order to exclude Palm from the marketplace in the future.*

Likewise, Microsoft has taken different positions inside and outside the courtroom. For example, an attorney for Microsoft stated that Microsoft had "zero deployments of its interactive TV middleware products connected to cable systems in the United States." However, Microsoft's marketing materials provide as follows:

> *Microsoft's multiple deployments around the world now including Charter-show Microsoft TV is ready to deploy now and set the standard for what TV can be.**

Explain why the executives had differing statements. For more information on the Microsoft antitrust cases, go to **http://www.usdoj.gov** or **http://www.microsoft.com**.

*Rebecca Buckman and Nicholas Kulish, "Microsoft Trial Prompts an Outbreak of Doublespeak," *Wall Street Journal*, April 15, 2002, B1, B3.

defendant conducts direct examination of the defendant's witnesses, and the plaintiff's lawyer can then cross-examine the defendant's witnesses.

directed verdict–a direction by the trial judge to the jury to return a verdict in favor of a specified party to the action.

summation–the attorney address that follows all the evidence presented in court and sums up a case and recommends a particular verdict be returned by the jury.

mistrial–a court's declaration that terminates a trial and postpones it to a later date; commonly entered when evidence has been of a highly prejudicial character or when a juror has been guilty of misconduct.

Motion for a Directed Verdict

A motion for a **directed verdict** asks the court to grant a verdict because even if all the evidence that has been presented by each side were true, there is either no basis for recovery or no defense to recovery.

For Example, suppose that a plaintiff company presented evidence that an employee who quit working for the company posted on his Facebook page, "I just wasn't happy there." The company might not feel good about the former employee's post, but there is no false statement and no breach of privacy. The evidence is true, but there is no legal right of recovery. The defendant employee would be entitled to a directed verdict. A directed verdict means that the party has not presented enough evidence to show that there is some right of recovery under the law.

Closing Arguments or Summation

After the witnesses for both parties have been examined and all the evidence has been presented, each attorney makes a closing argument. These statements are also called **summations;** they summarize the case and urge the jury to reach a particular verdict.

Motion for Mistrial

During the course of a trial, when necessary to avoid great injustice, the trial court may declare a **mistrial.** A mistrial requires a do-over, a new jury. A mistrial can be declared for jury or attorney misconduct. **For Example,** if a juror were caught fraternizing with one of the lawyers in the case, objectivity would be compromised and the court would most likely declare a mistrial. See also E-Commerce & Cyberlaw (Google's Impact on Trials) for more information on juror misconduct and case dismissals.

Jury Instructions and Verdict

instruction–summary of the law given to jurors by the judge before deliberation begins.

After the summation by the attorneys, the court gives the jurors **instructions** on the appropriate law to apply to the facts presented. The jury then deliberates and renders its verdict. After the jury verdict, the court enters a judgment. If the jury is deadlocked and unable to reach a verdict, known as a hung jury or a mistrial, the case is reset for a new trial at some future date.

Motion for New Trial; Motion for Judgment *n.o.v.*

judgment n.o.v.–or *non obstante veredicto* (notwithstanding the verdict), a judgment entered after verdict upon the motion of the losing party on the ground that the verdict is so wrong that a judgment should be entered the opposite of the verdict.

A court may grant a **judgment *non obstante veredicto*** or a **judgment *n.o.v.*** (notwithstanding the verdict) if the verdict is clearly wrong as a matter of law. The court can set aside the verdict and enter a judgment in favor of the other party. Perhaps one of the most famous judgments n.o.v. occurred in Boston in 1997 when a judge reversed the murder conviction of nanny Louise Woodward, who was charged with the murder of one of her young charges.

2-2e Post-trial Procedures

Recovery of Costs/Attorney Fees

Generally, the prevailing party is awarded costs. Costs include filing fees, service-of-process fees, witness fees, deposition transcript costs, and jury fees. Costs do not

ETHICS & THE LAW

Honesty, Lawyers, and BP Claims

Following the Deepwater Horizon oil spill in the Gulf of Mexico, BP established a $20 billion recovery fund. The purpose of the fund was to reimburse businesses and individuals who were affected by the spill, such as fishers, resorts, and boating companies that provided tours and other services.

Several lawyers and accountants were assigned to the Claims Administration Office (CAO) with the responsibilities for the receipt, evaluation, and payment of claims. In 2013, the federal judge overseeing the claims process became concerned about the conduct of those who were administering the trust. As a result, the judge appointed Louis Freeh, a former federal judge and director of the FBI, to investigate.

Among the many findings of the cases were conflicts, such as Lionel Sutton and Christine Reitano, husband and wife, two lawyers working at the CAO who had practiced law together in New Orleans as Sutton & Reitano. They referred a client, Casey Thonn, to Glen Lerner of AndryLerner, a law firm representing claimants to the CAO. Ms. Reitano then requested a referral fee from AndryLerner. The referral arrangement was never disclosed to the client, Casey Thonn, as Louisiana's code of professional ethics requires, nor the CAO office. Mr. Sutton continued his representation of Casey Thonn in a personal injury case but did not disclose that client relationship to anyone at the CAO. Mr. Sutton also did not disclose that he had a business relationship in a reclamation company, Crown LLC, and that he was one of two equity owners of that company, with Glen Lerner, a partner at AndryLerner, being the other owner. AndryLerner had a total of $7,908,460 in claims before the CAO. Mr. Sutton approved 496 of the claims.

On November 25, 2014, the U.S. Attorney for the Middle District of Florida announced 27 indictments against individuals who are alleged to have submitted fraudulent claims for reimbursement, ranging from $11,000 to $122,000, and totaling over $1,000,000.

BP began running full-page ads in major newspaper around the country with examples of the fraudulent claims. The judge is seeking restitution from many of the claimants.

What should the lawyers have done in their situations? Why did they not do it?

include compensation spent by a party for preparing the case or being present at trial, including the time lost from work because of the case and the fee paid to the attorney, although lost wages from an injury are generally part of damages.

Attorney fees may be recovered by a party who prevails if a statute permits the recovery of attorney fees or if the complaint involves a claim for breach of contract and the contract contains a clause providing for recovery of attorney fees.

execution–the carrying out of a judgment of a court, generally directing that property owned by the defendant be sold and the proceeds first be used to pay the execution or judgment creditor.

garnishment–the name given in some states to attachment proceedings.

Execution of Judgment

After a judgment has been entered or all appeals or appeal rights have ended, the losing party must pay that judgment. The winning party can also take steps to execute, or carry out, the judgment. The **execution** is accomplished by the seizure and sale of the losing party's assets by the sheriff according to a writ of execution or a writ of possession.

Garnishment is a common method of satisfying a judgment. When the judgment debtor is an employee, the appropriate judicial authority in the state garnishes (by written notice to the employer) a portion of the employee's wages on a regular basis until the judgment is paid.

2-3 Alternative Dispute Resolution (ADR)

Parties can use means other than litigation to resolve disagreements or disputes. Litigation takes significant time and money, so many businesses use alternative methods for resolving disputes. Those methods include arbitration, mediation, and several other formats. Figure 2-4 provides an overall view of alternative dispute resolution procedures.

2-3a Arbitration

arbitration–the settlement of disputed questions, whether of law or fact, by one or more arbitrators by whose decision the parties agree to be bound.

In **arbitration,** arbitrators (disinterested persons selected by the parties to the dispute) hear evidence and determine a resolution. Arbitration enables the parties to present the facts before trained experts familiar with the industry practices that may affect the nature and outcome of the dispute. Arbitration first reached extensive use in the field of commercial contracts and was encouraged as a means of avoiding expensive litigation and easing the workload of courts. However, over the past decade the popularity of arbitration has declined because of increasing procedural burdens and longer and more complex hearings. There have been an increasing number of cases in which arbitration clauses have been set aside as too onerous for a consumer or small business party to the agreement.[10]

A number of states have adopted the Uniform Arbitration Act.[11] Under this act and similar statutes, the parties to a contract may agree in advance that all disputes arising under it will be submitted to arbitration. In some instances, the contract will name the arbitrators for the duration of the contract. The uniform act requires a written agreement to arbitrate.[12]

The Federal Arbitration Act[13] provides that an arbitration clause in a contract relating to an interstate transaction is valid, irrevocable, and enforceable. When a contract subject to the Federal Arbitration Act provides for the arbitration of disputes, the parties are

[10] *College Park Pentecostal Holiness Church v. General Steel Corp.*, 847 F. Supp. 2d 807 (D. Md. 2012).

[11] On August 3, 2000, the National Conference of Commissioners on Uniform State Laws unanimously passed major revisions to the Uniform Arbitration Act (UAA). These revisions were the first major changes in 45 years to the UAA, which is the basis of arbitration law in 49 states, although not all states have adopted it in its entirety or most current form. Only 18 states and the District of Columbia have adopted the UAA 2000 revisions. John Lande, "A Framework for Advancing Negotiation Theory: Implications from a Study of How Lawyers Reach Agreement in Pretrial Litigation," 16 *Cardozo Journal of Conflict Resolution* 1 (2014).

[12] *Minkowitz v. Israeli*, 77 A.3d 1189 (N.J. Super. 2013).

[13] 9 U.S.C. §§114 *et seq.*

FIGURE 2-4 Dispute Resolution Procedures

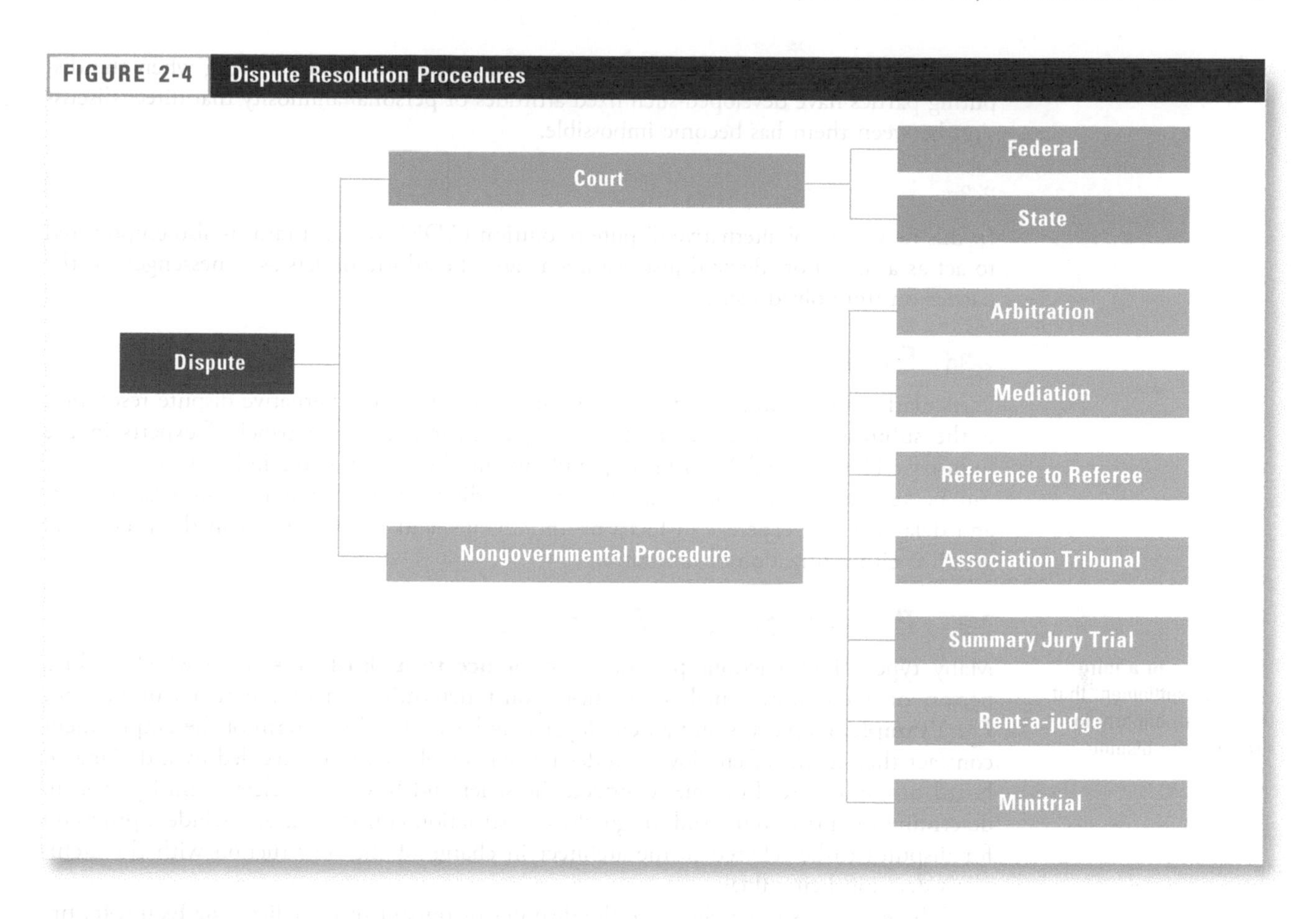

bound to arbitrate in accordance with the federal statute even if the agreement to arbitrate would not be binding under state law.

Mandatory Arbitration

In contrast with statutes that merely regulate arbitration when it is selected voluntarily by the parties, some statutes require that certain kinds of disputes be submitted to arbitration. In some states, by rule or statute, the arbitration of small claims is required.

Finality of Arbitration

Most parties provide, within their arbitration agreements, that the decision of the arbitrator will be final. Such a clause is binding on the parties, even when the decision seems to be wrong, and can be set aside only if there is clear proof of fraud, arbitrary conduct, or a significant procedural error.[14]

mediation–the settlement of a dispute through the use of a messenger who carries to each side of the dispute the issues and offers in the case.

2-3b Mediation

In **mediation,** a neutral person acts as a messenger between opposing sides of a dispute, carrying to each side the latest settlement offer made by the other. The mediator has no authority to make a decision, although in some cases the mediator may make suggestions that might ultimately be accepted by the disputing parties.

[14] *PoolRE Ins. Corp. v. Organizational Strategies, Inc.*, 2014 WL 1320188 (S.D. Tex. 2014).

The use of mediation has the advantage of keeping discussions going when the disputing parties have developed such fixed attitudes or personal animosity that direct discussion between them has become impossible.

2-3c MedArb

In this new form of alternative dispute resolution (ADR), the arbitrator is also empowered to act as a mediator. Beyond just hearing a case, the arbitrator acts as a messenger for the parties on unresolved issues.

2-3d Expert Panel

Particularly in the construction industry, one of the tools of alternative dispute resolution is the submission of a case, or perhaps a particular issue, to a panel of experts in the industry. This method has gained popularity in the construction industry where there can be technical questions about breach, including issues related to materials, process, and delays. These experts can focus on these issues and not be caught in the procedural grind of either litigation or arbitration.

2-3e Reference to a Third Person

reference to a third person–settlement that allows a nonparty to resolve the dispute.

Many types of transactions provide for **reference to a third person,** in which a third person or a committee makes an out-of-court determination of the rights of persons. **For Example,** employees and an employer may have agreed as a term of the employment contract that claims of employees under retirement plans will be decided by a designated board or committee. In a sales contract, the seller and buyer can select a third person to determine the price to be paid for goods. Construction contracts often include a provision for disputes to be referred to the architect in charge of the construction with the architect's decision being final.

These referrals often eliminate the disputes or pursuit of remedies. **For Example,** fire insurance policies commonly provide that if the parties cannot agree on the amount of the loss, each will appoint an appraiser, the two appraisers will appoint a third appraiser, and the three will determine the amount of the loss the insurer is required to pay.

2-3f Association Tribunals

association tribunal–a court created by a trade association or group for the resolution of disputes among its members.

Many disputes never reach the courts because both parties to a dispute belong to a group or an association, and the **association tribunal** created by the group or association disposes of the matter. Trade associations commonly require their members to employ out-of-court methods of dispute settlement. **For Example,** the National Association of Home Builders requires its member builders to use arbitration. The National Automobile Dealers Association provides for panels to determine warranty claims of customers. The decision of such panels is final as to the builder or dealer, but the consumer can still bring a regular lawsuit after losing before the panel. Members of an association must use the association tribunal, which means they cannot bypass the association tribunal and go directly to a law court.[15]

2-3g Summary Jury Trial

summary jury trial–a mock or dry-run trial for parties to get a feel for how their cases will play to a jury.

A **summary jury trial** is a dry-run or mock trial in which the lawyers present their claims before a jury of six persons. The object is to get the reaction of a sample jury. No evidence is presented before this jury, and it bases its opinion solely on what the lawyers state. The determination of the jury has no binding effect, but it has value in that it

[15] The securities industry follows this process as well.

gives the lawyers some idea of what a jury might think if there were an actual trial. This type of ADR has special value when the heart of a case is whether something is reasonable under all circumstances. When the lawyers and their clients see how the sample jury reacts, they may moderate their positions and reach a settlement.

2-3h Rent-A-Judge

rent-a-judge plan–dispute resolution through private courts with judges paid to be referees for the cases.

Under the **rent-a-judge plan,** the parties hire a judge to hear the case. In many states, the parties voluntarily choose the judge as a "referee," and the judge acts under a statute authorizing the appointment of referees. Under such a statute, the referee hears all evidence just as though there were a regular trial, and the rented judge's determination is binding on the parties unless reversed on appeal if such an appeal (like a court trial) is permitted under the parties' agreement.

2-3i Minitrial

minitrial–a trial held on portions of the case or certain issues in the case.

When only part of a case is disputed, the parties may stay within the framework of a lawsuit but agree that only the disputed issues will be taken to trial and submitted to a jury. **For Example,** if there is no real dispute over who is liable but the parties disagree as to the damages, the issue of damages alone may be submitted to the jury. This shortened trial is often called a **minitrial.** A minitrial may use a retired judge to make a decision on just the disputed issues. The parties may also specify whether this decision will be binding on the parties. As a practical matter, the evaluation of a case by a neutral person often brings the opposing parties together to reach a settlement.

2-3j Contract Provisions

The parties' contract may pave the way for the settlement of future disputes by including clauses that require the parties to use one of the means of ADR. Other provisions in contracts that serve to keep the parties calm with the hope of resolving differences without a lawsuit include waiting periods before a suit can be filed and obligations to continue performing even as they try to resolve differences and issues.

Make the Connection

Summary

Courts have been created to hear and resolve legal disputes. A court's specific power is defined by its jurisdiction. Courts of original jurisdiction are trial courts, and courts that review the decisions of trial courts are appellate courts. Trial courts may have general jurisdiction to hear a wide range of civil and criminal matters, or they may be courts of limited jurisdiction—such as a probate court or the Tax Court—with the subject matter of their cases restricted to certain areas.

The courts in the United States are organized into two different systems: the state and federal court systems. There are three levels of courts, for the most part, in each system, with trial courts, appellate courts, and a supreme court in each. The federal courts are federal district courts, federal courts of appeals, and the U.S. Supreme Court.

In the states, there may be specialized courts, such as municipal, justice, and small claims courts, for trial courts. Within the courts of original jurisdiction, there are rules for procedures in all matters brought before them. A civil case begins with the filing of a complaint by a plaintiff, which is then answered by a defendant. The parties may be represented by their attorneys. Discovery is the pretrial process used by the parties to find out the evidence in the case. The parties can use depositions, interrogatories, and document requests to uncover relevant information.

The case is managed by a judge and may be tried to a jury selected through the process of *voir dire*, with the parties permitted to challenge jurors on the basis of cause or through the use of their peremptory challenges. The trial begins following discovery and involves opening statements and the presentation of evidence, including the direct examination and cross-examination of witnesses. Once a judgment is entered, the party who has won can collect the judgment through garnishment and a writ of execution.

Alternatives to litigation for dispute resolution are available, including arbitration, mediation, MedArb, reference to a third party, association tribunals, summary jury trials, rent-a-judge plans, minitrials, and expert panels. Court dockets are relieved and cases consolidated using judicial triage, a process in which courts hear the cases involving the most serious medical issues and health conditions first. Triage is a blending of the judicial and alternative dispute resolution mechanisms.

Learning Outcomes

After studying this chapter, you should be able to clearly explain:

2-1 The Court System

LO.1 Explain the federal and state court systems

See Figure 2-1 and accompanying text, page 16.

See Figure 2-3 and accompanying text, page 19.

See the *Stanford* case on page 15 for a discussion of reversible error.

2-2 Court Procedure

LO.2 Describe court procedures

See the discussion of steps in litigation, pages 21–22.

See the *For Example* discussion of the Martha Stewart *voir dire* example, page 22.

See the Google jury issues box on page 23.

See the "Why Do We Require Sworn Testimony" box on page 24.

2-3 Alternative Dispute Resolution (ADR)

LO.3 List the forms of alternative dispute resolution and distinguish among them

See the discussion of arbitration, page 26.

See the discussion of other forms of ADR, mediation, minitrials, rent-a-judge, MedArb, judicial triage, and referral to a third party, pages 27–29.

See the discussion of employee and employer referrals of disputes to a designated board or committee, page 28.

Key Terms

admissibility
affirm
answer
appeal
appellate jurisdiction
arbitration
association tribunal
attorney-client privilege
complaint
counterclaim
court
cross-examination
defendant
demurrer
deposition
direct examination
directed verdict
discovery
en banc
execution
expert witness
federal district courts
garnishment
general jurisdiction
impeach
instructions
interrogatories
judge
judgment *n.o.v.* or judgment *non obstante veredicto*
jurisdiction
jury
limited (special) jurisdiction
mediation
minitrial
mistrial
motion for summary judgment
motion to dismiss
opening statements
original jurisdiction
plaintiff
pleadings
process
prosecutor
recross-examination
redirect examination
reference to a third person
remand
rent-a-judge plan
requests for production of documents
reverse
reversible error
small claims courts
subject matter jurisdiction
summary jury trial
summations
voir dire examination
writ of *certiorari*

Questions and Case Problems

1. List the steps in a lawsuit. Begin with the filing of the complaint, and explain the points at which there can be a final determination of the parties' rights in the case.
2. Explain why a business person would want to use alternative dispute resolution methods. Discuss the advantages. What disadvantages have you learned?
3. Ralph Dewey has been charged with a violation of the Electronic Espionage Act, a federal statute that prohibits the transfer, by computer or disk or other electronic means, of a company's proprietary data and information. Ralph is curious. What type of court has jurisdiction? Can you determine which court?
4. Jerry Lewinsky was called for jury duty. When *voir dire* began, Jerry realized that the case involved his supervisor at work. Can Jerry remain as a juror on the case? Why or why not?
5. Carolyn, Elwood, and Isabella are involved in a real estate development. The development is a failure, and Carolyn, Elwood, and Isabella want to have their rights determined. They could bring a lawsuit, but they are afraid the case is so complicated that a judge and jury not familiar with the problems of real estate development would not reach a proper result. What can they do?
6. Larketta Randolph purchased a mobile home from Better Cents Home Builders, Inc., and financed her purchase through Green Tree Financial Corporation. Ms. Randolph signed a standard form contract that required her to buy Vendor's Single Interest insurance, which protects the seller against the costs of repossession in the event of default. The agreement also provided that all disputes arising from the contract would be resolved by binding arbitration. Larketta found that there was an additional $15 in finance charges that were not disclosed in the contract. She and other Green Tree customers filed a class-action suit to recover the fees. Green Tree moved to dismiss the suit because Larketta had not submitted the issue to arbitration. Larketta protests, "But I want the right to go to court!" Does she have that right? What are the rights of parties under a contract with an arbitration clause? [*Green Tree Financial Corp. v. Randolph*, 531 U.S. 79]
7. John Watson invested $5,000,000 in SmartRead, Inc., a company that was developing an electronic reading device. Within a few months, the $5,000,000 was spent but SmartRead never developed the reading device. John filed suit against the directors of SmartRead for their failure to supervise SmartRead's CEO in his operation of the company. The directors used an expert on corporate governance to testify that the directors had done all that they could to oversee the company. The expert did not disclose that he had served as a director of a company and had been found to be negligent in his role there and had been required to pay $370,000 to shareholders. The directors won the case. Is there anything Watson can do?
8. Indicate whether the following courts are courts of original, general, limited, or appellate jurisdiction:
   a. Small claims court
   b. Federal bankruptcy court
   c. Federal district court
   d. U.S. Supreme Court
   e. Municipal court
   f. Probate court
   g. Federal court of appeals
9. The Nursing Home Pension Fund filed suit against Oracle Corporation alleging that Larry Ellison, the company's CEO, misled investors in 2001 about the true financial condition of the company. During the time of the alleged misrepresentation, Mr. Ellison was working with a biographer on his life story and there are videotapes of Mr. Ellison's interviews with his biographer as well as e-mails between the two that discuss Oracle. Could the Nursing Home Pension Fund have access to the tapes and e-mails? Explain how. [*Nursing Home Pension Fund, Local 144 v. Oracle Corp.*, 380 F.3d 1226 (9th Cir.)]
10. Mostek Corp., a Texas corporation, made a contract to sell computer-related products to North American Foreign Trading Corp., a New York corporation. North American used its own purchase order form, on which appeared the statement that any dispute arising out of an order would be submitted to arbitration, as provided in the terms set forth on the back of the order. Acting on the purchase order, Mostek delivered almost all of the goods but failed to deliver the final installment. North American then demanded that the matter be arbitrated. Mostek refused to do so. Was arbitration required? [*Application of Mostek Corp.*, 502 N.Y.S.2d 181 (App. Div.)]

11. Ceasar Wright was a longshoreman in Charleston, South Carolina, and a member of the International Longshoremen's Association (AFL-CIO). Wright used the union hiring hall. The collective bargaining agreement (CBA) of Wright's union provides for arbitration of all grievances. Another clause of the CBA states: "It is the intention and purpose of all parties hereto that no provision or part of this Agreement shall be violative of any Federal or State Law."

    On February 18, 1992, while Wright was working for Stevens Shipping and Terminal Company (Stevens), he injured his right heel and back. He sought permanent compensation from Stevens and settled his claims for $250,000 and another $10,000 in attorney fees. Wright was also awarded Social Security disability benefits.

    In January 1995, Wright, whose doctor had approved his return to work, returned to the hiring hall and asked to be referred for work. Wright did work between January 2 and January 11, 1995, but when the companies realized that Wright had been certified as permanently disabled, they deemed him not qualified for longshoreman work under the CBA and refused to allow him to work for them.

    Wright did not file a grievance under the union agreement but instead hired a lawyer and proceeded with a claim under the Americans with Disabilities Act. The district court dismissed the case because Wright had failed to pursue the grievance procedure provided by the CBA. Must Wright pursue the dispute procedure first, or can he go right to court on the basis of his federal rights under the Americans with Disabilities Act? [*Wright v. Universal Maritime Service Corp.*, 525 U.S. 70]

12. Winona Ryder was arrested for shoplifting from Saks Fifth Avenue in California. One of the members of the jury panel for her trial was Peter Guber, a Hollywood executive in charge of the production of three films in which Ms. Ryder starred, including *Bram Stoker's Dracula, The Age of Innocence*, and *Little Women*. If you were the prosecuting attorney in the case, how could you discover such information about this potential juror, and what are your options for excluding him from selection? [Rick Lyman, "For the Ryder Trial, a Hollywood Script," *New York Times*, November 3, 2002, SL-1]

13. Two doctors had a dispute over who was doing how much work at their clinic. Their dispute was submitted to arbitration and the arbitrator held in favor of the less experienced doctor. The senior doctor wants the arbitration set aside. Is it possible for the arbitrator's decision to be set aside?

14. Martha Simms is the plaintiff in a contract suit she has brought against Floral Supply, Inc., for its failure to deliver the green sponge Martha needed in building the floral designs she sells to exclusive home decorators. Martha had to obtain the sponge from another supplier and was late on seven deliveries. One of Martha's customers has been called by Martha's lawyer as a witness and is now on the witness stand, testifying about Martha's late performance and the penalty she charged. The lawyer for Floral Supply knows that Martha's customer frequently waives penalties for good suppliers. How can Floral Supply's lawyer get that information before the jury?

15. Saint Claire Adams was hired by Circuit City as a sales counselor. When he was hired he signed an employment contract that included a mandatory arbitration clause. Two years later he filed a suit against Circuit City for discrimination in the workplace. Circuit City moved to have the suit dismissed because of the arbitration requirement. Mr. Adams responded that he has certain rights under Title VII of the federal anti-discrimination laws that cannot be taken away through an arbitration clause. Is he correct? [*Circuit City Stores, Inc. v. Adams*, 532 U.S. 105]

CHAPTER 4

The Constitution as the Foundation of the Legal Environment

Learning Outcomes

After studying this chapter, you should be able to

LO.1 Describe the U.S. Constitution and the federal system

LO.2 Explain the relationship between the U.S. Constitution and the states

LO.3 Discuss interpreting and amending the Constitution

LO.4 List and describe the significant federal powers

LO.5 Discuss constitutional limitations on governmental power

4-1 The U.S. Constitution and the Federal System

federal system–the system of government in which a central government is given power to administer to national concerns while individual states retain the power to administer to local concerns.

The Constitution of the United States establishes the structure and powers of government but also the limitations on those powers. This Constitution forms the foundation of our legal environment. By establishing a central government to coexist with the governments of the individual states, the U.S. Constitution created a federal system. In a **federal system,** a central government has power to address national concerns while the individual states retain the power to handle local concerns.

4-1a What a Constitution Is

constitution–a body of principles that establishes the structure of a government and the relationship of the government to the people who are governed.

A **constitution** is the written document that establishes the structure of the government and its relationship to the people. The U.S. Constitution was adopted in 1789 by the 13 colonies that had won their independence from King George.[1]

4-1b The Branches of Government

tripartite–three-part division (of government).

legislative branch–the branch of government (e.g., Congress) formed to make the laws.

executive branch–the branch of government (e.g., the president) formed to execute the laws.

judicial branch–the branch of government (e.g., the courts) formed to interpret the laws.

bicameral–a two-house form of the legislative branch of government.

The U.S. Constitution establishes a **tripartite** (three-part) government: a **legislative branch** (Congress) to make the laws, an **executive branch** (the president) to execute or enforce the laws, and a **judicial branch** (courts) to interpret the laws.[2] The national legislature or Congress is a **bicameral** (two-house) body consisting of the Senate and the House of Representatives. Members of the Senate are popularly elected for a term of six years. Members of the House of Representatives are popularly elected for a term of two years. The president is elected by an electoral college whose membership is popularly elected. The president serves for a term of four years and is eligible for reelection for a second term. Judges of the United States are appointed by the president with the approval of the Senate and serve for life, subject to removal only by impeachment because of misconduct. (See Chapter 2 for a discussion of the federal court system.)

4-2 The U.S. Constitution and the States

The Constitution created certain powers within the national government that would have been exercised by the individual states, which are given their powers by the people of the state. Figure 4-1 illustrates the delegation of powers. Likewise, the states, as the power-granting authorities, reserved certain powers for themselves.

4-2a Delegated and Shared Powers

Delegated Powers

delegated powers–powers expressly granted the national government by the Constitution.

The powers given by the states to the national government are described as *delegated powers.* Some of these **delegated powers** are given exclusively to the national government. **For Example,** the national government alone may declare war or establish a currency.

[1] U.S. Const., Art 1, §8, cl 1. To read more of the U.S. Constitution, refer to Appendix 2, or go to **http://www.constitution.org** and click on "Founding Documents."

[2] *Free Enterprise Fund v. Public Company Accounting Oversight Board,* 561 U.S. 477 (2010).

FIGURE 4-1 Governments of the United States

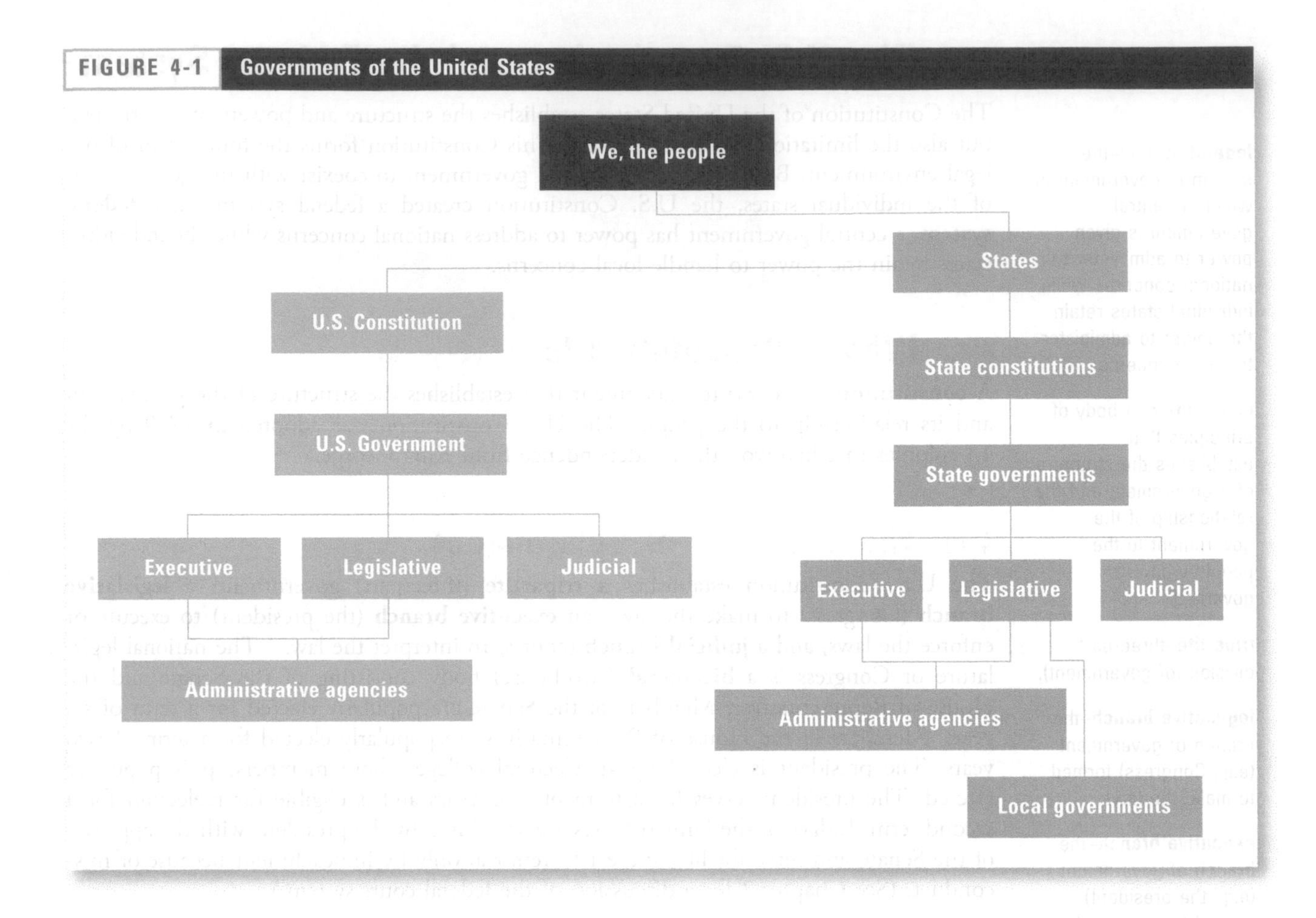

Shared Powers

shared powers–powers that are held by both state and national governments.

The powers delegated to the national government that may still be exercised by the states are **shared powers. For Example,** the grant of power to the national government to impose taxes did not destroy the state power to tax. In other cases, a state may provide regulation along with, but subject to the supremacy of, federal law. **For Example,** regulation of the use of navigable waterways within a state is an example of joint state and federal regulation.

4-2b Other Powers

police power–the power to govern; the power to adopt laws for the protection of the public health, welfare, safety, and morals.

***ex post facto* law**–a law making criminal an act that was lawful when done or that increases the penalty when done. Such laws are generally prohibited by constitutional provisions.

Police Power of the States

The states possess the power to adopt laws to protect the general welfare, health, safety, and morals of the people. This authority is called the **police power. For Example,** states may require that businesses be licensed with state agencies to protect persons dealing with the business. State exercise of the police power may not unreasonably interfere with federal powers.

Prohibited Powers

The Constitution also prohibits both states and the federal government from doing certain things. **For Example,** neither states nor the national government may adopt ***ex post facto* laws,** which make criminal an act that has already been committed but was not criminal when it was committed. Laws that increase the penalty for an act already committed above the penalty in force when the act was committed are also *ex post facto* laws.

4-2c Federal Supremacy

preemption–the federal government's superior regulatory position over state laws on the same subject area.

States cannot enact conflicting state regulation if the congressional intent to regulate exclusively can be inferred from the details of congressional regulation. **Preemption** means that the federal regulatory scheme is controlling.

Express Federal Regulation

The Constitution and statutes passed by Congress are the supreme law of the land. They cancel out any conflicting state law.[3] When a direct conflict exists between federal and state statutes, federal law prevails.

In some cases, however, no obvious conflict occurs because the federal statute covers only part of the subject matter. In such cases, the question becomes whether a state law can regulate the areas not regulated by Congress or whether the partial regulation made by Congress preempts, or takes over, the field so as to preclude state legislation.

CASE SUMMARY

Generic Preemption: Controlling Who Recovers for Pharma Injuries

FACTS: In 1978, the FDA approved an anti-inflammatory pain reliever called "sulindac" under the brand name of "Clinoril." When the patent expired, the FDA approved several generic versions of sulindac for sale, including one developed by Mutual Pharmaceutical (Petitioner). The warnings for Clinoril included the possibility of developing toxic epidermal necrolysis. Karen Bartlett (Respondent) took a generic form of sulindac in December 2004 and developed an acute case of toxic epidermal necrolysis. Sixty to sixty-five percent of Ms. Bartlett's body deteriorated, was burned off, or turned into an open wound. She spent months in a medically induced coma, underwent 12 eye surgeries, and was tube-fed for a year. She is now severely disfigured, has a number of physical disabilities, and is nearly blind.

At the time Ms. Bartlett got her sulindac prescription, the label did not refer to toxic epidermal necrolysis but warned that the drug could cause "severe skin reactions" and "fatalities." Toxic epidermal necrolysis was listed as a side effect in the package insert. After Ms. Bartlett was suffering from toxic epidermal necrolysis, the FDA did a comprehensive study and recommended that the product label include more explicit warnings about toxic epidermal necrolysis.

Ms. Bartlett sued Mutual in New Hampshire state court, and Mutual removed the case to federal court. Ms. Bartlett initially asserted both failure-to-warn and design-defect claims, but the District Court dismissed her failure-to-warn claim based on her doctor's "admi[ssion] that he had not read the box label or insert."

After a two-week trial on a design-defect claim, a jury found Mutual liable and awarded Ms. Bartlett over $21 million in damages. The Court of Appeals affirmed, and Mutual appealed. The U.S. Supreme Court granted *certiorari.*

DECISION: The court held that the federal law was clear that a generic manufacturer could not change the label, and it was the purpose of the law to provide a cheap way to get the drugs out there once the patent was expired. Generic manufacturers were to just use the same warnings provided by the brand name pharmaceutical company, without variation. Until there was a change in the label under FDA processes and standards, the generic manufacturer could not make additions or changes, and federal law preempted state laws on product liability recovery. ***[Mutual Pharmaceutical Co., Inc. v. Bartlett,* 133 S. Ct. 2466 (2013)]**

[3] U.S. Const., Art VI, cl 2 *PLIVA, Inc. v. Mensing,* 131 S. Ct. 2567 (2013).

Silence of Congress

In some situations, the silence of Congress in failing to cover a particular subject area indicates that Congress does not want any law on the matter. However, when national uniformity is essential, the silence of Congress generally means that the subject has been preempted for practical reasons by Congress and that no state law on the subject may be adopted.

Effect of Federal Deregulation

The fact that the federal government removes the regulations from a regulated industry does not automatically give the states the power to regulate that industry. If under the silence-of-Congress doctrine the states cannot regulate, they are still barred from regulating after deregulation. **For Example,** deregulation of banks in the 1980s did not mean that the states could step in and regulate those banks.[4]

4-3 Interpreting and Amending the Constitution

The Constitution as it is interpreted today has changed greatly from the Constitution as originally written. The change has been brought about by interpretation, amendment, and practice.

4-3a Conflicting Theories

Shortly after the Constitution was adopted, conflict arose over whether it was to be interpreted strictly, so as to give the federal government the least power possible, or broadly, so as to give the federal government the greatest power that the words would permit. These two views may be called the *bedrock view* and the *living-document view*, respectively.

bedrock view–a strict constructionist interpretation of a constitution.

living-document view–the term used when a constitution is interpreted according to changes in conditions.

In the **bedrock view,** or strict constructionist or originalist view, the purpose of a constitution is to state certain fundamental principles for all time. In the **living-document view,** a constitution is merely a statement of goals and objectives and is intended to grow and change with time.

Whether the Constitution is to be liberally interpreted under the living-document view or narrowly interpreted under the bedrock view has a direct effect on the Constitution. For the last century, the Supreme Court has followed the living-document view. This view has resulted in strengthening the power of the federal government, permitting the rise of administrative agencies, and expanding the protection of human rights.

One view is not selected to the exclusion of the other. As contradictory as these two views sound, the Constitution remains durable. We do not want a set of New Year's resolutions that will soon be forgotten. At the same time, we know that the world changes, and, therefore, we do not want a constitution that will hold us tied in a straitjacket of the past.

In terms of social forces that make the law, we are torn between our desire for stability and our desire for flexibility. We want a constitution that is stable. At the same time, we want one that is flexible.

[4] For a discussion of preemption of state regulation of airline advertising when federal regulation of air travel is so pervasive, see *New York v. Trans World Airlines,* 556 N.Y.S.2d 803 (1990) and *Pan American World Airways, Inc. v. Abrams,* 764 F. Supp. 864 (S.D.N.Y. 1991). See also footnote 3 for another case on pharmaceutical preemption and *People ex rel. Cuomo v. Greenberg,* 95 A.D.3d 474, 946 N.Y.S.2d 1 (N.Y.A.D. 2012).

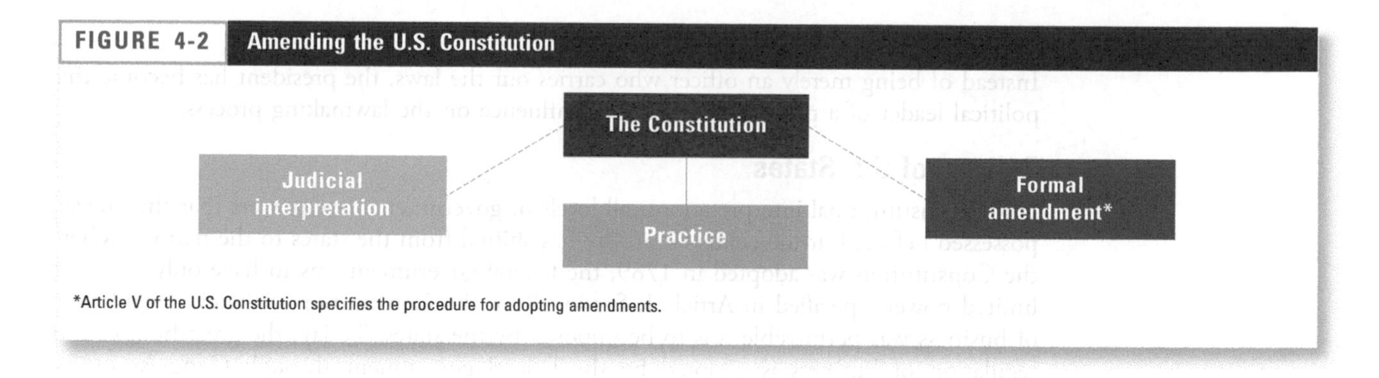

4-3b Amending the Constitution

The Constitution has been amended in three ways: (1) expressly, (2) by interpretation, and (3) by practice. Figure 4-2 illustrates these three methods of amendment.

Constitutional Method of Amending

Article V of the Constitution gives the procedure to be followed for amending the Constitution. Relatively few changes have been made to the Constitution by this formal process, although thousands of proposals have been made. Since the time of its adoption, there have been only 27 amendments to the Constitution.[5]

Amendment by Judicial Interpretation

The U.S. Supreme Court has made the greatest changes to the written Constitution by interpreting it. Generally, interpretation is used to apply the Constitution to a new situation that could not have been foreseen when the written Constitution was adopted.

Amendment by Practice

In practice, the letter of the Constitution is not always followed. Departure from the written Constitution began as early as 1793 when George Washington refused to make treaties as required by the Constitution, by and with the consent of the Senate. Washington began the practice of the president's negotiating a treaty with a foreign country and then submitting it to the Senate for approval. This practice has been followed since that time. Similarly, the electoral college was originally intended to exercise independent judgment in selecting the president, but it now automatically elects the official candidate of the party that elected the majority of the members of the electoral college.

4-3c The Living Constitution

The living Constitution has the following characteristics.

Strong Government

One of the characteristics of the new Constitution is strong government. Business enterprises are highly regulated and the economy is controlled through monetary policy.

[5] Gregory Watson, a University of Texas at Austin student who was doing research for a paper for a class on the U.S. Constitution, ran across a 1789 proposed amendment to the Constitution that had never been ratified by the states. Watson wrote a paper and got a "C" but through a successful letter-writing campaign was able to get the 27th Amendment passed. The amendment reads, "No law, varying the compensation for the services of the Senators and Representatives, shall take effect, until an election of Representatives shall have intervened."

Strong President

Instead of being merely an officer who carries out the laws, the president has become the political leader of a party, exerting strong influence on the lawmaking process.

Eclipse of the States

Under constitutional interpretations, all levels of government have powers that they never possessed before, but the center of gravity has shifted from the states to the nation. When the Constitution was adopted in 1789, the federal government was to have only the very limited powers specified in Article I, Section 8, of the Constitution. Whatever regulation of business was permissible was to be imposed by the states. Today, the great bulk of the regulation of business is adopted by the federal government through Congress or its administrative agencies. As the U.S. economy moved from the local community stage to the nationwide and then international stages, individual states could no longer provide effective regulation of business. Regulation migrated to the central government.

Administrative Agencies

These units of government were virtually unheard of in 1789, and the Constitution made no mention of them. The vast powers of the new Constitution are exercised to a very large degree by administrative agencies. They are in effect a fourth branch of the government, not provided for in the written Constitution. More importantly, the administrative agencies are the ones that come in contact with the majority of businesspersons and citizens.

Agencies have had a significant amount of power delegated to them. The members and heads of the agencies, boards, or commissions are not elected by the voters (see Chapter 6). They are appointed by the president and, at certain levels of appointment in the agency, must be approved by Congress.

4-4 Federal Powers

The federal government possesses powers necessary to administer matters of national concern.

4-4a The Power to Regulate Commerce

The desire to protect commerce from restrictions and barriers set up by the individual states was a prime factor leading to the adoption of the Constitution of 1789. To protect commerce, Congress was given Article I, Section 8, Clause 3—now known as the **commerce clause**—the power "to regulate commerce with foreign nations, and among the several states, and with the Indian tribes."[6]

commerce clause–that section of the U.S. Constitution allocating business regulation between federal and state governments.

Until 1937, the Supreme Court held that this provision gave Congress the power to control or regulate only that commerce crossing a state line, such as an interstate railway train or an interstate telegraph message.

The Commerce Power Becomes a General Welfare Power

In 1937, the Supreme Court began expanding the concept of interstate commerce. By 1946, the power to regulate interstate commerce had become very broad. By that year, the power had expanded to the point that it gave authority to Congress to adopt regulatory laws that were "as broad as the economic needs of the nation."[7] By virtue of this broad interpretation, Congress can regulate manufacturing, agriculture, mining, stock

[6] U.S. Const., Art 1, §8, cl 1. To read more of the U.S. Constitution, refer to Appendix 2, or go to **http://www.constitution.org** and click on "Founding Documents."
[7] *American Power & Light Co. v. Securities and Exchange Commission,* 329 U.S. 90 (1946).

exchanges, insurance, loan sharking, monopolies, and conspiracies in restraint of trade. The far reach of the interstate commerce power is seen in the Freedom of Access to Clinic Entrances Act,[8] which prohibits obstruction of entrances to clinics, as well as in the commerce clause challenges to the Affordable Health Care Act, also known as Obama Care.[9]

The case that was the beginning point in the transition of the commerce clause was *NLRB v. Jones & Laughlin Steel*, 301 U.S. 1 (1937). The "affectation" doctrine expanded the authority of the federal government under the commerce clause. At that time, the Court concluded, "If it is interstate commerce that feels the pinch, it does not matter how local the squeeze."

The Commerce Clause Today

Today, judicial review of the commerce clause typically finds some connection between the legislation and congressional authority. However, the U.S. Supreme Court has found some areas Congress may not regulate and has placed some limitations on the commerce clause. These constraints on the commerce clause focus on the nature of the underlying activity being regulated. So long as the federal regulation relates to economic/commercial activity, it is constitutional. If, however, the underlying activity is not economic and only may have an economic impact, the Supreme Court has imposed restrictions on congressional authority under the commerce clause. **For Example,** in *U.S. v. Morrison*, 529 U.S. 598 (2000), the Supreme Court held that the Violence Against Women Act was unconstitutional because the underlying activity being regulated was violence, an activity that was not economic. Regulation of economic activity is required in order to survive constitutional scrutiny under the commerce clause.

CASE SUMMARY

Mandating Health Insurance under the Commerce Clause

FACTS: Congress passed the Patient Protection and Affordable Care Act (also known as Obama Care) in order to increase the number of Americans covered by health insurance and decrease the cost of health care. One key provision in the law is the individual mandate, which requires most Americans to maintain "minimum essential" health insurance coverage. Attorneys general from several states, along with businesses, challenged this requirement (and other provisions of the law) as being unconstitutional under the commerce clause. From a series of federal court decisions below, some finding the law constitutional and others not, the affected parties appealed and the Supreme Court granted *certiorari.* Their cases were consolidated for the court's review.

DECISION: The court faced a new commerce clause issue of whether the federal government could require citizens to purchase a good or service because the lack of health insurance affected commerce. In the 5-4 decision, the court concluded, "The individual mandate, however, does not regulate existing commercial activity. It instead compels individuals to *become* active in commerce by purchasing a product, on the ground that their failure to do so affects interstate commerce. Construing the Commerce Clause to permit Congress to regulate individuals precisely *because* they are doing nothing would open a new and potentially vast domain to congressional authority. Every day individuals do not do an infinite number of things. In some cases they decide not to do something; in others they simply fail to do it. Allowing Congress to justify federal regulation by pointing to the effect of inaction on commerce would bring countless decisions an individual could *potentially* make within the scope of federal regulation, and—under the Government's theory—empower Congress to make those decisions for him." ***[National Federation of Independent Business v. Sebelius,* 132 S. Ct. 2566 (2012)] (Note: The law was still upheld.)**

[8] 18 U.S.C. §248.

[9] *United States v. Wilson,* 73 F.3d 675 (7th Cir. 1995), *cert. denied,* 519 U.S. 806 (1996), *Florida ex rel. National Federation of Independent Business v. Sebelius,* 132 S. Ct. 2566 (2012).

The Commerce Power as a Limitation on States

The federal power to regulate commerce not only gives Congress the power to act but also prevents states from acting in any way that interferes with federal regulation or burdens interstate commerce. **For Example,** if the federal government establishes safety device regulations for interstate carriers, a state cannot require different devices.

CASE SUMMARY

Minors in Maine and a Major Commerce Clause Decision

FACTS: Maine passed a law that prohibited anyone other than a Maine-licensed tobacco retailer from accepting an order for delivery of tobacco. The law required the retailer to arrange for delivery with a special receipt showing that someone over the age of 18 had received and signed for the tobacco products delivered. Out-of-state shippers and tobacco sellers challenged the law as one that favored Maine tobacco retailers. The state of Maine argued that its law was passed to prevent the public health hazard of minors becoming addicted to tobacco. The federal district court granted summary judgment for the shippers, and the court of appeals affirmed. The state of Maine appealed.

DECISION: In a 9 to 0 decision, the Court held that the Maine law may have been passed with health benefits in mind, but it clearly gave Maine businesses an economic benefit. In addition, other states had managed to fight teen smoking using programs other than discrimination between in-state and out-of-state tobacco retailers. **[*Rowe v. New Hampshire Motor Transport Association,* 552 U.S. 364 (2008)]**

States may not use their tax power for the purpose of discriminating against interstate commerce. **For Example,** a state cannot impose a higher tax on goods imported from another state than it imposes on the same kind of goods produced in its own territory.

State regulations designed to advance local interests may conflict with the commerce clause. Such regulations are invalid. For example, suppose a state has a health concern about having milk properly processed. One way to address the concern is to require all milk to be processed in-state. Such a regulation clearly favors that state's businesses and imposes a great burden on out-of-state milk producers. Such a regulation would be an unconstitutional exercise of state power because the state could simply require all milk sellers to be licensed. Licensing would allow the state to check the milk-processing procedures of all firms and accomplish the safety goal without imposing such a burden on out-of-state firms.[10] For example, in *Granholm v. Heald,* 544 U.S. 460 (2005), both New York and Michigan statutes prohibited out-of-state wine producers from selling their wines directly to consumers there. In-state wineries could sell directly to consumers. The impact of the prohibition on the out-of-state wine producers was that they were required to pay wholesaler fees and thus could not compete with in-state wine producers on direct-to-consumer sales.

The court held that state laws violated the commerce clause because they treated in-state and out-of-state economic interests differently with the result being that one benefits and the other is burdened. The mere fact that a wine producer is not a resident of the state should not foreclose access to markets there.[11]

[10] *Minnesota v. Clover Leaf Creamery,* 449 U.S. 456 (1981).

[11] *Missouri v. Harris,* 58 F. Supp. 3d 1059 (E.D. Cal. 2014) – in this case a federal judge dismissed a complaint brought by egg farmers in six states who are prohibited from selling their eggs in California unless they meet the nonconfinement standards of California's Proposition 2, which requires that chickens be able to lie down, stand up, and fully extend their limbs.

4-4b The Financial Powers

The financial powers of the federal government include the powers to tax and to borrow, spend, and coin money.

The Taxing Power

The federal Constitution provides that "Congress shall have power to lay and collect taxes, duties, imposts and excises, to pay the debts and provide for the common defence and general welfare of the United States."[12] Subject to the express and implied limitations arising from the Constitution, the states may impose such taxes as they desire and as their own individual constitutions and statutes permit. In addition to express constitutional limitations, both national and local taxes are subject to the unwritten limitation that they be imposed for a public purpose. Taxes must also be apportioned. A business cannot be taxed for all of its revenues in all 50 states. There must be apportionment of taxes, and there must be sufficient connection with the state.[13] **For Example,** in *Quill v. North Dakota,* 504 U.S. 298 (1992), Quill, an office equipment and supplies seller, did business in North Dakota through catalogs and flyers, advertisements in national periodicals, and telephone calls. Quill delivered all of its merchandise to its North Dakota customers by mail or common carriers from out-of-state locations. North Dakota imposed sales tax requirements on Quill. The U.S. Supreme Court held that the exercise of the taxing authority placed an undue burden on commerce and retailers such as Quill and that the standard of a company's presence in the state through property or personnel was required to impose taxes.

CASE SUMMARY

Booking Sales Tax Revenue Against BarnesandNoble.com

FACTS: The facts of this case are not in dispute. Barnesandnoble.com LLC (Bn.com) is a Delaware corporation that sells books, movies, and other media over the Internet. In 2006, the New Mexico Taxation and Revenue Department (the Department) assessed gross receipts tax against bn.com on its sales to New Mexico residents during a period from January 1998 through July 2005. Bn.com protested the assessment, and a hearing officer granted summary judgment to bn.com, finding that it lacked a substantial nexus with the state of New Mexico, and, therefore, it could not constitutionally be required to pay the tax. The Department appealed, and the Court of Appeals held that bn.com had a substantial nexus with the state. bn.com appealed.

DECISION: The court found the following interconnected activities of the stores (Booksellers): (1) Booksellers' promotion of bn.com through sales of gift cards redeemable at bn.com and bearing bn.com's name, (2) Booksellers' policy of sharing customers' e-mail addresses with bn.com, (3) Booksellers' implicit endorsement of bn.com through the companies' shared loyalty program and Booksellers' return policy, and (4) Booksellers' in-state use of Barnes & Noble logos and trademarks, which bn.com also used. Because Booksellers' activities in New Mexico were significantly associated with bn.com's ability to establish and maintain a market here, bn.com had a substantial nexus with the state of New Mexico. Therefore, New Mexico may collect gross receipts tax on bn.com's sales in the state without offending the commerce clause of the United States Constitution. Affirmed and remanded. ***[New Mexico Taxation and Revenue Department v. BarnesandNoble.com LLC,* 303 P.3d 824 (N.M. 2014)]**

[12] U.S. Const., Art 1, §8, cl 1. To read more of the U.S. Constitution, refer to Appendix 2, or go to **http://www.constitution.org** and click on "Founding Documents."

[13] *Polar Tankers, Inc. v. City of Valdez, Alaska,* 557 U.S. 1 (2009).

E-COMMERCE & CYBERLAW

Internet and Interstate

Collection of sales tax from Internet stores has been a stickler of an issue for businesses, state revenue officials, and the U.S. Supreme Court. All three were grappling with how to collect, what to collect, and whether anybody had any authority to collect. Internet sales represent a large, untapped source of revenue. A study from the Center for Business and Economic Research at the University of Tennessee estimated the lost tax revenue from untaxed Internet sales as $30 billion in 2011.

The merchants involved fell into different legal groups in terms of their theories on whether tax was owed and whether they should just pay it, with or without the states having the authority to tax:

1. Those stores with physical presences in states (Wal-Mart and J.C. Penney) that just collected sales tax as if they were collecting it in a store in that state where the Internet purchaser was located
2. Those stores without a physical presence (Amazon) that did collect taxes, particularly in those states known for taking a hard-line approach
3. Those stores without a physical presence that do not collect taxes and maintain that it is unconstitutional to do so
4. Those stores with or without a physical presence that have collected taxes but held them until everyone could figure out the legal status of the companies

What are the constitutional issues in this taxation question?

Amazon has negotiated with most states on sales tax issues and you can notice as a buyer that you pay some form of tax on your Amazon purchases now.

Source: Stu Woo, "Amazon Battles States Over Sales Tax," *Wall Street Journal*, August 3, 2011, p. A1.

The Spending Power

The federal government may use tax money and borrowed money "to pay the debts and provide for the common defence and general welfare of the United States."[14]

4-5 Constitutional Limitations on Government

The constitutional limitations discussed in the following sections afford protections of rights for both persons and businesses.

4-5a Due Process

The power of government is limited by both the Fifth and Fourteenth Amendments to the Constitution. Those amendments, respectively, prohibit the national government and state governments from depriving any person "of life, liberty, or property without due process of law."[15]

When Due Process Rights Arise

due process clause–a guarantee of protection against the loss of property or rights without the chance to be heard.

As a result of liberal interpretation of the Constitution, the **due process clause** now provides a guarantee of protection against the loss of property or rights without the chance to be heard. These amendments also guarantee that all citizens are given the same protections. **For Example,** the Supreme Court has extended the due process clause to protect

[14] U.S. Const., Art 1, §8, cl 1. To read more of the U.S. Constitution, refer to Appendix 2, or go to **http://www.constitution.org** and click on "Founding Documents."

[15] U.S. Const., Art 1, §8, cl 1. To read more of the U.S. Constitution, refer to Appendix 2, or go to **http://www.constitution.org** and click on "Founding Documents."

the record or standing of a student.[16] A student cannot lose credit in a course or be suspended or expelled without some form of a hearing.

Because there are so many areas in which due process rights exist and require a chance to be heard, speeding up due process has resulted in the creation of **quasi-judicial proceedings.** In these types of proceedings, the parties need not go through the complex, lengthy, and formal procedures of a trial (described in Chapter 2). Rather, these proceedings have a hearing officer or administrative law judge (see Chapter 6) who conducts an informal hearing in which the rules of evidence and procedure are relaxed.

quasi-judicial proceedings–forms of hearings in which the rules of evidence and procedure are more relaxed but each side still has a chance to be heard.

For Example, a student taking a grade grievance beyond a faculty member's decision will generally have his case heard by a panel of faculty and students as established by college or university rules. An employer appealing its unemployment tax rate will have the appeal heard by an administrative law judge.

What Constitutes Due Process?

Due process does not require a trial on every issue of rights. Shortcut procedures, such as grade grievance panels, have resulted as a compromise for providing the right to be heard along with a legitimate desire to be expeditious in resolving these issues. In *Horne v. U.S. Department of Agriculture*, 132 S. Ct. 2566 (2015), raisin farmers challenged the taking of their raisin crops by the Department of Agriculture in its efforts to stabilize the raisin market. The farmers' challenge was based on their lack of a hearing for the taking as well as compensation for the loss of their raisin crops and the imposition of penalties if they sold the raisins prohibited by the Department of Agriculture. The court held that the Fifth Amendment requires that the government pay just compensation when it takes personal property, just as when it takes real property. The government cannot make raisin growers relinquish their raisins without just compensation.

4-5b Equal Protection of the Law

The Constitution prohibits the states and the national government from denying any person the equal protection of the law.[17] This guarantee prohibits a government from treating one person differently from another when there is no reasonable ground for classifying them differently.

For Example, laws that make distinctions in the regulation of business, the right to work, and the right to use or enjoy property on the basis of race, national origin, or religion are invalid. Also invalid are laws that impose restrictions on some, but not all, persons without any justification for the distinction.[18] **For Example,** a state statute taxing out-of-state insurance companies at a higher rate than in-state insurance companies violates the equal protection clause.[19]

4-5c Privileges and Immunities

The U.S. Constitution declares that "the citizens of each state shall be entitled to all privileges and immunities of citizens in the several states."[20] The so-called **privileges and immunities clause** means that a person going into another state is entitled to make

privileges and immunities clause–a clause that entitles a person going into another state to make contracts, own property, and engage in business to the same extent as citizens of that state.

[16] That is, a student cannot be expelled without a chance to have his or her side of the story reviewed.

[17] U.S. Constitution, Fourteenth Amendment as to the states; modern interpretation of due process clause of the Fifth Amendment as to national government. Congress adopted the Civil Rights Act to implement the concept of equal protection.

[18] *Associated Industries of Missouri v. Lohman,* 511 U.S. 641 (1994).

[19] *Metropolitan Life Ins. Co. v. Ward,* 470 U.S. 869 (1985). But see a differing view on distinctive treatment of temporary bridge contractors vs. permanent bridge contractors, *Mabey Bridge & Shore, Inc. v. Schoch,* 666 F.3d 862 (3rd Cir. 2012).

[20] U.S. Const., Art 1, §8, cl 1. To read more of the U.S. Constitution, refer to Appendix 2, or go to **http://www.constitution.org** and click on "Founding Documents."

contracts, own property, and engage in business to the same extent as the citizens of that state. **For Example,** a state cannot bar someone who comes from another state from engaging in local business or from obtaining a hunting or fishing license merely because the person is not a resident of that state.

4-5d Protection of the Person

The Constitution has no general provision declaring that the government shall not impair rights of persons. The Constitution does not mention the phrase *unalienable right* that was part of the Declaration of Independence.[21] However, the Bill of Rights, the first 10 amendments to the Constitution, does provide protections for freedom of speech, jury trials, and freedom of religion and association.[22] The Bill of Rights provides for the due process protections discussed earlier as well as those that prohibit unlawful searches and seizures. The Second Amendment provides for the right to keep and bear arms, an issue that has resulted in some conflicting decisions that the U.S. Supreme Court has begun to address.[23]

During the last six decades, the Supreme Court has been interpreting the rights in these amendments and has been finding constitutional protection for a wide array of rights of the person that are not expressly protected by the Constitution. **For Example,** judicial interpretations have concluded that the Constitution provides for the right of privacy, the rights related to marriage,[24] protection from unreasonable zoning, protection of parental control, protection from discrimination because of poverty, and protection from gender discrimination.[25]

4-5e The Bill of Rights and Businesses as Persons

The Bill of Rights provides protections for individuals and also for corporations. **For Example,** the Fourth Amendment (see Chapter 7) provides protections against unreasonable searches. Individuals enjoy that protection in their homes, and corporations enjoy that protection with their files, offices, and business records. Businesses also enjoy freedom of speech protections under the First Amendment. The First Amendment provides that "Congress shall make no law … abridging the freedom of speech …"[26]

The U.S. Supreme Court has clarified the free speech rights of business through classification of the types of business speech. One form of business or commercial speech is advertising. This form of speech in which businesses tout their products is subject to regulation and restriction on form, content, and placement, and such regulation has been deemed constitutional. (See Chapters 24 and 32 for more information on the regulation of advertising.) However, there are other forms of commercial speech. Businesses do have the right to participate in political processes, such as creating

[21] The term *unalienable right* is employed in reference to natural right, fundamental right, or basic right. Apart from the question of scope of coverage, the adjective *unalienable* emphasizes the fact that the people still possess the right rather than having surrendered or subordinated it to the will of society. The word *alien* is the term of the old common law for transferring title or ownership. Today, we would say *transfer* and, instead of saying *unalienable* rights, would say *nontransferable* rights. Unalienable rights of the people were therefore rights that the people not only possessed but also could not give up even if they wanted to. Thus, these rights are still owned by everyone. It is important to note that the Declaration of Independence actually uses the word *unalienable* when describing the rights eventually placed in the Constitution as Amendments I–X, the Bill of Rights, not *inalienable.*

[22] *North Coast Women's Care Medical Group, Inc. v. San Diego County Superior Court,* 189 P.3d 959 (Ca. 2008).

[23] *District of Columbia v. Heller,* 554 U.S. 570 (2008).

[24] *U.S. v. Windsor,* 133 S. Ct. 2675 (2013).

[25] In some cases, the courts have given the due process and equal protection clauses a liberal interpretation in order to find a protection of the person; *Fisher v. University of Texas at Austin,* 133 S. Ct. 2411 (2013). *Certiorari* granted following a remand. 2015 WL 629286 (2015).

[26] For more on commercial speech, see Greater New Orleans Broadcasting Association, Inc., v. U.S., 527 U.S. 173 (1999) and *U.S. v. Philip Morris USA Inc.,* 566 F.3d 1095 (D.C. Cir. 2009). To read the full language of the First Amendment, go to Appendix 2, or to **http://www.constitution.org** and click on "Founding Documents."

political action committees and supporting or opposing ballot initiatives. Businesses often take positions and launch campaigns on ballot initiatives that will affect the taxes they will be required to pay. The courts are often balancing the power of corporate political speech, regulation of ads, and the right of corporations as citizens to speak.

CASE SUMMARY

The Case That Caused a Dust-Up between the President and a Justice

FACTS: In January 2008, Citizens United released a film entitled *Hillary: The Movie (Hillary)*, a 90-minute documentary about then-senator Hillary Clinton, who was a candidate in the Democratic Party's 2008 presidential primary elections. Most of the commentators in the film were quite critical of Senator Clinton. *Hillary* was released in theaters and on DVD, but Citizens United wanted to increase distribution by making it available through video-on-demand.

Citizens United produced two 10-second ads and one 30-second ad for *Hillary*. Each ad included a short, pejorative statement about Senator Clinton, followed by the name of the movie and the movie's Web site address. Citizens United wanted to run the advertisements on broadcast and cable television. The Federal Election Commission (FEC) wanted to stop Citizens United from running the ads and Citizens United brought suit, seeking a preliminary injunction against the FEC. The District Court denied Citizens United a preliminary injunction and granted the FEC summary judgment. Citizens United requested and was granted *certiorari.*

DECISION: The court held that the restrictions on running ads were unconstitutional as a prior restraint on speech as well as discrimination between and among speakers. The court held that requirements on disclosure of funding for ads was constitutional, an alternative to a ban on speech that was reasonable and allowed citizens to make their own determinations about the quality/bias of the speech (ads). President Obama spoke harshly of the decision in his State of the Union address in 2011, and Justice Samuel Alito mouthed, "Not true," in response to the president's remarks. [***Citizens United v. Federal Election Commission*, 558 U.S. 310 (2010)**]

THINKING THINGS THROUGH

Freedom of Speech and Our Headlights

Fed up with the warning signals and being outnumbered on the highways by drivers looking out for one another, police officers and state troopers began issuing tickets to those who send signals and warnings to drivers so that they can slow down and avoid being caught going above the speed limit. On November 17, 2012, a police officer pulled Michael Elli over and issued a citation for "[f]lashing lights on certain vehicles prohibited; warning of RADAR ahead."

In the case, *Elli v. City of Ellisville*, No. 4:13-CV-711 HEA (E.D. Mo. 2014), Mr. Elli was advised by the municipal judge that the standard punishment imposed in the City of Ellisville for using headlamps to communicate the presence of a speed trap is a $1,000 fine. Mr. Elli told the judge that he wanted to plead not guilty because he did not believe flashing headlamps violated §375.100 of the Ellisville city code. The judge became agitated and asked Mr. Elli if he had ever heard of "obstruction of justice." Mr. Elli then entered a plea of not guilty, and he was ordered to return to court on February 21, 2013. However, the prosecution terminated the case by dismissing the charge prior to the hearing date. Mr. Elli, with the help of the ACLU, filed a civil rights action in federal court.

Have Mr. Elli's rights been violated? Is flashing your headlights a form of speech? What do you think the courts decided?

Make the Connection

Summary

The U.S. Constitution created the structure of our national government and gave it certain powers. It also placed limitations on those powers. It created a federal system with a tripartite division of government and a bicameral national legislature.

The national government possesses some governmental powers exclusively while both the states and the federal government share other powers. In areas of conflict, federal law is supreme.

The U.S. Constitution is not a detailed document. It takes its meaning from the way it is interpreted. In recent years, liberal interpretation has expanded the powers of the federal government. Among the powers of the federal government that directly affect business are the power to regulate commerce; the power to tax and to borrow, spend, and coin money; and the power to own and operate businesses.

Among the limitations on government that are most important to business are the requirements of due process and the requirement of equal protection of the law. In addition, government is limited by the rights given to individuals such as freedom of speech, freedom of religion, and equal protection. The equal protection concept of the U.S. Constitution prohibits both the federal government and the state governments from treating one person differently from another unless there is a legitimate reason for doing so and unless the basis of classification is reasonable.

Learning Outcomes

After studying this chapter, you should be able to clearly explain:

4-1 The U.S. Constitution and the Federal System

LO.1 Describe the U.S. Constitution and the federal system

See the discussion of the tripartite (three-part) government, page 55.

4-2 The U.S. Constitution and the States

LO.2 Explain the relationship between the U.S. Constitution and the states

See the discussion of the federal system, page 55.

See Figure 4-1 for an illustration of the delegation of powers, page 56.

4-3 Interpreting and Amending the Constitution

LO.3 Discuss interpreting and amending the Constitution

See the discussion of the bedrock and living-document views, page 58.

4-4 Federal Powers

LO.4 List and describe the significant federal powers

See the *Bartlett* case, page 57.

See the discussion of the commerce power. See the *Sebelius* case, page 61.

See the discussion of the taxing power and the *Barnes & Noble* case, page 63.

4-5 Constitutional Limitations on Government

LO.5 Discuss constitutional limitations on governmental power

See the discussion of the Bill of Rights, page 66.

See the *Citizens United* case to understand First Amendment issues, page 67.

See the discussion of the Fourth Amendment, page 66.

See the discussion of due process, pages 64–65.

See the *For Example* discussion of a student taking a grade grievance beyond a faculty member's decision, page 65.

Key Terms

bedrock view
bicameral
commerce clause
constitution
delegated powers
due process clause
executive branch
ex post facto laws
federal system
judicial branch
legislative branch
living-document view
police power
preemption
privileges and immunities clause
quasi-judicial proceedings
shared powers
tripartite

Questions and Case Problems

1. Federal law requires most interstate truckers to obtain a permit that reflects compliance with certain federal requirements. The 1965 version of the law authorized states to require proof that a truck operator had such a permit. By 1991, 39 states had demanded such proof, requiring a $10 per truck registration fee and giving each trucker a stamp to affix to a multistate "bingo card" carried in the vehicle. Finding this scheme inefficient and burdensome, Congress created the current Single State Registration System (SSRS), which allows a trucking company to fill out one set of forms in one state, thereby registering in every participating state through which its trucks travel.

    A subsection of Michigan's Motor Carrier Act imposes on truck companies operating in interstate commerce an annual fee of $100 for each self-propelled motor vehicle operated by or on behalf of the motor carrier. The American Truckers Association (ATA) and others challenged the $100 fee as preempted by the extensive federal regulation of interstate trucking and trucking companies. The ATA and others appealed to the U.S. Supreme Court. What should the U.S. Supreme Court do? Be sure to discuss what portion of the Constitution applies to this issue. [*American Trucking Associations, Inc. v. Michigan Public Service Com'n*, 545 U.S. 429]

2. J.C. Penney, a retail merchandiser, has its principal place of business in Plano, Texas. It operates retail stores in all 50 states, including 10 stores in Massachusetts, and a direct mail catalog business. The catalogs illustrated merchandise available for purchase by mail order. The planning, artwork, design, and layout for these catalogs were completed and paid for outside of Massachusetts, primarily in Texas, and Penney contracted with independent printing companies located outside Massachusetts to produce the catalogs. The three major catalogs were generally printed in Indiana, while the specialty catalogs were printed in South Carolina and Wisconsin. Penney supplied the printers with paper, shipping wrappers, and address labels for the catalogs; the printers supplied the ink, binding materials, and labor. None of these materials was purchased in Massachusetts. Printed catalogs, with address labels and postage affixed, were transported by a common carrier from the printer to a U.S. Postal Service office located outside Massachusetts, where they were sent to Massachusetts addressees via third- or fourth-class mail. Any undeliverable catalogs were returned to Penney's distribution center in Connecticut.

    Purchases of catalog merchandise were made by telephoning or returning an order form to Penney at a location outside Massachusetts, and the merchandise was shipped to customers from a Connecticut distribution center. The Massachusetts Department of Revenue audited Penney in 1995 and assessed a use tax, penalty, and interest on the catalogs that had been shipped into Massachusetts. The position of the department was that there was a tax due of $314,674.62 on the catalogs that were used by Penney's Massachusetts customers. Penney said such a tax was unconstitutional in that it had no control or contact with the catalogs in the state. Can the state impose the tax? Why or why not? [*Commissioner of Revenue v. J.C. Penney Co., Inc.*, 730 N.E.2d 266 (Mass)]

3. Alfonso Lopez, Jr., a 12th-grade student at Edison High School in San Antonio, Texas, went to school carrying a concealed .38-caliber handgun and five bullets. School officials, acting on an anonymous tip, confronted Lopez. Lopez admitted that he had the gun. He was arrested and charged with violation of federal law, the Gun-Free School Zones Act of 1990. Lopez moved to dismiss his indictment on the grounds that the provision of the Gun-Free School Zones Act with which he was charged was unconstitutional in that it was beyond the power of Congress to legislate controls over public schools. The district court found the statute to be a constitutional exercise of congressional authority.

    Lopez was found guilty and sentenced to two years in prison. He appealed and challenged his conviction on the basis of the commerce clause. The Court of Appeals agreed with Lopez, found the Gun-Free School Zones Act an unconstitutional exercise of congressional authority, and reversed the conviction. The U.S. Attorney appealed. Who should win at the U.S. Supreme Court and why? [*United States v. Lopez*, 514 U.S. 549]

4. The University of Wisconsin requires all of its students to pay, as part of their tuition, a student activity fee. Those fees are used to support campus clubs and activities. Some students who objected to

the philosophies and activities of some of the student clubs filed suit to have the fees halted. What constitutional basis do you think they could use for the suit? [*Board of Regents of Wisconsin System v. Southworth,* 529 U.S. 217]

5. The Crafts' home was supplied with gas by the city gas company. Because of some misunderstanding, the gas company believed that the Crafts were delinquent in paying their gas bill. The gas company had an informal complaint procedure for discussing such matters, but the Crafts had never been informed that such a procedure was available. The gas company notified the Crafts that they were delinquent and that the company was shutting off the gas. The Crafts brought an action to enjoin the gas company from doing so on the theory that a termination without any hearing was a denial of due process. The lower courts held that the interest of the Crafts in receiving gas was not a property interest protected by the due process clause and that the procedures the gas company followed satisfied the requirements of due process. The Crafts appealed. Were they correct in contending that they had been denied due process of law? Why or why not? [*Memphis Light, Gas and Water Division v. Craft,* 436 U.S. 1]

6. In 2002, the Williamson family, riding in their 1993 Mazda minivan, was struck head-on by another vehicle. Thanh Williamson was sitting in a rear aisle seat, wearing a lap belt; she died in the accident. Delbert and Alexa Williamson were wearing lap-and-shoulder belts; they survived. Thanh's estate brought suit in a California state court to recover from Mazda for her wrongful death. The basis of the suit was that Mazda should have installed lap-and-shoulder belts on all seats, including the rear aisle seats, and that Thanh died because Mazda equipped her seat with only a lap belt instead. Federal safety requirements do not require lap-and-shoulder belts except for seats located next to doors and windows. Middle seats (aisle) can have a lap belt only. Mazda asked for a dismissal on the grounds that allowing Thanh's estate to recover would contradict federal law and that federal law preempts state tort laws on product liability. The trial court dismissed the suit as preempted by federal law, and the Court of Appeal affirmed. The U.S. Supreme Court granted *certiorari.* What should the court decide and why? [*Williamson v. Mazda Motor of America, Inc.,* 562 U.S. 323]

7. Montana imposed a severance tax on every ton of coal mined within the state. The tax varied depending on the value of the coal and the cost of production. It could be as high as 30 percent of the price at which the coal was sold. Montana mine operators and some out-of-state customers claimed that this tax was unconstitutional as an improper burden on interstate commerce. Decide. [*Commonwealth Edison Co. v. Montana,* 453 U.S. 609]

8. Ollie's Barbecue is a family-owned restaurant in Birmingham, Alabama, specializing in barbecued meats and homemade pies, with a seating capacity of 220 customers. It is located on a state highway 11 blocks from an interstate highway and a somewhat greater distance from railroad and bus stations. The restaurant caters to a family and white-collar trade, with a take-out service for "Negroes." (Note: This term is used by the Court in its opinion in the case.) In the 12 months preceding the passage of the Civil Rights Act, the restaurant purchased locally approximately $150,000 worth of food, $69,683 or 46 percent of which was meat that it bought from a local supplier who had procured it from outside the state. Ollie's has refused to serve Negroes in its dining accommodations since opening in 1927, and since July 2, 1964, it has been operating in violation of the Civil Rights Act. A lower court concluded that if it were required to serve Negroes, it would lose a substantial amount of business. The lower court found that the Civil Rights Act did not apply because Ollie's was not involved in "interstate commerce." Will the commerce clause permit application of the Civil Rights Act to Ollie's? [*Katzenbach v. McClung,* 379 U.S. 294]

9. Ellis was employed by the city of Lakewood. By the terms of his contract, he could be discharged only for cause. After working for six years, he was told that he was going to be discharged because of his inability to generate safety and self-insurance programs, because of his failure to win the confidence of employees, and because of his poor attendance. He was not informed of the facts in support of these conclusions and was given the option to resign. He claimed that he was entitled to a hearing. Is he entitled to one? Why or why not? [*Ellis v. City of Lakewood,* 789 P.2d 449 (Colo. App.)]

10. The Federal Food Stamp Act provided for the distribution of food stamps to needy households. In 1971, section 3(e) of the statute was amended to define households as limited to groups whose

members were all related to each other. This was done because of congressional dislike for the lifestyles of unrelated hippies who were living together in hippie communes. Moreno and others applied for food stamps but were refused them because the relationship requirement was not satisfied. An action was brought to have the relationship requirement declared unconstitutional. Is it constitutional? Discuss why or why not. [*USDA v. Moreno,* 413 U.S. 528]

11. New Hampshire adopted a tax law that in effect taxed the income of nonresidents working in New Hampshire only. Austin, a nonresident who worked in New Hampshire, claimed that the tax law was invalid. Was he correct? Explain. [*Austin v. New Hampshire,* 420 U.S. 656]

12. California passed a law that prohibited the sale or rental of "violent video games." The act defined violent video games as games "in which the range of options available to a player includes killing, maiming, dismembering, or sexually assaulting an image of a human being, if those acts are depicted" in a manner that "[a] reasonable person, considering the game as a whole, would find appeals to a deviant or morbid interest of minors." The association of video game manufacturers and developers brought suit, challenging the California statute as an unconstitutional violation of their First Amendment right and a violation of their due process rights because it is so vague. What should the U.S. Supreme Court hold on the constitutionality of the statute and why? [*Brown v. Entertainment Merchants Ass'n,* 131 S. Ct. 2729]

CHAPTER 5

Government Regulation of Competition and Prices

Learning Outcomes

After studying this chapter, you should be able to

LO.1 Explain the powers the government has to be sure free markets are working efficiently

LO.2 List the federal statutes that regulate horizontal markets and competition and give examples of each

LO.3 Describe the federal statutes that regulate the supply chain and vertical markets

LO.4 Discuss the remedies available to protect business competition

5-1 Power to Regulate Business

The federal government may regulate any area of business to advance the nation's national economic needs. Under the police power, states may regulate all aspects of business so long as they do not impose an unreasonable burden on interstate commerce or any activity of the federal government. (See Chapter 4 for a discussion of the protections and limits of the commerce clause.)

5-1a Regulation, Free Enterprise, and Deregulation

Milton Friedman, the Nobel economist, has written that government regulation of business interferes with the free enterprise system. Under a true free enterprise system, market forces would provide the necessary protections through the forces of demand and supply. Sometimes, however, the demand response, or market reaction, to problems or services is not rapid enough to prevent harm, and government regulation steps in to stop abuses. The antitrust laws step in when competitors create barriers to market entry or collude on prices or production in order to control prices.

5-1b Regulation of Unfair Competition

Each of the states and the federal government have statutes and regulations that prohibit unfair methods of competition. Unfair competition is controlled by both statutes and administrative agencies and regulations. The statutes that curb unfair competition are the Sherman Act, the Clayton Act, the Robinson-Patman Act, and the Federal Trade Commission Act.[1] Each of these statutes covers different types of anticompetitive behavior by competitors. There are horizontal restraints (those among competitors) and vertical restraints of trade (throughout the supply chain) and each is listed in Figure 5-1 and discussed in the sections that follow.

5-2 Regulation of Horizontal Markets and Competitors

Certain of the antitrust laws regulate the relationships between and among competitors, known as horizontal restraints. The goal of these laws is to be sure that firms that are

FIGURE 5-1 Types of Anticompetitive Behavior

HORIZONTAL RESTRAINTS	VERTICAL RESTRAINTS
Price-Fixing (Sherman Act)	Price Discrimination (Robinson-Patman Act)
Monopolization (Sherman Act)	Exclusive Dealings and Territories (Sherman Act)
Mergers among Competitors (Clayton Act)	Mergers along the Supply Chain (Clayton Act)
	Resale Price Maintenance (Sherman Act)
	Tying (Clayton Act)

[1] 15 U.S.C. §41 *et seq.* To review the Federal Trade Commission Act, go to **http://www.ftc.gov**.

gaining customers are doing so because they offer better products and better customer service and not because they are manipulating the markets or their prices.

CPA

5-2a Regulation of Prices

Governments, both national and state, may regulate prices. Prices in various forms are regulated, including not only what a buyer pays for goods but also through credit terms and other charges. The Sherman Act is the federal law that regulates this form of anticompetitive behavior among horizontal competitors.

CPA

Prohibition on Price-Fixing

Agreements among competitors, as well as "every contract, combination … or conspiracy" to fix prices, violate Section 1 of the Sherman Act.[2] Known as *horizontal price-fixing*, any agreement to charge an agreed-upon price or to set maximum or minimum prices between or among competitors are *per se*—in, through, or by themselves—is a violation of the Sherman Act. Price-fixing can involve competitors agreeing to not sell below a certain price, agreeing on commission rates, agreeing on credit terms, or exchanging cost information. Price is treated as a sensitive element of competition, and discussion among competitors has also been deemed to be an attempt to monopolize. An agreement among real estate brokers to never charge below a 6 percent commission is price-fixing.[3] **For Example,** in 2014, the Justice Department filed a civil antitrust suit against Apple and various e-book publishers for conspiracy to fix e-book prices. The publishers and Apple joined forces with the hope that they could prevent Amazon from taking hold of the e-book market with what one of the CEOs of a publishing firm called "the wretched $9.99 price point."[4] The CEOs met together and discussed prices in New York City. Apple had what was called "most favored nation" clauses in its contracts with the publishers; Apple had to be given the publishers' lowest price, thus preventing the publishers from dealing with Amazon. Three publishers settled their cases. Apple went to trial and was found guilty of a conspiracy to fix prices in the e-book market.

5-2b Monopolization

Monopolies and combinations that restrain trade are prohibited under the federal antitrust laws.

The Sherman Act

Sherman Antitrust Act–a federal statute prohibiting combinations and contracts in restraint of interstate trade, now generally inapplicable to labor union activity.

The **Sherman Antitrust Act** includes two very short sections that control monopolistic behavior. They provide:

> *[§1] Every contract, combination in the form of trust or otherwise, or conspiracy, in restraint of trade or commerce among the several states, or with foreign nations, is declared to be illegal.*
> *[§2] Every person who shall monopolize or attempt to monopolize, or combine or conspire with any other person or persons to monopolize any part of the trade or commerce among the several states, or with foreign nations, shall be deemed guilty of a felony.*[5]

[2] To view the full language of Section 1 of the Sherman Act, see 15 U.S.C. §1.

[3] *McClain v. Real Estate Board of New Orleans, Inc.*, 441 U.S. 942 (1980).

[4] *U.S. v. Apple, Inc.*, 12-CV-2826 (2012). **http://online.wsj.com/news/interactive/docid=120411161455-413f968a5c71466491205e6292975605%7Cfile=ebookssettle041112?ref=SB10001424052702304444604577337573054615152.** The other publishers also sued were Hachette Book Group, Inc., HarperCollins Publishers, The Penguin Group, and Simon & Schuster. *United States v. Apple Inc.*, 889 F. Supp. 2d 623 (S.D.N.Y. 2012), *U.S. v. Apple*, 791 F.3d 290 (2nd Cir. 2015).

[5] 15 U.S.C. §1. Free competition has been advanced by the Omnibus Trade and Competitiveness Act of 1988, 19 U.S.C. §2901 *et seq.*

CPA

The Sherman Act applies not only to buying and selling activities but also to manufacturing and production activities. Section 1 of the Sherman Act applies to agreements, conduct, or conspiracies to restrain trade, which can consist of price-fixing, tying, and monopolization. Section 2 prohibits monopolizing or attempting to monopolize by companies or individuals.

Monopolization

market power–the ability to control price and exclude competitors.

To determine whether a firm has engaged in monopolization or attempts to monopolize, the courts determine whether the firm has **market power,** which is the ability to control price and exclude competitors. Market power is defined by looking at both the geographic and product markets. **For Example,** a cereal manufacturer may have 65 percent of the nationwide market for its Crispy Clowns cereal (the product market), but it may have only 10 percent of the Albany, New York, market because of a local competitor, Crunchy Characters. Crispy Clowns may have market power nationally, but in Albany, it would not reach monopoly levels.

Having a large percentage of a market is not necessarily a monopoly.[6] The Sherman Act requires that the monopoly position be gained because of a superior product or consumer preference, not because the company has engaged in purposeful conduct to exclude competitors by other means, such as preventing a competitor from purchasing a factory. **For Example,** perhaps one of the best known monopolization cases involved Microsoft. In the case, the Justice Department alleged that because Microsoft had 90 percent of the market for operating systems, it had and used monopoly power to control and market and did so by refusing to sell its operating system to companies that installed Netscape in lieu of or in addition to the Microsoft Explorer browser.[7] Microsoft was found guilty of monopolization. Ironically, today, Microsoft has filed antitrust complaints against Google, alleging that Google drives those who use its search engine to its own specialized sites that compete with Microsoft and others.

THINKING THINGS THROUGH

Teeth Whitening and the Antitrust Laws

The market for teeth whitening began in the 1990s. North Carolina dentists grew a market for the application of concentrations of peroxide to teeth to create a chemical reaction that results in whiter teeth. In about 2003, non-dentists also started offering teeth-whitening services, often at a significantly lower price than the dentists. Day spas, chain whitening franchises, and other businesses offered the service. Shortly thereafter, dentists began complaining to the North Carolina State Board of Dental Examiners and sought to have the non-dentist whitening services shut down because allowing such services to be performed by non-dentists created public health, safety, and welfare concerns.

After receiving complaints from dentists, the Board opened an investigation into teeth-whitening services performed by non-dentists. As a result of the investigations, the Board issued 47 cease-and-desist letters to 29 non-dentist teeth-whitening providers. The letters were issued on official letterhead and noted that the companies were subject to misdemeanor charges for the unauthorized practice of dentistry if they did not cease and desist their operations. The result was that non-dentist teeth whiteners were eliminated from North Carolina.

The FTC filed a complaint against the Board charging it with unfair competition. The Board moved to dismiss the complaint. Who is correct in this situation?

[*North Carolina State Bd. of Dental Examiners v. F.T.C.*, 135 S. Ct. 1101 (2015)]

[6] *Bell Atlantic v. Twombly*, 550 U.S. 544 (2007).
[7] *United States v. Microsoft*, 253 F.2d 34 (D.C. Cir. 2001).

5-2c Boycotts and Refusals to Deal

Under the Sherman Act, competitors are not permitted to agree not to deal with certain buyers. Boycotts among competitors are *per se* violations of the Sherman Act, which means that there are no defenses to these kinds of controls by competitors on markets. Sometimes boycotts have the best of intentions, but they are still illegal. **For Example,** defense lawyers who went on strike in order to get a higher hourly rate for public defenders so that the indigent defendants would have quality representation still engaged in an illegal boycott.[8]

5-2d Mergers among Competitors

The Sherman Antitrust Act does not prohibit bigness. However, Section 7 of the Clayton Act provides that "no corporation ... shall acquire the whole or any part of the assets of another corporation ... where in any line of commerce in any section of the country, the effect of such acquisition may be substantially to lessen competition, or to tend to create a monopoly." If the Clayton Act is violated through ownership or control of competing enterprises, a court may order the violating defendant to dispose of such interests by issuing a decree called a **divestiture order.**[9] Courts examine market share and relevant markets to determine whether a merger would create a monopoly. **For Example,** the Justice Department filed suit to stop the proposed merger between Anheuser-Busch, InBev NV, the maker of Bud Light, and Modelo, the maker of Corona. The fears expressed in the suit were that the combination of the two companies

divestiture order–a court order to dispose of interests that could lead to a monopoly.

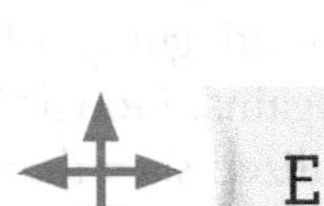

ETHICS & THE LAW

Toys Я Us and Horizontal/Vertical Controls on Distribution

Toys Я Us (TRU), a company that sells 20 percent of all the toys sold in the United States, coordinated informal agreements among toy manufacturers including Mattel and Hasbro that they would restrict the distribution of their products to warehouse club stores (such as Sam's and Costco). The toy market breaks out as follows:

TYPE OF RETAIL OUTLET	PRICE MARK-UP
Traditional toy and department stores	40–50%
Specialized discount toy stores (TRU)	30%
General discount (Wal-Mart/Kmart/Target)	22%
Warehouse/club	9%

To avoid the price competition, the informal TRU agreement was that the toy manufacturers would sell their products to warehouse clubs only if they were part of a more expensive package deal. For example, a Barbie doll could be purchased individually at Toys Я Us for $10.95, but the same Barbie doll could be purchased only as part of a package deal for $15.95 at the warehouse clubs. There were also some restrictions on the toys available to warehouse clubs. For example, Hall of Fame GI Joe was never sold at warehouse clubs. Mattel and Hasbro, fearful of losing Toys Я Us as a distribution tool, went along with the arrangement.

The Federal Trade Commission (FTC) filed suit against TRU to end the agreements.*

Walk through the antitrust laws and determine whether the conduct of TRU violated any of them. Then think through the ethics of TRU's actions. What about Mattel and Hasbro agreeing to the informal arrangement? Was their conduct in violation of the antitrust laws? Was it ethical?

******Toys "Я" Us, Inc. v. FTC* **(7th Cir. 2000). In re** ***Pool Products Distribution Market Antitrust Litigation*****, 988 F.Supp.2d 696 (E.D. La. 2013).**

[8] *FTC v. Superior Court Trial Lawyers Ass'n,* 493 U.S. 411 (1990).
[9] *California v. American Stores Co.,* 492 U.S. 1301 (1989).

E-COMMERCE & CYBERLAW

Steve Jobs's E-Mails in Apple's Antitrust Litigation

Apple faced its third antitrust trial related to the Internet in 2014, and the most damaging testimony against Apple came from the late Steve Jobs—through his e-mails. This third antitrust suit had been hanging around for 10 years and dealt with the issue of the workaround services that had developed to find a way to get music for the iPods loaded through sources other than Apple's iTunes. For example, in one e-mail, Mr. Jobs wrote, "We need to make sure that when Music Match launches their download music store they cannot use iPod. Is this going to be an issue?"* That would be the kind of language someone defending Apple against the antitrust allegations in this iPod case would not want to exist.

During the antitrust litigation over the e-book pricing wars, one of Mr. Jobs's e-mails read, "Throw in with Apple and see if we can all make a go of this to create a real mainstream e-books market at $12.99 and $14.99." The goal was to drive out Amazon from the market because Amazon e-book prices were cheaper.

E-mail is discoverable, admissible as evidence, and definitely not private. Employees should follow the admonition of one executive whose e-mail was used to fuel a million-dollar settlement by his company with a former employee: "If you wouldn't want anyone to read it, don't send it in e-mail."

*Brian X. Chen, "Star Witness In Apple Suit Is Still Jobs," *New York Times*, December 1, 2014, p. B1.

would result in their domination of the distribution chain and would result in price increases. At the time of the proposed merger, AB InBev NV held 39 percent of the beer market, Miller/Coors held 26 percent, Modelo held 7 percent, and Heineken, the last of the big four held 6 percent. Other beer makers combined hold the remaining 22 percent of the U.S. beer market. If Bud and Corona had merged as proposed, they would have held 46 percent of the country's beer market. The case was settled after Bud agreed to divestiture of certain brands that it sold that reduced its post-merger percentage of market share.

Clayton Act–a federal law that prohibits price discrimination.

Robinson-Patman Act–a federal statute designed to eliminate price discrimination in interstate commerce.

price discrimination–the charging practice by a seller of different prices to different buyers for commodities of similar grade and quality, resulting in reduced competition or a tendency to create a monopoly.

When large-size enterprises plan to merge, they must give written notice to the FTC and to the head of the Antitrust Division of the Department of Justice. This advance notice gives the department the opportunity to block the merger and thus avoid the loss that would occur if the enterprises merged and were then required to separate.[10] **For Example,** AT&T was required to notify the Justice Department when it proposed acquisition of T-Mobile because AT&T's market share was 37 percent and T-Mobile's was 16 percent. A merger (which was not approved) would have resulted in a company with a 51 percent share of the market.[11]

5-3 Regulation of the Supply Chain and Vertical Trade Restraints

5-3a Price Discrimination

The **Clayton Act** and **Robinson-Patman Act** prohibit price discrimination.[12] **Price discrimination** occurs when a seller charges different prices to different buyers for

[10] Antitrust Improvement Act of 1976, 15 U.S.C. §1311 *et seq.*

[11] Thomas Catan and Spencer A. Ante, "U.S. Sues to Stop AT&T Deal," *Wall Street Journal*, September 9, 2011, p. A1.

[12] 15 U.S.C. §§1, 2, 3, 7, 8.

"commodities of like grade and quality," with the result being reduced competition or a tendency to create a monopoly.[13]

Price discrimination prohibits charging different prices to buyers as related to marginal costs. That is, volume discounts are permissible because the marginal costs are different on the larger volume of goods. However, the Robinson-Patman Act makes it illegal to charge different prices to buyers when the marginal costs of the seller for those goods are the same. Any added incentives or bonuses are also considered part of the price.

For Example, offering one buyer free advertising while not offering it to another as an incentive to buy would be a violation of the Robinson-Patman Act. The Clayton Act makes both the giving and the receiving of any illegal price discrimination a crime.

CPA

Sellers cannot sell below cost to harm competitors or sell to one customer at a secret price that is lower than the price charged other customers when there is no economic justification for the lower price.[14] Some state statutes specifically permit sellers to set prices so that they can match competitive prices, but not to undercut a competitor's prices.[15]

CASE SUMMARY

Getting a Piece of the Pie Market

FACTS: Utah Pie Company is a Utah corporation that for 30 years has been baking pies in its plant in Salt Lake City and selling them in Utah and surrounding states. It entered the frozen pie business in 1957 and was immediately successful with its new line of frozen dessert pies—apple, cherry, boysenberry, peach, pumpkin, and mince.

Continental Baking Company, Pet Milk, and Carnation, all based in California, entered the pie market in Utah. When these companies entered the Utah market, a price war began. In 1958 Utah Pie was selling pies for $4.15 per dozen. By 1961, as all the pie companies competed, it was selling the same pies for $2.75 per dozen. Continental's price went from $5.00 per dozen in 1958 to $2.85 in 1961. Pet's prices went from $4.92 per dozen to $3.46, and Carnation's from $4.82 per dozen to $3.30.

Utah Pie filed suit, charging price discrimination. The district court found for Utah Pie. The Court of Appeals reversed, and Utah Pie appealed.

DECISION: There was price discrimination. Pet was selling its pies in Utah through Safeway at prices that were lower than its prices in other markets and also much lower than its own brand pie in the Salt Lake City market. Pet also introduced a 20-ounce economy pie under the Swiss Miss label and began selling the new pie in the Salt Lake market in August 1960 at prices ranging from $3.25 to $3.30 for the remainder of the period. This pie was at times sold at a lower price in the Salt Lake City market than it was sold in other markets. For 7 of the 44 months in question for price discrimination, Pet's prices in Salt Lake were lower than prices charged in the California markets. This was true even though selling in Salt Lake involved a 30- to 35-cent freight cost.

Also, Pet had predatory intent to injure Utah Pie. Pet admitted that it sent into Utah Pie's plant an industrial spy to seek information. Pet suffered substantial losses on its frozen pie sales during the greater part of time involved in this suit. Pet had engaged in predatory tactics in waging competitive warfare in the Salt Lake City market. Coupled with the price discrimination, Pet's behavior lessened competition and violated Robinson-Patman. [***Utah Pie Co. v. Continental Baking Co.,* 386 U.S. 685 (1967)**]

[13] 15 U.S.C. §13a. To read the full Clayton Act, go to **http://www.usdoj.gov** or **http://www.justice.gov** and plug in "Clayton Act" in a site search.

[14] In *Weyerhaeuser v. Ross-Simons,* 549 U.S. 212 (2007), the U.S. Supreme Court ruled that predatory bidding is also a price discrimination issue. In a monopsony, a buyer tries to control a market by overbidding all its competitors and thereby cornering the market for supplies it needs to produce goods. However, if the bidder is actually just in need of the goods and bids higher for them, there is no anticompetitive conduct.

[15] *Home Oil Company, Inc. v. Sam's East, Inc.,* 252 F. Supp. 2d 1302 (M.D. Ala. 2003).

Price discrimination is expressly permitted when it can be justified on the basis of (1) a difference in grade, quality, or quantity; (2) the cost of transportation involved in performing the contract; (3) a good-faith effort to meet competition; (4) differences in methods or quantities, that is, marginal cost differences; (5) deterioration of goods; or (6) a close-out sale of a particular line of goods. The Robinson-Patman Act[16] reaffirms the right of a seller to select customers and refuse to deal with anyone. The refusal, however, must be in good faith, not for the purpose of restraining trade.

5-3b Exclusive Dealings and Territories

Sometimes manufacturers have sole outlets. Sole outlets are not *per se* violations. For restrictions on territories and outlets to be legal, there must be enough interbrand competition to justify no intrabrand competition. **For Example,** Coca-Cola can have exclusive distributorships in cities because Pepsi will always be there providing consumers with competitive choices in soft drinks.

5-3c Resale Price Maintenance

Resale price maintenance is an attempt by manufacturers to control the prices that retailers can charge for their goods. A "suggested retail price" is just that, a suggestion, and is not a violation of the antitrust laws. However, some manufacturers have policies of terminating retailers when they charge too little or charge too much. For example, many Apple products are the same price wherever you buy them. Minimum prices are justified in a competitive sense because without them, some retailers would cut the price but not offer the customer service the manufacturer wants for its brand. Retailers who charge more can be stopped by manufacturers who do not want to gouge consumers on prices.

CASE SUMMARY

Bagging Customers for Having Sales

FACTS: Leegin Creative Leather Products, Inc., designs, manufactures, and distributes leather goods and accessories under the brand name "Brighton." The Brighton brand is sold across the United States in over 5,000 retail stores. PSKS, Inc., runs Kay's Kloset, a Brighton retailer in Lewisville, Texas, that carries about 75 different product lines but was known as the place in that area to go for Brighton.

Leegin's president, Jerry Kohl, who also has an interest in about 70 stores that sell Brighton products, believes that small retailers treat customers better, provide customers more services, and make their shopping experience more satisfactory than do larger, often impersonal retailers. In 1997, Leegin instituted the "Brighton Retail Pricing and Promotion Policy," which banished retailers that discounted Brighton goods below suggested prices.

In December 2002, Leegin discovered that Kay's Kloset had been marking down Brighton's entire line by 20 percent. When Kay's would not stop marking the Brighton products prices down, Leegin stopped selling to the store.

PSKS sued Leegin for violation of the antitrust laws. The jury awarded PSKS $1.2 million in damages and the judge trebled the damages and reimbursed PSKS for its attorney's fees and costs—for a judgment against Leegin of $3,975,000.80. The Court of Appeals affirmed. Leegin appealed.

DECISION: The Court held that the goal of providing customers with information and service through the smaller boutiques was a competitive strategy that offered consumers choices. It was not a *per se* violation for Leegin to require minimum prices. Resale price maintenance increases the choices consumers have by providing them with a full-service retailer. Each case on resale price maintenance requires examination of the market and the effect on competition, but it is not automatically anticompetitive. The decision was reversed. [***Leegin Creative Leather Products, Inc. v. PSKS, Inc.,*** **551 U.S. 877 (2007)**]

[16] 15 U.S.C. §§13, 21.

CASE SUMMARY

Fill It Up: The Price Is Right and Fixed

FACTS: Barkat U. Khan and his corporation entered into an agreement with State Oil to lease and operate a gas station and convenience store owned by State Oil. The agreement provided that Khan would obtain the gasoline supply for the station from State Oil at a price equal to a suggested retail price set by State Oil, less a margin of $3.25 per gallon. Khan could charge any price he wanted, but if he charged more than State Oil's suggested retail price, the excess went to State Oil. Khan could sell the gasoline for less than State Oil's suggested retail price, but the difference would come out of his allowed margin.

After a year, Khan fell behind on his lease payments, and State Oil gave notice of, and began, eviction proceedings. The court had Khan removed and appointed a receiver to operate the station. The receiver did so without the price constraints and received an overall profit margin above the $3.25 imposed on Khan.

Khan filed suit, alleging that the State Oil agreement was a violation of Section 1 of the Sherman Act because State Oil was controlling price. The district court held that there was no *per se* violation and that Khan had failed to demonstrate antitrust injury. The Court of Appeals reversed, and State Oil appealed.

DECISION: In what was a reversal of prior decisions, the Court held that vertical maximum prices (as in this case in which a retailer was prohibited from charging above a certain amount) are not a *per se* violation of the Sherman Act. The Court noted that benefits can come from retailers' not being able to charge above a certain amount. At a minimum, such controls on maximum prices were not an automatic violation of the Sherman Act and need to be examined in light of what happens to competition. In determining whether such prices might affect competition, the Court noted that maximum prices might have an impact on the survival of inefficient dealers, as was the case here. However, encouraging inefficiency is not the purpose of either the market or the laws on anticompetitive behavior. [***State Oil v. Khan*, 522 U.S. 3 (1997)**]

5-3d Tying

tying–the anticompetitive practice of requiring buyers to purchase one product in order to get another.

It is a violation of the Sherman Act to force "tying" sales on buyers. **Tying** occurs when the seller makes a buyer who wants to purchase one product buy an additional product that he or she does not want.

The essential characteristic of a tying arrangement that violates Section 1 of the Sherman Act is the use of control over the tying product within the relevant market to compel the buyer to purchase the tied article that either is not wanted or could be purchased elsewhere on better terms.

CASE SUMMARY

If You Want Our Cartridges, You Have to Use Our Ink

FACTS: Trident, Inc., and its parent, Illinois Tool Works Inc. (petitioners), manufacture and market printing systems that include: (1) a patented piezoelectric impulse ink jet printhead, (2) a patented ink container, consisting of a bottle and valve cap, which attaches to the printhead, and (3) specially designed, but unpatented, ink. These products are sold to original equipment manufacturers (OEMs) who are licensed to incorporate the printheads and containers into printers that are in turn sold to companies for use in printing barcodes on cartons and packaging materials. The OEMs agree that they will purchase their ink exclusively from Illinois, and that neither they nor their customers will refill the patented containers with ink of any kind.

Independent Ink, Inc., has developed an ink with the same chemical composition as the ink sold by Illinois. Independent Ink filed suit, alleging that Illinois's agreements with customers constituted an illegal tying and monopolization in violation of §§ 1 and 2 of the Sherman Act. 15 U.S.C. §§1, 2.

If You Want Our Cartridges, You Have to Use Our Ink continued

The federal district court granted summary judgment for Illinois, and Independent appealed. The appellate court reversed the decision and Illinois appealed.

DECISION: The court held that tying an unpatented product to a patented one was not a *per se* violation because there needed to be proof of market power in the patented product first. On remand, to establish tying, there must be proof that Illinois Tool has market power in the sale of its cartridges—such as a percentage of market share. You can only engage in tying through a tie of an unsuccessful product to a successful one—the more successful your product and the higher the demand, the more you lose the defense to tying. [***Illinois Tool Works Inc. v. Independent Ink, Inc.*, 547 U.S. 28 (2006)**]

5-3e Mergers along the Supply Chain

Vertical mergers occur between firms that have buyer and seller relationships. The Clayton Act also applies to vertical mergers. The test is whether the vertical merger will foreclose or lessen competition. **For Example,** Amazon is a retailer of both books and e-books, but it has begun its own publishing firm and has been recruiting authors. Other book publishers are watching closely as Amazon begins to obtain more power in the publishing part of the chain because of its dominance in the retail sales of books. During 2014, Amazon had a dust-up with Hachette Books because there were accusations that Amazon was holding up shipment of non-Amazon author books in order to affect sales and encourage more authors to sign with Amazon's publishing arm.

In addition to controlling business combinations, the federal government protects others. By statute or decision, associations of exporters, marine insurance associations, farmers' cooperatives, and labor unions are exempt from the Sherman Act with respect to agreements between their members. Certain pooling and revenue-dividing agreements between carriers are exempt from the antitrust law when approved by the appropriate federal agency. The Newspaper Preservation Act of 1970 grants an antitrust exemption to operating agreements entered into by newspapers to prevent financial collapse. The Soft Drink Interbrand Competition Act[17] grants the soft drink industry an exemption when it is shown that, in fact, substantial competition exists in spite of the agreements.

The general approach of the U.S. Supreme Court has been that these types of agreements should not be automatically, or *per se,* condemned as a restraint of interstate commerce merely because they create the power or potential to monopolize interstate commerce. It is only when the restraint imposed is unreasonable that the practice is unlawful. The Court applies the rule of reason in certain cases because the practice may not always harm competition.

SPORTS & ENTERTAINMENT LAW

Ticket Issues and Antitrust

The Justice Department took a very close look at whether the merger between Live Nation and Ticketmaster would be anticompetitive because the largest U.S. event promoter was proposing a merger with the largest primary and secondary ticket seller in the world. The merger was eventually approved because there were still thriving smaller ticket sellers.

[17] 15 U.S.C. §3501 *et seq.*

5-4 Remedies for Anticompetitive Behavior

5-4a Criminal Penalties

A violation of either section of the Sherman Act is punishable by fine or imprisonment, or both, at the discretion of the court. The maximum fine for a corporation is $100 million. A natural person can be fined a maximum of $1,000,000 or imprisoned for a maximum term of 10 years, or both.

5-4b Civil Remedies

In addition to these criminal penalties, the law provides for an injunction to stop the unlawful practices.

treble damages–three times the damages actually sustained.

Any individual or company harmed may bring a separate action for **treble damages** (three times the damages actually sustained). In addition to individual suits, there is the possibility that a state could bring a class-action suit if the antitrust violation has resulted in large numbers of buyers paying higher prices. **For Example,** Pilgrim's Pride agreed to pay $26 million in damages to dozens of poultry growers because of its closure of chicken-processing plants in order to bring down the price of chicken.

The attorney general of a state may bring a class-action suit to recover damages on behalf of those who have paid the higher prices. This action is called a *parens patriae* action on the theory that the state is suing as the parent of its people.

Make the Connection

Summary

Regulation by government has occurred primarily to protect one group from the improper conduct of another group. The police power is the basis for government regulation. Regulation is passed when the free enterprise system fails to control abuses, as when companies engage in unfair methods of competition.

There are horizontal and vertical forms of anticompetitive behavior. The Sherman Act focuses on horizontal anticompetitive behavior such as price-fixing, boycotts, refusals to deal, and monopolization achieved through means other than fair competition.

The Sherman Antitrust Act prohibits price-fixing among competitors, monopolies that do not result from superior skill or products, boycotts, and mergers that lessen competition. The Clayton Act prohibits mergers or the acquisition of the assets of another corporation when this conduct would tend to lessen competition or create a monopoly. The Justice Department requires premerger notification for proposed mergers. Violation of the federal antitrust statutes subjects the wrongdoer to criminal prosecution and possible civil liability that can include treble damages.

Vertical trade restraints include price discrimination, some exclusive dealings arrangements, resale price maintenance, and some mergers among companies positioned vertically in the supply chain.

Prices have been regulated both by prohibiting setting the exact price or a maximum price and discrimination in pricing. Price discrimination between buyers is prohibited when the effect of such discrimination could tend to create a monopoly or lessen competition. Price discrimination occurs when the prices charged different buyers are different despite the same marginal costs. Another vertical antitrust issue is resale price maintenance. Resale price maintenance is control by the manufacturer of the price of its goods as they flow through the supply chain. Resale price maintenance is not illegal *per se* if the control is for purposes of providing customer service.

Learning Outcomes

After studying this chapter, you should be able to clearly explain:

5-1 Power to Regulate Business

LO.1 Explain the powers the government has to be sure free markets are working efficiently

See the *For Example* about Crispy Clowns Cereal, page 75.

5-2 Regulation of Horizontal Markets and Competitors

LO.2 List the federal statutes that regulate horizontal markets and competition and give examples of each

See the Apple e-book pricing example, page 74.
See the Toys Я Us Ethics & the Law, page 76.
See the Thinking Things Through feature on teeth whitening, page 75.
See the Microsoft monopolization discussion, page 75.
See the Bud Light and Corona example on horizontal mergers, pages 76–77.

5-3 Regulation of the Supply Chain and Vertical Trade Restraints

LO.3 Describe the federal statutes that regulate the supply chain and vertical markets

See the *Utah Pie* case on predatory pricing, page 78.
See the *Khan* oil case on price controls, page 80.
See the *Leegin* case on resale price maintenance, page 79.
See the *Illinois Tool Works* case on tying, pages 80–81.
See the Sports & Entertainment Law feature on the merger in the event ticket market, page 81.

5-4 Remedies for Anticompetitive Behavior

LO.4 Discuss the remedies available to protect business competition

See a list of the penalties and remedies, page 82.

Key Terms

Clayton Act
divestiture order
market power
price discrimination
Robinson-Patman Act
Sherman Antitrust Act
treble damages
tying

Questions and Case Problems

1. American Crystal Sugar Co. was one of several refiners of beet sugar in northern California, and it distributed its product in interstate commerce. American Crystal and the other refiners had a monopoly on the seed supply and were the only practical market for the beets. In 1939, all of the refiners began using identical form contracts that computed the price paid to the sugar beet growers using a "factor" common to all the refiners. As a result, all refiners paid the same price for beets of the same quality. Though there was no hard evidence of an illegal agreement, the growers brought suit under the Sherman Act against the refiners, alleging that they conspired to fix a single uniform price among themselves to hold down the cost of the beets. The growers sued for the treble damages available under the Sherman Act. Can they recover? [*Mandeville Island Farms v. American Crystal Sugar Co.*, 334 U.S. 219]

2. Penny Stafford, the owner of Belvi Coffee and Tea Exchange, located in Bellevue, Washington, brought an antitrust suit against Starbucks. She alleged that through its exclusive leases, Starbucks bans other coffee shops from competing. Starbucks has a 73 percent market share, has $8.4 billion in annual sales in the United States, and owns 7,551 of the 21,400 coffeehouses located in the United States. However, if Dunkin' Donuts, KrispyKreme, and Tim Hortons are included in the gourmet coffee market, Starbucks holds only 43 percent of the coffee market. Starbucks purchased Seattle's Best Coffee (SBC) in 2003 and Torrefazione Italia the same year. Starbucks then closed one-half of all SBC stores and all of the Torrefazione outlets. Starbucks runs 59 stores within a two-mile radius of downtown Seattle. Stafford said that Starbucks has exclusive leases with landlords so that the landlords cannot lease space in the same building to another coffee shop. Does such an exclusive lease violate any antitrust laws, or are such clauses permitted under the law?

3. David Ungar holds a Dunkin' Donuts franchise. The terms of his franchise agreement require him to use only those ingredients furnished by Dunkin' Donuts. He is also required to buy its napkins, cups, and so on, with the Dunkin' Donuts trademark on them. Is

this an illegal tying arrangement? What if Dunkin' Donuts maintains that it needs these requirements to maintain its quality levels on a nationwide basis? [*Ungar v. Dunkin' Donuts of America, Inc.*, 429 U.S. 823]

4. During the 1980s, the NCAA, a voluntary unincorporated association of approximately 1,100 educational institutions, became concerned over the steadily rising costs of maintaining competitive athletic programs. As a way of containing those costs, the association imposed salary caps on college and university athletic coaches. The caps on salaries as well as limits on number and types of coaches were imposed pursuant to NCAA procedures and members' votes. A group of coaches filed suit, challenging the caps on salaries and hiring as being anticompetitive. The NCAA responded that it had a goal of containing athletic program costs as well as ensuring that entry-level coaching positions were available. Are the salary caps legal under the federal antitrust laws? [*Law v. National Collegiate Athletic Ass'n*, 134 F.3d 1010 (10th Cir.)]
5. Hines Cosmetic Co. sold beauty preparations nationally to beauty shops at a standard or fixed-price schedule. Some of the shops were also supplied with a free demonstrator and free advertising materials. The shops that were not supplied with them claimed that giving the free services and materials constituted unlawful price discrimination. Hines replied that there was no price discrimination because it charged everyone the same. What it was giving free was merely a promotional campaign that was not intended to discriminate against those who were not given anything free. Was Hines guilty of unlawful price discrimination? Explain.
6. Moore ran a bakery in Santa Rosa, New Mexico. His business was wholly intrastate. Meads Fine Bread Co., his competitor, engaged in an interstate business. Meads cut the price of bread in half in Santa Rosa but made no price cut in any other place in New Mexico or in any other state. This price-cutting drove Moore out of business. Moore then sued Meads for damages for violating the Clayton and Robinson-Patman Acts. Meads claimed that the price-cutting was purely intrastate and, therefore, did not constitute a violation of federal statutes. Was Meads correct? Why or why not? [*Moore v. Meads Fine Bread Co.*, 348 U.S. 115]
7. A&P Grocery Stores decided to sell its own brand of canned milk (referred to as *private label* milk). A&P asked its longtime supplier, Borden, to submit an offer to produce the private label milk. Bowman Dairy also submitted a bid, which was lower than Borden's. A&P's Chicago buyer then contacted Borden and said, "I have a bid in my pocket. You people are so far out of line it is not even funny. You are not even in the ballpark." The Borden representative asked for more details but was told only that a $50,000 improvement in Borden's bid "would not be a drop in the bucket." A&P was one of Borden's largest customers in the Chicago area. Furthermore, Borden had just invested more than $5 million in a new dairy facility in Illinois. The loss of the A&P account would result in underutilization of the plant. Borden lowered its bid by more than $400,000. The Federal Trade Commission charged Borden with price discrimination, but Borden maintained it was simply meeting the competition. Did Borden violate the Robinson-Patman Act? Does it matter that the milk was a private label milk, not its normal trade name Borden milk? [*Great Atlantic & Pacific Tea Co., Inc. v. FTC*, 440 U.S. 69]
8. Department 56 is a company that manufactures and sells collectible Christmas village houses and other replica items to allow collectors to create the whimsical "Snow Village" town or "Dickens Christmas." Department 56 has only authorized dealers. Sam's Club, a division of Wal-Mart Stores, Inc., began selling Department 56 pieces from the Heritage Village Collection. Susan Engel, president and CEO of Department 56, refused to sell Department 56 products to Wal-Mart. Does her refusal violate any antitrust laws?
9. Dr. Edwin G. Hyde, a board-certified anesthesiologist, applied for permission to practice at East Jefferson Hospital in Louisiana. An approval was recommended for his hiring, but the hospital's board denied him employment on grounds that the hospital had a contract with Roux & Associates for Roux to provide all anesthesiological services required by the hospital's patients. Dr. Hyde filed suit for violation of antitrust laws. Had the hospital done anything illegal? [*Jefferson Parish Hosp. Dist. No. 2 v. Hyde*, 466 U.S. 2]
10. BRG of Georgia, Inc. (BRG), and Harcourt Brace Jovanovich Legal and Professional Publications (HJB) are the nation's two largest providers of bar review materials and lectures. HJB began offering a Georgia bar review course on a limited basis in 1976 and was in direct, and often intense, competition

with BRG from 1977 to 1979 when the companies were the two main providers of bar review courses in Georgia. In early 1980, they entered into an agreement that gave BRG an exclusive license to market HJB's materials in Georgia and to use its trade name "Bar/Bri." The parties agreed that HJB would not compete with BRG in Georgia and that BRG would not compete with HJB outside of Georgia. Under the agreement, HJB received $100 per student enrolled by BRG and 40 percent of all revenues over $350. Immediately after the 1980 agreement, the price of BRG's course was increased from $150 to more than $400. Is their conduct illegal under federal antitrust laws? [*Palmer v. BRG of Georgia, Inc.*, 498 U.S. 46]

11. Favorite Foods Corp. sold its food to stores and distributors. It established a quantity discount scale that was publicly published and made available to all buyers. The top of the scale gave the highest discount to buyers purchasing more than 100 freight cars of food in a calendar year. Only two buyers, both national food chains, purchased in such quantities, and, therefore, they alone received the greatest discount. Favorite Foods was prosecuted for price discrimination in violation of the Clayton Act. Was it guilty?

12. Public Interest Corporation (PIC) owned and operated television station WTMV-TV in Lakeland, Florida. MCA Television Ltd. (MCA) owns and licenses syndicated television programs. In 1990, the two companies entered into a licensing contract for several first-run television shows. With respect to all but one of these shows, MCA exchanged the licenses on a "barter" basis for advertising time on WTMV. However, MCA conditioned this exchange on PIC's agreeing to license the remaining show, *Harry and the Hendersons*, for cash as well as for barter. *Harry and the Hendersons* was what some in the industry would call a "dog," a show that was not very good that attempted to capitalize on a hit movie. PIC agreed to this arrangement, although it did not want *Harry and the Hendersons*. The shows that PIC did want were *List of a Lifetime*, *List of a Lifetime II*, *Magnum P.I.*, and 17 other miscellaneous features. Is this an illegal tying arrangement? [*MCA Television Ltd. v. Public Interest Corp.*, 171 F.3d 1265 (11th Cir.)]

13. The Quickie brand wheelchair is the most popular customized wheelchair on the market. Its market share is 90 percent. Other manufacturers produce special-use wheelchairs that fold, that are made of mesh and lighter frames, and that are easily transportable. These manufacturers do not compete with Quickie on customized chairs. One manufacturer of the alternative wheelchairs has stated, "Look, it's an expensive market to be in, that Quickie market. We prefer the alternative chairs without the headaches of customizations." Another has said, "It is such a drain on cash flow in that market because insurers take so long to pay. We produce chairs that buyers purchase with their own money, not through insurers. Our sales are just like any other product." Quickie entered the market nearly 40 years ago and is known for its quality and attention to detail. Buying a Quickie custom chair, however, takes time, and the revenue stream from sales is slow but steady because of the time required to produce custom wheelchairs. Has Quickie violated the federal antitrust laws with its 90 percent market share? Discuss.

14. Gardner-Denver is the largest manufacturer of ratchet wrenches and their replacement parts in the United States. Gardner-Denver had two different lists of prices for its wrenches and parts. Its blue list had parts that, if purchased in quantities of five or more, were available for substantially less than its white list prices. Did Gardner-Denver engage in price discrimination with its two price lists? [*D. E. Rogers Assoc., Inc. v. Gardner-Denver Co.*, 718 F.2d 1431 (6th Cir.)]

15. The Aspen ski area consisted of four mountain areas. Aspen Highlands, which owned three of those areas, and Aspen Skiing, which owned the fourth, had cooperated for years in issuing a joint, multiple-day, all-area ski ticket. After repeatedly and unsuccessfully demanding an increased share of the proceeds, Aspen Highlands canceled the joint ticket. Aspen Skiing, concerned that skiers would bypass its mountain without some joint offering, tried a variety of increasingly desperate measures to re-create the joint ticket, even to the point of in effect offering to buy Aspen Highland's tickets at retail price. Aspen Highlands refused even that. Aspen Skiing brought suit under the Sherman Act, alleging that the refusal to cooperate was a move by Aspen Highlands to eliminate all competition in the area by freezing it out of business. Is there an antitrust claim here in the refusal to cooperate? What statute and violation do you think Aspen Skiing alleged? What dangers do you see in finding the failure to cooperate to be an antitrust violation? [*Aspen Skiing Co. v. Aspen Highlands Skiing Corp.*, 472 U.S. 585]

CHAPTER 6

Administrative Agencies

››› Learning Outcomes

After studying this chapter, you should be able to

LO.1 **Describe the nature and purpose of administrative agencies**

LO.2 **Discuss the legislative or rulemaking power of administrative agencies**

LO.3 **Explain the executive or enforcement function of administrative agencies**

LO.4 **Discuss the judicial power of administrative agencies including the rule on exhaustion of administrative remedies**

6-1 Nature of the Administrative Agency

Late in the nineteenth century, a new type of governmental structure began to develop to meet the highly specialized needs of government regulation of business: the administrative agency. The administrative agency is now typically the instrument through which government makes and carries out its regulations.

administrative agency–government body charged with administering and implementing legislation.

An **administrative agency** is a government body charged with administering and implementing legislation. An agency may be a department, an independent establishment, a commission, an administration, an authority, a board, or a bureau. Agencies exist on the federal and state levels. One example of a federal agency is the Federal Trade Commission (FTC), whose structure is shown in Figure 6-1.

6-1a Purpose of Administrative Agencies

Federal administrative agencies are created to carry out general policies specified by Congress. Federal agencies include the Securities Exchange Commission (SEC), the Consumer Product Safety Commission (CPSC), and the Food and Drug Administration (FDA). The law governing these agencies is known as **administrative law.**

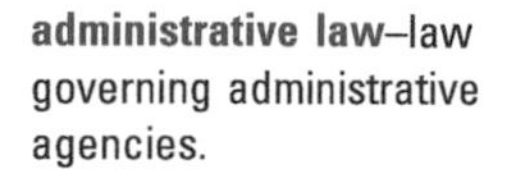

administrative law–law governing administrative agencies.

States also have administrative agencies that may have jurisdiction over areas of law affecting business, such as workers' compensation claims, real estate licensing, and unemployment compensation.

6-1b Uniqueness of Administrative Agencies

Administrative agencies differ from the legislative branch in that those who head up and operate are ordinarily appointed (in the case of federal agencies, by the president of the United States with the consent of the Senate).

In the tripartite structure of legislative, executive, and judicial branches, the judicial branch reviews actions of the executive and legislative branches to ensure that they have

FIGURE 6-1 Structure of the Federal Trade Commission

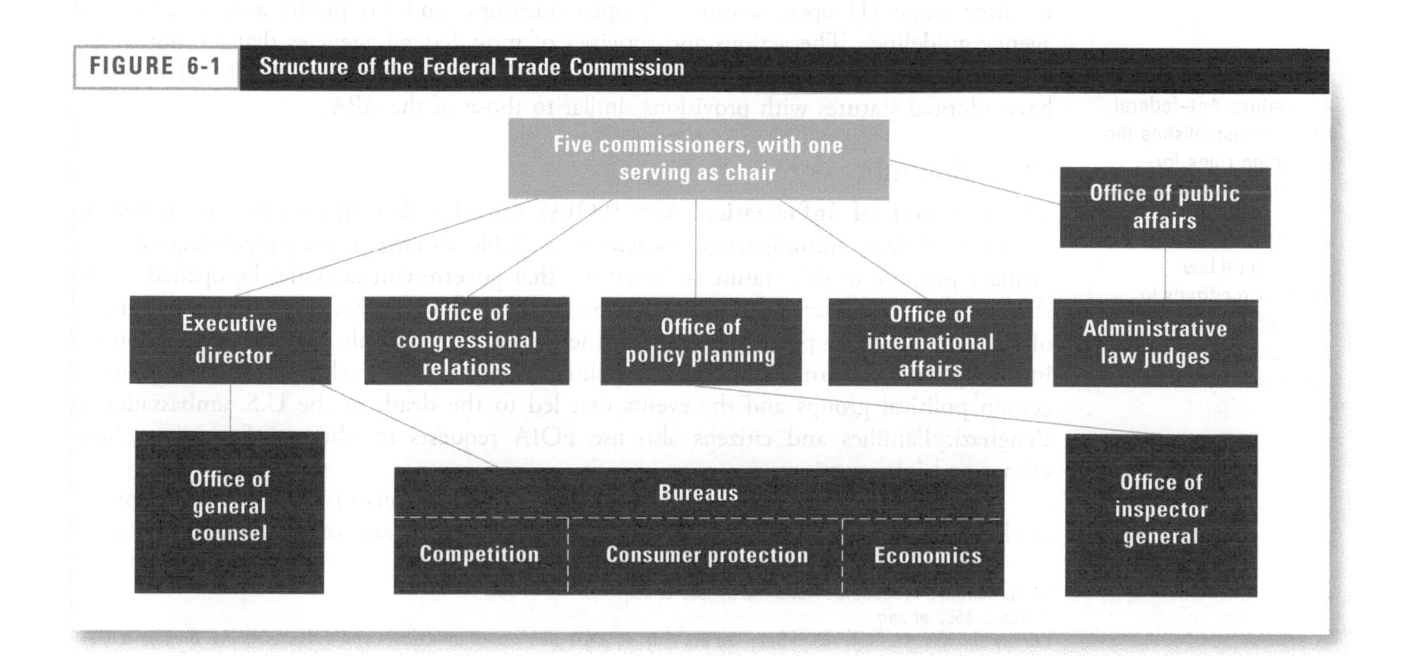

FIGURE 6-2 The Administrative Chain of Command

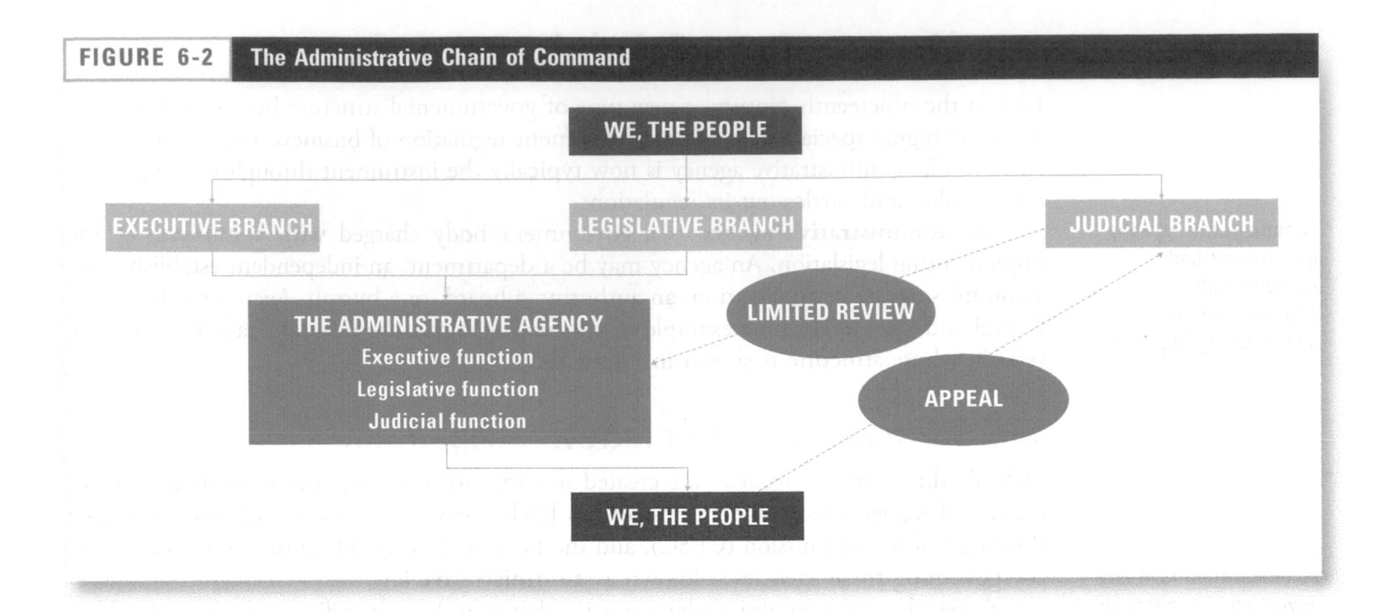

not exceeded their constitutional powers. However, governmental agencies combine legislative, executive, and judicial powers (Figure 6-2). These agencies make the rules, conduct inspections to see that the rules have been or are being obeyed, and determine whether there have been violations of their rules. Because agencies have such broad powers, they are subject to strict procedural rules as well as disclosure requirements (discussed in the following section).

6-1c Open Operation of Administrative Agencies

The public has ready access to the activity of administrative agencies. That access comes in three ways: (1) open records, (2) open meetings, and (3) public announcement of agency guidelines. The actions and activities of most federal agencies that are not otherwise regulated are controlled by the **Administrative Procedure Act** (APA).[1] Many states have adopted statutes with provisions similar to those of the APA.

Administrative Procedure Act–federal law that establishes the operating rules for administrative agencies.

Freedom of Information Act–federal law permitting citizens to request documents and records from administrative agencies.

Open Records

The **Freedom of Information Act**[2] (FOIA) provides that information contained in records of federal administrative agencies is available to citizens on proper request. The primary purpose of this statute is "to ensure that government activities be opened to the sharp eye of public scrutiny."[3] Over the past decade there has been an increasing number of FOIA requests by private groups and the media. For example, FOIA requests resulted in the release of information related to political controversies, such as the IRS targeting of certain political groups and the events that led to the death of the U.S. ambassador in Benghazi. Families and citizens also use FOIA requests to obtain information about crimes and investigations.

The Electronic Freedom of Information Act Amendments of 1996 extend the public availability of information to electronically stored data. The area of electronic government

[1] Administrative Procedures Act 5 U.S.C. §550 *et seq.*
[2] 5 U.S.C. §552 *et seq.*
[3] *Brady-Lunny v. Massey,* 185 F. Supp. 2d 928 (C.D. Ill. 2007). See also *Better Government Association v. Blagojevich,* 899 N.E.2d 382 (Ill. App. 2008).

activity has been a focus of FOIA requests. For example, in *Electronic Private Information Center v. Dept. of Homeland Security (DHS)*, 999 F. Supp. 2d 24 (2013), a private organization sought information about the authority of the DHS to shut down wireless network to prevent the detonation of explosive devices.

Because these requests can involve sensitive materials or issues of privacy, there are exceptions to this right of public scrutiny. These exceptions prevent individuals and companies from obtaining information that is not necessary to their legitimate interests and might harm the person or company whose information is being sought.[4] State statutes typically exempt from disclosure any information that would constitute an invasion of the privacy of others. **For Example,** when Sea World animal trainer, Dawn Brancheau, died as a result of an attack by a killer whale, OSHA conducted the investigation into her death because it was a workplace fatality. OSHA had taken photographs as part of the investigation and there were several FOIA requests for release of the investigation report, including the photos. Ms. Brancheau's family filed a "reverse FOI" suit to stop the disclosure of the information. However, as disturbing as the photos may have been, there is no FOIA exception for death scene materials.[5]

Freedom of information acts are broadly construed, and unless an exemption is clearly given, the information in question is subject to public inspection.[6] **For Example,** the Department of Justice is required to disclose materials related to an investigation of a member of Congress that has ended with no charges.[7] Moreover, the person claiming that there is an exemption that prohibits disclosure has the burden of proving that the exemption applies to the particular request made. Exemptions include commercial or financial information not ordinarily made public by the person or company that supplies the information to the agency as part of the agency's enforcement role.[8]

The FOIA's primary purpose is to subject agency action to public scrutiny. Its provisions are liberally interpreted, and agencies must make good-faith efforts to comply with its terms.

ETHICS & THE LAW

IRS Employees Who Snoop

In 1997, the Internal Revenue Service (IRS) disciplined employees who, out of curiosity, were looking up tax returns of famous people to see who made how much income. The IRS fired 23 employees, disciplined 349, and provided counseling for 472. In June 2013, another 349 IRS employees were disciplined, once again, for looking up tax returns of citizens without any authorization or work purpose for doing so. Is this practice so bad? What is wrong with just looking at data accessible at work?

Why are we concerned about selective research about private citizens? Does it matter that the information was not released to the public?

[4] Additional protection is provided by the Privacy Act of 1974, 5 U.S.C. §552a(b); *Doe v. U.S. Dept. of Treasury*, 706 F. Supp. 2d 1 (D.D.C. 2009) and protects government employees from disclosures about employer disciplinary actions.
[5] *Brancheau v. Secretary of Labor*, 2011 WL 4105047 (M.D. Fla.).
[6] Corporations have limited privacy rights. *FCC v. AT&T Inc.*, 562 U.S. 397 (2011).
[7] *Citizens for Responsibility and Ethics in Washington v. United States Department of Justice*, 48 F. Supp. 2d 40 (D.D.C. 2014).
[8] *Ayuda, Inc. v. Federal Trade Commission*, 70 F. Supp. 3d 247 (D.D.C. 2014); for a state law example, see *Oklahoma Public Employees Ass'n v. State ex rel. Oklahoma Office of Personnel Management*, 267 P.3d 838 (Okla. 2011).

Open Meetings

open meeting law–law that requires advance notice of agency meeting and public access.

Under the Sunshine Act of 1976,[9] called the **open meeting law,** the federal government requires most meetings of major administrative agencies to be open to the public. The Sunshine Act[10] applies to those meetings involving "deliberations" of the agency or those that "result in the joint conduct or disposition of official agency business." These statutes enable the public to know what actions agencies are taking and prevent administrative misconduct by having open meetings and public scrutiny. Many states also have enacted Sunshine laws.

Public Announcement of Agency Guidelines

To inform the public of the way administrative agencies operate, the APA, with certain exceptions, requires that each federal agency publish the rules, principles, and procedures that it follows.[11]

6-2 Legislative Power of the Agency

An administrative agency has the power to make laws and does so by promulgating regulations with public input.

6-2a Agency's Regulations as Law

An agency may adopt regulations within the scope of its authority. The power of an agency to carry out a congressional program "necessarily requires the formulation of policy and the making of rules to fill any gap left by Congress."[12] If the regulation is not authorized by the law creating the agency, anyone affected by it can challenge the regulation on the basis that the agency has exceeded its authority. (See the section "Beyond the Jurisdiction of the Agency" in this chapter.)

The authority of an agency is not limited to the technology in existence at the time the agency was created or assigned jurisdiction for enforcement of laws. The sphere in which an agency may act expands with new scientific developments.[13]

CASE SUMMARY

Can an Agency Regulate Hot Air?

FACTS: On October 20, 1999, a group of 19 private organizations (Petitioners) filed a rulemaking petition asking the EPA to regulate "greenhouse gas emissions from new motor vehicles under §202 of the Clean Air Act." These organizations argued that greenhouse gas emissions have significantly accelerated climate change, and that "carbon dioxide remains the most important contributor to [man-made] forcing of climate change."

Fifteen months after the petition was filed, the EPA requested public comment on "all the issues raised in [the] petition," adding a "particular" request for comments on "any scientific, technical, legal, economic or other aspect of

[9] The Government in the Sunshine Act can be found at 5 U.S.C. §552b.

[10] 5 U.S.C. §552b(a)(2).

[11] APA codified at 5 U.S.C. §552. See the section "Proposed Regulations" in this chapter for a description of the *Federal Register*, the publication in which these agency rules, principles, and procedures are printed.

[12] *National Elec. Mfrs. Ass'n v. U.S. Dept. of Energy*, 654 F.3d 496 (4th Cir. 2011); *King v. Burwell*, 759 F.3d 358 (4th Cir. 2014).

[13] *United States v. Midwest Video Corp.*, 406 U.S. 649 (1972).

Can an Agency Regulate Hot Air? continued

these issues that may be relevant to EPA's consideration of this petition, including whether there was global warming due to carbon emissions." The EPA received more than 50,000 comments over the next five months.

On September 8, 2003, the EPA entered an order denying the rulemaking petition because (1) the Clean Air Act does not authorize the EPA to issue mandatory regulations to address global climate change; and (2) even if the agency had the authority to set greenhouse gas emission standards, it would be unwise to do so at this time. Massachusetts, other states, and private organizations filed suit, challenging the EPA denial as arbitrary and capricious, violative of the APA, and *ultra vires* because of statutory mandates for EPA action.

The court of appeals dismissed the appeal from the agency denial and the Supreme Court granted *certiorari*.

DECISION: The Court held that greenhouse gases were a form of pollution and that the Clean Air Act required the EPA to take steps to curb those emissions. The Court found that any justification the EPA gave for inaction was not supported by either the statutory construction or the evidence on global warming. The decision was 5 to 4 in which the dissent maintained that no matter how strongly we feel about global warming, action is left to the executive and legislative branches, not the courts. The dissent also noted that agencies should be given great deference in making their decisions on whether to regulate certain issues and that the statute did not mandate regulation—it gave the EPA broad discretion and its discretion could include lack of scientific conclusions, deference to the president, or other agencies. [***Massachusetts v. EPA*, 549 U.S. 497 (2007)**]

When an agency's proposed regulation deals with a policy question that is not specifically addressed by statute, the agency that was created or given the discretion to administer the statute may establish new policies covering such issues.[14] **For Example,** the FCC has authority to deal with cell phones and cell phone providers even though when the agency was created, there were only the traditional types of land-line telephones.[15]

6-2b Agency Adoption of Regulations

Congressional Enabling Act

Before an agency can begin rulemaking proceedings, it must be given jurisdiction by congressional enactment in the form of a statute. **For Example,** Congress has enacted broad statutes governing discrimination in employment practices and has given authority to the Equal Employment Opportunity Commission (EEOC) to establish definitions, rules, and guidelines for compliance with those laws. Sometimes an existing agency is assigned the responsibility for new legislation implementation and enforcement. **For Example,** the Department of Labor has been assigned the responsibility to handle the whistle-blower protection provisions of Sarbanes-Oxley that provide protection against retaliation and/or termination to those who report financial chicanery at their companies. The Department of Labor has been in existence for almost a century, but it was assigned a new responsibility and given new jurisdiction by Congress.

Agency Research of the Problem

After jurisdiction is established, the agency has the responsibility to research the issues and various avenues of regulation for implementing the statutory framework. As the agency does so, it determines the cost and benefit of the problems, issues, and solutions. The study may be done by the agency itself, or it may be completed by someone hired by the agency. **For Example,** before red lights were required equipment in the rear windows

[14] *Anglers Conservation Network v. Pritzker*, 70 F. Supp. 3d 427 (D.D.C. 2014).
[15] *Fones4All Corp. v. F.C.C.*, 550 F.3d 811 (9th Cir. 2008).

E-COMMERCE & CYBERLAW

The Open Net, Net Neutrality, and the FCC's Authority

Several subscribers to Comcast's Internet services discovered that the company was interfering with their use of peer-to-peer networking applications. The subscribers asked the FCC to regulate the Internet management practices of Comcast. However, the court held that there was no statutory authority that permitted the FCC to regulate the internal practices of communication providers. **[*Comcast Corp. v. F.C.C.*, 600 F.3d 642 (C.A.D.C. 2010)**; see also ***Verizon v. FCC*, 740 F.3d 624 (D.C. Cir. 2014)].**

The case was the beginning of an ongoing legal battle for net neutrality. Net neutrality would mean that all data on the Internet would be treated equally. ISPs would not be able to charge differently depending on users, platform, etc. The ISPs claim that different treatment is necessary in order to ensure quality and access for all. The FCC has adopted a net neutrality standard, but the challenges continue.

of all cars, the Department of Transportation developed a study using taxicabs with the red lights in the rear windows and found that the accident rate for rear-end collisions with taxicabs was reduced dramatically. The study provided justification for the need for regulation as well as the type of regulation itself.

Proposed Regulations

Federal Register Act– federal law requiring agencies to make public disclosure of proposed rules, passed rules, and activities.

Federal Register– government publication issued five days a week that lists all administrative regulations, all presidential proclamations and executive orders, and other documents and classes of documents that the president or Congress direct to be published.

Following a study, the agency proposes regulations, which must be published. The **Federal Register Act**[16] requires that proposed administrative regulation be published in the ***Federal Register***. This is a government publication published five days a week that lists all administrative regulations, all presidential proclamations and executive orders, and other documents and classes of documents that the president or Congress directs to be published.

The Federal Register Act provides that printing an administrative regulation in the *Federal Register* is public notice of the contents of the regulation to persons subject to it or affected by it, but in addition, the Regulatory Flexibility Act,[17] passed during the Reagan administration, requires that all proposed rules be published in the trade journals of those trades that will be affected by the proposed rules. **For Example,** any changes in federal regulations on real property closings and escrows have to be published in real estate broker trade magazines. In addition to the public notice of the proposed rule, the agency must also include a "regulatory flexibility analysis" that "shall describe the impact of the proposed rule on small entities."[18] The goal of this portion of the APA was to be certain that small businesses were aware of proposed regulatory rules and their cost impact.

Public Comment Period

Following the publication of the proposed rules, the public has the opportunity to provide input on the proposed rules. Called the *public comment period,* this time must last at least 30 days (with certain emergency exceptions)[19] and can consist simply of letters written by

[16] 44 U.S.C. §1505 *et seq.*
[17] 5 U.S.C. §601 *et seq.*
[18] 5 U.S.C. §603(a).
[19] An emergency exemption for the 30-day comment period was made when airport security measures and processes were changed following the September 11, 2001, attacks on the World Trade Center and the Pentagon that were carried out using domestic, commercial airliners.

those affected that are filed with the agency or of hearings conducted by the agency in Washington, D.C., or at specified locations around the country. **For Example,** when the FAA was considering allowing cell phone usage during flights, the public, flight attendants, pilots, and airlines were concerned about the negative consequences of passengers using cell phones. From air rage, to safety concerns, to noise factors, the comments were almost unanimously against the proposal. The agency responded appropriately with a no-go on usage.

Options after Public Comment

After receiving the public input on the proposed rule, an agency can decide to pass, or promulgate, *the rule*. The agency can also decide to withdraw the rule. **For Example,** the EEOC had proposed rules on handling religious discrimination in the workplace. The proposed rules, which would have required employers to police those wearing a cross or other religious symbol, met with so much public and employer protest that they were withdrawn. Finally, the agency can decide to modify the rule based on comments and then promulgate or, if the modifications are extensive or material, modify and put the proposed rule back out for public comment again. A diagram of the rulemaking process can be found in Figure 6-3.

FIGURE 6-3 Steps in Agency Rulemaking

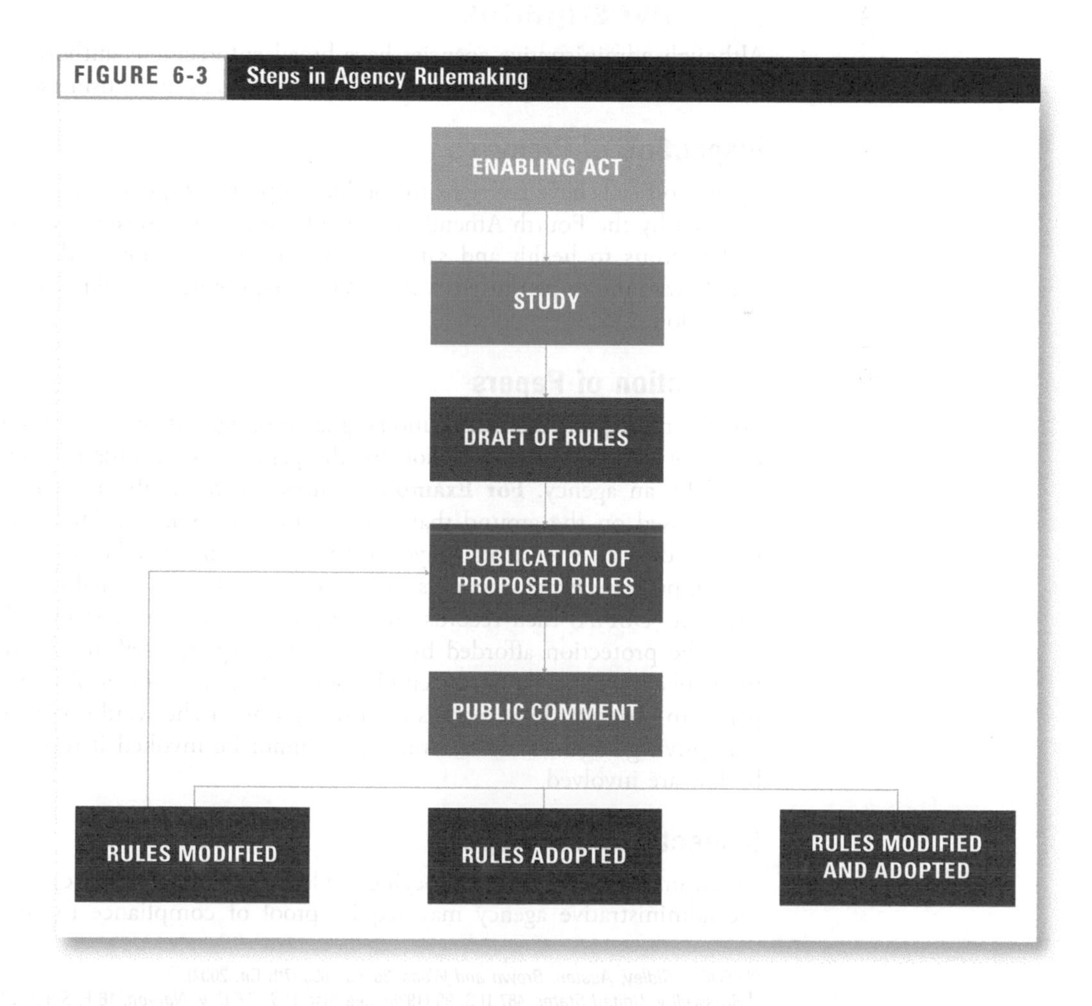

6-3 Executive Power of the Agency

The modern administrative agency has the power to execute the law and to bring proceedings against violators.

6-3a Enforcement or Execution of the Law

An agency has the power to investigate, to require persons to appear as witnesses, to require witnesses to produce relevant papers and records, and to bring proceedings against those who violate the law. In this connection, the phrase *the law* embraces regulations adopted by an agency as well as statutes and court decisions.

An agency may investigate to determine whether any violation of the law or of its rules generally has occurred. An agency may also investigate to determine whether additional rules need to be adopted, to ascertain the facts with respect to a particular suspected or alleged violation, and to see whether the defendant in a proceeding before it is complying with its final order. An agency may issue subpoenas to obtain information reasonably required by its investigation.[20]

6-3b Constitutional Limitations on Administrative Investigation

Although administrative agencies have broad enforcement authority, they remain subject to the constitutional protections afforded individuals and businesses.

Inspection of Premises

Agency officials have the right to conduct inspections, pursuant to the warrant protections afforded by the Fourth Amendment (see Chapter 7). However, when violation of the law is dangerous to health and safety, a workplace inspection without advance notice or a search warrant is permitted when such a requirement could defeat the purpose of the inspection.

Production of Papers

For the most part, the constitutional guarantee against unreasonable searches and seizures does not afford much protection for the papers and records of a business being investigated by an agency. **For Example,** a subpoena to testify or to produce records cannot be opposed on the ground that it is a search and seizure. The constitutional protection is limited to cases of actual physical search and seizure rather than obtaining information by compulsion. Employers must turn over to the Occupational Health and Safety Administration (OSHA) their records on workplace injuries and lost workdays.

The protection afforded by the guarantee against self-incrimination likewise cannot be invoked when a corporate employee or officer in control of corporate records is compelled to produce those records even though he or she would be incriminated by them.[21] The privilege against self-incrimination cannot be invoked if records required to be kept by law are involved.

Inspections and Reports

To ensure that a business is obeying the law, including an agency's regulations and orders, the administrative agency may require proof of compliance through the submission of

[20] *EEOC v. Sidley, Austen, Brown and Wood,* 35 F.3d 696 (7th Cir. 2002).

[21] *Braswell v. United States,* 487 U.S. 99 (1988); see also *U.S. S.E.C. v. Narvett,* 16 F. Supp. 3d 979 (E.D. Wis. 2014).

periodic reports. **For Example,** OSHA requires reports on injuries and fatalities in the workplace. **For Example,** at the local level, cities require that businesses have their tax licenses on display and that those licenses be up-to-date. An agency may also require the regulated person or enterprise to file reports in a specified form.[22]

Administrative agencies also have the right of inspection or the examination either of a building or plant or documents that businesses are required to retain. The element of surprise is important in administrative agency inspections. In fact, in some industries, it is a federal crime for company officers and managers to notify employees about the presence of federal inspectors at the business. **For Example,** following the Massey Energy Company's Upper Big Branch mine disaster that killed 29 miners, several managers and executives were criminally charged for notifying miners that inspectors were on the way and ordering miners to conceal hazards that would result in shut-downs or fines.[23] Three officials have entered guilty pleas or been convicted of the charges.[24] Don Blankenship, the CEO at the time, has also been charged with conspiring to violate safety standards.

6-4 Judicial Power of the Agency

Once the investigation of an agency reveals a potential violation of the law, an agency assumes its third role of judicial arbiter to conduct hearings on violations.

6-4a The Agency as a Specialized Court

An agency, although not a court by law, may be given power to sit as a court and to determine whether any violations of the law or of agency regulations have occurred. The National Labor Relations Board (NLRB) determines whether a prohibited labor practice has been committed.[25] The Securities Exchange Commission (SEC) acts as a court for determining violations of federal securities laws.

Beginning Enforcement—Preliminary Steps

Either a private individual or company or an agency may file a written complaint alleging some violation of law or regulation that is within the agency's jurisdiction. This complaint is then served on the company or individual named in the complaint, who then has the opportunity to file an answer to the allegations. There may be other phases of pleading between the parties and the agency, but, eventually, the matter comes before the agency to be heard. After a hearing, the agency makes a decision and enters an order either dismissing the complaint or directing remedies or resolutions.

The Administrative Hearing

To satisfy the requirements of due process, an agency handling a complaint must generally give notice and hold a hearing at which all persons affected may be present. A significant difference between an agency hearing and a court hearing is that there is no right of trial by jury before an agency. **For Example,** a workers' compensation board may decide a claim without any jury. Similarly, a case in which an employer protests the

[22] *United States v. Morton Salt Co.*, 338 U.S. 632 (1950).

[23] The federal agency involved was the Mine Safety and Health Administration (MSHA).

[24] *U.S. v. Stover*, 499 Fed. Appx. 267 (4th Cir. 2012).

[25] One of the requirements for a valid hearing by an agency is legal appointments of the commissioners to the agency. In *N.L.R.B. v. Noel Canning*, 134 S. Ct. 2550 (2014), the U.S. Supreme Court held that a National Labor Relations Board (NLRB) order was invalid because the president's recess appointments of several members of the board was not valid, and the commissioners had to be nominated and approved by Congress before their actions would be valid.

unemployment tax rate assigned to her company by a state agency has no right to a jury trial. The lack of a jury does not deny due process (see Chapter 4). An **administrative law judge (ALJ)** hears the complaint and has the authority to swear witnesses, take testimony, make evidentiary rulings, and make a decision to recommend to the agency heads for action.

administrative law judge–judicial figure who hears administrative agency actions.

An agency hearing is ordinarily not subject to the rules of evidence. The hearing tends to be more open, with discussion, as opposed to procedural processes that exclude some evidence.

Streamlined Procedure: Consent Decrees

Informal settlements or **consent decrees** are practical devices used to settle administrative law complaints after wrongdoer business is notified of that complaint. A consent decree is similar to a *nolo contendere* plea where there is no admission of guilt, but there are promises related to fines and cease and desists on activities.[26] The Administrative Dispute Resolution Act of 1990 encourages consent decrees and the use of other processes approaches such as alternative dispute resolution in order to expedite cases.[27] **For Example,** Kellogg's settled with the FTC on deceptive advertising charges related to health claims about its Rice Krispies®, Frosted Flakes®, and Special K® cereals. Without admitting any violation of the law, Kellogg's agreed to change the ads and package claims for the cereals. Kellogg's could no longer claim that its cereals increased the attentiveness of children.

informal settlements–negotiated disposition of a matter before an administrative agency, generally without public sanctions.

consent decrees–informal settlements of enforcement actions brought by agencies.

The Hearing Process

If the parties cannot reach an agreement through a consent decree, the questions of violations and penalties will go to an administrative hearing, which is quite different from the litigation described in Chapter 2. The defendant in an administrative law hearing is the person or company accused of a violation of an administrative regulation. The judge in these hearings is called an administrative law judge (ALJ) and at other levels of government is often called a **hearing examiner** or **hearing officer.**

Administrative hearings often have additional parties involved, parties with an interest in the case are permitted to participate, and are called **intervenors.** They enter the case through motions to intervene and are usually permitted to do so at any time before the start of a hearing. Typical intervenors are industry organizations. **For Example,** snowmobile manufacturers and the state of Wyoming, because of their economic interests in snowmobile activities, were intervenors in the national park cases challenging the Department of Interior snowmobile regulations for national parks.

hearing officer (or examiner)–another name for an administrative law judge.

intervenors–in administrative actions, third parties who have an interest in the issues being determined by an ALJ.

The Administrative Agency Decision

When an administrative agency makes a decision, it usually files an opinion that sets forth findings of facts and reasons for that decision. In some instances, a statute expressly requires this type of opinion, but agencies usually file opinions so that the parties and the court (in the event of an appeal) will understand the agency's action and reasoning.[28]

[26] The late comedian Johnny Carson said a defense decree is when a business says, "I didn't do anything, but I promise never to do it again."

[27] 5 U.S.C. §571 *et seq.*

[28] *Jordan v. Civil Service Bd., Charlotte*, 570 S.E.2d 912 (N.C. App. 2002).

6-4b Punishment and Enforcement Powers of Agencies

Penalty

Within the last few decades, agencies have increasingly been given the power to impose a penalty and to issue orders that are binding on a regulated party unless an appeal is taken to a court, which reverses the administrative decision. **For Example,** the Occupational Safety and Health Act of 1970 provides for the assessment of civil penalties against employers who fail to end dangerous working conditions when ordered to do so by the administrative agency created by that statute.[29] **For Example,** BP paid over $150 million in fines following the explosion at its Texas City refinery because the company had failed to address over 400 previously cited OSHA violations.

Cease-and-Desist Order

cease-and-desist order–order issued by a court or administrative agency to stop a practice that it decides is improper.

Environmental protection statutes adopted by states commonly give a state agency the power to assess a penalty for violating environmental protection regulations. As an illustration of the issuance of binding orders, the FTC can issue a **cease-and-desist order** to stop a practice that it decides is improper. This order to stop is binding unless reversed on an appeal. **For Example,** the FTC can order a company to stop making claims in ads that have been determined by that agency to be deceptive.

6-4c Exhaustion of Administrative Remedies

exhaustion of administrative remedies–requirement that an agency make its final decision before the parties can go to court.

The parties involved in an administrative agency action cannot obtain judicial review until the agency has made its final findings or decision in the case. The parties in administrative actions are required to go through the administrative process, something that is referred to the exhaustion of administrative remedies before they can take the action to court.

Exceptions to the **exhaustion of administrative remedies** requirement are: (1) available remedies that provide no genuine opportunity for adequate relief; (2) irreparable injury that could occur if immediate judicial relief is not provided; (3) an appeal to the administrative agency that would be useless; or (4) a substantial constitutional question that the plaintiff has raised.

6-4d Appeal from an Administrative Agency Action

There are several bases for challenging administrative agency actions. These bases are covered in the following sections.

Procedural Issues

If the procedure that an agency is to follow is specified by law, a decision of the agency that was made without following that procedure will be set aside and the matter sent back to the agency to proceed according to the required law.[30] An agency's actions, whether enforcement or rule promulgation, can be set aside if the agency has not followed the procedures required for rulemaking or, in the case of enforcement, the due process rights of the charged business or individual.

Substantive Law or Fact Issues

When the question that an agency decides is a question of law, a court will reverse the agency if the court disagrees with the legal interpretation.[31] Courts tend to accept the

[29] 29 U.S.C. §651 *et seq.*

[30] *Tingler v. State Board of Cosmetology,* 814 S.W.2d 683 (Mo. App. 1991).

[31] *Wallace v. Iowa State Bd. of Educ.,* 770 N.W.2d 344 (Iowa 2009).

agency's interpretation so long as it was reasonable even though it was not the only interpretation that could have been made.

A court will not reverse an agency's decision merely because the court would have made a different decision based on the same facts.[32] Courts assume that the agency has acted properly and those who appeal an agency decision must be able to show that the agency did not act on the basis of the facts or deliberately excluded facts.

Ultra Vires or Beyond the Jurisdiction of the Agency

The action of an agency can be set aside if what the agency has done is beyond the authority granted in the enabling statute for its creation. Several groups and businesses filed suit against the EPA challenging the Transport Rule, a rule designed to limit pollution across state lines. [*EME Homer City Generation, L.P. v. EPA*, 134 S. Ct. 1584 (2014)] The rule was challenged as *ultra vires* (beyond an agency's statutory authority). The court held that the Clean Air Act gave the EPA authority to determine how to allocate responsibility for a downwind state's excess pollution and that the Transport Rule was a permissible way for the EPA to construct the good neighbor concept.

Arbitrary and Capricious

When an agency changes its prior decisions and customary actions, it must give its reasons. In the absence of such an explanation, a reviewing court can set aside the agency action.[33]

CASE SUMMARY

Drilling Down to Arbitrary and Capricious Rules

FACTS: Hornbeck and others (plaintiffs) provide services to support offshore oil and gas drilling, exploration, and production activities in the Gulf of Mexico. Kenneth Salazar is the Secretary of the Department of Interior (DOI), a federal agency that includes the Minerals Management.

Following the BP Deepwater Horizon drilling platform explosion on April 20, 2010, and the resulting devastation and unprecedented disaster, President Obama asked DOI to conduct a study to determine what steps were needed to be taken to prevent another problem with oil rigs in the Gulf.

DOI did a 30-day study, consulting respected experts from state and federal governments, academic institutions, and industry and advocacy organizations. On May 27, 2010, DOI issued a Report that recommended a six-month moratorium on permits for new wells and an immediate halt to drilling operations on the 33 permitted wells in the Gulf of Mexico. The DOI report also stated that "the recommendations contained in this report have been peer-reviewed by seven experts identified by the National Academy of Engineering." The experts pointedly observed that this statement was misleading and called it a "misrepresentation." Although the experts agreed with the safety recommendations contained in the body of the main Report, five of the National Academy of Engineering experts and three of the other experts publicly stated that they "do not agree with the six month blanket moratorium" on floating drilling. They envisioned a more limited kind of moratorium, but a blanket moratorium was added after their final review and was never agreed to by them. The plaintiffs moved for a preliminary injunction against the moratorium.

DECISION: The court held that the experts balking at the conclusion of the report, the inconsistency of the moratorium with the report information, and the availability of alternatives made the moratorium unlikely to survive a challenge of the action being arbitrary and capricious and issued an injunction. [***Hornbeck Offshore Services, L.L.C. et al. v. Salazar*, 696 F. Supp. 2d 627 (E.D. La. 2010)**]

[32] *Dorchester Associates LLC v. District of Columbia Bd. of Zoning Adjustment,* 976 A.2d 200 (D.C. 2009).
[33] *Lorillard Tobacco Co. v. Roth,* 786 N.E.2d 7 (N.Y. App. 2003).

Constitutional Rights

Challenges to administrative agency rules and actions can also be based in constitutional rights.[34] **For Example,** agency restrictions on language or religious freedom have been successfully challenged in court. EEOC regulations on employees wearing religious jewelry (such as necklaces with crosses) were withdrawn after the agency realized through congressional actions that the regulations could not survive a constitutional challenge.

CASE SUMMARY

The Obscenity Case That Has Been Around as Long as Cher

FACTS: In a case that has been around almost as long as Cher, the U.S. Supreme Court, once again, issued a decision related to three FCC charges against Fox and ABC Television. First, in the 2002 Billboard Music Awards, broadcast by Fox Television, the singer Cher exclaimed during an unscripted acceptance speech: "I've also had my critics for the last 40 years saying that I was on my way out every year. Right. So f * * * 'em." At the 2003 Billboard Music Awards, Nicole Richie made the following unscripted remark while presenting an award: "Have you ever tried to get cow s* * * out of a Prada purse? It's not so f * * *ing simple." The third incident involved an episode of *NYPD Blue*, a regular television show broadcast by respondent ABC Television Network. The episode, broadcast on February 25, 2003, showed the nude buttocks of an adult female character for approximately seven seconds and for a moment the side of her breast. During the scene, in which the character was preparing to take a shower, a child portraying her boyfriend's son entered the bathroom. A moment of awkwardness followed. The FCC received indecency complaints about all three broadcasts.

After these incidents, but before the FCC issued Notices of Apparent Liability to Fox and ABC, it issued a decision sanctioning NBC for a comment made by the singer Bono during the 2003 Golden Globe Awards. Upon winning the award for Best Original Song, Bono exclaimed: "'This is really, really, f * * *ing brilliant. Really, really great.'" The FCC found that the use of the F-word was "one of the most vulgar, graphic and explicit descriptions of sexual activity in the English language," and found that "any use of that word or a variation, in any context, inherently" indecent. The FCC then found that both Fox and ABC had violated commission standards for decency.

The networks appealed the findings of indecency and their fines ($1.4 million each). The U.S. Supreme Court [*FCC v. Fox Television Stations, Inc.* (Fox 1), 556 U.S. 502 (2009)] held that the FCC's findings were not arbitrary nor capricious and remanded the case for findings related to the network's First Amendment challenges to the fines. On remand, the Court of Appeals found that the FCC indecency policy failed to give broadcasters sufficient notice of what would be considered indecent. The Court of Appeals found that the FCC was inconsistent as to which words it deemed patently offensive. The FCC standard was held to be void for vagueness. The FCC appealed.

DECISION: On appeal the U.S. Supreme Court held that the FCC failed to give Fox or ABC fair notice prior to the broadcasts in question that fleeting expletives and momentary nudity could be found indecent. Therefore, the FCC's standards, as applied to these broadcasts, were vague and void under the First Amendment. The Court set aside the FCC's findings as well as its orders and fines against the networks.

The FCC is free to create standards of decency for broadcasting programs. However, the standards must be established in advance of any charges of violations and those standards must be clear and applied consistently. Because the broadcasters would not have understood the standard at the time the violations occurred, the U.S. Supreme Court struck down the standards as void for vagueness. **[*F.C.C. v. Fox Television Stations, Inc.*, 132 S. Ct. 2307 (2012)]**

[34] *CBS Corp. v. F.C.C.*, 663 F.3d 122 (3rd Cir. 2011).

Make the Connection

Summary

The administrative agency is unique because it combines the three functions that are kept separate under our traditional governmental system: legislative, executive, and judicial. By virtue of legislative power, an agency adopts regulations that have the force of law, although agency members are not elected by those subject to the regulations. By virtue of the executive power, an agency carries out and enforces the regulations, makes investigations, and requires the production of documents. By virtue of the judicial power, an agency acts as a court to determine whether a violation of any regulation has occurred.

To some extent, an agency is restricted by constitutional limitations in inspecting premises and requiring the production of papers. These limitations, however, have a very narrow application in agency actions. When an agency acts as a judge, a jury trial is not required, nor must ordinary courtroom procedures be followed. Typically, an agency gives notice to the person claimed to be acting improperly, and a hearing is then held before the agency. When the agency has determined that there has been a violation, it may order that the violation stop. Under some statutes, the agency may go further and impose a penalty on the violator.

No appeal from an administrative agency's action can be made until every step available before the agency has been taken; that is, the administrative remedy must first be exhausted. An agency's actions can be reversed by a court if the agency exceeded its authority, the decision is not based in law or fact, the decision is arbitrary and capricious, the decision violates the laws or the rights of those affected by the agency's rule or actions, or, finally, the agency violated procedural steps.

Protection from secret government is provided by Sunshine laws that afford the right to know what most administrative agency records contain; by the requirement that most agency meetings be open to the public; by the invitation to the public to take part in rulemaking; and by publicity given, through publication in the *Federal Register* and trade publications, to the guidelines followed by the agency and the regulations it has adopted.

Learning Outcomes

After studying this chapter, you should be able to clearly explain:

6-1 Nature of the Administrative Agency

LO.1 Describe the nature and purpose of administrative agencies

See the discussion of the unique nature of agencies, pages 87–88.

See the discussion of obligations of administrative agencies, including APA and FOIA, page 88.

See Ethics & the Law on the IRS, page 89.

See the net neutrality Cyberlaw issue, page 92.

6-2 Legislative Power of the Agency

LO.2 Discuss the legislative or rulemaking power of administrative agencies

See the *Massachusetts v. EPA* case, pages 90–91.

6-3 Executive Power of the Agency

LO.3 Explain the executive or enforcement function of administrative agencies

See the *FCC* case, page 99.

See the Massey Energy example, page 95.

See the Kellogg's example on consent decrees, page 96.

6-4 Judicial Power of the Agency

LO.4 Discuss the judicial power of administrative agencies including the rule on exhaustion of administrative remedies

See the *Salazar* case, page 98.

Key Terms

administrative agency
administrative law
administrative law judge (ALJ)
Administrative Procedure Act
cease-and-desist order
consent decrees
exhaustion-of-administrative remedies
Federal Register
Federal Register Act
Freedom of Information Act
hearing examiner
hearing officer
informal settlements
intervenors
open meeting law

Questions and Case Problems

1. Following the events of September 11, 2001, in which four airplanes crashed as a result of the presence of terrorists on those flights, the FAA concluded that it needed to implement new procedures for airports and flights. The new procedures for security and flights took effect when the airports reopened five days later. Why did the FAA not need to go through the promulgation and public comment processes and time periods to have the new rules take effect?

2. The FDA was challenged by tobacco companies for its new rules that required the tobacco companies to put one of the FDA's 12 picture labels on its packaging. The tobacco companies argued that their First Amendment rights were violated by the rules, forcing them to speak in a certain way using government-mandated materials. The new labels were promulgated by both the FDA and the Department of Health and Human Services (HHS) pursuant to authority granted by Congress in 2009 under the Family Smoking Prevention and Tobacco Control Act.

   Under the law, the following nine textual statements were to be included on cigarette labels:

   WARNING: Cigarettes are addictive.

   WARNING: Tobacco smoke can harm your children.

   WARNING: Cigarettes cause fatal lung disease.

   WARNING: Cigarettes cause cancer.

   WARNING: Cigarettes cause strokes and heart disease.

   WARNING: Smoking during pregnancy can harm your baby.

   WARNING: Smoking can kill you.

   WARNING: Tobacco smoke causes fatal lung diseases in nonsmokers.

   WARNING: Quitting smoking now greatly reduces serious risks to your health.

   The act required that these warnings and graphic labels take up 50 percent of the cigarette package label and 20 percent of all cigarette ads.

   After publishing the proposed rule and receiving more than 1,700 comments, the FDA published its final rule in June 2011. Explain how the tobacco companies could challenge the rules. Discuss whether the rules will be set aside. [In the case of *R.J. Reynolds Tobacco Company et al. v. FDA et al.*, 696 F.3d 1205 (D.C. Cir.)]

3. The Tacoma-Pierce County Health Department conducted an investigation into the quality of care provided by ambulance service providers in its jurisdiction. On the basis of that investigation, the department issued a set of temporary rules and regulations that established minimum requirements for equipment, drugs, and service availability for ambulance service providers in Pierce County. The *Tacoma News* wanted to publish an article on the matter and sought discovery of everything that had led to the adoption of the regulations, including all details of the investigation made by the health department. The health department objected to disclosing the names of the persons who had volunteered information on which the department had based its action and the names of the ambulance companies. Were the names subject to a Freedom of Information Act (FOIA) request? [*Tacoma News, Inc. v. Tacoma-Pierce County Health Dept.*, 778 P.2d 1066 (Wash. App.)]

4. Congress adopted a law to provide insurance to protect wheat farmers. The agency in charge of the program adopted regulations to govern applications for this insurance. These regulations were published in the *Federal Register*. Merrill applied for insurance, but his application did not comply with the regulations. He claimed that he was not bound by the regulations because he never knew they had been adopted. Is he bound by the regulations? [*Federal Crop Ins. Corp. v. Merrill*, 332 U.S. 380]

5. Santa Monica adopted a rent control ordinance authorizing the Rent Control Board to set the amount of rents that could be charged. At a hearing before it, the board determined that McHugh was charging his tenants a rent higher than the maximum allowed. McHugh claimed that the action of the board was improper because there was no jury trial. Is McHugh correct? Why or why not? [*McHugh v. Santa Monica Rent Control Board*, 777 P.2d 911 (Cal.)]

6. New York City's charter authorized the New York City Board of Health to adopt a health code that it declared to have the force and effect of law. The board adopted a code that provided for the fluoridation of the public water supply. A suit was brought to enjoin the carrying out of this program on the grounds that it was unconstitutional and that money

could not be spent to carry out such a program in the absence of a statute authorizing the expenditure. It was also claimed that the fluoridation program was unconstitutional because there were other means of reducing tooth decay; fluoridation was discriminatory by benefiting only children; it unlawfully imposed medication on children without their consent; and fluoridation was or may be dangerous to health. Was the code's provision valid? [*Paduano v. City of New York*, 257 N.Y.S.2d 531]

7. What is the *Federal Register*? What role does it play in rulemaking? What is the difference between the *Federal Register* and the Code of Federal Regulations?
8. The Consumer Product Safety Commission is reconsidering a rule it first proposed in 1997 that would require child-resistant caps on household products, including cosmetics. When the rule was first proposed in 1997, it was resisted by the cosmetics industry and abandoned. However, in May 2001, a 16-month-old baby died after drinking baby oil from a bottle with a pull-tab cap.

   The proposed rule would cover products such as baby oil and suntan lotion and any products containing hydrocarbons such as cleansers and spot removers. The danger, according to the commission, is simply the inhalation by children, not necessarily the actual ingestion of the products. Five children have died from inhaling such fumes since 1993, and 6,400 children under the age of five were brought into emergency rooms and/or hospitalized for treatment after breathing in hydrocarbons. There is no medical treatment for the inhalation of hydrocarbons.

   Several companies in the suntan oil/lotion industry have supported the new regulations. The head of a consumer group has said, "We know these products cause death and injury. That is all we need to know."[35]

   What process must the CPSC follow to promulgate the rules? What do you think of the consumer group head's statement? Will that statement alone justify the rulemaking?
9. The *Federal Register* contained the following provision from the Environmental Protection Agency on January 14, 2002:

   We, the U.S. Fish and Wildlife Service (Service), announce the re-opening of the comment period on the proposed listing of Lomatium cookii *(Cook's lomatium) and* Limnanthes floccosa ssp. grandiflora *(large-flowered wooly meadowfoam) as endangered species under the Endangered Species Act of 1973, as amended (Act). We are re-opening the comment period to provide the public an opportunity to review additional information on the status, abundance, and distribution of these plants, and to request additional information and comments from the public regarding the proposed rule. Comments previously submitted need not be resubmitted as they will be incorporated into the public record as part of this extended comment period; all comments will be fully considered in the final rule.*

   DATES: We will accept public comments until March 15, 2002.

   What was the EPA doing and why? What could those who had concerns do at that point?
10. Macon County Landfill Corp. applied for permission to expand the boundaries of its landfill. Tate and others opposed the application. After a number of hearings, the appropriate agency granted the requested permission to expand. Tate appealed and claimed that the agency had made a wrong decision on the basis of the evidence presented. Will the court determine whether the correct decision was made? [*Tate v. Illinois Pollution Control Board*, 544 N.E.2d 1176 (Ill. App.)]
11. The planning commissioner and a real estate developer planned to meet to discuss rezoning certain land that would permit the real estate developer to construct certain buildings not allowed under the then-existing zoning law. A homeowners association claimed it had the right to be present at the meeting. This claim was objected to on the theory that the state's Open Meetings Act applied only to meetings of specified government units and did not extend to a meeting between one of them and an outsider. Was this objection valid?
12. The Michigan Freedom of Information Act declares that it is the state's policy to give all persons full information about the actions of the government and that "the people shall be informed so that they may participate in the democratic process." The union of clerical workers at Michigan State University requested the trustees of the university to give them the names and addresses of persons making monetary donations to the university. Michigan State objected because the disclosure of addresses was a violation of the right of privacy. Decide. [*Clerical-Technical*

[35] Julian E. Barnes, "Safety Caps Are Considered for Cosmetics," *New York Times*, October 10, 2001, C1, C8.

Union of Michigan State University v. Board of Trustees of Michigan State University, 475 N.W.2d 373 (Mich.)]

13. The Department of Health and Human Services has proposed new guidelines for the interpretation of federal statutes on gifts, incentives, and other benefits bestowed on physicians by pharmaceutical companies. The areas on which the interpretation focused follow:

    - Paying doctors to act as consultants or market researchers for prescription drugs
    - Paying pharmacies fees to switch patients to new drugs
    - Providing grants, scholarships, and anything more than nominal gifts to physicians for time, information sessions, and so on, on new drugs[36]

    The Office of Inspector General is handling the new rules interpretation and has established a public comment period of 60 days. Explain the purpose of the public comment period. What ethical issues do the regulations attempt to address?

14. San Diego Air Sports (SDAS) Center operates a sports parachuting business in Otay Mesa, California. SDAS offers training to beginning parachutists and facilitates recreational jumping for experienced parachutists. It indicates that the majority of SDAS jumps occur at altitudes in excess of 5,800 feet. The jump zone used by SDAS overlaps the San Diego Traffic Control Area (TCA). Although the aircraft carrying the parachutists normally operate outside the TCA, the parachutists themselves are dropped through it. Thus, the air traffic controllers must approve each jump.

    In July 1987, an air traffic controller in San Diego filed an Unsatisfactory Condition Report with the Federal Aviation Administration (FAA), complaining of the strain that parachuting was putting on the controllers and raising safety concerns. The report led to a staff study of parachute jumping within the San Diego TCA. This was followed by a letter in March 1988 from the FAA to SDAS, informing SDAS that "[e]ffective immediately parachute jumping within or into the San Diego TCA in the Otay Reservoir Jump Zone will not be authorized." The FAA stated that the letter was final and appealable. SDAS challenged the letter in federal court on grounds that it constituted rulemaking without compliance with required Administrative Procedure Act (APA) procedures. Who is correct in this dispute and why? [*San Diego Air Sports Center, Inc. v. FAA*, 887 F.2d 966 (9th Cir.)]

15. The Endangered Species Act (ESA) charges the National Marine Fisheries Service (a federal agency) with the duty to "ensure" that any proposed action by the Council does not "jeopardize" any threatened or endangered species. The Steller sea lion is on the list of endangered species. The agency developed a North Pacific marine fishery plan that permitted significant harvest of fish by commercial fisheries in the area. Greenpeace, an environmental group, challenged the agency on the grounds that the plan was not based on a sufficient number of biological studies on the impact of the allowed fishing on the Steller sea lion. Greenpeace's biologic opinion concluded that the fishery plan would reduce the level of food for the sea lions by about 40 percent to 60 percent, if the juvenile fish were not counted in that figure. Greenpeace's expert maintained that counting juvenile fish was misleading because they were not capable of reproducing and the government agency's figure was, as a result, much lower at 22 percent. What would Greenpeace need to show to be successful in challenging the agency's fishery plan? [*Greenpeace, American Oceans Campaign v. National Marine Fisheries Service*, 237 F. Supp. 2d 1181 (W.D. Wash.)]

[36]See 67 *Federal Register* 62057, October 3, 2002. Go to **http://www.oig.hhs.gov.** See also Robert Pear, "U.S. Warning to Drug Makers Over Payments," *New York Times*, October 1, 2002, A1, A23; Julie Appleby, "Feds Warn Drugmakers: Gifts to Doctors May Be Illegal," *USA Today*, October 2, 2002, 1A.

CHAPTER 7

Crimes

››› Learning Outcomes

After studying this chapter, you should be able to

LO.1 Discuss the nature and classification of crimes

LO.2 Describe the basis of criminal liability

LO.3 Identify who is responsible for criminal acts

LO.4 Explain the penalties for crimes and the sentencing for corporate crimes

LO.5 List examples of white-collar crimes and their elements

LO.6 Describe the common law crimes

LO.7 Discuss crimes related to computers

LO.8 Describe the rights of businesses charged with crimes and the constitutional protections afforded them

7-1 General Principles

Society sets certain standards of conduct and punishes a breach of those standards as a crime. This chapter introduces the means by which government protects people and businesses from prohibited conduct.

Detailed criminal codes and statutes define crimes and specify their punishment. Crimes vary from state to state but still show the imprint of a common law background through similar elements and structure.

7-1a Nature and Classification of Crimes

crime–violation of the law that is punished as an offense against the state or government.

misdemeanor–criminal offense with a sentence of less than one year that is neither treason nor a felony.

felony–criminal offense that is punishable by confinement in prison for more than one year or by death, or that is expressly stated by statute to be a felony.

A **crime** is conduct that is prohibited and punished by a government. Crimes are classified as *common law* or *statutory* according to their origin. Offenses punishable by less than one year in prison are called **misdemeanors.** More serious crimes are called **felonies,** including serious business crimes such as bribery and embezzlement, which are punishable by confinement in prison for more than one year. Misdemeanors include weighing goods with uninspected scales or operating without a sales tax license. An act may be a felony in one state and a misdemeanor in another.[1]

7-1b Basis of Criminal Liability

A crime generally consists of two elements: (1) a mental state (scienter or intent) and (2) an act or omission. Harm may occur as a result of a crime, but harm is not an essential element of a crime.

Mental State

Mental state, scienter, or intent, does not require an awareness or knowledge of guilt. In most crimes, the voluntary commission of the act is sufficient for proving mental state. Ignorance that a law is being broken does not mean there is not mental state. **For Example,** dumping waste without a permit is still a criminal act even when the party releasing the waste did not know about the permit requirement.

Act or Omission

Specific statutes define the conduct, or *actus reus*, that, when coupled with sufficient mental state, constitutes a crime. **For Example,** writing a check knowing you do not have the funds available is a crime. Likewise, the failure to file your annual income tax returns is also a crime.

CASE SUMMARY

Did I Know Pumping Gas Was a Crime?

FACTS: Ahmad owns a Spin-N-Market in Texas, a convenience store and gas station. One of the Spin-N-Market's gasoline tanks developed a leak. Jewel McCoy of CIT Environmental Services inspected the tank and said it needed to be drained and then pumped. McCoy gave Ahmad the cost of draining, and he suggested he would do it himself despite

[1] Some states further define crimes by seriousness with different degrees of a crime, such as first-degree murder, second-degree murder, and so on. Misdemeanors may be differentiated by giving special names to minor misdemeanors.

Did I Know Pumping Gas Was a Crime? continued

McCoy's warning about violations of the law. Ahmad rented a pump at the local hardware store and pumped over 5,000 gallons into a manhole near his store (4,690 of those gallons were gasoline). The gasoline made its way to the storm sewer system and then a creek as well as the city sewage treatment center. While firemen were working to divert the gasoline, the treatment center and two nearby schools had to be evacuated. Ahmad was charged with violation of the Clean Water Act and was convicted of two charges.

DECISION: The appeals court held that Ahmad did not have the intent to violate the statute, the CWA, because he thought that he was discharging water, not gasoline. There is more knowledge required for CWA violations; it is a criminal statute and there cannot be just strict liability—there still must be a showing of mental intent. [***United States v. Ahmad*, 101 F.3d 386 (5th Cir. 1996)**]

7-1c Responsibility for Criminal Acts

In some cases, persons who did not necessarily commit the criminal act itself are still held criminally responsible for acts committed by others.

Corporate Liability

Corporations are held responsible for the acts of their employees. A corporation may also be held liable for crimes based on the failure of its employees to act. In the past decade, some of the nation's largest corporations have paid fines for crimes based on employees' failure to take action or for the actions they did take. **For Example,** Siemens, an international company, paid the largest fine in the history of the Foreign Corrupt Practices Act for paying bribes in order to win contracts in countries around the world, a total of $1.6 billion in fines, including $350 million in the United States.

Officers and Agents of Corporations

One of the main differences between nonbusiness and business crimes is that more people in a company can be convicted for the same business crime. For nonbusiness crimes, only those who are actually involved in the act itself can be convicted of the crime. For business crimes, however, managers of firms whose employees commit criminal acts can be held liable if the managers authorized the conduct of the employees or knew about their conduct and did nothing or failed to act reasonably in their supervisory positions to prevent the employees from engaging in criminal conduct. **For Example,** the former security chief for Massey Energy was sentenced to three years in prison after being found guilty of notifying employees in advance of the arrival of federal mine inspectors at the company's mines.[2]

CASE SUMMARY

Rats in the Warehouse and a CEO with a Fine

FACTS: Acme Markets, Inc., was a national food retail chain headquartered in Philadelphia. John R. Park was president of Acme, which, in 1970, employed 36,000 people and operated 16 warehouses.

In 1970, the Food and Drug Administration (FDA) forwarded a letter to Park describing, in detail, problems with rodent infestation in Acme's Philadelphia warehouse facility. In December 1971, the FDA found the same types

[2] Ken Maher, "Ex-Massey Official Gets Three Years," *Wall Street Journal*, March 1, 2012, p. A3.

Rats in the Warehouse and a CEO with a Fine continued

of conditions in Acme's Baltimore warehouse facility. In January 1972, the FDA's chief of compliance for its Baltimore office wrote to Park about the inspection:

> *We note with much concern that the old and new warehouse areas used for food storage were actively and extensively inhabited by live rodents. Of even more concern was the observation that such reprehensible conditions obviously existed for a prolonged period of time without any detection, or were completely ignored.*
>
> *We trust this letter will serve to direct your attention to the seriousness of the problem and formally advise you of the urgent need to initiate whatever measures are necessary to prevent recurrence and ensure compliance with the law.*

After Park received the letter, he met with the vice president for legal affairs for Acme and was assured that he was "investigating the situation immediately and would be taking corrective action."

When the FDA inspected the Baltimore warehouse in March 1972, there was some improvement in the facility, but there was still rodent infestation. Acme and Park were both charged with violations of the federal Food, Drug and Cosmetic Act. Acme pleaded guilty. Park was convicted and fined $500; he appealed.

DECISION: Officers of a corporation can be held criminally liable for the conduct of others within the company if it can be shown that the officers knew of the issue and failed to take the steps necessary to eliminate the criminal activity. In this case, Park had been warned and had been given several opportunities to remedy the problem. Part of his responsibility as an officer is following up to be certain that tasks he has assigned are completed. Failure to follow through can be a basis for criminal liability. **[*United States v. Park*, 421 U.S. 658 (1975)]**

Federal Laws Targeting Officer and Director Criminal Responsibility

Following the Michael Milken and Ivan Boesky junk bond era on Wall Street in 1988, the Insider Trading and Securities Fraud Act of 1988 increased the criminal penalties for officers and directors who violated the law tenfold. In addition, the "white-collar kingpin" law imposed mandatory minimum sentences for corporate officers. Sarbanes-Oxley, which followed the 2000-era dot-com failures increased penalties for officers and directors from 5 years to 20 years, along with an increase in fines by 20 times. Under The Dodd-Frank Wall Street Reform and Consumer Protection Act, the types of white-collar executives covered under criminal laws increased to include brokers, insurers, and any financial services firms. In addition, Dodd-Frank created the Consumer Financial Protection Bureau (CFPB) that has the ability to refer cases to the Justice Department for prosecution. **For Example,** the CFPB would receive information about mortgage lenders, banks, and insurers from consumers that could then be turned over for possible criminal charges.

So-called honest services fraud has been refined by Dodd-Frank and court decisions.[3] Executives can no longer be convicted on the basis that something went wrong at their company. Proof of fraud requires something more than an officer just being an officer at the company—there must be active engagement in operations that led to the officer's committing fraud or some underlying crime, such as bribery that led to the company problems and loss in value.

Penalty for Crime: Forfeiture

When a defendant is convicted of a crime, the court may also declare that the defendant's rights in any property used or gained from a crime (an instrument of that crime) be confiscated. Some types of instruments of the crime are automatically forfeited, such as the tools of a crime. **For Example,** the U.S. government confiscated from confessed $50 billion Ponzi schemer, Bernie Madoff, everything from his yacht to his bank accounts

[3] *Skilling v. U.S.*, 561 U.S. 538 (2010).

to his seat on NASDAQ. Confiscation is, in effect, an increased penalty for the defendant's crime.

Penalties for Business and White-Collar Crimes

Most common law criminal penalties were created with "natural" persons in mind, as opposed to "artificial" or corporate persons. A $100,000 fine may be significant to an individual but to a corporation with $3 billion in assets and hundreds of millions in income, such a fine could be viewed as a minimal cost of doing business.

As a result of these fine amount realities, corporate penalties and processes have been reformed. Congress, prosecutors, and the courts are in continual processes of developing penalties for corporations and white-collar crimes so that the result is both a deterrent effect as well as changes in cultures of corporations to prevent additional violations.

Computing New Penalties for Corporations. Criminal penalties have been increased to allow judges to fine corporations according to how much a bad decision would cost. Rather than using fixed-amount fines for corporations, statutes and courts apply percentage of income, revenue, or profits penalties. **For Example,** a bad decision on a product line would cost a company 10 to 20 percent of its earnings. A criminal penalty could be imposed using that type of computation for the knowing sale of a defective product in this same percentage fashion with the idea that the company simply made a bad legal decision that should be reflected by an imposed earnings.

Corporate Integrity Agreements. Using a corporate integrity agreement (CIA), judges are able to, in effect, place corporations on probation. Under CIAs, companies are assigned monitors who are on-site and follow up to be sure the company is not committing any further violations. **For Example,** because of environmental law violations, ConEd was assigned a monitor from the National Resources Defense Council to observe the company's activities. Likewise, Apple has a monitor to prevent antitrust violations as a result of its civil charges of noncompetitive behavior. CIAs do not require an admission of guilt but generally require the payment of a fine and an agreement to "stay clean" for three to five years.

Federal Sentencing Guidelines. Another change in penalties for business and white-collar crimes has been the requirement for mandatory prison sentences for officers and directors who are convicted of crimes committed as they led their corporations. The human element of the corporation is then punished for the crimes that the business committed. The U.S. Sentencing Commission, established by Congress in 1984, has developed both federal sentencing guidelines and a carrot-and-stick approach to fighting business crime. If the managers of a company are involved and working to prevent criminal misconduct in the company and a crime occurs, the guidelines permit sentence reductions for the managers' efforts. If the managers do not adequately supervise conduct and do not encourage compliance with the law, the guidelines require judges to impose harsher sentences and fines. The guidelines, referred to as the **Federal Sentencing Guidelines** (or the *U.S. Sentencing Guidelines*), apply to federal crimes such as securities fraud, antitrust violations, racketeering, theft (embezzlement), Medicare fraud, and other business crimes. The sentencing guidelines permit a judge to place a guilty company on probation, with the length of the probation controlled by whether the company had prevention programs in place.

Federal Sentencing Guidelines–federal standards used by judges in determining mandatory sentence terms for those convicted of federal crimes.

Officer and Executive Banishment from Business Fields. One of the rapidly increasing forms of business crime punishment is barring executives and officers from working in their fields if they have a criminal conviction. **For Example,** the SEC can bar those who are convicted from the securities industry for a period of years or even for life (as in the case of junk bond king Michael Milken). In the health care field, federal agencies use the "responsible corporate officer" (RCO) doctrine to hold those who head up companies criminally responsible when their hospitals submit false Medicare claims or their drug firms misbrand prescription drugs. In addition to criminal sanctions for RCOs, agencies prosecuting the health care cases also seek to have the RCOs barred from the health care industry for periods that range from one year to life, with the typical time being 12 to 20 years.

Mandatory Sentences for Officers of Corporations Who Mastermind Crimes. The increased corporate and white-collar criminal penalties enacted under Sarbanes-Oxley (SOX) (see the next section for more discussion of SOX) also allow judges to consider the seriousness of the offense, the company's history of violations, its cooperation in the investigation, the effectiveness of its compliance program (often called an *ethics program*), and the role of senior management in the wrongdoing in determining fines and sentences. Corporate managers found to have masterminded any criminal activity must be sentenced to prison time.[4] Figure 7-1 is a summary of the current penalties for federal crimes. Under a U.S. Supreme Court decision, *U.S. v. Booker*, judges may only use the guidelines as just

FIGURE 7-1 Roster of White-Collar Criminal Charges

COMPANY/PERSON	ISSUE	STATUS
Boeing (2003)	Charges of illicit use of competitor's proprietary documents; charges of recruiting government official	Loss of 7 government contracts worth $250 million; $615 million fine; guilty plea by official who was wooed; 9-month sentence for that official
Countrywide Mortgage (2009)	Insider trading; securities fraud	Former CEO Angelo Mozilo charged with insider trading, CFO and COO charged with failure to disclose firm's relaxed lending standards; settled case for fines
Andrew Fastow, former CFO of Enron (2004)	Multimillion-dollar earnings from serving as principal in SPEs (special purpose entities) of Enron created to keep debts off the company books	Entered guilty plea to securities and wire fraud; sentenced to 6 years; helping plaintiffs in shareholder suits
Jeffrey Skilling, former CEO of Enron (2004)	Questions about his role in the Enron fraud; resigned just prior to company's collapse	Found guilty of securities fraud and sentenced to 24.4 years; U.S. Supreme Court partially reversed his conviction on honest services fraud; sentence reduced to 14 years
Galleon Group (2011)	Insider trading charges related to hedge fund's operations	23 executives, including the CEO, convicted or entered guilty pleas; Galleon's $3.7 billion fund liquidated; CEO (Raj Rajaratnam) sentenced to 11 years; a Goldman Sachs director (Rajat Gupta) also convicted of insider trading and sentenced to 2 years in prison for feeding information to Rajaratnam
HealthSouth (2003)	$2.7 billion accounting fraud; overstatement of revenues	16 former executives indicted; 5 guilty pleas

[4] *U.S. v. Booker*, 543 U.S. 220 (2005).

FIGURE 7-1 Roster of White-Collar Criminal Charges (continued)

COMPANY/PERSON	ISSUE	STATUS
Richard Scrushy, CEO of HealthSouth (2003)	85 federal felony counts, including violations of Sarbanes-Oxley financial certification provisions	Acquitted of financial fraud charges; found guilty of bribery and sentenced to 7 years
Martha Stewart, CEO of Martha Stewart Omnimedia and close friend of Sam Waksal, CEO of ImClone (2003)	Sold 5,000 shares of ImClone one day before public announcement of negative FDA action on Ebritux	Convicted of making false statements and conspiracy; served 5 months in prison, 5 months of home confinement, and two years of probation; fine of $30,000
KMPG (2006)	Tax shelter fraud	Settled with federal regulators by payment of $456 million penalty
Sotheby's (2003)	Price-fixing	Chairman given 1 year and 1 day in prison and a $7.5 million fine; CEO placed under house arrest for 1 year
WorldCom (2003)	Accounting issues centered on swaps—selling to other telecommunications companies and hiding expenses, thereby overstating revenue	WorldCom emerged from bankruptcy as MCI; 4 officers and managers entered guilty pleas; CEO Bernard Ebbers convicted and sentenced to 25 years
Bernie Madoff (2009)	$50 billion Ponzi scheme	Entered guilty plea to all charges; sentenced to 150 years (was 71 years old at time of sentencing); direct reports convicted
BP (2012)	Violation of Clean Air Act; willful failure to correct OSHA violations; manslaughter and obstruction	$50 million fine to EPA; $58 million fine to OSHA (largest in U.S. history) for pre–Deepwater Horizon explosion; $4 billion for crimes related to Deepwater Horizon explosion; $18 billion to settle suits
Stanford Securities (2012)	$9 billion Ponzi scheme	CEO convicted of mail, wire, and securities fraud and sentenced to 110 years; Laura Pendergest-Holt, the former chief investment officer, entered a guilty plea and was sentenced to 3 years; CFO entered a guilty plea
Massey Coal (2012)	Mine collapse resulting in the deaths of 29 miners	Three company officials entered guilty pleas and one was convicted of charges related to tipping off employees on mine inspections and destroying records to avoid government review; former CEO under indictment
Peanut Corporation of America (2013)	Indictments for producing and selling product without cleaning up salmonella issue at plant; falsifying tests that showed the salmonella was gone when it was not	Four company officers, including owner and CEO, convicted of criminal fraud and conspiracy
SAC Capital	Charges of insider trading; use of information from doctors about drug trial on new pharmaceuticals	Settled charges for $600 billion fine; 11 current and former employees convicted or entered guilty pleas

that, guidelines; the sentencing ranges are no longer mandatory for judges.[5] Going outside those ranges, however, is carefully reviewed by appellate courts.[6] Federal judges can consider evidence of prior convictions, but only if that evidence was presented at trial or if the defendant has a chance to present evidence about those convictions at the sentencing.[7]

White-Collar Crime Penalty Enhancement Act of 2002–federal reforms passed as a result of the collapses of companies such as Enron; provides for longer sentences and higher fines for both executives and companies.

Sarbanes-Oxley Reforms to Criminal Penalties. Part of SOX, passed by Congress following the collapses of Enron and WorldCom corporations, was the **White-Collar Crime Penalty Enhancement Act of 2002.**[8] This act increases penalties substantially. **For Example,** the penalties for mail and wire fraud are increased from a maximum of 5 years to a maximum of 20 years. Penalties for violation of pension laws increased from 1 year to 10 years and the fines increased from $5,000 to $100,000.[9] In addition, many federal statutes now require executives to reimburse their companies for any money earned as a result of illegal activity. **For Example,** the former CEO of UnitedHealth Group Inc. was required to pay back $448 billion in profits he had made from stock options that were granted illegally.[10]

THINKING THINGS THROUGH

Can a Pharmacy's License Be Revoked for Too Many Cash Sales of Oxycodone?

The Drug Enforcement Administration (DEA) has moved to revoke the controlled medication licenses of two pharmacies because the pharmacies were filling prescriptions for oxycodone (the painkiller) in excess of their monthly allowances for controlled substances. In addition, the DEA alleges that the pharmacies' corporate entities failed to conduct on-site inspections and failed to notice that 42 to 58 percent of all the sales of the substances were cash sales, something that is considered a red flag in the sale and distribution of controlled substances. In addition, the number of prescriptions filled continued to escalate.

The two pharmacies won an injunction against the revocation in federal district court. However, the DEA is hoping to persuade the judge to lift the injunction once it is able to show that the corporations should have known there was a problem. The rate of cash sales at these pharmacies was eight times the national rate for filling prescriptions with cash. Pharmacists at the drug stores, in interviews with the DEA agents, indicated that the customers paying cash for the oxycodone were "shady," and that they suspected that some of the prescriptions were not legitimate. One of the companies adjusted (increased) the levels of shipment of oxycodone to the pharmacies five times. In one on-site visit by a DEA agent, the following information emerged: one of every three cars that came to the drive-thru window had a prescription for oxycodone; many patients living at the same address had the same prescriptions for oxycodone from the same doctor.

Both companies, CVS and Cardinal Health, have indicated in court filings that they have changed their practices and provided training to pharmacy personnel so that they can spot these types of illegal prescriptions and report suspicious activity. Both pharmacy companies have terminated customers, meaning that they will no longer fill prescriptions for those customers.

The DEA seeks to hold the corporations responsible because of the lack of on-site presence and the failure to follow the numbers for sales and distribution at the pharmacies. Can the corporation be held liable when it was not actually participating in the distribution of the oxycodone?

Source: Timothy W. Martin and Devlin Barrett, "Red Flags Ignored, DEA Says," *Wall Street Journal,* February 21, 2012. p. B1.

[5] *U.S. v. Skilling,* 554 F.3d 529 (5th Cir. 2009).
[6] *Gall v. U.S.,* 552 U.S. 38 (2007).
[7] Miriam H. Baer, "Choosing Punishment," 92 *Boston Univ. Law Rev.* 577 (2010).
[8] 18 U.S.C. §1314 *et seq.*
[9] 18 U.S.C. §§1341 and 1343; 29 U.S.C. §1131.
[10] S. Almashat et al., "Rapidly Increasing Criminal and Civil Monetary Penalties Against the Pharmaceutical Industry: 1991 to 2010," *Public Citizen's Health Research Group,* December 16, 2010, available at **http://www.citizen.org/hrg1924.**

ETHICS & THE LAW

When Addictions Are Off and On Again

In 1994, Congress passed a law that permitted nonviolent convicts to reduce their sentences by up to 12 months if they completed a drug-rehab/counseling program. When the program was first created, 3,755 inmates entered the program. In 2008, 18,000 federal prisoners were in the program and there was a waiting list of 7,000 inmates.

Dr. Sam Waksal, the former CEO of ImClone, served nine fewer months than his original seven-year sentence because he participated in a prison rehab program for inmates who have a problem with substance abuse. However, when Dr. Waksal was interviewed for the presentencing report, he told the probation officer that he was a "social drinker" and had perhaps five glasses of wine per week. One month after the interview with the probation officer, Waksal's lawyers informed a federal judge that Waksal now had a "dependence on alcohol" and requested approval for Waksal's entry into a prison rehab program.

The former mayor of Atlanta, Bill Campbell, was admitted into a federal rehab program and, as a result, got a 9-month reduction on his 30-month sentence for tax evasion. He was admitted to rehab despite the fact that his lawyers argued at his sentencing hearing that he had no substance abuse problem and that he hated the taste of alcohol, therefore urging the judge to conclude that Campbell's imprisonment was not necessary.

The Bureau of Prisons indicates that it is cracking down on admissions to the program, looking more closely at doctors' letters and past histories of the inmates.

Evaluate the ethics of the inmates who feign addiction. Evaluate the ethics of the consulting firms that help them get into the program.

Source: Kai Falkenberg, "Time Off for Bad Behavior," *Forbes*, January 12, 2009, pp. 64–65.

Creative Penalties for White-Collar Crime. Federal judges are developing new types of sentences in order to use those convicted to convince businesspeople to avoid criminal conduct. **For Example,** in 2009, a federal judge required an executive who entered a guilty plea to spend his two years of probation writing a book about what he did and offer guidance to business executives so that they can avoid his missteps. He was required to publish and distribute the book.[11] In 2010, a federal agency agreed to defer penalties if an officer agreed to travel around the country and speak to companies and executives about the mistakes he had made in order to help them understand the need for vigilance in stopping missteps that lead to crimes.

7-1d Indemnification of Crime Victims

Penalties are paid to the government. Typically, the victim of a crime does not benefit from the criminal prosecution and conviction of the wrongdoer, although courts can order that restitution be paid to victims.

The Victims of Crime Act of 1984 creates a federal Crime Victims Fund.[12] Using the fines paid into the federal courts as well as other monies, the federal government makes grants to the states to assist them in financing programs to provide assistance for victims of crime.[13] The Victim and Witness Protection Act of 1982 authorizes the sentencing judge in a federal district court to order, in certain cases, that the defendant make restitution (restoration) to the victim or pay the victim the amount of medical expenses or loss of income caused by the crime.[14]

[11] Natasha Singer, "Judge Orders Former Bristol-Myers Executive to Write Book," *New York Times*, June 9, 2009, p. B3.
[12] 18 U.S.C. §3771. The act was amended in 2004 to include a type of bill of rights for crime victims, including assistance through the newly created Office for Victims of Crime.
[13] 18 U.S.C. §1401 *et seq.*
[14] 18 U.S.C. §3579, as amended by 18 U.S.C. §18.18; see *Hughey v. United States*, 495 U.S. 411 (1990). In 2002, Congress passed another victims' compensation statute, with this one providing relief and assistance to the victims of terrorist attacks in the United States. 42 U.S.C. §10603b.

7-2 White-Collar Crimes

white-collar crimes–crimes that do not use nor threaten to use force or violence or do not cause injury to persons or property.

White-collar crime is generally considered business crime, the type committed generally in the course of doing business and usually involving some form of deceit used to get gains.

7-2a Conspiracies

conspiracy–agreement between two or more persons to commit an unlawful act.

The crime of conspiracy is committed before the actual crime; it is the planning of the crime. A **conspiracy** is an agreement between two or more persons to commit an unlawful act or to use unlawful means to achieve an otherwise lawful result. Some conspiracy statutes do require that those charged must have done something to carry out the agreement before the crime of conspiracy is committed. Almost all white-collar criminal charges involve a count of conspiracy, something that results from the fact that individuals work together in corporations to accomplish frauds.

7-2b Money Laundering

The federal government has adopted a Money Laundering Control Act (MLCA).[15] The act prohibits the knowing and willful participation in a financial transaction when the transaction is designed to conceal or disguise the source of the funds. The so-called *USA Patriot Act* that was passed on October 26, 2001, less than two months after the destruction of the World Trade Center and the damage to the Pentagon on September 11, 2001, includes a substantial number of changes and amendments to the MLCA and the Bank Secrecy Act (BSA).[16] Both statutes have been used as means to control bribery, tax evasion, and money laundering. Their changes and amendments were designed to curb the funding of terrorist activities in the United States.

The Patriot Act expands the coverage of the law from banks and financial institutions to anyone involved in financial transactions, which includes securities brokers; travel agents; those who close real estate transactions; insurance companies; loan or finance companies; casinos; currency exchanges; check-cashing firms; auto, plane, and boat dealers; and branches and agencies of foreign banks located in the United States. The amendments make even small businesses subject to the requirements of disclosure under MLCA and BSA, such as reporting cash transactions in excess of $10,000.

In addition, the types of accounts covered have been expanded. The accounts covered are not only securities accounts but also money market accounts. Furthermore, banks are now more actively involved in supervising accounts and following through on government information furnished to the bank on suspicious transactions and activities as well as individuals. Banks are required to implement new policies to prevent the types of transactions tagged by the government and conduct internal investigations for suspicious transactions. Because of the required close-watch provisions of these laws, banks and others covered under the federal statutes have developed anti-money-laundering programs. These programs must include a "Know Your Customer" training segment that teaches employees how to spot suspicious customers and transactions.

7-2c Racketeering

Racketeer Influenced and Corrupt Organizations (RICO) Act–federal law, initially targeting organized crime that has expanded in scope and provides penalties and civil recovery for multiple criminal offenses, or a pattern of racketeering.

Congress passed the **Racketeer Influenced and Corrupt Organizations (RICO) Act**[17] in 1970 as part of the Organized Crime Control Act. The law was designed primarily to

[15] 18 U.S.C. §§1956–1957 (2000). *U.S. v. Prince*, 214 F.3d 740 (6th Cir. 2000).
[16] 31 U.S.C. §531(h).
[17] 18 U.S.C. §§1961–1968.

prevent individuals involved in organized crime from investing money obtained through racketeering in legitimate businesses. However, the broad language of the act, coupled with a provision that allows individuals and businesses to sue for treble damages, has resulted in an increasing number of lawsuits against ordinary business persons not associated with organized crime.

Criminal and Civil Applications

RICO authorizes criminal and civil actions against persons who use any income derived from racketeering activity to invest in, control, or conduct an enterprise through a pattern of *racketeering activity.*[18] In criminal and civil actions under RICO, a pattern of racketeering activity must be established by proving that at least two acts of racketeering activity—so-called *predicate acts*—have been committed within 10 years.[19] For example, the former Atlanta Public Schools administrators and teachers who were involved in the cheating scandal on the state's standardized tests were convicted of racketeering because they had engaged in fraud to obtain bonuses. Conviction under RICO's criminal provisions may result in a $25,000 fine and up to 20 years' imprisonment as well as forfeiture of the property involved. A successful civil plaintiff may recover three times the actual damages suffered and attorney fees.[20]

Expanding Usage

Civil RICO actions have been successful against business entities, such as accounting firms, labor unions, insurance companies, commercial banks, and stock brokerage firms. However, under the Private Securities Litigation Reform Act of 1995, securities fraud was eliminated as a **predicate act,** or a qualifying underlying offense, for private RICO actions, absent a prior criminal conviction.[21]

predicate act–qualifying underlying offense for RICO liability.

7-2d Bribery

Bribery is the act of giving money, property, or any benefit to a particular person to influence that person's judgment in favor of the giver.[22] At common law, the crime was limited to doing such acts to influence a public official.

The giving and the receiving of a bribe constitute separate crimes. In addition, the act of trying to obtain a bribe may be a crime of solicitation of bribery in some states, while in other states bribery is broadly defined to include solicitation of bribes.

[18] §1961. Definitions:
(1) "Racketeering activity" means any act or threat involving murder, kidnapping, gambling, arson, robbery, bribery, extortion, dealing in obscene matter, dealing in a controlled substance or listed chemical, or sports bribery; counterfeiting; theft from interstate shipment; embezzlement from pension and welfare funds; extortionate credit transactions; fraud; wire fraud; mail fraud; procurement of citizenship or nationalization unlawfully; reproduction of naturalization or citizenship papers; obstruction of justice; tampering with a witness, victim, or an informant; retaliating against a witness, victim, or an informant; false statement in application and use of passport; forgery or false use of passport; fraud and misuse of visas, permits, and other documents; racketeering; unlawful welfare fund payments; laundering of monetary instruments; use of interstate commerce facilities in the commission of murder-for-hire; sexual exploitation of children; interstate transportation of stolen motor vehicles; interstate transportation of stolen property; trafficking in counterfeit labels of phonorecords, computer programs or computer program documentation, or packaging and copies of motion pictures or other audiovisual works; criminal infringement of a copyright; trafficking in contraband cigarettes; and white slave traffic.

[19] Brian Slocum, "RICO and the Legislative Supremacy Approach to Federal Criminal Lawmaking," 31 *Loyola Univ. Chicago Law Journal* 639 (2000).

[20] *Criminal RICO: 18 U.S.C. 1961–1968: A Manual for Federal Prosecutors.* Washington, D.C.: U.S. Dept. of Justice, Criminal Division, Organized Crime and Racketeering Section [2013].

[21] 15 U.S.C. §78(a), (n)–(t).

[22] In re *Mangone,* 923 N.Y.S.2d 679 (2011).

7-2e Commercial Bribery

Commercial bribery is a form of bribery in which an agent for another is paid or given something of value in order to make a decision on behalf of his or her principal that benefits the party paying the agent. **For Example,** a napkin supplier who pays a restaurant agent $500 in exchange for that agent's decision to award the restaurant's napkin contract to that supplier has engaged in commercial bribery.[23]

7-2f Extortion and Blackmail

Extortion and *blackmail* are crimes in which money is exchanged for either specific actions or restraint in taking action.

Extortion

extortion–illegal demand by a public officer acting with apparent authority.

When a public officer makes an illegal demand, the officer has committed the crime of **extortion. For Example,** if a health inspector threatens to close down a restaurant on a false sanitation law charge unless the restaurant pays the inspector a sum of money, the inspector has committed extortion. (If the restaurant voluntarily offers the inspector the money to prevent the restaurant from being shut down because of actual violations of the sanitation laws, the crime committed would be bribery.)

Blackmail

blackmail–extortion demands made by a nonpublic official.

In jurisdictions where extortion is limited to the conduct of public officials, a nonofficial commits **blackmail** by making demands that would be extortion if made by a public official. Ordinarily, blackmail is the act of threatening someone with publicity about a matter that would damage the victim's personal or business reputation.

7-2g Corrupt Influence

Legislative bodies have increasingly outlawed certain practices that exert a corrupting influence on business transactions.

Improper Political Influence

At the federal and state levels, it is a crime for one who holds public office to hold a financial interest in or to receive money from an enterprise that seeks to do business with the government. Such conduct is a conflict of interest between the official's duty to citizens and his or her personal financial interests. **For Example,** the former governor of Illinois, Rod Blagojevich, was convicted of seeking funds, fundraisers, and positions in exchange for political favors. To keep officials' conduct transparent, lobbyists must register in Washington, D.C.,[24] and adhere to statutory limits on gifts and contributions to political campaigns. Public officials must file annual disclosure forms about their financial positions as well as provide a disclosure of all gifts and their value.

[23] Connecticut's commercial bribery statute is a good example. It provides: *A person is guilty of commercial bribery when he confers, or agrees to confer, any benefit upon any employee, agent or fiduciary without the consent of the latter's employer or principal, with intent to influence his conduct in relation to his employer's or principal's affairs.* CGSA §53a-160 (2014). Other examples of commercial bribery statues can be found at Minn. Stat Ann §609.86 (Minnesota 2014); NH Rev Stat §638:8 (New Hampshire 2014); Alaska Stat §11.45.670 (Alaska 2014); and Ala. Code §13A-11-120 (Alabama 2014). Mississippi prohibits commercial bribery as well as sports bribery, which is paying the agent of a sports team in order to influence the outcome of a sporting event. Miss. Code Ann §97-9-10 (2014).

[24] Foreign Agents Registration Act, 22 U.S.C. §611 *et seq.*, as amended.

Foreign Corrupt Practices Act

Foreign Corrupt Practices Act (FCPA)–federal law that makes it a felony to influence decision makers in other countries for the purpose of obtaining business, such as contracts for sales and services; also imposes financial reporting requirements on certain U.S. corporations.

The **Foreign Corrupt Practices Act (FCPA)** is a federal criminal statute that applies to businesses whose principal offices are in the United States; it is an antibribery and anticorruption statute covering these companies' international operations.[25] There is additional information on the FCPA in Chapter 10.

7-2h Counterfeiting

Counterfeiting is making, with fraudulent intent, a document or coin that appears to be genuine but is not because the person making it did not have the authority to make it. It is a federal crime to make, to possess with intent to transfer, or to transfer counterfeit coins, bank notes, or obligations or other securities of the United States. Various states also have statutes prohibiting the making and passing of counterfeit coins and bank notes. These statutes often provide, as does the federal statute, a punishment for the mutilation of bank notes or the lightening (of the weight) or mutilation of coins.

7-2i Forgery

forgery–fraudulently making or altering an instrument that apparently creates or alters a legal liability of another.

uttering–crime of issuing or delivering a forged instrument to another person.

Forgery consists of the fraudulent making or material altering of an instrument, such as a check, that attempts to create or changes a legal liability of another person.[26] Ordinarily, **forgery** consists of signing another's name with intent to defraud, but it may also consist of making an entire instrument or altering an existing one. It may also result from signing a fictitious name or using the identity of another in order to obtain funds or property. In lay language we talk about "identity theft," but it is a form of forgery because they are placing someone else's name and signature on documents.[27]

The issuing or delivery of a forged instrument to another person constitutes the crime of **uttering** a forged instrument. Sending a forged check through the channels of commerce or of bank collection constitutes an uttering of a forged instrument. The act of depositing a forged check into the forger's bank account by depositing it in an automatic teller machine constitutes uttering within the meaning of a forgery statute.[28]

7-2j Perjury

Perjury consists of knowingly giving false testimony in a judicial proceeding after having been sworn to tell the truth. Knowingly making false answers on any form filed with a government typically constitutes perjury or is subjected to the same punishment as perjury. In some jurisdictions, the false answers given in a situation other than in court or the litigation process is called the crime of *false swearing*. The penalties for perjury were increased substantially under SOX.

7-2k False Claims and Pretenses

Many statutes make it a crime to submit false claims or to obtain goods by false pretenses.

[25] 15 U.S.C. §78dd-1 *et seq.*

[26] Using another person's ID to obtain property or funds is a form of forgery. *Warlick v. State*, 330 P.3d 946 (Alas. App. 2014).

[27] *People v. Lloyd*, 987 N.Y.S.2d 672 (2014) (where defendants used stolen drivers' licenses and checks to forge checks and cash them).

[28] *Warren v. State*, 711 S.E.2d 108 (Ga. App. 2011).

False Claims

The federal false statement statute makes it a crime to knowingly and willfully make a false material statement about any matter within the jurisdiction of any department or agency of the United States. **For Example,** it is a crime to make false statements about income and assets on a student's application for federal financial aid.

SPORTS & ENTERTAINMENT LAW

Cycling Through Federal Funds

After cyclist Lance Armstrong admitted to doping during his cycling career, he was stripped of his seven Tour de France titles. However, the private punishment and disgrace pale in comparison to the action that the federal government is taking. The Justice Department has filed suit to collect from Mr. Armstrong the $40 million that the U.S. Postal Service paid to Mr. Armstrong's team during his career in exchange for the advertising and endorsements the USPS received. One-half of that money went to Mr. Armstrong. The suit alleges that the USPS was deceived into paying the money because Mr. Armstrong represented to the USPS that he was following the rules of cycling's governing bodies that prohibit the use of performance enhancing drugs.

A guilty verdict would mean that Mr. Armstrong would have to pay the USPS treble damages—the remedy afforded under the federal False Claims Act.

Obtaining Goods by False Pretenses

Almost all states have statutes that forbid obtaining money or goods under false pretenses.[29] An intent to defraud is an essential element of obtaining property by false pretenses.[30]

Examples of false pretense include delivering a check knowing that there is insufficient money in the bank account to cover the check.[31] False representations as to future profits in a business are also forms of false pretenses. Failing to perform on a contract is not a false pretense crime unless the contract had been entered into with the intent of not performing it.[32]

False Information Submitted to Banks

Knowingly making false statements in a loan application to a federally insured bank is a federal crime.[33] It is also a crime for a landowner to put a false value on land transferred to a bank as security for a loan.[34] **For Example,** many of the initial criminal charges in the subprime mortgage market collapse have involved mortgage brokers and appraisers who misrepresented property value or applicants' income in their mortgage applications for federally insured loans.

7-2l Bad Checks

Under a bad check statute, it is a crime to use or pass a check with the intent to defraud with the knowledge that there are insufficient funds in the bank to pay the check when it is presented for payment. Knowledge that the bad check will not be paid when presented

[29] *People v. Hussain*, 179 Cal. Rptr. 3d 679 (Cal. App. 2014).
[30] *U.S. v. Swisher*, 14 Cal. Daily Op. Serv. 12,314 (9th Cir. 2014)—wearing military uniform without actually having served in the military in order to obtain benefits was false pretense.
[31] *U.S. v. Tudeme*, 457 F.3d 577 (Fed. App. 2006).
[32] *Higginbotham v. State*, 356 S.W.3d 584 (Tex. App. 2011) and *People v. Headley*, 951 N.Y.S.2d 317 (2012).
[33] 18 U.S.C. §1014. See *U.S. v. Luis*, 765 F.3d 1061 (9th Cir. 2014).
[34] *U.S. v. Rizk*, 660 F.3d 1125 (9th Cir. 2011).

to the bank is an essential element of the crime. The bad check statutes typically provide that if the check is not made good within a specified number of days after payment by the bank is refused, it is presumed that the defendant acted with the intent to defraud.[35] For more information on checks, see Chapters 27 and 30.

7-2m Credit Card Crimes

It is a crime to steal a credit card and, in some states, to possess the credit card of another person without that person's consent. Using a credit card without the permission of the card owner is the crime of obtaining goods or services by false pretenses or with the intent to defraud. Likewise, a person who continues to use a credit card with the knowledge that it has been canceled is guilty of the crime of obtaining goods by false pretenses. Federal law also makes it a crime to use counterfeit credit cards for purposes of obtaining goods, services, or cash. The statute now covers the use of credit card numbers on the Internet in order to obtain goods and services.[36]

7-2n Embezzlement

embezzlement–statutory offense consisting of the unlawful conversion of property entrusted to the wrongdoer.

Embezzlement is the fraudulent conversion of another's property or money by a person to whom it has been entrusted.[37] Employees who take or sell their employer's property or funds for personal use have committed the crime of embezzlement. An agent employee commits embezzlement when he receives and keeps payments from third persons—payments the agent should have turned over to the principal. **For Example,** when an insured gives money to an insurance agent to pay the insurance company but the insurance agent uses the money to pay premiums on the policies of other persons, the agent is guilty of embezzlement. Generally, the intent to return the property or money embezzled or eventually actually returning it, is no defense.

7-2o Obstruction of Justice: Sarbanes-Oxley (SOX)

Another SOX provision clarifies what constitutes obstruction of justice and increases the penalties for such an act. The new section makes it a felony for anyone, including company employees, auditors, attorneys, and consultants,

> *to alter, destroy, mutilate, conceal, cover up, falsify or make a false entry with the "intent to impede, obstruct, or influence the investigation or proper administration of any matter within the jurisdiction of any department or agency of the United States."*[38]

The statute goes on to address audit records specifically and requires auditors to retain their work papers related to a client's audit for at least five years. Any destruction of documents prior to that time constitutes a felony and carries a penalty of up to 20 years. The statute was passed in response to the conduct of Arthur Andersen, the audit firm for the collapsed Enron Corporation. Many of the firm's audit papers on Enron were destroyed, but the firm and partner-in-charge escaped criminal liability because the government could not establish that the senior managers in Andersen were aware of the shredding.[39]

[35] *McMillan v. First Nat. Bank of Berwick,* 978 A.2d 370 (Pa. Super. 2009).
[36] 18 U.S.C. §1029. Fines for credit card fraud have been increased to between $50,000 and $100,000 per offense.
[37] *State v. Henry,* 73 So. 3d 958 (La. App. 2011); *Stern v. Epps,* 464 Fed. Appx. 388 (5th Cir. 2012).
[38] 18 U.S.C. §1519. *U.S. v. Hunt,* 526 F.3d 739 (11th Cir. 2008).
[39] *Arthur Andersen LLP v. U.S.,* 544 U.S. 696 (2005). The obstruction conviction of the firm was reversed because of insufficient proof of the firm's actual knowledge of document destruction.

7-2p Corporate Fraud: SOX

SOX also created a new form of mail and wire fraud. Ordinarily, mail or wire fraud consists of the use of the mail or telephones for purposes of defrauding someone of money and/or property. However, the SOX form of mail or wire fraud is based on new requirements imposed on corporate officers to certify their financial statements when they are issued. If a corporate officer fails to comply with all requirements for financial statement certification or certifies financial statements that contain false material information, the officer and company have committed corporate fraud with penalties that range from fines of $1,000,000 and/or 10 years to $5,000,000 and/or 20 years for willful violation of the certification requirements.

7-2q The Common Law Crimes

In contrast to white-collar crimes, *common law crimes* are crimes that involve the use of force or the threat of force or cause injury to persons or damage to property. The following sections discuss crimes of force and crimes against property that affect businesses.

Larceny

Larceny is the wrongful or fraudulent taking of the personal property of another by any person with fraudulent intent. Shoplifting is a common form of larceny. In many states, shoplifting is made a separate crime. In some states, all forms of larceny and robbery are consolidated into a statutory crime of theft. At common law, there was no crime known as theft.

Robbery

Robbery is the taking of personal property from the presence of the victim by use of force or fear. Most states have aggravated forms of robbery, such as robbery with a deadly weapon. Snatching a necklace from the neck of the victim involves sufficient force to constitute robbery. When the unlawful taking is not by force or fear, as when the victim does not know that the property is being taken, the offense is larceny, but it cannot be robbery.

Some statutes may be aimed at a particular kind of robbery. **For Example,** carjacking is a federal crime under the Anti-Car Theft Act of 1992.[40]

Burglary

At common law, *burglary* was the breaking and entering during the night into the dwelling house of another with the intent to commit a felony. Inserting the automatic teller card of another, without their knowledge or permission, into an automatic teller machine set in the wall of the bank may constitute an entry into the bank for the purpose of committing burglary.[41] Some states word their burglary *statutes*, however, so that there is no burglary in this automatic teller case. This act would be covered by other criminal statutes.

Modern statutes have eliminated many of the elements of the common law definition so that under some statutes it is now immaterial when or whether there was an entry to commit a felony. The elements of breaking and entering are frequently omitted. Under some statutes, the offense is aggravated and the penalty is increased, depending on the

[40] 18 U.S.C. §2119. See *U.S. v. Runyon*, 707 F.3d 475 (4th Cir. 2013).
[41] *People v. Cardwell*, 137 Cal. Rptr. 3d 525 (2012).

place where the offense was committed, such as a bank building, freight car, or warehouse. Related statutory offenses, such as the crime of possessing burglars' tools, have been created.

Arson

At common law, *arson* was the willful and malicious burning of another's dwelling. The law was originally designed to protect human life, although arson has been committed just with the burning of the building even if no one is actually hurt. In most states, arson is a felony, so if someone is killed in the resulting fire, the offense is considered a felony-murder. Under the felony-murder rule, homicide, however unintended, occurring in the commission of a felony is automatically classified as murder. Virtually every state has created a special offense of burning to defraud an insurer.

Riots and Civil Disorders

Damage to property in the course of a riot or civil disorder is ordinarily covered by other types of crimes such as the crime of larceny or arson. In addition, the act of assembling as a riotous mob and engaging in civil disorders is generally some form of crime in itself under either common law concepts of disturbing the peace or modern antiriot statutes, even without destruction or theft of property. However, statutes on civil disorders must be carefully drawn to avoid infringing on constitutionally protected free speech.

7-3 Criminal Law and the Computer

In some situations, ordinary crimes cover computer crime situations. In other situations, new criminal law statutes are required.

7-3a What Is a Computer Crime?

computer crimes– wrongs committed using a computer or with knowledge of computers.

Generally, the term **computer crime** is used to refer to a crime that can be committed only by a person having some knowledge of the operation of a computer. Just as stealing an automobile requires knowledge of how to operate and drive a car, so the typical computer crime requires the knowledge of how the computer works.

Because the more serious and costly wrongs relating to computers do not fit into the ordinary definitions of crime, there are now computer-specific criminal statutes: Computer crimes can be committed against the computer, using the computer, or through the computer.

7-3b The Computer as Victim

A traditional crime may be committed by stealing or intentionally damaging a computer.

Theft of Hardware

When a computer itself is stolen, the ordinary law relating to theft crimes should apply. Theft of a computer is subject to the same law as the theft of a truck or a desk.

Theft of Software

When a thief takes software, whether in the form of a program written on paper or a program on a disk or memory stick, something has been taken, but it is not tangible property as larceny requires. Virtually every state makes stealing software a crime.

Intentional Damage

The computer may be the "victim" of a crime when it is intentionally destroyed or harmed. In the most elementary form of damage, the computer could be harmed if it was smashed with an ax or destroyed in an explosion or a fire. In such cases, the purpose of the intentional damage is to cause the computer's owner the financial loss of the computer and the destruction of the information that is stored in it.

Intentional damage can result from more subtle means. Gaining access to the computer and then erasing or altering the data is also the crime of intentional damage. Likewise, interfering with the air conditioning so computers are damaged or malfunction would also be covered under intentional damage statutes. Planting a bug or virus in the software, causing a program to malfunction or to give incorrect output, is a form of intentional damage. Angry employees, former employees, and competitors have all been convicted of intentional damage.

7-3c Unauthorized Use of Computers

The unlawful use of a computer belonging to someone else is also a crime in some states. There are specific statutes at the state and federal levels that make it unlawful to use government computers without permission. One of the issues that is critical in criminal prosecution is whether the use was, in fact, "unauthorized." With Wi-Fi networks, the ease of access and openness has proven to be a challenge in prosecution for unauthorized use.[42] The key to prosecution in misuse of computer cases is proof that the access was not authorized.

CASE SUMMARY

Rifling Through Videos on Your Fellow Officers

FACTS: Sergeant Kenneth Riley used videos of a fellow officer, not for training purposes, but for purposes of getting a fellow officer disciplined. He showed the videos to those within the department who would not have authorization to view them. Riley was indicted for unauthorized use of a computer and unauthorized access and disclosure of computer data. Riley moved to have the indictment dismissed.

DECISION: Riley's access and use of computer data did not constitute the crime of unauthorized use of computers. The court held that what Riley did was a violation of workplace policies but did not fit within the criminal conduct intended to be covered by the statute. The judge was concerned about arbitrary definitions and enforcement and a criminal statute being used for retaliatory purposes. **[*New Jersey v. Riley*, 988 A.2d 1252 (N.J. 2009)]**

7-3d Computer Raiding

Taking information from a computer without the consent of the owner is a crime. Whether theft is accomplished by instructing the computer to make a printout of stored information or by tapping into its data bank by electronic means is not important. In some states, taking information is known as the crime of "computer trespass."[43]

[42] U.S.C. §1030(e)(6); for an article summarizing the issues, see Orin S. Kerr, "Cybercrime's Scope: Interpreting 'Access' and 'Authorization' in Computer Misuse Statutes," 78 *N.Y.U. L. Rev.* 1596, 1632–37 (2003).

[43] *Washington v. Riley*, 846 P.2d 1365 (Wash. 1993).

Both Congress and state legislatures have adopted statutes that make it a crime to gain unauthorized access to a computer or use information so gained to cause harm to the computer or its rightful user.[44] Again, the presence of Wi-Fi when there are unsecured users has complicated prosecutions for taking information.

7-3e Diverted Delivery by Computer

In many industries, a computer controls the delivery of goods. The person in charge of that computer or someone unlawfully gaining access to it may cause the computer to direct delivery to an improper place. That is, instead of shipping goods to the customers to whom they should go, the wrongdoer diverts the goods to a different place, where the wrongdoer or a confederate receives them.

Instructing the computer to give false directions can cause this fraudulent diversion of goods. Because the computer allows changes in delivery of goods through a mere keystroke, the depth of diversion cases is great. **For Example,** in one case, several hundred loaded freight cars disappeared. In another case, a loaded oil tanker was diverted to unload into a fleet of tank trucks operated by an accomplice of the computer operator.

7-3f Economic Espionage by Computer

Economic Espionage Act (EEA)–federal law that makes it a felony to copy, download, transmit, or in any way transfer proprietary files, documents, and information from a computer to an unauthorized person.

The **Economic Espionage Act (EEA)** is a federal law[45] passed in response to several cases in which high-level executives took downloaded proprietary information from their computers to their new employers. The EEA makes it a felony to steal, appropriate, or take a trade secret as well as to copy, duplicate, sketch, draw, photograph, download, upload, alter, destroy, replicate, transmit, deliver, send, mail, or communicate a trade secret. The penalties for EEA violations are up to $500,000 and 15 years in prison for individuals and $10 million for organizations. When employees take new positions with another

E-COMMERCE & CYBERLAW

They Were Bullies: Mean Girls in Cyberspace

On May 14, 2008, a federal grand jury indicted Lori Drew, 49, of Missouri, the first of what would become known as the cyber bully. Ms. Drew had created a MySpace site for Josh Evans, a fictitious teen boy she used as a means of getting information from Megan Meier, a 13-year-old girl with whom Ms. Drew's daughter had had a falling-out. Josh pretended to be interested in Megan, but then said that she was "fat" and that the world would be a better place without her. Megan hanged herself within an hour of receiving the final comments from "Josh." Ms. Drew was later charged and convicted of conspiracy and accessing computers without authorization.*

Since the time of that case, there have been a number of similar incidents in which friends, parents, and others harass individuals using the various sites available from Facebook to Instagram. States now have very specific cyberbullying statutes for prosecution. As one expert phrased it, we have to take responsibility for what we post online and the consequences that can stem from hurtful or fearsome comments. There are both civil and criminal statutes that provide curbs for victims. Civil remedies allow for injunctions, and criminal penalties are at a level that allows them to serve as a deterrent for the types of postings that began with the Drew case.

***U.S. v. Lori Drew*, 259 F.R.D. 449 (C.D. Cal. 2009).**

[44] The Counterfeit Access Device and Computer Fraud Act of 1984, 18 U.S.C. §1030 *et seq.*; Computer Fraud and Abuse Act of 1986, 18 U.S.C. §1001; Electronic Communications Privacy Act of 1986, 18 U.S.C. §2510; Computer Fraud Act of 1987, 15 U.S.C. §§272, 278, 40 U.S.C. §759; National Information Infrastructure Protection Act, 18 U.S.C. §1030 (protecting confidentiality and integrity on the Internet).

[45] 18 U.S.C. §1831.

company, their former employers are permitted to check the departing employees' computer e-mails and hard drives to determine whether the employees have engaged in computer espionage.

7-3g Electronic Fund Transfer Crimes

The Electronic Fund Transfers Act (EFTA)[46] makes it a crime to use any counterfeit, stolen, or fraudulently obtained card, code, or other device to obtain money or goods in excess of a specified amount through an electronic fund transfer system. The EFTA also makes it a crime to ship in interstate commerce devices or goods so obtained or to knowingly receive goods that have been obtained by means of the fraudulent use of the transfer system.

7-3h Circumventing Copyright Protection Devices Via Computer

The Digital Millennium Copyright Act (DMCA)[47] makes it a federal offense to circumvent or create programs to circumvent encryption devices that copyright holders place on copyrighted material to prevent unauthorized copying. Circumventing the encryption devices on software or CDs or DVDs is a violation of the DMCA. **For Example,** Dmitry Sklyarov, a Russian computer programmer, was the first person to be charged with a violation of the DMCA. Mr. Sklyarov was arrested in early 2002 at a computer show after giving a speech in Las Vegas at the Defcon convention on his product that he had developed to permit the circumvention of security devices on copyrighted materials. His program unlocked password-protected e-books and PDF files. He gave his speech and was returned to Russia in exchange for his agreement to testify in a case that will determine the constitutionality of DMCA.

The No Electronic Theft Act makes it a federal criminal offense to willfully infringe copyrighted material worth more than $1,000 using the Internet or other electronic devices even if the infringer does not profit from others' use of the material. **For Example,** sending along copyrighted articles on the Internet to friends, without permission from the site would be a violation even though there is no profit.

7-3i Spamming

Controlling the Assault of Non-Solicited Pornography and Marketing (CAN-SPAM) Act–allows private companies to bring suit against spammers for their unauthorized use of Internet Service Providers (ISPs).

Spamming, or the practice of sending out thousands of e-mails at once to many different computer users, is an ever-increasing problem. Congress passed the **Controlling the Assault of Non-Solicited Pornography and Marketing (CAN-SPAM) Act,** which allows private companies to bring suit against spammers for their unauthorized use of Internet Service Providers (ISPs).

For example, in March 2013, security experts said that we experienced what was "the biggest cyberattack in history." At the root of it was a fight over spam. Spamhaus, a Dutch company that fights spam, added Cyberbunker to its so-called blacklist. Spamhaus's blacklist consists of companies e-mail providers use as a screen to weed out spam. Cyberbunker is a Web-hosting service that, by its own description, will host any site except "child porn and anything related to terrorism."[48] Cyberbunker wants to spam and Spamhaus wants to protect e-mail servers from spam, so there is a war in

[46] 15 U.S.C. §1693(n).
[47] 17 U.S.C. §512 (2010).
[48] John Markoff and Nicole Perlroth, "Dispute on Spam Stirs Big Assault on the Internet," *New York Times*, March 27, 2013, p. A1.

cyberspace. Because of the international nature of these activities, prosecution is difficult, and authorities continue to investigate the combination of spamming and hacking crimes.

7-4 Criminal Procedure Rights for Businesses

The U.S. Constitution guarantees the protection of individual and corporate rights within the criminal justice system.

7-4a Fourth Amendment Rights for Businesses

Search and Seizure: Warrants

Fourth Amendment–privacy protection in the U.S. Constitution; prohibits unauthorized searches and seizures.

search warrant–judicial authorization for a search of property where there is the expectation of privacy.

The **Fourth Amendment** of the U.S. Constitution provides that "the right of the people to be secure in their persons, houses, papers, and effects, against unreasonable searches and seizures, shall not be violated." This amendment protects individual privacy by preventing unreasonable searches and seizures. Before a government agency can seize the property of individuals or businesses, it must obtain a valid **search warrant** issued by a judge or magistrate, based on probable cause, unless an exception to this warrant requirement applies. In other words, there must be good reason to search the location named. The Fourth Amendment applies equally to individuals and corporations. If an improper search is conducted, evidence obtained during the course of that search may be inadmissible in the criminal proceedings for the resulting criminal charges.[49]

Exceptions to the Warrant Requirement

Exceptions to the warrant requirement are emergencies, such as a burning building, and the "plain-view" exception, which allows law enforcement officials to take any property that anyone can see, for no privacy rights are violated when items and property are left in the open for members of the public to see. **For Example,** you have an expectation of privacy in the garbage in your garbage can when it is in your house. However, once you move that garbage can onto the public sidewalk for pickup, you no longer have the expectation of privacy because you have left your garbage out in plain view of the public. **For Example,** in *Dow Chemical Co. v. United States*, 476 U.S. 1819 (1986), the U.S. Supreme Court held that a company does not have a right of privacy from low-flying planes of its production facilities. Pictures taken from the airplanes of plant operations were not a violation of privacy.

Another exception allows officers to enter when they are needed to give aid because of an ongoing criminal act. **For Example,** officers who are able to see a fight through the windows of a house and resulting injuries can enter to render help. Another exception would be that the person who lives in the property to be searched has given permission for the search.

Privacy and Cyber Space: Access to Our Messages and Files. One of the questions related to privacy is how much of what we post online and put on our computers at work is protected by privacy rights that would require a warrant before law enforcement could examine the content. However, if employers have access to the information on your work computer and e-mails, you do not enjoy the protection of privacy.

[49] See *Arizona v. Gant*, 556 U.S. 332 (2009) in which the U.S. Supreme Court held that evidence obtained searching the vehicle of a suspect who is handcuffed and locked in a police car cannot be used. A search warrant is needed when the suspect has no access to the evidence to destroy it.

CASE SUMMARY

Shared Drive + Shared Access = NO PRIVACY

FACTS: In February 2003, while serving as a civilian contractor, Michael D. King resided in a dormitory at the Prince Sultan Air Base in Saudi Arabia. During his stay in the dormitory, King kept his personal laptop computer in his room and connected it to the base network. All users of the base network signed agreements indicating that they understood their communications over and use of the base network were subject to monitoring.

An enlisted airman was searching the base network for music files when he came across King's computer on the network. The airman was able to access King's hard drive because it was a "shared" drive. The airman discovered a pornographic movie and text files "of a pornographic nature." The airman reported his discovery to a military investigator, who, in turn, referred the matter to a computer specialist. This specialist located King's computer and hard drive on the base network and verified the presence of pornographic videos and explicit text files on the computer. She also discovered a folder on the hard drive labeled "pedophilia."

Military officials seized King's computer and also found CDs containing child pornography.

Two years later, the government obtained an indictment, charging King with possession of child pornography. After his arrest, the government searched his residence pursuant to a search warrant and found additional CDs and hard drives containing over 30,000 images of child pornography.

King entered a guilty plea and was sentenced to 108 months in prison. King then appealed his conviction on the grounds that there had been an illegal search and seizure of his computer and files.

DECISION: The court held that there was no Fourth Amendment violation because the investigators did not search King's files or computer initially to discover the pornographic materials. They merely had to access the universally accessible files of the military base. King had no expectation of privacy in whatever was posted on the shared drive. The search of his home computer and files in his room was with a warrant that was based on probable cause obtained from public access to the files. [***U.S. v. King*, 509 F.3d 1338 (11th Cir. 2007)**]

Business Records and Searches

In many business crimes, the records that prove a crime was committed are not in the hands of the person who committed that crime. Accountants, attorneys, and other third parties may have the business records in their possession. In addition to the Fourth Amendment issues involved in seizing these records (a warrant is still required), there may be protections for the business defendants. The next section covers those protections.

Protections for Privileged Records and Documents

All states recognize an attorney-client privilege, which means that an individual's conversations with her lawyer and the notes of those conversations are not subject to seizure unless the privilege is waived. In many of the prosecutions of companies, the Justice Department has asked companies to waive the attorney-client privilege so that it can have access to information that is then used to find other companies that may have participated in criminal activity.

Some states recognize an accountant-client privilege and other privileges, such as those between priest and parishioner or doctor and patient. A privileged relationship is one in which the records and notes resulting from the contact between individuals cannot be seized even with a warrant (with some exceptions).

7-4b Fifth Amendment Self-Incrimination Rights for Businesses

Self-Incrimination

Fifth Amendment–constitutional protection against self-incrimination; also guarantees due process.

The words "I take the Fifth" are used to invoke the constitutional protections against self-incrimination provided under the **Fifth Amendment** that prevents compelling a person to be a witness against himself. **For Example,** Mark McGwire, the former St. Louis baseball player, invoked the Fifth Amendment in his testimony during congressional hearings on steroid use. **For Example,** Edith O'Brien, an employee at the collapsed investment fund, MF Global, refused to answer questions before Congress, claiming her right against self-incrimination. Lois Lerner, a former administrator with the IRS, took the Fifth Amendment when she was subpoenaed to testify before Congress.

The Fifth Amendment protection applies only to individuals; corporations are not given Fifth Amendment protection. A corporation cannot prevent the disclosure of its books and records on the grounds of self-incrimination. The officers and employees of a corporation can assert the Fifth Amendment, but the records of the corporation belong to the corporation, not to them.

Miranda Rights

Miranda warnings–warnings required to prevent self-incrimination in a criminal matter.

The famous **Miranda warnings** come from a case interpreting the extent of Fifth Amendment rights. In *Miranda v. Arizona,*[50] the U.S. Supreme Court ruled that certain warnings must be given to persons who face custodial interrogation for the purposes of possible criminal proceedings. The warnings consist of an explanation to individuals that they have the right to remain silent; that if they do speak, anything they say can be used against them; that they have the right to have an attorney present; and that if they cannot afford an attorney, one will be provided for them. Failure to give the *Miranda* warnings means that any statements, including a confession, obtained while the individual was being interrogated cannot be used as evidence against that individual. The prosecution will have to rely on evidence other than the statements made in violation of *Miranda*, if such evidence exists.

7-4c Due Process Rights for Businesses

due process–the constitutional right to be heard, question witnesses, and present evidence.

Sixth Amendment–the U.S. constitutional amendment that guarantees a speedy trial.

Also included in the Fifth Amendment is the language of due process. **Due process** is the right to be heard, question witnesses, and present evidence before any criminal conviction can occur. Due process in criminal cases consists of an initial appearance at which the charges and the defendant's rights are outlined; a preliminary hearing or grand jury proceeding in which the evidence is determined to be sufficient to warrant a trial; an arraignment for entering a plea and setting a trial date when the defendant pleads innocent; a period of discovery for obtaining evidence; and a trial at which witnesses for the prosecution can be cross-examined and evidence presented to refute the charges. In addition to these procedural steps, the **Sixth Amendment** guarantees that the entire process will be completed in a timely fashion because this amendment guarantees a speedy trial.

[50] 384 U.S. 436 (1966).

Make the Connection

Summary

When a person does not live up to the standards set by law, this punishable conduct, called *crime*, may be common law or statutory in origin. Crimes are classified as *felonies*, which generally carry greater sentences and more long-term consequences, and *misdemeanors*.

Employers and corporations may be criminally responsible for their acts and the acts of their employees. The federal sentencing guidelines provide parameters for sentences for federal crimes and allow judges to consider whether the fact that a business promotes compliance with the law is a reason to reduce a sentence.

White-collar crimes include those relating to financial fraud. Sarbanes-Oxley reforms increased the penalties for financial fraud and added fraudulent financial statement certification as a crime. Other white-collar crimes include bribery, extortion, blackmail, and corrupt influence in politics and in business. Also included as white-collar crimes are counterfeiting, forgery, perjury, making false claims against the government, obtaining goods or money by false pretenses, using bad checks, false financial reporting, and embezzlement. The common law crimes include those that involve injury to person and/or property, such as arson and murder.

Statutes have expanded the area of criminal law to meet situations in which computers are involved. Both federal and state statutes make the unauthorized taking of information from a computer a crime. The diversion of deliveries of goods and the transfer of funds, the theft of software, and the raiding of computers are made crimes to some extent by federal laws. Newer federal statutes that apply to computers are the Economic Espionage Act, which prohibits downloading or copying information via computer to give to a competitor, and the Digital Millennium Copyright Act that prohibits circumventing or designing programs to circumvent encryption devices.

Criminal procedure is dictated by the Fourth, Fifth, and Sixth Amendments. The Fourth Amendment protects against unreasonable searches, the Fifth Amendment protects against self-incrimination and provides due process, and the Sixth Amendment guarantees a speedy trial.

Learning Outcomes

After studying this chapter, you should be able to clearly explain:

7-1 General Principles

LO.1 Discuss the nature and classification of crimes

See the discussion of crimes and misdemeanors, page 105.

LO.2 Describe the basis of criminal liability

See the *U.S. v. Ahmad* case, pages 105–106.

See the Massey Energy example, page 106.

LO.3 Identify who is responsible for criminal acts

See *U.S. v. Park*, pages 106–107.

See the discussion of CVS in Thinking Things Through, page 111.

LO.4 Explain the penalties for crimes and the sentencing for corporate crimes

See Figure 7-1, pages 109–110.

See the example on Michael Milken, page 109.

See the discussion of the sentencing guidelines and the various cases related to them, page 108.

See the Ethics & the Law feature, page 112.

7-2 White-Collar Crimes

LO.5 List examples of white-collar crimes and their elements

See the discussion on White Collar Crimes, pages 113–120.

See the *Andersen* example of obstruction, page 118.

LO.6 Describe the common law crimes

See the discussion on Common Law Crimes, pages 119–120.

See the Sports & Entertainment Law feature on Lance Armstrong and false claims, page 117.

See the E-Commerce & Cyberlaw discussion of cyber-bullying, page 122.

7-3 Criminal Law and the Computer

LO.7 Discuss crimes related to computers

See generally the section on Computer Crimes, page 120.

See the *New Jersey v. Riley* case for unauthorized access, page 121.

See the Cyberbunker-Spamhaus example for spamming, page 123.

7-4 Criminal Procedure Rights for Businesses

LO.8 Describe the rights of businesses charged with crimes and the constitutional protections afforded them

See the *U.S. v. King* case, page 125.

Key Terms

blackmail
computer crime
conspiracy
Controlling the Assault of Non-Solicited Pornography and Marketing (CAN-SPAM) Act
crime
due process
Economic Espionage Act (EEA)
embezzlement
extortion
Federal Sentencing Guidelines
felonies
Fifth Amendment
Foreign Corrupt Practices Act (FCPA)
forgery
Fourth Amendment
Miranda warnings
misdemeanors
predicate act
Racketeer Influenced and Corrupt Organizations (RICO) Act
search warrant
Sixth Amendment
uttering
white-collar crime
White-Collar Crime Penalty Enhancement Act of 2002

Questions and Case Problems

1. Bernard Flinn operated a business known as Harvey Investment Co., Inc./High Risk Loans. Flinn worked as a loan broker, matching those who came to him with lenders willing to loan them money given their credit history and the amount involved. From 1982 through 1985, Flinn found loans for five people. Indiana requires that persons engaged in the business of brokering loans obtain a license from the state. Flinn was prosecuted for brokering loans without having a license. He raised the defense that he did not know that a license was required and that, accordingly, he lacked the criminal intent to broker loans without having a license. Does Flinn have a good defense? [*Flinn v. Indiana*, 563 N.E.2d 536 (Ind.)]
2. H. J., Inc., and other customers of Northwestern Bell Corp. alleged that Northwestern Bell had furnished cash and tickets for air travel, plays, and sporting events and had offered employment to members of the Minnesota Public Utilities Commission in exchange for favorable treatment in rate cases before the commission. A Minnesota statute makes it a felony to bribe public officials. H. J. and other customers brought suit against Northwestern for violating the criminal bribery statute. Can the customers bring a criminal action? [*H. J., Inc. v. Northwestern Bell Corp.*, 420 N.W.2d 673 (Minn. App.)]
3. Baker and others entered a Wal-Mart store shortly after 3:00 A.M. by cutting through the metal door with an acetylene torch. They had moved some of the merchandise in the store to the rear door, but the police arrived before the merchandise could be taken from the store. Baker was prosecuted for larceny. He raised the defense that he was not guilty of larceny because no merchandise had ever left the store. Is there enough intent and action for a crime? [*Tennessee v. Baker*, 751 S.W.2d 154 (Tenn. App.)]
4. Gail drove her automobile after having had dinner and several drinks. She fell asleep at the wheel and ran over and killed a pedestrian. Prosecuted for manslaughter, she raised the defense that she did not intend to hurt anyone and because of the drinks did not know what she was doing. Was this a valid defense?
5. Dr. Doyle E. Campbell, an ophthalmologist, established his practice in southern Ohio in 1971. Many of Dr. Campbell's patients are elderly people who qualify for federal Medicare benefits and state Medicaid benefits. Under the existing financing system, a doctor who treats a Medicare patient is required to submit a "Medicare Health Insurance Claim Form" (HCFA Form 1500). The doctor is required to certify that "the services shown on this form were medically indicated and necessary for the health of the patient and were personally rendered by me or were rendered incident to my professional service by my employees." Claims Dr. Campbell submitted for his elderly patients ranged from $900 to $950, of which $530 to $680 were covered by the Medicare program. The government alleged that Dr. Campbell billed Medicare for several treatments that were either not performed or not necessary. Dr. Campbell was charged with fraud for the paperwork he submitted. Has he committed a crime? [*United States v. Campbell*, 845 F.2d 1374 (6th Cir.)]
6. In the late 1980s, Life Energy Resources, Ltd. (LER), a New York corporation, was a multilevel marketing network. LER's marketing plan provided that members of the general public could purchase its products

only through an official LER distributor or by becoming LER distributors themselves. Each potential distributor had to be sponsored by an existing distributor and was required to sign a distributorship agreement with LER stating that he or she would not make medical claims or use unofficial literature or marketing aids to promote LER products.

Ballistrea and his partner Michael Ricotta were at the top of the LER distribution network. Two products sold by LER were the REM SuperPro Frequency Generator (REM) and the Lifemax Miracle Cream (Miracle Cream). The REM, which sold for $1,350 to distributors, was a small box powered by electricity that ran currents through the feet and body of the user.

Ballistrea and Ricotta distributed literature and audiotapes to many potential downstream distributors and customers—some of whom were undercover government agents—touting the REM and the Miracle Cream. Other literature claimed that the Miracle Cream could alleviate the discomforts of premenstrual syndrome and reverse the effects of osteoporosis. The Food and Drug Administration charged Ballistrea and Ricotta with violating federal law for making medical claims concerning LER products. Their defense is that they never sold any of the products. They simply earned commissions as part of the marketing scheme and could not be held criminally liable on the charges. Are they correct? [*United States v. Ballistrea*, 101 F.3d 827 (2d Cir.)]

7. Carriage Homes, Inc. was a general contractor that built multifamily residential and land-development projects in Minnesota. John Arkell was Carriage Homes' chief executive officer, president, and sole shareholder. Carriage Homes built Southwinds, a condominium development of 38 residential units in Austin, Minnesota. The foundation elevations of some of the Southwinds units were lower than permitted under the State Building Code, causing storm water to pool in the units' driveways and garages. The city of Austin's development director sent Arkell a series of seven letters in 1999 and 2001 concerning the elevation problems, and Arkell gave the letters to the project managers, who failed to resolve the problems.

   Minnesota makes a violation of the State Building Code a misdemeanor. On May 30, 2001, the state charged Carriage Homes and Arkell with three misdemeanor counts each, alleging a violation of the Uniform Building Code (UBC).

   Carriage Homes pleaded guilty and was sentenced to a $1,000 fine. But Arkell pleaded not guilty, asserting that he could not be held criminally responsible for the violation. After a bench trial, the district court found Arkell guilty. He was sentenced to pay a fine, pay restitution to the condominium owners, and serve 90 days in jail, with 80 days stayed pending his compliance with sentencing conditions. Mr. Arkell appealed on the grounds that the employees and subcontractors had simply not followed his orders and he was not responsible for their failures. Is he correct? [*State v. Arkell*, 657 N.W.2d 883 (Minn. App.)]

8. James Durham runs an art gallery. He has several paintings from unknown artists that he has listed for sale. The paintings always sell at his weekly auction for $20,000 to $50,000 above what James believes them to be worth. James learns that the bidders at the auctions are employed by an olive distributor located near the shipping yards of the city. What concerns should Durham have about the art, the bidders, and the large purchase prices?

9. Jennings operated a courier service to collect and deliver money. The contract with his customers allowed him a day or so to deliver the money that had been collected. Instead of holding collections until delivered, Jennings made short-term investments with the money. He always made deliveries to the customers on time, but because he kept the profit from the investments for himself, Jennings was prosecuted for embezzlement. Was he guilty? [*New York v. Jennings*, 504 N.E.2d 1079 (N.Y.)]

10. In April 2006, a DC-9 aircraft landed in the port city of Ciudad del Carmen, located 500 miles east of Mexico City. When the plane's crew began directing security personnel away from the plane, the suspicious activity piqued the curiosity of local law enforcement officials. They decided to search the plane and found 128 suitcases packed with over 56 tons of cocaine. The cocaine was to have been delivered to Toluca, near Mexico City. In investigating the plane and individual involved, law enforcement agents discovered that the plane had been purchased with money that had been laundered through two U.S. banks, Wachovia Corp. and Bank of America Corp. Neither bank was actually aware that the money was being used to purchase a plane that would then be used for drug trafficking. Are the banks still criminally liable for breaking the rules?

Explain why or why not. What if the banks were aware of large sums of money being run through particular customers' accounts? Would that knowledge make a difference?

11. Grabert ran Beck's, an amusement center in Louisiana. He held a license for video gambling machines. Louisiana makes it illegal to allow a minor to play a video gambling machine. A mother came into Grabert's center carrying her 23-month-old baby in her arms. She sat at the video poker machine with her child on her lap and proceeded to play. State troopers witnessed the baby pushing the buttons on the machine at least three times. The Department of Public Safety and Corrections revoked Grabert's video gaming license because a minor had been allowed to play the machines, and Grabert sought judicial review. The trial court reversed, and the department appealed. Has Grabert committed the crime of allowing a minor to engage in gaming? Is this the crime of allowing a minor to gamble? [*Grabert v. Department of Public Safety & Corrections*, 680 So. 2d 764 (La. App.) *cert.* denied; *Grabert v. State through Dept. of Public Safety and Corrections*, 685 So. 2d 126 (La.)]

12. The Banco Central administered a humanitarian plan for the government of Ecuador. Fernando Banderas and his wife presented false claims that the bank paid. After the fraud was discovered, the bank sued Banderas and his wife for damages for fraud and treble damages under the Florida version of RICO. Banderas and his wife asserted that they were not liable for RICO damages because there was no proof that they were related to organized crime and because the wrong they had committed was merely ordinary fraud. They had not used any racketeering methods. Is involvement with organized crime a requirement for liability under RICO? [*Banderas v. Banco Central del Ecuador*, 461 So. 2d 265 (Fla. App.)]

13. Kravitz owned 100 percent of the stock of American Health Programs, Inc. (AHP). To obtain the Philadelphia Fraternal Order of Police as a customer for AHP, Kravitz paid money bribes to persons who he thought were officers of that organization but who in fact were federal undercover agents. He was prosecuted for violating RICO. He was convicted, and the court ordered the forfeiture of all of Kravitz's shares of AHP stock. Can a forfeiture be ordered? [*United States v. Kravitz*, 738 F.2d 102 (3d Cir.)]

14. Kathryn Erickson was the general manager of the Uintah Special Services District (USSD), an entity created to use federal-mineral-lease revenues for road projects. She, along with her secretary, Cheryl McCurdy, administered the USSD from a small office in Vernal, Utah. Ms. Erickson's authority was limited and she was not permitted to enter into or modify contracts for or to expend more than $1,000 of USSD funds, without board approval.

Mitchell Construction was a major contractor for USSD. In 1998, USSD awarded Mitchell Construction a contract to haul gravel from a site called Hamaker Bottoms and another contract to carry out small asphalt-paving projects. Both contracts were to be completed within the 1998 construction year.

During 1999 and 2000 Mitchell Construction continued to perform work on the projects covered by its 1998 contracts with USSD, despite their expiration. It submitted invoices to USSD and was paid for this work.

In June 1999 a federal grand jury began to investigate contracting irregularities at USSD and the Uintah County Road Department and issued a *subpoena duces tecum* to USSD requesting copies of "project contracts, invoices" between USSD and contractors.

While the office was preparing the response for the grand jury subpoena, Ms. McCurdy saw Ms. Erickson prepare a handwritten change order for the Hamaker Bottoms contract and saw Ms. Erickson and Gilman N. Mitchell both sign it. The change order, which was backdated to January 13, 1999, extended the contract through December 31, 2000.

Ms. McCurdy later discovered that two other change orders had been created and backdated. She spent a day copying documents for the grand jury and recording, on a handwritten list, all of the documents that she had copied. However, she left Ms. Erickson in the office while she was working on the list in order to go home for dinner. Ms. Erickson called her and told her not to come back because all the copying was done. Later, Ms. McCurdy found on Ms. Erickson's desk a photocopy of the grand jury document list and saw that two entries not in her handwriting had been added. These entries were for change orders for contracts between Mitchell Construction and USSD. Ms. McCurdy reported the change to the government.

Ms. Erickson and Mr. Mitchell were each indicted by a grand jury in the U.S. District Court for the District of Utah on three counts of obstruction of justice by knowingly falsifying a document with the knowledge and intent that the grand jury would rely on it. Are both the elements of mental intent (scienter) and action present for criminal convictions here? [*U.S. v. Erickson*, 561 F.3d 1150 (10th Cir.)]

CHAPTER 8

Torts

Learning Outcomes <<<

After studying this chapter, you should be able to

LO.1 Explain the difference between torts and crimes

LO.2 Distinguish between an assault and a battery

LO.3 Explain the three different torts of invasion of privacy

LO.4 Explain the torts of defamation and defenses

LO.5 Explain the elements of negligence and defenses

LO.6 Explain the tort of strict liability and why very few defenses are available

The law of torts permits individuals and companies to recover from other individuals and companies for wrongs committed against them. Tort law provides rights and remedies for conduct that meets the elements required to establish that a wrong has occurred.

8-1 General Principles

Civil, or noncriminal, wrongs that are not breaches of contract are governed by tort law. This chapter covers the types of civil wrongs that constitute torts and the remedies available for those wrongs.

8-1a What Is a Tort?

tort–civil wrong that interferes with one's property or person.

Tort comes from the Latin term *tortus*, which means "crooked, dubious, twisted." Torts are actions that are not straight but are crooked, or civil, wrongs. A tort is an interference with someone's person or property. **For Example,** entering someone's house without his or her permission is an interference and constitutes the tort of trespass. Causing someone's character to be questioned is a wrong against the person and is the tort of defamation. The law provides protection against these harms in the form of remedies awarded after the wrongs are committed. These remedies are civil remedies for the acts of interference by others.

8-1b Tort and Crime Distinguished

A *crime* is a wrong that arises from a violation of a public duty, whereas a *tort* is a wrong that arises from a violation of a private duty. A crime is a wrong of such a serious nature that the appropriate level of government steps in to prosecute and punish the wrongdoer to deter others from engaging in the same type of conduct. However, whenever the act that is committed as a crime causes harm to an identifiable person, that person may recover from the wrongdoer for monetary damages to compensate for the harm. For the person who experiences the direct harm, the act is called a *tort*; for the government, the same act is called a *crime*.

When the same act is both a crime and a tort, the government may prosecute the wrongdoer for a violation of criminal law, and the individual who experiences the direct harm may recover damages. **For Example,** O. J. Simpson was charged by the state of California with the murder of his ex-wife, Nicole Brown Simpson, and her friend Ron Goldman. A criminal trial was held in which O. J. Simpson was acquitted. Simpson was subsequently sued civilly by the families of Nicole Simpson and Ron Goldman for the tort of wrongful death. The jury in the civil case found Simpson civilly liable and the court ordered him to pay nearly $20 million in damages plus interest. Only $382,000 of this judgment was paid to the families.

8-1c Types of Torts

intentional tort–civil wrong that results from intentional conduct.

There are three types of torts: intentional torts, negligence, and strict liability. **Intentional torts** are those that occur when wrongdoers engage in intentional conduct. **For Example,** striking another person in a fight is an intentional act and would be the tort of battery and possibly also the crime of battery. Your arm striking another person's nose in a fast-moving crowd of people at a rock concert is not a tort or crime because your arm was pushed unintentionally by the force of the crowd. If you stretched out your arms in that crowd or began to swing your arms about and struck another person, you would be behaving carelessly in a crowd of people; and, although you may not have committed an intentional tort, it is possible that your careless conduct constitutes the tort of **negligence.** Careless actions, or actions taken without thinking through their consequences, constitute negligence. The harm to the other person's nose may not have been intended, but there is liability for these accidental harms under negligence. **For Example,** if you run a red light, hit another car, and injure its driver, you did not intend the result. However, your careless behavior of disregarding a traffic signal resulted in the injury, and you would have liability for your negligence to that driver.

negligence–failure to exercise due care under the circumstances in consequence of which harm is proximately caused to one to whom the defendant owed a duty to exercise due care.

In transmission of disease cases, depending on the facts, both intentional torts and negligence theories may apply. A person who knows or should know that he or she has herpes and fails to disclose that fact, or misrepresents that he or she is disease-free, may be liable to a sexual partner. The torts theories may include negligence, battery, intentional infliction of emotional distress, and fraud. In most cases, the three words "I have herpes" is fair notice of the danger of infection.[1] However, saying it is okay to have sex because the individual was not having an outbreak of the disease is actionable. **For Example,** Thomas R. disclosed to his girlfriend that he had herpes but nevertheless told her that it was "okay" to have sex with him because he was not then experiencing an outbreak of the disease. The jury's finding of negligence and fraudulent concealment in the transmission of the disease was upheld by the appeals court, and the plaintiff was awarded compensatory damages as well as $2.75 million in punitive damages.[2]

strict liability–civil wrong for which there is absolute liability because of the inherent danger in the underlying activity, for example, the use of explosives.

Strict liability is another type of tort that imposes liability without regard to whether there was any intent to harm or any negligence occurred. Strict liability is imposed without regard to fault. Strict or absolute liability is imposed because the activity involved is so dangerous that there must be full accountability. Nonetheless, the activity is necessary and cannot be prohibited. The compromise is to allow the activity but ensure that its dangers and resulting damages are fully covered through the imposition of full liability for all injuries that result. **For Example,** contractors often need to use dynamite to take a roadway through a mountainside or demolish a building that has become a hazard. When the dynamite is used, noise, debris, and possibly dangerous pieces of earth and building will descend on others' land and possibly on people. In most states, contractors are held strictly liable for the resulting damage from the use of dynamite. The activity is necessary and not illegal, but those who use dynamite must be prepared to compensate those who are injured as a result.

Other areas in which there is strict liability for activity include the storage of flammable materials and crop dusting. The federal government and the states have pure food laws that impose absolute liability on manufacturers who fail to meet the statutory standards for their products. Another area of strict liability is *product liability*, where a product is defective, and unreasonably dangerous, and has caused harm. **For Example,** Mr. Izell was awarded $6 million in compensatory damages and $18 million in punitive damages when he proved that exposure to inhalable asbestos fibers, supplied in part by Union Carbide, was a substantial factor in causing mesothelioma.[3] Product liability is covered in Chapter 24.

[1] *R.A.P. v. B.I.P.*, 428 N.W.2d 103, 108 (Minn. App. 1988).
[2] *Behr v. Redmond*, 123 Cal. Rptr. 3d 97 (Cal. App. 2011).
[3] *Izell v. Union Carbide Corp.*, 180 Cal. Rptr. 3d 382 (Cal. App. 2014).

8-2 Intentional Torts

8-2a Assault

An *assault* is intentional conduct that threatens a person with a well-founded fear of imminent harm coupled with the present ability to carry out the threat of harm. **For Example,** the angry assertion "I'm going to kick your butt" along with aggressive movement in the direction of the victim with the intent to carry out the threat is an assault, even though a third person intervenes to stop the intended action. Mere words, however, although insulting, are ordinarily insufficient to constitute an assault.

8-2b Battery

A *battery* is the intentional, wrongful touching of another person without that person's consent. Thus, a threat to use force is an assault, and the actual use of force is the battery. The single action of striking an individual can be both a crime and a tort. A lawsuit for the tort of battery provides a plaintiff with the opportunity to recover damages resulting from the battery. The plaintiff must prove damages, however.

CASE SUMMARY

An Exchange of Unpleasantries...

FACTS: Moore and Beye had an altercation after a public meeting regarding airport expansion. Moore owned a ranch near the airport and staunchly opposed expansion. Beye owned a flying service and avidly supports expansion. Moore and Beye exchanged unpleasantries while leaving the meeting. Beye then punched Moore on the left side of the jaw. Moore stumbled but caught himself before falling. He then exclaimed to the crowd, "You saw that. You are my witnesses. I've been assaulted. I want that man arrested." Ravalli County deputies took Beye into custody, and the state charged him with misdemeanor assault. Moore visited the hospital complaining of back and neck pain two days later and contended that he had injured his back while reeling from Beye's punch. He filed a civil complaint against Beye for damages. Moore's evidence mostly concerned his alleged back injury. Beye did not contest that he had punched Moore. His evidence countered that Moore's back problems had existed before the altercation. The judge instructed the jury that Beye had committed a battery as a matter of law and directed that they answer the question, "Was Moore damaged as a result of the battery?" The jury voted 11 to 1 that the battery did not injure Moore, and Moore appealed.

DECISION: Judgment for Beye. Beye presented the testimony of several eyewitnesses and a medical expert that Moore had sustained no damages. Although Moore presented considerable evidence to the contrary, it was not the court's function to agree or disagree with the verdict. Beye presented sufficient evidence to uphold the jury's verdict. **[*Moore v. Beye*, 122 P.3d 1212 (Mont. 2005)]**

8-2c False Imprisonment

false imprisonment– intentional detention of a person without that person's consent; called the *shopkeeper's tort* when shoplifters are unlawfully detained.

False imprisonment is the intentional detention of a person without that person's consent.[4] The detention need not be for any specified period of time, for any detention against one's will is false imprisonment. False imprisonment is often called the *shopkeeper's tort* because so much liability has been imposed on store owners for their unreasonable detention of customers suspected of shoplifting. Requiring a customer to sit in the manager's office or not allowing a customer to leave the store can constitute the tort of false

[4] *Forgie-Buccioni v. Hannaford Bros. Inc.*, 413 F.3d 175 (1st Cir. 2005).

shopkeeper's privilege–right of a store owner to detain a suspected shoplifter based on reasonable cause and for a reasonable time without resulting liability for false imprisonment.

imprisonment. Shop owners do, however, need the opportunity to investigate possible thefts in their stores. As a result, all states have some form of privilege or protection for store owners called a *shopkeeper's privilege.*

The **shopkeeper's privilege** permits the store owner to detain a suspected shoplifter based on reasonable suspicion for a reasonable time without resulting liability for false imprisonment to the accused customer.[5] The privilege applies even if the store owner was wrong about the customer being a shoplifter, so long as the store owner acted based on reasonable suspicions and treated the accused shoplifter in a reasonable manner.

CASE SUMMARY

A Can of Mousse: A Tote Bag of Trouble

FACTS: Patricia Holguin went to Sally's Beauty Supply Store carrying her "eco-friendly canvas shopping tote," a large bag that is conspicuous when used. Upon entering the store, there were no posted signs stating that shopping totes were not allowed. She picked up a can of mousse that was not exactly what she wanted and started to carry it in her tote toward the front counter to ask the cashier a question about it. As she walked toward the front of the store the assistant manager approached her and asked what was in the bag. She was detained by this manager, who told her that once she put the hair mousse in her tote bag, she was shoplifting. Holguin's lawsuit for false imprisonment against the store was dismissed with prejudice by the trial court. This court held that once she placed the merchandise in her bag, the store had probable cause to believe she was shoplifting and had a statutory conditional privilege to detain her, free from civil liability for false imprisonment, because she "willfully concealed merchandise." Holguin appealed.

DECISION: The court of appeals reversed the district court's decision. In general, merchants and their employees have a conditional privilege to detain a person free from civil liability based on probable cause, or reasonable grounds to believe that the individual "willfully concealed" merchandise without paying for it, provided the detention is for a reasonable time and conducted in a reasonable manner. "Willfully concealed," however, requires more than merely putting merchandise out of sight. In self-service stores customers have implied permission to pick up, handle, move, try on, replace, and carry about merchandise within the store. There must be circumstances which reflect that the purpose of the concealment is adverse to the store's right to be paid before the conclusion can be drawn that the merchandise was "willfully concealed" under the statute providing the conditional privilege to detain a customer. Placing the can of mousse in a reusable, personal canvas shopping bag to carry to the front of the store to ask a question, without more, did not constitute "willful concealment." ***[Holguin v. Sally's Beauty Supply, Inc.*, 264 P.3d 732 (N. Mex. App. 2011)]**

8-2d Intentional Infliction of Emotional Distress

intentional infliction of emotional distress–tort that produces mental anguish caused by conduct that exceeds all bounds of decency.

The **intentional infliction of emotional distress** (IIED) is a tort involving conduct that goes beyond all bounds of decency and produces mental anguish in the harmed individual. This tort requires proof of outrageous conduct and resulting emotional distress in the victim. **For Example,** Erica Schoen, a 16-year employee of Freightliner, returned to work on light duty after surgery for a work-related shoulder injury. She was assigned to work out of the nurse's station under two employees who intentionally worked her beyond her restrictions, assigned her to humiliating work, repeatedly called her worthless, and used her as a personal servant—ordering her to get snacks, sodas, and lunches for them and not reimbursing her. After five months of this treatment, Erica brought the matter to the human resources manager, who told her, in part, "Nobody wants you. You're

[5] *Limited Stores, Inc. v. Wilson-Robinson,* 876 S.W.2d 248 (Ark. 1994); see also *Wal-Mart Stores, Inc. v. Binns,* 15 S.W.3d 320 (Ark. 2000).

worthless. We build trucks down here…." Erica became hysterical and thereafter required psychiatric care. The jury awarded $250,000 for IIED, and the verdict was upheld on appeal because the repetitive misconduct and its duration, ratified by the human resource manager, was intolerable.[6]

8-2e Invasion of Privacy

invasion of privacy–tort of intentional intrusion into the private affairs of another.

The right to privacy is the right to be free of unreasonable intrusion into one's private affairs. The tort of **invasion of privacy** actually consists of three different torts: (1) public disclosure of private facts; (2) intrusion into the plaintiff's private affairs; and (3) appropriation of another's name, likeness, or image for commercial advantage.[7]

Public Disclosure of Private Facts

This tort involves public disclosure of a private fact, such as a business posting returned checks from customers near its cash registers in public display.

The first widely recognized call in American law for a right to privacy based on the common law and enforceable in a tort action was raised in an article by Samuel Warren and Louis Brandeis in *The Harvard Law Review* of 1890.[8] The authors recognized that the right to privacy must be subject to conditions if it is to coexist with freedom of speech, freedom of the press, and other established areas of the law. Accordingly they proposed limitations on the right such as it should not prevent publication of matters of general public interest. Or, if the person published the facts himself or consents, the facts are no longer private. The authors also speculated that the law would not grant redress for oral publications, where the injury would be so trifling that the law might well, in the interest of free speech, disregard it all together. Presently must a plaintiff in a right to privacy action produce documentation such as a writing, picture, or video to bring a common-law right-to-privacy action? The question is resolved in the *Yum! Brands, Inc.* decision.

CASE SUMMARY

Let's Get With It! The Town Crier Is No Longer the Principal Purveyor of News

FACTS: Melissa Ignat suffered from a bipolar disorder for which she was being treated with medications. Side effects of medication adjustments occasionally caused her to miss work. She alleged that after returning from one such absence her supervisor, Mary Shipma, informed her that she had told everyone in the department that Ignat was bipolar. Subsequently her coworkers avoided and shunned her, and one of them asked Shipma if Ignat was likely to "go postal" at work. Ignat brought suit for public disclosure of private facts, and the trial court granted summary judgment for Yum! Brands on the ground that the right of privacy can be violated only by a writing, not by word of mouth.

DECISION: Judgment reversed. Limiting liability for public disclosure of private facts to those recorded in a writing is contrary to the tort's purpose, which has been since its inception to allow a person to control the kind of information about himself made available to the public—in essence, to define his public persona. While the restriction may have made sense in the 1890s—when no one dreamed of talk

[6] *Schoen v. Freightliner LLC*, 199 P.3d 332 (Or. App. 2008).

[7] A fourth tort of invasion of privacy also exists, known as "invasion of privacy by false light," which is very similar to defamation discussed in this chapter. Like a claim of defamation, the plaintiff cannot succeed on a claim of invasion of privacy by false light if the alleged communication is accurate or true. See *Miller v. Central Indiana Community Foundation, Inc.* 11 N.E.3d 944 (Ind. App. 2014).

[8] S. D. Warren and L. D. Brandeis, *The Right to Privacy*, 4 *Harv. L. Rev.* 193 (1890); the following analysis is derived from the *Ignat v. Yum Brands, Inc.* decision, 154 Cal. Rptr. 3d 275, 278 (Cal. App. 2013).

Let's Get With It! The Town Crier Is No Longer the Principal Purveyor of News continued

radio or confessional television—it certainly makes no sense now. Private facts can be just as widely disclosed—if not more so—through oral media as through written ones. To allow a plaintiff redress for one kind of disclosure but not the other, when both can be equally damaging to privacy, is a rule better suited to an era when the town crier was the principal purveyor of news. It is long past time to discard this outmoded rule. **[*Ignat v. Yum! Brands, Inc.* 154 Cal. Rptr. 3d 275 (Cal. App. 2013)]**

Intrusion into the Plaintiff's Private Affairs

This tort involves intrusion into the plaintiff's private affairs or seclusion. An example would be planting a microphone in the plaintiff's office or home.

Appropriation of Another's Name, Likeness, or Image for Commercial Advantage

This form of invasion of privacy is generally referred to as the *right of publicity.* The elements of this tort are (1) appropriation of the plaintiff's name or likeness for the value associated with it, and not in an incidental manner or for a newsworthy purpose, (2) identification of the plaintiff in the publication, and (3) an advantage or benefit to the defendant. The right to publicity is designed to protect the commercial interest of celebrities in their identities. **For Example,** popular and critically acclaimed rock and roll musician Don Henley, the founder and member of the band The Eagles, successfully sued a department store chain that ran an international newspaper advertisement for its Henley shirt, which stated in large letters as the focus of the ad "This is Don's Henley." The ad (1) used the value associated with the famous name Don Henley to get consumers to read it, (2) the plaintiff was identifiable in the ad, and (3) the ad was created with the belief that use of the words "Don's Henley" would help sell the product.[9] A "newsworthiness defense" protects the act of publishing or reporting factual data on public affairs or sporting activities.[10]

Some states refer to the right of publicity as a cause of action for *commercial misappropriation of a name or likeness* and provide two vehicles a plaintiff can use to protect the economic value of one's name: a common law action or a statutory remedy. The *Schlein* case involved a breach of contract action and an action for commercial misappropriation of a doctor's name.

CASE SUMMARY

The Name Game: We Are Discontinuing Your Royalty on the "Schlein Ultra," Dr. Schlein

FACTS: Orthopedic Systems, Inc. (OSI), and Dr. Schlein entered into a contract, whereby OSI would manufacture and sell an unpatented product originally designed by Dr. Schlein called the "Schlein Shoulder Positioner," to be used in arthroscopic shoulder surgery. The contract called for a 5% royalty of the list price less discounts. Over the years OSI's marketing brochures thanked "Allen P. Schlein M.D. for his assistance in the development of the

[9] *Henley v. Dillard Department Stores,* 46 F. Supp. 2d 587 (N.D. Tex. 1999).
[10] *Dryer v. National Football League,* 2014 WL 5106738 (D. Minn. 2014).

The Name Game: We Are Discontinuing Your Royalty on the "Schlein Ultra," Dr. Schlein continued

product." OSI paid royalty checks from January 1991 to January 2005, when OSI paid its last royalty payment for the period ending December 2004. In January 2005, OSI sent a letter to Dr. Schlein stating that in light of the fact that there was no patent protection on the product, it would be discontinuing the royalty. From January 2005 until July 29, 2005, OSI continued to market and sell the product using Dr. Schlein's name. OSI sued Dr. Schlein for declaratory relief and reformation of the royalty contract. Dr. Schlein cross-complained for breach of contract and commercial misappropriation of his name. The jury awarded Dr. Schlein $616,043 for failure to pay royalties under the contract. OSI earned $1,220,000 in profits attributed to the use of Dr. Schlein's name during the period from January 1, 2005, to July 31, 2005, after which OSI stopped using Schlein's name. The trial court declined to award the profits to Schlein, and both parties appealed.

DECISION: The statutory remedy of Section 3444(a) requires the payment of the greater of $750, or the actual damages suffered as a result of the unauthorized use, and any profits for the unauthorized use that are attributable to use and are not taken into account in computing actual damages. The legislative history for the minimum $750 award was intended to fill the gap that existed in the common law tort of invasion of privacy as applied to noncelebrities whose names lacked commercial value on the open market. Unlike sports and entertainment stars, noncelebrities often could not prove damages under the common law; therefore, the statute established a concrete remedy for the little man with a minimum payment. An interpretation that limits damages to $750 as an alternative to all other damages would be contrary to the spirit of the statute. Judgment for Dr. Schlein, who is entitled as well to the $1,220,000 profits as a result of OSI's unauthorized use of his name. **[*Orthopedic Systems, Inc. v. Schlein*, 135 Cal. Rptr. 3d 200 (Cal. App. 2011)]**

8-2f Defamation

defamation–untrue statement by one party about another to a third party.

slander–defamation of character by spoken words or gestures.

libel–written or visual defamation without legal justification.

Defamation is a false statement by one party about another to a third party. **Slander** is spoken defamation.[11] **Libel** is a false publication by writing, printing, picture, or other fixed representation to the eye, which exposes any person to hatred, contempt, or ridicule, or which has a tendency to injure the individual in his or her occupation.[12] The elements of defamation are (1) the making of defamatory statement; (2) publication of the defamatory material; and (3) damages that result from the statement.

In cases in which the victim is a public figure, such as a well-known entertainer, a professional athlete, or a political figure, another element is required: the element of *malice*, which means that the statement was made by the defendant with knowledge that it was false, or with reckless disregard for whether it was true or false.[13] **For Example,** former wrestler and governor of Minnesota and former Navy SEAL Jesse Ventura sued Chris Kyle, the author of the bestselling autobiography entitled *American Sniper*, for defamation. Kyle, also a former Navy SEAL, wrote that a character named "Scruff Face," holding court in a Coronado, California, bar said, "he hates America," that the SEALS "were killing men and women and children and murdering," and that SEALS "deserve to lose a few"; at which point Kyle "punched him out." While not naming Ventura in the book, Kyle confirmed in television, radio, and in print interviews about the book, that "Scruff

[11] Regarding damages, where one publishes a slander that imputes to another a communicable disease, or would adversely affect that person's fitness for the proper conduct of a lawful business, trade, or profession, the words are actionable in themselves, and the law implies compensatory damages. Once compensatory damages are established the jury will assess punitive damages to punish the party who committed the wrong and to deter others from committing similar wrongs in the future. See *Tanner v. Ebbole*, 2011 WL 4425540 (Ala. App. 2011) where the jury returned "nominal" compensatory damages of $1 and punitive damages of $100,000 against Paul Averette, the owner of a competing tattoo business, for slanderous statements to several patrons that his competitor, Chassity Ebbole, had hepatitis, syphilis, gonorrhea, and AIDS and that she used "nasty needles."

[12] See *Wong v. Jing*, 117 Cal. Rptr. 3rd (Cal. App. 2010).

[13] See *New York Times Co. v. Sullivan*, 376 U.S. 254 (1964).

Face" was Ventura. Kyle was killed by a troubled veteran, and his wife, as executor of his estate, was substituted as defendant. The case, brought by public figure Jesse Ventura, boiled down to a creditability contest, with several witnesses testifying that Ventura's version of the events was true, while several other witnesses testified that Kyle's version of the events was true. The jury decided the case for Ventura, with the court concluding that in believing Ventura's version of the facts, then Kyle's writing and telling of the story of punching out Ventura was itself a basis for the jury to make a finding of actual malice. On the defamation claim the jury awarded $500,000 in damages. Some $1,345,477 in damages was assessed for unjust enrichment for the money made in defaming Ventura in the book *American Sniper.*[14]

The defenses to defamation include truth and privilege. Also defendants may assert their free speech rights under the First Amendment to express their opinions as they see fit; and the courts are required to distinguish between statements of fact and statements of opinion.

Online Issues

Internet and mobile platforms have radically changed how society consumes and shares news, opinions, and other content. Courts are faced with an increase in Internet defamation cases, many of which involve anonymous posts, which must initially be addressed by the courts.

Unveiling Identities of Offending Anonymous Posters. Interactive Web sites are immune from liability for content created by a third-party user unless the Web site actively edits the content.[15] It thus may be necessary for a "defamed" person to seek the identity of the anonymous poster through a court subpoena in a defamation lawsuit.

The First Amendment prohibits the government from abridging the freedom of speech and it also protects anonymous speech.[16] Courts must strike a balance between the right to anonymous speech and the right of those harmed by anonymous speech to seek legal redress. Before a plaintiff can compel disclosure of the identity of an anonymous Internet speaker, the plaintiff must demonstrate to a court that he or she has a credible claim, and the anonymous speaker must be given an opportunity to defend himself before the court will order the unveiling of his or her identity.[17] **For Example,** the Leshers filed a lawsuit against anonymous posters on the Internet forum Topix, who had accused the Leshers of being sexual deviants, molesters, and drug dealers. With a credible claim established, the court ordered Topix to turn over identifying information including Internet Protocol (IP) addresses, which led to the identity of the posters and, ultimately, a jury awarding $13.78 million in damages against the posters.[18]

Vigorous Criticism Versus Defamation. Legitimate customer complaints based on opinion are not actionable defamation. And, hyperbole, figurative language, and rhetoric expression is protected opinion such as a posting claiming "the worst wedding experience of my life." However, a factual assertion that "the bridal suite was a tool shed..." in context may be actionable in some courts.[19] Other courts are less willing to interpret comments as assertions of fact. **For Example,** a defendant using a concealing screen name on an Internet discussion forum, felt free to claim that a corporate president was part of a management team of "boobs, losers, and crooks" and "has fat thighs, a fake medical

[14] *Ventura v. Kyle*, 8 F. Supp. 3d 1115 (D. Minn. 2014).

[15] Section 203(c)(1) of the Communication Decency Act of 1996.

[16] *McIntyre v. Ohio Elections Comm'n*, 514 U.S. 334, 342 (1995). "Anonymity is a shield from the tyranny of the majority." *Id.* at 357.

[17] *Doe v. Coleman*, 436 S.W.3d 207 (Ky. App. 2014).

[18] Ki Mae Heussner and Susanna Kim, *'Anonymous' Posters to Pay $13 Million for Defamatory Comments*, abcnews.com (Apr. 24, 2012), **http://abcnews.go.com/Business/jury-awards-13-million-texas-defamation-suit-anonymous/print?id=16194071**.

[19] *Neumann v. Liles*, 261 Or. App. 567 (2014).

degree, ... and has poor ... hygiene." The plaintiff served a subpoena on the forum's host seeking the defendant's identity, and the defendant, appearing as "Doe 6," moved to quash. The appellate court, viewing the defendant's post in the context of what was a particularly "[h]eated" discussion forum in which numerous other posts questioned the defendant's credibility, and noting the defendant's "crude, ungrammatical" language, satirical tone, and vituperative, "juvenile name-calling," concluded that the defendant's railing was nonactionable opinion and ordered the subpoena quashed.[20]

Defenses: Truth and Privilege

The defenses to defamation include the truth. If the statement is true, even if it is harmful to the victim, it is not the tort of defamation.[21]

absolute privilege–complete defense against the tort of defamation, as in the speeches of members of Congress on the floor and witnesses in a trial.

Some statements are privileged, and this privilege provides a full or partial defense to the tort of defamation. **For Example,** members of Congress enjoy an **absolute privilege** when they are speaking on the floor of the Senate or the House because public policy requires a free dialogue on the issues pending in a legislative body. The same absolute privilege applies to witnesses in court proceedings to encourage witnesses with information to come forward and testify. Where a witness granted immunity from prosecution testifies before a governmental agency, the witness is entitled to immunity from defamation lawsuits. **For Example,** Roger Clemens sued his former trainer, Brian McNamee, for defamation, contending that McNamee falsely stated to a congressional committee that Clemens had used steroids during his professional baseball career. This defamation claim was dismissed because McNamee's statements were entitled to absolute immunity on the reasoning that the proper administration of justice requires full disclosure from witnesses without fear of retaliatory lawsuits.[22]

qualified privilege–media privilege to print inaccurate information without liability for defamation, so long as a retraction is printed and there was no malice.

The media enjoy a **qualified privilege** for stories that turn out to be false. Their qualified privilege is a defense to defamation so long as the information was released without malice and a retraction or correction is made when the matter is brought to their attention.

A *qualified privilege* to make a defamatory statement in the workplace exists when the statement is made to protect the interests of the private employer on a work-related matter, especially when reporting actual or suspected wrongdoing. **For Example,** Neda Lewis was fired from her job at Carson Oil Company for allegedly stealing toilet paper. The employee in charge of supplies noticed that toilet paper was regularly missing from the ladies room, and one evening from a third-floor window overlooking the parking lot, she observed that the plaintiff's bag contained two rolls of toilet paper. She reported the matter to the executive secretary, who reported it to both the president and the CEO of the firm, who decided to fire her. Two other employees were also informed. The employer was able to successfully raise the defense of a qualified privilege to Ms. Lewis' defamation action for "false accusations of theft" since all of the employees involved were participants in the investigation and termination of the employee.[23]

A new statutory privilege has been evolving with respect to letters of recommendation and references given by employers for employees who are applying for jobs at other companies. Most companies, because of concerns about liability for defamation, will only confirm that a former employee did work at their firm and will provide the time period during which the person was employed. Numerous states now have statutes that provide employers a qualified privilege with respect to references and recommendations. So long

[20] *Krinsky v. Doe*, 72 Cal. Rptr. 3d 231 (2008).
[21] See *Stark v. Zeta Phi Beta Sorority Inc.*, 587 F. Supp. 2d 170 (D.D.C. 2008).
[22] *Clemens v. McNamee*, 608 F. Supp. 2d 811 (S.D. Tex. 2009). On June 18, 2012, Clemens was acquitted of all six counts of lying to Congress.
[23] *Lewis v. Carson Oil Co.*, 127 P.3d 1207 (Or. App. 2006).

as the employer acts in good faith in providing information, there is no liability for defamation to the former employee as a result of the information provided.

8-2g Product Disparagement

slander of title–malicious making of false statements as to a seller's title.

trade libel–written defamation about a product or service.

product disparagement–false statements made about a product or business.

Although the comparison of products and services is healthy for competition, false statements about another's products constitute a form of slander called **slander of title** or libel called **trade libel;** collectively, these are known as **product disparagement,** which occurs when someone makes false statements about another business, its products, or its abilities.[24] The elements of product disparagement are (1) a false statement about a particular business product or about its service in terms of honesty, reputation, ability, or integrity; (2) communication of the statement to a third party; and (3) damages.

8-2h Wrongful Interference with Contracts

contract interference–tort in which a third party interferes with others' freedom to contract.

The tort of **contract interference** (or tortious interference with contracts) occurs when parties are not allowed the freedom to contract without interference from third parties. While the elements required to establish the tort of contract interference are complex, a basic definition is that the law affords a remedy when a third party intentionally causes another to break a contract already in existence.[25] **For Example,** Nikke Finke, a newspaper reporter who had a contract with the *New York Post* to write stories about the entertainment industry for the *Post's* business section, wrote two articles about a lawsuit involving a literary agent and the Walt Disney Company over merchandising rights to the Winnie-the-Pooh characters. Finke reported that the trial court sanctioned Disney for engaging in "misuse of the discovery process" and acting in "bad faith" and ordered Disney to pay fees and costs of $90,000. Disney's president, Robert Iger, sent a letter to the *Post's* editor-in-chief, Col Allan, calling Finke's reporting an "absolute distortion" of the record and "absolutely false." Approximately two weeks after the Pooh articles were published, the *Post* fired Finke; her editor told her she was being fired for the Pooh articles. She sued Disney on numerous tort theories, including interference with her contract with the *Post.* Disney sought to have the complaint dismissed, which motion was denied by the court. The Court of Appeals concluded that Finke demonstrated a reasonable probability of proving that Iger's allegations that she made false statements in her article were themselves false; and it concluded that a jury could find Disney liable for intentional interference with contractual relations based on circumstantial evidence and negligent interference with contractual relations because it was reasonably foreseeable to Disney that the nature of its accusations against Finke would result in her termination from employment.[26]

8-2i Trespass

trespass–unauthorized action with respect to person or property.

A **trespass** is an unauthorized action with respect to land or personal property. A *trespass to land* is any unpermitted entry below, on, across, or above the land of another. **For Example,** Joyce Ameral's home abuts the midway point of the 240-yard, par-4 ninth hole of the public Middlebrook Country Club. Balls sliced and hooked by golfers have damaged her windows and screens, dented her car, and made her deck too dangerous for daytime use. Her landscapers are forced to wear hard hats when cutting her lawn. In her lawsuit against the country club owner, the court ruled that the projection of golf balls onto Ameral's property constituted a continuing trespass and it enjoined the trespass.[27]

[24] *Sannerud v. Brantz,* 879 P.2d 341 (Wyo. 1994). See *Suzuki Motor Corp. v. Consumers Union,* 230 F.3d 1110 (9th Cir. 2003), *cert. denied* 540 U.S. 983 (2003), for an example of the complexity of a product disparagement action.

[25] See *Ventas, Inc. v. HCP, Inc.,* 647 F.3d 291 (6th Cir. 2011); *ASDI, Inc. v. Beard Research, Inc.,* 11 A.3d 749 (Del. 2010).

[26] *Finke v. The Walt Disney Co.,* 2 Cal. Rptr. 3d 436 (Cal. App. 2003).

[27] *Ameral v. Pray,* 831 N.E.2d 915 (Mass. App. 2005).

A *trespass to personal property* is the invasion of personal property without the permission of the owner. **For Example,** the use of someone's car without that person's permission is a trespass to personal property.

8-3 Negligence

The widest range of tort liability today arises in the field of negligence. Accidents happen! Property is damaged and/or injuries result. The fact that an individual suffers an injury does not necessarily mean that the individual will be able to recover damages for the injury. **For Example,** Rhonda Nichols was shopping in the outdoor garden center at a Lowe's Home Center when a "wild bird" flew into the back of her head, causing injuries. Her negligence lawsuit against Lowe's was dismissed because the owner did not have a duty to protect her from a wild bird attack because it was not reasonably foreseeable.[28] Jane Costa was passively watching a Boston Red Sox baseball game at Fenway Park when a foul ball struck her in the face, causing severe and permanent injuries. Her negligence lawsuit against the Boston Red Sox was unsuccessful because it was held that the owners had no duty to warn Ms. Costa of the obvious danger of foul balls being hit into the stands.[29] Although cases involving injury to spectators at baseball games in other jurisdictions have turned on other tort doctrines, injured fans, like Ms. Costa, are left to bear the costs of their injuries. Only when an injured person can demonstrate the following four elements of negligence is a right to recover established: (1) a duty, (2) breach of duty, (3) causation, and (4) damages.[30] Several defenses may be raised in a negligence lawsuit.

8-3a Elements of Negligence

Duty to Exercise Reasonable Care

The first element of negligence is a *duty*. There is a general duty of care imposed to act as a reasonably prudent person would in similar circumstances. **For Example,** Gustavo Guzman worked for a subcontractor as a chicken catcher at various poultry farms where a Tyson Foods employee, Brian Jones, operated a forklift and worked with the catchers setting up cages to collect birds for processing at a Tyson plant. Contrary to Tyson's instructions "never to allow catchers to move behind the forklift or otherwise out of sight," Brian moved his forklift and struck Guzman, who suffered a serious spinal injury. A general contractor, Tyson Foods, owes a duty to exercise reasonable care to a subcontractor's employee, Gustavo Guzman.[31]

malpractice–when services are not properly rendered in accordance with commonly accepted standards; negligence by a professional in performing his or her skill.

Professionals have a duty to perform their jobs at the level of a reasonable professional. For a professional such as an accountant, doctor, lawyer, dentist, or architect to avoid liability for **malpractice,** the professional must perform his or her skill in the same manner as, and at the level of, other professionals in the same field.

Those who own real property have a duty of care to keep their property in a condition that does not create hazards for guests. Businesses have a duty to inspect and repair their property so that their customers are not injured by hazards, such as spills on the

[28] *Nichols v. Lowe's Home Center, Inc.,* 407 F. Supp. 2d 979 (S.D. Ill. 2006).
[29] *Costa v. Boston Red Sox Baseball Club,* 809 N.E.2d 1090 (Mass. App. 2004).
[30] *Alfred v. Capital Area Soccer League, Inc.,* 669 S.E.2d 277 (N.C. App. 2008).
[31] *Tyson Foods Inc. v. Guzman,* 116 S.W.3d 233 (Tex. App. 2003). But see *Pippin v. Hill-Rom Co., Inc.,* 615 F.3d 886 (8th Cir. 2010), where a shipper's failure to load cargo onto an independent truck driver's trailer, as required by the transportation contract, did not give rise to a cause of action for negligence, where the driver was injured loading the truck by himself. The shipper owed no duty to the driver, who chose to load the truck by himself.

floor or uneven walking areas. When customer safety is a concern, businesses have a duty to provide adequate security, such as security patrols in mall parking lots.

Breach of Duty

The second element of negligence is the breach of duty imposed by statute or by the application of the reasonable person standard. The defendant's conduct is evaluated against what a reasonable person would have done under the circumstances. That is, when there is sufficient proof to raise a jury question, the jury decides whether the defendant breached the duty to the injured person from a reasonable person's perspective.[32] **For Example,** the jury in Guzman's lawsuit against Tyson Foods (the *Tyson* case), after weighing all of the facts and circumstances, determined that Tyson's employee's operation of the forklift constituted a breach of Tyson's duty of care to Guzman.

Causation

A third element of negligence is *causation*, the element that connects the duty and the breach of duty to the injuries to the plaintiff. **For Example,** in Guzman's lawsuit, the forklift operator's careless conduct was the cause in fact of this worker's injuries. A "but for" test for causation is used. *But for* Tyson employee Brian Jones's negligent conduct in moving the forklift under the circumstances surrounding the accident, Guzman would not have been injured.

Once the cause in fact is established, the plaintiff must establish *proximate cause.* That is, it must establish that the harm suffered by the injured person was a foreseeable consequence of the defendant's negligent actions. Foreseeability requires only the general danger to be foreseeable. In the *Tyson* case, the court determined that while there was some evidence that a jury could possibly infer that Tyson could not foresee an accident similar to the one involving Guzman, the evidence was legally sufficient to support the jury's finding that Tyson's negligence was foreseeable and the cause in fact of Guzman's injuries.

The landmark *Palsgraf v. Long Island Rail Road Co.* case established a limitation on liability for unforeseeable or unusual consequences following a negligent act.

CASE SUMMARY

The Scales Tipped on Causation

FACTS: Helen Palsgraf lived in Brooklyn. On a summer's day, she purchased tickets to travel to Rockaway Beach on the Long Island Rail Road (LIRR) with her two daughters. She was standing on a platform on the LIRR's East New York station when two men ran to catch another train. One of the men made it onto the train, but the other man, who was carrying a package, was unsteady as the train was about to pull out of the station. The LIRR conductor pulled him up, while the LIRR platform guard pushed him into the train, but in the process, he dropped the package. It contained fireworks and exploded! The concussion from the explosion caused the scales located next to

[32] A breach of duty may be established by the very nature of the harm to the plaintiff. The doctrine of *res ipsa loquitur* ("the event speaks for itself") provides a rebuttable presumption that the defendant was negligent when a defendant owes a duty to the plaintiff, the nature of the harm caused the plaintiff is such that it ordinarily does not happen in the absence of negligence, and the instrument causing the injury was in the defendant's exclusive control. An example of the doctrine is a lawsuit against a surgeon after a surgical device is discovered in a former patient months after the surgery by another physician seeking the cause of the patient's continuing pain subsequent to the operation.

The Scales Tipped on Causation continued

Mrs. Palsgraf to fall over, striking and injuring her. Mrs. Palsgraf sued LIRR for the negligence of the two employees who had assisted the passenger with the package to board the train. A jury awarded her $6,000, which was upheld 3-2 by the Appellate Division. Thereafter the state's highest court considered the railroad's appeal.

DECISION: Recovery for negligence is not available unless there has been some violation of a right. Helen Palsgraf was too remote in distance from the accident for any invasion of rights. To reach a different decision would mean that there could be no end to those who might be harmed. By helping someone onto a moving train, the train employees can anticipate that the passenger himself might be injured, that other passengers might be injured, and that those around the immediate scene might be injured. But Mrs. Palsgraf was too remote for her injuries to be reasonably foreseeable as a consequence of the action of helping a passenger onto a moving train. She was 25 to 30 feet away from the scene, and the explosion cannot be called the proximate cause of her concussion and other injuries. [***Palsgraf v. Long Island R. R. Co.*, 162 N.E. 99 (N.Y. 1928)**]

Damages

The plaintiff in a personal injury negligence lawsuit must establish the actual losses caused by the defendant's breach of duty of care and is entitled to be made whole for all losses. The successful plaintiff is entitled to compensation for (1) past and future pain and suffering (mental anguish), (2) past and future physical impairment, (3) past and future medical care, and (4) past and future loss of earning capacity. Life and work life expectancy are critical factors to consider in assessing damage involving permanent disabilities with loss of earning capacity. Expert witnesses are utilized at trial to present evidence based on worklife tables and present value tables to deal with these economic issues. The jury considers all of the evidence in the context of the elements necessary to prove negligence and all defenses raised, and it renders a verdict. **For Example,** in the *Tyson* case, the defendant presented evidence and argued that Gustavo Guzman was himself negligent regarding the accident. The jury found that both parties were negligent and attributed 80 percent of the fault to Tyson and 20 percent to Guzman (this is called *comparative negligence* and is discussed in the following section). The jury awarded Guzman $931,870.51 in damages ($425,000.00 for past physical pain and mental anguish, $150,000.00 for future physical pain and mental anguish, $10,000.00 for past physical impairment, $10,000.00 for future physical impairment, $51,870.51 for past medical care, $5,000.00 for future medical care, $70,000.00 for past lost earning capacity, and $210,000.00 for future lost earning capacity). After deducting 20 percent of the total jury award for Guzman's own negligence, the trial court's final judgment awarded Guzman $745,496.41.

In some situations, the independent actions of two defendants occur to cause harm. **For Example,** Penny Shipler was rendered a quadriplegic as a result of a Chevrolet S-10 Blazer rollover accident. She sued the driver Kenneth Long for negligence and General Motors for negligent design of the Blazer's roof. She was awarded $18.5 million in damages. Because two causes provided a single indivisible injury, the two defendants were held jointly and severally liable.[33] Under *joint and several liability*, each defendant may be held liable to pay the entire judgment. However, should one defendant pay the entire judgment, that party may sue the other for "contribution" for its proportionate share.

In some cases in which the breach of duty was shocking, plaintiffs may be awarded *punitive damages*. However, punitive (also called *exemplary*) damages are ordinarily applied

[33] *Shipler v. General Motors Corp.*, 710 N.W.2d 807 (Neb. 2006).

when the defendant's tortious conduct is attended by circumstances of fraud, malice, or willful or wanton conduct.[34]

contributory negligence–negligence of the plaintiff that contributes to injury and at common law bars recovery from the defendant although the defendant may have been more negligent than the plaintiff.

8-3b Defenses to Negligence

Contributory Negligence

A plaintiff who is also negligent gives the defendant the opportunity to raise the defense of **contributory negligence,** which the defendant establishes by utilizing the elements of negligence previously discussed, including the plaintiff's duty to exercise reasonable care for his or her own safety, the breach of that duty, causation, and harm. Under common law, the defense of contributory negligence, if established, is a complete bar to recovery of damages from the defendant.

CASE SUMMARY

Keep Your Eye on the Ball in Sports: Keep Your Eye on the 300-Pound Boxes in Trucking

FACTS: Lawrence Hardesty is an over-the-road tractor-trailer truck driver who picked up a load of stadium seating equipment for the NFL stadium under construction in Baltimore. The equipment was packaged in large corrugated cardboard boxes weighing several hundred pounds. The shipper, American Seating Co., loaded the trailer while Hardesty remained in the cab of his truck doing "paperwork" and napping. Considerable open space existed between the boxes and the rear door of the trailer. The evidence showed that Hardesty failed to properly examine the load bars used to secure the boxes from movement during transit. When Hardesty arrived at the Baltimore destination, he opened the rear trailer door and boxes at the end of the trailer fell out and injured him. Hardesty brought a personal injury negligence action against the shipper. American Seating Co. responded that Hardesty was contributorily negligent, thus barring his negligence claim.

DECISION: Judgment for American Seating Co. because the claim is barred by Hardesty's contributory negligence. His decision to ignore the loading process by remaining in his truck, oblivious to the manner and means of the loading of the trailer, coupled with his own failure to examine the load bars sufficiently to confirm that they would "adequately secure" the cargo, together with his decision, in the face of his prior omissions, to open the doors of the trailer upon his arrival in Baltimore while standing within the zone of danger created by the possibility (of which he negligently failed to inform himself) of injury from cargo falling out of the trailer, cohered to rise to the level of a cognizable breach of duty—contributory negligence. [***Hardesty v. American Seating Co.*, 194 F. Supp. 2d 447 (D. Md. 2002)**]

The contributory negligence defense has given way to the defense of comparative negligence in most states.[35]

Comparative Negligence

Because contributory negligence produced harsh results with no recovery of damages for an injured plaintiff, most states have adopted a fairer approach to handling situations in which both the plaintiff and the defendant are negligent; it is called *comparative*

[34] See *Eden Electrical, Ltd. v. Amana Co.*, 370 F.3d 824 (8th Cir. 2004); and *University of Colorado v. American Cyanamid Co.*, 342 F.3d 1298 (Fed. Cir. 2003).

[35] Alabama, the District of Columbia, Maryland, North Carolina, and Virginia are pure contributory negligence states, which hold that the damaged party cannot recover any damages even if it is just 1 percent at fault. See *RGR, LLC v. Settle*, 758 S.E.2d 215 (Va. 2014) where the Virginia Supreme Court set aside a $2.5 million judgment finding that the plaintiff was contributorily negligent as a matter of law.

negligence. Comparative negligence is a defense that permits a negligent plaintiff to recover some damages but only in proportion to the defendant's degree of fault.[36] **For Example,** in the *Tyson* case, both the defendant and the plaintiff were found to be negligent. The jury attributed 80 percent of the fault for the plaintiff's injury to Tyson and 20 percent of the fault to the plaintiff, Guzman. While Guzman's total damages were $931,870, they were reduced by 20 percent, and the final judgment awarded Guzman was $745,496.

Some comparative negligence states refuse to allow the plaintiff to recover damages if the plaintiff's fault was more than 50 percent of the cause of the harm.[37]

Assumption of the Risk

The assumption of the risk defense has two categories. *Express assumption of the risk* involves a written exculpatory agreement under which a plaintiff acknowledges the risks involved in certain activities and releases the defendant from prospective liability for personal injuries sustained as a result of the defendant's negligent conduct. Examples include ski lift tickets, white water rafting contracts, permission for high school cheerleading activities, and parking lot claim checks. In most jurisdictions these agreements are enforceable as written. However, in some jurisdictions they may be considered unenforceable because they violate public policy. **For Example,** Gregory Hanks sued the Powder Ridge Ski Resort for negligence regarding serious injuries he sustained while snowtubing at the defendant's facility. He had signed a release, which explicitly provided that the snowtuber: *["fully] assume[s] all risks associated with [s]nowtubing,* even if due to the NEGLIGENCE" of the defendants [emphasis in original]. The Supreme Court of Connecticut found that the release was unenforceable because it violated the public policy by shifting the risk of negligence to the weaker bargainer.[38]

Implied primary assumption of the risk arises when a plaintiff has impliedly consented, often in advance of any negligence by the defendant, to relieve a defendant of a duty to the plaintiff regarding specific known and appreciated risks. It is a subjective standard, one specific to the plaintiff and his or her situation. **For Example,** baseball mom Delinda Taylor took her two boys to a Seattle Mariners baseball game and was injured during the pregame warm-up when a ball thrown by José Mesa got past Freddie Garcia, striking Taylor in the face and causing serious injuries. The defendant baseball team successfully raised the affirmative defense of implied primary assumption of the risk by showing that Mrs. Taylor had full subjective understanding of the specific risk of getting hit by a thrown baseball, and she voluntarily chose to encounter that risk.[39] However, John Coomer, a spectator at a Kansas City Royals baseball game was struck in the eye by a hotdog thrown by the team's mascot, Slugger, during a "Hotdog Launch," causing Coomer to suffer a detached retina. The Supreme Court of Missouri held that being injured by Slugger's hotdog toss was not a risk inherent in watching a Royals baseball game.[40]

A number of states have either abolished the defense of assumption of the risk, reclassifying the defense as comparative negligence so as not to completely bar a plaintiff's recovery of damages, or have eliminated the use of the assumption of the risk terminology to handle cases under the duty, breach of duty, causation, and harm elements of negligence previously discussed.[41]

[36] *City of Chicago v. M/V Morgan,* 375 F.3d 563 (7th Cir. 2004).
[37] *Davenport v. Cotton Hope Plantation,* 482 S.E.2d 569 (S.C. App. 1997).
[38] *Hanks v. Powder Ridge,* 885 A.2d 734 (Conn. 2005).
[39] *Taylor v. Baseball Club of Seattle,* 130 P.3d 835 (Wash. App. 2006).
[40] *Coomer v. K.C. Royals Baseball Corp.,* 437 S.W.3d 184 (Mo. 2014).
[41] See, for example, *Costa v. The Boston Red Sox Baseball Club,* 809 N.E.2d 1090 (Mass. App. 2004), where the court cites state precedent that "... the abolishment of assumption of the risk as an affirmative defense did not alter the plaintiff's burden ... to prove the defendant owed [the plaintiff] a duty of care ... and thus left intact the open and obvious damages rule, which operates to negate the existence of a duty to care."

SPORTS & ENTERTAINMENT LAW

Liability for Injuries under the Sports Exception Doctrine

Charles "Booby" Clark played football for the Cincinnati Bengals as a running back on offense. Dale Hackbart played defensive free safety for the Denver Broncos. As a consequence of an interception by the Broncos, Hackbart became an offensive player, threw a block, and was watching the play with one knee on the ground when Clark "acting out of anger and frustration, but without a specific intent to injure," stepped forward and struck a blow to the back of Hackbart's head and neck, causing a serious neck fracture. Is relief precluded for injuries occurring during a professional football game? The answer is no. While proof of mere negligence is insufficient to establish liability during such an athletic contest, liability must instead be premised on heightened proof of reckless or intentional conduct on the part of the defendant. In the *Hackbart* case, the court determined that if the evidence established that the injury was the result of acts of Clark that were in reckless disregard of Hackbart's safety, Hackbart is entitled to damages.* Why didn't Hackbart pursue recovery under negligence law, contending that Clark had a general duty of care to act as a reasonably prudent person would in similar circumstances? Because football and other contact sports contain within the rules of the games inherent *unreasonable* risks of harm, a negligence theory is not applicable. What contact sports do you believe qualify under this "sports exception" doctrine for which proof of negligence is insufficient to establish liability for injuries sustained during the athletic contest? Is softball a contact sport for players? What about coaching or officiating decisions made in the middle of a fast-moving game?**

PGA golfer Walter Mallin sued PGA golfer John Paesani for injuries that Mallin sustained while competing in a PGA golf tournament when Paesani drove a golf ball that struck Mallin in the head on his right temple. Paesani contends that the "sports exception" doctrine applies and the negligence case must be dismissed. How would you decide this case?***

***Hackbart v. Cincinnati Bengals, Inc.*, 601 F.2d 516 (10th Cir. 1979).**
See ***Guillo v. DeKamp Junction, Inc.*, 959 N.E.2d 215 (Ill. App. 2011).
*****Mallin v. Paesani*, 892 A.2d 1043 (Conn. Super. 2005).**

Immunity

Governments are generally immune from tort liability.[42] This rule has been eroded by decisions and in some instances by statutes, such as the Federal Tort Claims Act. Subject to certain exceptions, this act permits the recovery of damages from the United States for property damage, personal injury, or death action claims arising from the negligent act or omission of any employee of the United States under such circumstances that the United States, if a private person, would be liable to the claimant in accordance with the law of the place where the act or omission occurred. A rapidly growing number of states have abolished governmental immunity, although many still recognize it.

Until the early 1900s, charities were immune from tort liability, and children and parents and spouses could not sue each other. These immunities are fast disappearing. **For Example,** if a father's negligent driving of his car causes injuries to his minor child passenger, the child may recover from the father for his injuries.[43]

8-4 Strict Liability

The final form of tort liability is known as *strict liability*. When the standards of strict liability apply, very few defenses are available. Strict liability was developed to provide guaranteed protection for those who are injured by conduct the law deems both serious and inexcusable.

[42] *Kirby v. Macon County*, 892 S.W.2d 403 (Tenn. 1994).
[43] *Cates v. Cates*, 588 N.E.2d 330 (Ill. App. 1992); see also *Doe v. McKay*, 700 N.E.2d 1018 (Ill. 1998).

THINKING THINGS THROUGH

Torts and Public Policy

Over a decade ago, a jury awarded 81-year-old Stella Liebeck nearly $3 million because she was burned after she spilled a cup of McDonald's coffee on her lap. Based on these limited facts, a national discussion ensued about a need for tort reform, and to this day "Stella Awards" are given on Web sites for apparently frivolous or excessive lawsuits. Consider the following additional facts and the actual damages awarded Stella Liebeck. Decide whether her recovery was just.

- McDonald's coffee was brewed at 195 to 205 degrees.
- McDonald's quality assurance manager "was aware of the risk [of burns] ... and had no plans to turn down the heat."
- Mrs. Liebeck spent seven days in the hospital with third-degree burns and had skin grafts. Gruesome photos of burns of the inner thighs, groin, and buttocks were entered as evidence.
- The compensatory damages were $200,000, which were reduced to $160,000 because Mrs. Liebeck was determined to be 20 percent at fault.
- The jury awarded $2.7 million in punitive damages. The trial court judge reduced this amount to $480,000.
- The total recovery at the trial court for Mrs. Liebeck was $640,000. Both parties appealed, and a settlement was reached at what is believed to be close to the $640,000 figure.

Tort remedies have evolved because of public policy incentives for the protection of individuals from physical, mental, and economic damage. Tort remedies provide economic motivation for individuals and businesses to avoid conduct that could harm others.

The amount of the compensation and the circumstances in which compensation for torts should be paid are issues that courts, juries, and legislatures review. Many legislatures have examined and continue to review the standards for tort liability and damages.

The U.S. Supreme Court devoted several decisions in recent years to dealing with excessive punitive damages in civil litigation, and it has set "guideposts" to be used by courts in assessing punitive damages.* In *State Farm Mutual Automobile Insurance Co. v. Campbell*, compensatory damages for the plaintiffs at the trial court level were $1 million, and punitive damages, based in part on evidence that State Farm's nationwide policy was to underpay claims regardless of merit to enhance profits, were assessed at $145 million. The Supreme Court concluded that the facts of *Campbell* would likely justify a punitive damages award only at or near the amount of compensatory damages. Thus, even those who act very badly as State Farm Insurance did have a constitutionally protected right under the due process clause of the Fourteenth Amendment to have civil law damages assessed in accordance with the Supreme Court's guideposts.

******BMW of North America v. Gore***, 517 U.S. 559 (1996); *Cooper Industries v. Leatherman Tool Group, Inc.*, 532 U.S. 424 (2001); *State Farm Insurance v. Campbell*, 538 U.S. 408 (2003); *Exxon Shipping Co. v. Baker*, 544 U.S. 471 (2008).**

8-4a What Is Strict Liability?

Strict liability is an absolute standard of liability imposed by the law in circumstances the courts or legislatures have determined require a high degree of protection. When strict liability is imposed, the result is that the company or person who has caused injury or damages by the conduct will be required to compensate for those damages in an absolute sense. Few, if any, defenses apply in a situation in which the law imposes a strict liability standard. **For Example,** as noted earlier in the chapter, engaging in ultrahazardous activities, such as using dynamite to excavate a site for new construction, results in strict liability for the contractor performing the demolition. Any damages resulting from the explosion are the responsibility of that contractor, so the contractor is strictly liable.

8-4b Imposing Strict Liability

Strict liability arises in a number of different circumstances, but the most common are in those situations in which a statutory duty is imposed and in product liability. **For Example,** at both the state and federal levels, there are requirements for the use, transportation, and sale of radioactive materials, as well as the disposal of biomedical materials and tools. Any violation of these rules and regulations would result in strict liability for the company or person in violation.

Product liability, while more fully covered in Chapter 24, is another example of strict liability. A product that is defective through its design, manufacture, or instructions and that injures someone results in strict liability for the manufacturer.

Make the Connection

Summary

A *tort* is a civil wrong that affords recovery for damages that result. The three forms of torts are intentional torts, negligence, and strict liability. A tort differs from a crime in the nature of its remedy. Fines and imprisonment result from criminal violations, whereas money damages are paid to those who are damaged by conduct that constitutes a tort. An action may be both a crime and a tort, but the tort remedy is civil in nature.

Selected intentional torts are false imprisonment, defamation, product disparagement, contract interference or tortious interference, and trespass. False imprisonment is the detention of another without his or her permission. False imprisonment is often called the *shopkeeper's tort* because store owners detain suspected shoplifters. Many states provide a privilege to store owners if they detain shoplifting suspects based on reasonable cause and in a reasonable manner. Defamation is slander (oral) or libel (written) and consists of false statements about another that damage the person's reputation or integrity. With an increase in Internet cases, some of which involve anonymous posts, courts may compel disclosure of identity only if the plaintiff can demonstrate a credible claim and the anonymous speaker is given the opportunity to defend before the unveiling of his or her name. Truth is an absolute defense to defamation, and there are some privileges that protect against defamation, such as those for witnesses at trial and for members of Congress during debates on the floor. There is a developing privilege for employers when they give references for former employees. Invasion of privacy is intrusion into private affairs; public disclosure of private facts; or appropriation of someone's name, image, or likeness for commercial purposes.

To establish the tort of negligence, one must show that there has been a breach of duty in the form of a violation of a statute or professional competency standards or of behavior that does not rise to the level of that of a reasonable person. That breach of duty must have caused the foreseeable injuries to the plaintiff, and the plaintiff must be able to quantify the damages that resulted. Possible defenses to negligence include contributory negligence, comparative negligence, and assumption of risk.

Strict liability is absolute liability with few defenses.

Learning Outcomes

After studying this chapter, you should be able to clearly explain:

8-1 General Principles

LO.1 Explain the difference between torts and crimes

See the discussion on wrongs that are a violation of a private duty as torts, and wrongs that are a violation of a public duty as crimes, page 132.

See the O. J. Simpson example of his acquittal of the crime of murder and his civil liability for the torts of wrongful death, page 132.

8-2 Intentional Torts

LO.2 Distinguish between an assault and a battery

See the "kick your butt" threat example of an assault, page 134.

LO.3 Explain the three different torts of invasion of privacy

See the discussion of the intrusion into a person's private affairs, public disclosure of private facts, and right of publicity torts, pages 136–137.

See the *Ignat* case, which determined that a right of privacy can be violated by word of mouth, pages 136–137.

See the *Schlein* case involving commercial misappropriation of one's name, pages 137–138.

LO.4 Explain the torts of defamation and defenses

See the discussion of slander, libel, and trade libel beginning, pages 138 and 141.

See the *Ventura* case involving the requirement of the enhanced element of malice for cases in which the victim is a public figure, page 138.

See the discussion involving unveiling the identity of offending anonymous posters of defamatory remarks on the Internet, page 139.

8-3 Negligence

LO.5 Explain the elements of negligence and defenses

See the discussion of the elements of negligence: duty, breach of duty, and causation and damages, pages 142–144.

See the discussion of the defenses of contributory negligence, comparative negligence, assumption of risk, and immunity, pages 145–147.

8-4 Strict Liability

LO.6 Explain the tort of strict liability and why very few defenses are available

See the dynamite excavation example, holding the contractor liable for any damages with no defenses because of the hazardous activity, page 148.

See the product liability example, page 149.

Key Terms

absolute privilege
contract interference
contributory negligence
defamation
false imprisonment
intentional infliction of emotional distress
intentional torts
invasion of privacy
libel
malpractice
negligence
product disparagement
qualified privilege
shopkeeper's privilege
slander
slander of title
strict liability
tort
trade libel
trespass

Questions and Case Problems

1. Christensen Shipyards built a 155-foot yacht for Tiger Woods at its Vancouver, Washington, facilities. It used Tiger's name and photographs relating to the building of the yacht in promotional materials for the shipyard without seeking his permission. Was this a right of publicity tort because Tiger could assert that his name and photos were used to attract attention to the shipyard to obtain commercial advantage? Did the shipyard have a First Amendment right to present the truthful facts regarding its building of the yacht and the owner's identity as promotional materials? Does the fact that the yacht was named *Privacy* have an impact on this case? Would it make a difference as to the outcome of this case if the contract for building the yacht had a clause prohibiting the use of Tiger's name or photo without his permission?

2. ESPN held its Action Sports and Music Awards ceremony in April, at which celebrities in the fields of extreme sports and popular music such as rap and heavy metal converged. Well-known musicians Ben Harper and James Hetfield were there, as were popular rappers Busta Rhymes and LL Cool J. Famed motorcycle stuntman Evel Knievel, who is commonly thought of as the "father of extreme sports," and his wife, Krystal, were photographed. The photograph depicted Evel, who was wearing a motorcycle jacket and rose-tinted sunglasses, with his right arm around Krystal and his left arm around another young woman. ESPN published the photograph on its "extreme sports" Web site with a caption that read "Evel Knievel proves that you're never too old to be a pimp." The Knievels brought suit against ESPN, contending that the photograph and caption were defamatory because they accused Evel of soliciting prostitution and implied that Krystal was a prostitute. ESPN contends that the caption was a figurative and slang usage and was not defamatory as a matter of law. Decide. [*Knievel v. ESPN*, 393 F.3d 1068 (9th Cir.)]

3. While snowboarding down a slope at Mammoth Mountain Ski Area (Mammoth), 17-year-old David Graham was engaged in a snowball fight with his 14-year-old brother. As he was "preparing to throw a snowball" at his brother, David slammed into Liam Madigan, who was working as a ski school instructor for Mammoth, and injured him. Madigan sued Graham for damages for reckless and dangerous

behavior. The defense contended that the claim was barred under the doctrine of assumption of the risk, applicable in the state, arising from the risk inherent in the sport that allows for vigorous participation and frees a participant from a legal duty to act with due care. Decide. [*Mammoth Mountain Ski Area v. Graham*, 38 Cal. Rptr. 3d 422 (Cal. App.)]

4. Following a visit to her hometown of Coalinga, Cynthia wrote "An Ode to Coalinga" (Ode) and posted it in her online journal on MySpace.com. Her last name did not appear online. Her page included her picture. The Ode opens with "The older I get, the more I realize how much I despise Coalinga" and then proceeds to make a number of extremely negative comments about Coalinga and its inhabitants. Six days later, Cynthia removed the Ode from her journal. At the time, Cynthia was a student at UC Berkeley, and her parents and sister were living in Coalinga. The Coalinga High School principal, Roger Campbell, submitted the Ode to the local newspaper, the *Coalinga Record*, and it was published in the Letters to the Editor section, using Cynthia's full name. The community reacted violently to the Ode, forcing the family to close its business and move. Cynthia and her family sued Campbell and the newspaper on the right-of-privacy theory of public disclosure of private facts. What are the essential elements of this theory? Was Cynthia and her family's right of privacy violated? [*Moreno v. Hanford Sentinel, Inc.*, 91 Cal. Rptr. 3d 858 (Cal. App.)]

5. Catherine Bosley worked as a television news anchor for WKBN Channel 27 in Youngstown, Ohio. While on vacation with her husband in Florida she participated in a "wet t-shirt" contest, which was videotaped without her consent by DreamGirls, Inc. and licensed to Marvad Corp., which runs a Web site for adult entertainment through a subscription service on the Internet. Marvad used depictions of her in advertisements to promote the materials and services it markets. Web site searches related to Catherine Bosley in 2004 were the most popular search on the World Wide Web. Due to the publicity, she resigned from her position at WKBN. Bosley sought an injunction against the defendants from using her image in any manner that promotes the sale of their goods or services. The defendants contend that an injunction would violate their First Amendment rights. What legal theory did Bosley rely on to seek the injunction? Would an injunction be in violation of the defendant's First Amendment's rights? Decide. [*Bosley v. Wildwett.com*, 310 F. Supp. 2d 914 (N.D. Ohio)]

6. Juanita DeJesus was seriously injured when hit on the head by a foul ball at a minor league baseball game and sued the stadium operators for negligence and premises liability. The case progressed to the Indiana Supreme Court where the Indianapolis Indians urged the State Supreme Court to dispose of the premises liability and negligence claims in one fell swoop by adopting the so-called Baseball Rule, which provides that:

   a ballpark operator that provides screening behind home plate sufficient to meet ordinary demand for protected seating has fulfilled its duty with respect to screening and cannot be subjected to liability for injuries resulting to a spectator by an object leaving the playing field.

   Should the Court adopt this clear and unambiguous rule for the national pastime? Does the Court have authority to make such a ruling? How would you decide her negligence claim? [*South Shore Baseball, LLC v. DeJesus*, 11 N.E.3d 903 (Ind.)]

7. Mallinckrodt produces nuclear and radioactive medical pharmaceuticals and supplies. Maryland Heights Leasing, an adjoining business owner, claimed that low-level radiation emissions from Mallinckrodt damaged its property and caused a loss in earnings. What remedy should Maryland Heights have? What torts are involved here? [*Maryland Heights Leasing, Inc. v. Mallinckrodt, Inc.*, 706 S.W.2d 218 (Mo. App.)]

8. An owner abandoned his van in an alley in Chicago. In spite of repeated complaints to the police, the van was allowed to remain in the alley. After several months, it was stripped of most of the parts that could be removed. Jamin Ortiz, age 11, was walking down the alley when the van's gas tank exploded. The flames from the explosion set fire to Jamin's clothing, and he was severely burned. Jamin and his family brought suit against the city of Chicago to recover damages for his injuries. Could the city be held responsible for injuries caused by property owned by someone else? Why or why not? [*Ortiz v. Chicago*, 398 N.E.2d 1007 (Ill. App.)]

9. Carrigan, a district manager of Simples Time Recorder Co., was investigating complaints of mismanagement of the company's Jackson office. He called at the home of Hooks, the secretary of that office, who expressed the opinion that part of the trouble was caused by the theft of parts and

equipment by McCall, another employee. McCall was later discharged and sued Hooks for slander. Was she liable? [*Hooks v. McCall*, 272 So. 2d 925 (Miss.)]

10. Defendant no. 1 parked his truck in the street near the bottom of a ditch on a dark, foggy night. Iron pipes carried in the truck projected nine feet beyond the truck in back. Neither the truck nor the pipes carried any warning light or flag, in violation of both a city ordinance and a state statute. Defendant no. 2 was a taxicab owner whose taxicab was negligently driven at an excessive speed. Defendant no. 2 ran into the pipes, thereby killing the passenger in the taxicab. The plaintiff brought an action for the passenger's death against both defendants. Defendant no. 1 claimed he was not liable because it was Defendant no. 2's negligence that had caused the harm. Was this defense valid? [*Bumbardner v. Allison*, 78 S.E.2d 752 (N.C.)]

11. Carl Kindrich's father, a member of the Long Beach Yacht Club before he died, expressed a wish to be "buried at sea." The Yacht Club permitted the Kindrich family the use of one of its boats, without charge, for the ceremony, and Mr. Fuller—a good friend of Carl's father—piloted the boat. Portable stairs on the dock assisted the attendees in boarding. Upon returning, Fuller asked for help to tie up the boat. The steps were not there, and Carl broke his leg while disembarking to help tie up the boat. Carl sued the Yacht Club for negligence in failing to have someone on the dock to ensure that the portable steps were available. The Yacht Club contended that it was not liable because Carl made the conscious decision to jump from the moving vessel to the dock, a primary assumption of risk in the sport of boating. The plaintiff contended that he was not involved in the sport of boating, and at most his actions constituted minimal comparative negligence, the type that a jury could weigh in conjunction with the defendant's negligence in assessing damages. Decide. [*Kindrich v. Long Beach Yacht Club*, 84 Cal. Rptr. 3d 824 (Cal. App.)]

12. Hegyes was driving her car when it was negligently struck by a Unjian Enterprises truck. She was injured, and an implant was placed in her body to counteract the injuries. She sued Unjian, and the case was settled. Two years later Hegyes became pregnant. The growing fetus pressed against the implant, making it necessary for her doctor to deliver the child 51 days prematurely by Cesarean section. Because of its premature birth, the child had a breathing handicap. Suit was brought against Unjian Enterprises for the harm sustained by the child. Was the defendant liable? [*Hegyes v. Unjian Enterprises, Inc.*, 286 Cal. Rptr. 85 (Cal. App.)]

13. Kendra Knight took part in a friendly game of touch football. She had played before and was familiar with football. Michael Jewett was on her team. In the course of play, Michael bumped into Kendra and knocked her to the ground. He stepped on her hand, causing injury to a little finger that later required its amputation. She sued Michael for damages. He defended on the ground that she had assumed the risk. Kendra claimed that assumption of risk could not be raised as a defense because the state legislature had adopted the standard of comparative negligence. What happens if contributory negligence applies? What happens if the defense of comparative negligence applies?

14. A passenger on a cruise ship was injured by a rope thrown while the ship was docking. The passenger was sitting on a lounge chair on the third deck when she was struck by the weighted end of a rope thrown by an employee of Port Everglades, where the boat was docking. These ropes, or heaving lines, were being thrown from the dock to the second deck, and the passenger was injured by a line that was thrown too high.

    The trial court granted the cruise line's motion for directed verdict on the ground there was no evidence that the cruise line knew or should have known of the danger. The cruise line contended that it had no notice that this "freak accident" could occur. What is the duty of a cruise ship line to its passengers? Is there liability here? Does it matter that an employee of the port city, not the cruise lines, caused the injury? Should the passenger be able to recover? Why or why not? [*Kalendareva v. Discovery Cruise Line Partnership*, 798 So. 2d 804 (Fla. App.)]

15. Blaylock was a voluntary psychiatric outpatient treated by Dr. Burglass, who became aware that Blaylock was violence prone. Blaylock told Dr. Burglass that he intended to do serious harm to Wayne Boynton, Jr., and shortly thereafter he killed Wayne. Wayne's parents then sued Dr. Burglass on grounds that he was liable for the death of their son because he failed to give warning or to notify the police of Blaylock's threat and nature. Was a duty breached here? Should Dr. Burglass be held liable? [*Boynton v. Burglass*, 590 So. 2d 446 (Fla. App.)]

PART 2

Contracts

CHAPTER 11

Nature and Classes of Contracts: Contracting on the Internet

Learning Outcomes <<<

After studying this chapter, you should be able to

LO.1 Explain the meaning and importance of privity of a contract

LO.2 Describe the way in which a contract arises

LO.3 Distinguish between bilateral and unilateral contracts

LO.4 Explain the reasoning behind quasi-contract recovery

LO.5 Explain how Internet contracts involve the same types of issues as offline contracts

Practically every business transaction affecting people involves a contract.

11-1 Nature of Contracts

This introductory chapter will familiarize you with the terminology needed to work with contract law. In addition, the chapter introduces quasi contracts, which are not true contracts but obligations imposed by law.

11-1a Definition of a Contract

contract–a binding agreement based on the genuine assent of the parties, made for a lawful object, between competent parties, in the form required by law, and generally supported by consideration.

A **contract** is a legally binding agreement.[1] By one definition, "a contract is a promise or a set of promises for the breach of which the law gives a remedy, or the performance of which the law in some way recognizes as a duty."[2] Contracts arise out of agreements, so a contract may be defined as an agreement creating an obligation.

The substance of the definition of a contract is that by mutual agreement or assent, the parties create enforceable duties or obligations. That is, each party is legally bound to do or to refrain from doing certain acts.

11-1b Elements of a Contract

The elements of a contract are (1) an agreement (2) between competent parties (3) based on the genuine assent of the parties that is (4) supported by consideration, (5) made for a lawful objective, and (6) in the form required by law, if any. These elements will be considered in the chapters that follow.

11-1c Subject Matter of Contracts

The subject matter of a contract may relate to the performance of personal services, such as contracts of employment to work developing computer software or to play professional football. A contract may provide for the transfer of ownership of property, such as a house (real property) or an automobile (personal property), from one person to another.

11-1d Parties to a Contract

promisor–person who makes a promise.

promisee–person to whom a promise is made.

obligor–promisor.

obligee–promisee who can claim the benefit of the obligation.

privity–succession or chain of relationship to the same thing or right, such as privity of contract, privity of estate, privity of possession.

privity of contract–relationship between a promisor and the promisee.

The person who makes a promise is the **promisor,** and the person to whom the promise is made is the **promisee.** If the promise is binding, it imposes on the promisor a duty or obligation, and the promisor may be called the **obligor.** The promisee who can claim the benefit of the obligation is called the **obligee.** The parties to a contract are said to stand in **privity** with each other, and the relationship between them is termed **privity of contract.** **For Example,** when the state of North Carolina and the architectural firm of O'Brien/Atkins Associates executed a contract for the construction of a new building at the University of North Carolina, Chapel Hill, these parties were in privity of contract. However, a building contractor, RPR & Associates, who worked on the project did not have standing to sue on the contract between the architect and the state because the contractor was not in privity of contract.[3]

[1] The Uniform Commercial Code defines *contract* as "the total legal obligation which results from the parties' agreement as affected by [the UCC] and any other applicable rules of law." U.C.C. §1–201(11).

[2] Restatement (Second) of Contracts §1.

[3] *RPR & Associates v. O'Brien/Atkins Associates, PA,* 24 F. Supp. 2d 515 (M.D.N.C. 1998). See also *Roof Techs Int Inc. v. State,* 57 P.3d 538 (Kan. App. 2002), where a layer of litigation was avoided regarding lawsuits involving the renovation of the Farrell Library at Kansas State University. The state was the only party in privity of contract with the architectural firm and would thus have to bring claims against the architectural firm on behalf of all of the contractors. Two subcontractors, the general contractor, and the owner of the library, the state of Kansas, used a settlement and liquidation agreement assigning all of the state's claims against the architect to the general contractor.

In written contracts, parties may be referred to by name. More often, however, they are given special names that better identify each party. For example, consider a contract by which one person agrees that another may occupy a house upon the payment of money. The parties to this contract are called *landlord* and *tenant*, or *lessor* and *lessee*, and the contract between them is known as a *lease*. Parties to other types of contracts also have distinctive names, such as *vendor* and *vendee* for the parties to a sales contract, *shipper* and *carrier* for the parties to a transportation contract, and *insurer* and *insured* for the parties to an insurance policy.

A party to a contract may be an individual, a partnership, a limited liability company, a corporation, or a government.[4] One or more persons may be on each side of a contract. Some contracts are three-sided, as in a credit card transaction, which involves the company issuing the card, the holder of the card, and the business furnishing goods and services on the basis of the credit card.

If a contract is written, the persons who are the parties and who are bound by it can ordinarily be determined by reading what the document says and seeing how it is signed. A contract binds only the parties to the contract. It cannot impose a duty on a person who is not a party to it. Ordinarily, only a party to a contract has any rights against another party to the contract.[5] In some cases, third persons have rights on a contract as third-party beneficiaries or assignees. A person cannot be bound, however, by the terms of a contract to which that person is not a party. **For Example,** in approximately 1995 Jeff and Mark Bass signed Marshall B. Mathers III, better known as rapper Eminem, to an exclusive record deal with FBT Productions LLC (FBT), their production company. In 2000 Aftermath Records entered into a direct contractual relationship with Eminem, transferring Eminem's recording services from FBT directly to Aftermath. Under the contract FBT became a "passive income participant," retaining a right to royalty income from Eminem's recordings. A dispute occurred regarding percentages of royalties due. Aftermath entered into an agreement with Eminem in 2009, setting the royalties for Eminem's *Recovery* and *Relapse* albums, asserting that all royalties, including royalties owed FBT were dictated by this 2009 agreement. FBT was not a party to the 2009 agreement and as such cannot be bound by it. A contract cannot bind a nonparty. Therefore, Aftermath was required to pay FBT royalties for the two albums at a higher rate in accordance with an earlier agreement.[6]

CPA

11-1e How a Contract Arises

offeror–person who makes an offer.

offeree–person to whom an offer is made.

A contract is based on an agreement. An agreement arises when one person, the **offeror,** makes an offer and the person to whom the offer is made, the **offeree,** accepts. There must be both an offer and an acceptance. If either is lacking, there is no contract.

11-1f Intent to Make a Binding Agreement

Because a contract is based on the consent of the parties and is a legally binding agreement, it follows that the parties must have an intent to enter into an agreement that is binding. Sometimes the parties are in agreement, but their agreement does not produce a contract. Sometimes there is merely a preliminary agreement, but the parties never actually make a contract, or there is merely an agreement as to future plans or intentions without any contractual obligation to carry out those plans or intentions.

[4] See *Purina Mills, LLC v. Less*, 295 F. Supp. 2d 1017 (N.D. Iowa 2003) in which the pig-seller plaintiff, which converted from a corporation to a limited liability company (LLC) while the contract was in effect, was a proper party in interest and could maintain a contract action against defendant buyers.

[5] *Hooper v. Yakima County*, 904 P.2d 1193 (Wash. App. 1995).

[6] *F.B.T. Productions, LLC v. Aftermath Records*, 2011 WL 5174766 (C.D. Cal. Oct. 31, 2011).

11-1g Freedom of Contract

In the absence of some ground for declaring a contract void or voidable, parties may make such contracts as they choose. The law does not require parties to be fair, or kind, or reasonable, or to share gains or losses equitably.

formal contracts–written contracts or agreements whose formality signifies the parties' intention to abide by the terms.

11-2 Classes of Contracts

Contracts may be classified according to their form, the way in which they were created, their binding character, and the extent to which they have been performed.

CPA

11-2a Formal and Informal Contracts

Contracts can be classified as formal or informal.

contract under seal–contract executed by affixing a seal or making an impression on the paper or on some adhering substance such as wax attached to the document.

recognizance–obligation entered into before a court to do some act, such as to appear at a later date for a hearing. Also called a *contract of record*.

informal contract–simple oral or written contract.

Formal Contracts

Formal contracts are enforced because the formality with which they are executed is considered sufficient to signify that the parties intend to be bound by their terms. Formal contracts include (1) **contracts under seal** where a person's signature or a corporation's name is followed by a scroll, the word *seal*, or the letters *L.S.*;[7] (2) contracts of record, which are obligations that have been entered before a court of record, sometimes called a **recognizance**; and (3) negotiable instruments.

Informal Contracts

All contracts other than formal contracts are called **informal** (or simple) **contracts** without regard to whether they are oral or written. These contracts are enforceable, not because of the form of the transaction but because they represent agreement of the parties.

11-2b Express and Implied Contracts

Simple contracts may be classified as *express contracts* or *implied contracts* according to the way they are created.

express contract–agreement of the parties manifested by their words, whether spoken or written.

implied contract–contract expressed by conduct or implied or deduced from the facts.

Express Contracts

An **express contract** is one in which the terms of the agreement of the parties are manifested by their words, whether spoken or written.

Implied Contracts

An **implied contract** (or, as sometimes stated, a *contract implied in fact*) is one in which the agreement is shown not by words, written or spoken, but by the acts and conduct of the parties.[8] Such a contract arises when (1) a person renders services under circumstances indicating that payment for them is expected and (2) the other person, knowing such circumstances, accepts the benefit of those services. **For Example,** when a building owner requests a professional roofer to make emergency repairs to the roof of a building, an obligation arises to pay the reasonable value of such services, although no agreement has been made about compensation.

[7] Some authorities explain L.S. as an abbreviation for *locus sigilium* (place for the seal).

[8] *Lindquist Ford, Inc. v. Middleton Motors, Inc.*, 557 F.3d 469, 481 (7th Cir. 2009). See also *Dynegy Marketing and Trade v. Multiut Corp.*, 648 F.3d 506 (7th Cir. 2011).

An implied contract cannot arise when there is an existing express contract on the same subject.[9] However, the existence of a written contract does not bar recovery on an implied contract for extra work that was not covered by the contract.

To prevail on a cause of action for breach of an implied-in-fact contract based on an idea submission, plaintiffs must show (1) they conditioned the submission of their ideas on an obligation to pay for any use of the ideas; (2) the defendants voluntarily accepted the submission of ideas; and (3) the defendants actually used these ideas, rather than their own ideas with other sources. In an idea submission case where similarities exist, it is a complete defense for the defendants to show that they independently created their product. **For Example,** in 1977, Anthony Spinner a highly regarded television producer and writer, submitted drafts of his script entitled "Lost" to ABC. ABC decided to pass on the proposal for it would be too expensive to produce. In 2004, ABC premiered a pilot for LOST in September, and the series ran for six years. Spinner's subsequent implied-in-fact idea submission lawsuit was unsuccessful because ABC demonstrated that the script for the LOST series was created independently.[10]

CPA

11-2c Valid and Voidable Contracts and Void Agreements

Contracts may be classified in terms of enforceability or validity.

valid contract– agreement that is binding and enforceable.

voidable contract– agreement that is otherwise binding and enforceable but may be rejected at the option of one of the parties as the result of specific circumstances.

Valid Contracts

A **valid contract** is an agreement that is binding and enforceable.

Voidable Contracts

A **voidable contract** is an agreement that is otherwise binding and enforceable, but because of the circumstances surrounding its execution or the lack of capacity of one of the parties, it may be rejected at the option of one of the parties. **For Example,** a person who has been forced to sign an agreement that that person would not have voluntarily signed may, in some instances, avoid the contract.

FIGURE 11-1 Contractual Liability

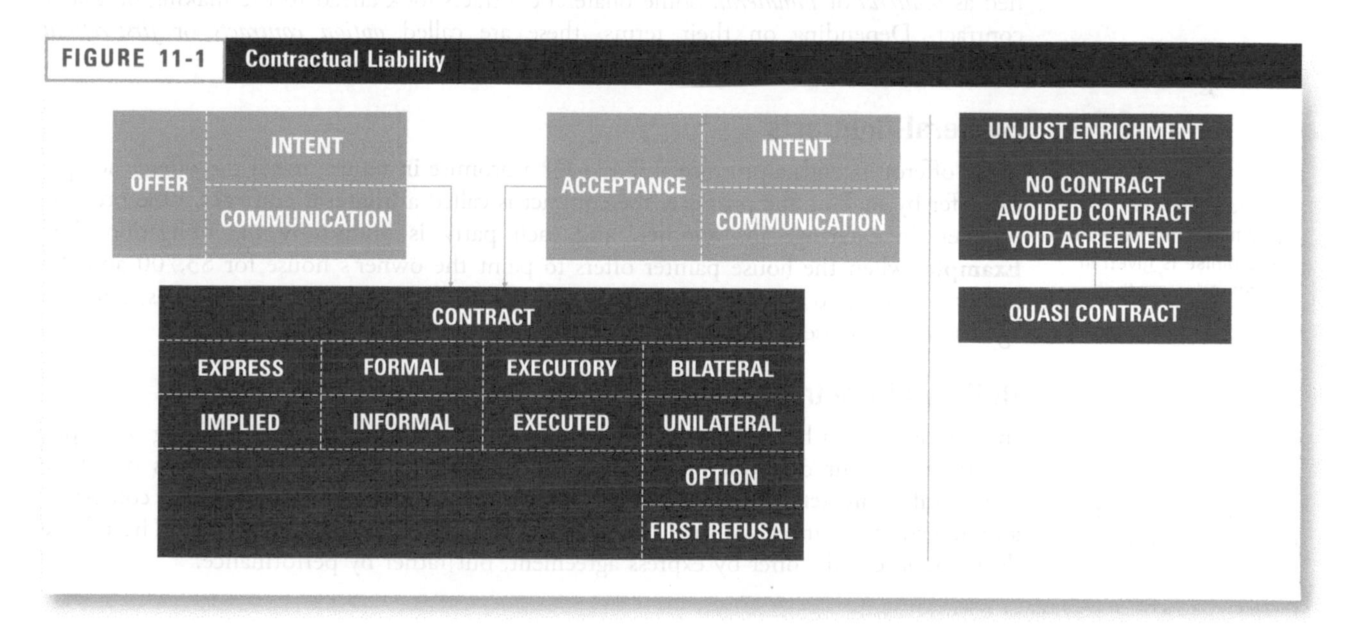

[9] *Pepsi-Cola Bottling Co. of Pittsburgh, Inc., v. PepsiCo, Inc.*, 431 F.3d 1241 (10th Cir. 2000).
[10] *Spinner v. American Broadcasting Companies, Inc.*, 155 Cal. Rptr. 3d 32 (Cal. App. 2013).

Void Agreements

void agreement–agreement that cannot be enforced.

A **void agreement** is without legal effect. An agreement that contemplates the performance of an act prohibited by law is usually incapable of enforcement; hence it is void. Likewise, it cannot be made binding by later approval or ratification.

11-2d Executed and Executory Contracts

Contracts may be classified as *executed contracts* and *executory contracts* according to the extent to which they have been performed.

Executed Contracts

executed contract–agreement that has been completely performed.

An **executed contract** is one that has been completely performed. In other words, an executed contract is one under which nothing remains to be done by either party.[11] A contract may be executed immediately, as in the case of a cash sale, or it may be executed or performed in the future.

Executory Contracts

executory contract–agreement by which something remains to be done by one or both parties.

In an **executory contract,** something remains to be done by one or both parties.[12] **For Example,** on July 10, Mark agreed to sell to Chris his Pearl drum set for $600, the terms being $200 upon delivery on July 14, with $200 to be paid on July 21, and the final $200 being due July 28. Prior to the July 14 delivery of the drums to Chris, the contract was entirely executory. After the delivery by Mark, the contract was executed as to Mark and executory as to Chris until the final payment was received on July 28.

11-2e Bilateral and Unilateral Contracts

In making an offer, the offeror is in effect extending a promise to do something, such as pay a sum of money, if the offeree will do what the offeror requests. Contracts are classified as *bilateral* or *unilateral.* Some bilateral contracts look ahead to the making of a later contract. Depending on their terms, these are called *option contracts* or *first-refusal contracts.*

CPA

Bilateral Contracts

bilateral contract–agreement under which one promise is given in exchange for another.

If the offeror extends a promise and asks for a promise in return and if the offeree accepts the offer by making the promise, the contract is called a **bilateral contract.** One promise is given in exchange for another, and each party is bound by the obligation. **For Example,** when the house painter offers to paint the owner's house for $3,700 and the owner promises to pay $3,700 for the job, there is an exchange of promises, and the agreement gives rise to a bilateral contract.

Unilateral Contracts

unilateral contract–contract under which only one party makes a promise.

In contrast with a bilateral contract, the offeror may promise to do something or to pay a certain amount of money only when the offeree does an act.[13] Examples of where **unilateral contracts** commonly appear are when a reward is offered, a contest is announced, or changes are made and disseminated in an employee manual. The offeree does not accept the offer by express agreement, but rather by performance.

[11] *Marsh v. Rheinecker,* 641 N.E.2d 1256 (Ill. App. 1994).

[12] *DiGennaro v. Rubbermaid, Inc.,* 214 F. Supp. 2d 1354 (S.D. Fla. 2002).

[13] See *Young v. Virginia Birth-Related Neurological Injury Compensation Program,* 620 S.E.2d 131 (Va. App. 2005).

CASE SUMMARY

Unilateral Contract: Pretty Good Bonus!

FACTS: Aon Risk Services, Inc. (ARS Arkansas), and Combined Insurance Companies are subsidiaries of Aon Corporation. The parent corporation issued an "Interdependency Memo" dated February 2000, which encouraged ARS brokerage offices to place insurance business with Aon-affiliated companies. It also set up a bonus pool for revenues generated under the plan, with Combined agreeing to pay "30% of annualized premium on all life products over 15-year term plus 15% 1st year for all other products." John Meadors saw the memo in February 2000, and believed it would entitle him to this compensation over and above his employment contract. Meadors put Combined in touch with Dillard's Department Stores and on March 24, 2000, Dillard's and Combined executed a five-year agreement whereby Dillard's employees could purchase life, disability, and other insurance policies through workplace enrollment. When Meadors did not receive bonus-pool money generated by the transaction, he sued his employer for breach of a unilateral contract. The employer's defense was that the memo was not sufficiently definite to constitute an offer.

DECISION: Judgment for Meadors for $2,406,522.60. A unilateral contract is composed of an offer that invites acceptance in the form of actual performance. For example, in the case of a reward, the offeree accepts by performing the particular task, such as the capture of the fugitive for which the reward is offered. In this case the offer contained in the Interdependency Memo set out specific percentages of provisions that would go into the bonus pool, and required that the pool be distributed annually. It was sufficiently definite to constitute an offer. Meadors was responsible for the production of the Dillard's account, and was entitled to the bonus promised in the memo. [***Aon Risk Services Inc. v. Meadors*, 267 S.W.3d 603 (Ark. App. 2007)**]

Option and First-Refusal Contracts

option contract–contract to hold an offer to make a contract open for a fixed period of time.

right of first refusal–right of a party to meet the terms of a proposed contract before it is executed, such as a real estate purchase agreement.

The parties may make a contract that gives a right to one of them to enter into a second contract at a later date. If one party has an absolute right to enter into the later contract, the initial contract is called an **option contract.** Thus, a bilateral contract may be made today, giving one of the parties the right to buy the other party's house for a specified amount. This is an option contract because the party with the privilege has the freedom of choice, or option, to buy or not buy. If the option is exercised, the other party to the contract must follow the terms of the option and enter into the second contract. If the option is never exercised, no second contract ever arises, and the offer protected by the option contract merely expires.

In contrast with an option contract, a contract may merely give a **right of first refusal.** This imposes only the duty to make the first offer to the party having the right of first refusal.

11-2f Quasi Contracts

quasi contract–court-imposed obligation to prevent unjust enrichment in the absence of a contract.

In some cases, a court will impose an obligation even though there is no contract.[14] Such an obligation is called a **quasi contract,** which is an obligation imposed by law.

Prevention of Unjust Enrichment

A quasi contract is not a true contract reflecting all of the elements of a contract set forth previously in this chapter. The court is not seeking to enforce the intentions of the parties contained in an agreement. Rather, when a person or enterprise receives a benefit from another, even in the absence of a promise to pay for the benefit, a court may impose an obligation to pay for the reasonable value of that benefit, to avoid *unjust enrichment*.

[14] *Thayer v. Dial Industrial Sales, Inc.*, 85 F. Supp. 2d 263 (S.D.N.Y. 2000).

FIGURE 11-2 Contract

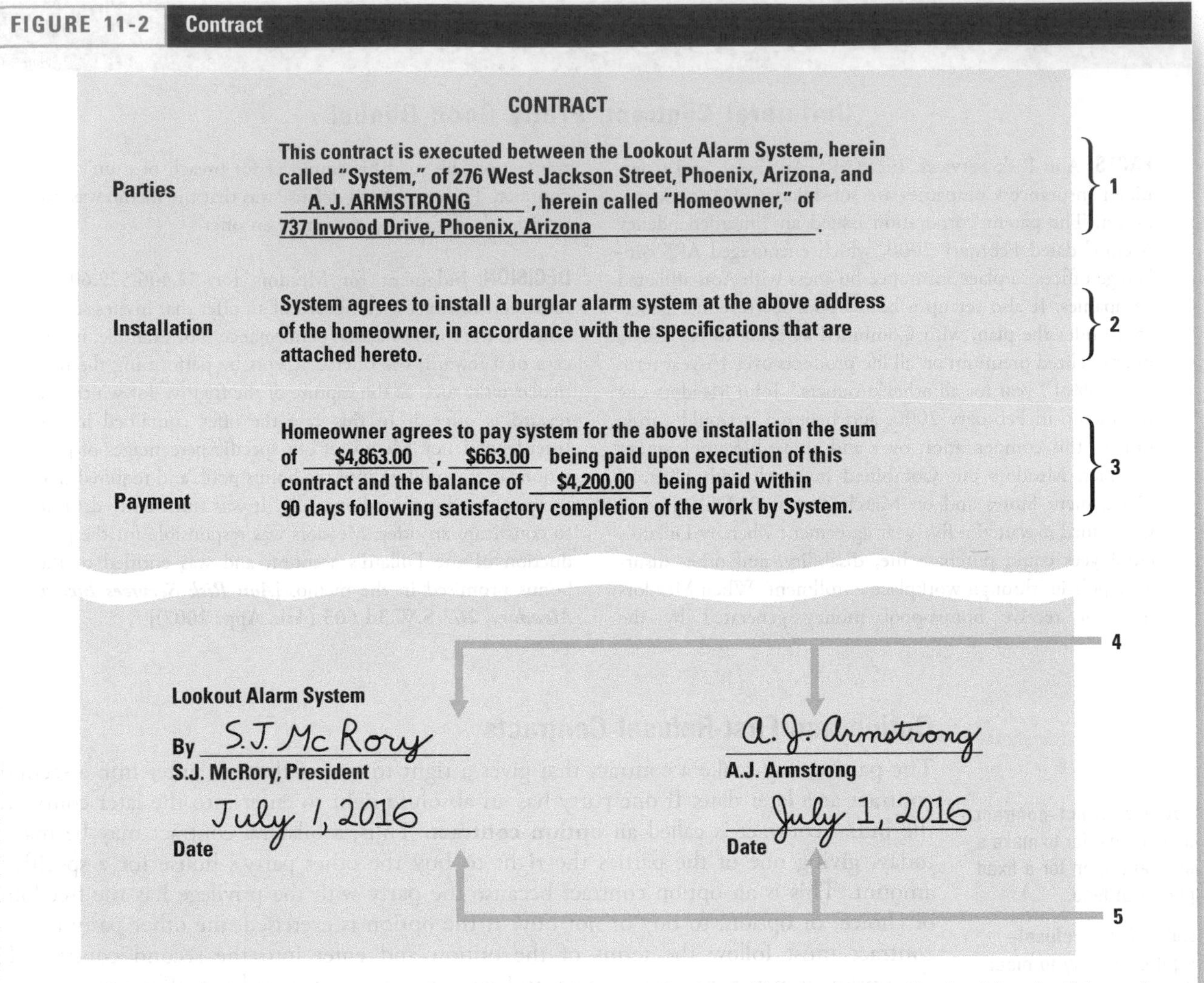

CONTRACT

Parties

This contract is executed between the Lookout Alarm System, herein called "System," of 276 West Jackson Street, Phoenix, Arizona, and A. J. ARMSTRONG, herein called "Homeowner," of 737 Inwood Drive, Phoenix, Arizona.

Installation

System agrees to install a burglar alarm system at the above address of the homeowner, in accordance with the specifications that are attached hereto.

Payment

Homeowner agrees to pay system for the above installation the sum of $4,863.00, $663.00 being paid upon execution of this contract and the balance of $4,200.00 being paid within 90 days following satisfactory completion of the work by System.

Lookout Alarm System

By S.J. McRory
S.J. McRory, President

July 1, 2016
Date

A.J. Armstrong
A.J. Armstrong

July 1, 2016
Date

Note that this contract includes the following important information: (1) the name and address of each party, (2) the promise or consideration of the seller, (3) the promise or consideration of the buyer, (4) the signature of the two parties, and (5) the date.

The spirit behind the law of unjust enrichment is to apply the law "outside the box" and fill in the cracks where common civil law and statutes fail to achieve justice.[15]

A successful claim for unjust enrichment usually requires (1) a benefit conferred on the defendant, (2) the defendant's knowledge of the benefit, and (3) a finding that it would be unjust for the defendant to retain the benefit without payment. The burden of proof is on the plaintiff to prove all of the elements of the claim. **For Example,** Hiram College sued Nicholas Courtad for $6,000 plus interest for tuition and other expenses. Because no evidence of a written contract was produced, the court considered it an unjust enrichment claim by the college. Courtad had attended classes for a few weeks and had not paid his tuition due to a problem with his financial aid package. Because he did not receive any credit hours toward a degree, which is the ultimate benefit

[15] *Hernandez v. Lopez,* 103 Cal. Rptr. 3d 376, 381 (Cal. App. 2009).

of attending college, the court found that he did not receive a benefit and that a finding of unjust enrichment was not appropriate.[16]

Sometimes a contract may be unenforceable because of a failure to set forth the contract in writing in compliance with the statute of frauds or a consumer protection act.[17] In other circumstances, no enforceable contract exists because of a lack of definite and certain terms. Yet in both situations, one party may have performed services for the benefit of the other party and the court will require payment of the reasonable value of services to avoid the unjust enrichment of the party receiving the services without paying for them. These damages are sometimes referred to as *restitution damages*. Some courts refer to this situation as an action or recovery in ***quantum meruit*** (as much as he or she deserved).

quantum meruit–as much as deserved; an action brought for the value of the services rendered the defendant when there was no express contract as to the purchase price.

For Example, Arya Group, Inc. (Arya), sued the entertainer Cher for unjust enrichment. In June 1996, Cher negotiated an oral agreement with Arya to design and construct a house on her Malibu property for $4,217,529. The parties' oral agreement was set forth in a written contract with an August 1997 date and was delivered to Cher in October 1997. She never signed it. Between June 1996 and November 1997, Arya performed and received payment for a number of services discharged under the unsigned contract. In August 1997, Cher requested Arya to meet with a home designer named Bussell who had previously worked with Cher on a Florida project, and Arya showed Bussell the plans and designs for the Malibu property and introduced her to his subcontractors. In November 1997, Cher terminated her agreement with Arya without paying the balance then due, as asserted by Arya, of $415,169.41. Arya claims that Cher and Bussell misappropriated the plans and designs Arya had prepared. Cher and the other defendants demurred to Arya's unjust enrichment complaint, pointing out that construction contracts must be evidenced in a writing signed by both parties under state law in order to be enforceable in a court of law. The appeals court determined that Arya's noncompliance with the state law requiring a signed written contract did not absolutely foreclose Arya from seeking damages for unjust enrichment if he could prove the assertions in the complaint that Cher was a sophisticated homeowner with previous involvement in residential construction who had legal representation in negotiating the agreement with Arya, and that Cher would be unjustly enriched if she were not required to compensate Arya for the reasonable value of the work already performed.[18]

CASE SUMMARY

No Free Rides

FACTS: PIC Realty leased farmland to Southfield Farms. After Southfield harvested its crop, it cultivated the land in preparation for the planting in the following year. However, its lease expired, so it did not plant that crop. It then sued PIC for reimbursement for the reasonable value of the services and materials used in preparing the land because this was a benefit to PIC. There was evidence that it was customary for landlords to compensate tenants for such work.

DECISION: Southfield was entitled to recover the reasonable value of the benefit conferred upon PIC. This was necessary in order to prevent the unjust enrichment of PIC. [***PIC Realty Corp. v. Southfield Farms, Inc.*****, 832 S.W.2d 610 (Tex. App. 1992)]**

[16] *Hiram College v. Courtad*, 834 N.E.2d 432 (Ohio App. 2005).

[17] See *Shafer Electric & Construction v. Mantia*, 96 A.3d 989 (Pa. 2014) where the Supreme Court of Pennsylvania determined that the state's Home Improvement Consumer Protection Act did not preclude the common law equitable remedy of *quantum meruit* when a contractor fails to fully comply with the Consumer Protection Act.

[18] *Arya Group, Inc. v. Cher*, 91 Cal. Rptr. 2d 815 (Cal. App. 2000). See also *Fischer v. Flax*, 816 A.2d 1 (2003).

A situation may arise over the mistaken conferrence of a benefit. **For Example,** Nantucket Island has a few approved colors for houses in its historic district. Using the approved gray color, Martin Kane and his crew began painting Sheldon Adams's house in the historic district as the result of a mistaken address. Adams observed the initiation of the work from his office across the street but did nothing to stop the painters. At the end of the day when the work was done, Adams refused to pay for the work, saying, "I signed no contract and never approved this work." The law deems it inequitable that Adams should have received the benefit of this work, having observed the benefit being conferred and knowing that the painters expected payment. Adams would be unjustly enriched if he were allowed to retain the benefit without payment for the reasonable value of the work. If Adams did not have knowledge that the work was being done and thus that payment was expected, quasi-contractual liability would not be imposed.

The mistake that benefits the defendant may be the mistake of a third party.

Preclusion by an Express Contract

Courts award relief based on quasi-contractual principles, implying by law a contract where one did not exist in fact. Thus, where an express contract exists, it precludes an unjust enrichment claim.[19]

CASE SUMMARY

When in Doubt, Write It Out

FACTS: Facing financial turbulence, Philippine Airlines (PAL) sought to renegotiate its aircraft lease contract (ALC) with World Airlines (WA). WA refused to negotiate with PAL. PAL retained John Sununu, the former Governor of New Hampshire and the former Chief of Staff to President George H. W. Bush and Sununu's partner Victor Frank to represent it. Sununu and Frank sent a contract proposal to PAL, which included a proposed "success fee" of $600,000 if they persuaded WA to accept a modification of the lease contract. PAL gave Sununu and Frank a verbal go-ahead but did not sign the proposed contract. Thereafter PAL sent a contract that was different from that proposed by Sununu and Frank, containing a success fee of 4 percent of savings if they were able to reach a settlement to reduce the remaining obligation of PAL to WA in accordance with either of two very specific settlement offers. Caught up in the actual intense settlement negotiations with WA on behalf of PAL Sununu and Frank signed the contract. Thereafter, they were successful in obtaining an amendment to the lease contract, saving PAL $12.8 million. PAL refused to pay a success fee of $520,000 because the actual settlement did not meet the contractual criteria, which was limited to just the two specific settlement offers. Sununu and Frank sued PAL for unjust enrichment and other contract theories.

DECISION: Judgment for PAL. Sununu and Frank conferred a benefit on PAL through their efforts to persuade WA to negotiate with PAL; and PAL accepted and retained the benefit for the renegotiated lease. There can be no claim, however, for unjust enrichment when an express contract exists between two parties. A court awards relief based on quasi-contractual principles, implying by law a contract, only where one did not exist in fact. The court stated:

> *To grant PALs summary judgment motion is not to condone its conduct. The airline can rightly be accused of stinginess for enforcing the formalistic terms of the contract in spite of the plaintiffs' earnest efforts on its behalf ... PAL may have violated Sununu and Frank's trust, but it did not violate the law.*
>
> *... Sununu and Frank seem to have done their best to serve their client, but they made a reckless bet by trusting PAL. They were accustomed to*

[19] However, if the parties have abandoned following the written provisions of the contract, it is proper for a court to allow recovery on the basis of *quantum meruit* on an implied contract. See *Geoscience Group Inc. v. Waters Construction Co. Inc.*, 759 S.E.2d 696 (N.C. App. 2014).

When in Doubt, Write It Out continued

handshake deals in which personal relationships count for more than legal documents, so they made little effort to put their understanding with PAL on paper. When they ran into a client who didn't play by the same rules, they paid the price.

The lesson is one that should be taught in law and business schools across America: When in doubt, write it out.

[*Sununu v. Philippine Airlines, Inc.*, 792 F. Supp. 2d 39 (D. D.C. 2011)]

Extent of Recovery

When recovery is allowed in quasi contract, the plaintiff recovers the reasonable value of the benefit conferred on the defendant,[20] or the fair and reasonable[21] value of the work performed, depending on the jurisdiction and the circumstances of the case itself. The customary method of calculating damages in construction contract cases is actual job costs plus an allowance for overhead and profits minus amount paid.[22]

THINKING THINGS THROUGH

Twelve Years of Litigation

Brown University accepted the bid of Marshall Contractors, Inc. (Marshall), to build the Pizzitola Sports Facility on its Providence, Rhode Island, campus. The parties intended to execute a formal written contract. Brown decided to pay $7,157,051 for the project, but Marshall sought additional payment for items it deemed extras and not contemplated in its bid. Because the parties were unable to agree on the scope of the project as compared to the price Brown was willing to pay, they never executed the formal written contract. Nevertheless, in the context of this disagreement over terms and price, construction began in May 1987. When the parties could not resolve their disagreements as the project neared completion in January 1989, Marshall sued Brown University, seeking to recover the costs for what it deemed "changes." Brown asserted that an implied-in-fact contract existed for all work at the $7,157,051 figure because the contractor went ahead with the project knowing the money Brown would pay. The litigation ended up in the Supreme Court of Rhode Island, and in 1997, the court concluded that no express or implied-in-fact contract had ever been reached by the parties concerning the scope of the project and what costs were to be included in the price stipulated by Brown. The case was remanded to the trial court for a new trial. After a trial on the theories of *quantum meruit* and unjust enrichment, a jury awarded Marshall $1.2 million dollars, which was some $3.1 million less than Marshall sought. Brown University appealed, and on November 21, 2001, the Supreme Court of Rhode Island affirmed the jury verdict for the contractor, determining that the proper measure of damages on unjust enrichment and *quantum meruit* theories was "the reasonable value of the work done."*

In May 1987 when the parties could not reach agreement enabling the execution of a formal written contract, Thinking Things Through at that point in time should have exposed the potential for significant economic uncertainties to both parties in actually starting the building process under such circumstances. In the spring of 1987 when all parties were unable to reach agreement, mediation or expedited arbitration by construction experts may well have resolved the controversy and yielded an amicable written contract with little or no delay to the project. Instead, the unsettled cost issues during the building process could have had an adverse impact on the "job chemistry" between the contractor and the owner, which may have adversely affected the progress and quality of the job. The 12 years of litigation that, with its economic and human resource costs, yielded just $1.2 million for the contractor was a no-win result for both sides. A primary rule for all managers in projects of this scope is to make sure the written contracts are executed before performance begins! Relying on "implied-in-fact" or quasi-contract legal theories is simply a poor management practice.

***_ADP Marshall, Inc. v. Brown University_, 784 A.2d 309 (R.I. 2001).**

[20] *Ramsey v. Ellis*, 484 N.W.2d 331 (Wis. 1992).
[21] *ADP Marshall, Inc. v. Brown University*, 784 A.2d 309 (R.I. 2001).
[22] *Miranco Contracting, Inc. v. Pelel*, 871 N.Y.S.2d 310 (A.D. 2008).

11-3 Contracting on the Internet

Doing business online for consumers is very similar to doing business through a catalog purchase or by phone. Before placing an order, a buyer is commonly concerned about the reputation of the seller. The basic purchasing principle of *caveat emptor* still applies: buyer beware! The Internet provides valuable tools to allow a buyer to research the reputation of the seller and its products. Online evaluations of companies and their products can be found at Web sites, such as Consumer Reports (**http://www.consumerreports.org**), Consumers Digest (**http://www.consumersdigest.com**), or the Better Business Bureau (**http://www.bbb.org**). E-consumers may have access to categorized histories of comments by other e-consumers, such as Planet Feedback ratings at **http://www.planetfeedback.com.**

The intellectual property principles set forth in Chapter 9—as well as the contractual principles, the law of sales, and privacy laws you are about to study—all apply to e-commerce transactions. When you are purchasing an item online, you must carefully read all of the terms and conditions set forth on the seller's Web site when assessing whether to make a contemplated purchase. The proposed terms may require that any disputes be litigated in a distant state or be resolved through arbitration with restricted remedies, or there may be an unsatisfactory return policy, warranty limitations, or limitation of liability. Generally, the Web site terms become the contract of the parties and are legally enforceable.

The laws you have studied that prevent deceptive advertising by brick-and-mortar businesses also apply to Internet sites.[23] If an in-state site is engaging in false advertising, you may be able to exercise consumer protection rights through your state's attorney general's office, or you may find some therapeutic relief by reporting the misconduct to the Internet Scambusters site (**http://www.scambusters.com**).

From a seller's perspective, it is exceedingly helpful to have as much information as possible on your potential customers' buying habits. Federal law prohibits the collection of personal information from children without parental consent, and some states restrict the unauthorized collection of personal information. European Union countries have strict laws protecting the privacy of consumers. Sellers intending to collect personal information should obtain the consent of their customers, make certain that children are excluded, and make sure that the information is stored in a secure environment.

Advanced encryption technology has made the use of credit card payments through the Internet very safe. No computer system connected to the Internet is totally secure, however. In the worst-case scenario, credit card issuers will not charge a user for more than the first $50 of unauthorized activity.

Internet contracts involve the same types of issues that are addressed in contracts offline but with certain technology-related nuances. The parties to the e-contracts must still negotiate their obligations in clear and unambiguous language, including such terms as quantity, quality, and price as well as warranties, indemnification responsibilities, limitations on liability, and termination procedures. The federal Electronic Signatures in Global and National Commerce Act (E-Sign) and the Uniform Electronic Transactions Act (UETA) mandate parity between paper and electronic contracts. The basic legal rules that govern contracts offline are the very same rules that govern online contracts, and basic civil procedure rules apply. **For Example,** California buyer Paul Boschetto bought a 1964 Ford Galaxy that had been advertised on eBay to be "in awesome condition" from a Milton, Wisconsin, resident, J. Hansing, for $34,106. On delivery Boschetto discovered

[23] See *MADCAP I, LLC v. McNamee*, 712 N.W.2d 16 (Wis. App. 2005) in which the court found genuine issues of material fact as to whether a business Web site falsely represented the size and nature of its business to induce the public to purchase products and services described on its Web site in violation of the state's fraudulent representations statute.

that the car had rust, extensive dents, and would not start. His lawsuit against Hansing in U.S. District Court in California was dismissed for lack of personal jurisdiction.[24] (The formation of a contract with a nonresident defendant was not, standing alone, sufficient to create personal jurisdiction in California.)

Boxes identifying special Internet e-commerce topics are strategically placed throughout these chapters.

Make the Connection

Summary

A contract is a binding agreement between two or more parties. A contract arises when an offer is accepted with contractual intent (the intent to make a binding agreement).

Contracts may be classified in a number of ways according to form, the way in which they were created, validity, and obligations. With respect to form, a contract may be either informal or formal, such as those under seal or those appearing on the records of courts. Contracts may be classified by the way they were created as those that are expressed by words—written or oral—and those that are implied or deduced from conduct. The question of validity requires distinguishing between contracts that are valid, those that are voidable, and those that are not contracts at all but are merely void agreements. Contracts can be distinguished on the basis of the obligations created as executed contracts, in which everything has been performed, and executory contracts, in which something remains to be done. The bilateral contract is formed by exchanging a promise for a promise, so each party has the obligation of thereafter rendering the promised performance. In the unilateral contract, which is the doing of an act in exchange for a promise, no further performance is required of the offeree who performed the act.

In certain situations, the law regards it as unjust for a person to receive a benefit and not pay for it. In such a case, the law of quasi contracts allows the performing person to recover the reasonable value of the benefit conferred on the benefited person even though no contract between them requires any payment. Unjust enrichment, which a quasi contract is designed to prevent, sometimes arises when there was never any contract between the persons involved or when there was a contract, but for some reason it was avoided or held to be merely a void agreement.

Learning Outcomes

After studying this chapter, you should be able to clearly explain:

11-1 Nature of Contracts

LO.1 Explain the meaning and importance of privity of a contract

See the example of the subcontractor, RPR & Associates, who worked on a project but could not sue the owner for payment, pages 206–207.

See the example involving rapper Eminem, FBT, and Aftermath Records, where FBT was not a party to the contract and thus not bound by it, page 207.

LO.2 Describe the way in which a contract arises

See the discussion on offer and acceptance, page 207.

11-2 Classes of Contracts

LO.3 Distinguish between bilateral and unilateral contracts

See the example of the Nantucket painters, pages 213–214.

See the *AON Risk Services* case where an insurance agent won his case based on a unilateral contract theory, page 211.

[24] *Boschetto v. Hansing,* 539 F.3d 1011 (9th Cir. 2008).

LO.4 Explain the reasoning behind quasi-contract recovery

See the example whereby Cher had to pay a home designer for certain work even though there was no contract, page 213.

11-3 Contracting on the Internet

LO.5 Explain how Internet contracts involve the same types of issues as offline contracts

See the eBay example, page 217.

Key Terms

bilateral contract
contract
contract under seal
executed contract
executory contract
express contract
formal contract
implied contract
informal contract
obligee
obligor
offeree
offeror
option contract
privity
privity of contract
promisee
promisor
quantum meruit
quasi contract
recognizance
right of first refusal
unilateral contracts
valid contract
void agreement
voidable contract

Questions and Case Problems

1. What is a contract?
2. Fourteen applicants for a city of Providence, Rhode Island, police academy training class each received from the city a letter stating that it was a "conditional offer of employment" subject to successful completion of medical and psychological exams. The 14 applicants passed the medical and psychological exams. However, these applicants were replaced by others after the city changed the selection criteria. Can you identify an offer and acceptance in this case? Can you make out a bilateral or unilateral contract? [*Ardito et al. v. City of Providence*, 213 F. Supp. 2d 358 (D.R.I.)]
3. Compare an implied contract with a quasi contract.
4. The Jordan Keys law firm represented the Greater Southeast Community Hospital of Washington, D.C., in a medical malpractice suit against the hospital. The hospital was self-insured for the first $1,000,000 of liability and the St. Paul Insurance Co. provided excess coverage up to $4,000,000. The law firm was owed $67,000 for its work on the malpractice suit when the hospital went into bankruptcy. The bankruptcy court ordered the law firm to release its files on the case to St. Paul to defend under the excess coverage insurance, and the Jordan Keys firm sued St. Paul for its legal fees of $67,000 expended prior to the bankruptcy under an "implied-in-fact contract" because the insurance company would have the benefit of all of its work. Decide. [*Jordan Keys v. St. Paul Fire*, 870 A.2d 58 (D.C.)]
5. Beck was the general manager of Chilkoot Lumber Co. Haines sold fuel to the company. To persuade Haines to sell on credit, Beck signed a paper by which he promised to pay any debt the lumber company owed Haines. He signed this paper with his name followed by "general manager." Haines later sued Beck on this promise, and Beck raised the defense that the addition of "general manager" showed that Beck, who was signing on behalf of Chilkoot, was not personally liable and did not intend to be bound by the paper. Was Beck liable on the paper? [*Beck v. Haines Terminal and Highway Co.*, 843 P.2d 1229 (Alaska)]
6. *A* made a contract to construct a house for *B*. Subsequently, *B* sued *A* for breach of contract. *A* raised the defense that the contract was not binding because it was not sealed. Is this a valid defense? [*Cooper v. G. E. Construction Co.*, 158 S.E.2d 305 (Ga. App.)]
7. Edward Johnson III, the CEO and principal owner of the world's largest mutual fund company, Fidelity Investments, Inc., was a longtime tennis buddy of Richard Larson. In 1995, Johnson asked Larson, who had construction experience, to supervise the construction of a house on Long Pond, Mount Desert Island, Maine. Although they had no written contract, Larson agreed to take on the project for $6,700 per month plus lodging. At the end of the project in 1997, Johnson made a $175,000 cash payment to Larson, and he made arrangements for

Larson to live rent-free on another Johnson property in the area called Pray's Meadow in exchange for looking after Johnson's extensive property interests in Maine. In the late summer of 1999, Johnson initiated a new project on the Long Pond property. Johnson had discussions with Larson about doing this project, but Larson asked to be paid his former rate, and Johnson balked because he had already hired a project manager. According to Johnson, at a later date he again asked Larson to take on the "shop project" as a favor and in consideration of continued rent-free use of the Pray's Meadow home. Johnson stated that Larson agreed to do the job "pro bono" in exchange for the use of the house, and Johnson acknowledged that he told Larson he would "take care" of Larson at the end of the project, which could mean as much or as little as Johnson determined. Larson stated that Johnson told him that he would "take care of" Larson if he would do the project and told him to "trust the Great Oracle" (meaning Johnson, the highly successful businessperson). Larson sought payment in March 2000 and asked Johnson for "something on account" in April. Johnson offered Larson a loan. In August during a tennis match, Larson again asked Johnson to pay him. Johnson became incensed, and through an employee, he ended Larson's participation in the project and asked him to vacate Pray's Meadow. Larson complied and filed suit for payment for work performed at the rate of $6,700 per month. Did Larson have an express contract with Johnson? What legal theory or theories could Larson utilize in his lawsuit? How would you decide this case if you believed Larson's version of the facts? How would you decide the case if you believed Johnson's version of the facts? [*Larson v. Johnson*, 196 F. Supp. 2d 38 (D. Me. 2002)]

8. While Clara Novak was sick, her daughter Janie helped her in many ways. Clara died, and Janie then claimed that she was entitled to be paid for the services she had rendered her mother. This claim was opposed by three brothers and sisters who also rendered services to the mother. They claimed that Janie was barred because of the presumption that services rendered between family members are gratuitous. Janie claimed that this presumption was not applicable because she had not lived with her mother but had her own house. Was Janie correct? [In re *Estate of Novak*, 398 N.W.2d 653 (Minn. App.)]

9. Dozier and his wife, daughter, and grandson lived in the house Dozier owned. At the request of the daughter and grandson, Paschall made some improvements to the house. Dozier did not authorize these, but he knew that the improvements were being made and did not object to them. Paschall sued Dozier for the reasonable value of the improvements, but Dozier argued that he had not made any contract for such improvements. Was he obligated to pay for such improvements?

10. When Harriet went away for the summer, Landry, a house painter, painted her house. He had a contract to paint a neighbor's house but painted Harriet's house by mistake. When Harriet returned from vacation, Landry billed her for $3,100, which was a fair price for the work. She refused to pay. Landry claimed that she had a quasi-contractual liability for that amount. Was he correct?

11. Margrethe and Charles Pyeatte, a married couple, agreed that she would work so that he could go to law school and that when he finished, she would go back to school for her master's degree. After Charles was admitted to the bar and before Margrethe went back to school, the two were divorced. She sued Charles, claiming that she was entitled to quasi-contractual recovery of the money that she had paid for Charles's support and law school tuition. He denied liability. Was she entitled to recover for the money she spent for Charles's maintenance and law school tuition? [*Pyeatte v. Pyeatte*, 661 P.2d 196 (Ariz. App.)]

12. Carriage Way was a real estate development of approximately 80 houses and 132 apartments. The property owners were members of the Carriage Way Property Owners Association. Each year, the association would take care of certain open neighboring areas, including a nearby lake, that were used by the property owners. The board of directors of the association would make an assessment or charge against the property owners to cover the cost of this work. The property owners paid these assessments for a number of years and then refused to pay any more. In spite of this refusal, the association continued to take care of the areas in question. The association then sued the property owners and claimed that they were liable for the benefit that had been conferred on them. Were the owners liable? [*Board of Directors of Carriage Way Property Owners Ass n v. Western National Bank*, 487 N.E.2d 974 (Ill. App.)]

13. When improvements or buildings are added to real estate, the real estate tax assessment is usually increased to reflect the increased value of the property. Frank Partipilo and Elmer Hallman owned neighboring tracts of land. Hallman made improvements to his land, constructing a new building and driveway on the tract. The tax assessor made a mistake about the location of the boundary line between Partipilo's and Hallman's land and thought the improvements were made on Partipilo's property. Instead of increasing the taxes on Hallman's land, the assessor wrongly increased the taxes on Partipilo's land. Partipilo paid the increased taxes for three years. When he learned why his taxes had been increased, he sued Hallman for the amount of the increase that Partipilo had been paying. Hallman raised the defense that he had not done anything wrong and that the mistake had been the fault of the tax assessor. Decide. [*Partipilo v. Hallman*, 510 N.E.2d 8 (Ill.App.)]

14. When a college student complained about a particular course, the vice president of the college asked the teacher to prepare a detailed report about the course. The teacher did and then demanded additional compensation for the time spent in preparing the report. He claimed that the college was liable to provide compensation on an implied contract. Was he correct? [*Zadrozny v. City Colleges of Chicago*, 581 N.E.2d 44 (Ill. App.)]

15. Smith made a contract to sell automatic rifles to a foreign country. Because the sale of such weapons to that country was illegal under an act of Congress, the U.S. government prosecuted Smith for making the contract. He raised the defense that because the contract was illegal, it was void and there is no binding obligation when a contract is void; therefore, no contract for which he could be prosecuted existed. Was he correct?

CPA Question

1. Kay, an art collector, promised Hammer, an art student, that if Hammer could obtain certain rare artifacts within two weeks, Kay would pay for Hammer's postgraduate education. At considerable effort and expense, Hammer obtained the specified artifacts within the two-week period. When Hammer requested payment, Kay refused. Kay claimed that there was no consideration for the promise. Hammer would prevail against Kay based on:

   a. Unilateral contract.

   b. Unjust enrichment.

   c. Public policy.

   d. Quasi contract.

CHAPTER 12

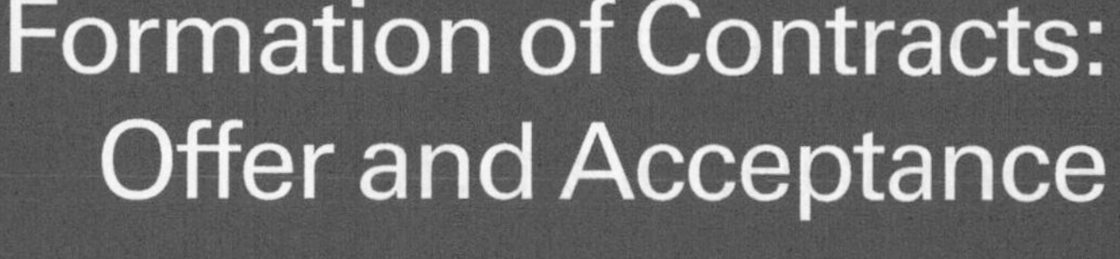

Formation of Contracts: Offer and Acceptance

Learning Outcomes ❮❮❮

After studying this chapter, you should be able to

LO.1 **Decide whether an offer contains definite and certain terms**

LO.2 **Explain the exceptions the law makes to the requirement of definiteness**

LO.3 **Explain all the ways an offer can be terminated**

LO.4 **Explain what constitutes the acceptance of an offer**

LO.5 **Explain the implications of failing to read a clickwrap agreement**

A *contract* consists of enforceable obligations that have been voluntarily assumed. Thus, one of the essential elements of a contract is an agreement. This chapter explains how the basic agreement arises, when there is a contract, and how there can be merely unsuccessful negotiations without a resulting contract.

12-1 Requirements of an Offer

offer–expression of an offeror's willingness to enter into a contractual agreement.

An **offer** expresses the willingness of the offeror to enter into a contractual agreement regarding a particular subject. It is a promise that is conditional upon an act, a forbearance (a refraining from doing something one has a legal right to do), or a return promise.

CPA

12-1a Contractual Intention

To make an offer, the offeror must appear to intend to create a binding obligation. Whether this intent exists is determined by objective standards.[1] This intent may be shown by conduct. **For Example,** when one party signs a written contract and sends it to the other party, such action is an offer to enter into a contract on the terms of the writing.

There is no contract when a social invitation is made or when an offer is made in obvious jest or excitement. A reasonable person would not regard such an offer as indicating a willingness to enter into a binding agreement. The test for a valid, binding offer is whether it induces a reasonable belief in the offeree that he or she can, by accepting it, bind the offeror, as developed in the *Wigod* case.

CASE SUMMARY

A Valid Offer!

FACTS: The U.S. Department of the Treasury implemented the federal Home Affordable Mortgage Program (HAMP) to help homeowners avoid foreclosure amidst the sharp decline in the nation's housing market in 2008. In 2009, Wells Fargo Bank issued Lori Wigod a four-month "trial" loan modification under a Trial Period Plan (TPP). After the trial period, if the borrower complied with all of the terms of the TPP agreement, including making all required payments and providing all required documentation, and if the borrower's representations remained true and correct, the servicer, Well Fargo, had to offer a permanent mortgage modification. Wigod alleged that she complied with these requirements and that Wells Fargo refused to grant a permanent modification. Wells Fargo contended that the TPP contained no valid offer.

DECISION: Judgment for Wigod. A person can prevent his submission from being treated as an offer by using suitable language conditioning the formation of a contract on some further step, such as approval by corporate headquarters. It is when the promisor conditions a promise on *his own* future action or approval that there is no binding offer. Here, the TTP spelled out two conditions precedent to Wells Fargo's obligation to offer a permanent modification. Wigod had to comply with the requirements of the TPP, and her financial representations had to be true and accurate. These conditions had to be satisfied by the promisee (Wigod). Here a reasonable person in Wigod's position would read the TPP as a default offer that she could accept so long as she satisfied the two conditions. [***Wigod v. Wells Fargo Bank,* 673 F.3d 547 (7th Cir. 2012)**]

Invitation to Negotiate

The first statement made by one of two persons is not necessarily an offer. In many instances, there may be a preliminary discussion or an invitation by one party to the

[1] *Glass Service Co. v. State Farm Mutual Automobile Ins. Co.,* 530 N.W.2d 867 (Minn. App. 1995).

other to negotiate or to make an offer. Thus, an inquiry by a school as to whether a teacher wished to continue the following year was merely a survey or invitation to negotiate and was not an offer that could be accepted. Therefore, the teacher's affirmative response did not create a contract.

Ordinarily, a seller sending out circulars or catalogs listing prices is not regarded as making an offer to sell at those prices. The seller is merely indicating a willingness to consider an offer made by a buyer on those terms. The reason for this rule is, in part, the practical consideration that because a seller does not have an unlimited supply of any commodity, the seller cannot possibly intend to make a contract with everyone who sees the circular. The same principle is applied to merchandise that is displayed with price tags in stores or store windows and to most advertisements. An advertisement in a newspaper is ordinarily considered an invitation to negotiate and is not an offer that can be accepted by a reader of the paper.[2] However, some court decisions have construed advertisements as offers that called for an act on the part of the customer, thereby forming a unilateral contract, such as the advertisement of a reward for the return of lost property.

Quotations of prices, even when sent on request, are likewise not offers unless the parties have had previous dealings or unless a trade custom exists that would give the recipient of the quotation reason to believe that an offer was being made. Whether a price quotation is to be treated as an offer or merely an invitation to negotiate is a question of the intent of the party giving the quotation.[3]

Agreement to Make a Contract at a Future Date

No contract arises when the parties merely agree that at a future date they will consider making a contract or will make a contract on terms to be agreed on at that time. In such a case, neither party is under any obligation until the future contract is made. Unless an agreement is reached on all material terms and conditions and nothing is left to future negotiations, a contract to enter a contract in the future is of no effect. **For Example,** Hewitt Associates provided employee benefits administrative services to Rollins, Inc., under a contract negotiated in 2001 to run through 2006. Prior to its expiration, the parties negotiated—seeking to agree to a multiyear extension of the 2001 agreement. They agreed to all of the material terms of the contract, except that Rollins balked at a $1.8 million penalty clause. Rollins's employees told Hewitt that the extension "was going to be signed." However, Rollins did not sign and the 2001 agreement expired. Hewitt's contention that the agreement was enforceable at the moment Rollins told Hewitt it was going to sign the new agreement was rejected by the court, stating that an agreement to reach an agreement is a contradiction in terms and imposes no obligation on the parties.[4]

Contracts to Negotiate

Regarding modern transactions involving significant up-front investments in deal structuring and due diligence, compelling reasons exist for parties to exchange binding promises protective of the deal-making process and why the courts may deem it socially beneficial to enforce them. Without any legal protection a counter-party may attempt to hijack the deal. Parties may wish to build in safeguards that operate early in the bargaining process to allow investing resources in a deal, but without inextricably locking themselves into a transaction that is still in a partially formulated state. *Contracts to negotiate* can satisfy this need.[5] **For Example,** David Butler, an inventor of safety technology

[2] *Zanakis-Pico v. Cutter, Dodge, Inc.*, 47 P.2d 1222 (Haw. 2002).

[3] Statutes prohibiting false or misleading advertising may require adherence to advertised prices.

[4] *Hewitt Associates, LLC v. Rollins, Inc.*, 669 S.E.2d 551 (Ga. App. 2008).

[5] New York, Illinois, Pennsylvania, California, and Delaware have recognized this doctrine. Mississippi and Washington have repudiated it.

for cutting tools was allowed to pursue his claim of breach of contract to negotiate against Shiraz Balolia.[6]

12-1b Definiteness

An offer, and the resulting contract, must be definite and certain so that it is capable of being enforced.[7]

CASE SUMMARY

Definite and Certain Terms

FACTS: ServiceMaster, as the general contractor hired to restore the Cleveland Brown Stadium in time for the Browns' first pre-season football game, hired subcontractor Novak to perform restoration and construction work. Novak sued for $37,158.82 for work performed on the August 2, 2007, severe rainstorm project, referred to as Loss 2. ServiceMaster contended that Novak was bound by a written but unsigned subcontractor agreement, and that Novak's alleged oral contract was lacking any definite terms to be enforceable. From a judgment for Novak, ServiceMaster appealed.

DECISION: Judgment for Novak. The record contained sufficient evidence of definite terms to enforce the oral contract. Novak V.P. Pinchot credibly testified that Novak's "time and materials" billing on the final invoice contained the hours worked at the published union rate plus the cost of materials, plus 10 percent, which method of pricing is widely understood in the construction industry. Novak is entitled to $37,158.82 plus an 18% penalty for violation of the state Prompt Payment Statute. [***Frank Novak & Sons, Inc. v. A-Team, LLC, dba ServiceMaster*, 6 N.E.3d 1242 (Ohio App. 2014)**]

If an offer is indefinite or vague or if an essential provision is lacking,[8] no contract arises from an attempt to accept it. Courts are not in the business of writing contracts and will not supply terms unless the parties' obligations and intents are clearly implied. Thus, an offer to conduct a business for as long as it is profitable is too vague to be a valid offer. The acceptance of such an offer does not result in a contract that can be enforced. Statements by a bank that it was "with" the debtors and would "support" them in their proposed business venture were too vague to be regarded as a promise by the bank to make necessary loans to the debtors.

CASE SUMMARY

What Is the Meaning of an Agreement for a "Damn Good Job"?

FACTS: Larry Browneller made an oral contract with Hubert Plankenhorn to restore a 1963 Chevrolet Impala convertible. The car was not in good condition. Hubert advised the owner that his work would not yield a car of "show" quality because of the condition of the body, and he accordingly believed that the owner merely wanted a presentable car. Larry, on the other hand, having told Hubert that he wanted a "damn good job," thought this statement would yield a car that would be competitive at the small amateur car shows he attended. When the finished car had what Larry asserted

[6] *Butler v. Balolia*, 736 F.3d 609 (1st Cir. 2013).
[7] *Norton v. Correctional Medicare, Inc.*, 2010 WL 4103016 (N.D.N.Y. Oct. 18, 2010).
[8] *Peace v. Doming Holdings Inc.*, 554 S.E.2d 314 (Ga. App. 2001).

What Is the Meaning of an Agreement for a "Damn Good Job"? continued

were "waves" in the paint as a result of an uneven surface on the body, Larry brought suit against Hubert for breach of the oral contract.

DECISION: There was clearly a misunderstanding between the parties over the quality of work that could and would be obtained. *Quality* was a material term of the oral contract between the parties, on which there was no shared understanding. Accordingly, a court will not find an individual in breach of a term of the contract where the term did not exist. **[In re *Plankenhorn*, 228 B.R. 638 (N.D. Ohio 1998)]**

The fact that minor, ministerial, and nonessential terms are left for future determination does not make an agreement too vague to be a contract.[9] **For Example,** John McCarthy executed an offer to purchase (OTP) real estate from Ana Tobin on a printed form generated by the local Real Estate Board. The OTP stated that "McCarthy hereby offers to buy" and Tobin's signature indicates that "this offer is hereby accepted". The OTP also detailed the amount to be paid and when and described the property title requirements and the time and place for closing. Above the signature line it stated: "NOTICE: This is a legal document that creates binding obligations. If not understood, consult an attorney". The OTP also required the parties to execute a standard form Purchase and Sale Agreement (PSA). Subsequently Tobin received a much higher offer for the property, which she accepted, asserting that she was free to do so because she had not signed the PSA. The court held that the OTP was a firm offer that bound Tobin to sell to McCarthy.[10]

The law does not favor the destruction of contracts because that would go against the social force of carrying out the intent of the parties.[11] Consequently, when it is claimed that a contract is too indefinite to be enforced, a court will do its best to find the intent of the parties and thereby reach the conclusion that the contract is not too indefinite. **For Example,** boxing promoter Don King had both a Promotional Agreement and a Bout Agreement with boxer Miguel Angel Gonzalez. The Bout Agreement for a boxing match with Julio Cesar Chavez gave King the option to promote the next four of Gonzalez's matches. The contract made clear that if Gonzalez won the Chavez match, he would receive at least $75,000 for the next fight unless the parties agreed otherwise, and if he lost, he would receive at least $25,000 for the subsequent fight unless otherwise agreed. The agreement did not explicitly state the purse for the subsequent match in the event of a draw. The Chavez match ended in a draw, and Gonzalez contended that this omission rendered the contract so indefinite that it was unenforceable. The court disagreed, stating that striking down a contract as indefinite and in essence meaningless is at best a last resort. The court held that although the contract was poorly drafted, the Promotional Agreement contained explicit price terms for which a minimum purse for fights following a draw may be inferred.[12] A court may not, however, rewrite the agreement of the parties in order to make it definite.

[9] *Hsu v. Vet-A-Mix, Inc.*, 479 N.W.2d 336 (Iowa App. 1991). But see *Ocean Atlantic Development Corp. v. Aurora Christian Schools, Inc.*, 322 F.3d 983 (7th Cir. 2003), where letter offers to purchase (OTP) real estate were signed by both parties, but the offers conditioned the purchase and sale of each property upon the subsequent execution of a purchase and sale agreement. The court held that the parties thus left themselves room to walk away from the deal under Illinois law, and the OTPs were not enforced.

[10] *McCarthy v. Tobin*, 706 N.E.2d 629 (Mass. 1999). But see [FN 9].

[11] *Mears v. Nationwide Mut., Inc. Co.*, 91 F.3d 1118 (8th Cir. 1996).

[12] *Gonzalez v. Don King Productions, Inc.*, 17 F. Supp. 2d 313 (S.D.N.Y. 1998); see also *Echols v. Pelullo*, 377 F.3d 272 (3rd Cir. 2004).

THINKING THINGS THROUGH

The Rules of Negotiations

Business agreements are often reached after much discussion, study, and posturing by both sides. Many statements may be made by both sides about the price or value placed on the subject of the transaction. Withholding information or presenting selective, self-serving information may be perceived by a party to the negotiations as protective self-interest. Does the law of contracts apply a duty of good faith and fair dealing in the negotiation of contracts? Does the Uniform Commercial Code provide for a general duty of good faith in the negotiation of contracts? Are lawyers under an ethical obligation to inform opposing counsel of relevant facts? The answer to all of these questions is no.

The Restatement (Second) of Contracts applies the duty of good faith and fair dealing to the performance and enforcement of contracts, not their negotiation;* so also does the UCC.** The American Bar Association's Model Rules of Professional Conduct, Rule 4.1 Comment 1, requires a lawyer to be "truthful" when dealing with others on a client's behalf, but it also states that generally a lawyer has "no affirmative duty to inform an opposing party of relevant facts."*** Comment 2 to Rule 4.1 contains an example of a "nonmaterial" statement of a lawyer as "estimates of price or value placed on the subject of a transaction."

The legal rules of negotiations state that—in the absence of fraud, special relationships, or statutory or contractual duties—negotiators are not obligated to divulge pertinent information to the other party to the negotiations. The parties to negotiations themselves must demand and analyze pertinent information and ultimately assess the fairness of the proposed transaction. Should a party conclude that the elements of a final proposal or offer are excessive or dishonest, that party's legal option is to walk away from the deal. Generally, the party has no basis to bring a lawsuit for lack of good faith and fair dealing in negotiations.

However, Thinking Things Through, the ethical standards for negotiations set forth in Chapter 3 indicate that establishing a reputation for trustworthiness, candor, and reliability often leads to commercial success for a company's continuing negotiations with its customers, suppliers, distributors, lenders, unions, and employees.****

*Restatement (Second) of Contracts §105, comment (c).
**Uniform Commercial Code §1-203.
***American Bar Association Model Rule of Professional Conduct 4.1(a) Comment 1.
****For a contrary example, consider the following story. The Atlanta Braves baseball team's general manager Frank Wren negotiated with free agent baseball player Rafael Furcal's agent Paul Kinzer. When all terms had been negotiated, Kinzer asked for a written terms-of-agreement sheet signed by the Braves, which to Wren meant an agreement had been reached. Kinzer took the sheet to the L.A. Dodgers, who then reached an agreement to sign the shortstop. Braves President John Schuerholz said, "The Atlanta Braves will no longer do business with that company—ever. I told Arn Tellem that we can't trust them to be honest and forthright." "Braves GM Blasts Furcal's Agents," Associated Press, *The Boston Globe*, December 20, 2008, C-7.

Definite by Incorporation

An offer and the resulting contract that by themselves may appear "too indefinite" may be made definite by reference to another writing. **For Example,** a lease agreement that was too vague by itself was made definite because the parties agreed that the lease should follow the standard form with which both were familiar. An agreement may also be made definite by reference to the prior dealings of the parties and to trade practices.

Implied Terms

Although an offer must be definite and certain, not all of its terms need to be expressed. Some omitted terms may be implied by law. **For Example,** an offer "to pay $400" for a certain Movado timepiece does not state the terms of payment. A court, however, would not condemn this provision as too vague but would hold that it required that cash be paid and that the payment be made on delivery of the watch. Likewise, terms may be implied from conduct. As an illustration, when borrowed money was given to the borrower by a check on which the word *loan* was written, the act of the borrower in endorsing the check constituted an agreement to repay the amount of the check.

FIGURE 12-1 Offer and Acceptance

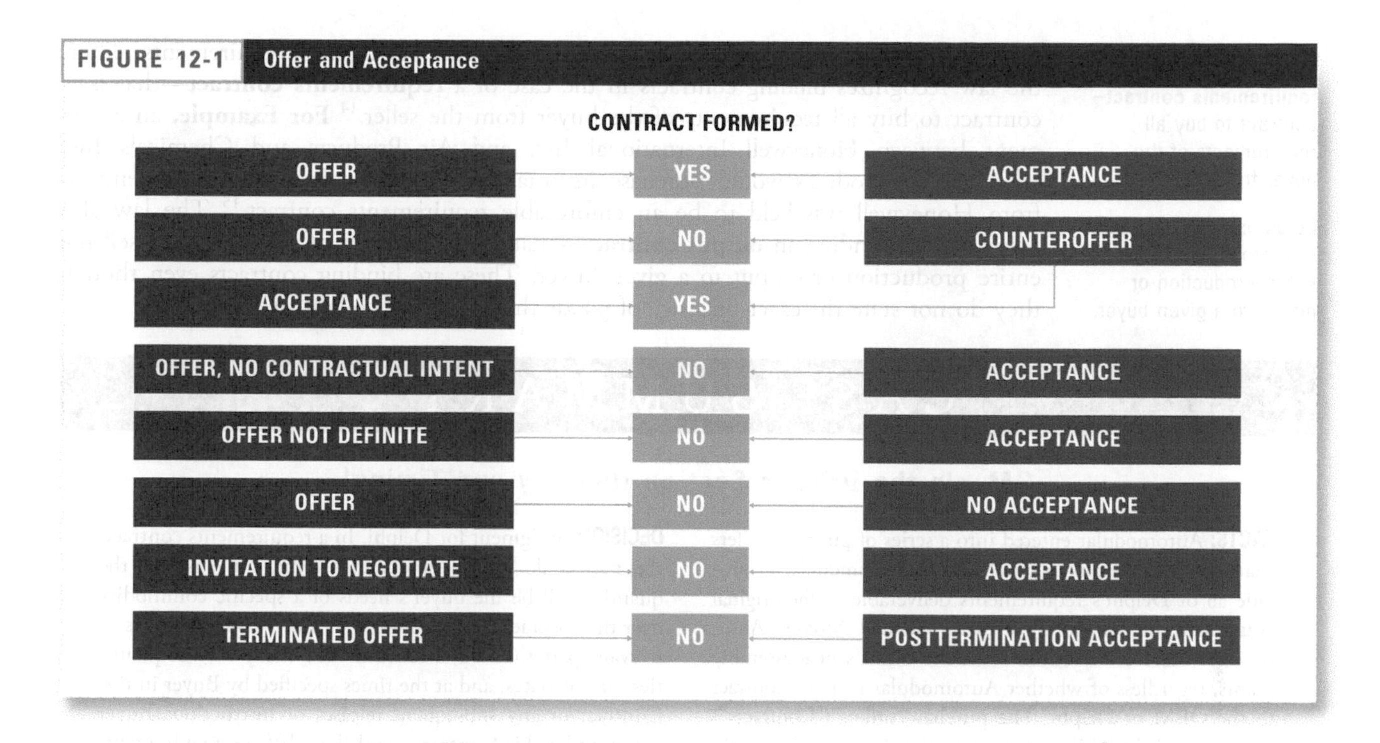

"Best Efforts" Clauses

While decades ago it was generally accepted that a duty defined only in terms of "best efforts" was too indefinite to be enforced, such a view is no longer widely held. **For Example,** Thomas Hinc, an inventor, executed a contract with Lime-O-Sol Company (LOS) for LOS to produce and distribute Hinc's secret ingredient Stain Remover. Under the contract, Hinc was to receive $10 per gallon sold. The contract contained a clause obligating both parties to use their "best efforts" to market the product "in a manner that seems appropriate." Ultimately, LOS never produced, marketed, or sold Stain Remover for the duration of the contract. The court rejected the defense that the "best efforts" provision was vague and unenforceable stating "[b]est efforts, as commonly understood, means, at the very least *some* effort. It certainly does not mean *zero* effort—the construction LOS urges here to escape any obligation under its contract."[13]

Divisible Contracts

divisible contract–agreement consisting of two or more parts, each calling for corresponding performances of each part by the parties.

When the agreement consists of two or more parts and calls for corresponding performances of each part by the parties, the agreement is a **divisible contract.** Thus, in a promise to buy several separate articles at different prices at the same time, the agreement may be regarded as separate or divisible promises for the articles.

Exceptions to Definiteness

The law has come to recognize certain situations in which the practical necessity of doing business makes it desirable to have a contract, yet the situation is such that it is impossible to adopt definite terms in advance. In these cases, the indefinite term is often tied to some independent factor that will be definitely ascertainable at some time in the future. The

[13] *Hinc v. Lime-O-Sol Company*, 382 F.3d 716 (7th Cir. 2004). See also *Olsenhaus Pure Vegan, LLC v. Electric Wonderland, Inc.*, 983 N.Y.S.2d 506 (A.D. 2014).

requirements contract–contract to buy all requirements of the buyer from the seller.

output contract–contract of a producer to sell its entire production or output to a given buyer.

indefinite term might be tied to market price, production, or sales requirements. Thus, the law recognizes binding contracts in the case of a **requirements contract**—that is, a contract to buy all requirements of the buyer from the seller.[14] **For Example,** an agreement between Honeywell International Inc. and Air Products and Chemicals Inc. whereby Air Products would purchase its total requirements of wet process chemicals from Honeywell was held to be an enforceable requirements contract.[15] The law also recognizes as binding an **output contract**—that is, the contract of a producer to sell the entire production or output to a given buyer. These are binding contracts even though they do not state the exact quantity of goods that are to be bought or sold.

CASE SUMMARY

GM—In the Driver's Seat on Quantity and Timing!

FACTS: Automodular entered into a series of purchase orders that obligated Delphi to purchase and Automodular to provide all of Delphi's requirements deliverable to the original equipment manufacturer (OEM), General Motors. Automodular receives directions from the OEM's final assembly plants, regardless of whether Automodular is under contract to the OEM or Delphi. The purchase orders ("Contracts") incorporated Delphi's terms that the Buyer, GM, could require Automodular to implement changes to the specifications or design of the goods or to the scope of any services covered by the Contracts. GM informed Automodular that it needed fewer components and directed Automodular to, among other requirements, reduce shifts, change the assembly line speed, and change the length of workers' shifts. As a result, Automodular requested a price increase per unit assembled from Delphi because Automodular believed that such an increase was warranted pursuant to the Contract's change-in-scope provision. Delphi, however, refused to negotiate any price increase and the matter was litigated.

DECISION: Judgment for Delphi. In a requirements contract, the parties do not fix a quantity term, but instead, the quantity will be the buyer's needs of a specific commodity over the contract's life. Section 2.5 of the Contract states in relevant part that "[d]eliveries will be made in the quantities, on the dates, and at the times specified by Buyer in this Contract or any subsequent releases or instructions Buyer issues under this Contract," and that "[i]f the requirements of Buyer's customers or market, economic or other conditions require changes in delivery schedules, Buyer may change the rate of scheduled shipments or direct temporary suspension of scheduled shipments without entitling [Automodular] to a price adjustment or other compensation." This provision demonstrates the intent of the parties to allow the buyer to effectively control the timing and quantity of deliveries without entitling Automodular to an adjustment in price. **[In re *Delphi Corp.*, 2009 WL 803598 (S.D.N.Y. 2009)]**

CPA 12-1c Communication of Offer to Offeree

An offer must be communicated to the offeree. Otherwise, the offeree cannot accept even though knowledge of the offer has been indirectly acquired. Internal management communications of an enterprise that are not intended for outsiders or employees do not constitute offers and cannot be accepted by them. Sometimes, particularly in the case of unilateral contracts, the offeree performs the act called for by the offeror without knowing of the offer's existence. Such performance does not constitute an acceptance. Thus, without knowing that a reward is offered for information leading to the arrest of a particular criminal, a person may provide information that leads to the arrest of the criminal. In most states, if that person subsequently learns of the reward, the reward cannot be recovered.[16]

[14] *Simcala v. American Coal Trade, Inc.*, 821 So. 2d 197 (Ala. 2001).

[15] *Honeywell International Inc. v. Air Products and Chemicals, Inc.*, 872 A.2d 944 (Sup. Ct. Del. 2005).

[16] With respect to the offeror, it should not make any difference, as a practical matter, whether the services were rendered with or without knowledge of the existence of the offer. Only a small number of states have adopted this view, however.

Not only must the offer be communicated but also it must be communicated by the offeror or at the offeror's direction.

CPA 12-2 Termination of Offer

An offeree cannot accept a terminated offer. Offers may be terminated by revocation, counteroffer, rejection, lapse of time, death or disability of a party, or subsequent illegality.

CPA 12-2a Revocation of Offer by Offeror

Ordinarily, an offeror can revoke the offer before it is accepted. If this is done, the offeree cannot create a contract by accepting the revoked offer. **For Example,** Bank of America (BOA) contended that it had reached a valid settlement agreement on December 17, 2010, with Jonathan Davidoff concerning his lawsuit against BOA seeking damages for slander of credit and breach of contract. At 3:08 P.M. on December 17, 2010, Davidoff revoked his offer to settle the matter. A few minutes later BOA counsel sent by e-mail the settlement agreements signed by the defendants and asked if Mr. Davidoff would "rescind his rejection." Davidoff clearly revoked the settlement offer prior to BOA's delivery of acceptance of the offer and no contract was formed.[17]

An ordinary offer may be revoked at any time before it is accepted even though the offeror has expressly promised that the offer will be good for a stated period and that period has not yet expired.

The fact that the offeror expressly promised to keep the offer open has no effect when no consideration was given for that promise.

What Constitutes a Revocation?

No particular form or words are required to constitute a revocation. Any words indicating the offeror's termination of the offer are sufficient. A notice sent to the offeree that the property that is the subject of the offer has been sold to a third person is a revocation of the offer. A customer's order for goods, which is an offer to purchase at certain prices, is revoked by a notice to the seller of the cancellation of the order, provided that such notice is communicated before the order is accepted.

Communication of Revocation

A revocation of an offer is ordinarily effective only when it is made known to the offeree.[18] Until it is communicated to the offeree, directly or indirectly, the offeree has reason to believe that there is still an offer that may be accepted, and the offeree may rely on this belief. A letter revoking an offer made to a particular offeree is not effective until the offeree receives it. It is not a revocation when the offeror writes it or even when it is mailed or dispatched. A written revocation is effective, however, when it is delivered to the offeree's agent or to the offeree's residence or place of business under such circumstances that the offeree may be reasonably expected to be aware of its receipt.

It is ordinarily held that there is a sufficient communication of the revocation when the offeree learns indirectly of the offeror's revocation. This is particularly true in a land sale when the seller-offeror, after making an offer to sell the land to the offeree, sells the land to a third person and the offeree indirectly learns of such sale. The offeree necessarily realizes that the seller cannot perform the original offer and therefore must be considered to have revoked it.

[17] *Davidoff v. Bank of America*, 2011 WL 999564 (S.D. Fla. Oct. 18, 2010).
[18] *MD Drilling and Blasting, Inc. v. MLS Construction, LLC*, 889 A.2d 850 (Conn. App. 2006).

If the offeree accepts an offer before it is effectively revoked, a valid contract is created.

Option Contracts

An *option contract* is a binding promise to keep an offer open for a stated period of time or until a specified date. An option contract requires that the promisor receive consideration—that is, something, such as a sum of money—as the price for the promise to keep the offer open. In other words, the option is a contract to refrain from revoking an offer.

Firm Offers

firm offer–offer stated to be held open for a specified time, under the UCC, with respect to merchants.

As another exception to the rule that an offer can be revoked at any time before acceptance, statutes in some states provide that an offeror cannot revoke an offer prior to its expiration when the offeror makes a firm offer. A **firm offer** is an offer that states that it is to be irrevocable, or irrevocable for a stated period of time. Under the Uniform Commercial Code, this doctrine of firm offer applies to a merchant's signed, written offer to buy or sell goods but with a maximum of three months on its period of irrevocability.[19]

12-2b Counteroffer by Offeree

counteroffer–proposal by an offeree to the offeror that changes the terms of, and thus rejects, the original offer.

The offeree rejects the offer when it ignores the original offer and replies with a different offer.[20] If the offeree purports to accept an offer but in so doing makes any change to the terms of the offer, such action is a **counteroffer** that rejects the original offer. An "acceptance" that changes the terms of the offer or adds new terms is a rejection of the original offer and constitutes a counteroffer.[21]

Ordinarily, if *A* makes an offer, such as to sell a used automobile to *B* for $3,000, and *B* in reply makes an offer to buy at $2,500, the original offer is terminated. *B* is in effect indicating refusal of the original offer and in its place is making a different offer. Such an offer by the offeree is known as a *counteroffer*. No contract arises unless the original offeror accepts the counteroffer.

Counteroffers are not limited to offers that directly contradict the original offers. Any departure from or addition to the original offer is a counteroffer even though the original offer was silent on the point added by the counteroffer.

CASE SUMMARY

The Counteroffer Serves as a Rejection

FACTS: While riding her motorcycle Amy Kemper was struck by a vehicle driven by Brown. She suffered serious injuries and Brown was charged with DUI. Kemper sent a demand letter to Brown's insurance claim's administrator Statewide, which stated in part:

> *Please send all the insurance money that Mr. Brown had under his insurance policy. In exchange, I will agree to sign a limited release.*
>
> *The release must not have any language saying that I will have to pay Mr. Brown or his insurance company any of their incurred costs.*
>
> .... *If you fail to meet my demand, I will be forced to hire an attorney and sue Mr. Brown and your company. Please do not contact me, or my friends[,] as this demand is very simple.*

Statewide sent a letter to Kemper agreeing to settle her claims for the limits of Brown's liability insurance. Attached

[19] U.C.C. §2-205.

[20] *Bourque v. FDIC*, 42 F.3d 704 (1st Cir. 1994).

[21] *Hardy Corp. v. Rayco Industrial, Inc.*, 143 So. 3d 172 (Ala. 2013).

The Counteroffer Serves as a Rejection continued

to the letter was a $25,000 check and a two-page limited liability release form. The letter stated, in part,

> *[i]n concluding the settlement, we are entrusting that you place money in an escrow account in regards to any and all liens pending. This demand is being asserted to protect the lien's interest[.]*

Ms. Kemper rejected Statewide's "counteroffer" and filed suit. Brown filed a motion to enforce the "settlement agreement."

DECISION: Judgment for Kemper. To establish a contract the offer must be accepted unequivocally and without variance of any sort. Statewide demanded that Kemper place the settlements funds into an escrow account to protect against any pending liens. Its response was a counteroffer rather than an unconditional and unequivocal acceptance. No binding settlement agreement was formed. **[*Kemper v. Brown*, 754 S.E.2d 141 (Ga. App. 2014)]**

12-2c Rejection of Offer by Offeree

If the offeree rejects the offer and communicates this rejection to the offeror, the offer is terminated. Communication of a rejection terminates an offer even though the period for which the offeror agreed to keep the offer open has not yet expired. It may be that the offeror is willing to renew the offer, but unless this is done, there is no longer any offer for the offeree to accept.

12-2d Lapse of Time

When the offer states that it is open until a particular date, the offer terminates on that date if it has not yet been accepted. This is particularly so when the offeror declares that the offer shall be void after the expiration of the specified time. Such limitations are strictly construed. **For Example,** Landry's Restaurant Minnesota Inc. extended a written, signed offer to Starlite L.P. to lease Starlite's real estate for a period of 20 years. The written offer stated that if a fully executed acceptance of the lease is not returned to Landry's Minnesota Inc. within six days of the written offer dated April 30, 1998, "the offer to lease ... shall be deemed withdrawn and this lease shall be deemed null and void." Starlite signed and returned the lease agreement on May 11, 1998, five days after the May 6 deadline. Landry's Minnesota occupied the property and built a restaurant on it but vacated the property after nine years. Starlite sued the restaurant's parent corporation, Landry's Restaurants Inc., as guarantor of the lease, seeking payment for past due and ongoing rent. Starlite's lawsuit was not successful as no valid lease agreement existed because no contract could be properly formed when acceptance occurred after the written offer had expired.[22]

If the offer contains a time limitation for acceptance, an attempted acceptance after the expiration of that time has no effect and does not give rise to a contract.[23] When a specified time limitation is imposed on an option, the option cannot be exercised after the expiration of that time, regardless of whether the option was exercised within what would have been held a reasonable time if no time period had been specified.

If the offer does not specify a time, it will terminate after the lapse of a reasonable time. What constitutes a reasonable time depends on the circumstances of each case—that is, on the nature of the subject matter, the nature of the market in which it is sold, the time of

[22] *Starlite Limited Partnership v. Landry's Restaurants, Inc.*, 780 N.W.2d 396 (Minn. App. 2010).
[23] *Century 21 Pinetree Properties, Inc. v. Cason*, 469 S.E.2d 458 (Ga. App. 1996).

year, and other factors of supply and demand. If a commodity is perishable or fluctuates greatly in value, the reasonable time will be much shorter than if the subject matter is of a stable value. An offer to sell a harvested crop of tomatoes would expire within a very short time. When a seller purports to accept an offer after it has lapsed by the expiration of time, the seller's acceptance is merely a counteroffer and does not create a contract unless the buyer accepts that counteroffer.

12-2e Death or Disability of Either Party

If either the offeror or offeree dies or becomes mentally incompetent before the offer is accepted, the offer is automatically terminated. **For Example,** Chet Wilson offers to sell his ranch to Interport, Inc., for $2.5 million. Five days later, Chet is killed in an aviation accident. Interport, Inc., subsequently writes to Chet Wilson Jr., an adult, that his father's offer is accepted. No contract is formed because the offer made by Chet died with him.

CPA

12-2f Subsequent Illegality

If the performance of the contract becomes illegal after the offer is made, the offer is terminated. **For Example,** if an offer is made to sell six semiautomatic handguns to a commercial firing range for $550 per weapon but a new law prohibiting such sales is enacted before the offer is accepted, the offer is terminated.

CPA

12-3 Acceptance of Offer

acceptance–unqualified assent to the act or proposal of another; as the acceptance of a draft (bill of exchange), of an offer to make a contract, of goods delivered by the seller, or of a gift or deed.

An **acceptance** is the assent of the offeree to the terms of the offer. Objective standards determine whether there has been an agreement of the parties.

12-3a What Constitutes an Acceptance?

No particular form of words or mode of expression is required, but there must be a clear expression that the offeree agrees to be bound by the terms of the offer. If the offeree reserves the right to reject the offer, such action is not an acceptance.[24]

12-3b Privilege of Offeree

Ordinarily, the offeree may refuse to accept an offer. If there is no acceptance, by definition there is no contract. The fact that there had been a series of contracts between the parties and that one party's offer had always been accepted before by the other does not create any legal obligation to continue to accept subsequent offers.

CPA

12-3c Effect of Acceptance

The acceptance of an offer creates a binding agreement or contract,[25] assuming that all of the other elements of a contract are present. Neither party can subsequently withdraw from or cancel the contract without the consent of the other party. **For Example,** James Gang refused to honor an oral stock purchase agreement he made with Moshen Sadeghi under terms he assented to and that were announced on the record to a court as a mutual

[24] *Pantano v. McGowan*, 530 N.W.2d 912 (Neb. 1995).
[25] *Ochoa v. Ford*, 641 N.E.2d 1042 (Ind. App. 1994).

settlement of a dispute. Gang was not allowed subsequently to withdraw from the agreement, because it was an enforceable contract.[26]

CPA 12-3d Nature of Acceptance

An *acceptance* is the offeree's manifestation of intent to enter into a binding agreement on the terms stated in the offer. Whether there is an acceptance depends on whether the offeree has manifested an intent to accept. It is the objective or outward appearance that is controlling rather than the subjective or unexpressed intent of the offeree.[27]

In the absence of a contrary requirement in the offer, an acceptance may be indicated by an informal "okay," by a mere affirmative nod of the head, or in the case of an offer of a unilateral contract, by performance of the act called for.

The acceptance must be absolute and unconditional. It must accept just what is offered.[28] If the offeree changes any terms of the offer or adds any new term, there is no acceptance because the offeree does not agree to what was offered.

When the offeree does not accept the offer exactly as made, the addition of any qualification converts the "acceptance" into a counteroffer, and no contract arises unless the original offeror accepts such a counteroffer.

CPA 12-3e Who May Accept?

Only the person to whom an offer is directed may accept it. If anyone else attempts to accept it, no agreement or contract with that person arises.

If the offer is directed to a particular class rather than a specified individual, anyone within that class may accept it. If the offer is made to the public at large, any member of the public at large having knowledge of the existence of the offer may accept it.

When a person to whom an offer was not made attempts to accept it, the attempted acceptance has the effect of an offer. If the original offeror is willing to accept this offer, a binding contract arises. If the original offeror does not accept the new offer, there is no contract.

CASE SUMMARY

There's No Turning Back

FACTS: As a lease was about to expire, the landlord, CRA Development, wrote the tenant, Keryakos Textiles, setting forth the square footage and the rate terms on which the lease would be renewed. Keryakos sent a reply stating that it was willing to pay the proposed rate but wanted different cancellation and option terms in the renewal contract. CRA rejected Keryakos's terms, and on learning this, Keryakos notified CRA that it accepted the terms of its original letter. CRA sought to evict Keryakos from the property, claiming that no lease contract existed between it and Keryakos.

DECISION: The lease contract is governed by ordinary contract law. When the tenant offered other terms in place of those made by the landlord's offer, the tenant made a counteroffer. This had the effect of rejecting or terminating the landlord's offer. The tenant could not then accept the rejected offer after the tenant's counteroffer was rejected. Therefore, there was no contract. [***Keryakos Textiles, Inc. v. CRA Development, Inc.*, 563 N.Y.S.2d 308 (App. Div. 1990)**]

[26] *Sadeghi v. Gang*, 270 S.W.3d 773 (Tex. App. 2008).
[27] *Cowan v. Mervin Mewes, Inc.*, 546 N.W.2d 104 (S.D. 1996).
[28] *Jones v. Frickey*, 618 S.E.2d 29 (Ga. App. 2005).

CPA 12-3f Manner and Time of Acceptance

The offeror may specify the manner and time for accepting the offer. When the offeror specifies that there must be a written acceptance, no contract arises when the offeree makes an oral acceptance. If the offeror calls for acceptance by a specified time and date, a late acceptance has no legal effect, and a contract is not formed. Where no time is specified in the offer, the offeree has a reasonable period of time to accept the offer. After the time specified in the offer or a reasonable period of time expires (when no time is specified in the offer), the offeree's power to make a contract by accepting the offer "lapses."

When the offeror calls for the performance of an act or of certain conduct, the performance thereof is an acceptance of the offer and creates a unilateral contract.

When the offeror has specified a particular manner and time of acceptance, generally, the offeree cannot accept in any other way. The basic rule applied by the courts is that the offeror is the master of the offer![29]

CPA Silence as Acceptance

In most cases, the offeree's silence and failure to act cannot be regarded as an acceptance. Ordinarily, the offeror is not permitted to frame an offer in such a way as to make the silence and inaction of the offeree operate as an acceptance. Nor can a party to an existing contract effect a modification of that agreement without the other party's actual acceptance or approval. **For Example,** H. H. Taylor made a contract with Andy Stricker, a civil engineer, to design a small hotel. The parties agreed on an hourly rate with "total price not to exceed $7,200," and required that additional charges be presented to Taylor prior to proceeding with any changes. Andy was required to dedicate more hours to the project than anticipated but could not present the additional charges to Taylor because Taylor would not return his phone calls. He billed Taylor $9,035 for his services. Taylor's failure to act in not returning phone calls is not a substitute for the assent needed to modify a contract. Stricker is thus only entitled to $7,200.[30]

Unordered Goods and Tickets

Sometimes a seller writes to a person with whom the seller has not had any prior dealings, stating that unless notified to the contrary, the seller will send specified merchandise and the recipient is obligated to pay for it at stated prices. There is no acceptance if the recipient of the letter ignores the offer and does nothing. The silence of the person receiving the letter is not an acceptance, and the sender, as a reasonable person, should recognize that none was intended.

This rule applies to all kinds of goods, books, magazines, and tickets sent through the mail when they have not been ordered. The fact that the items are not returned does not mean that they have been accepted; that is, the offeree is required neither to pay for nor to return the items. If desired, the recipient of the unordered goods may write "Return to Sender" on the unopened package and put the package back into the mail without any additional postage. The Postal Reorganization Act provides that the person who receives unordered mailed merchandise from a commercial sender has the right "to retain, use, discard, or dispose of it in any manner the recipient sees fit without any obligation

[29] See *1-800 Contacts, Inc. v. Weigner,* 127 P.3d 1241 (Utah App. 2005).
[30] *Stricker v. Taylor,* 975 P.2d 930 (Or. App. 1999).

whatsoever to the sender."[31] It provides further that any unordered merchandise that is mailed must have attached to it a clear and conspicuous statement of the recipient's right to treat the goods in this manner.

CPA 12-3g Communication of Acceptance

Acceptance by the offeree is the last step in the formation of a bilateral contract. Intuitively, the offeror's receipt of the acceptance should be the point in time when the contract is formed and its terms apply. When the parties are involved in face-to-face negotiations, a contract is formed upon the offeror's receipt of the acceptance. When the offeror hears the offeree's words of acceptance, the parties may shake hands, signifying their understanding that the contract has been formed.

E-COMMERCE & CYBERLAW

Contract Formation on the Internet

It is not possible for an online service provider or seller to individually bargain with each person who visits its Web site. The Web site owner, therefore, as offeror, places its proposed terms on its Web site and requires visitors to assent to these terms in order to access the site, download software, or purchase a product or service.

In a written contract, the parties sign a paper document indicating their intention to be bound by the terms of the contract. Online, however, an agreement may be accomplished by the visitor-offeree simply typing the words "I Accept" in an onscreen box and then clicking a "send" or similar button that indicates acceptance. Or the individual clicks an "I Agree" or "I Accept" icon or check box. Access to the site is commonly denied those who do not agree to the terms. Such agreements have come to be known as *clickwrap* agreements and in the case of software license agreements, *SLAs*. The agreements contain fee schedules and other financial terms and may contain terms such as a notice of the proprietary nature of the material contained on the site and of any limitations on the use of the site and the downloading of software. Moreover, the clickwrap agreements may contain limitations on liability, including losses associated with the use of downloaded software or products or services purchased from the site.

To determine whether a clickwrap agreement is enforceable, courts apply traditional principles of contract law and focus on whether the plaintiffs had reasonable notice of and manifested assent to the clickwrap agreement. Failure to read an enforceable clickwrap agreement, as with any binding contract, will not excuse compliance with its terms.

In *Specht v. Netscape Communications Corp.*,* the Internet users were urged to click on a button to download free software, but the offer did not make clear to the user that clicking the download button would signify assent to restrictive contractual terms and conditions. The court, in its 2002 decision, declined to enforce this clickwrap agreement. Internet sellers and service providers generally learned from the *Specht* decision, and most clickwrap agreements now provide sufficient notice and means for clear assent. For example, in *Feldman v. Google, Inc.*,** decided in 2007, the user was unsuccessful in challenging the terms of Google's "AdWords" Program clickwrap agreement. In order to activate an AdWords account, the user had to visit a Web page that displayed the agreement in a scrollable text box. The text of the agreement was immediately visible to the user, as was a prominent admonition in boldface to read the terms and conditions carefully, and with instructions to indicate assent if the user agreed to the terms.

Unlike the impermissible agreement in *Specht*, the user here had to take affirmative action and click the "Yes, I agree to the above terms and conditions" button in order to proceed to the next step. Clicking "Continue" without clicking the "Yes" button would have returned the user to the same Web page. If the user did not agree to all of the terms, he could not have activated his account, placed ads, or incurred charges.

*306 F.3d 17 (2d Cir. 2002).

***Feldman v. Google, Inc.*, 513 F. Supp. 2d 229 (E.D. Pa. 2007).** See also ***A.V. v. Iparadigms, LLC*, 554 F. Supp. 2d 473 (E.D. Va. 2008).**

[31] Federal Postal Reorganization Act §3009.

CPA

Mailbox Rule

When the parties are negotiating at a distance from each other, special rules have developed as to when the acceptance takes effect based on the commercial expediency of creating a contract at the earliest period of time and the protection of the offeree. Under the so-called *mailbox rule*, a properly addressed, postage-paid mailed acceptance takes effect when the acceptance is placed into the control of the U.S. Postal Service[32] or, by judicial extension, is placed in the control of a private third-party carrier such as Federal Express or United Parcel Service.[33] That is, the acceptance is effective upon dispatch even before it is received by the offeror.

CASE SUMMARY

When the Mailbox Bangs Shut

FACTS: The Thoelkes owned land. The Morrisons mailed an offer to the Thoelkes to buy their land. The Thoelkes agreed to this offer and mailed back a contract signed by them. While this letter was in transit, the Thoelkes notified the Morrisons that their acceptance was revoked. Were the Thoelkes bound by a contract?

DECISION: The acceptance was effective when mailed, and the subsequent revocation of the acceptance had no effect. **[*Morrison v. Thoelke*, 155 So. 2d 889 (Fla. App. 1963)]**

The offeror may avoid the application of this rule by stating in the offer that acceptance shall take effect upon receipt by the offeror.

CPA

Determining the Applicable Means of Communication

The modern rule on the selection of the appropriate medium of communication of acceptance is that unless otherwise unambiguously indicated in the offer, it shall be construed as inviting acceptance in any manner and by any medium reasonable under the circumstances.[34] A medium of communication is normally reasonable if it is one used by the offeror or if it is customary in similar transactions at the time and place the offer is received. Thus, if the offeror uses the mail to extend an offer, the offeree may accept by using the mail. Indeed, acceptance by mail is ordinarily reasonable when the parties are negotiating at a distance even if the offer is not made by mail.

CPA

Telephone and Electronic Communication of Acceptance

Although telephonic communication is very similar to face-to-face communication, most U.S. courts, nevertheless, have applied the mailbox rule, holding that telephoned acceptances are effective where and when dispatched.

[32] See *Adams v. Lindsell*, 106 Eng. Rep. 250 (K.B. 1818). Common law jurisdictions have unanimously adopted the mailbox rule, as has the Restatement (Second) of Contracts §63, and the U.C.C. [see U.C.C. §1-201(26),(38)].

[33] But see *Baca v. Trejo*, 902 N.E.2d 1108 (Ill App. 2009) whereby an Illinois court determined that a statute deeming a document to be filed with a state court on the date shown by the U.S. Postal Service cancellation mark—the mailbox rule—does not apply to documents consigned to a private carrier, UPS. The court reasoned that courts should not have the task of deciding which carriers are acceptable.

[34] Restatement (Second) of Contracts §30; U.C.C. §2-206(1) (a).

The courts have yet to address the applicability of the mailbox rule to e-mail. However, when the offeree's server is under the control of an independent entity, such as an online service provider, and the offeree cannot withdraw the message, it is anticipated that the courts will apply the mailbox rule, and acceptance will take effect on proper dispatch. In the case of companies that operate their own servers, the acceptance will take effect when the message is passed onto the Internet.

Facsimile transmissions are substantially instantaneous and could be treated as face-to-face communications. However, it is anticipated that U.S. courts, when called upon to deal with this issue, will apply the mailbox acceptance-upon-dispatch rule as they do with telephoned acceptances.

Effects of the Mailbox Rule

If an offer requires that acceptance be communicated by a specific date and the acceptance is properly dispatched by the offeree on the final date, the acceptance is timely and the contract is formed, even though the offeror actually receives the acceptance well after the specified date has passed. **For Example,** by letter dated February 18, 1999, Morton's of Chicago mailed a certified letter to the Crab House accepting the Crab House's offer to terminate its restaurant lease. The Crab House, Inc., sought to revoke its offer to terminate the lease in a certified letter dated February 18, 1999, and by facsimile transmission to Morton's dated February 19, 1999. On February 22, 1999, the Crab House received Morton's acceptance letter; and on the same date Morton's received Crab House's letter revoking the offer to terminate the lease. Acceptance of an offer is effective upon dispatch to the Postal Service, and the contract springs into existence at the time of the mailing. Offers, revocations, and rejections are generally effective only upon the offeree's receipt. Morton's dispatch of its acceptance letter on February 18 formed an agreement to terminate the lease, and the fax dispatched on February 19 was too late to revoke the offer to terminate the lease.[35]

12-3h Auction Sales

At an auction sale, the statements made by the auctioneer to draw forth bids are merely invitations to negotiate. Each bid is an offer, which is not accepted until the auctioneer indicates that a particular offer or bid is accepted. Usually, this is done by the fall of the auctioneer's hammer, indicating that the highest bid made has been accepted.[36] Because a bid is merely an offer, the bidder may withdraw the bid at any time before it is accepted by the auctioneer.

Ordinarily, the auctioneer who is not satisfied with the amounts of the bids that are being made may withdraw any article or all of the property from the sale. Once a bid is accepted, however, the auctioneer cannot cancel the sale. In addition, if it had been announced that the sale was to be made "without reserve," the property must be sold to the person making the highest bid regardless of how low that bid may be.

In an auction "with reserve," the auctioneer takes bids as agent for the seller with the understanding that no contract is formed until the seller accepts the transaction.[37]

[35] *Morton's of Chicago v. Crab House Inc.*, 746 N.Y.S.2d 317 (2002). *Kass v. Grais*, 2007 WL 2815498 (N.Y. Sup. Sept. 4, 2007).

[36] *Dry Creek Cattle Co. v. Harriet Bros. Limited Partnership*, 908 P.2d 399 (Wyo. 1995).

[37] *Marten v. Staab*, 543 N.W.2d 436 (Neb. 1996). Statutes regulate auctions and auctioneers in all states. For example, state of Maine law prohibits an auctioneer from conducting an auction without first having a written contract with the consignor of any property to be sold, including (1) whether the auction is with reserve or without reserve, (2) the commission rate, and (3) a description of all items to be sold. See *Street v. Board of Licensing of Auctioneers*, 889 A.2d 319 ([Me.] 2006).

Make the Connection

Summary

Because a contract arises when an offer is accepted, it is necessary to find that there was an offer and that it was accepted. If either element is missing, there is no contract.

An offer does not exist unless the offeror has contractual intent. This intent is lacking if the statement of the person is merely an invitation to negotiate, a statement of intention, or an agreement to agree at a later date. Newspaper ads, price quotations, and catalog prices are ordinarily merely invitations to negotiate and cannot be accepted.

An offer must be definite. If an offer is indefinite, its acceptance will not create a contract because it will be held that the resulting agreement is too vague to enforce. In some cases, an offer that is by itself too indefinite is made definite because some writing or standard is incorporated by reference and made part of the offer. In some cases the offer is made definite by implying terms that were not stated. In other cases, the indefinite part of the offer is ignored when that part can be divided or separated from the balance of the offer.

Assuming that there is in fact an offer that is made with contractual intent and that it is sufficiently definite, it still does not have the legal effect of an offer unless it is communicated to the offeree by or at the direction of the offeror.

In some cases, there was an offer but it was terminated before it was accepted. By definition, an attempted acceptance made after the offer has been terminated has no effect. The offeror may revoke the ordinary offer at any time. All that is required is the showing of the intent to revoke and the communication of that intent to the offeree. The offeror's power to revoke is barred by the existence of an option contract under common law or a firm offer under the Uniform Commercial Code. An offer is also terminated by the express rejection of the offer or by the making of a counteroffer, by the lapse of the time stated in the offer or of a reasonable time when none is stated, by the death or disability of either party, or by a change of law that makes illegal a contract based on the particular offer.

When the offer is accepted, a contract arises. Only the offeree can accept an offer, and the acceptance must be of the offer exactly as made without any qualification or change. Ordinarily, the offeree may accept or reject as the offeree chooses.

The acceptance is any manifestation of intent to agree to the terms of the offer. Ordinarily, silence or failure to act does not constitute acceptance. The recipient of unordered goods and tickets may dispose of the goods or use the goods without such action constituting an acceptance. An acceptance does not exist until the words or conduct demonstrating assent to the offer is communicated to the offeror. Acceptance by mail takes effect at the time and place when and where the letter is mailed or the fax is transmitted.

In an auction sale, the auctioneer asking for bids makes an invitation to negotiate. A person making a bid is making an offer, and the acceptance of the highest bid by the auctioneer is an acceptance of that offer and gives rise to a contract. When the auction sale is without reserve, the auctioneer must accept the highest bid. If the auction is not expressly without reserve, the auctioneer may refuse to accept any of the bids.

Learning Outcomes

After studying this chapter, you should be able to clearly explain:

12-1 Requirements of an Offer

LO.1 Decide whether an offer contains definite and certain terms

See the *Novak* case for an example of an oral contract with definite enforceable terms, page 224.

See the *Plankenhorn* case for the meaning of a "damn good job," page 225.

See the legal impact of a party's statement that the contract "was going to be signed" in the *Hewitt* example, page 223.

See the *Wigod* case that discusses the test for a valid, binding offer, page 222.

12-2 Termination of Offer

LO.2 Explain the exceptions the law makes to the requirement of definiteness

See the *Delphi* case on requirements contracts, page 228.

LO.3 Explain all the ways an offer can be terminated
See the discussion of revocation, counteroffer, rejection, lapse of time, death or disability of a party, or subsequent illegality, pages 229–232.
See the *Davidoff* example of a revocation communicated to the offeree prior to acceptance, page 229.
See the *Landry's Restaurants* example that illustrates the effect of an "acceptance" signed just a few days after the written offer had expired, page 231.
See the *Kemper* case showing that a counteroffer serves as a rejection, page 231.

12-3 Acceptance of Offer

LO.4 Explain what constitutes the acceptance of an offer
See the *Sadeghi* example where acceptance of an offer created a binding contract, pages 232–233.
See the *Keryakos Textiles* case on the impact of a counteroffer, page 233.

LO.5 Explain the implications of failing to read a clickwrap agreement
See the *Feldman* case as an example of an enforceable clickwrap agreement containing notice and manifested assent, page 235.

Key Terms

acceptance
counteroffer
divisible contract
firm offer
offer
output contract
requirements contract

Questions and Case Problems

1. Bernie and Phil's Great American Surplus store placed an ad in the *Sunday Times* stating, "Next Saturday at 8:00 A.M. sharp, 3 brand new mink coats worth $5,000 each will be sold for $500 each! First come, first served." Marsha Lufklin was first in line when the store opened and went directly to the coat department, but the coats identified in the ad were not available for sale. She identified herself to the manager and pointed out that she was first in line in conformity with the store's advertised offer and that she was ready to pay the $500 price set forth in the store's offer. The manager responded that a newspaper ad is just an invitation to negotiate and that the store decided to withdraw "the mink coat promotion." Review the text on unilateral contracts in the section titled "Bilateral and Unilateral Contracts" in Chapter 11. Decide.
2. Brown made an offer to purchase Overman's house on a standard printed form. Underneath Brown's signature was the statement: "ACCEPTANCE ON REVERSE SIDE." Overman did not sign the offer on the back but sent Brown a letter accepting the offer. Later, Brown refused to perform the contract, and Overman sued him for breach of contract. Brown claimed there was no contract because the offer had not been accepted in the manner specified by the offer. Decide. [*Overman v. Brown*, 372 N.W.2d 102 (Neb.)]
3. Katherine mailed Paul an offer with definite and certain terms and that was legal in all respects stating that it was good for 10 days. Two days later she sent Paul a letter by certified mail (time stamped by the Postal Service at 1:14 P.M.) stating that the original offer was revoked. That evening Paul e-mailed acceptance of the offer to Katherine. She immediately phoned him to tell him that she had revoked the offer that afternoon, and that he would surely receive it in tomorrow's mail. Was the offer revoked by Katherine?
4. Nelson wanted to sell his home. Baker sent him a written offer to purchase the home. Nelson made some changes to Baker's offer and wrote him that he, Nelson, was accepting the offer as amended. Baker notified Nelson that he was dropping out of the transaction. Nelson sued Baker for breach of contract. Decide. What social forces and ethical values are involved? [*Nelson v. Baker*, 776 S.W.2d 52 (Mo. App.)]
5. Lessack Auctioneers advertised an auction sale that was open to the public and was to be conducted with reserve. Gordon attended the auction and bid $100 for a work of art that was worth much more. No higher bid, however, was made. Lessack refused to sell the item for $100 and withdrew the item from the sale. Gordon claimed that because he was the highest bidder, Lessack was required to sell the item to him. Was he correct?

6. Willis Music Co. advertised a television set at $22.50 in the Sunday newspaper. Ehrlich ordered a set, but the company refused to deliver it on the grounds that the price in the newspaper ad was a mistake. Ehrlich sued the company. Was it liable? Why or why not? [*Ehrlich v. Willis Music Co.*, 113 N.E.2d 252 (Ohio App.)]
7. When a movement was organized to build Charles City College, Hauser and others signed pledges to contribute to the college. At the time of signing, Hauser inquired what would happen if he should die or be unable to pay. The representative of the college stated that the pledge would then not be binding and that it was merely a statement of intent. The college failed financially, and Pappas was appointed receiver to collect and liquidate the assets of the college corporation. He sued Hauser for the amount due on his pledge. Hauser raised the defense that the pledge was not a binding contract. Decide. What ethical values are involved? [*Pappas v. Hauser*, 197 N.W.2d 607 (Iowa)]
8. Maria Cantu was a special education teacher under a one-year contract with the San Benito School district for the 1990–1991 school year. On Saturday, August 18, just weeks before fall-term classes were to begin, she hand delivered a letter of resignation to her supervisor. Late Monday afternoon the superintendent put in the mail a properly stamped and addressed letter to Cantu accepting her offer of resignation. The next morning at 8:00, before the superintendent's letter reached her, Cantu hand delivered a letter withdrawing her resignation. The superintendent refused to recognize the attempted rescission of the resignation. Decide. [*Cantu v. Central Education Agency*, 884 S.W.2d 563 (Tex. App.)]
9. A. H. Zehmer discussed selling a farm to Lucy. After a 40-minute discussion of the first draft of a contract, Zehmer and his wife, Ida, signed a second draft stating: "We hereby agree to sell to W. O. Lucy the Ferguson farm complete for $50,000 title satisfactory to buyer." Lucy agreed to purchase the farm on these terms. Thereafter, the Zehmers refused to transfer title to Lucy and claimed they had made the contract for sale as a joke. Lucy brought an action to compel performance of the contract. The Zehmers claimed there was no contract. Were they correct? [*Lucy v. Zehmer*, 84 S.E.2d 516 (Va. App.)]
10. Wheeler operated an automobile service station, which he leased from W. C. Cornitius, Inc. The lease ran for three years. Although the lease did not contain any provision for renewal, it was in fact renewed six times for successive three-year terms. The landlord refused to renew the lease for a seventh time. Wheeler brought suit to compel the landlord to accept his offer to renew the lease. Decide. [*William C. Cornitius, Inc. v. Wheeler*, 556 P.2d 666 (Or.)]
11. Buster Cogdill, a real estate developer, made an offer to the Bank of Benton to have the bank provide construction financing for the development of an outlet mall, with funds to be provided at prime rate plus two percentage points. The bank's president Julio Plunkett thanked Buster for the proposal and said, "I will start the paperwork." Did Cogdill have a contract with the Bank of Benton? [*Bank of Benton v. Cogdill*, 454 N.E.2d 1120 (Ill. App.)]
12. Ackerley Media Group, Inc., claimed to have a three-season advertising Team Sponsorship Agreement (TSA) with Sharp Electronics Corporation to promote Sharp products at all Seattle Supersonics NBA basketball home games. Sharp contended that a valid agreement did not exist for the third season (2000–2001) because a material price term was missing, thus resulting in an unenforceable "agreement to agree." The terms of the TSA for the 2000–2001 third season called for a base payment of $144,200 and an annual increase "not to exceed 6% [and] to be mutually agreed upon by the parties." No "mutually agreed" increase was negotiated by the parties. Ackerley seeks payment for the base price of $144,200 only. Sharp contends that since no price was agreed upon for the season, the entire TSA is unenforceable, and it is not obligated to pay for the 2000–2001 season. Is Sharp correct? [*Ackerley Media Group, Inc. v. Sharp Electronics Corp.*, 170 F. Supp. 2d 445 (S.D.N.Y.)]
13. L. B. Foster invited Tie and Track Systems Inc. to submit price quotes on items to be used in a railroad expansion project. Tie and Track responded by e-mail on August 11, 2006, with prices for 9 items of steel ties. The e-mail concluded, "The above prices are delivered/Terms of Payment—to be agreed/ Delivery—to be agreed/We hope you are successful with your bid. If you require any additional information please call." Just 3 of the 9 items listed in Tie and Track's price quote were "accepted" by the project. L. B. Foster demanded that Tie and Track provide the items at the price listed in the quote. Tie and Track refused. L. B. Foster sued for breach of contract. Did the August 11 e-mail constitute an offer, acceptance of which could bind the supplier to

a contract? If so, was there a valid acceptance? [*L. B. Foster v. Tie and Track Systems, Inc.*, 2009 WL 900993 (N.D. Ill.)]

14. On August 15, 2003, Wilbert Heikkila signed an agreement with Kangas Realty to sell eight parcels of Heikkila's property. On September 8, 2003, David McLaughlin met with a Kangas agent who drafted McLaughlin's offer to purchase three of the parcels. McLaughlin signed the offer and gave the agent checks for each parcel. On September 9 and 10, 2003, the agent for Heikkila prepared three printed purchase agreements, one for each parcel. On September 14, 2003, David's wife, Joanne McLaughlin, met with the agent and signed the agreements. On September 16, 2003, Heikkila met with his real estate agent. Writing on the printed agreements, Heikkila changed the price of one parcel from $145,000 to $150,000, the price of another parcel from $32,000 to $45,000, and the price of the third parcel from $175,000 to $179,000. Neither of the McLaughlins signed an acceptance of Heikkila's changes to the printed agreements before Heikkila withdrew his offer to sell. The McLaughlins learned that Heikkila had withdrawn his offer on January 1, 2004, when the real estate agent returned the checks to them. Totally shocked at Heikkila's conduct, the McLaughlins brought action to compel specific performance of the purchase agreement signed by Joanne McLaughlin on their behalf. Decide. [*McLaughlin v. Heikkila*, 697 N.W.2d 231 (Minn. App.)]

CPA Questions

1. Able Sofa, Inc., sent Noll a letter offering to sell Noll a custom-made sofa for $5,000. Noll immediately sent a telegram to Able purporting to accept the offer. However, the telegraph company erroneously delivered the telegram to Abel Soda, Inc. Three days later, Able mailed a letter of revocation to Noll, which was received by Noll. Able refused to sell Noll the sofa. Noll sued Able for breach of contract. Able:
   a. Would have been liable under the deposited acceptance rule only if Noll had accepted by mail.
   b. Will avoid liability since it revoked its offer prior to receiving Noll's acceptance.
   c. Will be liable for breach of contract.
   d. Will avoid liability due to the telegraph company's error (Law, #2, 9911).

2. On September 27, Summers sent Fox a letter offering to sell Fox a vacation home for $150,000. On October 2, Fox replied by mail agreeing to buy the home for $145,000. Summers did not reply to Fox. Do Fox and Summers have a binding contract?
   a. No, because Fox failed to sign and return Summers's letter.
   b. No, because Fox's letter was a counteroffer.
   c. Yes, because Summers's offer was validly accepted.
   d. Yes, because Summers's silence is an implied acceptance of Fox's letter (Law, #2, 0462).

3. On June 15, Peters orally offered to sell a used lawn mower to Mason for $125. Peters specified that Mason had until June 20 to accept the offer. On June 16, Peters received an offer to purchase the lawn mower for $150 from Bronson, Mason's neighbor. Peters accepted Bronson's offer. On June 17, Mason saw Bronson using the lawn mower and was told the mower had been sold to Bronson. Mason immediately wrote to Peters to accept the June 15 offer. Which of the following statements is correct?
   a. Mason's acceptance would be effective when received by Peters.
   b. Mason's acceptance would be effective when mailed.
   c. Peters's offer had been revoked and Mason's acceptance was ineffective.
   d. Peters was obligated to keep the June 15 offer open until June 20 (Law, #13, 3095).

CHAPTER 13

Capacity and Genuine Assent

Learning Outcomes

After studying this chapter, you should be able to

LO.1 Define contractual capacity

LO.2 Explain the extent and effect of avoidance of a contract by a minor

LO.3 Distinguish unilateral mistakes and mutual mistakes

LO.4 Explain the difference between intentional misrepresentation, negligent misrepresentation, and puffery

LO.5 Explain the difference between undue influence and duress

A *contract* is a binding agreement. This agreement must be made between parties who have the capacity to do so. They must also truly agree so that all parties have really consented to the contract. This chapter explores the elements of contractual capacity of the parties and the genuineness of their assent.

13-1 Contractual Capacity

Some persons lack contractual capacity, a lack that embraces both those who have a status incapacity, such as minors, and those who have a factual incapacity, such as persons who are insane.

13-1a Contractual Capacity Defined

contractual capacity–ability to understand that a contract is being made and to understand its general meaning.

Contractual capacity is the ability to understand that a contract is being made and to understand its general meaning. However, the fact that a person does not understand the full legal meaning of a contract does not mean that contractual capacity is lacking. Everyone is presumed to have capacity unless it is proven that capacity is lacking or there is status incapacity.[1] **For Example,** Jacqueline, aged 22, entered into a contract with Sunrise Storage Co. but later claimed that it was not binding because she did not understand several clauses in the printed contract. The contract was binding. No evidence supported her claim that she lacked capacity to contract or to understand its subject. Contractual capacity can exist even though a party does not understand every provision of the contract.

Status Incapacity

Over the centuries, the law has declared that some classes of persons lack contractual capacity. The purpose is to protect these classes by giving them the power to get out of unwise contracts. Of these classes, the most important today is the class identified as minors.

Until recent times, some other classes were held to lack contractual capacity in order to discriminate against them. Examples are married women and aliens. Still other classes, such as persons convicted of and sentenced for a felony, were held to lack contractual capacity in order to punish them. Today, these discriminatory and punitive incapacities have largely disappeared. Married women have the same contractual capacity as unmarried persons.

By virtue of international treaties, the discrimination against aliens has been removed.

CASE SUMMARY

We Really Mean Equal Rights

FACTS: An Alabama statute provided that a married woman could not sell her land without the consent of her husband. Montgomery made a contract to sell land she owned to Peddy. Montgomery's husband did not consent to the sale. Montgomery did not perform the contract and Peddy sued her. The defense was raised that the contract was void and could not be enforced because of the statute. Peddy claimed that the statute was unconstitutional.

DECISION: The statute was unconstitutional. Constitutions, both federal and state, guarantee all persons the equal protection of the law. Married women are denied this equal protection when they are treated differently than married men and unmarried women. The fact that such unequal treatment had once been regarded as proper does not justify its modern continuation. **[*Peddy v. Montgomery*, 345 So. 2d 988 (Ala. 1991)]**

[1] In re *Adoption of Smith*, 578 So. 2d 988 (La. App. 1991).

Factual Incapacity

A *factual incapacity* contrasts with incapacity imposed because of the class or group to which a person belongs. A factual incapacity may exist when, because of a mental condition caused by medication, drugs, alcohol, illness, or age, a person does not understand that a contract is being made or understand its general nature. However, mere mental weakness does not incapacitate a person from contracting. It is sufficient if the individual has enough mental capacity to understand, to a reasonable extent, the nature and effect of what he is doing.[2]

13-1b Minors

Minors may make contracts.[3] To protect them, however, the law has always treated minors as a class lacking contractual capacity.

Who Is a Minor?

At common law, any person, male or female, under 21 years of age was a minor. At common law, minority ended the day before the 21st birthday. The "day before the birthday" rule is still followed, but the age of majority has been reduced from 21 years to 18 years.

CPA

Minor's Power to Avoid Contracts

With exceptions that will be noted later, a contract made by a minor is voidable at the election of the minor. **For Example,** Adorian Deck, a minor, created a Twitter feed titled "@OMGFacts." The feed collected and republished interesting and trivial facts from other sources on the Internet. It was subscribed to by over 300,000 Twitter users, including some celebrities. Spatz, Inc., entered into a joint venture with Deck as described in a written contract signed by both parties, under which Spatz would expand the Twitter feed into a suite of Internet products, including a Web site and a Youtube.com video channel. In an "OMG-moment" prior to his 18th birthday, Deck notified Spatz, Inc., that he wished to disaffirm the parties' agreement. This disaffirmation by a minor rescinded the entire contract, rendering it a nullity.[4] The minor may affirm or ratify the contract on attaining majority by performing the contract, by expressly approving the contract, or by allowing a reasonable time to lapse without avoiding the contract.

CPA **What Constitutes Avoidance?** A minor may avoid or *disaffirm* a contract by any expression of an intention to repudiate the contract. Any act inconsistent with the continuing validity of the contract is also an avoidance.

CPA **Time for Avoidance.** A minor can disaffirm a contract only during minority and for a reasonable time after attaining majority. After the lapse of a reasonable time, the contract is deemed ratified and cannot be avoided by the minor.

CPA **Minor's Misrepresentation of Age.** Generally, the fact that the minor has misrepresented his or her age does not affect the minor's power to disaffirm the contract. Some states hold that such fraud of a minor bars contract avoidance. Some states permit the minor

[2] *Fisher v. Schefers*, 656 N.W.2d 591 (Minn. App. 2003).
[3] *Buffington v. State Automobile Mut. Ins. Co.*, 384 S.E.2d 873 (Ga. App. 1989).
[4] *Deck v. Spatz, Inc.*, 2011 WL 775067 (E.D. Cal. Sept. 27, 2011).

to disaffirm the contract in such a case but require the minor to pay for any damage to the property received under the contract.

In any case, the other party to the contract may disaffirm it because of the minor's fraud.

CPA

Restitution by Minor after Avoidance

When a minor disaffirms a contract, the question arises as to what the minor must return to the other contracting party.

Original Consideration Intact. When a minor still has what was received from the other party, the minor, on avoiding the contract, must return it to the other party or offer to do so. That is, the minor must put things back to the original position or, as it is called, restore the **status quo ante.**

status quo ante–original positions of the parties.

Original Consideration Damaged or Destroyed. What happens if the minor cannot return what has been received because it has been spent, used, damaged, or destroyed? The minor's right to disaffirm the contract is not affected. The minor can still disaffirm the contract and is required to return only what remains. The fact that nothing remains or that what remains is damaged does not bar the right to disaffirm the contract. In states that follow the common law rule, minors can thus refuse to pay for what has been received under a contract or can get back what had been paid or given even though they do not have anything to return or return property in a damaged condition. There is, however, a trend to limit this rule.

Recovery of Property by Minor on Avoidance

When a minor disaffirms a contract, the other contracting party must return the money received. Any property received from the minor must also be returned. If the property has been sold to a third person who did not know of the original seller's minority, the minor cannot get the property back. In such cases, however, the minor is entitled to recover the property's monetary value or the money received by the other contracting party.

CPA

Contracts for Necessaries

A minor can disaffirm a contract for necessaries but must pay the reasonable value for furnished necessaries.

What Constitutes Necessaries? Originally, **necessaries** were limited to those things absolutely necessary for the sustenance and shelter of the minor. Thus limited, the term would extend only to food, clothing, and lodging. In the course of time, the rule was relaxed to extend generally to things relating to the health, education, and comfort of the minor. Thus, the rental of a house used by a married minor is a necessary.

necessaries–things indispensable or absolutely necessary for the sustenance of human life.

Liability of Parent or Guardian. When a third person supplies the parents or guardian of a minor with goods or services that the minor needs, the minor is not liable for these necessaries because the third person's contract is with the parent or guardian, not with the minor.

When necessary medical care is provided a minor, a parent is liable at common law for the medical expenses provided the minor child. However, at common law, the child can be held contractually liable for her necessary medical expenses when the parent is unable or unwilling to pay.

CASE SUMMARY

The Concussion and Legal Repercussions

FACTS: Sixteen-year-old Michelle Schmidt was injured in an automobile accident and taken to Prince George's Hospital. Although the identities of Michelle and her parents were originally unknown, the hospital provided her emergency medical care for a brain concussion and an open scalp wound. She incurred hospital expenses of $1,756.24. Ms. Schmidt was insured through her father's insurance company. It issued a check to be used to cover medical expenses. However, the funds were used to purchase a car for Ms. Schmidt. Since she was a minor when the services were rendered, she believed that she had no legal obligation to pay. After Ms. Schmidt attained her eighteenth birthday and failed to pay the hospital, it brought suit against her.

DECISION: Judgment for the hospital. The prevailing modern rule is that minors' contracts are voidable except for necessaries. The doctrine of necessaries states that a minor may be held liable for necessaries, including medical necessaries when parents are unwilling to pay. The court concluded that Ms. Schmidt's father demonstrated a clear unwillingness to pay by using the insurance money to purchase a car rather than pay the hospital. The policy behind the necessaries exception is for the benefit of minors because the procurement of such is essential to their existence, and if they were not permitted to bind themselves, they might not be able to obtain the necessaries. [***Schmidt v. Prince George's Hospital*, 784 A.2d 1112 (Md. 2001)**]

CPA Ratification of Former Minor's Voidable Contract

A former minor cannot disaffirm a contract that has been ratified after reaching majority.[5]

CPA **What Constitutes Ratification?** Ratification consists of any words or conduct of the former minor manifesting an intent to be bound by the terms of a contract made while a minor.

CPA **Form of Ratification.** Generally, no special form is required for ratification of a minor's voidable contract, although in some states a written ratification or declaration of intention is required.

CPA **Time for Ratification.** A person can disaffirm a contract any time during minority and for a reasonable time after that but, of necessity, can ratify a contract only after attaining majority. The minor must have attained majority, or the ratification would itself be regarded as voidable.

Contracts That Minors Cannot Avoid

Statutes in many states deprive a minor of the right to avoid an educational loan;[6] a contract for medical care; a contract made while running a business; a contract approved by a court; a contract made in performance of a legal duty; and a contract relating to bank accounts, insurance policies, or corporate stock.

Liability of Third Person for a Minor's Contract

The question arises as to whether parents are bound by the contract of their minor child. The question of whether a person cosigning a minor's contract is bound if the contract is avoided also arises.

[5] *Fletcher v. Marshall*, 632 N.E.2d 1105 (Ill. App. 1994).

[6] A Model Student Capacity to Borrow Act makes educational loans binding on minors in Arizona, Mississippi, New Mexico, North Dakota, Oklahoma, and Washington. This act was reclassified from a uniform act to a model act by the Commissioners on Uniform State Law, indicating that uniformity was viewed as unimportant and that the matter was primarily local in character.

Liability of Parent. Ordinarily, a parent is not liable on a contract made by a minor child. The parent may be liable, however, if the child is acting as the agent of the parent in making the contract. Also, the parent is liable to a seller for the reasonable value of necessaries supplied by the seller to the child if the parent had deserted the child.

Liability of Cosigner. When the minor makes a contract, another person, such as a parent or a friend, may sign along with the minor to make the contract more acceptable to the third person.

With respect to the other contracting party, the cosigner is bound independently of the minor. Consequently, if the minor disaffirms the contract, the cosigner remains bound by it. When the debt to the creditor is actually paid, the obligation of the cosigner is discharged.

If the minor disaffirms a sales contract but does not return the goods, the cosigner remains liable for the purchase price.

13-1c Mentally Incompetent Persons

A person with a mental disorder may be so disabled as to lack capacity to make a contract. An individual seeking to avoid the consequences of a contract due to incompetency must demonstrate that at the time the agreement was executed he or she was suffering from a mental illness or defect, which rendered the party incapable of comprehending the nature of the transaction, or that by reason of mental illness the party was unable to control his or her conduct.[7] **For Example,** a guardian established that Ms. Brunson suffered from a mental illness at the time the challenged mortgage documents were executed, and the contract was set aside by the court.[8] However, where a guardian's evidence was insufficient to demonstrate that at the time two mortgage transactions occurred, one in 1999 for $212,000 and a second in 2003 for $7,628.08, that Mr. and Mrs. Haedrich were incompetent or that Washington Mutual Bank knew or was put on notice of their purported incapacity, the court refused to vacate the judgments of foreclosure.[9]

Effect of Incompetency

An incompetent person may ordinarily avoid a contract in the same manner as a minor. Upon the removal of the disability (that is, upon becoming competent), the formerly incompetent person can either ratify or disaffirm the contract.

A mentally incompetent person or his estate is liable for the reasonable value of all necessaries furnished that individual.

A current trend in the law is to treat an incompetent person's contract as binding when its terms and the surrounding circumstances are reasonable and the person is unable to restore the other contracting party to the status quo ante.

CASE SUMMARY

Friends Should Tell Friends about Medical Leaves

FACTS: Wilcox Manufacturing Group, Inc., did business under the name of Superior Automation Co., and Howard Wilcox served as Superior's president. As part of a loan "lease agreement" of $50,000 executed on December 5, 2000, Superior was to repay Marketing Services of Indiana (MSI) $67,213.80 over the course of 60 months. Wilcox gave a

[7] *Horrell v. Horrell,* 900 N.Y.S.2d 666 (2d Dept. 2010).

[8] In re *Doar,* 900 N.Y.S.2d 593 (Sup. Ct. Queens Co., Dec. 18, 2009).

[9] *JP Morgan Chase Bank v. Haedrich,* 918 N.Y.S.2d 398 (Sup. Ct. Nassau County, Oct. 15, 2010).

Friends Should Tell Friends about Medical Leaves continued

personal guarantee for full and prompt payment. Wilcox had been a patient of psychiatrist Dr. Shaun Wood since May 21, 1999, and was diagnosed as suffering from bipolar disorder during the period from June 2000 to January 2001. On June 9, 2000, Wilcox told Dr. Wood he was having problems functioning at work, and Dr. Wood determined that Wilcox was experiencing lithium toxicity, which lasted for 10 months, during which time he suffered from impaired cognitive functions that limited his capacity to understand the nature and quality of his actions and judgments. Superior made monthly payments though to October 28, 2003, and the balance owed at that time was $33,031.37. MSI sued Wilcox personally and the corporation for breach of contract. The defendants raised the defense of lack of capacity and contended that they were not liable on the loan signed by the corporate president when he was incapacitated.

DECISION: Judgment for MSI. The acts or deeds of a person of unsound mind whose condition has not been judicially ascertained and who is not under guardianship are voidable and not absolutely void. The acts are subject to ratification or disaffirmance on removal of the disability. The latest Wilcox could have been experiencing the effects of lithium toxicity was October 2001. Wilcox thus regained his capacity by that date. No attempt was made to disaffirm the contract. Rather, monthly payments continued to be made for a year and one-half before the payments ceased. The contract was thus ratified by the conduct of the president of Superior after he recovered his ability to understand the nature of the contract. [***Wilcox Manufacturing, Inc., v. Marketing Services of Indiana, Inc.***, **832 N.E.2d 559 (Ind. App. 2005)**]

Appointment of Guardian

If a court appoints a guardian for the incompetent person, a contract made by that person before the appointment may be ratified or, in some cases, disaffirmed by the guardian. If the incompetent person makes a contract after a guardian has been appointed, the contract is void and not merely voidable.

13-1d Intoxicated Persons

The capacity of a party to contract and the validity of the contract are not affected by the party's being impaired by alcohol at the time of making the contract so long as the party knew that a contract was being made.

If the degree of intoxication is such that a person does not know that a contract is being made, the contract is voidable by that person. On becoming sober, the individual may avoid or rescind the contract. However, an unreasonable delay in taking steps to set aside a known contract entered into while intoxicated may bar the intoxicated person from asserting this right.[10]

Excessive intoxication is a viable defense to contracts arising between casinos and their patrons. Thus, when a casino comes to court to enforce a marker debt against a patron, it seeks to enforce a contractual debt, and the patron is entitled to raise the common law defense that his capacity to contract was impaired by voluntary intoxication.[11]

The courts treat impairment caused by the use of drugs the same as impairment caused by the excessive use of alcohol.

CPA

13-2 Mistake

The validity of a contract may be affected by the fact that one or both of the parties made a mistake. In some cases, the mistake may be caused by the misconduct of one of the parties.

[10] *Diedrich v. Diedrich*, 424 N.W.2d 580 (Minn. App. 1988).
[11] See *Adamar of New Jersey v. Luber*, 2011 WL 1325978 (D. N.J. Mar. 30, 2011).

13-2a Unilateral Mistake

A *unilateral mistake*—that is, a mistake by only one of the parties—as to a fact does not affect the contract when the mistake is unknown to the other contracting party.[12] When a contract is made on the basis of a quoted price, the validity of the contract is not affected by the fact that the party furnishing the quotation made a mathematical mistake in computing the price if there was no reason for the other party to recognize that there had been a mistake.[13] The party making the mistake may avoid the contract if the other contracting party knew or should have known of the mistake.

CASE SUMMARY

Bumper Sticker: "Mistakes Happen!" (or words to that effect)

FACTS: Lipton-U City, LLC (Lipton), and Shurgard Storage Centers discussed the sale of a self-storage facility for approximately $7 million. Lipton became concerned about an existing environmental condition and, as a result, the parties agreed to a lease with an option to buy rather than an outright sale. The contract specified a 10-year lease with an annual rent starting at $636,000 based on a property valuation of $7 million. Section 2.4 of the contract contained the purchase option. Shurgard representatives circulated an e-mail with a copy to Lipton representatives that a purchase option price would be based on six months of *annualized* net operating income. When the lease was submitted to Lipton, inexplicably any language regarding multiplying by 2 or annualizing the net income was omitted. Donn Lipton announced to his attorneys that the lease reflected his successful negotiation of a purchase option based on six months of *unannualized* net operating income. Eight months after signing the lease, Lipton sought to exercise the purchase option under Section 2.4 and stated a price of $2,918,103. Shurgard rejected the offer and filed suit for rescission, citing the misunderstanding about the price terms.

DECISION: Judgment for Shurgard. Under state law, if a material mistake made by one party is known to the other party or is of such a character or circumstances that the other party should know of it, the mistaken party has a right to rescission. Lipton knew or should have known of the mistake of the lessor (Shurgard) in believing that the purchase price would be based on a full year of net operating income rather than six months of net operating income. Lipton was notified by e-mail that the six-month figure was to be annualized and knew that the property was valued at approximately $7 million. [***Shurgard Storage Centers v. Lipton-U City, LLC*, 394 F.3d 1041 (8th Cir. 2005)**]

13-2b Mutual Mistake

When both parties enter into a contract under a mutually mistaken understanding concerning a basic assumption of fact or law on which the contract is made, the contract is voidable by the adversely affected party if the mistake has a material effect on the agreed exchange.[14]

A contract based on *a mutual mistake in judgment* is not voidable by the adversely affected party. **For Example,** if both parties believe that a colt is not fast enough to develop into a competitive race horse and effect a sale accordingly, when the animal later develops into the winner of the Preakness as a three-year-old, the seller cannot rescind the contract based on mutual mistake because the mutual mistake was a mistake in judgment. In contrast, when two parties to a contract believe a cow to be barren at the time they contract for its sale, but before delivery of the animal to the buyer, it is discovered that the assumption was mistaken, such is a mutual mistake of fact making the contract void.[15]

[12] *Truck South Inc. v. Patel*, 528 S.E.2d 424 (S.C. 2000).
[13] *Procan Construction Co. v. Oceanside Development Corp.*, 539 N.Y.S.2d 437 (App. Div. 2d 1989).
[14] See *Browning v. Howerton*, 966 P.2d 367 (Wash. App. 1998).
[15] See *Sherwood v. Walker*, 66 Mich. 568 (1887).

13-2c Mistake in the Transcription or Printing of the Contract: Reformation

In some instances, the parties make an oral agreement, and in the process of committing it to writing or printing it from a manuscript, a phrase, term, or segment is inadvertently left out of the final, signed document. The aggrieved party may petition the court to **reform** the contract to reflect the actual agreement of the parties. However, the burden of proof is heightened to clear and convincing evidence that such a mistake was made. **For Example,** Jewell Coke Co. used an illustration to explain a complex pricing formula in its negotiations with the ArcelMittal steel mill in Cleveland, Ohio, for a long-term contract for the supply of blast furnace coke. The multiplier in the illustration was the actual intent of the parties, according to ArcelMittal, but during the drafting process the multiplier was accidently inverted, resulting in an overpayment of $100,000,000 when discovered, and which potentially could result in an overpayment of over $1 billion over the life of the contract. If proven, the court will reform the contract to reflect the intentions of the parties at the time the contract was made.[16]

reformation–remedy by which a written instrument is corrected when it fails to express the actual intent of both parties because of fraud, accident, or mistake.

13-3 Deception

One of the parties may have been misled by a fraudulent statement. In such situations, there is no true or genuine assent to the contract, and it is voidable at the innocent party's option.

FIGURE 13-1 Avoidance of Contract

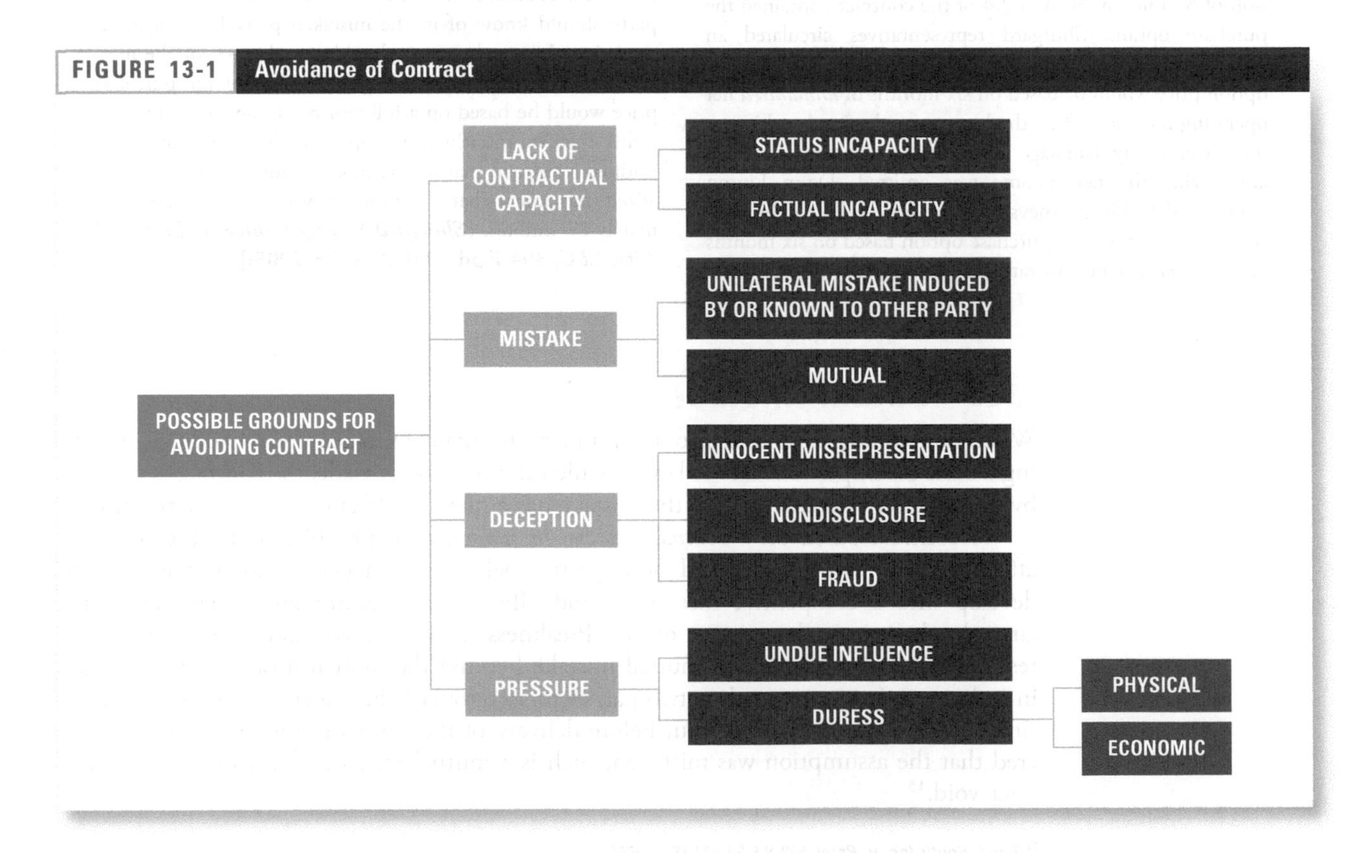

[16] *ArcelMittal Cleveland, Inc. v. Jewell Coke Co,* 750 F. Supp. 2d 839 (N.D. Ohio 2010).

13-3a Intentional Misrepresentation

Fraud is a generic term embracing all multifarious means that human ingenuity can devise and that are resorted to by one individual to get advantage over another. It is classified in the law as a *tort*. However, where a party is induced into making a contract by a material misrepresentation of fact, this form of fraudulent activity adversely affects the genuineness of the assent of the innocent party, and this type of fraud is the focus of our discussion in the chapters on contracts.

13-3b Fraud

fraud–making of a false statement of a past or existing fact, with knowledge of its falsity or with reckless indifference as to its truth, with the intent to cause another to rely thereon, and such person does rely thereon and is harmed thereby.

Fraud is the making of a material misrepresentation (or false statement) of fact with (1) knowledge of its falsity or reckless indifference to its truth, (2) the intent that the listener rely on it, (3) the result that the listener does so rely, and (4) the consequence that the listener is harmed.[17]

To prove fraud, there must be a material misrepresentation of fact. Such a misrepresentation is one that is likely to induce a reasonable person to assent to a contract. **For Example,** Traci Hanson-Suminski purchased a used Honda Civic from Arlington Acura for $10,899. On a test drive with salesperson Mike Dobin, Traci noticed a vibration in the steering wheel and asked if the car had been in an accident. Dobin said, "No, it's fine." The dealer put new tires on the car and Traci bought it. Traci testified that she would not have purchased the car if she had known it had been in an accident. Eight months later when she sought to trade the car for another car, she was shown a Carfax Vehicle History Report, which indicated the car had been in an accident. The dealer testified that all its sales associates are trained to respond to questions about vehicle history with "I don't know." It asserted that Dobin's statement was mere puffery. The court found that Dobin's statement was a material misrepresentation of the car's history, inducing the plaintiff to purchase the car. It rejected outright the dealer's assertion of puffery, which it defined as meaningless superlatives that no reasonable person would take seriously.[18]

Statement of Opinion or Value

Ordinarily, matters of opinion of value or opinions about future events are not regarded as fraudulent. Forecasts about the future state of financial or real estate markets must be regarded not as fact, but as predictions or speculations.

A statement of opinion may be fraudulent when the speaker knows of past or present facts that make the opinion false. **For Example,** Biff Williams, the sales manager of Abrasives International (AI), sold an exclusive dealership selling AI products to Fred Farkas for $100,000 down and a 3 percent royalty on all gross proceeds. Williams told Farkas, "You have the potential to earn $300,000 to $400,000 a year in this territory." He later added, "We have four dealerships making that kind of money today." Farkas was thus persuaded by the business potential of the territory and executed the purchase contract. He later found out that AI had a total of just four distributorships at that time, and that the actual earnings of the highest producer was $43,000. Assertions of opinions about the future profit potential alone may not amount to fraud, but the assertion of present fact—that four dealerships were presently earning $300,000 to $400,000 a year—was a material misstatement of fact that made the forecast sales potential for Farkas's territory a

[17] *Maack v. Resource Design & Construction, Inc.*, 875 P.2d 570 (Utah 1994); *Bortz v. Noon*, 729 A.2d 555 (Pa. 1999).
[18] *Hanson-Suminski v. Rohrman Midwest Motors Inc.*, 858 N.E.2d 194 (Ill. App. 2008).

material misstatement of fact as well. Because there were reliance and damages, Farkas can rescind the contract based on fraud and recover all damages resulting from it.[19]

CASE SUMMARY

Remember This One: Mere Opinions Are Not Actionable at All!

FACTS: In approximately July 2005 a loan broker and an appraiser working for a subsidiary of Bank of America appraised the Cansinos home at a fair market value of $620,000. Based on that appraisal and other representations by lending personnel, the Cansinos elected to refinance their home with a $496,000 adjustable rate mortgage. Lending personnel told them their home would appreciate and they would be able to sell or refinance the home at a later date before having to make higher monthly loan payments. In 2010, the Cansinos discovered that their home was valued between $350,000 and $400,000. Soon thereafter they stopped making payments on the 2005 loan. As of March 2012 the monthly payments were approximately $1,960, the balance due on the loan was approximately $626,000, and the fair market value of the home was approximately $350,000. The trial court dismissed the Cansinos fraud action against B of A, and they appealed.

DECISION: Judgment against the Cansinos. Concerning B of A's representation on the future appreciation of the Cansinos' home, such statements or predictions regarding future events are deemed to be mere opinions, which are not actionable. And, any financial market forecast must be regarded not as a fact but as prediction or speculation. While the Casinos state the home was valued between $350,000 and $400,000 in 2010, this does not support their claim that the 2005 appraisal of $620,000 was a misrepresentation. [***Cansinos v. Bank of America*, 169 Cal. Rptr. 3d 619 (Cal. App. 2014)**]

Justifiable Reliance on Statement

A fraudulent statement made by one party has no importance unless the other party relies on the statement's truth. **For Example,** after making thorough tests of Nagel Company's pump, Allstate Services Company ordered 100 pumps. It later sued Nagel on the ground that advertising statements made about the pumps were false. Allstate Services cannot impose fraud liability on Nagel for the advertisements, even if they were false, because it had not relied on them in making the purchase but had acted on the basis of its own tests.

Disclaimer of reliance clauses are common in commerce these days. Trusting the honesty of salespersons or their disarming statements, an individual may knowingly or obliviously agree in a sales agreement containing a disclaimer of reliance clause that no representations have been made to him or her, while at the same time believing and relying upon representations, which in fact have been made and in fact are false and but for which the individual would not have made the agreement. Ordinarily, purchasers cannot assert justifiable reliance on statements made by sellers that directly contradict clear and specific terms of their written contracts.[20]

[19] The Federal Trade Commission and state agencies have franchise disclosure rules that will penalize the franchisor in this case. See Chapter 40.

[20] But see *Italian Cowboy Partners, Ltd. v. Prudential Insurance*, 341 S.W.3d 323 (Tex. 2011) where a split decision of the Texas Supreme Court determined that the following contract language was not a disclaimer of reliance to negate the "justifiable reliance" element of a fraud claim.

> *Tenant acknowledges that neither Landlord nor Landlord's agents, employees or contractors have made any representations or promises with respect to the Site, the Shopping Center or this lease except as expressly set forth herein.*

The court determined that the property manager's representations to the future tenant that the building was problem free; no problems had been experienced by the prior tenant; and the building was a perfect restaurant site were false statements of fact known to be false when made. Testimony indicated that the manager herself had personally experienced a sewer gas odor in the prior tenant's restaurant she described as "almost unbearable" and "ungodly."

CASE SUMMARY

Are Disclaimer of Reliance Clauses a License to Lie?

FACTS: David Sarif and seven other purchasers (Purchasers) each bought a unit at the 26-story Twelve Atlantic Station (Twelve) condominiums in 2005 and 2006. They sued the developers and the brokers for fraud in the inducement and negligent misrepresentation. They alleged that at the time of their purchases, the developers were advertising "spectacular city views" of Atlanta while they had already undertaken to develop the 46-story Atlantic Station tower directly across the street, and that their brokers were advising the Purchasers that any future development to the south of Twelve would be low- to mid-rise office buildings. Purchasers allege that they paid substantial premiums for their views of the city from the south side of the building, which is now blocked by the 46-story building. Each Purchaser signed an agreement containing a provision stating that "[t]he views from and natural light available to the Unit may change over time due to, among other circumstances, additional development and the removal or addition of landscaping"; a disclaimer at the top of the first page as required by the Georgia Condominium Act stating that "ORAL REPRESENTATIONS CANNOT BE RELIED UPON AS CORRECTLY STATING THE REPRESENTATIONS OF SELLER"; an express disclaimer in which Purchasers affirmed that they did not rely upon any representations or statements of the brokers; and a comprehensive merger clause.

DECISION: Set forth in the written contract of the parties, all of the Purchasers signed agreements that expressly stated that views may change over time, and oral representations of the sellers could not be relied on. Justifiable reliance is an essential element of a fraud or negligent misrepresentation claim. Since the Purchasers are estopped from relying on representations outside their agreements, they cannot sustain a case that requires justifiable reliance. [***Novare Group, Inc. v. Sarif,*** **718 S.E.2d 304 (Ga. 2011)**]

Proof of Harm

For an individual to recover damages for fraud, proof of harm to that individual is required. The injured party may recover the actual losses suffered as a result of the fraud as well as punitive damages when the fraud is gross or oppressive. The injured party has the right to have the court order the rescission or cancellation of the contract that has been induced by fraud.[21]

13-3c Negligent Misrepresentation

While fraud requires the critical element of a known or recklessly made falsity, a claim of negligent misrepresentation contains similar elements except it is predicated on a negligently made false statement. That is, the speaker failed to exercise due care regarding material information communicated to the listener but did not intend to deceive. When the negligent misrepresentation of a material fact that the listener relies on results in harm to the listener, the contract is voidable at the option of the injured party. If fraud is proven, as opposed to misrepresentation, recovery of punitive damages in addition to actual damages can occur. Because it may be difficult to prove the intentional falsity required for fraud, it is common for a lawsuit to allege both a claim of fraud and a claim of negligent misrepresentation. **For Example,** Marshall Armstrong worked for Fred Collins, owner of Collins Entertainment, Inc., a conglomerate that owns and operates video games. Collins Entertainment's core product, video poker, was hurt by a court ruling that prohibited cash payouts, which adversely affected its business and resulted in a debt of $13 to $20 million to SouthTrust bank. Chief operating officer Armstrong, on his

[21] *Paden v. Murray,* 523 S.E.2d 75 (Ga. App. 2000).

own time, came up with the idea of modifying bingo machines as a new venture. To exploit this idea, Collins agreed to form a corporation called Skillpins Inc., that was unencumbered by the SouthTrust debt and to give Armstrong a 10 percent ownership interest. After a period, with some 300 Skillpins machines producing income, Armstrong discovered the revenues from the new venture on the debt-laden Collins Entertainment profit and loss statement, not that of Skillpins, Inc. Armstrong's suit for both fraud and intentional misrepresentation was successful. In addition to actual damages, he received $1.8 million in punitive damages for fraud.[22]

13-3d Nondisclosure

Under certain circumstances, nondisclosure serves to make a contract voidable, especially when the nondisclosure consists of active concealment.

General Rule of Nonliability

Ordinarily, a party to a contract has no duty to volunteer information to the other party. **For Example,** if Fox does not ask Tehan any questions, Tehan is not under any duty to make a full statement of material facts. Consequently, the nondisclosure of information that is not asked for does not impose fraud liability or impair the validity of a contract.

CASE SUMMARY

Welcome to the Seesaw: Buyer versus Seller

FACTS: Dalarna Management Corporation owned a building constructed on a pier on a lake. There were repeated difficulties with rainwater leaking into the building, and water damage was visible in the interior of the building. Dalarna made a contract to sell the building to Curran. Curran made several inspections of the building and had the building inspected twice by a licensed engineer. The engineer reported there were signs of water leaks. Curran assigned his contract to Puget Sound Service Corporation, which then purchased the building from Dalarna. Puget Sound spent approximately $118,000 attempting to stop the leaks. Puget Sound then sued Dalarna for damages, claiming that Dalarna's failure to disclose the extent of the water leakage problem constituted fraud.

DECISION: Judgment for Dalarna. Curran was aware there was a water leakage problem, and therefore the burden was on the buyer to ask questions to determine the extent of the problem. There was no duty on the seller to volunteer the extent of the water damage merely because it had been a continuing problem that was more than just a simple leak. The court reached this conclusion because the law "balances the harshness of the former rule of caveat emptor [let the buyer beware] with the equally undesirable alternative of courts standing in loco parentis [in the place of a parent] to parties transacting business." **[*Puget Sound Service Corp. v. Dalarna Management Corp.*, 752 P.2d 1353 (Wash. App. 1988)]**

Exceptions

The following exceptions to the general rule of nonliability for nondisclosure exist.

Unknown Defect or Condition. A duty may exist in some states for a seller who knows of a serious defect or condition to disclose that information to the other party where the defect or condition is unknown to the other person and is of such a nature that it is unlikely that the other person would discover it. However, a defendant who had no knowledge of the defect cannot be held liable for failure to disclose it.[23]

[22] *Armstrong v. Collins,* 621 S.E.2d 368 (S.C. App. 2005).
[23] *Nesbitt v. Dunn,* 672 So. 2d 226 (La. App. 1996).

confidential relationship–relationship in which, because of the legal status of the parties or their respective physical or mental conditions or knowledge, one party places full confidence and trust in the other.

Confidential Relationship. If parties stand in a **confidential relationship,** failure to disclose information may be regarded as fraudulent. **For Example,** in an attorney-client relationship,[24] the attorney has a duty to reveal anything that is material to the client's interest when dealing with the client. The attorney's silence has the same legal consequence as a knowingly made false statement that there was no material fact to be told the client.

Active Concealment. Nondisclosure may be more than the passive failure to volunteer information. It may consist of a positive act of hiding information from the other party by physical concealment, or it may consist of knowingly or recklessly furnishing the wrong information. Such conduct constitutes fraud. **For Example,** when Nigel wanted to sell his house, he covered the wooden cellar beams with plywood to hide extensive termite damage. He sold the house to Kuehne, who sued Nigel for damages on later discovering the termite damage. Nigel claimed he had no duty to volunteer information about the termites, but by covering the damage with plywood, he committed active fraud as if he had made a false statement that there were no termites.

13-4 Pressure

What appears to be an agreement may not in fact be voluntary because one of the parties entered into it as the result of undue influence or physical or economic duress.

CPA

13-4a Undue Influence

An aged parent may entrust all business affairs to a trusted child; a disabled person may rely on a nurse; a client may follow implicitly whatever an attorney recommends. The relationship may be such that for practical purposes, one person is helpless in the hands of the other. When such a confidential relationship exists, it is apparent that the parent, the disabled person, or the client is not exercising free will in making a contract suggested by the child, nurse, or attorney but is merely following the will of the other person. Because of the great possibility of unfair advantage, the law presumes that the dominating person exerts **undue influence** on the other person whenever the dominating person obtains any benefit from a contract made with the dominated person.[25] The contract is then voidable. It may be set aside by the dominated person unless the dominating person can prove that, at the time the contract was made, no unfair advantage had been taken.

undue influence–influence that is asserted upon another person by one who dominates that person.

The class of confidential relationships is not well defined. It ordinarily includes the relationships of parent and child, guardian and ward, physician and patient, and attorney and client, and any other relationship of trust and confidence in which one party exercises a control or influence over another.

Whether undue influence exists is a difficult question for courts (ordinarily juries) to determine. The law does not regard every influence as undue.

An essential element of undue influence is that the person making the contract does not exercise free will. In the absence of a recognized type of confidential relationship, such as that between parent and child, courts are likely to take the attitude that the person who claims to have been dominated was merely persuaded and there was therefore no undue influence.

[24] In re *Boss Trust,* 487 N.W.2d 256 (Minn. App. 1992).
[25] *Ayers v. Shaffer,* 748 S.E.2d 83 (Va. 2013).

CASE SUMMARY

Cards and Small Talk Sometimes Make the Sale

FACTS: John Lentner owned the farm adjacent to the Schefers. He moved off the farm to a nursing home in 1999. In the fall of 2000, Kristine Schefers visited Lentner at the nursing home some 15 times, engaging in small talk and watching him play cards. In the spring of 2001, Lentner agreed to sell his farm to Kristine and her husband Thomas for $50,000 plus $10,000 for machinery and tools. Kristine drove Lentner to the bank to get the deed from his safe deposit box. She also took him to the abstractor who drafted the transfer documents. Soon after the sale, Earl Fisher was appointed special conservator of Lentner. Fisher sought to set aside the transaction, asserting that Kristine's repeated visits to the nursing home and her failure to involve Lentner's other family members in the transaction unduly influenced Lentner.

DECISION: Judgment for Thomas and Kristine Schefers. Undue influence is shown when the person making the contract ceased to act of his own free volition and became a mere puppet of the wielder of that influence. Mere speculation alone that Lentner was a "puppet" acting according to the wishes of Schefers is insufficient to set aside the sale. Undue influence was not established. **[*Fisher v. Schefers*, 656 N.W.2d 592 (Minn. App. 2003)]**

CPA

13-4b Duress

A party may enter into a contract to avoid a threatened danger. The danger threatened may be a physical harm to person or property, called **physical duress,** or it may be a threat of financial loss, called **economic duress.**

physical duress–threat of physical harm to person or property.

economic duress–threat of financial loss.

duress–conduct that deprives the victim of free will and that generally gives the victim the right to set aside any transaction entered into under such circumstances.

Physical Duress

A person makes a contract under **duress** when there is such violence or threat of violence that the person is deprived of free will and makes the contract to avoid harm. The threatened harm may be directed either at a near relative of the contracting party or against the contracting party. If a contract is made under duress, the resulting agreement is voidable at the victim's election.

Agreements made to bring an end to mass disorder or violence are ordinarily not binding contracts because they were obtained by duress.

One may not void a contract on grounds of duress merely because it was entered into with great reluctance and proves to be very disadvantageous to that individual.[26]

Economic Duress

Economic duress is a condition in which one is induced by a wrongful act or threat of another to make a contract under circumstances that deprive one of the exercise of his own free will.[27] **For Example,** Richard Case, an importer of parts used to manufacture high-quality mountain bicycles, had a contractual duty to supply Katahdin Manufacturing Company's needs for specifically manufactured stainless steel brakes for the 2016 season. Katahdin's president, Bill Read, was in constant contact with Case about the delay in delivery of the parts and the adverse consequences it was having on Katahdin's relationship with its retailers. Near the absolute deadline for meeting orders for the 2016 season, Case called Read and said, "I've got the parts in, but I'm not sure I'll be able to send

[26] *Miller v. Calhoun/Johnson Co*, 497 S.E.2d 397 (Ga. App. 1998).
[27] *Hurd v. Wildman, Harrold, Allen, and Dixon*, 707 N.E.2d 609 (Ill. App. 1999).

them to you because I'm working on next year's contracts, and you haven't signed yours yet." Case's 2017 contract increased the cost of parts by 38 percent. Read signed the contract to obtain the delivery but later found a new supplier and gave notice to Case of this action. The defense of economic duress would apply in a breach of contract suit brought by Case on the 2017 contract because Case implicitly threatened to commit the wrongful act of not delivering parts due under the prior contract, and Katahdin Company had no means available to obtain parts elsewhere to prevent the economic loss that would occur if it did not receive those parts.

Make the Connection

Summary

An agreement that otherwise appears to be a contract may not be binding because one of the parties lacks contractual capacity. In such a case, the contract is ordinarily voidable at the election of the party who lacks contractual capacity. In some cases, the contract is void. Ordinarily, contractual incapacity is the inability, for mental or physical reasons, to understand that a contract is being made and to understand its general terms and nature. This is typically the case when it is claimed that incapacity exists because of insanity, intoxication, or drug use. The incapacity of minors arises because society discriminates in favor of that class to protect them from unwise contracts.

The age of majority is 18. Minors can disaffirm most contracts. If a minor received anything from the other party, the minor, on avoiding the contract, must return what had been received from the other party if the minor still has it.

When a minor disaffirms a contract for a necessary, the minor must pay the reasonable value of any benefit received.

Minors only are liable for their contracts. Parents of a minor are not liable on the minor's contracts merely because they are the parents. Frequently, an adult enters into the contract as a coparty of the minor and is then liable without regard to whether the minor has avoided the contract.

The contract of an insane person is voidable to much the same extent as the contract of a minor. An important distinction is that if a guardian has been appointed for the insane person, a contract made by the insane person is void, not merely voidable.

An intoxicated person lacks contractual capacity if the intoxication is such that the person does not understand that a contract is being made.

The consent of a party to an agreement is not genuine or voluntary in certain cases of mistake, deception, or pressure. When this occurs, what appears to be a contract can be avoided by the victim of such circumstances or conduct.

As to mistake, it is necessary to distinguish between unilateral mistakes that are unknown to the other contracting party and those that are known. Mistakes that are unknown to the other party usually do not affect the binding character of the agreement. A unilateral mistake of which the other contracting party has knowledge or has reason to know makes the contract avoidable by the victim of the mistake.

The deception situation may be one of negligent misrepresentation or fraud. The law ordinarily does not attach any significance to nondisclosure. Contrary to this rule, there is a duty to volunteer information when a confidential relationship exists between the possessor of the knowledge and the other contracting party.

When concealment goes beyond mere silence and consists of actively taking steps to hide the truth, the conduct may be classified as fraud. A statement of opinion or value cannot ordinarily be the basis for fraud liability.

The voluntary character of a contract may be lacking because the agreement had been obtained by pressure. This may range from undue influence through the array of threats of extreme economic loss (called *economic duress*) to the threat of physical force that would cause serious personal injury or damage to property (called *physical duress*). When the voluntary character of an agreement has been destroyed by deception, or pressure, the victim may avoid or rescind the contract or may obtain money damages from the wrongdoer.

Learning Outcomes

After studying this chapter, you should be able to clearly explain:

13-1 Contractual Capacity

LO.1 Define contractual capacity

See the example where Jacqueline, age 22, did not understand parts of a storage contract, page 243.

LO.2 Explain the extent and effect of avoidance of a contract by a minor

See the *Adorian Deck* example where the creator of a Twitter feed, a minor, disaffirmed his joint venture contract, page 244.

See the *Prince George's Hospital* case where a minor had to pay for medical necessaries, page 246.

13-2 Mistake

LO.3 Distinguish unilateral mistakes and mutual mistakes

See the *Shurgard Storage* case where the "other party" should have known of the unilateral mistake, page 249.

See the *Jewell Coke Co.* example of a remedy for a billion dollar mistake, page 250.

See the example of the mutual mistake of fact regarding the fertility of a cow, page 249.

13-3 Deception

LO.4 Explain the difference between intentional misrepresentation, negligent misrepresentation, and puffery

See the example of the purchase of the used Honda, where the misrepresentation was found to be fraud, not puffery, page 251.

See the *Novare Group, Inc.*, decision on the enforceability of disclaimer-of-liability clauses, page 253.

13-4 Pressure

LO.5 Explain the difference between undue influence and duress

See the *Fisher v. Schefers* undue influence litigation, page 256.

See the Katahdin bicycle example on economic duress, page 256.

Key Terms

confidential relationship
contractual capacity
duress
economic duress
fraud
necessaries
physical duress
reformation
status quo ante
undue influence

Questions and Case Problems

1. Lester purchased a used automobile from MacKintosh Motors. He asked the seller if the car had ever been in a wreck. The MacKintosh salesperson had never seen the car before that morning and knew nothing of its history but quickly answered Lester's question by stating: "No. It has never been in a wreck." In fact, the auto had been seriously damaged in a wreck and, although repaired, was worth much less than the value it would have had if there had been no wreck. When Lester learned the truth, he sued MacKintosh Motors and the salesperson for damages for fraud. They raised the defense that the salesperson did not know the statement was false and had not intended to deceive Lester. Did the conduct of the salesperson constitute fraud?
2. Helen, age 17, wanted to buy a Harley-Davidson "Sportster" motorcycle. She did not have the funds to pay cash but persuaded the dealer to sell the cycle to her on credit. The dealer did so partly because Helen said that she was 22 and showed the dealer an identification card that falsely stated her age as 22. Helen drove the motorcycle away. A few days later, she damaged it and then returned it to the dealer and stated that she disaffirmed the contract because she was a minor. The dealer said that she could not because (1) she had misrepresented her age and (2) the motorcycle was damaged. Can she avoid the contract?
3. Paden signed an agreement dated May 28 to purchase the Murrays' home. The Murrays accepted Paden's offer the following day, and the sale closed on June 27. Paden and his family moved into the home on July 14, 1997. Paden had the home inspected prior to closing. The report listed four minor repairs needed by the home, the cost of which

was less than $500. Although these repairs had not been completed at the time of closing, Paden decided to go through with the purchase. After moving into the home, Paden discovered a number of allegedly new defects, including a wooden foundation, electrical problems, and bat infestation. The sales agreement allowed extensive rights to inspect the property. The agreement provided:

> *Buyer … shall have the right to enter the property at Buyer's expense and at reasonable times … to thoroughly inspect, examine, test, and survey the Property.… Buyer shall have the right to request that Seller repair defects in the Property by providing Seller within 12 days from Binding Agreement Date with a copy of inspection report(s) and a written amendment to this agreement setting forth the defects in the report which Buyer requests to be repaired and/or replaced.… If Buyer does not timely present the written amendment and inspection report, Buyer shall be deemed to have accepted the Property "as is."*

Paden sued the Murrays for fraudulent concealment and breach of the sales agreement. If Mr. Murray told Paden on May 26 that the house had a concrete foundation, would this be fraud? Decide. [*Paden v. Murray*, 523 S.E.2d 75 (Ga. App.)]

4. High-Tech Collieries borrowed money from Holland. High-Tech later refused to be bound by the loan contract, claiming the contract was not binding because it had been obtained by duress. The evidence showed that the offer to make the loan was made on a take-it-or-leave-it basis. Was the defense of duress valid? [*Holland v. High-Tech Collieries, Inc.*, 911 F. Supp. 1021 (N.D. W.Va.)]
5. Thomas Bell, a minor, went to work in the Pittsburgh beauty parlor of Sam Pankas and agreed that when he left the employment, he would not work in or run a beauty parlor business within a 10-mile radius of downtown Pittsburgh for a period of two years. Contrary to this provision, Bell and another employee of Pankas's opened a beauty shop three blocks from Pankas's shop and advertised themselves as Pankas's former employees. Pankas sued Bell to stop the breach of the noncompetition, or restrictive, covenant. Bell claimed that he was not bound because he was a minor when he had agreed to the covenant. Was he bound by the covenant? [*Pankas v. Bell*, 198 A.2d 312 (Pa.)]
6. Aldrich and Co. sold goods to Donovan on credit. The amount owed grew steadily, and finally Aldrich refused to sell any more to Donovan unless Donovan signed a promissory note for the amount due. Donovan did not want to but signed the note because he had no money and needed more goods. When Aldrich brought an action to enforce the note, Donovan claimed that the note was not binding because it had been obtained by economic duress. Was he correct? [*Aldrich & Co. v. Donovan*, 778 P.2d 397 (Mont.)]
7. James Fitl purchased a 1952 Mickey Mantle Topps baseball card from baseball card dealer Mark Strek for $17,750 and placed it in a safe deposit box. Two years later, he had the card appraised, and he was told that the card had been refinished and trimmed, which rendered it valueless. Fitl sued Strek and testified that he had relied on Strek's position as a sports card dealer and on his representations that the baseball card was authentic. Strek contends that Fitl waited too long to give him notice of the defects that would have enabled Strek to contact the person who sold him the card and obtain relief. Strek asserts that he therefore is not liable. Advise Fitl concerning possible legal theories that apply to his case. How would you decide the case? [See *Fitl v. Strek*, 690 N.W.2d 605 (Neb.)]
8. Willingham proposed to obtain an investment property for the Tschiras at a "fair market price," lease it back from them, and pay the Tschiras a guaranteed return through a management contract. Using a shell corporation, The Wellingham Group bought a commercial property in Nashville for $774,000 on December 14, and the very same day sold the building to the Tschiras for $1,985,000. The title insurance policy purchased for the Tschiras property by Willingham was for just $774,000. Willingham believes that the deal was legitimate in that they "guaranteed" a return on the investment. The Tschiras disagree. In a lawsuit against Willingham, what theory will the Tschiras rely on? Decide. [*Tschiras v. Willingham*, 133 F.3d 1077 (6th Cir.)]
9. Blubaugh was a district manager of Schlumberger Well Services. Turner was an executive employee of Schlumberger. Blubaugh was told that he would be fired unless he chose to resign. He was also told that if he would resign and release the company and its employees from all claims for wrongful discharge, he would receive about $5,000 in addition to his regular severance pay of approximately $25,000 and would

be given job-relocation counseling. He resigned, signed the release, and received about $40,000 and job counseling. Some time thereafter, he brought an action claiming that he had been wrongfully discharged. He claimed that the release did not protect the defendants because the release had been obtained by economic duress. Were the defendants protected by the release? [*Blubaugh v. Turner*, 842 P.2d 1072 (Wyo.)]

10. Sippy was thinking of buying Christich's house. He noticed watermarks on the ceiling, but the agent showing the house stated that the roof had been repaired and was in good condition. Sippy was not told that the roof still leaked and that the repairs had not been able to stop the leaking. Sippy bought the house. Some time later, heavy rains caused water to leak into the house, and Sippy claimed that Christich was liable for damages. What theory would he rely on? Decide. [*Sippy v. Christich*, 609 P.2d 204 (Kan. App.)]

11. CEO Bernard Ellis sent a memo to shareholders of his Internet-related services business some four days before the expiration of a lock-up period during which these shareholders had agreed not to sell their stock. In the memo, he urged shareholders not to sell their stock on the release date because in the event of a massive sell-off "our stock could plummet." He also stated *"I think our share price will start to stabilize and then rise as our company's strong performance continues."* Based on Ellis' "strong performance" statement, a major corporate shareholder did not sell. The price of the stock fell from $40 a share to 29 cents a share over the subsequent nine-month period. The shareholder sued Ellis for fraud, seeking $27 million in damages. Analyze the italicized statement to see if it contains an actionable misrepresentation of fact and a basis of fraud liability. [*New Century Communications v. Ellis*, 318 F.3d 1023 (11th Cir.)]

12. Office Supply Outlet, Inc., a single-store office equipment and supply retailer, ordered 100 model RVX-414 computers from Compuserve, Inc. A new staff member made a clerical error on the order form and ordered a quantity that was far in excess of what Office Supply could sell in a year. Office Supply realized the mistake when the delivery trucks arrived at its warehouse. Its manager called Compuserve and explained that it had intended to order just 10 computers. Compuserve declined to accept the return of the extra machines. Is the contract enforceable? What additional facts would allow the store to avoid the contract for the additional machines?

13. The Printers International Union reached agreement for a new three-year contract with a large regional printing company. As was their practice, the union negotiators then met with Sullivan Brothers Printers, Inc., a small specialty shop employing 10 union printers, and Sullivan Brothers and the union agreed to follow the contractual pattern set by the union and the large printing company. That is, Sullivan Brothers agreed to give its workers all of the benefits negotiated for the employees of the large printing company. When the contract was typed, a new benefit of 75 percent employer-paid coverage for a dental plan was inadvertently omitted from the final contract the parties signed. The mistake was not discovered until six months after the contract took effect. Sullivan Brothers Printers, Inc., is reluctant to assume the additional expense. It contends that the printed copy, which does not cover dental benefits, must control. The union believes that clear and convincing evidence shows an inadvertent typing error. Decide.

14. The city of Salinas entered into a contract with Souza & McCue Construction Co. to construct a sewer. City officials knew unusual subsoil conditions (including extensive quicksand) existed that would make performance of the contract unusually difficult. This information was not disclosed when city officials advertised for bids. The advertisement for bids directed bidders to examine carefully the site of the work and declared that the submission of a bid would constitute evidence that the bidder had made an examination. Souza & McCue was awarded the contract, but because of the subsoil conditions, it could not complete on time and was sued by Salinas for breach of contract. Souza & McCue counterclaimed on the basis that the city had not revealed its information on the subsoil conditions and was thus liable for the loss. Was the city liable? [*City of Salinas v. Souza & McCue Construction Co.*, 424 P.2d 921 (Cal. App. 3d)]

15. Vern Westby inherited a "ticket" from Anna Sjoblom, a survivor of the sinking of the *Titanic*, which had been pinned to the inside of her coat. He also inherited an album of postcards, some of which related to the *Titanic*. The ticket was a one-of-a-kind item in good condition. Westby needed cash and went to the biggest antique dealer in Tacoma, operated by Alan Gorsuch and his family, doing business

as Sanford and Sons, and asked about the value of these items. Westby testified that after Alan Gorsuch examined the ticket, he said, "It's not worth nothing." Westby then inquired about the value of the postcard album, and Gorsuch advised him to come back later. On Westby's return, Gorsuch told Westby, "It ain't worth nothing." Gorsuch added that he "couldn't fetch $500 for the ticket." Since he needed money, Westby asked if Gorsuch would give him $1,000 for both the ticket and the album, and Gorsuch did so.

Six months later, Gorsuch sold the ticket at a nationally advertised auction for $110,000 and sold most of the postcards for $1,200. Westby sued Gorsuch for fraud. Testimony showed that Gorsuch was a major buyer in antiques and collectibles in the Puget Sound area and that he would have had an understanding of the value of the ticket. Gorsuch contends that all elements of fraud are not present since there was no evidence that Gorsuch intended that Westby rely on the alleged representations, nor did Westby rely on such. Rather, Gorsuch asserts, it was an arm's-length transaction and Westby had access to the same information as Gorsuch. Decide. [*Westby v. Gorsuch*, 50 P.3d 284 (Wash. App.)]

CPA Questions

1. A building subcontractor submitted a bid for construction of a portion of a high-rise office building. The bid contained material computational errors. The general contractor accepted the bid with knowledge of the errors. Which of the following statements best represents the subcontractor's liability?
   a. Not liable, because the contractor knew of the errors.
   b. Not liable, because the errors were a result of gross negligence.
   c. Liable, because the errors were unilateral.
   d. Liable, because the errors were material (5/95, Law, #17, 5351).
2. Egan, a minor, contracted with Baker to purchase Baker's used computer for $400. The computer was purchased for Egan's personal use. The agreement provided that Egan would pay $200 down on delivery and $200 thirty days later. Egan took delivery and paid the $200 down payment. Twenty days later, the computer was damaged seriously as a result of Egan's negligence. Five days after the damage occurred and one day after Egan reached the age of majority, Egan attempted to disaffirm the contract with Baker. Egan will:
   a. Be able to disaffirm despite the fact that Egan was *not* a minor at the time of disaffirmance.
   b. Be able to disaffirm only if Egan does so in writing.
   c. Not be able to disaffirm because Egan had failed to pay the balance of the purchase price.
   d. Not be able to disaffirm because the computer was damaged as a result of Egan's negligence (11/93, Law, #21, 4318).

CHAPTER 14

Consideration

Learning Outcomes

After studying this chapter, you should be able to

LO.1 **Explain what constitutes consideration**

LO.2 **Distinguish between a "preexisting legal obligation" and "past consideration"**

LO.3 **Explain why promises based on moral obligations lack consideration**

LO.4 **List the exceptions to the requirement of consideration**

LO.5 **Explain the "fundamental idea" underlying promissory estoppel**

Will the law enforce every promise? Generally, a promise will not be enforced unless something is given or received for the promise.

14-1 General Principles

As a general rule, one of the elements needed to make an agreement binding is consideration.

14-1a Consideration Defined and Explained

consideration–promise or performance that the promisor demands as the price of the promise.

Consideration is what each party to a contract gives up to the other in making their agreement.

Bargained-for Exchange

Consideration is the bargained-for exchange between the parties to a contract. In order for consideration to exist, something of value must be given or promised in return for the performance or promise of performance of the other.[1] The value given or promised can be money, services, property, or the forbearance of a legal right.

For Example, Beth offers to pay Kerry $100 for her used skis, and Kerry accepts. Beth has promised something of value, $100, as consideration for Kerry's promise to sell the skis, and Kerry has promised Beth something of value, the skis, as consideration for the $100. If Kerry offered to *give* Beth the used skis and Beth accepted, these parties would have an agreement but not an enforceable contract because Beth did not provide any consideration in exchange for Kerry's promise of the skis. There was no *bargained-for exchange* because Kerry was not promised anything of value from Beth.

Benefit-Detriment Approach

Some jurisdictions analyze consideration from the point of view of a *benefit-detriment approach*, defining *consideration* as a benefit received by the promisor or a detriment incurred by the promisee.[2]

As an example of a unilateral contract analyzed from a benefit-detriment approach to consideration, Mr. Scully, a longtime summer resident of Falmouth, states to George Corfu, a college senior, "I will pay you $3,000 if you paint my summer home." George in fact paints the house. The work of painting the house by George, the promisee, was a legal detriment to him. Also, the painting of the house was a legal benefit to Scully, the promisor. There was consideration in this case, and the agreement is enforceable.

14-1b Gifts

Promises to make a gift are unenforceable promises under the law of contracts because of lack of consideration, as illustrated previously in the scenario of Kerry promising to give her used skis to Beth without charge. There was no bargained-for exchange because Kerry was not promised anything of value from Beth. A completed gift, however, cannot be rescinded for lack of consideration.[3]

Charitable subscriptions by which individuals make pledges to finance the construction of a college building, a church, or another structure for charitable purposes are binding to the extent that the donor (promisor) should have reasonably realized that the charity was relying on the promise in undertaking the building program. Some states require proof that the charity has relied on the subscription.[4]

[1] *Brooksbank v. Anderson*, 586 N.W.2d 789 (Minn. App. 1998).
[2] *Sullo Investments, LLC v. Moreau*, 95 A.3d 1144 (Ct. 2014).
[3] *Homes v. O'Bryant*, 741 So. 2d 366 (Miss. App. 1999).
[4] *King v. Trustees of Boston University*, 647 N.E.2d 1176 (Ma. 1995).

An agreement to give property for the consideration of love and affection does not transfer the property to the donee nor secure for the donee a right to sue to compel the completion of the contract. Love and affection alone have not been recognized as consideration for a contract.

CASE SUMMARY

What's Love Got to Do With It...

FACTS: Amber Williams and Frederick Ormsby lived together in a nonmarital relationship in a house deeded to Ormsby in 2004. The couple separated and attended couples counseling. Amber refused to move back into the house unless Frederick granted her a one-half interest in the property. On June 2, 2005, they signed a document purportedly making themselves equal partners in the home. Amber ended the relationship in September 2007, and she sought specific performance of the June 2, 2005, contract giving her a half-interest in the property. Frederick defended that "love and affection is insufficient consideration for a contract."

DECISION: Judgment for Ormsby. The only consideration offered by Amber for the June 2, 2005, agreement was her resumption of a romantic relationship with Frederick. Essentially this agreement amounts to a gratuitous promise by Frederick to give Amber an interest in property based solely on the consideration of love and affection. This June 2005 document is not an enforceable contract because it fails for want of consideration. [***Williams v. Ormsby*, 966 N.E.2d 255 (Ohio 2012)**]

14-1c Adequacy of Consideration

Ordinarily, courts do not consider the adequacy of the consideration given for a promise. The fact that the consideration supplied by one party is slight when compared with the burden undertaken by the other party is immaterial. It is a matter for the parties to decide when they make their contract whether each is getting a fair return. It is not a function of a court to review the amount of the consideration passed unless the amount is so grossly inadequate as to shock the conscience of the court.

CASE SUMMARY

A Good Neighbor Shocks the Conscience of the Court

FACTS: Dr. George Dohrmann made a contract with his very elderly childless neighbor, Mrs. Virginia Rogers, wherein she agreed to transfer to Dr. Dohrmann upon her death her valuable condominium and its contents and $4,000,000 in cash in exchange for Dohrmann incorporating the name of Rogers into the names of his two children to help perpetuate the Rogers names after her death. Dr. Dohrmann performed by taking the legal action necessary to add the Rogers name into the legal names of his two boys. From a judgment against Dohrmann on his breach of contract action against the Rogers estate, he appealed.

DECISION: Judgment against Dohrmann. He did not change the boys' surnames to Rogers, nor even change their middle names to Rogers. He merely added Rogers after their middle names. This can hardly be said to perpetuate the Rogers name after Mrs. Rogers' death. Dohrmann's argument that it is improper for a court to consider the relative value or adequacy of the consideration is rejected in this particular case. While the statement is generally true, in cases such as the one at bar it will not be applied where the consideration is so grossly inadequate as to shock the conscience of the court. [***Dohrmann v. Swaney*, 14 N.E.3d 605 (Ill. App. 2014)**]

The fact that the consideration turns out to be disappointing does not affect the binding character of the contract. Thus, the fact that a business purchased by a group of investors proves unprofitable does not constitute a failure of consideration that releases the buyers from their obligation to the seller.

14-1d Forbearance as Consideration

forbearance–refraining from doing an act.

In most cases, consideration consists of the performance of an act, such as providing a service, or the making of a promise to provide a service or goods, or paying money.[5] Consideration may also consist of **forbearance,** which is refraining from doing an act that an individual has a legal right to do, or it may consist of a promise of forbearance. In other words, the promisor may desire to buy the inaction or a promise of inaction of the other party.

The giving up of any legal right can be consideration for the promise of the other party to a contract. Thus, the relinquishment of a right to sue for damages will support a promise for the payment of money given in return for the promise to relinquish the right, if such is the agreement of the parties.

The promise of a creditor to forbear collecting a debt is consideration for the promise of the debtor to modify the terms of the transaction.

14-1e Illusory Promises

illusory promise–promise that in fact does not impose any obligation on the promisor.

In a bilateral contract, each party makes a promise to the other. For a bilateral contract to be enforceable, there must be *mutuality of obligation.* That is, both parties must have created obligations to the other in their respective promises. If one party's promise contains either no obligation or only an apparent obligation to the other, this promise is an **illusory promise.** The party making such a promise is not bound because he or she has made no real promise. The effect is that the other party, who has made a real promise, is also not bound because he or she has received no consideration. It is said that the contract fails for lack of mutuality.

Consider the example of the Jacksonville Fire soccer team's contract with Brazilian soccer star Edmundo. Edmundo signed a contract to play for the Jacksonville franchise of the new International Soccer League for five years at $25 million. The extensive document signed by Edmundo set forth the details of the team's financial commitment and the details of Edmundo's obligations to the team and its fans. On page 4 of the document, the team inserted a clause reserving the right "to terminate the contract and team obligations at any time in its sole discretion." During the season, Edmundo received a $40 million five-year offer to play for Manchester United of the English Premier League, which he accepted. Because Jacksonville had a free way out of its obligation by the unrestricted cancellation provision in the contract, it thus made its promises to Edmundo illusory. Edmundo was not bound by the Jacksonville contract as a result of a lack of mutuality and was free to sign with Manchester United.

Cancellation Provisions

cancellation provision–crossing out of a part of an instrument or a destruction of all legal effect of the instrument, whether by act of party, upon breach by the other party, or pursuant to agreement or decree of court.

Although a promise must impose a binding obligation, it may authorize a party to cancel the agreement under certain circumstances on giving notice by a certain date. Such a provision does not make this party's promise illusory, for the party does not have a free way out and is limited to living up to the terms of the **cancellation provision. For Example,** actress Zsa Zsa Gabor made a contract with Hollywood Fantasy Corporation to appear at a fantasy vacation in San Antonio, Texas, on May 2–4, for a $10,000 appearance fee plus itemized (extravagant) expenses. The last paragraph of the agreement stated: "It is agreed that if a significant acting opportunity in a film comes up, Ms. Gabor will have the right to cancel her appearance in San Antonio by advising Hollywood Fantasy in writing by April 15, 1991." Ms. Gabor sent a telegram on April 15, 1991, canceling her appearance. During the May 2 through 4 period, Ms. Gabor's only acting activity was a 14-second cameo role during the opening credits of *Naked Gun 2½.* In a lawsuit for breach of

[5] *Prenger v. Baumhoer,* 914 S.W.2d 413 (Mo. App. 1996).

contract that followed, the jury saw this portion of the movie and concluded that Ms. Gabor had not canceled her obligation on the basis of a "significant acting opportunity," and she was held liable for breach of contract.[6]

Conditional Promises

A *conditional promise* is a promise that depends on the occurrence of a specified condition in order for the promise to be binding. **For Example,** Mary Sparks, in contemplation of her signing a lease to take over a restaurant at Marina Bay, wanted to make certain that she had a highly qualified chef to run the restaurant's food service. She made a contract with John "Grumpy" White to serve as executive chef for a one-year period at a salary of $150,000. The contract set forth White's responsibilities and was conditioned on the successful negotiation of the restaurant lease with Marina Bay Management. Both parties signed it. Although the happening of the condition was within Mary's control because she could avoid the contract with Grumpy White by not acquiring the restaurant lease, she limited her future options by the contract with White. Her promise to White was not illusory because after signing the contract with him, if she acquired the restaurant lease, she was bound to hire White as her executive chef. Before signing the contract with White, she was free to sign any chef for the position. The contract was enforceable.

CPA 14-2 Special Situations

The following sections analyze certain common situations in which a lawsuit turns on whether the promisor received consideration for the promise sued on.

14-2a Preexisting Legal Obligation

Ordinarily, doing or promising to do what one is already under a legal obligation to do is not consideration.[7] Similarly, a promise to refrain from doing what one has no legal right to do is not consideration. This preexisting duty or legal obligation can be based on statute, on general principles of law, on responsibilities of an office held, or on a preexisting contract.

For Example, Officer Mary Rodgers is an undercover police officer in the city of Pasadena, California, assigned to weekend workdays. Officer Rodgers promised Elwood Farnsworth that she would diligently patrol the area of the Farnsworth estate on weekends to keep down the noise and drinking of rowdy young persons who gathered in this area, and Mr. Farnsworth promised to provide a $500 per month gratuity for this extra service. Farnsworth's promise is unenforceable because Officer Rodgers has a preexisting official duty as a police officer to protect citizens and enforce the antinoise and public drinking ordinances.

CPA Completion of Contract

Suppose that a contractor refuses to complete a building unless the owner promises a payment or bonus in addition to the sum specified in the original contract, and the owner promises to make that payment. The question then arises as to whether the owner's promise is binding. Most courts hold that the second promise of the owner is without consideration.

[6] *Hollywood Fantasy Corp. v. Gabor*, 151 F.2d 203 (5th Cir. 1998).

[7] *Willamette Management Associates, Inc. v. Palczynski*, 38 A.3d 1212 (Conn. App. 2012).

CASE SUMMARY

You're Already Under Contract

FACTS: Crookham & Vessels had a contract to build an extension of a railroad for the Little Rock Port Authority. It made a contract with Larry Moyer Trucking to dig drainage ditches. The ditch walls collapsed because water would not drain off. This required that the ditches be dug over again. Larry Moyer refused to do this unless extra money was paid. Crookham & Vessels agreed to pay the additional compensation, but after the work was done, it refused to pay. Larry Moyer sued for the extra compensation promised.

DECISION: Judgment against Moyer. Moyer was bound by its contract to dig the drainage ditches. Its promise to perform that obligation was not consideration for the promise of Crookham & Vessels to pay additional compensation. Performance of an obligation is not consideration for a promise by a party entitled to that performance. The fact that performance of the contract proved more difficult or costly than originally contemplated does not justify making an exception to this rule. [***Crookham & Vessels, Inc. v. Larry Moyer Trucking, Inc.*, 699 S.W.2d 414 (Ark. App. 1985)**]

If the promise of the contractor is to do something that is not part of the first contract, then the promise of the other party is binding. **For Example,** if a bonus of $5,000 is promised in return for the promise of a contractor to complete the building at a date earlier than that specified in the original agreement, the promise to pay the bonus is binding.

CPA

Good-Faith Adjustment. A current trend is to enforce a second promise to pay a contractor a higher amount for the performance of the original contract when there are extraordinary circumstances caused by unforeseeable difficulties and when the additional amount promised the contractor is reasonable under the circumstances.

CASE SUMMARY

"You Had a Preexisting Legal Obligation," Said the Public Guardian, Mr. Angel

FACTS: John Murray was director of finance of the city of Newport. A contract was made with Alfred Maher to remove trash. Later, Maher requested that the city council increase his compensation. Maher's costs were greater than had been anticipated because 400 new dwelling units had been put into operation. The city council voted to pay Maher an additional $10,000 a year. After two such annual payments had been made, Angel and other citizens of the city sued Murray and Maher for a return of the $20,000. They said that Maher was already obligated by his contract to perform the work for the contract sum, and there was, accordingly, no consideration for the payment of the increased compensation. From a decision in favor of the plaintiffs, the city and Maher appealed.

DECISION: Judgment for the city and Maher. When a promise modifying an original contract is made before the contract is fully performed on either side due to unanticipated circumstances that prompt the modification, and the modification is fair and equitable, such a good faith adjustment will be enforced. The unanticipated increase in the number of new units from 20 to 25 per year to 400 units in the third year of this five-year contract, which prompted the additional yearly payments of $10,000, was a voluntary good faith adjustment. It was not a "hold up" by a contractor refusing to complete an unprofitable contract unless paid additional compensation, where the preexisting duty rule would apply. [***Angel v. Murray*, 322 A.2d 630 (R.I. 1974)**]

Contract for Sale of Goods. When the contract is for the sale of goods, any modification made in good faith by the parties to the contract is binding without regard to the existence of consideration for the modification.

CPA Compromise and Release of Claims

The rule that doing or promising to do what one is already legally bound to do is not consideration applies to a part payment made in satisfaction of an admitted or *liquidated debt.* Thus, a promise to pay part of an amount that is admittedly owed is not consideration for a promise to discharge the balance. It will not prevent the creditor from demanding the remainder later. **For Example,** John owes Mark $100,000, which was due on March 1, 2016. On March 15, John offers to pay back $80,000 if Mark will agree to accept this amount as the discharge of the full amount owed. Mark agrees to this proposal, and it is set forth in writing signed by the parties. However, Mark later sues for the $20,000 balance. Mark will be successful in the lawsuit because John's payment of the $80,000 is not consideration for Mark's promise to discharge the full amount owed because John was doing only what he had a preexisting legal duty to do.

If the debtor pays the part payment before the debt is due, there is consideration because, on the day when the payment was made, the creditor was not entitled to demand any payment. Likewise, if the creditor accepts some article (even of slight value) in addition to the part payment, consideration exists.

A debtor and creditor may have a bona fide dispute over the amount owed or whether any amount is owed. Such is called an *unliquidated debt.* In this case, payment by the debtor of less than the amount claimed by the creditor is consideration for the latter's agreement to release or settle the claim. It is generally regarded as sufficient if the claimant believes in the merit of the claim.[8]

Part-Payment Checks

When there is a good-faith dispute about the amount of a debt and the debtor tenders a check that states on its face "paid in full" and references the transaction in dispute, but the amount of the check is less than the full amount the creditor asserts is owed, the cashing of the check by the creditor discharges the entire debt.

Composition of Creditors

composition of creditors–agreement among creditors that each shall accept a part payment as full payment in consideration of the other creditors doing the same.

In a **composition of creditors,** the various creditors of one debtor mutually agree to accept a fractional part of their claims in full satisfaction of the claims. Such agreements are binding and are supported by consideration. When creditors agree to extend the due date of their debts, the promise of each creditor to forbear is likewise consideration for the promise of other creditors to forbear.

14-2b Past Consideration

past consideration–something that has been performed in the past and which, therefore, cannot be consideration for a promise made in the present.

A promise based on a party's past performance lacks consideration.[9] It is said that **past consideration** is no consideration. **For Example,** Fred O'Neal came up with the idea for the formation of the new community bank of Villa Rica and was active in its formation. Just prior to the execution of the documents creating the bank, the organizers discussed that once the bank was formed, it would hire O'Neal, giving him a three-year contract in inflation adjusted figures of $104,000 the first year, $107,000 the second year, and $110,000 the third. In a lawsuit against the bank for breach of contract, O'Neal testified that the consideration he gave in exchange for the three-year contract was his past effort to organize the bank. The court stated that past consideration generally will not support a subsequent promise and that the purported consideration was not rendered to the bank, which had not yet been established when his promotion and

[8] *F. H. Prince & Co. v. Towers Financial Corp.,* 656 N.E.2d 142 (Ill. App. 1995).
[9] *Smith v. Locklear,* 906 So. 2d 1273 (Fla. App. 2005).

ETHICS & THE LAW

Alan Fulkins, who owns a construction company that specializes in single-family residences, is constructing a small subdivision with 23 homes. Tretorn Plumbing, owned by Jason Tretorn, was awarded the contract for the plumbing work on the homes at a price of $4,300 per home.

Plumbing contractors complete their residential projects in three phases. Phase one consists of digging the lines for the plumbing and installing the pipes that are placed in the foundation of the house. Phase two consists of installing the pipes within the walls of the home, and phase three is installing of the surface plumbing, such as sinks and tubs. However, industry practice dictates that the plumbing contractor receive one-half of the contract amount after completion of phase one.

Tretorn completed the digs of phase one for Fulkins and received payment of $2,150. Tretorn then went to Fulkins and demanded an additional $600 per house to complete the work. Fulkins said, "But you already have a contract for $4,300!" Tretorn responded, "I know, but the costs are killing me. I need the additional $600."

Fulkins explained the hardship of the demand, "Look, I've already paid you half. If I hire someone else, I'll have to pay them two-thirds for the work not done. It'll cost me $5,000 per house."

Tretorn responded, "Exactly. I'm a bargain because the additional $600 I want only puts you at $4,900. If you don't pay it, I'll just lien the houses and then you'll be stuck without a way to close the sales. I've got the contract all drawn up. Just sign it and everything goes smoothly."

Should Fulkins sign the agreement? Does Tretorn have the right to the additional $600? Was it ethical for Tretorn to demand the $600? Is there any legal advice you can offer Fulkins?

organization work took place.[10] The presence of a bargained-for exchange is not present when a promise is made in exchange for a past benefit.[11]

14-2c Moral Obligation

In most states, promises made to another based on "moral obligation" lack consideration and are not enforceable.[12] They are considered gratuitous promises and unenforceable. **For Example,** Robert Lewis and his brother Lewis Lester had an agreement under which Robert would provide help for his uncle Floyd and serve as his power of attorney and the brothers would split the uncle's estate equally. Floyd left his estate to Lewis Lester. Robert's suit against his brother to enforce their agreement failed for lack of consideration. Services performed by one family member on behalf of another family member are presumed to have been rendered in obedience to a moral obligation without expectation of compensation.[13]

14-3 Exceptions to the Laws of Consideration

The ever-changing character of law clearly appears in the area of consideration as part of the developing law of contracts.

14-3a Exceptions to Consideration

By statute or decision, traditional consideration is not required in these situations:

[10] *O'Neal v. Home Town Bank of Villa Rica*, 514 S.E.2d 669 (Ga. App. 1999); *Lee v. Choi*, 754 S.E.2d 371 (Ga. App. 2013).

[11] But see *United Resource Recovery Corp v. Ranko Venture Management Inc.*, 854 F. Supp. 2d 645 (S.D.N.Y. 2008) where a past work agreement was unenforceable because it was based on past consideration—however, the individual could recover under a signed consulting agreement for which no compensation had been paid. See also *Travis v. Paepke*, 3 So. 3d 131 (Miss. App. 2009).

[12] *Production Credit Ass'n of Manaan v. Rub*, 475 N.W.2d 532 (N.D. 1991). As to the Louisiana rule of moral consideration, see *Thomas v. Bryant*, 596 So. 2d 1065 (La. App. 1992).

[13] *Lewis v. Lester*, 760 N.E.2d 91 (N.C. App. 2014).

FIGURE 14-1 Consideration and Promises

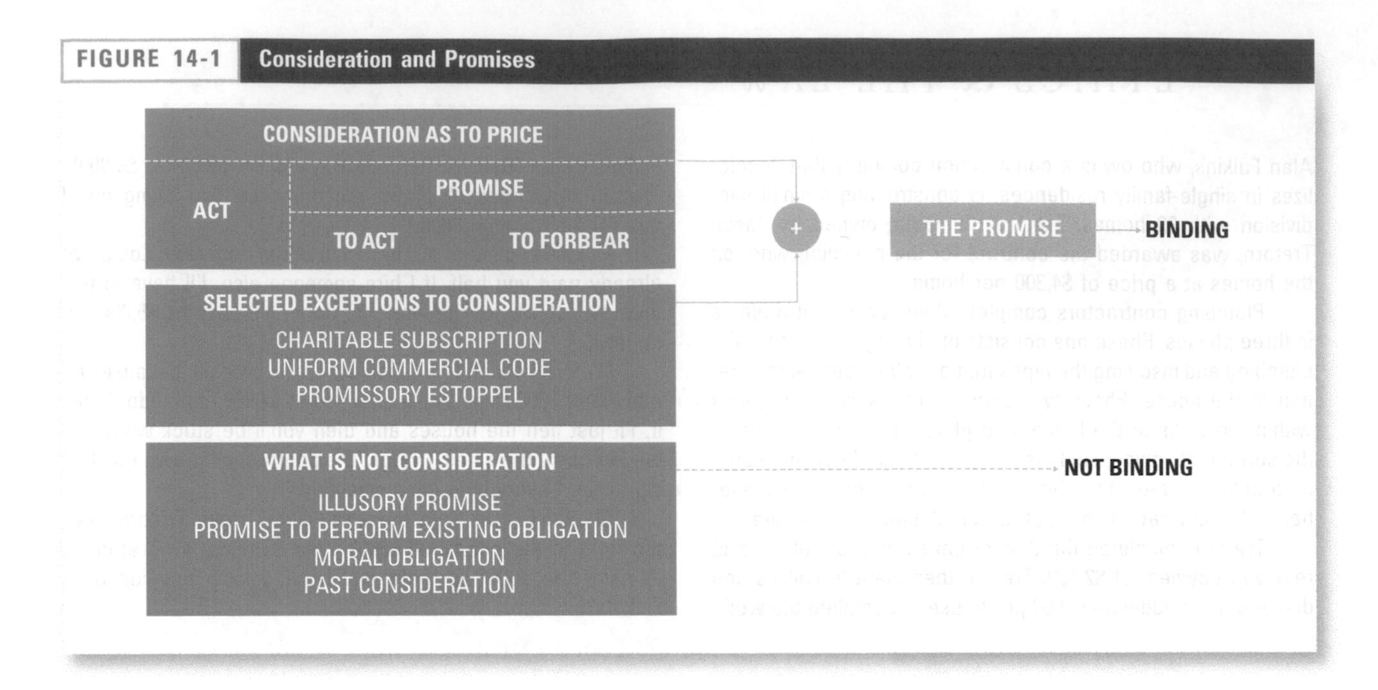

Charitable Subscriptions

Where individuals made pledges to finance the construction of buildings for charitable purposes, consideration is lacking according to technical standards applied in ordinary contract cases. For public policy reasons, the reliance of the charity on the pledge in undertaking the project is deemed a substitute for consideration.

Uniform Commercial Code

In some situations, the Uniform Commercial Code abolishes the requirement of consideration. **For Example,** under the Code, consideration is not required for (1) a merchant's written, firm offer for goods stated to be irrevocable, (2) a written discharge of a claim for an alleged breach of a commercial contract, or (3) an agreement to modify a contract for the sale of goods.[14]

promissory estoppels–doctrine that a promise will be enforced although it is not supported by consideration when the promisor should have reasonably expected that the promise would induce action or forbearance of a definite and substantial character on the part of the promised and injustice can be avoided only by enforcement of the promise.

Promissory Estoppel

Under the doctrine of **promissory estoppel,** a promisor may be prevented from asserting that his or her promise is unenforceable because the promisee gave no consideration for the promise.[15] This doctrine, sometimes called the *doctrine of detrimental reliance*, is applicable when (1) the promisor makes a promise that lacks consideration, (2) the promisor intends or should reasonably expect that the promisee will rely on the promise, (3) the promisee in fact relies on the promise in some definite and substantial manner, and (4) enforcement of the promise is the only way to avoid injustice.[16]

Damages recoverable in a case of promissory estoppel are not the profits that the promisee expected, but only the amount necessary to restore the promisee to the position he or she would have been in had the promisee not relied on the promise.[17]

[14] U.C.C. §2-209(1).
[15] See *Weiss v. Smulders,* 96 A.3d 1175 (Conn. 2014).
[16] *Neuhoff v. Marvin Lumber and Cedar Co.,* 370 F.3d 197 (1st Cir. 2004).
[17] *Medistar Corp. v. Schmidt,* 267 S.W.3d 150 (Tex. App. 2008).

Legal difficulties often arise because parties take certain things for granted. Frequently, they will be sure that they have agreed to everything and that they have a valid contract. Sometimes, however, they do not. The courts are then faced with the problem of leaving them with their broken dreams or coming to their rescue when promissory estoppel can be established.

CASE SUMMARY

Brits Rescued by Promissory Estoppel

FACTS: Portman Lamborghini, Ltd. (Portman), was owned by Chaplake Holdings, Ltd., a United Kingdom company, which was owned by David Jolliffe and David Lakeman as equal shareholders. Between 1984 and 1987, Portman sold approximately 30 new Lamborghinis each year through its exclusive concession contract with the car maker. It was then the largest Lamborghini dealer in the world since Lamborghini's production was just 250 cars per year. These cars sold at a retail price between $200,000 and $300,000. In 1987, Chrysler Corporation bought Lamborghini, and its chairman, Lee Iacocca, presented a plan to escalate production to 5,000 units within five years. The plan included the introduction of a new model, the P140, with a retail price of $70,000. Between 1987 and 1991, *all* of the Chrysler/Lamborghini top executives with whom Jolliffe and Lakeman and their top advisors came in contact provided the same message to them: Chrysler was committed to the Expansion Plan, and in order for Portman to retain its exclusive U.K. market, it must expand its operational capacity from 35 cars in 1987 to 400 cars by 1992. Accordingly, Portman acquired additional financing, staff, and facilities and built a new distribution center. An economic downturn in the United States and major development and production problems at Lamborghini led Chrysler to reduce its expansion investment by two-thirds. Factory production delays eroded Portman's profitability and success, and it entered into receivership in April 1992. Suit was brought on behalf of the Portman and Chaplake entities on a promissory estoppel theory against Chrysler, a Delaware corporation.

DECISION: Judgment for Portman and Chaplake on the promissory estoppel theory. (1) A promise was made by Chrysler that the Lamborghini line would expand tenfold and that Portman would retain its exclusivity deal *only* if it expanded its operational capacity. (2) The promisor, Chrysler, should have reasonably expected that Portman would rely on this promise. (3) Lakeman and Jolliffe were given the same message and promise by *all* of the top executives involved, and it was therefore not unreasonable for them to rely upon the promises made by these executives and to undertake the detriment of major expansion activity that would have been unnecessary but for the Expansion Plan and the role they were promised. (4) The prevention of injustice is the "fundamental idea" underlying the doctrine of promissory estoppel, and injustice can be avoided in this case only by the enforcement of Chrysler's promise. Portman is entitled to £ 569,321 for its costs to implement its Expansion Plan, and Chaplake is entitled to £ 462,686 for its investment in Portman's expansion. [***Chrysler Corp. v. Chaplake Holdings, Ltd.*, 822 A.2d 1024 (Del. 2003)**]

Make the Connection

Summary

A promise is not binding if there is no consideration for the promise. Consideration is what the promisor requires as the price for his promise. That price may be doing an act, refraining from the doing of an act, or merely promising to do or to refrain. In a bilateral contract, it is necessary to find that the promise of each party is supported by consideration. If either promise is not so supported, it is not binding, and the agreement of the parties is not a contract.

Consequently, the agreement cannot be enforced. When a promise is the consideration, it must be a binding promise. The binding character of a promise is not affected by the circumstance that there is a condition precedent to the performance promised. A promise to do what one is already obligated to do is not consideration, although some exceptions are made. Such exceptions include the rendering of a partial performance or a modified performance accepted as a good-faith adjustment to a changed situation, a compromise and release of claims, a part-payment check, and a compromise of creditors. Because consideration is the price that is given to obtain the promise, past benefits conferred on the promisor cannot be consideration.

A promise to refrain from doing an act can be consideration. A promise to refrain from suing or asserting a particular claim can be consideration. When consideration is forbearance to assert a claim, it is immaterial whether the claim is valid as long as the claim has been asserted in the good-faith belief that it was valid.

When the promisor obtains the consideration specified for the promise, the law is not ordinarily concerned with the value or adequacy of that consideration.

Under the doctrine of promissory estoppel a court may enforce a promise lacking consideration where it is the only way to avoid injustice.

Learning Outcomes

After studying this chapter, you should be able to clearly explain:

14-1 General Principles

LO.1 Explain what constitutes consideration

See the *Williams v. Ormsby* case, which determined that love and affection is not recognized as consideration, page 264.

See the "bargained for exchange" example involving Beth and Kerry, page 263.

See the "benefit-detriment" approach to consideration example, page 263.

See the discussion on forbearance as consideration, page 265.

14-2 Special Situations

LO.2 Distinguish between a "preexisting legal obligation" and "past consideration"

See the preexisting duty example involving Officer Rodgers, page 266.

See the *Angel v. Murray* case involving a good-faith adjustment exception to the preexisting duty rule, page 267.

See the example involving Fred O'Neal where he found out the past consideration is no consideration rule, page 268.

LO.3 Explain why promises based on moral obligations lack consideration

See the example of the gratuitous deeds of Robert Lewis, page 269.

14-3 Exceptions to the Laws of Consideration

LO.4 List the exceptions to the requirement of consideration

See the discussion on charitable subscriptions, the UCC, and promissory estoppel, pages 270–271.

LO.5 Explain the "fundamental idea" underlying promissory estoppel

See the *Chaplake Holdings* case where the court enforced Chrysler's promise in order to correct an injustice, page 271.

Key Terms

cancellation provision
composition of creditors
consideration
forbearance
illusory promise
past consideration
promissory estoppel

Questions and Case Problems

1. Sarah's house caught on fire. Through the prompt assistance of her neighbor Odessa, the fire was quickly extinguished. In gratitude, Sarah promised to pay Odessa $1,000. Can Odessa enforce this promise?

2. William E. Story agreed to pay his nephew, William E. Story II, a large sum of money (roughly equivalent to $75,000 in 2016 dollars) "if he would refrain from drinking liquor, using tobacco, swearing, and

playing cards or billiards for money until he should come to be 21 years of age." William II had been using tobacco and occasionally drank liquor but refrained from using these stimulants over several years until he was 21 and also lived up to the other requirements of his uncle's offer. Just after William II's 21st birthday, Story acknowledged that William II had fulfilled his part of the bargain and advised that the money would be invested for him with interest. Story died, and his executor, Sidway, refused to pay William II because he believed the contract between Story and William II was without consideration. Sidway asserted that Story received no benefit from William II's performance and William II suffered no detriment (in fact, by his refraining from the use of liquor and tobacco, William II was not harmed but benefited, Sidway asserted). Is there any theory of consideration that William II can rely on? How would you decide this case? [*Hamer v. Sidway*, 124 N.Y. 538]

3. Dale Dyer, who was employed by National By-Products, Inc., was seriously injured at work as the result of a job-related accident. He agreed to give up his right to sue the employer for damages in consideration of the employer's giving him a lifetime job. The employer later claimed that this agreement was not binding because Dyer's promise not to sue could not be consideration for the promise to employ on the ground that Dyer in fact had no right to sue. Dyer's only remedy was to make a claim under workers' compensation. Was the agreement binding? [*Dyer v. National By-Products, Inc.*, 380 N.W.2d 732 (Iowa)]
4. Charles Sanarwari retained Stan Gissel to prepare his income tax return for the year 2014. The parties agreed on a fee of $400. Charles had done a rough estimate based on last year's return and believed he would owe the IRS approximately $2,000. When Stan's work was completed, it turned out that Charles would receive a $2,321 tax refund. Charles paid for Stan's services and was so pleased with the work that he promised to pay Stan an additional $400 for the excellent job on the tax return when he received his tax refund. Thereafter, Charles had a falling out with Stan over a golf tournament snub. Stan was not paid the $400 promised for doing an excellent job on the tax return, and he sued Charles as a matter of principle. Decide.
5. Medistar is a real estate development company specializing in the development of medical facilities. Dr. Schmidt, the team physician for the San Antonio Spurs basketball team, sought to develop "The Texas Center for Athletes" medical center next to the Spurs facility and urged Medistar to obtain the real estate and develop the project on his group's behalf. Medistar spent more than $1 million and thousands of man-hours on the project from 2000 to July 12, 2004, when Dr. Schmidt's new group of investors purchased the property next to the Spur's facility for the project; subsequently, Medistar was informed that it would have no role in the project. Medistar asserts that it relied on Dr. Schmidt's assurances that it would be the developer of the project—and after four years and the $1 million in time and expenses it spent, it is unconscionable to be excluded from the project. Dr. Schmidt and associates contend that Medistar has presented no contractual agreement tying it to any legal obligation to Medistar. Is there a viable legal theory available to Medistar? If so what is the remedy? [*Medistar v. Schmidt*, 267 S.W.3d 150 (Tex. App.)]
6. While on a fishing trip, Tom Snyder met an elderly couple living in near-destitute conditions in a rural area of Texas. He returned to the area often, and he regularly purchased groceries for the couple and paid for their medical needs. Some two years later, the couple's son, David, discovered what Tom had been doing and promised to reimburse Snyder for what he had furnished his parents. He failed to do so and Tom sued David for breach of his promise to reimburse Snyder. Tom has receipts for most of the purchases. What defense, if any, does David have? Decide.
7. The Aqua Drilling Company made a contract to drill a well for the Atlas Construction Company. It was expected that this would supply water for a home being constructed by Atlas. Aqua did not make any guarantee or warranty that water would be produced. Aqua drilled the well exactly as required by the contract, but no water was produced. Atlas refused to pay. It asserted that the contract was not binding on the theory that there had been a failure of consideration because the well did not produce water. Was the contract binding? [*Atlas Construction Co., Inc. v. Aqua Drilling Co.*, 559 P.2d 39 (Wyo.)]
8. Sears, Roebuck and Co. promised to give Forrer permanent employment. Forrer sold his farm at a loss to take the job. Shortly after beginning work, he was discharged by Sears, which claimed that the contract could be terminated at will. Forrer claimed

that promissory estoppel prevented Sears from terminating the contract. Was he correct? [*Forrer v. Sears, Roebuck & Co.*, 153 N.W.2d 587 (Wis.)]

9. Kemp leased a gas filling station from Baehr. Kemp, who was heavily indebted to Penn-O-Tex Oil Corp., transferred to it his right to receive payments on all claims. When Baehr complained that the rent was not paid, he was assured by the corporation that the rent would be paid to him. Baehr did not sue Kemp for the overdue rent but later sued the corporation. The defense was raised that there was no consideration for the promise of the corporation. Decide. [*Baehr v. Penn-O-Tex Corp.*, 104 N.W.2d 661 (Minn.)]

10. John Blackwell was seriously injured in an auto accident. His wife was Korean and spoke little English and needed help communicating with Blackwell's doctor. The Blackwells hired Choi as an interpreter in 1997 and over time Mr. Choi assisted with the family finances and other matters. In 2010 Blackwell's wife fired Choi and later the parties signed an agreement agreeing to pay Choi $450,000 "for the work Choi had done for Blackwell." Choi sued to obtain payment. Was he successful? [*Lee v. Choi*, 754 S.E.2d 371 (Ga. App.)]

11. Kelsoe worked for International Wood Products, Inc., for a number of years. One day Hernandez, a director and major stockholder of the company, promised Kelsoe that the corporation would give her 5 percent of the company's stock. This promise was never kept, and Kelsoe sued International for breach of contract. Had the company broken its contract? [*Kelsoe v. International Wood Products, Inc.*, 588 So. 2d 877 (Ala.)]

12. Kathy left her classic 1978 Volkswagen convertible at Freddie's Service Station, requesting a "tune-up." When she returned that evening, Freddie's bill was $374. Kathy stated that Firestone and Sears advertise tune-ups for $70, and she asked Freddie, "How can you justify this bill?" Freddie responded, "Carburator work." Kathy refused to pay the bill and left. That evening, when the station closed, she took her other set of keys and removed her car, after placing a check in the station's mail slot. The check was made out to Freddie's Service Station for $200 and stated on its face: "This check is in full payment of my account with you regarding the tune-up today on my 1978 Volkswagen convertible." Freddie cashed the check in order to meet his business expenses and then sued Kathy for the difference owed. What result?

13. On the death of their mother, the children of Jane Smith gave their interests in their mother's estate to their father in consideration of his payment of $1 to each of them and his promise to leave them the property on his death. The father died without leaving them the property. The children sued their father's second wife to obtain the property in accordance with the agreement. The second wife claimed that the agreement was not a binding contract because the amount of $1 and future gifts given for the children's interests were so trivial and uncertain. Decide.

14. Radio Station KSCS broadcast a popular music program. It announced that it would pay $25,000 to any listener who detected that it did not play three consecutive songs. Steve Jennings listened to and heard a program in which two songs were followed by a commercial program. He claimed the $25,000. The station refused to pay on the ground that there was no consideration for its promise to pay that amount. Was the station liable? [*Jennings v. Radio Station KSCS*, 708 S.W.2d 60 (Tex. App.)]

15. Hoffman wanted to acquire a franchise for a Red Owl grocery store. (Red Owl was a corporation that maintained a system of chain stores.) An agent of Red Owl informed Hoffman and his wife that if they would sell their bakery in Wautoma, acquire a certain tract of land in Chilton (another Wisconsin city), and put up $6,000, they would be given a franchise. In reliance on the agent's promise, Hoffman sold his business and acquired the land in Chilton, but he was never granted a franchise. He and his wife sued Red Owl. Red Owl raised the defense that there had been only an assurance that Hoffman would receive a franchise, but because there was no promise supported by consideration, there was no binding contract to give him a franchise. Decide. [*Hoffman v. Red Owl Stores, Inc.*, 133 N.W.2d 267 (Wis.)]

C H A P T E R 15

Legality and Public Policy

15-1 General Principles
- 15-1a Effect of Illegality
- 15-1b Exceptions to Effect of Illegality
- 15-1c Partial Illegality
- 15-1d Crimes and Civil Wrongs
- 15-1e Good Faith and Fairness
- 15-1f Unconscionable Clauses

15-2 Agreements Affecting Public Welfare
- 15-2a Agreements Contrary to Public Policy
- 15-2b Gambling, Wagers, and Lotteries

15-3 Regulation of Business
- 15-3a Effect of Violation
- 15-3b Statutory Regulation of Contracts
- 15-3c Licensed Callings or Dealings
- 15-3d Contracts in Restraint of Trade
- 15-3e Agreements Not to Compete
- 15-3f Usurious Agreements

Learning Outcomes ⟨⟨⟨

After studying this chapter, you should be able to

LO.1 **Explain the general contract principles on "illegality"**

LO.2 **Explain the implied obligation on all parties of good faith and fair dealing**

LO.3 **Understand that it is only in unusual situations that a contract provision will be unenforceable because it is unconscionable**

LO.4 **Explain the rationale for requiring licenses to carry on as a business, trade, or profession**

LO.5 **Distinguish between noncompete clauses after the sale of a business and noncompete clauses in employment contracts**

A court will not enforce a contract if it is illegal, contrary to public policy, or unconscionable.

15-1 General Principles

An agreement is illegal either when its formation or performance is a crime or a tort or when it is contrary to public policy or unconscionable.

15-1a Effect of Illegality

Ordinarily, an illegal agreement is void. When an agreement is illegal, the parties are usually not entitled to the aid of the courts. Examples of illegal contracts where the courts have left the parties where they found them include a liquor store owner not being allowed to bring suit for money owed for goods (liquor) sold and delivered on credit in violation of statute and an unlicensed home improvement contractor not being allowed to enforce his contract for progress payments due him. If the illegal agreement has not been performed, neither party can sue the other to obtain performance or damages. If the agreement has been performed, neither party can sue the other to obtain damages or to set the agreement aside.[1]

CASE SUMMARY

The Illegal Paralegal

FACTS: Brian Neiman was involved in the illegal practice of law for over seven years. Having been found guilty of illegally practicing law, he sought to collect disability benefits under his disability insurance policy with Provident Life due to an alleged bipolar disorder, the onset of which occurred during the pendency of criminal and bar proceedings against him. Neiman contends that his bipolar disorder prevents him from working as a paralegal. Provident contends that Neiman should not be indemnified for the loss of income generated from his illegal practice of law.

DECISION: Because all of Neiman's income was derived from the unlawful practice of law in the seven years preceding his claim, as a matter of public policy, a court will not enforce a disability benefits policy that compensates him for his loss of income he was not entitled to earn. Neiman's own wrongdoing caused the contract to be void. Accordingly, Neiman was *in pari delicto* [equally guilty], if not more at fault than the insurance company, in causing the contract to be void and will recover neither benefits nor the premiums he paid. The court must leave the parties where it found them. [***Neiman v. Provident Life & Accident Insurance Co.***, **217 F. Supp. 2d 1281 (S.D. Fla. 2002)**]

Even if a contract appears to be legal on its face, it may be unenforceable if it was entered into for an illegal purpose. **For Example,** if zoning regulations in the special-purpose district of Washington, D.C., require that only a professional can lease space in a given building, and the rental agent suggests that two nonprofessionals take out the lease in their attorney's name but all parties realize that the premises will be used only by the nonprofessionals, then the lease in question is illegal and unenforceable.[2]

15-1b Exceptions to Effect of Illegality

To avoid hardship, exceptions are made to the rules stated previously in the section titled "Effect of Illegality."

[1] *Sabia v. Mattituck Inlet Marina, Inc.,* 805 N.Y.S.2d 346 (A.D. 2005).
[2] *McMahon v. A, H, & B,* 728 A.2d 656 (D.C. 1999).

Protection of One Party

When the law that the agreement violates is intended to protect one of the parties, that party may seek relief. **For Example,** when, in order to protect the public, the law forbids the issuance of securities by certain classes of corporations, a person who has purchased them may recover the money paid.

Unequal Guilt

in pari delicto–equally guilty; used in reference to a transaction as to which relief will not be granted to either party because both are equally guilty of wrongdoing.

When the parties are not ***in pari delicto***—equally guilty—the least guilty party is granted relief when public interest is advanced by doing so. **For Example,** when a statute is adopted to protect one of the parties to a transaction, such as a usury law adopted to protect borrowers, the person to be protected will not be deemed to be *in pari delicto* with the wrongdoer when entering into a transaction that the statute prohibits.

15-1c Partial Illegality

An agreement may involve the performance of several promises, some of which are illegal and some legal. The legal parts of the agreement may be enforced provided that they can be separated from the parts that are illegal.

When the illegal provision of a contract may be ignored without defeating the contract's basic purpose, a court will merely ignore the illegal provision and enforce the balance of the contract. Consequently, when a provision for the payment of an attorney's fee in a car rental agreement was illegal because a local statute prohibited it, the court would merely ignore the fee provision and enforce the balance of the contract.[3]

Contracts that involve both unlawful and lawful provisions may be enforced if the illegal portion is severable from the legal. **For Example,** where two separate funds were provided to Watkins by Kyablue, one for gambling purposes and the other in the form of a loan for personal expenses, Kyablue was allowed to recover the repayment of the personal loan, which was severable from the arguably illegal portion relating to gambling-related contracts.[4]

15-1d Crimes and Civil Wrongs

An agreement is illegal, and therefore void, when it calls for the commission of any act that constitutes a crime. To illustrate, one cannot enforce an agreement by which the other party is to commit an assault, steal property, burn a house, or kill a person. A contract to obtain equipment for committing a crime is illegal and cannot be enforced. Thus, a contract to manufacture and sell illegal slot machines is void.

An agreement that calls for the commission of a civil wrong is also illegal and void. Examples are agreements to slander a third person; defraud another; infringe another's patent, trademark, or copyright; or fix prices.

15-1e Good Faith and Fairness

good faith–absence of knowledge of any defects or problems.

Every contract has an implied obligation that neither party shall do anything that will have the effect of destroying or injuring the right of the other party to receive the fruits of the contract. This means that in every contract there exists an implied covenant of **good faith** and fair dealing. **For Example,** Katy Lesser entered into a 10-year lease of retail space to operate a natural food store in South Burlington, Vermont. Her business prospered and in April 1999 she signed a lease for additional space. For five years, the

[3] *Harbour v. Arelco, Inc.,* 678 N.E.2d 381 (Ind. 1997).

[4] *Kyablue v. Watkins,* 149 Cal. Rptr. 3d 156 (Cal. App. 2012).

landlord continually rebuffed her efforts to meet and discuss plans to renovate the 1999 space to expand the grocery store, motivated solely by a desire to pressure the tenant to pay a portion of his legal fees in an unrelated zoning case. The court found that the landlord breached the obligation of good faith and fair dealing, causing the 1999 space to be essentially unusable from 1999 to 2004. The court awarded the tenant the rent she paid for this period less a storage fee adjustment.[5]

15-1f Unconscionable Clauses

Ordinarily, a court will not consider whether a contract is fair or unfair, is wise or foolish, or operates unequally between the parties. **For Example,** the Kramper Family Farm agreed to sell 17.59 acres of land to Dakota Industrial Development, Inc. (DID), for $35,000 per acre if the buyer constructed a paved road along the property by December 31. The contract also provided that if the road was not completed by the date set forth in the contract, the price per acre would be $45,000. When the road was not completed by the December 31 date, Family Farm sued DID for the additional $10,000 per acre. DID defended that to apply the contract according to its plain language would create an unconscionable result and was an unenforceable penalty provision contrary to public policy. The court refused to allow DID to escape its contractual obligations on the pretext of unconscionability and public policy arguments. The parties are at liberty to contract as they see fit, the court concluded, and, generally, a court will not inquire into the adequacy of consideration inasmuch as the value of property is a matter of personal judgment by the parties to the contract. In this case, the price consisted of either $45,000 per acre, or $35,000 per acre with the road by a certain date.[6]

However, in certain unusual situations, the law may hold a contract provision unenforceable because it is too harsh or oppressive to one of the parties. This principle may be applied to invalidate a clause providing for the payment by one party of an excessive penalty on the breaking of a contract or a provision inserted by the dominant party that it shall not be liable for the consequences of intentional torts, fraud, or gross negligence. This principle is extended in connection with the sale of goods to provide that "if the court ... finds the contract or any clause of the contract to have been unconscionable at the time it was made, the court may refuse to enforce the contract, or it may enforce the remainder of the contract without the unconscionable clause, or it may so limit the application of any unconscionable clause as to avoid any unconscionable result."[7]

What Constitutes Unconscionability?

A provision in a contract that gives what the court believes is too much of an advantage over a buyer may be held void as unconscionable.

Determination of Unconscionability

Some jurisdictions analyze unconscionability as having two separate elements: procedural and substantive. Both elements must be present for a court to refuse to enforce a contract provision. Other jurisdictions analyze unconscionability by considering the doctrine of adhesion and whether the clause in question is unduly oppressive.

Procedural unconscionability has to do with matters of freedom of assent resulting from inequality of bargaining power and the absence of real negotiations and meaningful

[5] *Century Partners, LP v. Lesser Goldsmith Enterprises,* 958 A.2d 627 (Vt. 2008).
[6] *Kramper Family Farm v. Dakota Industrial Development, Inc.,* 603 N.W.2d 463 (Neb. App. 1999).
[7] U.C.C. §2-302(1).

contract of adhesion–contract offered by a dominant party to a party with inferior bargaining power on a take-it-or-leave-it basis.

choice or a surprise resulting from hiding a disputed term in an unduly long document or fine print. Companywide standardized form contracts imposed on a take-it-or-leave-it basis by a party with superior bargaining strength are called **contracts of adhesion,** and they may sometimes be deemed procedurally unconscionable.

Substantive unconscionability focuses on the actual terms of the contract itself. Such unconscionability is indicated when the contract terms are so one-sided as to shock the conscience or are so extreme as to appear unconscionable according to the mores and business practices of the time and place.

The U.S. Supreme Court has made clear that arbitration is an acceptable forum for the resolution of employment disputes between employees and their employers, including employment-related claims based on federal and state statutes.[8] The controlling arbitration agreement language is commonly devised and implemented by the employer. Under the Federal Arbitration Act (FAA), the employer can obtain a court order to stay court proceedings and compel arbitration according to the terms of the controlling arbitration agreement. The Supreme Court also made clear that in agreeing to arbitration of a statutory claim, a party does not forgo substantive rights afforded by the statute. In a growing number of court decisions, in effect employers are finding that courts will not enforce arbitration agreements in which the employer has devised an arbitration agreement that functions as a thumb on the employer's side of the scale.[9]

When a court finds that a contract or any clause of a contract was unconscionable at the time it was made, it may enforce the remainder of the contract without the unconscionable clause or refuse to enforce the entire agreement if the agreement is permeated by unconscionability. **For Example,** two provisions of a premarital agreement between Jeffrey and Nancy Facter waiving the right to spousal and child support upon the dissolution of the marriage were found to be unconscionable. The invalid provisions were deleted and the remainder of the agreement was enforced.[10] An arbitration agreement may be substantively unconscionable if fees and costs are so excessive as to deny the litigant the ability to pursue a claim. **For Example,** an arbitration agreement was found to be substantively unconscionable because the plaintiff John Clark, a retired senior citizen

THINKING THINGS THROUGH

Legality and Public Policy

Karl Llewellyn, the principal drafter of the law that governs nearly all sales of goods in the United States—the Uniform Commercial Code (UCC)—once wrote, "Covert tools are never reliable tools." He was referring to unfairness in a contract or between the contracting parties.

The original intent of declaring certain types of contracts void because of issues of imbalance was based in equity. Courts stepped in to help parties who found themselves bound under agreements that were not fair and open in both their written terms and the communications between the parties. One contracts scholar wrote that the original intent could be described as courts stepping in to help "presumptive sillies like sailors and heirs..." and others who, if not crazy, are "pretty peculiar."

However, as the sophistication of contracts and commercial transactions increased, the importance of accuracy, honesty, and fairness increased. Unconscionability is a contracts defense that permits courts to intervene where contracts, if enforced, would "affront the sense of decency." Unconscionability is a term of ethics or moral philosophy used by courts to prevent exploitation and fraud.

[8] *Gilmer v. Interstate/Johnson Lane Corp.,* 500 U.S. 20 (1991); *Circuit City Stores, Inc. v. Adams,* 532 U.S. 105 (2001).
[9] See *Vassi/Kouska v. Woodfield Nissan Inc.,* 830 N.E.2d 619 (Ill. App. 2005).
[10] In re *the Marriage of Facter,* 152 Cal. Rptr. 3d 79 (Cal. App. 2013).

living on a fixed income, could not afford to pay the projected $22,800 in arbitrators' fees to arbitrate his medical negligence and abuse and neglect of a vulnerable adult action against the defendant nursing home, where the arbitration agreement did not provide for a waiver/reduction of fees based on financial hardship.[11]

15-2 Agreements Affecting Public Welfare

Agreements that may harm the public welfare are condemned as contrary to public policy and are not binding. Agreements that interfere with public service or the duties of public officials, obstruct legal process, or discriminate against classifications of individuals may be considered detrimental to public welfare and, as such, are not enforceable.

15-2a Agreements Contrary to Public Policy

A given agreement may not violate any statute but may still be so offensive to society that the courts feel that enforcing the contract would be contrary to public policy.

public policy–certain objectives relating to health, morals, and integrity of government that the law seeks to advance by declaring invalid any contract that conflicts with those objectives even though there is no statute expressly declaring such a contract illegal.

Public policy cannot be defined precisely but is loosely described as protection from that which tends to be injurious to the public or contrary to the public good or which violates any established interest of society. Contracts that may be unenforceable as contrary to public policy frequently relate to the protection of the public welfare, health, or safety; to the protection of the person; and to the protection of recognized social institutions. **For Example,** a woman entered into a services contract with a male in exchange for financial support. The record disclosed, however, that the association between the parties was one founded upon the exchange of money for sex. The court determined that the agreement for financial support in exchange for illicit sexual relations was violative of public policy and thus was unenforceable.[12] Courts are cautious in invalidating a contract on the ground that it is contrary to public policy because courts recognize that, on the one hand, they are applying a very vague standard and, on the other hand, they are restricting the freedom of the contracting parties to contract freely as they choose.[13]

15-2b Gambling, Wagers, and Lotteries

lottery–any plan by which a consideration is given for a chance to win a prize; it consists of three elements: (1) there must be a payment of money or something of value for an opportunity to win, (2) a prize must be available, and (3) the prize must be offered by lot or chance.

Gambling contracts are illegal. Largely as a result of the adoption of antigambling statutes, wagers or bets are generally illegal. Private **lotteries** involving the three elements of prize, chance, and consideration (or similar affairs of chance) are also generally held illegal. In many states, public lotteries (lotteries run by a state government) have been legalized by statute. Raffles are usually regarded as lotteries. In some states, bingo games, lotteries, and raffles are legalized by statute when the funds raised are used for a charitable purpose.

Sales promotion schemes calling for the distribution of property according to chance among the purchasers of goods are held illegal as lotteries without regard to whether the scheme is called a *guessing contest*, a *raffle*, or a *gift*.

Giveaway plans and games are lawful so long as it is not necessary to buy anything or give anything of value to participate. If participation is free, the element of consideration is lacking, and there is no lottery.

An activity is not gambling when the result is solely or predominantly a matter of skill. In contrast, it is gambling when the result is solely a matter of luck. Rarely is any activity 100 percent skill or 100 percent luck.

[11] *Clark v. Renaissance West*, LLC, 307 P.3d 77 (Ariz. App. 2013).
[12] *Anonymous v. Anonymous*, 740 N.Y.S.2d 341 (App. Div. 2002).
[13] *Beacon Hill Civic Ass'n v. Ristorante Toscano, Inc.*, 662 N.E.2d 1015 (Mass. 1996).

ETHICS & THE LAW

Public Policy Issues Regarding Surrogacy Contracts

William Stern and his wife were unable to have children. The Sterns entered into a surrogacy contract with Mary Beth Whitehead though the Infertility Center of New York (ICNY). William Stern and the Whiteheads (husband and wife) signed a contract for Mary Beth to be artificially inseminated and carry Stern's child to term, for which Stern was to pay Mary Beth $10,000 and ICNY $7,500.

Mary Beth was successfully artificially inseminated in 1985, and "Baby M" was born on March 27, 1986. On March 30, 1986, Mary Beth turned Baby M over to the Sterns. Subsequently, Mary Beth became so emotionally distraught that the Sterns allowed her to take Baby M for one week to help her adjust. The Whiteheads fled to New Jersey with the baby, and the search and return of Baby M attracted national attention and brought forth the national discussion of the legality of surrogacy contracts. The Supreme Court of New Jersey invalidated the surrogacy contract as against public policy but affirmed the trial court's use of "the best interests of the child" analysis,* and on remand the trial court awarded the Sterns custody and visitation rights to Mary Beth Whitehead.

Assisted Reproductive Technology (ART) has created ways for people to have children regardless of their reproductive capacity, including traditional and gestational categories. The ability to create a family using ART has seemingly outpaced legislative responses to the legal questions presented. In *Rosecky v. Schissel*, the Wisconsin Supreme Court determined that a surrogacy agreement was a valid and largely enforceable contract except for the language requiring the surrogate mother to terminate her parental rights.**

Chief Justice Shirley Abrahamson in her concurring opinion disagreed with the majority opinion's authorization of people to contract out the State's traditional, statutory oversight role in the protection of children. She points out numerous public policy issues regarding the validity of surrogacy agreements including:

*Must the agreement be in writing; should compensated agreements be allowed and what are the limits on compensation; should the availability of surrogacy be limited to married couples or to infertile intended parents; should the age of any party be limited; should a spouse be required either to consent or to be made party to the contract; must each individual involved be represented by counsel; should the State require that information about each individual's legal rights be provided; what provisions are valid regarding who makes decisions about health care and termination of the pregnancy; how and when may the agreement be terminated; and must any party to the agreement be given the opportunity to change his or her mind before or after the birth of the child.****

What is your opinion?

***Matter of Baby M.*, 537 A.2d 1227 (N.J. 1988).**

****Rosecky v. Schissel*, 833 N.W.2d 634 (Wis. 2013).**

****Id.* at 126 FN.2.

15-3 Regulation of Business

Local, state, and national laws regulate a wide variety of business activities and practices.

15-3a Effect of Violation

Whether an agreement made in connection with business conducted in violation of the law is binding or void depends on how strongly opposed the public policy is to the prohibited act. Some courts take the view that the agreement is not void unless the statute expressly specifies this. In some instances, a statute expressly preserves the validity of the contract. **For Example,** if someone fails to register a fictitious name under which a business is conducted, the violator, after registering the name as required by statute, is permitted to sue on a contract made while illegally conducting business.

15-3b Statutory Regulation of Contracts

To establish uniformity or to protect one of the parties to a contract, statutes frequently provide that contracts of a given class must follow a statutory model or must contain specified provisions. **For Example,** statutes commonly specify that particular clauses must be included in insurance policies to protect the persons insured and their beneficiaries. Other statutes require that contracts executed in connection with credit buying and loans contain particular provisions designed to protect the debtor.

Consumer protection legislation gives the consumer the right to rescind the contract in certain situations. Laws relating to truth in lending, installment sales, and home improvement contracts commonly require that an installment-sale contract specify the cash price, the down payment, the trade-in value (if any), the cash balance, the insurance costs, and the interest and finance charges.

CPA 15-3c Licensed Callings or Dealings

Statutes frequently require that a person obtain a license, certificate, or diploma before practicing certain professions, such as law and medicine.[14] A license may also be required before carrying on a particular business or trade, such as that of a real estate broker, stockbroker, hotel keeper, or pawnbroker.

If a license is required to protect the public from unqualified persons, a contract made by an unlicensed person is unenforceable. **For Example,** a corporation that does not hold a required real estate broker's license cannot sue to recover fees for services as a broker. An unlicensed insurance broker who cannot recover a fee because of the absence of a license cannot evade the statutory requirement by having a friend who is a licensed broker bill for the services and collect the payment for him.

CASE SUMMARY

How Much for a Brokerage License? How Much Commission Was Lost?

FACTS: Thompson Halbach & Associates, Inc., an Arizona corporation, entered into an agreement with Meteor Motors, Inc., the owner of Palm Beach Acura, to find a buyer for the dealership, and Meteor agreed to pay a 5 percent commission based on the closing price of the sale. Working out of Scottsdale, Arizona, Thompson solicited potential Florida purchasers for the Florida business by phone, fax, and e-mail. Among those contacted was Craig Zinn Automotive Group, which ultimately purchased Palm Beach Acura from Meteor Motors for $5,000,000. Thompson was not paid its $250,000 commission and brought suit against Meteor for breach of contract. Meteor defended that Thompson was an unlicensed broker and that a state statute declares a contract for a commission with an unlicensed broker to be invalid. Thompson responded that the Florida state statute did not apply because it worked out of Scottsdale.

DECISION: Judgment for Meteor. The Florida statute clearly applies to a foreign broker who provides brokerage activities in Florida. Thompson solicited potential Florida purchasers for the Florida business and that purchaser was a Florida corporation. [***Meteor Motors v. Thompson Halbach & Associates*, 914 So. 2d 479 (Fla. App. 2005)**]

In some states an unlicensed contractor can neither enforce a home improvement contract against an owner nor seek recovery in *quantum meruit.* **For Example,** a contractor who performed work on Adam Gottbetter's apartment in New York City and was not paid for its work was barred from pursuing its claim against the owner.[15]

However, if the statute does not provide expressly that its violation will deprive the parties of their right to sue on the contract, and the denial of relief is wholly out of proportion to the requirements of public policy, the right to recover will not be denied. **For Example,** an unlicensed contractor who installed water pumps on Staten Island little

[14] *Hakimi v. Cantwell,* 855 N.Y.S.2d 273 (App. Div. 2008).
[15] *Orchid Construction Corp. v. Gottbetter,* 932 N.Y.S.2d 100 (A.D. 2011).

league fields was not barred from recovering $18,316.59 for the work in question, which was not home improvement work.[16]

CPA 15-3d Contracts in Restraint of Trade

An agreement that unreasonably restrains trade is illegal and void on the ground that it is contrary to public policy. Such agreements take many forms, such as a combination to create a monopoly or to obtain a corner on the market or an association of merchants to increase prices. In addition to the illegality of the agreement based on general principles of law, statutes frequently declare monopolies illegal and subject the parties to various civil and criminal penalties.[17]

CPA 15-3e Agreements Not to Compete

In the absence of a valid restrictive covenant, the seller of a business may compete with the buyer, or an ex-employee may solicit customers of the former employer. Restrictive covenants not to compete are disfavored (but not prohibited) in many states as a trade restraint because they may prevent an employee from earning a living, adversely restrain the mobility of employees, and may be overly protective of the interests of employers at the expense of employees. A noncompete provision may be enforceable, however, if (1) it is narrowly drawn to protect the employer's legitimate business interests, (2) it is not unduly burdensome on the employee's ability to earn a living, (3) the geographic restriction is not overly broad, and (4) a reasonable time limitation is given. Reasonably necessary noncompete clauses in the sale of a business are enforced in all states.

Sale of Business

When a going business is sold, it is commonly stated in the contract that the seller shall not go into the same or a similar business again within a certain geographic area or for a certain period of time, or both. In early times, such agreements were held void because they deprived the public of the service of the person who agreed not to compete, reduced competition, and exposed the public to monopoly. To modern courts, the question is whether, under the circumstances, the restriction imposed on one party is reasonably necessary to protect the other party. If the restriction is reasonable, it is valid and enforceable. **For Example,** when Scott Gaddy, the majority stockholder of GWC Insurance Brokers sold his business to Alliant for $4.1 million he agreed to refrain from competing in the insurance business in California for five years. Under California law contracts not to compete are void, except for noncompetition covenants in connection with the sale of a business. The reason for the exception is to prevent the seller from depriving the buyer of the full value of the acquisition, including the sold company's goodwill. The court enforced the covenant against Gaddy.[18]

Employment Contract

Employers rely on noncompete clauses to protect their businesses from employees who leave after receiving expensive training or engineers, scientists, or other professionals or

[16] *Del Carlo v. Staten Island Little League, Inc.*, 993 N.Y.S.2d 435 (A.D. 2014).

[17] Sherman Antitrust Act, 15 U.S.C. §§1–7; Clayton Act, 15 U.S.C. §§12–27; Federal Trade Commission Act, 15 U.S.C. §§41–58.

[18] Cal. Rptr. 3d 259 (Cal. App. 2008). Aside from the sale of a business, under California law, any "contract by which anyone is restrained from engaging in a lawful profession, trade or business is to that extent void." Cal B&P Code §16600. A noncompete provision is permitted, however, when "necessary to protect the employer's trade secrets." See *Lotono v. Aetna U.S. Healthcare Inc.*, 82 F. Supp. 2d 1089 (C.D. Cal. 1999), where Aetna was liable for wrongful termination when it fired a California employee for refusing to sign a noncompete agreement.

nonprofessionals who leave firms or businesses to join competitors. Employers enforce these clauses by notifying the new employer and threatening litigation,[19] or seeking a preliminary injunction prohibiting the violation of the noncompete agreement.[20] The burden of proof is on the employer to show that the provision is narrowly drawn to protect the employer's legitimate business interests as to time, place, and activities. Employers have legitimate protectable business interests including maintaining their goodwill with existing customers, their confidential information, and trade secrets. If the noncompete provision is overly broad, however, it will be unenforceable. **For Example,** Home Paramount Pest Control's noncompete clause with Justin Shaffer that prohibited him from working in the pest control industry in any capacity, barring him "in any manner whatsoever," was overly broad and unenforceable.[21] Geographic restrictions are also at issue. **For Example,** Illinois manufacturer Arcor's noncompete clause, which had a restricted area of "the United States and Canada" precluding competition by a former employee for a one-year period, was found to be unenforceable as an industry-wide ban that constituted a "blanket prohibition on competition."[22] Overly broad and unreasonable restrictive covenants will not be enforced.

CASE SUMMARY

Unreasonable and Unenforceable

FACTS: On December 12, 2012, Defendants Contreras, Senn, Verduzco, and VanderWeerd, inseminated cows at several dairy farms in Sunnyside, Washington, on behalf of their employer, Genex Cooperative, Inc. ("Genex"). The very next day, they inseminated cows at the same dairy farms—but this time on behalf of CRV USA ("CRV"), a Genex rival. Jilted by its former employees and spurned by its customers, Genex filed suit to enforce non-competition agreements against three of the defendants. Although the individual contracts varied in terms, Contreras, Senn, and Verduzco contended the agreements were unenforceable. Mr. VanderWeerd had not signed an agreement.

DECISION: Judgment against Genex. Verduzco's noncompete covenant prohibited him from contacting any dairy farm, which he had sought either new or increased business from in the last eighteen months. Under Wisconsin law, applicable to Verduzco's agreement, prohibiting an employee from soliciting any customer the employee has tried but failed to do business with for the former employer is a violation of state law.

Senn's restrictive agreement was governed by Washington law and found to be unreasonable because it was not limited to soliciting or serving former clients. It appeared to the court that Genex actually used restrictive covenants to eliminate legitimate competition or to strong-arm employees to accept ever-dwindling wages and restrict their freedom to work.

Contreras—who cannot read or write English—was a low-level agricultural worker with an employment-at-will relationship with Genex. An at-will employee may be terminated without any cause and then be prohibited from seeking new employment in his line of work. Genex did not meet its burden to establish the reasonableness of its covenant with Contreras, and the noncompete agreement was thus unenforceable. [***Genex Cooperative, Inc. v. Contreras,* 39 IER Cases 294 (E.D. Wash. 2014)**]

[19] In *Socko v. Mid-Atlantic Systems of CPA, Inc.,* 99 A.3d 928 (Pa. Super. 2014), the employer notified the new employer and threatened litigation. Socko successfully challenged this action, with the court deciding that the agreement was unenforceable for lack of consideration because it was entered into after the commencement of Socko's employment with Mid-Atlantic.

[20] A motion for a preliminary injunction is heard expeditiously by the court and is ordinarily used to preserve the status quo pending a trial on the merits. However, in noncompete cases, the validity of the time limitation is "clothed with immediacy." Decisions at the preliminary injunction stage become, in effect, a determination on the merits. See *Horner International Co. v. McCoy,* 754 S.E.2d 852 (2014).

[21] *Home Paramount Pest Control Companies, Inc. v. Shaffer,* 718 S.E.2d 762 (Va. 2011).

[22] *Arcor, Inc. v. Haas,* 842 N.E.2d 265 (Ill. App. 2005).

Effect of Invalidity

When a restriction of competition agreed to by the parties is invalid because its scope as to time or geographic area is too great, how does this affect the contract? Some courts trim the restrictive covenant down to a scope they deem reasonable and require the parties to abide by that revision.[23] This rule is nicknamed the "blue-pencil rule." **For Example,** Julie Murray signed a noncompete agreement, which was validly assigned to the purchaser of the Accounting Center of Luca County, Inc. When the new owner changed from an hourly wage to commission pay for her tax preparation work, she objected and was terminated. The court found that the 24-month noncompete restriction exceeded what was reasonable to protect the employer's legitimate business interests and modified the time period to one year.[24] In the *Arcor* case, the court refused to "blue-pencil" the covenant because to render the clause reasonable, the court would in effect be writing a new agreement, which is inappropriate.[25] Other courts refuse to apply the blue-pencil rule and hold that the restrictive covenant is void or that the entire contract is void.[26] There is also authority that a court should refuse to apply the blue-pencil rule when the restrictive covenant is manifestly unfair and would virtually keep the employee from earning a living.

15-3f Usurious Agreements

usury–lending money at an interest rate that is higher than the maximum rate allowed by law.

Usury is committed when money is loaned at a higher rate of interest than the law allows. Most states prohibit by statute charging more than a stated amount of interest. These statutes provide a maximum annual contract rate of interest that can be exacted under the law of a given state. In many states, the usury law does not apply to loans made to corporations.

THINKING THINGS THROUGH

Noncompete Clauses, Cause for Concern?

Several states do not enforce noncompete clauses in employment contracts, according to the research of Matt Marx, who dedicated his doctoral studies at Harvard to this topic. The states are (from west to east): California, Nevada, Montana, North Dakota, Minnesota, Oklahoma, West Virginia, and Connecticut. (New York, Washington, and Oregon have significantly limited their applicability.) Marx had naively signed a two-year noncompete agreement out of MIT at SpeechWorks, a voice recognition start-up, and when he wanted to leave and continue in the voice recognition field, his options were to sit out the two-year noncompete period or go to work at a California firm, which he did. He is now researching whether enforcing noncompetes in a state can spur inventors, engineers, and entrepreneurs to move elsewhere to pursue development of their ideas.*

Does a state's innovation suffer when noncompete clauses handcuff employees to an employer, or force employees to take an unpaid leave for the noncompete period before continuing in their field with a new or start-up employer? Thinking Things Through, prospective employees should carefully consider the impact noncompetes would have on their lives, and if they must sign one, carefully negotiate its duration and scope.**

*See Scott Kirsner, "Why 'Noncompete' Means 'Don't Thrive,'" *Boston Globe,* December 30, 2007, E–1; Scott Kirsner, "Start-ups Stifled by Noncompetes," *Boston Globe,* June 21, 2009, G–1.
**For a comprehensive study of the strength of noncompetition enforcement rankings by state, see Norman D. Bishara, "Fifty Ways to Leave Your Employer: Relative Enforcement of Covenants Not to Compete, Trends and Implications for Employee Mobility Policy," 13 *U. Pa. J. Bus. L.* 751 (2011).

[23] *Keeley v. CSA, P.C.,* 510 S.E.2d 880 (Ga. App. 1999).
[24] *Murray v. Accounting Center of Lucas County, Inc.,* 898 N.E.2d 89 (Ohio App. 2008).
[25] *Arcor, Inc. v. Hass* 842 N.E.2d 265 (Ill. App. 2005).
[26] *Volcen Steel Structures, Inc. v. McCarty,* 764 S.E.2d 458 (Ga. App. 2014).

When a lender incurs expenses in making a loan, such as the cost of appraising property or making a credit investigation of the borrower, the lender will require the borrower to pay the amount of such expenses. Any fee charged by a lender that goes beyond the reasonable expense of making the loan constitutes "interest" for the purposes of determining whether the transaction is usurious.[27]

Penalites for violating usury laws vary from state to state, with a number of states restricting the lender to the recovery of the loan but no interest whatsoever; other states allow recovery of the loan principal and interest up to the maximum contract rate. Some states also impose a penalty on the lender such as the payment of double the interest paid on a usurious loan.

CASE SUMMARY

Would You Recommend Karen Canzoneri as an Investment Advisor?

FACTS: Karen Canzoneri entered into two agreements with Howard Pinchuck. Under the first agreement, Canzoneri advanced $50,000 to be repaid at 12 percent per month for 12 consecutive months "as an investment profit." The second agreement required "$36,000 to be repaid on or before 6/1/01 with an investment profit of $36,000, total being $72,000." The annualized rate of return for the first transaction was 144 percent and for the second transaction was 608 percent. The civil penalty for violating the state's maximum interest rate of 25 percent per annum is forfeiture of the entire principal amount. Canzoneri contends that the transactions were investments not subject to the usury law.

DECISION: Judgment for Pinchuck. The four elements of a usurious transaction are present: (1) the transaction was a loan, (2) the money loaned required that it be returned, (3) an interest rate higher than allowed by law was required, and (4) a corrupt intention to take more than the legal rate for the use of the money loaned exists. Even though the terms called for "profit," not "interest," the courts looked to the substance, not the form of the transaction. [***Pinchuck v. Canzoneri*, 920 So. 2d 713 (Fla. App. 2006)**]

Make the Connection

Summary

When an agreement is illegal, it is ordinarily void and no contract arises from it. Courts will not allow one party to an illegal agreement to bring suit against the other party. There are some exceptions to this, such as when the parties are not equally guilty or when the law's purpose in making the agreement illegal is to protect the person who is bringing suit. When possible, an agreement will be interpreted as being lawful. Even when a particular provision is held unlawful, the balance of the agreement may be saved so that the net result is a contract minus the clause that was held illegal.

The term *illegality* embraces situations in unconscionable contract clauses in which the courts hold that contract provisions are unenforceable because they are too harsh or oppressive to one of the parties to a transaction. If the clause is part of a standard form contract drafted by the party having superior bargaining power and is presented on a take-it-or-leave-it basis (a contract of adhesion) and the substantive terms of the clause itself are unduly oppressive, the clause will be found to be unconscionable and not enforced.

[27] *Lentimo v. Cullen Center Bank and Trust Co.*, 919 S.W.2d 743 (Tex. App. 1996).

Whether a contract is contrary to public policy may be difficult to determine because public policy is not precisely defined. That which is harmful to the public welfare or general good is contrary to public policy. Contracts condemned as contrary to public policy include those designed to deprive the weaker party of a benefit that the lawmaker desired to provide, agreements injuring public service, and wagers and private lotteries. Statutes commonly make the wager illegal as a form of gambling. The private lottery is any plan under which, for a consideration, a person has a chance to win a prize.

Illegality may consist of the violation of a statute or administrative regulation adopted to regulate business. An agreement not to compete may be illegal as a restraint of trade except when reasonable in its terms and when it is incidental to the sale of a business or to a contract of employment.

The charging by a lender of a higher rate of interest than allowed by law is usury. Courts must examine transactions carefully to see whether a usurious loan is disguised as a legitimate transaction.

Learning Outcomes

After studying this chapter, you should be able to clearly explain:

15-1 General Principles

LO.1 Explain the general contract principles on "illegality"

See the unenforceable illegal lease to nonprofessionals example, page 276.

See the example where a contract to manufacture and sell illegal slot machines is void, page 277.

LO.2 Explain the implied obligation on all parties of good faith and fair dealing

See the example of the Vermont landlord who deprived a tenant of her rights under a lease, page 278.

15-2 Agreements Affecting Public Welfare

LO.3 Understand that it is only in unusual situations that a contract provision will be unenforceable because it is unconscionable

See the *Kramper Family Farm* example where the court refused to consider whether the contract was fair or unfair, wise or foolish, page 278.

But see *John Clark's* case, illustrating an unconscionable arbitration clause, page 280.

15-3 Regulation of Business

LO.4 Explain the rationale for requiring licenses to carry on as a business, trade, or profession

See the discussion requiring licenses to protect the public from unqualified persons, page 282.

LO.5 Distinguish between noncompete clauses after the sale of a business and noncompete clauses in employment contracts

See the example where the California court enforced a five-year noncompete clause against the seller of a business, page 283.

See the example involving Julie Murray's noncompete clause and why it was modified from 24 months to one year, page 285.

See the *Genex* case that illustrates a trend barring enforcement of overly broad and unreasonable noncompetition clauses, page 284.

Key Terms

contracts of adhesion	*in pari delicto*	public policy
good faith	lotteries	usury

Questions and Case Problems

1. When are the parties to an illegal agreement *in pari delicto?*

2. John Iwen sued U.S. West Direct because of a negligently constructed yellow pages advertisement. U.S. West Direct moved to stay litigation and compel arbitration under the yellow pages order form, which required advertisers to resolve all controversies through arbitration, but allowed U.S. West (the publisher) to pursue judicial remedies to collect amounts due it. Under the arbitration provision, Iwen's sole remedy was a pro rata reduction or refund of the cost of the advertisement. The order

form language was drafted by U.S. West Direct on a take-it-or-leave-it basis and stated in part:

> *Any controversy or claim arising out of or relating to this Agreement, or breach thereof, other than an action by Publisher for the collection of amounts due under this Agreement, shall be settled by final, binding arbitration in accordance with the Commercial Arbitration rules of the American Arbitration Association.*

If forced to arbitration, Iwen would be unable to recover damages for the negligently constructed yellow pages ad, nor could he recover damages for infliction of emotional distress and punitive damages related to his many efforts to adjust the matter with the company, which were ignored or rejected. Must Iwen have his case resolved through arbitration rather than a court of law? [*Iwen v. U.S. West Direct*, 977 P.2d 989 (Mont.)]

3. Sutcliffe Banton, dba Nemard Construction, furnished labor and materials (valued at $162,895) for improving Vicky Deafeamkpor's New York City residential property. She paid only $41,718, leaving $121,987 unpaid. Banton sued her and the jury awarded $90,000 in damages. Deafeamkpor moved for an order setting aside the jury's verdict because Banton was not properly licensed by New York City. Under NYC Code an unlicensed contractor may neither enforce a home improvement contract against an owner or recover in *quantum meruit.* The jury heard all the evidence regarding the materials and labor expended on Deafeamkpor's residence and concluded that the plaintiff performed satisfactory work valued at $90,000 for which he was not paid. Should the court allow the owner to take advantage of Banton and his employees and suppliers? What public policy would support such an outcome? Decide. [*Nemard Construction Corp. v. Deafeamkpor*, 863 N.Y.S.2d 846]

4. Eugene McCarthy left his position as director of sales for Nike's Brand Jordan division in June 2003 to become vice president of U.S. footwear sales and merchandising at Reebok, one of Nike's competitors. Nike sought a preliminary injunction to prevent McCarthy from working for Reebok for a year, invoking a noncompete agreement McCarthy had signed in Oregon in 1997 when Nike had promoted him to his earlier position as a regional footwear sales manager. The agreement stated in pertinent part:

> *During EMPLOYEE'S employment by NIKE… and for one (1) year thereafter, ("the Restriction Period"), EMPLOYEE will not directly or indirectly … be employed by, consult for, or be connected in any manner with, any business engaged anywhere in the world in the athletic footwear, athletic apparel or sports equipment and accessories business, or any other business which directly competes with NIKE or any of its subsidiaries or affiliated corporations.*

McCarty contends that such a contract is a restraint of trade and should not be enforced. Nike contends that the agreement is fair and should be enforced. Decide. [*Nike, Inc. v. McCarthy*, 379 F.3d 576 (9th Cir.)]

5. Ewing was employed by Presto-X-Co., a pest exterminator. His contract of employment specified that he would not solicit or attempt to solicit customers of Presto-X for two years after the termination of his employment. After working several years, his employment was terminated. Ewing then sent a letter to customers of Presto-X stating that he no longer worked for Presto-X and that he was still certified by the state. Ewing set forth his home address and phone number, which the customers did not previously have. The letter ended with the statement, "I thank you for your business throughout the past years." Presto-X brought an action to enjoin Ewing from sending such letters. He raised the defense that he was prohibited only from soliciting and there was nothing in the letters that constituted a seeking of customers. Decide. What ethical values are involved? [*Presto-X-Co. v. Ewing*, 442 N.W.2d 85 (Iowa)]

6. The Minnesota adoption statute requires that any agency placing a child for adoption make a thorough investigation and not give a child to an applicant unless the placement is in the best interests of the child. Tibbetts applied to Crossroads, Inc., a private adoption agency, for a child to adopt. He later sued the agency for breach of contract, claiming that the agency was obligated by contract to supply a child for adoption. The agency claimed that it was required only to use its best efforts to locate a child and was not required to supply a child to Tibbetts unless it found him to be a suitable parent. Decide. [*Tibbetts v. Crossroads, Inc.*, 411 N.W.2d 535 (Minn. App.)]

7. Siddle purchased a quantity of fireworks from Red Devil Fireworks Co. The sale was illegal, however, because Siddle did not have a license to make the purchase, which the seller knew because it had been so informed by the attorney general of the state. Siddle did not pay for the fireworks, and Red Devil

sued him. He defended on the ground that the contract could not be enforced because it was illegal. Was the defense valid? [*Red Devil Fireworks Co. v. Siddle*, 648 P.2d 468 (Wash. App.)]

8. Justin Shaffer, while an employee of the Home Paramount Pest Control Companies Inc., signed an employment agreement providing that:

   The Employee will not engage directly or indirectly or concern himself/herself in any manner whatsoever in the carrying on or conducting the business of exterminating, pest control, termite control and/or fumigation services as an owner, agent, servant, representative, or employee, and/or as a member of a partnership and/or as an officer, director or stockholder of any corporation, or in any manner whatsoever, in any city, cities, county or counties in the state(s) in which the Employee works and/or in which the Employee was assigned during the two (2) years next preceding the termination of the Employment Agreement and for a period of two (2) years from and after the date upon which he/she shall cease for any reason whatsoever to be an employee of [Home Paramount].

   Shaffer resigned from Home Paramount and became an employee of Connor's Termite and Pest Control Inc. Home Paramount sued Shaffer and Connor's, claiming that Shaffer's employment by Connor's violated the contract. The defendants contended that the provision was overboard and unenforceable. Decide. [*Home Paramount Pest Control Companies, Inc. v. Shaffer*, 718 S.E.2d 762 (Va.)]

9. Smith was employed as a salesman for Borden, Inc., which sold food products in 63 counties in Arkansas, 2 counties in Missouri, 2 counties in Oklahoma, and 1 county in Texas. Smith's employment contract prohibited him from competing with Borden after leaving its employ. Smith left Borden and went to work for a competitor, Lady Baltimore Foods. Working for this second employer, Smith sold in 3 counties of Arkansas. He had sold in 2 of these counties while he worked for Borden. Borden brought an injunction action against Smith and Lady Baltimore to enforce the noncompete covenant in Smith's former contract. Was Borden entitled to the injunction? [*Borden, Inc. v. Smith*, 478 S.W.2d 744 (Ark.)]

10. All new employees of Circuit City Stores were required to sign a Dispute Resolution Agreement (DRA) mandating that employees submit all employment-related disputes to arbitration. Under the DRA Circuit City was not obligated to arbitrate its claims against employees and may bring lawsuits against employees. Remedies are limited under the DRA, including a one-year back pay limit and a two-year front pay limit, with cap on punitive damages of an amount up to the greater of the amount of back pay and front pay awarded or $5,000. In a civil lawsuit under state law a plaintiff is entitled to all forms of relief. The DRA requires that employees split the cost of the arbitrator's fees with the employer. An individual is not required to pay for the services of a judge. Adams filed a sexual harassment case against his employer in state court. Circuit City filed a petition in federal court to compel arbitration. Decide. [*Circuit City Stores, Inc. v. Adams*, 274 F.3d 889 (9th Cir.)]

11. Vodra was employed as a salesperson and contracting agent for American Security Services. As part of his contract of employment, Vodra signed an agreement that for three years after leaving this employment, he would not solicit any customer of American. Vodra had no experience in the security field when he went to work for American. To the extent that he became known to American's customers, it was because of being American's representative rather than because of his own reputation in the security field. After some years, Vodra left American and organized a competing company that solicited American's customers. American sued him to enforce the restrictive covenant. Vodra claimed that the restrictive covenant was illegal and not binding. Was he correct? [*American Security Services, Inc. v. Vodra*, 385 N.W.2d 73 (Neb.)]

12. Potomac Leasing Co. leased an automatic telephone system to Vitality Centers. Claudene Cato signed the lease as guarantor of payments. When the rental was not paid, Potomac Leasing brought suit against Vitality and Cato. They raised the defense that the rented equipment was to be used for an illegal purpose—namely, the random sales solicitation by means of an automatic telephone in violation of state statute; that this purpose was known to Potomac Leasing; and that Potomac Leasing could therefore not enforce the lease. Was this defense valid? [*Potomac Leasing Co. v. Vitality Centers, Inc.*, 718 S.W.2d 928 (Ark.)]

13. The English publisher of a book called *Cambridge* gave a New York publisher permission to sell that book any place in the world except in England. The New York publisher made several bulk sales of the book to buyers who sold the book throughout the world, including England. The English publisher

sued the New York publisher and its customers for breach of the restriction prohibiting sales in England. Decide.

14. Sandra Menefee sued Geographic Expeditions, Inc. (GeoEx), for the wrongful death of her son while on a GeoEx expedition up Mount Kilimanjaro. GeoEx moved to compel arbitration under the parties' limitation of liability contract. GeoEx designed its arbitration clause to limit the plaintiffs' recovery and required them to indemnify GeoEx for its legal costs and fees if they unsuccessfully pursued any claim covered by the release agreement. Moreover, GeoEx required that plaintiffs pay half of any mediation fees and arbitrate in San Francisco, GeoEx's choice of venue, as opposed to the plaintiffs' home in Colorado. Should the court require the Menefees to arbitrate? If any component of the arbitration clause is found to be unconscionable, should the court simply sever the objectionable provision and enforce the remainder of the arbitration clause? [*Lhotka v. Geographic Expeditions, Inc.*, 104 Cal. Rptr. 3d 844 (Cal. App. 2010)]

15. Yarde Metals, Inc., owned six season tickets to New England Patriots football games. Gillette Stadium, where the games are played, had insufficient men's restrooms in use for football games at that time, which was the subject of numerous newspaper columns. On October 13, 2002, a guest of Yarde Metals, Mikel LaCroix, along with others, used available women's restrooms to answer the call of nature. As LaCroix left the restroom, however, he was arrested and charged with disorderly conduct. The Patriots organization terminated all six of Yarde's season ticket privileges, incorrectly giving as a reason that LaCroix was ejected "for throwing bottles in the seating section." Yarde sued, contending that "by terminating the plaintiff's season tickets for 2002 and for the future arbitrarily, without cause and based on false information," the Patriots had violated the implicit covenant of good faith and fair dealing of the season tickets contract. The back of each Patriots ticket states:

    This ticket and all season tickets are revocable licenses. The Patriots reserve the right to revoke such licenses, in their sole discretion, at any time and for any reason.

    How would you decide this case? [*Yarde Metals, Inc. v. New England Patriots Ltd.*, 834 N.E.2d 1233 (Mass. App.)]

CPA Questions

1. West, an Indiana real estate broker, misrepresented to Zimmer that West was licensed in Kansas under the Kansas statute that regulates real estate brokers and requires all brokers to be licensed. Zimmer signed a contract agreeing to pay West a 5 percent commission for selling Zimmer's home in Kansas. West did not sign the contract. West sold Zimmer's home. If West sued Zimmer for nonpayment of commission, Zimmer would be:
   a. Liable to West only for the value of services rendered.
   b. Liable to West for the full commission.
   c. Not liable to West for any amount because West did not sign the contract.
   d. Not liable to West for any amount because West violated the Kansas licensing requirements (5/92, Law, #25).

2. Blue purchased a travel agency business from Drye. The purchase price included payment for Drye's goodwill. The agreement contained a covenant prohibiting Drye from competing with Blue in the travel agency business. Which of the following statements regarding the covenant is *not* correct?
   a. The restraint must be *no* more extensive than is reasonably necessary to protect the goodwill purchased by Blue.
   b. The geographic area to which it applies must be reasonable.
   c. The time period for which it is to be effective must be reasonable.
   d. The value to be assigned to it is the excess of the price paid over the seller's cost of all tangible assets (11/87, Law, #2).

CHAPTER 16

Writing, Electronic Forms, and Interpretation of Contracts

Learning Outcomes <<<

After studying this chapter, you should be able to

- **LO.1** Explain when a contract must be evidenced by a writing
- **LO.2** Explain the effect of noncompliance with the statute of frauds
- **LO.3** Explain the parol evidence rule and the exceptions to this rule
- **LO.4** Understand the basic rule of contract construction that a contract is enforced according to its terms
- **LO.5** State the rules for interpreting ambiguous terms in a contract

When must a contract be written? What is the effect of a written contract? These questions lead to the statute of frauds and the parol evidence rule.

16-1 Statute of Frauds

A *contract* is a legally binding agreement. Must the agreement be evidenced by a writing?

16-1a Validity of Oral Contracts

In the absence of a statute requiring a writing, a contract may be oral or written. Managers and professionals should be more fully aware that their oral communications, including telephone conversations and dinner or breakfast discussions, may be deemed legally enforceable contracts. **For Example,** suppose that Mark Wahlberg, after reviewing a script tentatively entitled *The Bulger Boys*, meets with Steven Spielberg to discuss Mark's playing mobster James "Whitey" Bulger in the film. Steven states, "You *are* Whitey, Marky! The nuns at Gate of Heaven Grammar School in South Boston—or maybe it was St. Augustine's—they don't send for the Boston Police when they are troubled about drug use in the schools; they send for you to talk to the kids. Nobody messes with you, and the kids know it. This is true stuff, I think, and this fugitive's brother Bill comes out of the Southie projects to be president of U Mass." Mark likes the script. Steven and Mark block out two months of time for shooting the film this fall. They agree on Mark's usual fee and a "piece of the action" based on a set percentage of the net income from the film. Thereafter, Mark's agent does not like the deal. He believes there are better scripts for Mark. And with Hollywood accounting, a percentage of the "net" take is usually of little value. However, all of the essential terms of a contract have been agreed on, and such an oral agreement would be legally enforceable. As set forth in the following text, no writing is required for a services contract that can be performed within one year after the date of the agreement.

Certain contracts, on the other hand, must be evidenced by a writing to be legally enforceable. These contracts are covered by the **statute of frauds.**[1]

statute of frauds–statute that, in order to prevent fraud through the use of perjured testimony, requires that certain kinds of transactions be evidenced in writing in order to be binding or enforceable.

Because many oral contracts are legally enforceable, it is a good business practice in the preliminary stages of discussions to stipulate that no binding agreement is intended to be formed until a written contract is prepared and signed by the parties.

16-1b Contracts That Must Be Evidenced by a Writing

The statute of frauds requires that certain kinds of contracts be evidenced by a writing or they cannot be enforced. This means that either the contract itself must be in writing and signed by both parties or there must be a sufficient written memorandum of the oral contract signed by the person being sued for breach of contract. A *part performance* doctrine

[1] The name is derived from the original Statute of Frauds and Perjuries, which was adopted in 1677 and became the pattern for similar legislation in America. The 17th section of that statute governed the sale of goods, and its modern counterpart is §2-201 of the UCC. The 4th section of the English statute provided the pattern for U.S. legislation with respect to contracts other than for the sale of goods described in this section of the chapter. The English statute was repealed in 1954 except as to land sale and guarantee contracts. The U.S. statutes remain in force, but the liberalization by U.C.C. §2-201 of the pre-Code requirements with respect to contracts for the sale of goods lessens the applicability of the writing requirement. Additional movement away from the writing requirement is seen in the 1994 Revision of Article 8, Securities, which abolishes the statute of frauds provision of the original U.C.C. §8-319 and goes beyond by declaring that the one-year performance provision of the statute of frauds is not applicable to contracts for securities. U.C.C. §8-113 [1994 Revision].

or exception to the statute of frauds may exist when the plaintiff's part performance is "unequivocally referable" to the oral agreement.[2]

Agreement That Cannot Be Performed within One Year After the Contract Is Made

A writing is required when the contract, by its terms or subject matter, cannot be performed within one year after the date of the agreement. An oral agreement to supply a line of credit for two years cannot be enforced because of the statute of frauds.

CASE SUMMARY

Not a Good Move, Doctor

FACTS: Despite not having an executed employment agreement, Dr. William Bithoney sold his home in New York and moved to Atlanta in early October in anticipation of his October 15 start work date as an executive at Grady Memorial Hospital. But the night before his anticipated start, he was informed that Grady's governing body, the Fulton-DeKalb Hospital Authority, did not approve his hiring and would not permit him to commence work. He sued the Authority for breach of an oral contract for severance, claiming that he and Grady's CEO, Otis Story, had agreed that he would receive "a severance payment of 15 months salary if Grady terminated his employment without cause." Bithoney had received a draft employment contract from Grady, which included a provision that, in the event Bithoney was terminated without cause, he would receive "full severance payment," which would be "payable for 15 months from the effective date of said termination."

DECISION: Judgment for the hospital. If the oral severance agreement were to be paid in a lump sum after termination, the oral agreement would not fall within the statute of frauds. Because the draft employment agreement provided that the severance "shall be payable for 15 months from the effective date of said termination," it was found to be a 15-month payment term barred by the statute of frauds. [***Bithoney v. Fulton-DeKalb Hospital Authority*, 721 S.E.2d 577 (Ga. App. 2011)**]

The year runs from the time the oral contract is made rather than from the date when performance is to begin. In computing the year, the day on which the contract was made is excluded.

No *part performance* exception exists to validate an oral agreement not performable within one year. **For Example,** Babyback's Foods negotiated a multiyear oral agreement to comarket its barbecue meat products with the Coca-Cola Co. nationwide and arranged to have several coolers installed at area grocery stores in Louisville under the agreement. Babyback's faxed to Coca-Cola a contract that summarized the oral agreement but Coca-Cola never signed it. Because Coca-Cola did not sign and no part performance exception exists for an oral agreement not performable within one year, Babyback's lawsuit was unsuccessful.[3]

When no time for performance is specified by the oral contract and complete performance could "conceivably occur" within one year, the statute of frauds is not applicable to the oral contract.[4]

When a contract may be terminated at will by either party, the statute of frauds is not applicable because the contract may be terminated within a year. **For Example,** David Ehrlich was hired as manager of Gravediggaz pursuant to an oral management agreement that was terminable at will by either Ehrlich or the group. He was entitled to

[2] *Carey & Associates v. Ernst*, 802 N.Y.S.2d 160 (A.D. 2005).

[3] *Coca-Cola Co. v. Babyback's International Inc.*, 841 N.E.2d 557 (Ind. 2006).

[4] *De John v. Speech Language & Communication Assoc.*, 974 N.Y.S.2d 725 (A.D. 2013).

FIGURE 16-1 Hurdles in the Path of a Contract

WRITING REQUIRED	
STATUTE OF FRAUDS	EXCEPTIONS
MORE THAN ONE YEAR TO PERFORM SALE OF LAND ANSWER FOR ANOTHER'S DEBT OR DEFAULT PERSONAL REPRESENTATIVE TO PAY DEBT OF DECEDENT FROM PERSONAL FUNDS PROMISE IN CONSIDERATION OF MARRIAGE SALE OF GOODS FOR $500 OR MORE MISCELLANEOUS	PART PERFORMANCE PROMISOR BENEFIT DETRIMENTAL RELIANCE
PAROL EVIDENCE RULE	EXCEPTIONS
EVERY COMPLETE, FINAL WRITTEN CONTRACT	INCOMPLETE CONTRACT AMBIGUOUS TERMS FRAUD, ACCIDENT, OR MISTAKE TO PROVE EXISTENCE OR NONBINDING CHARACTER OF CONTRACT MODIFICATION OF CONTRACT ILLEGALITY

receive 15 percent of the gross earnings of the group and each of its members, including rap artist Robert Diggs, professionally known as RZA, for all engagements entered into while he was manager under this oral agreement. Such an at-will contract is not barred by the statute of frauds.[5]

Agreement to Sell or a Sale of an Interest in Land

All contracts to sell land, buildings, or interests in land, such as mortgages, must be evidenced by a writing.[6] Leases are also interests in land and must be in writing, except in some states where leases for one year or less do not have to be in writing.[7] **For Example,**

[5] See *Ehrlich v. Diggs*, 169 F. Supp. 2d 124 (E.D.N.Y. 2001). See also *Sterling v. Sterling*, 800 N.Y.S.2d 463 (A.D. 2005), in which the statute of frauds was no bar to an oral partnership agreement, deemed to be at will, that continued for an indefinite period of time.

[6] *Magnum Real Estate Services, Inc. v. Associates, LLC*, 874 N.Y.S.2d 435 (A.D. 2009).

[7] See, however, *BBQ Blues Texas, Ltd. v. Affiliated Business*, 183 S.W.3d 543 (Tex. App. 2006), in which Eddie Calagero of Affiliated Business and the owners of BBQ Blues Texas, Ltd., entered an oral commission agreement to pay a 10 percent commission if he found a buyer for the restaurant, and he did so. The oral agreement was held to be outside the statute of frauds because the activity of finding a willing buyer did not involve the transfer of real estate. The second contract between the buyer and seller of the restaurant, which involved the transfer of a lease agreement, was a separate and distinct agreement over which Calagero had no control.

if Mrs. O'Toole orally agrees to sell her house to the Gillespies for $250,000 and, thereafter, her children convince her that she could obtain $280,000 for the property if she is patient, Mrs. O'Toole can raise the defense of the statute of frauds should she be sued for breach of the oral agreement. Under the *part performance doctrine*, an exception exists by which an oral contract for the sale of land will be enforced by a court of equity in a suit for specific performance if the buyer has taken possession of the land under an oral contract and has made substantial improvements, the value of which cannot easily be ascertained, or has taken possession and paid part of the purchase price.

Promise to Answer for the Debt or Default of Another

suretyship–undertaking to pay the debt or be liable for the default of another.

If an individual *I* promises a creditor *C* to pay the debt of *D* if *D* does not do so, *I* is promising to answer for the debt of another. Such a promise is sometimes called a **suretyship** contract, and it must be in writing to be enforceable. *I*, the promisor, is obligated to pay only if *D* does not pay. *I*'s promise is a *collateral* or *secondary* promise, and such promises must be in writing under the statute of frauds.[8]

Main Purpose of Exception. When the main purpose of the promisor's promise to pay the debt of another is to benefit the promisor, the statute of frauds is not applicable, and the oral promise to pay the debt is binding.

For Example, an individual *I* hires a contractor *C* to repair *I*'s building, and the supplier *S* is unwilling to extend credit to *C*. In an oral promise by *I* to pay *S* what is owed for the supplies in question if *C* does not pay, *I* is promising to pay for the debt of another, *C*. However, the *main purpose* of *I*'s promise was not to aid *C* but to get his own house repaired. This promise is not within the statute of frauds.[9]

CASE SUMMARY

"I Personally Guarantee" Doesn't Mean I'm Personally Liable, Does It?

FACTS: Joel Burgower owned Material Partnerships Inc. (MPI), which supplied Sacos Tubulares del Centro, S.A. de C.V. (Sacos), a Mexican bag manufacturer, essential materials to make its products. When MPI was not paid for shipments, it insisted that Jorge Lopez, Sacos's general manager, personally guarantee all past and future obligations to MPI. In a letter to Burgower dated September 25, 1998, Lopez wrote:

> *I ... want to certify you [sic] that I, personally, guaranty all outstanding [sic] and liabilities of Sacos Tubulares with Material Partnerships as well as future shipments.*

Lopez drafted the letter himself and signed it over the designation "Jorge Lopez Venture, General Manager."

After receiving the September 25th letter, MPI resumed shipping product to Sacos, sending additional shipments valued at approximately $200,000. MPI subsequently received one payment of approximately $60,000 from Sacos. When Sacos did not pay for the additional shipments, MPI stopped shipping to it. The Sacos plant closed, and MPI brought suit in a Texas court against Lopez, claiming he was individually liable for the corporate debt of more than $900,000 under the terms of the personal guarantee. Lopez contended that he signed the letter in his capacity as general manager of Sacos as a corporate guarantee and that it was not an enforceable personal guarantee. MPI contended that the letter was a clear personal guarantee.

[8] See *Martin Printing, Inc. v. Sone*, 873 A.2d 232 (Conn. App. 2005), in which James Kuhe, in writing, personally guaranteed Martin Printing, Inc., to pay for printing expenses of *Pub Links Golfer Magazine*, if his corporation, Abbey Inc., failed to do so. When Abbey, Inc., failed to pay, the court enforced Kuhe's promise to pay.

[9] See *Christian v. Smith*, 759 N.W.2d 447 (Neb. 2008).

"I Personally Guarantee" Doesn't Mean I'm Personally Liable, Does It? continued

DECISION: The essential terms of a guarantee agreement required by the statute of frauds were present in this case. Lopez stated in his September 25th letter that "I, personally, guaranty," manifesting an intent to guarantee, and described the obligation being guaranteed as "all outstandings and liabilities of Sacos," as well as "future shipments." Lopez's signature over his corporate office does not render the document ambiguous because the clear intent was expressed in the word "personally." [***MPI v. Jorge Lopez Ventura*, 102 S.W.2d 252 (Tex. App. 2003)**]

Promise by the Executor or Administrator of a Decedent's Estate to Pay a Claim Against the Estate from Personal Funds

personal representative–administrator or executor who represents decedents under UPC.

executor, executrix–person (man, woman) named in a will to administer the estate of the decedent.

administrator, administratrix–person (man, woman) appointed to wind up and settle the estate of a person who has died without a will.

decedent–person whose estate is being administered.

The **personal representative (executor** or **administrator)** has the duty of handling the affairs of a deceased person, paying the debts from the proceeds of the estate and distributing any balance remaining. The executor or administrator is not personally liable for the claims against the estate of the **decedent.** If the personal representative promises to pay the decedent's debts with his or her own money, the promise cannot be enforced unless it is evidenced by a writing.

If the personal representative makes a contract on behalf of the estate in the course of administering the estate, a writing is not required. The representative is then contracting on behalf of the estate. Thus, if the personal representative employs an attorney to settle the estate or makes a burial contract with an undertaker, no writing is required.

Promises Made in Consideration of Marriage

Promises to pay a sum of money or give property to another in consideration of marriage must be in writing under the statute of frauds.

For Example, if Mr. John Bradley orally promises to provide Karl Radford $20,000 on Karl's marriage to Mr. Bradley's daughter Michelle—and Karl and Michelle marry—the agreement is not enforceable under the statute of frauds because it was not in writing.

Prenuptial or *antenuptial* agreements are entered into by the parties before their marriage. After full disclosure of each party's assets and liabilities, and in some states, income,[10] the parties set forth the rights of each partner regarding the property and, among other things, set forth rights and obligations should the marriage end in a separation or divorce. Such a contract must be in writing.

For Example, when Susan DeMatteo married her husband M. J. DeMatteo in 1990, she had a 1977 Nova and $5,000 in the bank. M. Joseph DeMatteo was worth as much as $112 million at that time, and he insisted that she sign a prenuptial agreement before their marriage. After full disclosure of each party's assets, the prenuptial agreement was signed and videotaped some five days before their marriage ceremony. The agreement gave Susan $35,000 a year plus cost-of-living increases, as well as a car and a house, should the marriage dissolve. After the couple divorced, Susan argued before the state's highest court that the agreement was not "fair or reasonable" because it gave her less than 1 percent of her former husband's wealth. The court upheld the agreement, however, pointing out that Susan was fully informed about her fiancé's net worth and was represented by counsel.[11] When there is full disclosure and representation, prenuptial agreements, like other contracts, cannot be set aside unless they are unconscionable, which in a domestic relations setting means leaving a former spouse unable to support herself or himself.

[10] See FLA. STAT. §732–702 (2).

[11] *DeMatteo v. DeMatteo*, 762 N.E.2d 797 (Mass. 2002). See also *Waton v. Waton*, 887 So. 2d 419 (Fla. App. 2004).

Sale of Goods

As will be developed in Chapter 22, Nature and Form of Sales, contracts for the sale of goods priced at $500 or more must ordinarily be in writing under U.C.C. §2-201.[12]

Promissory Estoppel

The statute of frauds may be circumvented when the party seeking to get around the statute of frauds is able to prove an enhanced promissory estoppel. While one element of a routine promissory estoppel case requires that the promisee rely on the promise in some definite and substantial manner, an enhanced level of reasonable reliance is necessary in order to have enhanced promissory estoppel, along with proof of an unconscionable injury or unjust enrichment. **For Example,** an Indiana bakery, Classic Cheesecake Inc., was able to interest several hotels and casinos in Las Vegas in buying its products. On July 27, 2004, its principals sought a loan from a local branch office of J. P. Morgan Chase Bank in order to establish a distribution center in Las Vegas. On September 17, local bank officer Dowling told Classic that the loan was a "go." When credit quality issues surfaced, Dowling continued to make assurances that the loan would be approved. On October 12, however, she told Classic that the loan had been turned down. Classic claimed that the bank's breach of its oral promise to make the loan and Classic's detrimental reliance on the promise caused it to lose more than $1 million. The Indiana statute of frauds requires agreements to lend money to be in writing. Classic contended that the oral agreement in this case must be enforced on the basis of promissory estoppel and the company's unconscionable injury. Judge Posner of the Seventh Circuit upheld the dismissal of the claim, writing (in part):

> *... For the plaintiff to treat the bank loan as a certainty because they were told by the bank officer whom they were dealing with that it would be approved was unreasonable, especially if, as the plaintiffs' damages claim presupposes, the need for the loan was urgent. Rational businessmen know that there is many a slip "twixt cup and lips," that a loan is not approved until it is approved, that if a bank's employee tells you your loan application will be approved that is not the same as telling you it has been approved, and that if one does not have a loan commitment in writing yet the need for the loan is urgent one had better be negotiating with other potential lenders at the same time....*[13]

CPA 16-1c Note or Memorandum

The statute of frauds requires a writing to evidence those contracts that come within its scope. This writing may be a note or memorandum as distinguished from a contract.[14] The statutory requirement is, of course, satisfied if there is a complete written contract signed by both parties.

Signing

The note or memorandum must be signed by the party sought to be bound by the contract. **For Example,** in the previous scenario involving Mark Wahlberg and Steven Spielberg, suppose the parties agreed to do the film according to the same terms but agreed to begin shooting the film a year from next April, and Mark wrote the essential terms on a napkin, dated it, and had Steven sign it "to make sure I got it right." Mark

[12] As will be presented in Chapter 22, under Revised Article 2, §2-201, the $500 amount is increased to $5,000. This revision has not yet been adopted by any state.

[13] *Classic Cheesecake Co. Inc. v. J. P. Morgan Chase Bank,* 546 F.3d 839 (7th Cir. 2008).

[14] *McLinden v. Coco,* 765 N.E.2d 606 (Ind. App. 2002).

then placed the napkin in his wallet for his records. Because the contract could not be performed within one year after the date of the agreement, a writing would be required. If Steven thereafter decided not to pursue the film, Mark could enforce the contract against him because the napkin-note had been signed by the party to be bound or "sought to be charged," Steven. However, if Mark later decided not to appear in the film, the agreement to do the film could not be enforced against Mark because no writing existed signed by Mark, the party sought to be charged. The signature may be an ordinary one or any symbol that is adopted by the party as a signature. It may consist of initials, figures, or a mark. In the absence of a local statute that provides otherwise, a signature may be made by pencil, pen, typewriter, print, or stamp. It is unlikely that a logo can constitute a legal signature. **For Example,** University of South Carolina sports fans claimed that a university brochure contained a signed writing sufficient to satisfy the statute of frauds supportive of their rights to continued premium seating at the new basketball arena. The presence or absence of the university's signature turned on whether the university logo on the brochures suffices for a legal signature. The court majority found that the logo did not constitute a legal signature. However, Justice Pleicones admonished the court majority to be more circumspect in holding that a logo can never constitute a signature for the purposes of the statute of frauds.[15]

Electronic Signature. Electronic signatures have parity with on-paper signatures under the Uniform Electronic Transactions Act (UETA).[16] The act treats e-signatures and e-records as if they were handwritten. The parties themselves determine how they will determine each other's identity such as by a credit card, a password or pin, or other secure means. Certain documents and records are exempt under the act, such as wills, trusts, and commercial law matters.

Content

The note or memorandum must contain all of the essential terms of the contract so the court can determine just what was agreed. If any essential term is missing, the writing is not sufficient. A writing evidencing a sale of land that does not describe the land or identify the buyer does not satisfy the statute of frauds. The subject matter must be identified either within the writing itself or in other writings to which it refers. A deposit check given by the buyer to the seller does not take an oral land sales contract out of the statute of frauds. This is so because the check does not set forth the terms of the sale. The note or memorandum may consist of one writing or of separate papers, such as letters, or a combination of such papers. Separate writings cannot be considered together unless they are linked. Linkage may be by express reference in each writing to the other or by the fact that each writing clearly deals with the same subject matter. An exchange of e-mails may constitute an enforceable agreement if the writings include all of the agreement's essential terms. **For Example,** three e-mails were determined to be a binding integrated fee agreement limiting the Kasowitz law firm to a flat $1 million fee and rejecting a higher success fee sought from the client. On September 8, 2006, Kasowitz (by attorney Goldberg) e-mailed a proposed fee arrangement to the client's in-house counsel, Bergman, which provided in relevant part:

> *We can do the Cardtronics case for a flat $1 million, payable over 10 months as you suggested (exclusive of disbursements), plus 20% of amounts recovered above some number, as opposed to a percentage payable from dollar one.*

[15] *Springolo v. University of South Carolina*, 757 S.E.2d 384 (S.C. 2014).

[16] Forty-seven states and the District of Columbia have adopted the UETA. The remaining three states, Illinois, New York, and Washington, are subject to the federal Electronic Signatures in Global and National Commerce Act (E-Sign), 15 U.S.C.§7001, which is consistent with the UETA in many respects.

Based on the numbers we have, which obviously are approximations, we actually think the damages could be between $10 and $11 million over the life of the contract. So I'm thinking of 20% of everything above $4 million as the success fee portion...

On September 19, 2006, Goldberg sent an e-mail to Bergman in which he stated, in relevant part,

I would love to have our fee arrangement in place by then so I can just tear into these guys.

In an e-mail response to Kasowitz that same day, Bergman wrote:

Go.

The recovery amounted to $1.75 million, and no success fee was called for under the agreement evident from the e-mails.[17]

16-1d Effect of Noncompliance

The majority of states hold that a contract that does not comply with the statute of frauds is not enforceable.[18] If an action is brought to enforce the contract, the defendant can raise the defense that the alleged contract is not enforceable because it is not evidenced by a writing, as required by the statute of frauds.

Recovery of Value Conferred

In most instances, a person who is prevented from enforcing a contract because of the statute of frauds is nevertheless entitled to recover from the other party the value of any services or property furnished or money given under the oral contract. Recovery is not based on the terms of the contract but on a quasi-contractual obligation. The other party is to restore to the plaintiff what was received in order to prevent unjust enrichment at the plaintiff's expense. **For Example,** when an oral contract for services cannot be enforced because of the statute of frauds, the person performing the work may recover the reasonable value of the services rendered.

Who May Raise the Defense of Noncompliance?

Only a party to the oral contract may raise a defense that it is not binding because there is no writing that satisfies the statute of frauds. Third persons, such as an insurance company or the Internal Revenue Service, cannot claim that a contract is void because the statute of frauds was not satisfied.

16-2 Parol Evidence Rule

When the contract is evidenced by a writing, may the contract terms be changed by the testimony of witnesses?

16-2a Exclusion of Parol Evidence

The general rule is that parol or extrinsic evidence will not be allowed into evidence to add to, modify, or contradict the terms of a written contract that is fully integrated

[17] *Kasowitz, Benson, Torres & Friedman, LLP v. Reade*, 950 N.Y.S.2d 8 (A.D. 2012); but see *Dahan v. Weiss*, 991 N.Y.S.2d 119 (A.D. 2014), where e-mail messages failed to express the full intentions of the parties.

[18] The UCC creates several statutes of frauds of limited applicability, in which it uses the phrase "not enforceable": §1-206 (sale of intangible personal property); §2-201 (sale of goods); and §8-319 (sale of securities).

or complete on its face.[19] Evidence of an alleged earlier oral or written agreement within the scope of the fully integrated written contract or evidence of an alleged contemporaneous oral agreement within the scope of the fully integrated written contract is inadmissible as *parol evidence.*

Parol evidence is admissible, however, to show fraud, duress, or mistake and under certain other circumstances to be discussed in the following paragraphs.

parol evidence rule–rule that prohibits the introduction into evidence of oral or written statements made prior to or contemporaneously with the execution of a complete written contract, deed, or instrument, in the absence of clear proof of fraud, accident, or mistake causing the omission of the statement in question.

The **parol evidence rule** is based on the theory that either there never was an oral agreement or, if there was, the parties abandoned it when they reached the stage in negotiations of executing their written contract. The social objective of the parol evidence rule is to give stability to contracts and to prevent the assertion of terms that did not exist or did not survive the bargaining of the parties so as to reach inclusion in the final written contract.

For Example, *L* (landlord), the owner of a new development containing a five-store mall, discusses leasing one of the stores to *T* (tenant), who is viewing the property with his sister *S*, a highly credible poverty worker on leave from her duties in Central America. *L*, in the presence of *S*, agrees to give *T* the exclusive right to sell coffee and soft drinks in the five-store mall. Soon *L* and *T* execute a detailed written lease for the store, which makes no provision for *T's* exclusive right to sell soft drinks and coffee in the mall. Subsequently, when two of the mall's new tenants begin to sell soft drinks and coffee, *T* brings suit against *L* for the breach of the oral promise granting him exclusive rights to sell soft drinks and coffee. *T* calls *S* as his first witness to prove the existence of the oral promise. *L*, through his attorney, will object to the admission of any evidence of a prior oral agreement that would add to or amend the fully integrated written lease, which set forth all restrictions on the landlord and tenant as to uses of the premises. After study of the matter, the court, based on the parol evidence rule, will not hear testimony from either *S* or *T* about the oral promise *L* made to *T*. In order to preserve his exclusive right to sell the drinks in question, *T* should have made certain that this promise was made part of the lease. His lawsuit will not be successful.

16-2b When the Parol Evidence Rule Does Not Apply

The parol evidence rule will not apply in certain cases. The most common of these are discussed in the following paragraphs.

Ambiguity

ambiguous–having more than one reasonable interpretation.

If a written contract is **ambiguous** or may have two or more different meanings, parol evidence may generally be admitted to clarify the meaning.[20]

Parol evidence may also be admitted to show that a word used in a contract has a special trade meaning or a meaning in the particular locality that differs from the common meaning of that word.

Fraud, Duress, or Mistake

A contract apparently complete on its face may have omitted a provision that should have been included. Parol evidence may be admitted to show that a provision was omitted as the result of fraud, duress, or mistake and to further show what that provision stated. Parol evidence is admissible to show that a provision of the written contract was a mutual mistake even though the written provision is unambiguous. When one party claims to

[19] *Mayday v. Grathwohl*, 805 N.W.2d 285 (Minn. App. 2011).

[20] *Berg v. Hudesman*, 801 P.2d 222 (Wash. 1990). This view is also followed by U.C.C. §2-202(a), which permits terms in a contract for the sale of goods to be "explained or supplemented by a course of dealing or usage of trade ... or by course of performance." Such evidence is admissible not because there is an ambiguity but "in order that the true understanding of the parties as to the agreement may be reached." Official Code Comment to §2-202.

have been fraudulently induced by the other to enter into a contract, the parol evidence rule does not bar proof that there was a fraud. **For Example,** the parol evidence rule does not bar proof that the seller of land intentionally misrepresented that the land was zoned to permit use as an industrial park. Such evidence does not contradict the terms of the contract but shows that the agreement is unenforceable.[21]

Modification of Contract

The parol evidence rule prohibits only the contradiction of a complete written contract. It does not prohibit proof that the contract was thereafter modified or terminated.

CASE SUMMARY

All Sail and No Anchor

FACTS: On April 2, 1990, Christian Bourg hired Bristol Boat Co., Inc., and Bristol Marine Co. (defendants) to construct and deliver a yacht on July 1, 1990. However, the defendants did not live up to their promises and the contract was breached. On October 22, 1990, the defendants executed a written settlement agreement whereby Bourg agreed to pay an additional sum of $135,000 for the delivery of the yacht and to provide the defendants a loan of $80,000 to complete the construction of the vessel. Referencing the settlement agreement, the defendants at the same time executed a promissory note obliging them to repay the $80,000 loan plus interest in annual installments due on November 1 of each year, with the final payment due on November 1, 1994. The court stated in presenting the facts: "However, like the yacht itself, the settlement agreement soon proved to be just another hole in the water into which the plaintiff threw his money." Bourg sued the defendants after they failed to make certain payments on the note, and the court granted a motion for summary judgment in favor of Bourg for $59,081. The defendants appealed.

DECISION: Judgment for Bourg. Because the defendants' affidavit recites that an alleged oral side agreement was entered into at the same time as the settlement agreement and promissory note—the oral side agreement allegedly stated "that the note would be paid for by services rendered by the defendants"—the oral side agreement would have constituted a contemporaneous modification that would merge into the integrated promissory note and settlement agreement and thus be barred from admission into evidence under the parol evidence rule. Although parties to an integrated written contract can modify their understanding by a subsequent oral pact, to be legally effective, there must be evidence of mutual assent to the essential terms of the modification and adequate consideration. Here the defendants adduced no competent evidence of either mutual assent to particular terms or a specific consideration that would be sufficiently definite to constitute an enforceable subsequent oral modification to the parties' earlier written agreements. Thus, legally this alleged oral agreement was all sail and no anchor. [***Bourg v. Bristol Boat Co.,*** **705 A.2d 969 (R.I. 1998)**]

16-3 Rules of Construction and Interpretation

In interpreting contracts, courts are aided by certain rules.

16-3a Intention of the Parties

When persons enter into an agreement, it is to be presumed that they intend for their agreement to have some effect. A court will strive to determine the intent of the parties and to give effect to it. A contract, therefore, is to be enforced according to its terms.[22] A court cannot remake or rewrite the contract of the parties under the pretense of interpreting.[23]

[21] *Edwards v. Centrex Real Estate Corp.,* 61 Cal. Rptr. 518 (Cal. App. 1997).
[22] See *Greenwald v. Kersh,* 621 S.E.2d 463 (Ga. App. 2005).
[23] *Abbot v. Schnader, Harrison, Segal & Lewis, LLP,* 805 A.2d 547 (Pa. Super. 2002).

No particular form of words is required, and any words manifesting the intent of the parties are sufficient. In the absence of proof that a word has a peculiar meaning or that it was employed by the parties with a particular meaning, a common word is given its ordinary meaning.

Meaning of Words

Ordinary words are to be interpreted according to their ordinary meaning.[24] **For Example,** when a contract requires the gasoline dealer to pay the supplier for "gallons" supplied, the term *gallons* is unambiguous and does not require that an adjustment of the gallonage be made for the temperature.[25] When a contract calls for a businessperson to pay a builder for the builder's "costs," the term *costs* is unambiguous, meaning actual costs, not a lesser amount based on the builder's bid.[26]

If there is a common meaning to a term, that meaning will be followed even though the dictionary may contain additional meanings. If technical or trade terms are used in a contract, they are to be interpreted according to the area of technical knowledge or trade from which the terms are taken.

Incorporation by Reference

The contract may not cover all of the agreed terms. The missing terms may be found in another document. Frequently, the parties executing the contract for storage will simply state that a storage contract is entered into and that the contract applies to the goods listed in the schedule attached to and made part of the contract. Likewise, a contract for the construction of a building may involve plans and specifications on file in a named city office. The contract will simply state that the building is to be constructed according to those plans and specifications that are "incorporated herein and made part of this contract." When there is such an **incorporation by reference,** the contract consists of both the original document and the detailed statement that is incorporated in it.

incorporation by reference–contract consisting of both the original or skeleton document and the detailed statement that is incorporated in it.

When a contract refers to another document, however, the contract must sufficiently describe the document or so much of it as is to be interpreted as part of the contract.

16-3b Whole Contract

The provisions of a contract must be construed as a whole in such a way that every part is given effect.

Every word of a contract is to be given effect if reasonably possible. The contract is to be construed as a whole, and if the plain language of the contract thus viewed solves the dispute, the court is to make no further analysis.[27]

CASE SUMMARY

When You Permanently Reduced the Shipping Spots to Zero, You "Terminated" the Contract, Silly

FACTS: C.A. Acquisition Newco LLC is a successor in interest to Cyphermint, Inc. ("CI"), a New York corporation specializing in software development for self-service kiosks. DHL Express (USA), Inc., is an Ohio corporation with a principal place of business in Florida. It is a division of DHL International GmbH, a Deutsche Post Company and express carrier

[24] *Thorton v. D.F.W. Christian Television, Inc.*, 925 S.W.2d 17 (Tex. App. 1995).
[25] *Hopkins v. BP Oil, Inc.*, 81 F.3d 1070 (11th Cir. 1996).
[26] *Batzer Construction, Inc. v. Boyer*, 125 P.3d 773 (Or. App. 2006).
[27] *Covensky v. Hannah Marine Corp.*, 903 N.E.2d 422 (Ill. App. 2009).

When You Permanently Reduced the Shipping Spots to Zero, You "Terminated" the Contract, Silly continued

of documents and freight. Until 2008, DHL provided express pick-up and delivery, including same-day air delivery of letters and packages throughout the United States.

DHL entered into an agreement with Cyphermint, hoping to expand its customer base by offering domestic shipping services in retail locations, such as Walgreens and OfficeMax, via kiosks, or "Shipping Spots." Customers were able to use the kiosks' touch screen to pay for shipping costs and print shipping labels. The contract provided for an initial three-year term (August 1, 2006, through July 31, 2009) that automatically renewed for two more years unless either party gave notice of its election not to renew 90 days before the end of the initial contract. Under the contract, Cyphermint agreed to provide interactive software, enabling customers to use DHL's services from the shipping spots. Section 10.5 of the contract governs termination fees:

> *There shall be no termination fees for any termination by either party, irrespective of the reason for such termination, except for a "Material Breach" or as provided pursuant to the "Statement of Work" (SOW).*

The SOW contains the following provision concerning termination fees:

> *Should DHL terminate this agreement for any reason other than a material breach by Cyphermint before its termination date DHL agrees to compensate CI in the amount of $50,000 per month for each month remaining in the initial term.*

In November 2008, DHL decided to end all domestic delivery service within the United States. CI requested early termination fees under Section 10.5 of the contract of $413,333.33. DHL refused to pay, contending that Section 2.8 of the contract gave DHL the discretion to control the number and placement of the shipping spots, and when it ended U.S. domestic operations, it exercised its discretion to reduce shipping spots to zero.

DECISION: Judgment for CI. In reviewing a document, a court must consider the document as a whole, rather than attempting to isolate certain parts of it. Even if the court were to accept DHL's argument that Section 2.8 gave it blanket authority to reduce or eliminate the shipping spot project altogether, the outcome would remain the same. The relevant provision in the contract provides for termination fees without regard to whether the termination was authorized. The only restriction placed on the recovery of such fees is that they will not be available in the case of a material breach by Cyphermint. DHL failed to explain how reducing the shipping spots to zero was in any way different from "terminating" the contract. **[*C.A. Acquisition Newco, LLC v. DHL Express (USA), Inc.*, 795 F. Supp. 2d 140 (D. Mass. 2011)]**

16-3c Contradictory and Ambiguous Terms

One term in a contract may conflict with another term, or one term may have two different meanings. It is then necessary for the court to determine whether there is a contract and, if so, what the contract really means.

CASE SUMMARY

Who Pays the Piper?

FACTS: Olander Contracting Co., developer Gail Wachter, and the City of Bismarck, North Dakota, entered into a water and sewer construction contract including, among other things, connecting a 10-inch sewer line from Wachter's housing development to the city's existing 36-inch concrete sewer main and installing a manhole at the connection, to be paid for by Wachter. Olander installed the manhole, but it collapsed within a few days. Olander installed a second manhole, with a large base supported by pilings, but it too failed a few days after it was installed. Olander then placed a rock bedding under the city's sewer main, replaced 78 feet of the existing concrete pipe with PVC pipe, and installed a manhole a third time on a larger base. Olander sued Wachter and the City of Bismarck for damages of

Who Pays the Piper? continued

$456,536.25 for extra work it claims it was required to perform to complete its contract. Both defendants denied they were responsible for the amount sued under the contract. The jury returned a special verdict, finding that Olander performed "extra work/unforeseen work ... for which it is entitled to be compensated in excess of the contract price" in the amount of $220,849.67, to be paid by the City of Bismarck. Appeals were taken.

DECISION: Judgment for Olander. The trial judge properly made the initial determination that the contract language was ambiguous. That is, the language used by the parties could support good arguments for the positions of both parties. This resolved a question of law. Once this determination had been made, the judge allowed extrinsic evidence from all parties as to what they meant when they negotiated the contract. This evidence related to the questions of fact, which were left to the jury. Testimony was taken from the parties who negotiated the contract, and testimony was also heard about the role of each of the parties in the actual construction of the manhole, the cause for the collapses, and why the contractor had to replace the city's existing concrete pipe with PVC pipe and the city's role in making this determination. The jury then fulfilled its role answering the question whether or not Olander had performed extra work in the affirmative, concluding that the city was required to pay for it. [***Olander Contracting v. Wachter*, 643 N.W.2d 29 (2002)**]

If the language within the four corners of the contract is unambiguous, the parties' intentions are determined from the plain meaning of the words, used in the contract, as a matter of law, by the judge. A contract term or provision is *ambiguous* if it is capable of more than one reasonable interpretation because of the uncertain meaning of terms or missing terms. A finding of ambiguity is justified only if the language of the contract reasonably supports the competing interpretations.[28] It is the role of the judge—a question of law—to initially determine whether a contract is ambiguous. If the contract is ambiguous, it is the role of the jury—a question of fact—to determine which party's position is correct with the aid of extrinsic evidence.

Nature of Writing

When a contract is partly a printed form or partly typewritten and partly handwritten and the written part conflicts with the printed or typewritten part, the written part prevails. When there is a conflict between a printed part and a typewritten part, the latter prevails. Consequently, when a clause typewritten on a printed form conflicts with what is stated by the print, the conflicting print is ignored and the typewritten clause controls. This rule is based on the belief that the parties had given greater thought to what they typed or wrote for the particular contract as contrasted with printed words already in a form designed to cover many transactions. Thus, a typewritten provision to pay 90 cents per unit overrode a preprinted provision setting the price as 45 cents per unit.

When there is a conflict between an amount or quantity expressed both in words and figures, as on a check, the amount or quantity expressed in words prevails. Words control because there is less danger that a word will be wrong than a number.

Ambiguity

A contract is ambiguous when the intent of the parties is uncertain and the contract is capable of more than one reasonable interpretation.[29] The background from which the contract and the dispute arose may help in determining the intention of the parties. **For Example,** when suit was brought in Minnesota on a Canadian insurance policy, the

[28] *QEP Energy Co. v. Sullivan*, 444 Fed. Appx. 284 (10th Cir. 2011).
[29] *Kaufman & Stewart v. Weinbrenner Shoe Co.*, 589 N.W.2d 499 (Minn. App. 1999).

question arose whether the dollar limit of the policy referred to Canadian or U.S. dollars. The court concluded that Canadian dollars were intended. Both the insurer and the insured were Canadian corporations; the original policy, endorsements to the policy, and policy renewals were written in Canada; over the years, premiums had been paid in Canadian dollars; and a prior claim on the policy had been settled by the payment of an amount computed on the basis of Canadian dollars.

Strict Construction Against Drafting Party

An ambiguous contract is interpreted strictly against the party who drafted it.[30] **For Example,** an insurance policy containing ambiguous language regarding coverage or exclusions is interpreted against the insurer and in favor of the insured when two interpretations are reasonably possible. This rule is a secondary rule that may be invoked only after all of the ordinary interpretive guides have been exhausted. The rule basically assigns the risk of an unresolvable ambiguity to the party creating it.[31]

16-3d Implied Terms

In some cases, a court will imply a term to cover a situation for which the parties failed to provide or, when needed, to give the contract a construction or meaning that is reasonable.

The court often implies details of the performance of a contract not expressly stated in the contract. In a contract to perform work, there is an implied promise to use such skill as is necessary to properly perform the work.

CASE SUMMARY

Read the Contract Your Honor. Where Did We Promise the Holguins That Their Satellite Dish Would Be Properly Installed?

FACTS: The Holguins ordered a bundle of services from AT&T and affiliates DISH California and EchoStar consisting of telephone, Internet, and satellite television services, with Deborah Holguin signing up with the AT&T sales agents. The installation process did not go as planned. The DISH technician drilled through a sewer pipe in the Holguins' wall, fed a satellite television cable through it, and patched the wall without repairing the sewer pipe. The improper installation was not discovered until 14 months later, and the damaged pipe leaked sewer water into the surrounding wall cavity and caused mold buildup in the Holguins' home. As a result, the Holguins suffered respiratory problems and other health issues. The repair efforts were a nightmare causing the Holguins to hire their own contractor to complete the remediation work. The Holguins sued AT&T, DISH, and EchoStar for breach of contract. From a judgment for the Holguins for $109,000 in compensatory damages and attorney fees, the defendants appealed. AT&T, DISH, and EchoStar contend that the trial court erred in interpreting the Holguins' contract to contain an implied term requiring the Holguins' satellite television equipment to be properly installed.

DECISION: Judgment for the Holguins. It is a well-settled principle that express contractual terms give rise to implied duties, violations of which may themselves constitute breaches of contract. Accompanying every contract is a common-law duty to perform with care, skill, reasonable expedience, and faithfulness the thing agreed to be done, and a negligent failure to observe any of these conditions is a tort, as well as a breach of the contract. There was no error applying the implied contractual term that the equipment be properly installed. **[*Holguin v. Dish Network, LLC*, 178 Cal. Rptr. 3d 100 (Cal. App. 2014)]**

[30] *Idaho Migrant Council, Inc. v. Warila*, 89 P.2d 39 (Wyo. 1995).
[31] *Premier Title Co. v. Donahue*, 765 N.E.2d 513 (Ill. App. 2002).

In every contract, there is an implied obligation that neither party shall do anything that will have the effect of destroying or injuring the right of the other party to receive the fruits of the contract. This means that in every contract there exists an implied covenant of **good faith** and fair dealing. When a contract may reasonably be interpreted in different ways, a court should make the interpretation that is in harmony with good faith and fair dealing. **For Example,** when a contract is made subject to the condition that one of the parties obtain financing, that party must make reasonable, good-faith efforts to obtain financing. The party is not permitted to do nothing and then claim that the contract is not binding because the condition has not been satisfied. Likewise, when a contract requires a party to obtain government approval, the party must use all reasonable means to obtain it.[32]

good faith–absence of knowledge of any defects or problems.

The Uniform Commercial Code imposes an obligation of good faith in the performance or enforcement of every contract.[33]

16-3e Conduct and Custom

The conduct of the parties and the customs and usages of a particular trade may give meaning to the words of the parties and thus aid in the interpretation of their contract.

Conduct of the Parties

The conduct of the parties in carrying out the terms of a contract is the best guide to determine the parties' intent. When performance has been repeatedly tendered and accepted without protest, neither party will be permitted to claim that the contract was too indefinite to be binding. **For Example,** a travel agent made a contract with a hotel to arrange for trips to the hotel. After some 80 trips had already been arranged and paid for by the hotel at the contract price without any dispute about whether the contract obligation was satisfied, any claim by the travel agent that it could charge additional fees must be rejected.

Custom and Usage of Trade

The customs and **usages of trade** or commercial activity to which the contract relates may be used to interpret the terms of a contract.[34] **For Example,** when a contract for the construction of a building calls for a "turn-key construction," industry usage is admissible to show what this means: a construction in which all the owner needs to do is to turn the key in the lock to open the building for use and in which all construction risks are assumed by the contractor.[35]

usage of trade–language and customs of an industry.

Custom and usage, however, cannot override express provisions of a contract that are inconsistent with custom and usage.

16-3f Avoidance of Hardship

As a general rule, a party is bound by a contract even though it proves to be a bad bargain. If possible, a court will interpret a contract to avoid hardship. Courts will, if possible, interpret a vague contract in a way to avoid any forfeiture of a party's interest.

When hardship arises because the contract makes no provision for the situation that has occurred, the court will sometimes imply a term to avoid the hardship.

[32] *Kroboth v. Brent,* 625 N.Y.S.2d 748 (A.D. 1995).
[33] U.C.C. §§1-201(19), 1-203.
[34] *Affiliated FM Ins. Co. v. Constitution Reinsurance Corp.,* 626 N.E.2d 878 (Mass. 1994).
[35] *Blue v. R.L. Glossen Contracting, Inc.,* 327 S.E.2d 582 (Ga. App. 1985).

Make the Connection

Summary

An oral agreement may be a contract unless it is the intention of the parties that they should not be bound by the agreement without a writing executed by them. Certain contracts must be evidenced by a writing, however, or else they cannot be enforced. The statutes that declare this exception are called *statutes of frauds*. Statutes of frauds commonly require that a contract be evidenced by writing in the case of (1) an agreement that cannot be performed within one year after the contract is made, (2) an agreement to sell any interest in land, (3) a promise to answer for the debt or default of another, (4) a promise by the executor or administrator of a decedent's estate to pay a claim against the estate from personal funds, (5) a promise made in consideration of marriage, and (6) a contract for the sale of goods for a purchase price of $500 or more.

To evidence a contract to satisfy a statute of frauds, there must be a writing of all essential terms. The writing must be signed by the defendant against whom suit is brought for enforcement of the contract.

If the applicable statute of frauds is not satisfied, the oral contract cannot be enforced. To avoid unjust enrichment, a plaintiff barred from enforcing an oral contract may in most cases recover from the other contracting party the reasonable value of the benefits conferred by the plaintiff on the defendant.

When there is a written contract, the question arises whether that writing is the exclusive statement of the parties' agreement. If the writing is the complete and final statement of the contract, parol evidence as to matters agreed to before or at the time the writing was signed is not admissible to contradict the writing. This is called the *parol evidence rule*. In any case, the parol evidence rule does not bar parol evidence when (1) the writing is ambiguous, (2) the writing is not a true statement of the agreement of the parties because of fraud, duress, or mistake, or (3) the existence, modification, or illegality of a contract is in controversy.

Because a contract is based on the agreement of the parties, courts must determine the intent of the parties manifested in the contract. The intent that is to be enforced is the intent as it reasonably appears to a third person. This objective intent is followed.

In interpreting a contract, ordinary words are to be given their ordinary meanings. If trade or technical terms have been used, they are interpreted according to their technical meanings. The court must consider the whole contract and not read a particular part out of context. When different writings are executed as part of the same transaction, or one writing refers to or incorporates another, all of the writings are to be read together as the contract of the parties.

When provisions of a contract are contradictory, the court will try to reconcile or eliminate the conflict. If this cannot be done, the conclusion may be that there is no contract because the conflict makes the agreement indefinite as to a material matter. In some cases, conflict is solved by considering the form of conflicting terms. Handwriting prevails over typing and a printed form, and typing prevails over a printed form. Ambiguity will be eliminated in some cases by the admission of parol evidence or by interpreting the provision strictly against the party preparing the contract, particularly when that party has significantly greater bargaining power.

Learning Outcomes

After studying this chapter, you should be able to clearly explain:

16-1 Statute of Frauds

LO.1 Explain when a contract must be evidenced by a writing

See the discussion and examples illustrated throughout this chapter beginning on page 292.

LO.2 Explain the effect of noncompliance with the statute of frauds

See the *Bithoney* case where a doctor's oral contract for severance was barred by the statute of frauds, page 293.

See the example in which an oral contract cannot be enforced because it is not in writing, but the plaintiff may recover the reasonable value of the services rendered, page 299.

16-2 Parol Evidence Rule

LO.3 Explain the parol evidence rule and the exceptions to this rule

See the example in which the tenant is not allowed to call a witness to testify about a prior oral agreement that would add to and alter the written lease, page 300.

See the exceptions based on ambiguity, fraud, duress, and mistake, pages 300–301.

16-3 Rules of Construction and Interpretation

LO.4 Understand the basic rule of contract construction that a contract is enforced according to its terms

See the example of the interpretation of the word "costs," page 302.

See the *DHL Express* case that illustrates the judicial common sense of interpreting the contract as a whole rather than a strained construction contrary to the contract's intent, pages 302–303.

LO.5 State the rules for interpreting ambiguous terms in a contract

See the discussion on the nature of the writing, page 304.

Key Terms

administrator
ambiguous
decedent
executor
good faith
incorporation by reference
parol evidence rule
personal representative
statute of frauds
suretyship
usages of trade

Questions and Case Problems

1. Kelly made a written contract to sell certain land to Brown and gave Brown a deed to the land. Thereafter, Kelly sued Brown to get back a 20-foot strip of the land. Kelly claimed that before making the written contract, it was agreed that Kelly would sell all of his land to Brown to make it easier for Brown to get a building permit, but after that was done, the 20-foot strip would be reconveyed to Kelly. Was Kelly entitled to the 20-foot strip? What ethical values are involved? [*Brown v. Kelly*, 545 So. 2d 518 (Fla. App.)]
2. Martin made an oral contract with Cresheim Garage to work as its manager for two years. Cresheim wrote Martin a letter stating that the oral contract had been made and setting forth all of its terms. Cresheim later refused to recognize the contract. Martin sued Cresheim for breach of the contract and offered Cresheim's letter in evidence as proof of the contract. Cresheim claimed that the oral contract was not binding because the contract was not in writing and the letter referring to the contract was not a contract but only a letter. Was the contract binding?
3. Lawrence loaned money to Moore, who died without repaying the loan. Lawrence claimed that when he mentioned the matter to Moore's widow, she promised to pay the debt. She did not pay it, and Lawrence sued her on her promise. Does she have any defense? [*Moore v. Lawrence*, 480 S.W.2d 941 (Ark.)]
4. Jackson signed an agreement to sell 79 acres of land to Devenyns. Jackson owned 80 acres and was apparently intending to keep for himself the acre on which his home was located. The written agreement also stated that "Devenyns shall have the option to buy on property ___," but nothing was stated in the blank space. Devenyns sued to enforce the agreement. Was it binding? [In re *Jackson's Estate*, 892 P.2d 786 (Wyo.)]
5. Boeing Airplane Co. contracted with Pittsburgh–Des Moines Steel Co. for the latter to construct a supersonic wind tunnel. R.H. Freitag Manufacturing Co. sold materials to York-Gillespie Co., which subcontracted to do part of the work. To persuade Freitag to keep supplying materials on credit, Boeing and the principal contractor both assured Freitag that he would be paid. When Freitag was not paid by the subcontractor, he sued Boeing and the contractor. They defended on the ground that the assurances given Freitag were not written. Decide. What ethical values are involved? [*R.H. Freitag Mfg. Co. v. Boeing Airplane Co.*, 347 P.2d 1074 (Wash.)]
6. Louise Pulsifer owned a farm that she wanted to sell and ran an ad in the local newspaper. After Russell Gillespie agreed to purchase the farm, Pulsifer wrote him a letter stating that she would not sell it. He

sued her to enforce the contract, and she raised the defense of the statute of frauds. The letter she had signed did not contain any of the terms of the sale. Gillespie, however, claimed that the newspaper ad could be combined with her letter to satisfy the statute of frauds. Was he correct? [*Gillespie v. Pulsifer*, 655 S.W.2d 123 (Mo.)]

7. In February or March, Corning Glass Works orally agreed to retain Hanan as management consultant from May 1 of that year to April 30 of the next year for a present value fee of $200,000. Was this agreement binding? Is this decision ethical? [*Hanan v. Corning Glass Works*, 314 N.Y.S.2d 804 (A.D.)]

8. Catherine (wife) and Peter (husband) Mallen had lived together unmarried for some four years when Catherine got pregnant and a marriage was arranged. Peter asked Catherine to sign a prenuptial agreement. Although his financial statement attached to the agreement did not state his income at $560,000 per year, it showed he was wealthy, and she had lived with him for four years and knew from their standard of living that he had significant income. Catherine contends that failure to disclose Peter's income was a nondisclosure of a material fact when the agreement was drawn up and that accordingly the agreement is not valid. Peter contends that he fully disclosed his net worth and that Catherine was well aware of his significant income. Further, he contends that disparities in the parties' financial status and business experience did not make the agreement unconscionable. Decide. [*Mallen v. Mallen*, 622 S.E.2d 812 (Ga. Sup. Ct.)]

9. Panasonic Industrial Co. (PIC) created a contract making Manchester Equipment Co., Inc. (MECI), a nonexclusive wholesale distributor of its products. The contract stated that PIC reserved the unrestricted right to solicit and make direct sales of the products to anyone, anywhere. The contract also stated that it contained the entire agreement of the parties and that any prior agreement or statement was superseded by the contract. PIC subsequently began to make direct sales to two of MECI's established customers. MECI claimed that this was a breach of the distribution contract and sued PIC for damages. Decide. What ethical values are involved? [*Manchester Equipment Co. Inc. v. Panasonic Industrial Co.*, 529 N.Y.S.2d 532 (App. Div.)]

10. A contract made for the sale of a farm stated that the buyer's deposit would be returned "if for any reason the farm cannot be sold." The seller later stated that she had changed her mind and would not sell, and she offered to return the deposit. The buyer refused to take the deposit back and brought suit to enforce the contract. The seller contended that the "any reason" provision extended to anything, including the seller's changing her mind. Was the buyer entitled to recover? [*Phillips v. Rogers*, 200 S.E.2d 676 (W. Va.)]

11. Integrated, Inc., entered into a contract with the state of California to construct a building. It then subcontracted the electrical work to Alec Fergusson Electrical Contractors. The subcontract was a printed form with blanks filled in by typewriting. The printed payment clause required Integrated to pay Fergusson on the 15th day of the month following the submission of invoices by Fergusson. The typewritten part of the contract required Integrated to pay Fergusson "immediately following payment" (by the state) to the general contractor. When was payment required? [*Integrated, Inc. v. Alec Fergusson Electrical Contractors*, 58 Cal. Rptr. 503 (Cal. App.)]

12. Consolidated Credit Counseling Services, Inc. (Consolidated), sued Affinity Internet, Inc., doing business as SkyNetWEB (Affinity), for breach of its contract to provide computer and Web hosting services. Affinity moved to compel arbitration, and Consolidated argued that the contract between the parties did not contain an arbitration clause. The contract between the parties stated in part: "This contract is subject to all of SkyNetWEB's terms, conditions, user and acceptable use policies located at **http://www.skynetweb.com/company/legal/legal.php.**" An arbitration provision can be found by going to the Web site and clicking to paragraph 17 of the User Agreement. The contract itself makes no reference to an agreement to arbitrate, nor was paragraph 17 expressly referred to or described in the contract. Nor was a hard copy of the information on the Web site either signed by or furnished to Consolidated. Was Consolidated obligated to arbitrate under the clear language of paragraph 17? [*Affinity Internet v. Consolidated Credit*, 920 So. 2d 1286 (Fla. App.)]

13. Physicians Mutual Insurance Co. issued a policy covering Brown's life. The policy declared that it did not cover any deaths resulting from "mental disorder, alcoholism, or drug addiction." Brown was killed when she fell while intoxicated. The insurance company refused to pay because of the quoted provision. Her executor, Savage, sued the insurance company.

Did the insurance company have a defense? [*Physicians Mutual Ins. Co. v. Savage*, 296 N.E.2d 165 (Ind. App.)]

14. The Dickinson Elks Club conducted an annual Labor Day golf tournament. Charbonneau Buick-Pontiac offered to give a new car as a prize to anyone making "a hole in one on hole no. 8." The golf course of the club was only nine holes. To play 18 holes, the players would go around the course twice, although they would play from different tees or locations for the second nine holes. On the second time around, what was originally the eighth hole became the seventeenth hole. Grove was a contestant in the tournament. He scored 3 on the no. 8 hole, but on approaching it for the second time as the seventeenth hole, he made a hole in one. He claimed the prize car from Charbonneau. The latter claimed that Grove had not won the prize because he did not make the hole in one on the eighth hole. Decide. [*Grove v. Charbonneau Buick-Pontiac, Inc.*, 240 N.W.2d 8533 (N.D.)]

15. Tambe Electric Inc. entered into a written agreement with Home Depot to provide copper wire to Tambe at a price set forth in the writing, and allowing the contractor the option of paying for the wire over a period of time. Home Depot did not fulfill this written agreement and Tambe sued for $68,598, the additional cost it had to subsequently pay to obtain copper wire for its work. Home Depot defended that it had made an oral condition precedent requiring payment in full by Tambe at the time it accepted the price quoted in the written agreement. Decide. [*Tambe Electric v. Home Depot*, 856 N.Y.S.2d 373]

CPA Questions

1. Which of the following statements is true with regard to the statute of frauds?
   a. All contracts involving consideration of more than $500 must be in writing.
   b. The written contract must be signed by all parties.
   c. The statute of frauds applies to contracts that can be fully performed within one year from the date they are made.
   d. The contract terms may be stated in more than one document.

2. With regard to an agreement for the sale of real estate, the statute of frauds:
   a. Requires that the entire agreement be in a single writing.
   b. Requires that the purchase price be fair and adequate in relation to the value of the real estate.
   c. Does *not* require that the agreement be signed by all parties.
   d. Does *not* apply if the value of the real estate is less than $500.

3. In negotiations with Andrews for the lease of Kemp's warehouse, Kemp orally agreed to pay one-half of the cost of the utilities. The written lease, later prepared by Kemp's attorney, provided that Andrews pay all of the utilities. Andrews failed to carefully read the lease and signed it. When Kemp demanded that Andrews pay all of the utilities, Andrews refused, claiming that the lease did not accurately reflect the oral agreement. Andrews also learned that Kemp intentionally misrepresented the condition of the structure of the warehouse during the negotiations between the parties. Andrews sued to rescind the lease and intends to introduce evidence of the parties' oral agreement about sharing the utilities and the fraudulent statements made by Kemp. Will the parol evidence rule prevent the admission of evidence concerning each of the following?

	Oral agreement regarding who pays the utilities	*Fraudulent statements by Kemp*
a.	Yes	Yes
b.	No	Yes
c.	Yes	No
d.	No	No

CHAPTER 18

Discharge of Contracts

Learning Outcomes <<<

After studying this chapter, you should be able to

LO.1 List the three types of conditions that affect a party's duty to perform

LO.2 Explain the on-time performance rule

LO.3 Explain the adequacy of performance rules

LO.4 Explain four ways a contract can be discharged by agreement of the parties

LO.5 State the effect on a contract of the death or disability of one of the contracting parties

LO.6 Explain when impossibility or impracticability may discharge a contract

In the preceding chapters, you studied how a contract is formed, what a contract means, and who has rights under a contract. In this chapter, attention is turned to how a contract is ended or discharged. In other words, what puts an end to the rights and duties created by a contract?

18-1 Conditions Relating to Performance

As developed in the body of this chapter, the ordinary method of discharging obligations under a contract is by performance. Certain promises may be less than absolute and instead come into effect only upon the occurrence of a specified event, or an existing obligation may be extinguished when an event happens. These are conditional promises.

18-1a Classifications of Conditions

condition–stipulation or prerequisite in a contract, will, or other instrument.

When the occurrence or nonoccurrence of an event, as expressed in a contract, affects the duty of a party to the contract to perform, the event is called a **condition.** Terms such as *if, provided that, when, after, as soon as, subject to*, and *on the condition that* indicate the creation of a condition.[1] Conditions are classified as *conditions precedent, conditions subsequent*, and *concurrent conditions.*

Condition Precedent

condition precedent–event that if unsatisfied would mean that no rights would arise under a contract.

A **condition precedent** is a condition that must occur before a party to a contract has an obligation to perform under the contract. **For Example,** a condition precedent to a contractor's (MasTec's) obligation to pay a subcontractor (MidAmerica) under a "pay-if-paid" by the owner (PathNet) clause in their subcontract agreement is the receipt of payment by MasTec from PathNet. The condition precedent—payment by the owner—did not occur due to bankruptcy, and, therefore, MasTec did not have an obligation to pay MidAmerica.[2]

CASE SUMMARY

A Blitz on Offense?

FACTS: Richard Blitz owns a piece of commercial property at 4 Old Middle Street. On February 2, 1998, Arthur Subklew entered into a lease with Blitz to rent the rear portion of the property. Subklew intended to operate an auto sales and repair business. Paragraph C of the lease was a zoning contingency clause that stated, "Landlord [plaintiff] will use Landlord's best efforts to obtain a written verification that Tenant can operate [an] Auto Sales and Repair Business at the demised premises. If Landlord is unable to obtain such commitment from the municipality, then this agreement shall be deemed null and void and Landlord shall immediately return deposit monies to Tenant." The zoning board approved the location only as a general repair business. When Subklew refused to occupy the premises, Blitz sued him for breach of contract.

[1] *Harmon Cable Communications v. Scope Cable Television, Inc.*, 468 N.W.2d 350 (Neb. 1990).

[2] *MidAmerica Construction Management, Inc. v. MasTec North America, Inc.*, 436 F.3d 1257 (10th Cir. 2006). But see *International Engineering Services, Inc. v. Scherer Construction Co.*, 74 So. 3d 53 (Fla. App. 2011), where a "pay-when-paid" provision was found to be ambiguous, resulting in the general contractor being liable for the payment to the subcontractor.

A Blitz on Offense? continued

DECISION: Judgment for Subklew. A condition precedent is a fact or event that the parties intend must exist before there is right to a performance. If the condition is not fulfilled, the right to enforce the contract does not come into existence. Blitz's obligation to obtain written approval of a used car business was a condition precedent to the leasing agreement. Since it was not obtained, Blitz cannot enforce the leasing agreement. [***Blitz v. Subklew*, 810 A.2d 841 (Conn. App. 2002)**]

Condition Subsequent

condition subsequent– event whose occurrence or lack thereof terminates a contract.

The parties to a contract may agree that a party is obligated to perform a certain act or pay a certain sum of money, but the contract contains a provision that relieves the obligation on the occurrence of a certain event. That is, on the happening of a **condition subsequent,** such an event extinguishes the duty to thereafter perform. **For Example,** Chad Newly served as the weekend anchor on *Channel 5 News* for several years. The station manager, Tom O'Brien, on reviewing tapes in connection with Newly's contract renewal, believed that Newly's speech on occasion was slightly slurred, and he suspected that it was from alcohol use. In the parties' contract discussions, O'Brien expressed his concerns about an alcohol problem and offered help. Newly denied there was a problem. O'Brien agreed to a new two-year contract with Newly at $190,000 for the first year and $220,000 for the second year with other benefits subject to "the condition" that the station reserved the right to make four unannounced drug-alcohol tests during the contract term; and should Newly test positive for drugs or alcohol under measurements set forth in the contract, then all of Channel 5's obligations to Newly under the contract would cease. When Newly subsequently failed a urinalysis test three months into the new contract, the happening of this event extinguished the station's obligation to employ and pay him under the contract. Conditions subsequent are strictly construed, and where ambiguous, are construed against forfeiture.[3]

SPORTS & ENTERTAINMENT LAW

Endorsement Contracts

Sports marketing involves the use of famous athletes to promote the sale of products and services in our economy. Should an athlete's image be tarnished by allegations of immoral or illegal conduct, a company could be subject to financial losses and corporate embarrassment. Endorsement contracts may extend for multiyear periods, and should a "morals" issue arise, a company would be well served to have had a broad morals clause in its contract that would allow the company at its sole discretion to summarily terminate the endorsement contract. Representatives of athletes, on the other hand, seek narrow contractual language that allows for termination of endorsement contracts only upon the indictment for a crime, and they seek the right to have an arbitrator, as opposed to the employer, make the determination as to whether the morals clause was violated. John Daly's endorsement contract with Callaway Golf was terminated by the company when he violated his good conduct clause that restricted gambling and drinking activities; and NFL running back Adrian Peterson's endorsement contracts were canceled after he injured his four-year-old son by spanking him with a wooden switch. Nike, RadioShack, and other sponsors ended their relationships (with an estimated value of $10 million a year) with cyclist Lance Armstrong after he admitted taking performance enhancing drugs.

Can the courts be utilized to resolve controversies over whether a "morals clause" has been violated? If so, is the occurrence of a morals clause violation a condition precedent or a condition subsequent?

[3] *Cardone Trust v. Cardone,* 8 A.3d 1 (N.H. 2010).

Concurrent Condition

In most bilateral contracts, the performances of the parties are *concurrent conditions.* That is, their mutual duties of performance under the contract are to take place simultaneously. **For Example,** concerning a contract for the sale and delivery of certain goods, the buyer must tender to the seller a certified check at the time of delivery as set forth in the contract, and the seller must tender the goods to the buyer at the same time.

18-2 Discharge by Performance

When it is claimed that a contract is discharged by performance, questions arise as to the nature, time, and sufficiency of the performance.

18-2a Normal Discharge of Contracts

A contract is usually discharged by the performance of the terms of the agreement. In most cases, the parties perform their promises and the contract ceases to exist or is thereby discharged. A contract is also discharged by the expiration of the time period specified in the contract.[4]

18-2b Nature of Performance

Performance may be the doing of an act or the making of payment.

Tender

tender–goods have arrived, are available for pickup, and the buyer is notified.

An offer to perform is known as a **tender.** If performance of the contract requires the doing of an act, the refusal of a tender discharges the party offering to perform and is a basis for that party to bring a lawsuit.

A valid tender of payment consists of an unconditional offer of the exact amount due on the date when due. A tender of payment is not just an expression of willingness to pay; it must be an actual offer to perform by making payment of the amount owed.

Payment

When the contract requires payment, performance consists of the payment of money.

Application of Payments. If a debtor owes more than one debt to the creditor and pays money, a question may arise as to which debt has been paid. If the debtor specifies the debt to which the payment is to be applied and the creditor accepts the money, the creditor is bound to apply the money as specified.[5] Thus, if the debtor specifies that a payment is to be made for a current purchase, the creditor may not apply the payment to an older balance.

Payment by Check. Payment by commercial paper, such as a check, is ordinarily a conditional payment. A check merely suspends the debt until the check is presented for payment. If payment is then made, the debt is discharged; if not paid, the suspension terminates, and suit may be brought on either the debt or the check. Frequently, payment must be made by a specified date. It is generally held that the payment is made on time if it is mailed on or before the final date for payment.

[4] *Washington National Ins. Co. v. Sherwood Associates,* 795 P.2d 665 (Utah App. 1990).
[5] *Oakes Logging, Inc. v. Green Crow, Inc.,* 832 P.2d 894 (Wash. App. 1992).

CASE SUMMARY

The Mailed-Check Payment

FACTS: Thomas Cooper was purchasing land from Peter and Ella Birznieks. Cooper was already in possession of the land but was required to pay the amount owed by January 30; otherwise, he would have to vacate the property. The attorney handling the transaction for the Birznieks told Cooper that he could mail the payment to him. On January 30, Cooper mailed to the attorney a personal check drawn on an out-of-state bank for the amount due. The check arrived at the Birznieks' attorney's office on February 1. The Birznieks refused to accept the check on the grounds that it was not a timely payment and moved to evict Cooper from the property.

DECISION: Because of the general custom to regard a check mailed to a creditor as paying the bill that is owed, payment was made by Cooper on January 30 when he mailed the check. Payment was therefore made within the required time even though received after the expiration of the required time. **[*Birznieks v. Cooper*, 275 N.W.2d 221 (Mich. 1979)]**

18-2c Time of Performance

When the date or period of time for performance is specified in the contract, performance should be made on that date or within that time period.

No Time Specified

When the time for performance is not specified in the contract, an obligation to perform within a reasonable time is implied.[6] The fact that no time is specified neither impairs the contract on the ground that it is indefinite nor allows an endless time in which to perform. What constitutes a reasonable time is determined by the nature of the subject matter of the contract and the facts and circumstances surrounding the making of the contract.

When Time Is Essential

If performance of the contract on or within the exact time specified is vital, it is said that "time is of the essence." Time is of the essence when the contract relates to property that is perishable or that is fluctuating rapidly in value. When a contract fixes by unambiguous language a time for performance and where there is no evidence showing that the parties did not intend that time should be of the essence, failure to perform within the specified time is a breach of contract entitling the innocent party to damages. **For Example,** Dixon and Gandhi agreed that Gandhi would close on the purchase of a motel as follows: "Closing Date. The closing shall be held … on the date which is within twenty (20) days after the closing of Nomura Financing." Gandhi did not close within the time period specified, and Dixon was allowed to retain $100,000 in prepaid closing costs and fees as liquidated damages for Gandhi's breach of contract.[7]

When Time Is Not Essential

Unless a contract so provides, time is ordinarily not of the essence, and performance within a reasonable time is sufficient. In the case of the sale of property, time is not

[6] *First National Bank v. Clark,* 447 S.E.2d 558 (W. Va. 1994).
[7] *Woodhull Corp. v. Saibaba Corp.,* 507 S.E.2d 493 (Ga. App. 1998).

regarded as of the essence when there has not been any appreciable change in the market value or condition of the property and when the person who delayed does not appear to have done so for the purpose of speculating on a change in market price.

Waiver of Essence of Time Limitation

A provision that time is of the essence may be waived. It is waived when the specified time has expired but the party who could complain requests the delaying party to take steps necessary to perform the contract.

18-2d Adequacy of Performance

When a party renders exactly the performance called for by the contract, no question arises as to whether the contract has been performed. In other cases, there may not have been a perfect performance, or a question arises as to whether the performance satisfies the standard set by the contract.

CPA

Substantial Performance

substantial performance–equitable rule that if a good-faith attempt to perform does not precisely meet the terms of the agreement, the agreement will still be considered complete if the essential purpose of the contract is accomplished.

Perfect performance of a contract is not always possible when dealing with construction projects. A party who in good faith has provided **substantial performance** of the contract may sue to recover the payment specified in the contract.[8] However, because the performance was not perfect, the performing party is subject to a counterclaim for the damages caused the other party. When a building contractor has substantially performed the contract to construct a building, the contractor is responsible for the cost of repairing or correcting the defects as an offset from the contract price.[9]

The measure of damages under these circumstances is known as "cost of completion" damages.[10] If, however, the cost of completion would be unreasonably disproportionate to the importance of the defect, the measure of damages is the diminution in value of the building due to the defective performance.

Whether there is substantial performance is a question of degree to be determined by all of the facts, including the particular type of structure involved, its intended purpose, and the nature and relative expense of repairs.

For Example, a certain building contractor (BC) and a certain owner (O) made a contract to construct a home overlooking Vineyard Sound on Martha's Vineyard according to plans and specifications that clearly called for the use of General Plumbing Blue Star piping. The contract price was $1,100,000. Upon inspecting the work before making the final $400,000 payment and accepting the building, O discovered that BC had used Republic piping throughout the house. O explained to BC that his family had made its money by investing in General Plumbing, and he, therefore, would not make the final payment until the breach of contract was remedied. BC explained that Republic pipes were of the same industrial grade and quality as the Blue Star pipes. Moreover, BC estimated that it would cost nearly $300,000 to replace all of the pipes because of the destruction of walls and fixtures necessary to accomplish such a task. BC may sue O for $400,000 for breach of contract, claiming he had substantially performed the contract, and O may counterclaim for $300,000, seeking an offset for the cost of remedying the breach. The court will find in favor of the contractor and will not allow the $300,000 offset but will allow a "nominal" offset of perhaps $100 to $1,000 for the amount by

[8] *Gala v. Harris,* 77 So. 3d 1065 (La. App. 2012).

[9] Substantial performance is not a defense to a breach of contract claim, however. See *Bentley Systems Inc. v. Intergraph Corp.,* 922 So. 2d 61 (Ala. 2005).

[10] *Hammer Construction Corp. v. Phillips,* 994 So. 2d 1135 (Fla. App. 2008).

FIGURE 18-1 Causes of Contract Discharge

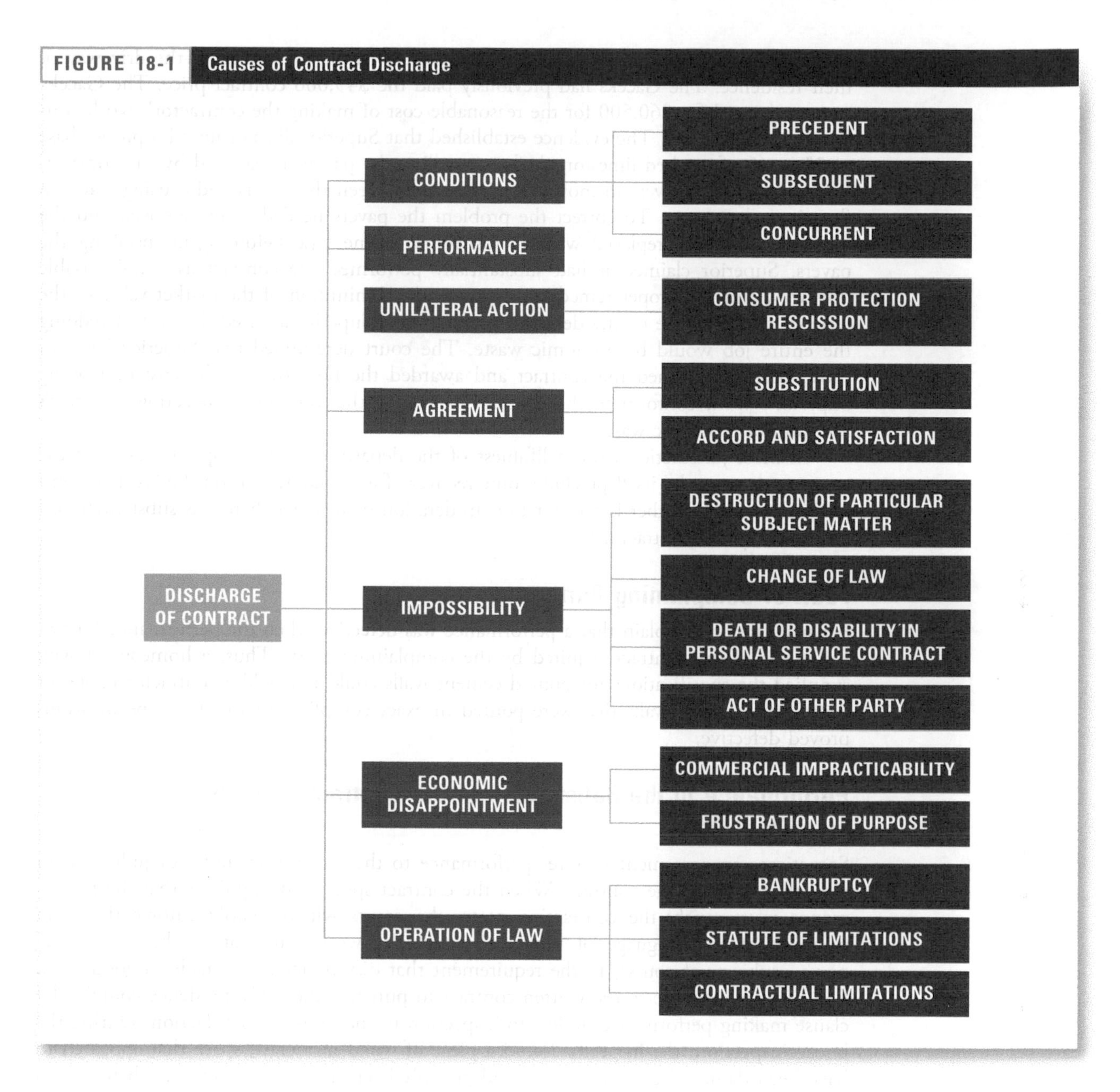

which the Republic pipes diminished the value of the building. To have required the pipes to be replaced would amount to economic waste.[11]

When a contractor does not substantially perform its obligations under a contract, not only will the contractor not prevail in a breach of contract claim against a homeowner for extra work beyond the contract price but the contractor is liable for the reasonable cost of making the contractor's work conform to the contract. **For Example,** Superior Wall and Paver, LLC, sued homeowners Pamela and Mark Gacek for $14,350 it claimed

[11] See *Jacob & Youngs, Inc. v. Kent,* 230 N.Y. 239 (1921).

was still owed Superior as extra work, for concrete pavers it installed in the driveway of their residence. The Gaceks had previously paid the $45,000 contract price. The Gaceks counterclaimed for $60,500 for the reasonable cost of making the contractor's work conform to the contract. The evidence established that Superior did not install a proper base of 3″ to 4″ of crushed limestone before installing the pavers as required by the contract, which caused the pavers to move, creating gaps between the pavers and causing water to flow into the garage. To correct the problem the pavers needed to be removed and the area excavated and replaced with a crushed limestone base before again installing the pavers. Superior claimed it had substantially performed the contract as a fully usable driveway, and the proper remedy, if any, was the diminution of the market value of the Gaceks' property due to any defective performance. Superior asserted the cost of redoing the entire job would be economic waste. The court determined that Superior had not substantially performed the contract and awarded the homeowners the cost of making Superior's work conform to the contract by having the job redone, rejecting Superior's assertion of economic waste.[12]

In most jurisdictions, the willfulness of the departure from the specifications of the contract does not by itself preclude some recovery for the contractor on the "cost of completion" basis but rather is a factor in consideration of whether there was substantial performance by the contractor.[13]

Fault of Complaining Party

A party cannot complain that a performance was defective when the performance follows the terms of the contract required by the complaining party. Thus, a homeowner who supplied the specifications for poured cement walls could not hold a contractor liable for damages when the walls that were poured in exact compliance with those specifications proved defective.

Performance to the Satisfaction of the Contracting Party or a Third Party

Sometimes an agreement requires performance to the satisfaction, taste, or judgment of the other party to the contract. When the contract specifically stipulates that the performance must satisfy the contracting party, the courts will ordinarily enforce the plain meaning of the language of the parties and the work must satisfy the contracting party—subject, of course, to the requirement that dissatisfaction be made in good faith. **For Example,** the Perrones' written contract to purchase the Hills' residence contained a clause making performance subject to inspection to the Perrones' satisfaction. During the house inspection, the inspector found a piece of wood in a crawl space that appeared to have been damaged by termites and had possibly been treated some 18 years before with chlordane. At the end of the inspection Mr. Perrone indicated that he would perform on the contract. Thereafter, he went on the Internet and found that chlordane is a highly toxic pesticide now banned from use as a termite treatment. As a result, the Perrones rescinded the contract under the buyer satisfaction clause. The Hills sued, believing that speculation about a pesticide treatment 18 years ago was absurd. They contended that the Perrones had breached the contract without a valid reason. The court decided for the

[12] *Superior Wall and Paver, LLC v. Gacek,* 73 So. 3d (Ala. App. 2011).

[13] But see *USX Corp. v. M. DeMatteo Construction Co.,* 315 F.3d 43 (1st Cir. 2002), for application of a common law rule that prohibits a construction contractor guilty of a willful breach of contract from maintaining any suit on the contract against the other party.

Perrones, since they exercised the "satisfaction clause" in good faith.[14] Good-faith personal satisfaction is generally required when the subject matter of the contract is personal, such as interior design work, tailoring, or the painting of a portrait.

With respect to things mechanical or routine performances, courts require that the performance be such as would satisfy a reasonable person under the circumstances.

When work is to be done subject to the approval of an architect, an engineer, or another expert, most courts apply the reasonable person test of satisfaction.

18-3 Discharge by Action of Parties

Contracts may be discharged by the joint action of both contracting parties or, in some cases, by the action of one party alone.

18-3a Discharge by Unilateral Action

rescission–action of one party to a contract to set the contract aside when the other party is guilty of a breach of the contract.

substitution–substitution of a new contract between the same parties.

accord and satisfaction–agreement to substitute for an existing debt some alternative form of discharging that debt, coupled with the actual discharge of the debt by the substituted performance.

release–an instrument by which the signing party (releasor) relinquishes claims or potential claims against one or more persons (releasees) who might otherwise be subject to liability to the releasor.

waiver–release or relinquishment of a known right or objection.

Ordinarily, a contract cannot be discharged by the action of either party alone. In some cases, however, the contract gives one of either party the right to cancel the contract by unilateral action, such as by notice to the other party. Insurance policies covering loss commonly provide that the insurer may cancel the policy upon giving a specified number of days' notice.

Consumer Protection Rescission

A basic principle of contract law is that once made, a contract between competent persons is a binding obligation. Consumer protection legislation introduces into the law a contrary concept—that of giving the consumer a chance to think things over and to rescind the contract. Thus, the federal Consumer Credit Protection Act (CCPA) gives the debtor the right to rescind a credit transaction within three business days when the transaction would impose a lien on the debtor's home. **For Example,** a homeowner who mortgages his or her home to obtain a loan may cancel the transaction for any reason by notifying the lender before midnight of the third full business day after the loan is made.[15]

A Federal Trade Commission regulation gives the buyer three business days in which to cancel a home-solicited sale of goods or services costing more than $25.[16]

18-3b Discharge by Agreement

A contract may be discharged by the operation of one of its provisions or by a subsequent agreement. Thus, there may be a discharge by (1) the terms of the original contract, such as a provision that the contract should end on a specified date; (2) a mutual cancellation, in which the parties agree to end their contract; (3) a mutual **rescission,** in which the parties agree to annul the contract and return both parties to their original positions before the contract had been made; (4) the **substitution** of a new contract between the same parties; (5) a novation or substitution of a new contract involving a new party;[17] (6) an **accord and satisfaction;** (7) a **release;** or (8) a **waiver.**

[14] *Hill v. Perrones,* 42 P.3d 210 (Kan. App. 2002).

[15] If the owner is not informed of this right to cancel, the three-day period does not begin until that information is given. Consumer Credit Protection Act §125, 15 U.S.C. §1635(a), (e), (f).

[16] C.F.R. §429.1.

[17] *Eagle Industries, Inc. v. Thompson,* 900 P.2d 475 (Or. 1995). In a few jurisdictions, the term *novation* is used to embrace the substitution of any new contract, whether between the original parties or not.

Substitution

The parties may decide that their contract is not the one they want. They may then replace it with another contract. If they do, the original contract is discharged by substitution.[18]

Accord and Satisfaction

When the parties have differing views as to the performance required by the terms of a contract, they may agree to a different performance. Such an agreement is called an *accord.* When the accord is performed or executed, there is an accord and satisfaction, which discharges the original obligation. To constitute an accord and satisfaction, there must be a bona fide dispute, a proposal to settle the dispute, and performance of the agreement.

CASE SUMMARY

A Full Court Press to No Avail

FACTS: In September 2002, La Crosse Litho Supply, LLC (La Crosse), entered into a distribution agreement with MKL Pre-Press Electronics (MKL) for the distribution of a printing system. La Crosse purchased a 7000 System unit from MKL for its end user Printing Plus. MKL technicians were to provide service and training for the unit. The 7000 System at Printing Plus failed on three occasions, and ultimately repairs were unsuccessful. On September 30, 2003, La Crosse canceled the distribution agreement. On October 2, 2003, La Crosse sent a letter to MKL's sales vice president Bill Landwer setting forth an itemized accounting of what it owed MKL Pre-Press with deductions for the purchase price of the failed 7000 System and other offsets. MKL sent a subsequent bill for repairs and services, to which La Crosse objected and stated that it would not pay. MKL's attorney sent a demand letter for $26,453.31. La Crosse's president, Randall Peters, responded by letter dated December 30, 2003, explaining that with an offset for training and warranty work it had performed, "we are sending you the final payment in the amount of $1,696.47." He added, "[w]ith this correspondence, we consider all open issues between La Crosse Litho Supply and MKL Pre-Press closed." Enclosed with the letter was a check for $1,696.47 payable to MKL Pre-Press. In the remittance portion of the check, under the heading "Ref," was typed "FINAL PAYM." The check was endorsed and deposited on either January 26 or 27, 2004. MKL sued La Crosse for $24,756.84. La Crosse defended that the tender and subsequent deposit of the check for $1,696.47 constituted an accord and satisfaction. Jill Fleming, MKL's office manager, stated that it was her duty to process checks and that she did not read Peters' letter. From a judgment for La Crosse, MKL appealed.

DECISION: Judgment for La Crosse. There was an honest dispute as to the amount owed, as evident from the exchange of letters. La Crosse tendered an amount with the explicit understanding that it was the "final payment" of all demands, and the creditor MKL's acceptance and negotiation of a check for that amount constitutes an accord and satisfaction. Ms. Fleming had the authority to endorse checks and deposit them, and her doing so can and should be imputed to her employer, thereby constituting an accord and satisfaction. [***MKL Pre-Press Electronics v. La Crosse Litho Supply, LLC*, 840 N.E.2d 687 (Ill. App. 2005)**]

Release

A release is an instrument by which the signing party (releasor) relinquishes claims or potential claims against one or more persons (releasees) who might otherwise be subject to liability to the releasor. The existence of a valid release is a complete defense to a tort action against the releasee. **For Example,** Heriberto Rodriguez, while driving a Hertz rental car, was injured in a collision with a vehicle operated by Takeshi Oto, who was

[18] See *Foti Fuels, Inc. v. Kurrle Corp.,* 90 A.3d 885 (Vt. 2013).

on company related business for his employer Toshiba of America. Heriberto settled with Hertz for $25,000.00, the limit of the Hertz coverage of the vehicle and signed a written release in favor of Hertz and Oto "and all other persons, firms, corporations, associations or partnerships." Later, Rodriquez filed a negligence action against Oto and Toshiba of America. The settlement releasing "all persons … and corporations" applied to Oto and Toshiba and was a complete defense in this case.[19]

18-4 Discharge by External Causes

Circumstances beyond the control of the contracting parties may discharge the contract.

18-4a Discharge by Impossibility

To establish impossibility a party must show (1) the unexpected occurrence of an intervening act; (2) that the risk of the unexpected occurrence was not allocated by agreement or custom; and (3) that the occurrence made performance impossible. The doctrine of impossibility relieves nonperformance only in extreme circumstances.[20] The party asserting the defense of impossibility bears the burden of proving "a real impossibility and not a mere inconvenience or unexpected difficulty."[21] Moreover, courts will generally only excuse nonperformance where performance is objectively impossible—that is, incapable performance by anyone. Financial inability to perform a contract that a party voluntarily entered into will rarely, if ever, excuse nonperformance. **For Example,** Ms. Robinson was employed by East Capital Community Development Group under a written employment contract for one year but was terminated early for lack of funding. The contract did not reference that her continued employment was contingent on continued grant funding. The contract was objectively capable of performance. The defense of impossibility was rejected by the court.[22]

Destruction of Particular Subject Matter

When parties contract expressly for, or with reference to, a particular subject matter, the contract is discharged if the subject matter is destroyed through no fault of either party. When a contract calls for the sale of a wheat crop growing on a specific parcel of land, the contract is discharged if that crop is destroyed by blight.

On the other hand, if there is merely a contract to sell a given quantity of a specified grade of wheat, the seller is not discharged when the seller's crop is destroyed by blight. The seller had made an unqualified undertaking to deliver wheat of a specified grade. No restrictions or qualifications were imposed as to the source. If the seller does not deliver the goods called for by the contract, the contract is broken, and the seller is liable for damages.

Change of Law

A contract is discharged when its performance is made impossible, impractical, or illegal by a subsequent change in the law. A contract to construct a nonfireproof building at a particular place is discharged by the adoption of a zoning law prohibiting such a building within that area. Mere inconvenience or temporary delay caused by the new law, however, does not excuse performance.

[19] *Rodriquez v. Oto,* 151 Cal. Rptr. 3d 667 (Cal. App. 2013).
[20] *Island Development Corp. v. District of Columbia,* 933 A.2d 340, 350 (D.C. 2007).
[21] *Bergmann v. Parker,* 216 A.2d 581 (D.C. 1966).
[22] *East Capital View Community Development Corp. v. Robinson,* 941 A.2d 1036 (D.C. 2008).

CASE SUMMARY

If you're fond of sand dunes, and salty air...
... served by a window with an ocean view
You're not at the Petrozzi's house in Ocean City

FACTS: To rectify seashore protection problems, the City of Ocean City in 1989 participated in a beach replenishment and sand dunes restoration program. The Army Corps of Engineers required Ocean City to have access rights where sand was to be placed. To ease property owners' concerns over their beach front views, Ocean City proposed easements under which it would construct and maintain the dune system with height limitations of no greater than three feet above the average elevation of block bulkheads. From May 1992 to December 1995 Ocean City acquired the necessary easements. Between 1992 and 2000 natural accretion caused the dunes to grow in height and width. After 1994 the Coastal Area Facilities Review Act (CAFRA) required municipalities to receive written authorization from the Department of Environmental Protection (DEP) for dunes maintenance. Ocean City's permit applications to reduce the height of existing sand dunes was denied by the DEP. Owners of the beach front properties sued for breach of its easement agreements. From the dismissal of their claims by the trial court, certain owners appealed.

DECISION: Decision for the property owners. The 1994 CAFRA amendments rendered impossible Ocean City's performance under the easement agreements in question. Impossibility or impracticability of performance are compete defenses where a fact essential to performance is assumed by the parties but does not exist at the time of performance. Yet the fact remains that the plaintiffs gave up their rights to compensation in reliance on Ocean City's promise to protect their ocean views. The owners are entitled to damages for the loss of their ocean views. [***Petrozzi v. City of Ocean City*, 433 N.J. Super. 290 (App. Div. 2013)**]

Death or Disability

When the contract obligates a party to render or receive personal services requiring peculiar skill, the death, incapacity, or illness of the party that was either to render or receive the personal services excuses both sides from a duty to perform. It is sometimes said that "the death of either party is the death of the contract."

The rule does not apply, however, when the acts called for by the contract are of such a character that (1) the acts may be as well performed by others, such as the promisor's personal representatives, or (2) the contract's terms contemplate continuance of the obligations after the death of one of the parties. **For Example,** Lynn Jones was under contract to investor Ed Jenkins to operate certain Subway sandwich shops and to acquire new franchises with funding provided by Jenkins. After Jenkins's death, Jones claimed that he was no longer bound under the contract and was free to pursue franchise opportunities on his own. The contract between Jones and Jenkins expressed that it was binding on the parties' "heirs and assigns" and that the contract embodied property rights that passed to Jenkins's widow. The agreement's provisions thus established that the agreement survived the death of Jenkins, and Jones was therefore obligated to remit profits from the franchise he acquired for himself after Jenkins's death.[23]

Act of Other Party

Every contract contains "an implied covenant of good faith and fair dealing." As a result of this covenant, a promisee is under an obligation to do nothing that would interfere with the promisor's performance. When the promisee prevents performance or otherwise makes performance impossible, the promisor is discharged from the contract. Thus, a

[23] *Jenkins Subway, Inc. v. Jones,* 990 S.W.2d 713 (Tenn. App. 1998).

subcontractor is discharged from any obligation when it is unable to do the work because the principal contractor refuses to deliver the material, equipment, or money required by the subcontract. When the default of the other party consists of failing to supply goods or services, the duty may rest on the party claiming a discharge of the contract to show that substitute goods or services could not be obtained elsewhere.

18-4b Developing Doctrines

Commercial impracticability and frustration of purpose may excuse performance.

Commercial Impracticability

The doctrine of *commercial impracticability* was developed to deal with the harsh rule that a party must perform its contracts unless it is absolutely impossible. However, not every type of impracticability is an excuse for nonperformance. **For Example,** I. Patel was bound by his franchise agreement with Days Inn, Inc., to maintain his 60-room inn on old Route 66 in Lincoln, Illinois, to at least minimum quality assurance standards. His inn failed five consecutive quality inspections over two years, with the inspector noting damaged guest rooms, burns in the bedding, and severely stained carpets. Patel's defense when his franchise was canceled after the fifth failed inspection was that bridge repairs on the road leading from I-55 to his inn had adversely affected his business and made it commercially impractical to live up to the franchise agreement. The court rejected his defense, determining that while the bridge work might have affected patronage, it had no effect on his duty to comply with the quality assurance standards of his franchise agreement.[24] Commercial impracticability is available only when the performance is made impractical by the subsequent occurrence of an event whose nonoccurrence was a basic assumption on which the contract was made.[25]

The defense of commercial impracticability will not relieve sophisticated business entities from their contractual obligations due to an economic downturn, even one as drastic and severe as the recent recession. **For Example,** real estate developer Beemer Associates was not excused under this doctrine of commercial impracticability from performance of its construction loan payment obligation of $5,250,000 plus interest and fees where unanticipated changes in the financial and real estate markets made it unable to secure tenants at the expected rate.[26] Economic downturns and other market shifts do not constitute unanticipated circumstances in a market economy.[27]

Frustration of Purpose Doctrine

Because of a change in circumstances, the purpose of the contract may have no value to the party entitled to receive performance. In such a case, performance may be excused if both parties were aware of the purpose and the event that frustrated the purpose was unforeseeable.[28]

For Example, National Southern Bank rents a home near Willowbend Country Club on the southeastern shore of North Carolina for $75,000 a week to entertain business guests at the Ryder Cup matches scheduled for the week in question. Storm damage

[24] *Days Inn of America, Inc. v. Patel,* 88 F. Supp. 2d 928 (C.D. Ill. 2000).
[25] See Restatement (Second) of Contracts §261; U.C.C. §2-615.
[26] *LSREF2 Baron, LLC v. Beemer,* 2011 WL 6838163 (M.D. Fla. Dec. 29, 2011).
[27] *Flathead-Michigan I, LLC v. Peninsula Dev., LLC,* 2011 WL 940048 (E.D. Mich. March 16, 2011).
[28] The defense of frustration of purpose, or commercial frustration, is very difficult to invoke because the courts are extremely reluctant to allow parties to avoid obligations to which they have agreed. See *Wal-Mart Stores, Inc. v. AIG Life Insurance Co.,* 872 A.2d 611 (Del. Ch. 2005), denying application of the commercial frustration doctrine when the supervening event, the invalidation of hundreds of millions in tax deductions by the IRS, was reasonably foreseeable and could have been provided for in the contract.

from Hurricane David the week before the event caused the closing of the course and the transfer of the tournament to another venue in a different state. The bank's duty to pay for the house may be excused by the doctrine of *frustration of purpose*, because the transfer of the tournament fully destroyed the value of the home rental, both parties were aware of the purpose of the rental, and the cancellation of the golf tournament was unforeseeable.

Comparison to Common Law Rule

The traditional common law rule refuses to recognize commercial impracticability or frustration of purpose. By the common law rule, the losses and disappointments against which commercial impracticability and frustration of purpose give protection are merely the risks that one takes in entering into a contract. Moreover, the situations could have been guarded against by including an appropriate condition subsequent in the contract. A condition subsequent declares that the contract will be void if a specified event occurs.[29] The contract also could have provided for a readjustment of compensation if there was a basic change of circumstances. The common law approach also rejects these developing concepts because they weaken the stability of a contract.

An indication of a wider recognition of the concept that "extreme" changes of circumstances can discharge a contract is found in the Uniform Commercial Code (UCC). The UCC provides for the discharge of a contract for the sale of goods when a condition that the parties assumed existed, or would continue, ceases to exist.[30]

Force Majeure

To avoid litigation over impossibility and impracticability issues, modern contracting parties often contract around the doctrine of impossibility, specifying the failures that will excuse performance in their contracts. The clauses in which they do this are called *force majeure*—uncontrollable event—clauses. And they are enforced by courts as written.

18-4c Temporary Impossibility

Ordinarily, a temporary impossibility suspends the duty to perform. If the obligation to perform is suspended, it is revived on the termination of the impossibility. If, however, performance at that later date would impose a substantially greater burden on the party obligated to perform, some courts discharge the obligor from the contract.

After the September 11, 2001, terrorist attack on the World Trade Center, New York City courts followed wartime precedents that had developed the law of temporary impossibility. Such impossibility, when of brief duration, excuses performance until it subsequently becomes possible to perform rather than excusing performance altogether. Thus, an individual who was unable to communicate her cancellation of travel 60 days prior to her scheduled travel as required by her contract, which needed to occur on or before September 14, 2001, could expect relief from a cancellation penalty provision in the contract based on credible testimony of attempted phone calls to the travel agent on and after September 12, 2001, even though the calls did not get through due to communication problems in New York City.[31]

Weather

Acts of God, such as tornadoes, lightning, and floods, usually do not terminate a contract even though they make performance difficult. Thus, weather conditions constitute a risk

[29] *Wermer v. ABI*, 10 S.W.3d 575 (Mo. App. 2000).
[30] U.C.C. §2-615.
[31] See *Bugh v. Protravel International, Inc.*, 746 N.Y.S.2d 290 (Civ. Ct. N.Y.C. 2002).

that is assumed by a contracting party in the absence of a contrary agreement. Consequently, extra expense sustained by a contractor because of weather conditions is a risk that the contractor assumes in the absence of an express provision for additional compensation in such a case. **For Example,** Danielo Contractors made a contract to construct a shopping mall for the Rubicon Center, with construction to begin November 1. Because of abnormal cold and blizzard conditions, Danielo was not able to begin work until April 1 and was five months late in completing the construction of the project. Rubicon sued Danielo for breach of contract by failing to perform on schedule. Danielo is liable. Because the contract included no provision covering delay caused by weather, Danielo bore the risk of the delay and resulting loss.

Modern contracts commonly contain a "weather clause" and reflect the parties' agreement on this matter. When the parties take the time to discuss weather issues, purchasing insurance coverage is a common resolution.

operation of law–attaching of certain consequences to certain facts because of legal principles that operate automatically as contrasted with consequences that arise because of the voluntary action of a party designed to create those consequences.

bankruptcy–procedure by which one unable to pay debts may surrender all assets in excess of any exemption claim to the court for administration and distribution to creditors, and the debtor is given a discharge that releases him from the unpaid balance due on most debts.

18-4d Discharge by Operation of Law

A contract is discharged by **operation of law** by (1) an alteration or a material change made by a party, (2) the destruction of the written contract with intent to discharge it, (3) bankruptcy, (4) the operation of a statute of limitations, or (5) a contractual limitation.

Bankruptcy

As set forth in the chapter on bankruptcy, even though all creditors have not been paid in full, a discharge in **bankruptcy** eliminates ordinary contract claims against the debtor.

CPA

statute of limitations–statute that restricts the period of time within which an action may be brought.

Statute of Limitations

A **statute of limitations** provides that after a certain number of years have passed, a contract claim is barred. The time limitation provided by state statutes of limitations varies widely. The time period for bringing actions for breach of an oral contract is two to three years. The period may differ with the type of contract—ranging from a relatively short time for open accounts (ordinary customers' charge accounts) to four years for sales of goods.[32] A somewhat longer period exists for bringing actions for breach of written contracts (usually 4 to 10 years). **For Example,** Prate Installations, Inc., sued homeowners Richard and Rebecca Thomas for failure to pay for a new roof installed by Prate. Prate had sent numerous invoices to the Thomases over a four-year period seeking payment to no avail. The Thomases moved to dismiss the case under a four-year limitation period. However, the court concluded that the state's 10-year limitations period on written contracts applied.[33] The maximum period for judgments of record is usually 10 to 20 years.

A breach of contract claim against a builder begins to run when a home's construction is substantially complete. **For Example,** a breach of contract claim against home builder Stewart Brockett was time barred under a state's six-year statute of limitations for breach of contract actions inasmuch as the home in question was substantially completed in September 2001 and the breach of contract action commenced on June 17, 2008.[34] A breach of contract claim not founded upon an instrument of writing may be governed by a two-year statute of limitations.

[32] U.C.C. §2-725(1).

[33] *Prate Installations, Inc. v. Thomas,* 842 N.E.2d 1205 (Ill. App. 2006).

[34] *New York Central Mutual Fire Insurance Co. v. Gilder Oil Co.,* 936 N.Y.S.2d 815 (Sup. Ct. A.D. 2011).

CASE SUMMARY

Tempus Fugit: File It on Time or Loose It!

FACTS: Larry Montz and Daena Smoller, the real parties in interest (RPIs) in this case pitched a concept for a television program entitled *Ghost Expeditions Haunted* (Concepts) to NBCUniversal Media, LLC (NBC) from 1996 to 2001. The RPIs claim that, after NBC informed them they were not interested in Concepts, NBC teamed up with another company to misappropriate and exploit their concepts by producing the hit series *Ghost Hunters* without permission or compensation. The *Ghost Hunters* show premiered on the Syfy cable channel on October 6, 2004. The RPIs filed their first lawsuit on November 8, 2006. The Superior Court denied NBC's motion for summary judgment, which asserted the claims were time-barred by the applicable two-year statute of limitations, and NBC appealed this decision.

DECISION: Judgment for NBC. The statute of limitations for implied contracts in California is two years from the time the last element of a cause of action is complete. In this case a suit for breach of an implied contract not to exploit an idea without paying for it arises with the sale or exploitation of the idea. Here, the accrual date is the date on which the work is released to the general public on television on October 6, 2004. Thus RPIs had until October 5, 2006, to file their lawsuit. They did not do so until November 8, 2006, resulting in the action being time-barred. While the "discovery rule" may operate to delay accrual of a cause of action where professionals such as a doctor or lawyer breaches a duty of care, for a layperson would lack ability to observe, evaluate or detect the wrongdoing; but such a rule is inapplicable here because the offending work was publicly televised. **[*NBCUniversal Media, LLC v. Superior Court*, 171 Cal. Rptr. 3d 1 (Cal. App. 2014)]**

Contractual Limitations

Some contracts, particularly insurance contracts, contain a time limitation within which suit must be brought. This is in effect a private statute of limitations created by the agreement of the parties.

A contract may also require that notice of any claim be given within a specified time. A party who fails to give notice within the time specified by the contract is barred from suing on the contract.

A contract provision requiring that suit be brought within one year does not violate public policy, although the statute of limitations would allow two years in the absence of such a contract limitation.[35]

Make the Connection

Summary

A party's duty to perform under a contract can be affected by a condition precedent, which must occur before a party has an obligation to perform; a condition subsequent, that is, a condition or event that relieves the duty to thereafter perform; and concurrent conditions, which require mutual and often simultaneous performance.

Most contracts are discharged by performance. An offer to perform is called a *tender of performance*. If a tender of performance is wrongfully refused, the duty of the tenderer to perform is terminated. When the performance called for by the contract is the payment of money, it must be legal tender that is offered. In actual practice, it is

[35] *Keiting v. Skauge,* 543 N.W.2d 565 (Wis. App. 1995).

common to pay and to accept payment by checks or other commercial paper.

When the debtor owes the creditor on several accounts and makes a payment, the debtor may specify which account is to be credited with the payment. If the debtor fails to specify, the creditor may choose which account to credit.

When a contract does not state when it is to be performed, it must be performed within a reasonable time. If time for performance is stated in the contract, the contract must be performed at the time specified if such time is essential (is of the essence). Ordinarily, a contract must be performed exactly in the manner specified by the contract. A less-than-perfect performance is allowed if it is a substantial performance and if damages are allowed the other party.

A contract cannot be discharged by unilateral action unless authorized by the contract itself or by statute, as in the case of consumer protection rescission.

Because a contract arises from an agreement, it may also be terminated by an agreement. A contract may also be discharged by the substitution of a new contract for the original contract; by a novation, or making a new contract with a new party; by accord and satisfaction; by release; or by waiver.

A contract is discharged when it is impossible to perform. Impossibility may result from the destruction of the subject matter of the contract, the adoption of a new law that prohibits performance, the death or disability of a party whose personal action was required for performance of the contract, or the act of the other party to the contract. Some courts will also hold that a contract is discharged when its performance is commercially impracticable or there is frustration of purpose. Temporary impossibility, such as a labor strike or bad weather, has no effect on a contract. It is common, though, to include protective clauses that excuse delay caused by temporary impossibility.

A contract may be discharged by operation of law. This occurs when (1) the liability arising from the contract is discharged by bankruptcy, (2) suit on the contract is barred by the applicable statute of limitations, or (3) a time limitation stated in the contract is exceeded.

Learning Outcomes

After studying this chapter, you should be able to clearly explain:

18-1 Conditions Relating to Performance

LO.1 List the three types of conditions that affect a party's duty to perform

See the "pay-if-paid" condition-precedent example in the section titled "Condition Precedent," page 328.

See the TV anchor's "failed urinalysis test" condition subsequent example, page 329.

18-2 Discharge by Performance

LO.2 Explain the on-time performance rule

See the "mailed-check payment" example, page 331.

See the "time is of the essence" example, page 331.

LO.3 Explain the adequacy of performance rules

See the application of the substantial performance rule to the nonconforming new home piping example, page 332.

See the effect of failure to substantially perform a contract in the *Superior Wall and Paver* case, pages 333–334.

18-3 Discharge by Action of Parties

LO.4 Explain four ways a contract can be discharged by agreement of the parties

See the text discussion on rescission, cancellation, substitution, and novation in the section titled "Discharge by Agreement," page 335.

18-4 Discharge by External Causes

LO.5 State the effect on a contract of the death or disability of one of the contracting parties

See the Subway sandwich shops example, page 338.

LO.6 Explain when impossibility or impracticability may discharge a contract

See the Ryder Cup frustration-of-purpose example, pages 339–340.

See the *Ocean City* impossibility case, which provided a remedy, page 338.

Key Terms

accord and satisfaction
bankruptcy
condition
condition precedent
condition subsequent
operation of law
release
rescission
statute of limitations
substantial performance
substitution
tender
waiver

Questions and Case Problems

1. CIT entered into a sale/leaseback contract with Condere Tire Corporation for 11 tire presses at Condere's tire plant in Natchez, Mississippi. Condere ceased making payments on these presses owned by CIT, and Condere filed for Chapter 11 bankruptcy. CIT thereafter contracted to sell the presses to Specialty Tires Inc. for $250,000. When the contract was made, CIT, Condere, and Specialty Tire believed that CIT was the owner of the presses and was entitled to immediate possession. When CIT attempted to gain access to the presses to have them shipped, Condere changed its position and refused to allow the equipment to be removed from the plant. When the presses were not delivered, Specialty sued CIT for damages for nondelivery of the presses, and CIT asserted the defense of impracticability. Decide. [*Specialty Tires, Inc. v. CIT*, 82 F. Supp. 2d 434 (W.D. Pa.)]
2. Lymon Mitchell operated a Badcock Home Furnishings dealership, under which as dealer he was paid a commission on sales and Badcock retained title to merchandise on display. Mitchell sold his dealership to another and to facilitate the sale, Badcock prepared a summary of commissions owed with certain itemized offsets it claimed that Mitchell owed Badcock. Mitchell disagreed with the calculations, but he accepted them and signed the transfer documents, closing the sale on the basis of the terms set forth in the summary, and was paid accordingly. After pondering the offsets taken by Badcock and verifying the correctness of his position, he brought suit for the additional funds owed. What defense would you expect Badcock to raise? How would you decide the case? Explain fully. [*Mitchell v. Badcock Corp.*, 496 S.E.2d 502 (Ga. App.)]
3. American Bank loaned Koplik $50,000 to buy equipment for a restaurant about to be opened by Casual Citchen Corp. The loan was not repaid, and Fast Foods, Inc., bought out the interest of Casual Citchen. As part of the transaction, Fast Foods agreed to pay the debt owed to American Bank, and the parties agreed to a new schedule of payments to be made by Fast Foods. Fast Foods did not make the payments, and American Bank sued Koplik. He contended that his obligation to repay $50,000 had been discharged by the execution of the agreement providing for the payment of the debt by Fast Foods. Was this defense valid? [*American Bank & Trust Co. v. Koplik*, 451 N.Y.S.2d 426 (A. D.)]
4. Metalcrafters made a contract to design a new earth-moving vehicle for Lamar Highway Construction Co. Metalcrafters was depending on the genius of Samet, the head of its research department, to design a new product. Shortly after the contract was made between Metalcrafters and Lamar, Samet was killed in an automobile accident. Metalcrafters was not able to design the product without Samet. Lamar sued Metalcrafters for damages for breach of the contract. Metalcrafters claimed that the contract was discharged by Samet's death. Is it correct?
5. The Tinchers signed a contract to sell land to Creasy. The contract specified that the sales transaction was to be completed in 90 days. At the end of the 90 days, Creasy requested an extension of time. The Tinchers refused to grant an extension and stated that the contract was terminated. Creasy claimed that the 90-day clause was not binding because the contract did not state that time was of the essence. Was the contract terminated? [*Creasy v. Tincher*, 173 S.E.2d 332 (W. Va.)]
6. Christopher Bloom received a medical school scholarship created by the U.S. Department of Health and Human Services to increase the number of doctors serving rural areas. In return for this assistance, Bloom agreed to practice four years in a region identified as being underserved by medical professionals. After some problem with his postgraduation assignment, Bloom requested a repayment schedule from the agency. Although no terms were offered, Bloom tendered to the agency two checks totaling $15,500 and marked "Final Payment." Neither check was cashed, and the government sued Bloom for $480,000, the value of the assistance provided. Bloom claimed that by tendering the checks to the agency, his liability had been discharged by an accord and satisfaction. Decide. [*United States v. Bloom*, 112 F.3d 200 (7th Cir.)]
7. Dickson contracted to build a house for Moran. When it was approximately 25 percent to 40 percent completed, Moran would not let Dickson work anymore because he was not following the building plans and specifications and there were many defects. Moran hired another contractor to correct the defects and finish the building. Dickson sued Moran for

breach of contract, claiming that he had substantially performed the contract up to the point where he had been discharged. Was Dickson correct? [*Dickson v. Moran*, 344 So. 2d 102 (La. App.)]

8. A lessor leased a trailer park to a tenant. At the time, sewage was disposed of by a septic tank system that was not connected with the public sewage system. The tenant knew this, and the lease declared that the tenant had examined the premises and that the landlord made no representation or guarantee as to the condition of the premises. Sometime thereafter, the septic tank system stopped working properly, and the county health department notified the tenant that he was required to connect the septic tank system with the public sewage system or else the department would close the trailer park. The tenant did not want to pay the additional cost involved in connecting with the public system. The tenant claimed that he was released from the lease and was entitled to a refund of the deposit that he had made. Was he correct? [*Glen R. Sewell Street Metal v. Loverde*, 451 P.2d 721 (Cal. App.)]

9. Oneal was a teacher employed by the Colton Consolidated School District. Because of a diabetic condition, his eyesight deteriorated so much that he offered to resign if he would be given pay for a specified number of "sick leave" days. The school district refused to do this and discharged Oneal for nonperformance of his contract. He appealed to remove the discharge from his record. Decide. What ethical values are involved? [*Oneal v. Colton Consolidated School District*, 557 P.2d 11 (Wash. App.)]

10. Northwest Construction, Inc., made a contract with the state of Washington for highway construction. Part of the work was turned over under a subcontract to Yakima Asphalt Paving Co. The contract required that any claim be asserted within 180 days. Yakima brought an action for damages after the expiration of 180 days. The defense was that the claim was too late. Yakima replied that the action was brought within the time allowed by the statute of limitations and that the contractual limitation of 180 days was therefore not binding. Was Yakima correct?

11. Farmer William Weber sued the North Loup Irrigation District for breach of contract because North Loup failed to deliver water to his farm during the 2010 season as a result of the destruction of a diversion dam caused by catastrophic flooding in June 2010. The contract between the parties stated that irrigation charges must be paid by December of the year preceding the irrigation season. At the time of the flood Weber had not yet paid his 2010 irrigation charges; and he paid the 2010 charge under protest on April 13, 2011. Weber explained, "I've never wrote a check for $10,000 in my life that I didn't get something for." Did North Loup breach its contractual duties to Weber? Was payment by December 2009 a condition precedent to North Loup's duty to deliver water? Decide. [*Weber v. North Loup River Power and Irrigation District*, 854 N.W.2d 263 (Neb.)]

12. Suburban Power Piping Corp., under contract to construct a building for LTV Steel Corp., made a subcontract with Power & Pollution Services, Inc., to do some of the work. The subcontract provided that the subcontractor would be paid when the owner (LTV) paid the contractor. LTV went into bankruptcy before making the full payment to the contractor, who then refused to pay the subcontractor on the ground that the "pay-when-paid" provision of the subcontract made payment by the owner a condition precedent to the obligation of the contractor to pay the subcontractor. Was the contractor correct? [*Power & Pollution Services, Inc. v. Suburban Power Piping Corp.*, 598 N.E.2d 69 (Ohio App.)]

13. Union Pacific Railroad's long-term coal-hauling contract with electric utility WEPCO provided that if the railroad is prevented by "an event of Force Majeure" from reloading empty coal cars (after it has delivered coal to WEPCO) with iron ore destined for Geneva, Utah, it can charge the higher rate that the contract makes applicable to shipments that do not involve backhauling. The iron ore that the railroad's freight trains would have picked up in Minnesota was intended for a steel mill in Utah. The steel company was bankrupt in 1999 when the parties signed the contract. In November 2001 the steel mill shut down and closed for good in February 2004. Thereafter, the railroad wrote WEPCO to declare "an event of Force Majeure," and that henceforth it would be charging WEPCO the higher rate applicable to shipments without a backhaul. WEPCO sued the railroad for breach of the force majeure provision in the contract, contending that the railroad waited over two plus years to increase rates. The railroad contends that the clause should be interpreted as written. Decide. [*Wisconsin Electric Power Co. v. Union Pacific Railroad Co.*, 557 F.3d 504 (7th Cir.)]

14. Beeson Company made a contract to construct a shopping center for Sartori. Before the work was

fully completed, Sartori stopped making the payments to Beeson that the contract required. The contract provided for liquidated damages of $1,000 per day if Beeson failed to substantially complete the project within 300 days of the beginning of construction. The contract also provided for a bonus of $1,000 for each day Beeson completed the project ahead of schedule. Beeson stopped working and sued Sartori for the balance due under the contract, just as though it had been fully performed. Sartori defended on the ground that Beeson had not substantially completed the work. Beeson proved that Sartori had been able to rent most of the stores in the center. Was there substantial performance of the contract? If so, what would be the measure of damages? [*J.M. Beeson Co. v. Sartori*, 553 So. 2d 180 (Fla. App.)]

15. New Beginnings provides rehabilitation services for alcohol and drug abuse to both adults and adolescents. New Beginnings entered into negotiation with Adbar for the lease of a building in the city of St. Louis and subsequently entered into a three-year lease. The total rent due for the three-year term was $273,000. After the lease was executed, the city denied an occupancy permit because Alderman Bosley and residents testified at a hearing in vigorous opposition to the presence of New Beginnings in the neighborhood. A court ordered the permit issued. Alderman Bosley thereafter contacted the chair of the state's appointment committee and asked her to pull the agency's funding. He received no commitment from her on this matter. After a meeting with the state director of Alcohol and Drug Abuse where it was asserted that the director said the funding would be pulled if New Beginnings moved into the Adbar location, New Beginnings' board decided not to occupy the building. Adbar brought suit for breach of the lease, and New Beginnings asserted that it was excused from performance because of commercial impracticability and frustration of purpose. Do you believe the doctrine of commercial impracticability should be limited in its application so as to preserve the certainty of contracts? What rule of law applies to this case? Decide. [*Adbar v. New Beginnings*, 103 S.W.2d 799 (Mo. App.)]

CPA Questions

1. Parc hired Glaze to remodel and furnish an office suite. Glaze submitted plans that Parc approved. After completing all the necessary construction and painting, Glaze purchased minor accessories that Parc rejected because they did not conform to the plans. Parc refused to allow Glaze to complete the project and refused to pay Glaze any part of the contract price. Glaze sued for the value of the work performed. Which of the following statements is correct?
   a. Glaze will lose because Glaze breached the contract by not completing performance.
   b. Glaze will win because Glaze substantially performed and Parc prevented complete performance.
   c. Glaze will lose because Glaze materially breached the contract by buying the accessories.
   d. Glaze will win because Parc committed anticipatory breach.

2. Ordinarily, in an action for breach of a construction contract, the statute of limitations time period would be computed from the date the contract is:
   a. Negotiated.
   b. Breached.
   c. Begun.
   d. Signed.

3. Which of the following will release all original parties to a contract but will maintain a contractual relationship?

	Novation	*Substituted contract*
a.	Yes	Yes
b.	Yes	No
c.	No	Yes
d.	No	No

CHAPTER 19

Breach of Contract and Remedies

Learning Outcomes <<<

After studying this chapter, you should be able to

LO.1 Explain what constitutes a breach of contract and an anticipatory breach of contract

LO.2 Describe the effect of a waiver of a breach

LO.3 Explain the range of remedies available for breach of contract

LO.4 Explain when liquidated damages clauses are valid and invalid

LO.5 State when liability-limiting clauses and releases are valid

What can be done when a contract is broken?

19-1 What Constitutes a Breach of Contract?

The question of remedies does not become important until it is first determined that a contract has been violated or breached.

19-1a Definition of Breach

breach–failure to act or perform in the manner called for in a contract.

A **breach** is the failure to act or perform in the manner called for by the contract. When the contract calls for performance, such as painting an owner's home, the failure to paint or to paint properly is a *breach of contract.* If the contract calls for a creditor's forbearance, the creditor's action in bringing a lawsuit is a breach of the contract.

19-1b Anticipatory Breach

When the contract calls for performance, a party may make it clear before the time for performance arrives that the contract will not be performed. This is referred to as an **anticipatory breach.**

anticipatory breach–promisor's repudiation of the contract prior to the time that performance is required when such repudiation is accepted by the promisee as a breach of the contract.

anticipatory repudiation–repudiation made in advance of the time for performance of the contract obligations.

Anticipatory Repudiation

When a party expressly declares that performance will not be made when required, this declaration is called an **anticipatory repudiation** of the contract. To constitute such a repudiation, there must be a clear, absolute, unequivocal refusal to perform the contract according to its terms. **For Example,** Procter & Gamble (P&G) sought payment on four letters of credit issued by a Serbian bank, Investbanka. P&G presented two letters by June 8, prior to their expiration dates, with the necessary documentation for payment to Beogradska Bank New York, Investbanka's New York agent. A June 11 letter from Beogradska Bank broadly and unequivocally stated that the bank would not pay the letters of credit. Two additional letters of credit totaling $20,000 issued by Investbanka that expired by June 30 were not thereafter submitted to the New York agent bank by P&G. However, a court found that the bank had anticipatorily breached its obligations under those letters of credit by its broad renouncements in the June 11 letter, and judgments were rendered in favor of P&G.[1]

CASE SUMMARY

Splitting Tips—Contract Price Less Cost of Completion

FACTS: Hartland Developers, Inc., agreed to build an airplane hangar for Robert Tips of San Antonio for $300,000, payable in three installments of $100,000, with the final payment due upon the completion of the building and the issuance of a certificate of completion by the engineer representing Tips. The evidence shows that Tips's representative, Mr. Lavelle, instructed Hartland to cease work on the building because Tips could no longer afford to make payments. Hartland ceased work as instructed before the final completion of the building, having been paid $200,000 at the time. He sued Tips for breach of contract. On May 6, 1996, the trial court allowed Hartland the amount owing on the contract, $100,000, less the cost of completing the building according to the contract, $65,000, plus attorney fees and prejudgment interest. Tips appealed, pointing out, among other assertions, that he was required to

[1] *Procter & Gamble v. Investbanka,* 2000 WL 520630 (S.D.N.Y. 2000).

Splitting Tips—Contract Price Less Cost of Completion continued

spend $23,000 to provide electrical outlets for the hangar, which were contemplated in the contract.

DECISION: Judgment for Tips, subject to offsets. The trial judge based his damages assessment on anticipatory repudiation of contract. The evidence that Tips's representative, Lavelle, instructed Hartland to cease work on the project because Tips no longer could afford to make payments was sufficient to support this finding. However, Tips is entitled to an offset for electrical connections of $23,000 under a breach of contract theory. [***Tips v. Hartland Developers, Inc.*****, 961 S.W.2d 618 (Tex. App. 1998)]**

A refusal to perform a contract that is made before performance is required, unless the other party to the contract does an act or makes a concession that is not required by the contract, is an anticipatory repudiation of the contract.[2] However, a firmly stated request for additional payment under an existing contract without refusal to perform until the additional payment is made is not a repudiation of a contract. **For Example,** Sunesis Trucking Company's August 14, 2009, letter to Thistledown Racetrack seeking additional payment for hauling straw and manure from the raceway's horse stalls stating "accept this as notice that we will haul your manure at the following fees" was held not to be a notice of termination and did not establish an anticipatory breach excusing Thistledown from its obligations under the contract.[3]

Anticipatory Repudiation by Conduct

The anticipatory repudiation may be expressed by conduct that makes it impossible for the repudiating party to perform subsequently. **For Example,** while the Town of Mammoth Lakes, California, was claiming a willingness to move forward with a hotel/condominium project under its contract with the developer, in actuality, the evidence established that town officials refused to move forward and actively sought to undermine the developer's rights under the development contract. The court affirmed a judgment of $30 million in damages and attorneys' fees.[4]

19-2 Waiver of Breach

The breach of a contract may have no importance because the other party to the contract waives the breach.

19-2a Cure of Breach by Waiver

waiver–release or relinquishment of a known right or objection.

The fact that one party has broken a contract does not necessarily mean that there will be a lawsuit or a forfeiture of the contract. For practical business reasons, one party may be willing to ignore or waive the breach. When it is established that there has been a **waiver** of a breach, the party waiving the breach cannot take any action on the theory that the contract was broken. The waiver, in effect, erases the past breach. The contract continues as though the breach had not existed.

The waiver may be express or it may be implied from the continued recognition of the existence of the contract by the aggrieved party.[5] When the conduct of a party shows an intent to give up a right, it waives that right.[6]

[2] See *Black Diamond Energy, Inc. v. Encana Oil and Gas (USA) Inc.*, 326 P.3d 904 (Wyo. 2014).
[3] *Sunesis Trucking Co. v. Thistledown Racetrack, LLC,* 13 N.E.3d 727 (Ohio App. 2014).
[4] *Mammoth Lakes Land Acquisition, LLC v. Town of Mammoth Lakes,* 120 Cal. Rptr. 3d 797 (Cal. Ct. of App. 3d Dist. 2010).
[5] *Huger v. Morrison,* 809 So. 2d 1140 (La. App. 2002).
[6] *Stronghaven Inc. v. Ingram,* 555 S.E.2d 49 (Ga. App. 2001).

19-2b Existence and Scope of Waiver

It is a question of fact whether there has been a waiver.

CASE SUMMARY

Have You Driven a Ford Lately, Jennifer?

FACTS: In 1995, Northland Ford Dealers, an association of dealerships, offered to sponsor a "hole in one" contest at Moccasin Creek Country Club. A banner announced that a hole in one would win a car but gave no other details, and the local dealer parked a Ford Explorer near the banner. Northland paid a $4,602 premium to Continental Hole-In-One, Inc., to ensure the award of the contest prize. The insurance application stated in capital letters that "ALL AMATEUR MEN AND WOMEN WILL UTILIZE THE SAME TEE." And Continental established the men/women yardage for the hole to be 170 yards but did not make this known to the participants. Jennifer Harms registered for the tournament and paid her entrance fee. At the contest hole, she teed off from the amateur women's red marker, which was a much shorter distance to the pin than the 170 yards from the men's marker—and she made a hole in one. When she inquired about the prize, she was told that because of insurance requirements, all amateurs had to tee off from the amateur men's tee box, and because she had not done so, she was disqualified. Harms, a collegiate golfer at Concordia College, returned there to complete her last year of athletic eligibility and on graduation sued Northland for breach of contract. Northland contends that under NCAA rules, accepting a prize or agreeing to accept a prize would have disqualified Harms from NCAA competition. It also asserts that her continuation of her NCAA competition evinced intent to waive acceptance of the car.

DECISION: Judgment for Harms. Northland must abide by the rules it announced, not by the ones it left unannounced that disqualified all amateur women from the contest. This was a vintage unilateral contract with performance by the offeree as acceptance. Harms earned the prize when she sank her winning shot. Waiver is a volitional relinquishment, by act or word, of a known existing right conferred in law or contract. Harms could not disclaim the prize; it was not hers to refuse. She was told her shot from the wrong tee disqualified her. One can hardly relinquish what was never conferred. Northland's waiver defense is devoid of merit. [***Harms v. Northland Ford Dealers*, 602 N.W.2d 58 (S.D. 1999)**]

Existence of Waiver

A party may express or declare that the breach of a contract is waived. A waiver of a breach is more often the result of an express forgiving of a breach. Thus, a party allowing the other party to continue performance without objecting that the performance is not satisfactory waives the right to raise that objection when sued for payment by the performing party.

For Example, a contract promising to sell back a parcel of commercial property to Jackson required Jackson to make a $500 payment to Massey's attorney on the first of the month for five months, December through April. It was clearly understood that the payments would be "on time without fail." Jackson made the December payment on time. New Year's Day, a holiday, fell on a Friday, and Jackson made the second payment on January 4. He made $500 payments on February 1, March 1, and March 31, respectively, and the payments were accepted and a receipt issued on each occasion. However, Massey refused to convey title back to Jackson because "the January 4 payment was untimely and the parties' agreement had been breached." The court held that the doctrine of waiver applied due to Massey's acceptance of the late payment and the three subsequent payments without objection, and the court declared that Jackson was entitled to possession of the land.[7]

[7] *Massey v. Jackson*, 726 So. 2d 656 (Ala. App. 1998).

Scope of Waiver

The waiver of a breach of contract extends only to the matter waived. It does not show any intent to ignore other provisions of the contract.

Antimodification Clause

Modern contracts commonly specify that the terms of a contract shall not be deemed modified by waiver as to any breaches. This means that the original contract remains as agreed to. Either party may therefore return to, and insist on, compliance with the original contract.

In the example involving Jackson and Massey's contract, the trial court reviewed the contract to see whether the court was restricted by the contract from applying the waiver. It concluded: "In this case, the parties' contract did not contain any terms that could prevent the application of the doctrine of waiver to the acceptance of late payments."[8]

19-2c Reservation of Rights

It may be that a party is willing to accept a defective performance but does not wish to surrender any claim for damages for the breach. **For Example,** Midwest Utilities, Inc., accepted 20 carloads of Powder River Basin coal (sometimes called *Western coal*) from its supplier, Maney Enterprises, because its power plants were in short supply of coal. Midwest's requirements contract with Maney called for Appalachian coal, a low-sulfur, highly efficient fuel, which is sold at a premium price per ton. Midwest, in accepting the tendered performance with a **reservation of rights,** gave notice to Maney that it reserved all rights to pursue damages for the tender of a nonconforming shipment.

reservation of rights–assertion by a party to a contract that even though a tendered performance (e.g., a defective product) is accepted, the right to damages for nonconformity to the contract is reserved.

remedy–action or procedure that is followed in order to enforce a right or to obtain damages for injury to a right.

19-3 Remedies for Breach of Contract

One or more **remedies** may be available to the innocent party in the case of a breach of contract. There is also the possibility that arbitration or a streamlined out-of-court alternative dispute resolution procedure is available or required for determining the rights of the parties.

19-3a Remedies Upon Anticipatory Repudiation

When an anticipatory repudiation of a contract occurs, the aggrieved person has several options. The individual may (1) do nothing beyond stating that performance at the proper time will be required, (2) regard the contract as having been definitively broken and bring a lawsuit against the repudiating party without waiting to see whether there will be proper performance when the performance date arrives, or (3) regard the repudiation as an offer to cancel the contract. This offer can be accepted or rejected. If accepted, there is a discharge of the original contract by the subsequent cancellation agreement of the parties.

19-3b Remedies in General and the Measure of Damages

Courts provide a *quasi-contractual* or *restitution* remedy in which a contract is unenforceable because it lacked definite and certain terms or was not in compliance with the statute of frauds, yet one of the parties performed services for the other. The measure of damages in these and other quasi-contract cases is the reasonable value of the services performed, not an amount derived from the defective contract.

[8] *Id.* at 659.

FIGURE 19-1 What Follows the Breach

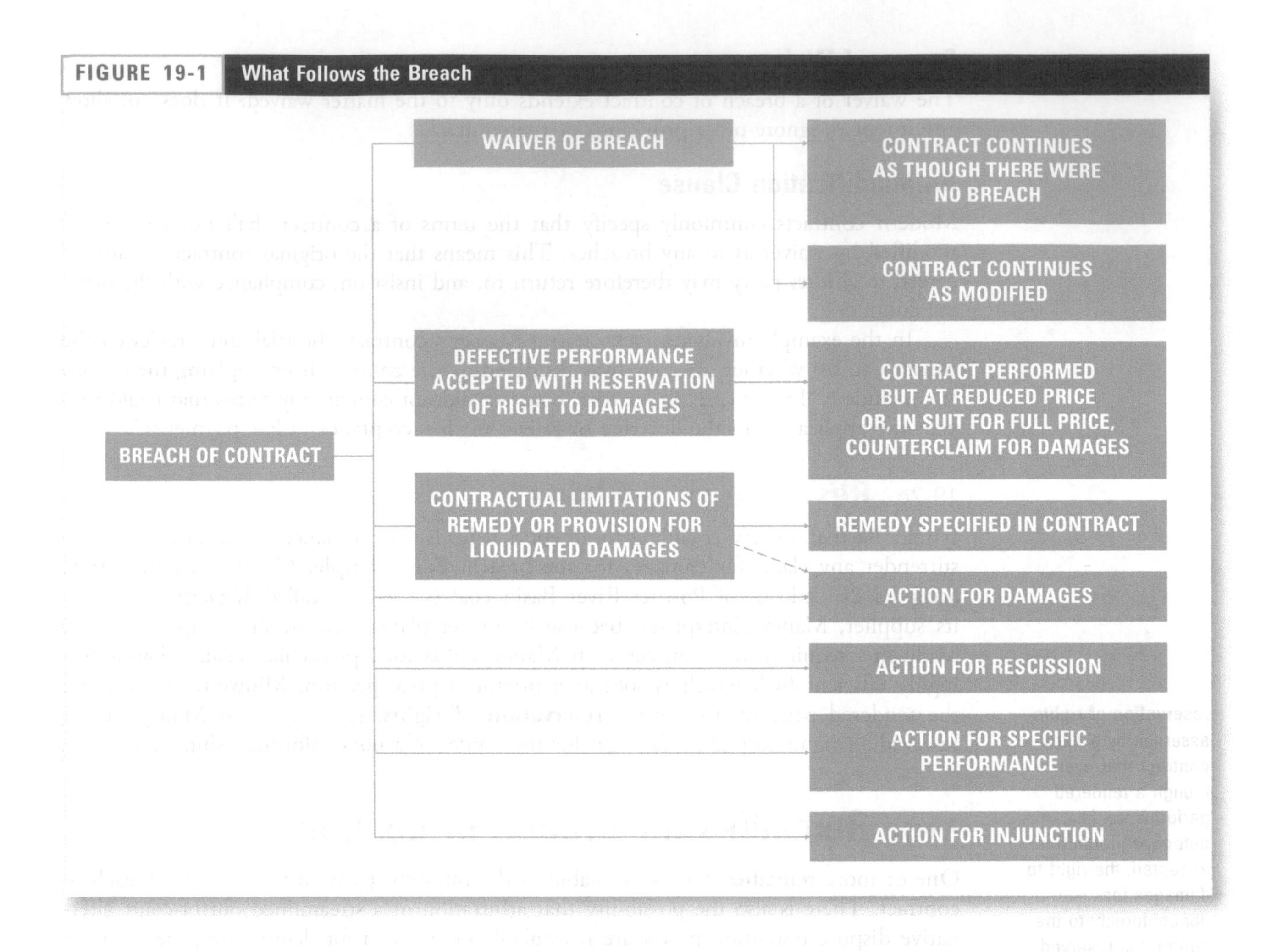

In cases when a person retains money or when a contemplated contract is not properly formed and no work is performed, the party retaining the benefit is obligated to make restitution to the person conferring the benefit. **For Example,** Kramer Associates, Inc. (KAI), a Washington D.C., consulting firm, accepted $75,000 from a Ghana-based corporation, Ikam, Ltd., to secure financing for a Ghana development project. No contract was ever executed, and KAI did virtually nothing to secure financing for the project. Restitution of the $75,000 was required.[9]

When there is a breach of contract, the regular remedy is an award of *monetary damages.* In unusual circumstances, when monetary damages are inadequate, the injured party may obtain **specific performance,** whereby the court will order that the contract terms be carried out.

specific performance–action brought to compel the adverse party to perform a contract on the theory that merely suing for damages for its breach will not be an adequate remedy.

The measure of monetary damages when there has been a breach of contract is the sum of money that will place the injured party in the same position that would have been attained if the contract had been performed.[10] That is, the injured party will be given the *benefit of the bargain* by the court. As seen in the *Tips v. Hartland Developers* case, the nonbreaching party, Hartland, was awarded the contract price less the cost of completion of the project, which had the effect of giving the builder the benefit of the bargain.

[9] *Kramer Associates, Inc. v. Ikam, Ltd.,* 888 A.2d 247 (D.C. 2005).
[10] *Leingang v. City of Mandan,* 468 N.W.2d 397 (N.D. 1991).

19-3c Monetary Damages

compensatory damages–sum of money that will compensate an injured plaintiff for actual loss.

nominal damages–nominal sum awarded the plaintiff in order to establish that legal rights have been violated although the plaintiff in fact has not sustained any actual loss or damages.

Monetary damages are commonly classified as compensatory damages, nominal damages, and punitive damages. **Compensatory damages** compensate the injured party for the damages incurred as a result of the breach of contract. Compensatory damages have two branches, *direct damages* and *consequential* (or *special*) *damages*.

Injured parties that do not sustain an actual loss because of a breach of contract are entitled to a judgment of a small sum of money such as $1; these damages are called **nominal damages.**

Damages in excess of actual loss, imposed for the purpose of punishing or making an example of the defendant, are known as **punitive damages** or *exemplary damages.* In contract actions, punitive damages are not ordinarily awarded.[11]

Direct and Consequential Damages

Direct damages (sometimes called *general damages*) are those that naturally flow from the given type of breach of contract involved and include *incidental damages*, which are extra expenditures made by the injured party to rectify the breach or mitigate damages.[12] **Consequential damages** (sometimes called *special damages*) are those that do not necessarily flow from the type of breach of contract involved but happen to do so in a particular case as a result of the injured party's particular circumstances.[13]

CASE SUMMARY

Who Pays the Expenses?

FACTS: Jerry Birkel was a grain farmer. Hassebrook Farm Service, Inc., made a contract with Jerry to sell to him and install a grain storage and drying bin. Jerry traded in his old dryer to the seller. The new equipment did not work properly, and Jerry had to pay other persons for drying and storing his grain. Jerry sued Hassebrook for damages and claimed the right to be repaid what he had paid to others for drying and storage.

DECISION: Jerry was entitled to recover what he had paid others for drying and storage. Because Jerry had traded in his old dryer to the seller, it was obvious to the seller that if the new equipment did not work properly, Jerry would be forced to pay for alternative drying and storage to prevent the total loss of his crops. The cost of such an alternative was therefore within the seller's contemplation when the contract was made, and so the buyer could recover this cost as an element of damages for the seller's breach of contract. **[*Birkel v. Hassebrook Farm Service, Inc.*, 363 N.W.2d 148 (Neb. 1985)]**

punitive damages–damages, in excess of those required to compensate the plaintiff for the wrong done, that are imposed in order to punish the defendant because of the particularly wanton or willful character of wrongdoing; also called *exemplary damages.*

Consequential damages may be recovered only if it was reasonably foreseeable to the defendant that the kind of loss in question could be sustained by the nonbreaching party if the contract were broken.

For Example, in early August, Spencer Adams ordered a four-wheel-drive GMC truck with a rear-end hydraulic lift for use on his Aroostook County, Maine, potato farm. The contract price was $63,500. He told Brad Jones, the owner of the dealership, that he had to have the truck by Labor Day so he could use it to bring in his crop from the fields before the first frost, and Brad nodded that he understood. The truck did not arrive by

[11] A party who is not awarded actual damages but wins nominal damages can be considered a "prevailing party" for the purposes of a contractual attorney fee-shifting provision. *Brock v. King,* 629 S.E.2d 829 (Ga. App. 2006).

[12] In New York State, the courts utilize the terms *general* and *special* damages as opposed to the terms *direct* and *consequential* damages. See *Biotronik A.G. v. Connor Medsystems Ireland, Ltd.,* 988 N.Y.S.2d 527 (Ct. App. 2014).

[13] See *Powell Electrical Systems, Inc. v. Hewlett Packard Co.,* 356 S.W.3d 113 (Tex. App. 2011).

direct damages–losses that are caused by breach of a contract.

consequential damages–damages the buyer experiences as a result of the seller's breach with respect to a third party; also called *special damages.*

Labor Day as promised in the written contract. After a two-week period of gradually escalating recriminations with the dealership, Adams obtained the same model GMC truck at a dealership 40 minutes away in Houlton but at the cost of $65,500. He was also able to rent a similar truck from the Houlton dealer for $250 for the day while the new truck was being prepared. Farmhands had used other means of harvesting, but because of the lack of the truck, their work was set back by five days. As a result of the delays, 30 percent of the crop was still in the fields when the first frost came, causing damages expertly estimated at $320,000. The *direct damages* for the breach of contract in this case would be the difference between the contract price for the truck of $63,500 and the market price of $65,500, or $2,000. These direct damages naturally flow from the breach of contract for the purchase of a truck. Also, the *incidental damages* of $250 for the truck rental are recoverable direct damages. The $320,000 loss of the potato crop was a consequence of not having the truck, and this sum is arguably recoverable by Spencer Adams as *consequential* or *special damages.* Adams notified Brad Jones of the reason he needed to have the truck by Labor Day, and it should have been reasonably foreseeable to Jones that loss of a portion of the crop could occur if the truck contract was breached. However, because of Spencer Adams's obligation to mitigate damages (as discussed next), it is unlikely that Adams will recover the full consequential damages. Truck rental availability or the lack of availability within the rural area, alternative tractor usage, and the actual harvesting methods used by Adams all relate to the mitigation issue to be resolved by the jury.

Mitigation of Damages

The injured party is under the duty to mitigate damages if reasonably possible.[14] In other words, damages must not be permitted to increase if an increase can be prevented by reasonable efforts. This means that the injured party must generally stop any performance under the contract to avoid running up a larger bill. The duty to mitigate damages may require an injured party to buy or rent elsewhere the goods that the wrongdoer was obligated to deliver under the contract. In the case of breach of an employment contract by the employer, the employee is required to seek other similar employment. The wages earned from other employment must be deducted from the damages claimed. The discharged employee, however, is not required to take employment of less-than-comparable work.

Effect of Failure to Mitigate Damages. The effect of the requirement of mitigating damages is to limit recovery by the nonbreaching party to the damages that would have been sustained had this party mitigated the damages where it was possible to do so.

CASE SUMMARY

The Opposite of a Win-Win Situation

FACTS: On February 4, 2006, the Heymanns agreed to buy a condominium from Gayle Fischer for $315,000. Both parties signed a purchase and sale agreement. The Agreement authorized the Heymanns to terminate if Fischer refused to fix any "major defect" discovered upon inspection but did not permit them to terminate if Fischer refused to perform "routine maintenance" or make "minor repair[s]." On February 10, 2006, the Heymanns demanded Fischer fix an electrical problem after an inspection report revealed that electricity was not flowing to three power outlets. The Heymanns thought this was a "major defect" under the Agreement and conditioned their purchase on Fischer's timely response. Fischer failed to timely respond to their demand—even though she eventually fixed the problem

[14] *West Pinal Family Health Center, Inc. v. McBryde,* 785 P.2d 66 (Ariz. App. 1989).

The Opposite of a Win-Win Situation continued

for $117 on February 20 by having an electrician push the reset button on three outlets and change a light bulb. The Heymanns tendered a mutual release to void the Agreement. Fischer refused to sign the release and sued for specific performances or damages. The case progressed to the trial court, the court of appeals, back to the trial court, and ultimately to the Supreme Court of Indiana.

After the deal fell through in 2006 Fischer attempted to mitigate damages by selling the condo but the housing market entered a major downturn. On February 13, 2007, she received an offer to purchase the condo for $240,000 but her counter-offer of $286,000 was rejected. She eventually sold the condo in November 2011 for $180,000. Fischer seeks damages for the difference between the Heymann purchase price of $315,000 and the sale in 2011 of $180,000, plus the cost of maintaining the condo from 2006 through 2011, and attorney's fees for a total of $306,616.

DECISION: Fischer's failure to respond to the Heymann's demand for electrical repairs was not a basis to void the contract. Rather the $117 repair consisting of pushing the reset button on three outlets and the change of a light bulb was not a "major defect" which would allow for the voiding of a contract. Accordingly, the Heymanns were in breach of the Purchase Agreement. The duty to mitigate damages is a common law duty independent of contract terms requiring the non-breaching party to make a reasonable effort to decrease the damage caused by the breach. Fischer acted unreasonably when she could have mitigated damages and sold the condo for $240,000, in 2007, instead of waiting until 2011. Accordingly, her compensatory damages are $75,000, the difference between $315,000 and $240,000 plus $15,109 in carrying cost to the 2007 offer date and reasonable attorney fees of $3,862 incurred up to the 2007 date for a total of $93,977. **[*Fischer v. Heymann*, 12 N.E.3d 867 (Ind. 2014)]**

19-3d Rescission

When one party commits a material breach of the contract, the other party may rescind the contract; if the party in default objects, the aggrieved party may bring an action for rescission. A breach is *material* when it is so substantial that it defeats the object of the parties in making the contract.[15]

CASE SUMMARY

The Buck Doesn't Stop Here (at Slip B1)

FACTS: Edgar Buck owns *Rookie IV*, a $6 million 61-foot boat requiring a dock slip 20 feet in width. Buck's daughter Susanne owns ZAN, LCC, and Buck has authority to act on behalf of ZAN. Susanne wanted a waterfront lot to build a home, and Buck wanted a boat slip out of the Intercoastal Waterway where the boat regularly sustained damage. ZAN (Buck) agreed to purchase a slip for Buck's boat and lot 3 for Susanne. Just prior to the closing, Buck discovered that the slip designated as B1 was actually two slips, B1 and B2 and *Rookie IV* would not fit into B1. Buck was informed by Ripley Cove's agent and later its closing attorney Dan David that the sellers owned B2 and that it would be no problem to give Buck the 20 foot clearance he needed and to place two pilings in the adjoining slip. Buck then agreed to close on the property. It was later discovered that at the time of the closing, Ripley Cove no longer owned B2. Since *Rookie IV* could not fit into the slip, ZAN sued for rescission of the contract for the lot and slip and damages. The trial court determined that ZAN proved its claims, awarded $10,000 for breach of contract and negligent misrepresentation but refused to rescind the contract. ZAN appealed.

DECISION: Judgment for ZAN. The main purpose of the contract was to provide Buck with a slip for *Rookie IV*. Thus ZAN was entitled to rescission of the contract *in toto*, both the slip and the land, despite the parties' lack of dispute regarding the upland parcel. A breach of contract claim warranting rescission of the contract must be so substantial and fundamental as to defeat the purpose of the contract. Such was the nature of the breach in this case. **[*ZAN, LLC v. Ripley Cove, LLC*, 751 S.E.2d 664 (S.C. App. 2013)]**

[15] *Greentree Properties, Inc. v. Kissee*, 92 S.W.3d 289 (Mo. App. 2003).

An injured party who rescinds a contract after having performed services may recover the reasonable value of the performance rendered under restitutionary or quasi-contractual damages. Money paid by the injured party may also be recovered. **For Example,** the Sharabianlous signed a purchase agreement to buy a building owned by Berenstein Associates for $2 million. Thereafter the parties learned of environmental contamination on the property. Faced with uncertainty about the scope of the problem and the cost of the cleanup, the deal fell through and litigation ensued. The trial court rescinded the agreement based on mutual mistake of fact because neither party knew the full extent of the environmental hazard at the property. Damages available to parties upon mistake are more limited than those available in cases in which rescission is based on fault. The Sharabianlous were awarded $61,423.82 in expenses and an order returning their $115,000 deposit.[16]

The purpose of rescission is to restore the injured party to the position occupied before the contract was made. However, the party seeking restitutionary damages must also return what this party has received from the party in default.

For Example, Pedro Morena purchased real estate from Jason Alexander after Alexander had assured him that the property did not have a flooding problem. In fact, the property regularly flooded after ordinary rainstorms. Morena was entitled to the return of the purchase price and payment for the reasonable value of the improvements he made to the property. Alexander was entitled to a setoff for the reasonable rental value of the property during the time Morena was in possession of this property.

19-3e Action for Specific Performance

Under special circumstances, an injured party may obtain the equitable remedy of specific performance, which compels the other party to carry out the terms of a contract. Specific performance is ordinarily granted only if the subject matter of the contract is "unique," thereby making an award of money damages an inadequate remedy. Contracts for the purchase of land will be specifically enforced.[17]

Specific performance of a contract to sell personal property can be obtained only if the article is of unusual age, beauty, unique history, or other distinction. **For Example,** Maurice owned a rare Revolutionary War musket that he agreed to sell to Herb. Maurice then changed his mind because of the uniqueness of the musket. Herb can sue and win, requesting the remedy of specific performance of the contract because of the unique nature of the goods.

When the damages sustained by the plaintiff can be measured in monetary terms, specific performance will be refused. Consequently, a contract to sell a television station will not be specifically enforced when the buyer had made a contract to resell the station to a third person; the damages caused by the breach of the first contract would be the loss sustained by being unable to make the resale, and such damages would be adequate compensation to the original buyer.[18]

Ordinarily, contracts for the performance of personal services are not specifically ordered. This is because of the difficulty of supervision by the court and the restriction of the U.S. Constitution's Thirteenth Amendment prohibiting involuntary servitude except as criminal punishment.

injunction–order of a court of equity to refrain from doing (negative injunction) or to do (affirmative or mandatory injunction) a specified act.

19-3f Action for an Injunction

When a breach of contract consists of doing an act prohibited by the contract, a possible remedy is an **injunction** against doing the act. **For Example,** when the obligation in an employee's contract is to refrain from competing after resigning from the company and

[16] *Sharabianlou v. Karp,* 105 Cal. Rptr. 3d 300 (Cal. App. 2010).
[17] *English v. Muller,* 514 S.E.2d 195 (Ga. 1999).
[18] *Miller v. LeSea Broadcasting, Inc.,* 87 F.3d 224 (7th Cir. 1996).

the obligation is broken by competing, a court may order the former employee to stop competing. Similarly, when a vocalist breaks a contract to record exclusively for a particular label, she may be enjoined from recording for any other company. This may have the indirect effect of compelling the vocalist to record for the plaintiff.

19-3g Reformation of Contract by a Court

At times, a written contract does not correctly state the agreement already made by the parties. When this occurs, either party may seek to have the court reform or correct the writing to state the agreement actually made.

A party seeking reformation of a contract must clearly prove both the grounds for reformation and what the agreement actually was.[19] This burden is particularly great when the contract to be reformed is written. This is so because the general rule is that parties are presumed to have read their written contracts and to have intended to be bound by them when they signed the contracts.

When a unilateral mistake is made and it is of such consequence that enforcing the contract according to its terms would be unconscionable, a court may reform the contract to correct the mistake.

CASE SUMMARY

Will a Court Correct a Huge Mistake?

FACTS: New York Packaging Corp. (NYPC) manufactured plastic sheets used by Owens Corning (OC) at its asphalt plants throughout the country as dividers to separate asphalt containers and prevent them from sticking to one another. Janet Berry, a customer service representative at Owens Corning, called and received a price from NYPC of "$172.50 per box," with a box containing 200 plastic sheets. Ms. Berry put the information into OC's computer systems, which in turn generated a purchase order. She mistakenly believed that the unit of measurement designated as "EA" on the purchase order was per box when it in fact was per sheet. As a result, the purchase orders likewise reflected a price of $172.50 per sheet rather than per box. The computer automatically calculated the total price of the purchase order and faxed it to NYPC as $1,078,195, without Ms. Berry seeing the huge total price. NYPC filled the order, which included overrun sheets, and billed OC $1,414,605.60. NYPC sought payment at the contract price of $172.50 per sheet. It points out that the purchase order contained a "no oral modification" clause and, by its terms, the order was binding when NYPC accepted. The buyer contends that NYPC is attempting to take advantage of this huge and obvious mistake and that the contract should be reformed.

DECISION: Ms. Berry made a unilateral mistake that was, or should have been, known by NYPC. OC used the sheets after its offer to return them to NYPC was refused. Therefore, the contract could not be rescinded. The drafting error in this case was so huge that to enforce the written contract would be unconscionable. Accordingly, the unit of measurement is amended to read "per box" rather than "EA"; the "Order Qty" is amended to read "41 boxes of 200 sheets per box"; and the overall price is modified to read $7,072.50, not $1,078,195. **[In re *Owens Corning et al., Debtors in Possession*, 291 B.R. 329 (2003)]**

19-4 Contract Provisions Affecting Remedies and Damages

The contract of the parties may contain provisions that affect the remedies available or the recovery of damages.

[19] The evidence must be "clear, unequivocal and decisive," *First Chatham Bank v. Liberty Capital, LLC*, 755 S.E.2d 219 (Ga. App. 2014).

19-4a Limitation of Remedies

The contract of the parties may limit the remedies of the aggrieved parties. **For Example,** the contract may give one party the right to repair or replace a defective item sold or to refund the contract price. The contract may require both parties to submit any dispute to arbitration or another streamlined out-of-court dispute resolution procedure.

19-4b Liquidated Damages

liquidated damages–provision stipulating the amount of damages to be paid in the event of default or breach of contract.

The parties may stipulate in their contract that a certain amount should be paid in case of a breach. This amount is known as liquidated damages and may be variously measured by the parties. When delay is possible, **liquidated damages** may be a fixed sum, such as $1,000 for each day of delay. When there is a total default, damages may be a percentage of the contract price or the amount of the down payment.

Validity

liquidated damages clause–specification of exact compensation in case of a breach of contract.

To be valid, a **liquidated damages clause** must satisfy two requirements: (1) The situation must be one in which it is difficult or impossible to determine the actual damages and (2) the amount specified must not be excessive when compared with the probable damages that would be sustained.[20] The validity of a liquidated damages clause is determined on the basis of the facts existing when the clause was agreed to.

Effect

When a liquidated damages clause is held valid, the injured party cannot collect more than the amount specified by the clause. The defaulting party is bound to pay such damages once the fact is established that there has been a default. The injured party is not required to make any proof as to damages sustained, and the defendant is not permitted to show that the damages were not as great as the liquidated sum.

Invalid Clauses

If the liquidated damages clause calls for the payment of a sum that is clearly unreasonably large and unrelated to the possible actual damages that might be sustained, the clause will be held to be void as a penalty. **For Example,** a settlement agreement between 27 plaintiffs seeking recovery for injuries resulting from faulty breast implants and the implants' manufacturer, Dow Corning Corp., called for seven $200,000 payments to each plaintiff. The agreement also called for a $100 per day payment to each plaintiff for any time when the payments were late as "liquidated damages." The court held that the $100 per day figure was not a reasonable estimate of anticipated damages. Rather, it was an unenforceable "penalty" provision.[21]

When a liquidated damages clause is held invalid, the effect is merely to erase the clause from the contract, and the injured party may proceed to recover damages for breach of the contract. Instead of recovering the liquidated damages amount, the injured party will recover whatever actual damages he can prove. **For Example,** Richard Goldblatt and his wife Valerie breached a five-year restrictive covenant in a settlement agreement with the medical devices corporation that Goldblatt had cofounded, C.P. Motion, Inc. A liquidated damages provision in the settlement agreement that obligated Goldblatt and his wife to pay $250,000 per breach of the restrictive covenant was unenforceable as a penalty clause. The appeals court set aside a $4,969,339 judgment against the Goldblatts, determining that the parties could have agreed to arrive at actual damages by

[20] *Southeast Alaska Construction Co. v. Alaska,* 791 P.2d 339 (Alaska 1990).

[21] *Bear Stearns v. Dow Corning Corp.,* 419 F.3d 543 (6th Or. 2005). See *Boone Coleman Construction, Inc. v. Village of Piketon,* 13 N.E.3d 1190 (Ohio App. 2014).

calculating a percentage of lost profits of specific lost clients or reclaiming any profits gained by the breaching parties. Because the liquidated damages clause was a penalty provision, C.P. Motion, Inc., may only recover the actual damages filed and proven at trial.[22]

19-4c Attorneys' Fees

Attorneys' fees are a very significant factor in contract litigation. In Medistar Corporation's suit against Dr. David Schmidt, the jury awarded it $418,069 in damages under its promissory estoppel claim and in addition thereto the trial court judge allowed Medistar to recover $408,412 for its attorneys' fees. A state statute allows recovery of attorneys' fees for the prevailing party in a breach of partnership claim. On appeal the recovery of $408,412 in attorneys' fees was reversed since the jury awarded zero damages on Medistars' breach of partnership claim. The net result after payment of attorneys' fees—and not counting attorneys' fees for the appeal—was $9,657 for Medistar, after four years of "successful" litigation.[23]

The so-called American rule states that each party is responsible for its own attorneys' fees in the absence of an express contractual or statutory provision to the contrary.[24] Even in the event of a valid contractual provision for attorneys' fees, a trial court has the discretion to exercise its equitable control to allow only such sum as is reasonable, or the court may properly disallow attorneys' fees altogether on the basis that such recovery would be inequitable. **For Example,** although Evergreen Tree Care Services was awarded some monetary damages in its breach of contract suit against JHL, Inc., it was unsuccessful in its claim for attorneys' fees under a provision for attorneys' fees in the contract because the trial court exercised its equitable discretion, finding that both parties to the litigation came to court with "unclean hands," and that Evergreen failed to sufficiently itemize and exclude fees to discovery abuses.[25]

19-4d Limitation of Liability Clauses

A contract may contain a provision stating that one of the parties shall not be liable for damages in case of breach. Such a provision is called an **exculpatory clause,** or when a monetary limit to damages for breach of contract is set forth in the contract, it may be referred to as a **limitation-of-liability clause.**

exculpatory clause–provision in a contract stating that one of the parties shall not be liable for damages in case of breach; also called a *limitation-of-liability clause.*

limitation-of-liability clause–provision in a contract stating that one of the parties is not liable for damages in case of breach; also called *exculpatory clause.*

Content and Construction

If an exculpatory clause or a limitation-of-liability clause limits liability for damages caused only by negligent conduct, liability is neither excluded nor limited if the conduct alleged is found to be grossly negligent, willful, or wanton. **For Example,** Security Guards Inc. (SGI) provided services to Dana Corporation, a truck frame manufacturer under a contract that contained a limitation-of-liability clause capping losses at $50,000 per occurrence for damages "caused solely by the negligence" of SGI or its employees. When a critical alarm was activated by a fire in the paint shop at 5:39 P.M., the SGI guard on duty did not follow appropriate procedures, which delayed notification to the fire department for 15 minutes. Royal Indemnity Co., Dana's insurer, paid Dana $16,535,882 for the fire loss and sued SGI for $7 million, contending that the SGI guard's actions were grossly negligent and caused the plant to suffer increased damages. The court held that if SGI were to be found grossly negligent, the liability would not be limited to $50,000, and a jury could find damages far exceeding that amount.[26]

[22] *Goldblatt v. C. P. Motion, Inc.,* 77 So. 3d 798 (Fla. App. 2011).
[23] *Medistar Corp. v. Schmidt,* 267 S.W.3d 150 (Tex. App. 2008).
[24] *Centimark v. Village Manor Associates, Ltd.,* 967 A.2d 550 (Conn. App. 2009).
[25] *Stafford v. JHL, Inc.,* 194 P.3d 315 (Wyo. 2008). See also *FNBC v. Jennessey Group, LLC,* 759 N.W.2d 808 (Iowa App. 2008).
[26] *Royal Indemnity Co. v. Security Guards, Inc,* 255 F. Supp. 2d 497 (E.D. Pa. 2003).

Validity

While contracts that exculpate persons from liability are not favored by the court because they encourage lack of care and are therefore strictly construed against the person or entity seeking to escape liability, nevertheless when the language of the contract and the intent of the parties are clearly exculpatory, the contract will be upheld. This principle arises out of the broad policy of the law, which accords to contracting parties' freedom to bind themselves as they see fit. **For Example,** the exculpatory clause in a rental contract that David Hyatt signed with Mini Storage On the Green, which was clearly exculpatory, relieved Mini Storage of liability for injuries Hyatt suffered when the unit door he was pulling down with some extra force came off its tracks and injured him.[27]

Releases

Release forms signed by participants in athletic and sporting events declaring that the sponsor, proprietor, or operator of the event shall not be liable for injuries sustained by participants because of its negligence are generally binding.[28]

CASE SUMMARY

How to Handle a Risky Business

FACTS: Chelsea Hamill attended Camp Cheley for three years. Before attending camp each summer her parents signed a liability/risk release form. In July 2004, when Hamill was 15 years old, she fell off a Cheley horse and broke her arm. Chelsea brought a negligence and gross negligence lawsuit against the summer camp. Hamill's mother testified at her deposition that she voluntarily signed the release after having "skimmed" it. At her deposition, the mother testified as follows:

> Attorney: And, you know, you knew that someone such as Christopher Reeve had been tragically injured falling off a horse?
>
> Ms. Hamill: Yes.
>
> Attorney: Did you personally know Mr. Reeve?
>
> Ms. Hamill: Yes.
>
> Attorney: And so you were aware that there were significant risks associated with horseback riding?
>
> Ms. Hamill: Yes.
>
> Attorney: And you were aware that your daughter was going to be doing a significant amount of horseback riding?
>
> Ms. Hamill: Yes.

Hamill's mother's interpretation of the release was that prospective negligent claims were not waived. The camp disagreed. The release stated in part:

> *I, on behalf of myself and my child, hereby release and waive* any claim of liability against Cheley ... *occurring to my child while he/she participates in any and all camp programs and activities.*
>
> *I give my permission for my child to participate in all camp activities, including those described above. I acknowledge and assume the risks involved in these activities, and for any damages, illness,* injury or death ... *resulting from such risks for myself and my child.*
>
> *(Emphasis Added.)*

DECISION: Judgment for Camp Cheley. The release did not need to include an exhaustive list of particularized injury scenarios to be effective. Hamill's mother had more than sufficient information to allow her to assess the extent of injury possible in horseback riding and to make an "informed" decision before signing the release. The mother was informed of the intent to release "all claims," including prospective negligence claims. While exculpatory agreements are not a bar to civil liability for gross negligence, the record is devoid of evidence of gross negligence. [***Hamill v. Cheley Colorado Camps, Inc.*, 262 P.3d 945 (Colo. App. 2011)**]

[27] *Hyatt v. Mini Storage On the Green,* 763 S.E.2d 166 (N.C. App. 2014).

[28] But see *Woodman v. Kera, LLC,* 760 N.W.2d 641 (Mich. App. 2008) where the Court of Appeals of Michigan held that a preinjury waiver signed by a parent on behalf of a five-year-old child was invalid. See also *Brooten v. Hickok Rehabilitation Services, LLC,* 831 N.W.2d 445 (Wis. App. 2013) where the court held that the release was impermissibly broad, well beyond negligence claims.

Make the Connection

Summary

When a party fails to perform a contract or performs improperly, the other contracting party may sue for damages caused by the breach. What may be recovered by the aggrieved person is stated in terms of being direct or consequential damages. Direct damages are those that ordinarily will result from the breach. Direct damages may be recovered on proof of causation and amount. Consequential damages can be recovered only if, in addition to proving causation and amount, it is shown that they were reasonably within the contemplation of the contracting parties as a probable result of a breach of the contract. The right to recover consequential damages is lost if the aggrieved party could reasonably have taken steps to avoid such damages. In other words, the aggrieved person has a duty to mitigate or reduce damages by reasonable means.

In any case, the damages recoverable for breach of contract may be limited to a specific amount by a liquidated damages clause.

In a limited number of situations, an aggrieved party may bring an action for specific performance to compel the other contracting party to perform the acts called for by the contract. Specific performance by the seller is always obtainable for the breach of a contract to sell land or real estate on the theory that such property has a unique value. With respect to other contracts, specific performance will not be ordered unless it is shown that there was some unique element present so that the aggrieved person would suffer a damage that could not be compensated for by the payment of money damages.

The aggrieved person also has the option of rescinding the contract if (1) the breach has been made concerning a material term and (2) the aggrieved party returns everything to the way it was before the contract was made.

Although there has been a breach of the contract, the effect of this breach is nullified if the aggrieved person by word or conduct waives the right to object to the breach. Conversely, an aggrieved party may accept a defective performance without thereby waiving a claim for breach if the party makes a reservation of rights. A reservation of rights can be made by stating that the defective performance is accepted "without prejudice," "under protest," or "with reservation of rights."

Learning Outcomes

After studying this chapter, you should be able to clearly explain:

19-1 What Constitutes a Breach of Contract?

LO.1 Explain what constitutes a breach of contract and an anticipatory breach of contract

See the illustration of a painting contractor's failure to properly paint a house, page 348.

See the *Tips* case in which damages are assessed for anticipatory repudiation of a contract, pages 348–349.

See the racetrack example of a "request," not an anticipatory breach, page 349.

See the *Mammoth Lakes* example involving anticipatory repudiation by conduct, page 349.

19-2 Waiver of Breach

LO.2 Describe the effect of a waiver of a breach

See the application of the waiver doctrine as applied in the Massey example, page 350.

19-3 Remedies for Breach of Contract

LO.3 Explain the range of remedies available for breach of contract

See Figure 19-1, "What Follows the Breach," page 352.

See the Spencer Adams example involving a range of monetary damages, pages 353–354.

See the boat slip for *Rookie IV* case involving rescission of a contract, page 355.

See the rare Revolutionary War musket example of specific performance, page 356.

19-4 Contract Provisions Affecting Remedies and Damages

LO.4 Explain when liquidated damages clauses are valid and invalid

See the Dow Corning faulty breast implants settlement agreement example in which liquidated damages of a $100 per day late payment were found to be unenforceable penalty provision, page 358.

LO.5 State when liability-limiting clauses and releases are valid

See the *Cheley Camps* case that illustrates how the camp successfully raised a signed parental exculpatory release as a defense in a horseback riding injury case, page 360.

Key Terms

anticipatory breach
anticipatory repudiation
breach
compensatory damages
consequential damages
direct damages
exculpatory clause
injunction
limitation-of-liability clause
liquidated damages
liquidated damages clause
nominal damages
punitive damages
remedies
reservation of rights
specific performance
waiver

Questions and Case Problems

1. The Forsyth School District contracted with Textor Construction, Inc., to build certain additions and alter school facilities, including the grading of a future softball field. Under the contract, the work was to be completed by August 1. Various delays occurred at the outset of the project attributable to the school district, and the architect's representative on the job, Mr. Hamilton, told Textor's vice president, William Textor, not to be concerned about a clause in the contract of $250 per day liquidated damages for failure to complete the job by August 1. Textor sued the school district for breach of contract regarding payment for the grading of the softball field, and the District counterclaimed for liquidated damages for 84 days at $250 per day for failure to complete the project by the August 1 date. What legal basis exists for Textor to defend against the counterclaim for failure to complete the job on time? Was it ethical for the school district to bring this counterclaim based on the facts before you? [*Textor Construction, Inc. v. Forsyth R-III School District*, 60 S.W.3d 692 (Mo. App.)]

2. Self-described "sports nut" Gary Baker signed up for a three-year club-seat "package" that entitled him and a companion to tickets for 41 Boston Bruin hockey games and 41 Boston Celtic basketball games at the New Boston Garden Corporation's Fleet Center for approximately $18,000 per year. After one year, Baker stopped paying for the tickets thinking that he would simply lose his $5,000 security deposit. New Boston sued Baker for breach of contract, seeking the balance due on the tickets of $34,866. At trial, Baker argued to the jury that although he had breached his contract, New Boston had an obligation to mitigate damages, for example, by treating his empty seats and those of others in the same situation as "rush seats" shortly before game time and selling them at a discount. New Boston argued that just as a used luxury car cannot be returned for a refund, a season ticket cannot be canceled without consequences. Decide.

3. Rogers made a contract with Salisbury Brick Corp. that allowed it to remove earth and sand from land he owned. The contract ran for four years with provision to renew it for additional four-year terms up to a total of 96 years. The contract provided for compensation to Rogers based on the amount of earth and sand removed. By an unintentional mistake, Salisbury underpaid Rogers the amount of $863 for the months of November and December 1986. Salisbury offered this amount to Rogers, but he refused to accept it and claimed that he had been underpaid in other months. Rogers claimed that he was entitled to rescind the contract. Was he correct? [*Rogers v. Salisbury Brick Corp.*, 882 S.E.2d 915 (S.C.)]

4. Manny Fakhimi agreed to buy an apartment complex for $697,000 at an auction from David Mason. Fakhimi was obligated to put up 10 percent of the agreed-to price at the auction as a deposit. The agreement allowed Mason to keep this deposit should Fakhimi fail to come up with the remaining 90 percent of the auction price as liquidated damages for the default. Shortly after the auction, Fakhimi heard a rumor that the military base located near the apartment complex might be closing. Fakhimi immediately stopped payment on the check and defaulted on the agreement. Mason sued Fakhimi for the liquidated damages specified in the sales contract. Decide. [*Mason v. Fakhimi*, 865 P.2d 333 (Neb.)]

5. Protein Blenders, Inc., made a contract with Gingerich to buy from him the shares of stock of a small corporation. When the buyer refused to take and pay for the stock, Gingerich sued for specific performance of the contract on the ground that the value of the stock was unknown and could not be readily ascertained because it was not sold on the general market. Was he entitled to specific performance? [*Gingerich v. Protein Blenders, Inc.*, 95 N.W.2d 522 (Iowa)]

6. The buyer of real estate made a down payment. The contract stated that the buyer would be liable for damages in an amount equal to the down payment if the buyer broke the contract. The buyer refused to go through with the contract and demanded his down payment back. The seller refused to return it and claimed that he was entitled to additional damages from the buyer because the damages that he had suffered were more than the amount of the down payment. Decide. [*Waters v. Key Colony East, Inc.*, 345 So. 2d 367 (Fla. App.)]
7. Kuznicki made a contract for the installation of a fire detection system by Security Safety Corp. for $498. The contract was made one night and canceled at 9:00 the next morning. Security then claimed one-third of the purchase price from Kuznicki by virtue of a provision in the contract that "in the event of cancellation of this agreement … the owner agrees to pay 33⅓ percent of the contract price, as liquidated damages." Was Security Safety entitled to recover the amount claimed? [*Security Safety Corp. v. Kuznicki*, 213 N.E.2d 866 (Mass.)]
8. FNBC is a business brokerage firm that assists in the purchase and sale of businesses. Jennings and Hennessey were independent contractors working for FNBC. They left FNBC, and FNBC sued them for breach of their contracts with FNBC. The trial court issued a permanent injunction prohibiting the former contractors from using proprietary information and the court awarded attorneys' fees under a clause in the contract that would obligate Jennings and Hennessey to indemnify FNBC against claims "brought by persons not a party to the provision." Jennings and Hennessey appealed the decision on attorneys' fees. Decide. [*FNBC v. Jennessey Group, LLC*, 759 N.W.2d 808 (Iowa App.)]
9. Melodee Lane Lingerie Co. was a tenant in a building that was protected against fire by a sprinkler and alarm system maintained by the American District Telegraph Co. (ADT). Because of the latter's fault, the controls on the system were defective and allowed the discharge of water into the building, which damaged Melodee's property. When Melodee sued ADT, its defense was that its service contract limited its liability to 10 percent of the annual service charge made to the customer. Was this limitation valid? [*Melodee Lane Lingerie Co. v. American District Telegraph Co.*, 218 N.E.2d 661 (N.Y.)]
10. JRC Trading Corp (JRC) bought computer software and hardware from Progressive Data Systems (PDS) for $167,935, which it paid in full, to track movement of its trucks with inventory and to process transactions. The purchase agreement also called for a $7,500 per year licensing fee for an 18-year period, and it stated that in the event of default PDS could "accelerate and declare all obligations of Customer as a liquidated sum." A dispute arose between the parties, and when the case was litigated the only actual contract charges owed PDS were the license fees of $7,500 for two years. The application of the liquidated damages clause would yield an additional $120,000 cash for PDS for the future fees for 16 years without any reduction for expenses or the present cash value for the not-yet-earned fees. JRC contends that actual damages were clearly ascertainable and that the liquidated damages clause was a penalty provision that should not be enforced. Progressive argued that the court must interpret the contract as written, stating that the court has no power to rewrite the contract. Decide. [*Jefferson Randolf Corp. v. PDS*, 553 S.E.2d 304 (Ga. App.)]
11. Ken Sulejmanagic, aged 19, signed up for a course in scuba diving taught by Madison at the YMCA. Before the instruction began, Ken was required to sign a form releasing Madison and the YMCA from liability for any harm that might occur. At the end of the course, Madison, Ken, and another student went into deep water. After Ken made the final dive required by the course program, Madison left him alone in the water while he took the other student for a dive. When Madison returned, Ken could not be found, and it was later determined that he had drowned. Ken's parents sued Madison and the YMCA for negligence in the performance of the teaching contract. The defendants raised the defense that the release Ken signed shielded them from liability. The plaintiffs claimed that the release was invalid. Who was correct? [*Madison v. Superior Court*, 250 Cal. Rptr. 299 (Cal. App.)]
12. Wassenaar worked for Panos under a three-year contract stating that if the contract were terminated wrongfully by Panos before the end of the three years, he would pay as damages the salary for the remaining time that the contract had to run. After three months, Panos terminated the contract, and Wassenaar sued him for pay for the balance of the contract term. Panos claimed that this amount could not be recovered because the contract provision for the payment was a void penalty. Was this provision valid? [*Wassenaar v. Panos*, 331 N.W.2d 357 (Wis.)]

13. Soden, a contractor, made a contract to build a house for Clevert. The sales contract stated that "if either party defaults in the performance of this contract," that party would be liable to the other for attorneys' fees incurred in suing the defaulter. Soden was 61 days late in completing the contract, and some of the work was defective. In a suit by the buyer against the contractor, the contractor claimed that he was not liable for the buyer's attorneys' fees because he had made only a defective performance and because "default" in the phrase quoted meant "nonperformance of the contract." Was the contractor liable for the attorneys' fees? [*Clevert v. Soden*, 400 S.E.2d 181 (Va.)]

14. Protection Alarm Co. made a contract to provide burglar alarm security for Fretwell's home. The contract stated that the maximum liability of the alarm company was the actual loss sustained or $50, whichever was the lesser, and that this provision was agreed to "as liquidated damages and not as a penalty." When Fretwell's home was burglarized, he sued for the loss of approximately $12,000, claiming that the alarm company had been negligent. The alarm company asserted that its maximum liability was $50. Fretwell claimed that this was invalid because it bore no relationship to the loss that could have been foreseen when the contract was made or that in fact "had been sustained." Decide.

15. Shepherd-Will made a contract to sell Emma Cousar:

    5 acres of land adjoining property owned by the purchaser and this being formerly land of Shepherd-Will, Inc., located on north side of Highway 223. This 5 acres to be surveyed at earliest time possible at which time plat will be attached and serve as further description on property.

    Shepherd-Will owned only one 100-acre tract of land that adjoined Emma's property. This tract had a common boundary with her property of 1,140 feet. Shepherd-Will failed to perform this contract. Emma sued for specific performance of the contract. Decide. [*Cousar v. Shepherd-Will, Inc.*, 387 S.E.2d 723 (S.C. App.)]

CPA Questions

1. Master Mfg., Inc., contracted with Accur Computer Repair Corp. to maintain Master's computer system. Master's manufacturing process depends on its computer system operating properly at all times. A liquidated damages clause in the contract provided that Accur pay $1,000 to Master for each day that Accur was late responding to a service request. On January 12, Accur was notified that Master's computer system had failed. Accur did not respond to Master's service request until January 15. If Master sues Accur under the liquidated damages provision of the contract, Master will:
    a. Win, unless the liquidated damage provision is determined to be a penalty.
    b. Win, because under all circumstances liquidated damages provisions are enforceable.
    c. Lose, because Accur's breach was *not* material.
    d. Lose, because liquidated damage provisions violate public policy (5/93, Law, #25).

2. Jones, CPA, entered into a signed contract with Foster Corp. to perform accounting and review services. If Jones repudiates the contract prior to the date performance is due to begin, which of the following is *not* correct?
    a. Foster could successfully maintain an action for breach of contract after the date performance was due to begin.
    b. Foster can obtain a judgment ordering Jones to perform.
    c. Foster could successfully maintain an action for breach of contract prior to the date performance is due to begin.
    d. Foster can obtain a judgment for the monetary damages it incurred as a result of the repudiation (5/89, Law, #35).

3. Which of the following concepts affect(s) the amount of monetary damages recoverable by the nonbreaching party when a contract is breached?

	Forseeability of damages	*Mitigation of damages*
a.	Yes	Yes
b.	Yes	No
c.	No	Yes
d.	No	No

CHAPTER 34

Bankruptcy

Learning Outcomes <<<

After studying this chapter, you should be able to

LO.1 List the requirements for the commencement of a voluntary bankruptcy case and an involuntary bankruptcy case

LO.2 Explain the procedure for the administration of a debtor's estate

LO.3 List a debtor's duties and exemptions

LO.4 Explain the significance of a discharge in bankruptcy

LO.5 Explain when a business reorganization plan or an extended-time payment plan might be used

34-1 Bankruptcy Law

What can a person or business do when overwhelmed by debts? Bankruptcy proceedings can provide temporary and sometimes permanent relief from those debts.

Bankruptcy is a statutory proceeding with detailed procedures and requirements.

34-1a The Federal Law

Bankruptcy law is based on federal statutes that have been refined over the years. In October 2005, Congress passed the Bankruptcy Abuse Prevention and Consumer Protection Act of 2005 (BAPCPA), the law that is still in effect.[1]

Jurisdiction over bankruptcy proceedings is in courts of special jurisdiction called **bankruptcy courts,** which operate under the umbrella of the federal district courts.

bankruptcy courts–court of special jurisdiction to determine bankruptcy issues.

34-1b Types of Bankruptcy Proceedings

There are three types of bankruptcy proceedings.

CPA

Liquidation or Chapter 7 Bankruptcy

Chapter 7 bankruptcy–liquidation form of bankruptcy under federal law.

liquidation–process of converting property into money whether of particular items of property or of all the assets of a business or an estate.

A **Chapter 7 bankruptcy** is one in which all of the debtor's assets (with some exemptions) will be **liquidated** to pay debts. Those debts that remain unpaid or are paid only partially are discharged, with some exceptions. The debtor who declares Chapter 7 bankruptcy begins again with a nearly clean slate.

Chapter 7 bankruptcy is available to individuals, partnerships, and corporations. However, farmers, insurance companies, savings and loans, municipalities, Small Business Administration companies, and railroads are not entitled to declare Chapter 7 bankruptcy because they are specifically governed by other statutes or specialized sections of the Bankruptcy Code.[2]

Under the BAPCPA, consumers generally cannot go directly to a Chapter 7 liquidation bankruptcy because they must demonstrate that they do not have the means to repay the debts before they can do a Chapter 7 liquidation.[3] The means test, which is discussed later, considers the disposable income that is available after the bankruptcy court has deducted allowable expenses that are listed as part of the means section of the BAPCPA, including items such as health insurance and child support.

CPA

Reorganization or Chapter 11 Bankruptcy

Chapter 11 bankruptcy–reorganization form of bankruptcy under federal law.

Chapter 11 bankruptcy is a way for a debtor to reorganize and continue a business with protection from overwhelming debts and without the requirement of liquidation. Abercrombie & Fitch, Fuddruckers, the Chicago Cubs, Chrysler, General Motors, the Sharper Image, United Airlines, and Delta are all examples of companies that have gone through Chapter 11 bankruptcies. Stockbrokers, however, are not eligible for Chapter 11 bankruptcy.

[1] The act is codified at 11 U.S.C. §101 *et seq.*

[2] For example, the Small Business Investment Act governs the insolvency of small business investment companies, 11 U.S.C. §109(b). Municipalities' bankruptcies are governed by Chapter 9 of the Bankruptcy Code, and farmers' bankruptcies are covered under Chapter 11. Following the 2008 market collapse, there were a series of municipal bankruptcies because of excessive debt and pension obligations.

[3] 11 U.S.C. §707(C)(2)(a). There are exceptions to the requirements of establishing no means, such as those who incurred their debts while on active military service.

ETHICS & THE LAW

Bankruptcy Records

According to **http://www.bankruptcydata.com**, the following are the largest bankruptcies in the history of the United States:

Company	*Date*	*Amount*
Lehman Brothers	09/15/2008	$640,000,000 billion
Washington Mutual (WaMu)	09/26/2008	$327,900,000 billion
WorldCom	07/21/2002	$103,900,000 billion
General Motors	06/01/2009	$91,000,000 billion
CIT	11/01/2009	$80,400,000 billion
Enron	12/02/2001	$65,500,000 billion
Conseco	12/02/2002	$61,300,000 billion
MF Global	10/31/2011	$41,000,000 billion
Chrysler	04/20/2009	$39,300,000 billion
Thornburg Mortgage	05/05/2009	$36,500,000 billion

Total bankruptcy filings in the United States from 2008 to 2014 were as follows. Note the spike following 2008 because of the economic crisis.

Year	*Total*	*Nonbusiness*	*Business*
2014	936,795	909,812	26,983
2013	1,071,932	1,038,720	33,212
2012	1,221,091	1,181,016	40,075
2011	1,410,653	1,362,847	47,806
2010	1,593,081	1,536,799	56,282
2009	1,473,675	1,412,838	60,837
2008	1,117,641	1,074,108	43,533

Is there an ethical component to declaring bankruptcy? For example, actor Gary Busey's agent referred to bankruptcy as a business strategy. What are the risks of using bankruptcy as a business strategy?

CPA

Chapter 13 Bankruptcy or Payment Plans or Consumer Debt Adjustment Plans

Chapter 13 bankruptcy–proceeding of consumer debt readjustment plan bankruptcy.

Chapter 13 of the federal Bankruptcy Code provides consumers an individual form of reorganization. Chapter 13 works with consumer debtors to develop a plan to repay debt. To be eligible for **Chapter 13 bankruptcy,** the individual must owe unsecured debts of less than $383,175 and secured debts of less than $1,149.525 and have regular income.[4] Chapter 13 plays an expanded role in bankruptcy because reforms require debtors with the means to pay their debts to go first into Chapter 13 bankruptcy rather than automatically declaring Chapter 7 bankruptcy.

34-2 How Bankruptcy Is Declared

Bankruptcy can be declared in different ways. The federal Bankruptcy Code spells out the requirements and process for declaration.

CPA

34-2a Declaration of Voluntary Bankruptcy

voluntary bankruptcy–proceeding in which the debtor files the petition for relief.

A **voluntary bankruptcy** is begun when the debtor files a petition with the bankruptcy court. A joint petition may be filed by a husband and wife. When a voluntary case is

[4] 11 U.S.C. §109(e). These amounts were automatically increased in 2013 and are in effect for three years (through April 2016).

begun, the debtor must file a schedule of current income and current expenditures unless the court excuses this filing.

means test–new standard under the Reform Act that requires the court to find that the debtor does not have the means to repay creditors; goes beyond the past requirement of petitions being granted on the simple assertion of the debtor saying, "I have debts."

A court can dismiss an individual debtor's (consumer's) petition for abuse if the debtor does not satisfy the **means test,** which measures the debtor's ability to pay by computing the debtor's disposable income. Only those debtors who fall below their state's median disposable income will be able to continue in a Chapter 7 proceeding. Individual debtors who meet the means test are required to go into Chapter 13 bankruptcy because they have not qualified for Chapter 7 bankruptcy. The formula for applying the means test is as follows:

Debtor's current monthly income less
Allowable expenses under the Bankruptcy Code = Disposable income × 60

The debtor commits bankruptcy abuse if this number is not less than the lower of the following:

- 25 percent of the debtor's unsecured claims or $7,475, whichever is greater; or
- $12,475

A finding of abuse means that the debtor's Chapter 7 voluntary petition is dismissed.[5]

Under the BAPCPA, the bankruptcy judge also has the discretion to order the debtor's lawyer to reimburse the trustee for costs and attorney's fees and to assess a civil penalty against the lawyer if the court finds that the lawyer has not acted in good faith in filing the debtor's bankruptcy petition.[6] Lawyers are required to declare themselves (in public ads as well as in any individual meetings with clients) to be "debt relief agencies" or state that they "help people file for relief under the Bankruptcy Code." Debt relief organizations must disclose that bankruptcy may be part of what is required for relief from their debts. Lawyers who advertise their credit/bankruptcy expertise are subject to the laws and regulations that apply to debt relief agencies. If the agency/lawyer advises them to do something that causes the court to declare that there has been bankruptcy abuse, the lawyer/debt relief agency is responsible as well. As part of their role as debt counselors, lawyers are prohibited from advising clients to undertake more debt in contemplation of filing bankruptcy.[7]

Debtors are required to undergo credit counseling (from an approved nonprofit credit counseling agency) within the 180 days prior to declaring a bankruptcy. In addition, the court applies the means test described earlier to determine whether the debtor qualifies for bankruptcy.[8]

There is significant disagreement among the bankruptcy courts about the meaning of "projected income." The disagreement results from the differing situations of the debtors. **For Example,** how do courts deal with debtors who are about to experience a large drop in disposable income? And do courts then consider what happens when debtors'

[5] 11 U.S.C. §707(b). Debtor using bankruptcy to stall a lawsuit who filled out the bankruptcy forms inaccurately was held to have acted in bad faith. In re *Crest By The Sea*, 522 B.R. 540 (D.N.J. 2014). Debtors who failed to disclose their income from a rental property were guilty of bad faith. In re *Fox*, 521 B.R. 520 (D. Md. 2004).
[6] 11 U.S.C. §707(b)(4).
[7] 11 U.S.C. §§526-528. *Milavetz, Gallop & Milavetz, P.A. v. U.S.*, 559 U.S. 229 (2010).
[8] 11 U.S.C. §109(h)(2). There are exceptions to the counseling requirements; for example, active military duty, disability, and emergencies. 11 U.S.C. 111(a) is the counseling provision. The counseling must be completed prior to filing for bankruptcy or the petition can be dismissed, In re *Alvarado*, 496 B.R. 200 (N.D. Cal. 2013). However, being in prison is not an excuse for not going through counseling, and the petition may be dismissed. In re *Gordon*, 467 B.R. 639 (W.D. Ky. 2012) and In re *Kerr*, 2014 WL 6747112 (N.D. Ohio 2014).

incomes are expected to go up? If the projected income test used is applied, the bankruptcy could be dismissed. Debtors and creditors take different positions depending on which way the income goes, and the courts continue to debate the definition of projected income.[9]

CASE SUMMARY

Lawyer/Debtor in the Hoosegow: Still Eligible for Chapter 13?

FACTS: Topous obtained a judgment against Clarence Kenyon Gomery, a lawyer (Debtor), and his law firm, Gomery and Associates, PLLC. That case arose from Mr. Gomery's representation of Topous in various business transactions, including the purchase of property referred to as the Old Mitchell Creek Golf Course. Topous alleged that Mr. Gomery drafted an Operating Agreement creating a limited liability company, T & G Real Estate Development, LLC, to purchase and hold the Mitchell Creek property. Although Topous paid the full purchase price to acquire the property, Mr. Gomery defrauded Topous in the transaction by surreptitiously giving himself a one-half ownership interest in T & G in the Operating Agreement he drafted. The jury awarded ownership of the Mitchell Creek property to Topous and ordered Mr. Gomery to pay Topous damages in the net amount of $11,622.22 and imposed sanctions for Frivolous Defense and for Spoliation of Evidence (see Chapter 2) against Mr. Gomery and his law firm, jointly and severally, for $314,629.27.

Unable to pay the judgment, Mr. Gomery filed a voluntary petition under Chapter 13 on April 2, 2014.

In July 2014, Mr. Gomery was arrested and charged with solicitation of murder. Detective Gomez testified about a recorded conversation between Mr. Gomery and Dale Fisher. During the course of the recorded conversation, Mr. Gomery offered Mr. Fisher $20,000 to kill Christopher K. Cooke, the attorney who represented Topous. Detective Gomez also testified that Mr. Gomery paid Mr. Fisher $1,000 during the recorded conversation, purportedly to purchase the weapon that would be used in committing the crime. Mr. Gomery is currently incarcerated and awaiting trial on these criminal charges.

Mr. Gomery seeks confirmation of his Chapter 13 Plan. The Trustee and Topous have objected to the Plan on the grounds that the Plan is not feasible, and that neither the Plan nor the petition was filed in good faith. The Trustee has also requested that Mr. Gomery's case be converted to Chapter 7 due to the Debtor's lack of good faith.

DECISION: The Debtor's schedules failed to disclose significant and valuable assets. For example, JACCK Enterprises, LLC, in which the Debtor had an interest, appeared on the Debtor's own individual tax returns for 2009 through 2013, along with the returns of JACCK itself. Those returns reflect his income from JACCK and show him as having a one-half ownership interest in the LLC. But he did not disclose JACCK.

The Debtor's Schedules did not disclose that he owned any firearms.

Chapter 13 relief is reserved for the 'honest but unfortunate debtor.'

The court found that the Debtor had not been fair in his treatment of his creditors and was not been forthright in his dealings with the Trustee, the creditors, and this Bankruptcy Court. Under the circumstances, the court found that the Debtor had not acted in good faith.

The Court held that conversion to Chapter 7, which would allow these matters to be investigated by a Chapter 7 trustee, was in the best interests of creditors in this case.

The Debtor offered no explanation, let alone evidence, of the source of the funds he proposed to use to make the $100 monthly payments required under his proposed Plan. The Debtor was incarcerated at the time of the bankruptcy proceedings and had offered no evidence of any current income. Although the Debtor's Plan proposed increasing his payments in the future, the Debtor's attorney admitted that it is unlikely that the Debtor will resume his legal practice in the future. Because the Debtor had no current income, and limited prospects for income in the future, the Court concluded that the Debtor is not eligible to be a debtor under Chapter 13. The Debtor's case was converted to a Chapter 7 proceeding. **[In re *Gomery*, 523 B.R. 773 (W.D. Mich. 2015)]**

[9] In re *Turner*, 425 B.R. 918 (S.D. Ga. 2010); In re *Hilton*, 395 B.R. 433 (E.D. Wis. 2008); In re *Anstett*, 383 B.R. 380 (D.S.C. 2008); In re *Colclasure*, 383 B.R. 463 (E.D. Ark. 2008); and In re *Justice*, 418 B.R. 342 (W.D. Mo. 2009).

CPA

34-2b Declaration of Involuntary Bankruptcy

Eligibility

involuntary bankruptcy– proceeding in which a creditor or creditors file the petition for relief with the bankruptcy court.

An **involuntary bankruptcy** is begun when creditors file a petition with the bankruptcy court. An involuntary case may be commenced against any individual, partnership, or corporation, except those excluded from filing voluntary petitions. Nonprofit corporations are also exempt from involuntary proceedings.[10]

CPA

Number and Claims of Petitioning Creditors

If there are 12 or more creditors, at least 3 of those creditors whose unsecured and undisputed claims total $15,325 or more must sign the involuntary petition.[11] If there are fewer than 12 creditors, excluding employees or insiders (that is, the debtor's relatives,

THINKING THINGS THROUGH

Means Test Justifying the End of Debt

The following excerpt is a hypothetical case an experienced bankruptcy attorney worked through to illustrate the application of the means test.

The Brokes, a married couple in their early 40s, have two children in private schools. They are residents of Memphis, Shelby County, Tennessee; their annual gross income is $86,496. Like many debtors, the Brokes lost their home following an unsuccessful Chapter 13 case three years ago. They now rent a house for $2,000 a month. They owe back federal taxes in the amount of $9,000. They have secured debt on two cars with remaining balances of $10,000 and $6,000 and unsecured, consumer debt totaling $28,000. They desire to seek relief under Chapter 7 of the Bankruptcy Code.

The Brokes' gross monthly income is $7,208. After deducting taxes and other mandatory payroll deductions of $1,509, the couple has $5,699 in monthly income. The means test requires several additional deductions from the Brokes' gross monthly income. Section 707(b)(A)(2)(ii) provides a deduction for living and housing expenses using National Standards and Local Standards and additional Internal Revenue Service (IRS) figures. Allowable living expenses for a family of four in Ura and Ima Brokes' income bracket, based on national standards, total $1,564, while housing and utility figures for Shelby County, Tennessee, allow $1,354. In addition, there are allowable expenses for transportation. Based on IRS figures, the Brokes can subtract national ownership costs of $475 for the first car and $338 for the second, as well as regional operating and public transportation costs of $242 and $336, respectively. They can also deduct their reasonably necessary health insurance costs, here the sum of $600, and $250 a month for private school tuition. Subtracting all of these figures from the Brokes' monthly income leaves $540.

Under §707(b)(2)(A)(iii), the Brokes can subtract payments on secured debt. The amount contractually due on their two automobiles over the next 60 months is $16,000. After dividing this total by 60 and rounding to the nearest dollar, the monthly allowable deduction for secured debt is $267. Subtracting this amount from $540 leaves $273.

Next come priority claim deductions. The Brokes are not subject to any child support or alimony claims, but they do owe $9,000 in back taxes. Again, dividing this amount by 60 yields a deductible amount of $150. Subtracting this from $273 leaves $123 in disposable monthly income. This figure would be multiplied by 60, amounting to a total of $7,380 in disposable income over the five-year period. Abuse is thus statutorily presumed because the debtors' current monthly income reduced by allowable amounts is not less than either $7,000 (25 percent of their nonpriority unsecured claims of $28,000) or $6,000. The Brokes' Chapter 7 case will therefore be dismissed (or they will be allowed voluntarily to convert their Chapter 7 case to a case under Chapter 13).

Does the means test make it more difficult for debtors to declare bankruptcy?*

*Robert J. Landry III and Nancy Hisey Mardis, "Consumer Bankruptcy Reform: Debtors' Prison without Bars or 'Just Desserts' for Deadbeats?" 36 *Golden Gate U. L Rev.* 91 (2006). Reprinted with permission.

[10] 11 U.S.C. §303(a). In re *C.W. Min. Co.*, 431 B.R. 307 (Utah 2009). These amounts are adjusted periodically by statutory formulas.

[11] 11 U.S.C. §303.

partners, directors, and controlling persons), any creditor whose unsecured claim is at least $15,325 may sign the petition. In the case of involuntary consumer petitions, there is disagreement as to whether the debtor will still be required to complete the credit counseling requirement prior to the granting of the automatic stay.

bona fide–in good faith; without any fraud or deceit.

If a creditor holds security for a claim, only the amount of the claim in excess of the value of the security is counted. The holder of a claim that is the subject of a **bona fide** dispute may not be counted as a petitioning creditor.[12] **For Example,** David, a CPA, is an unsecured creditor of Arco Company for $16,000. Arco has a total of 10 creditors, all of whom are unsecured. Arco has not paid any of the creditors for three months. The debtor has fewer than 12 creditors. Any one of the creditors may file the petition if the unsecured portion of the amount due that creditor is at least $15,325. Because David is owed $16,000 in unsecured debts, he may file the petition alone.

CPA

Grounds for Relief for Involuntary Case

The mere filing of an involuntary case petition does not result in an order of relief. The debtor may contest the bankruptcy petition. If the debtor does not contest the petition, the court will enter an order of relief if at least one of the following grounds exists: (1) The debtor is generally not paying debts as they become due or (2) within 120 days before the filing of the petition, a custodian has been appointed for the debtor's property.

CPA

34-2c Automatic Stay

automatic stay–order to prevent creditors from taking action such as filing suits or seeking foreclosure against the debtor.

Just the filing of either a voluntary or an involuntary petition operates as an **automatic stay,** which prevents creditors from taking action, such as filing suits or foreclosure actions, against the debtor.[13] The stay freezes all creditors in their filing date positions so that no one creditor gains an advantage over other creditors. This automatic stay ends when the bankruptcy case is closed or dismissed (for example, on a finding of abuse by the debtor who has failed to survive the means-to-pay test) or when the debtor is granted a discharge. An automatic stay means that all activity by creditors with respect to collection must stop, with some exceptions incorporated for child support and other family support issues. All litigation with the debtor is halted, and any judgments in place cannot be executed.[14]

34-2d If the Creditors Are Wrong: Rights of Debtor in an Involuntary Bankruptcy

If an involuntary petition is dismissed other than by consent of all petitioning creditors and the debtor, the court may award costs, reasonable attorney fees, or damages to the debtor. The damages are those that were caused by taking possession of the debtor's property. The debtor may also recover damages against any creditor who filed the petition in bad faith.

Figure 34-1 provides a summary of the requirements for declaration of bankruptcy and the standards for relief.

[12] 11 U.S.C. §303(b)(1). *Farmers & Merchants State Bank v. Turner,* 518 B.R. 642 (N.D. Fla. 2014).
[13] 11 U.S.C. §362. In re *Taggart,* 522 B.R. 627 (D. Or. 2014). Proceeding with the foreclosure on a home after a stay is entered is a violation of the stay order. In re *Betchan,* 524 B.R. 830 (E.D. Wash. 2015).
[14] In re *Hill,* 523 B.R. 704 (D. Mont. 2014).

FIGURE 34-1 Declaration of Bankruptcy

	Chapter 7	Chapter 11	Chapter 13
Trustee	Yes	No	Yes
Eligible persons: Individuals Partnerships Corporations	 Yes (consumer restrictions) Yes Yes	 Yes (individual restrictions) Yes Yes	 Yes (consumer restrictions) No No
Voluntary	Yes	Yes	Yes
Involuntary	Yes, except for farmers and nonprofits**	Yes, except for farmers and nonprofits	No
Exemptions	S & L's, credit unions, SBA, railroads, municipalities	Same as Chapter 7 plus stockbrokers*	Only individuals allowed
Requirements-Voluntary	Debts; means test applies to consumers	Debts; means test applies to consumers	Income plus <$383,175 unsecured debt; <$1,149,525 secured debt
Requirements-Involuntary	<12 = 1/$15,325 ≥12 = 3/$15,325	<12 = 1/$15,325 ≥12 = 3/$15,325	N/A

*Railroads are eligible
**Chapter 9 — Municipalities; Chapter 12 — Farmers

34-3 Administration of the Bankruptcy Estate

The administration of the bankruptcy estate varies according to the type of bankruptcy declared. This section of the chapter focuses on the process for liquidation or Chapter 7 bankruptcy. Figure 34-2 provides a flowchart view of the Chapter 7 liquidation process.

34-3a The Order of Relief

order of relief–the order from the bankruptcy judge that starts the protection for the debtor; when the order of relief is entered by the court, the debtor's creditors must stop all proceedings and work through the bankruptcy court to recover debts (if possible). Court finding that creditors have met the standards for bankruptcy petitions.

The **order of relief** is granted by the bankruptcy court and is the procedural step required for the case to proceed in bankruptcy court.[15] An order of relief is entered automatically in a voluntary case and in an involuntary case when those filing the petition have established that the debtor is unable to pay his, her, or its debts as they become due. In consumer cases and Chapter 11 cases that involve an individual, the bankruptcy court must apply the means test to determine whether the individual is eligible for declaring bankruptcy or whether there has been an abuse of the bankruptcy court and system.

34-3b List of Creditors

It is the debtor's responsibility to furnish the bankruptcy court with a list of creditors. Although imposing the responsibility for disclosing debts on the debtor may not seem to be effective, the debtor has an incentive for full disclosure. Those debts not disclosed by the debtor will not be discharged in bankruptcy.

[15] 11 U.S.C. §301.

SPORTS & ENTERTAINMENT LAW

From Millions to Nada: Celebrity Bankruptcies

- Michael Vick, who was one of the highest paid NFL players, filed for bankruptcy in 2008, from prison. Mr. Vick could not afford to pay his bills as well as the fines that were imposed when he entered a guilty plea on charges related to a dog-fighting operation. The fines were not discharged, but he was relieved of his other debts related to his personal property.
- MC Hammer, the "Hammer Time" mega star of the early 1990s, declared bankruptcy in 1996 with $9.6 million in assets and $13.7 million in debts. Mr. Hammer's problem was that he had salary costs of $500,000 per month in order to maintain his entourage.
- Kim Basinger, actress, had to declare bankruptcy after settling a contract suit by Main Line Pictures for $3.8 million for backing out of a movie deal with the company.
- Willie Nelson, Country Western singer, declared bankruptcy in 1990, a necessary result of his owing $16.7 million in taxes because the IRS won its case on Nelson's tax shelters, which were fraudulent. Mr. Nelson also said that he had too many hangers-on that he was supporting. Mr. Nelson was not able to get all of his tax debt discharged because not all tax debts are fully dischargeable and there is no discharge allowed for tax debts that resulted from fraud.
- Walt Disney declared bankruptcy in Kansas City before he moved to Hollywood. Mr. Disney ran a small animation studio there and when his only customer went bankrupt, Mr. Disney tried to continue on, living in his office and eating only canned beans. He eventually gave up, declared bankruptcy, and moved to Hollywood, where he founded an empire.
- Sir Elton John is the quintessential profligate spender whose purchases landed him in bankruptcy. By the time he declared bankruptcy in 2002, Sir Elton had credit card charges of $400,000 per month. His total debt per month was $2,000,000.
- Sinbad, the comedian, failed to pay taxes on his earnings from *Jingle All the Way.* California's Department of Revenue filed a $2.5 million lien on his home and he and his wife declared bankruptcy shortly after in 2009.
- Meat Loaf, singer, declared bankruptcy following a lawsuit filed by a former partner who wrote songs with him.
- Dionne Warwick, singer, filed for bankruptcy because of $10 million in back taxes and negligent financial management.

What are the causes of bankruptcy? What advice would you give to celebrities and athletes about management of their income and bills?

34-3c Trustee in Bankruptcy

trustee in bankruptcy–impartial person elected to administer the debtor's estate.

The **trustee in bankruptcy** is elected by the creditors. The court or the U.S. trustee will appoint an interim trustee if the creditors do not elect a trustee.

The trustee automatically becomes the owner of all of the debtor's property in excess of the property to which the debtor is entitled under exemption laws. The trustee holds all of the rights formerly owned by the debtor.

CPA

34-3d The Bankrupt's Estate

All of the debtor's property, with certain exceptions discussed later, is included in the *bankrupt's estate.* Property inherited by the debtor within six months after the filing of the petition also passes to the trustee.

preferences–transfers of property by a debtor to one or more specific creditors to enable these creditors to obtain payment for debts owed.

In many cases, when a debtor knows that insolvency is a problem and bankruptcy is imminent, the debtor attempts to hang onto property or reputation by making transfers of assets to friends, relatives, and creditors. However, trustees have the authority to set aside or void (1) transfers by the debtor that a creditor holding a valid claim under state law could have avoided at the commencement of the bankruptcy case, (2) **preferences,** that is, transfers of property by the debtor to a creditor, the effect of which is to enable

FIGURE 34-2 Anatomy of Bankruptcy Case

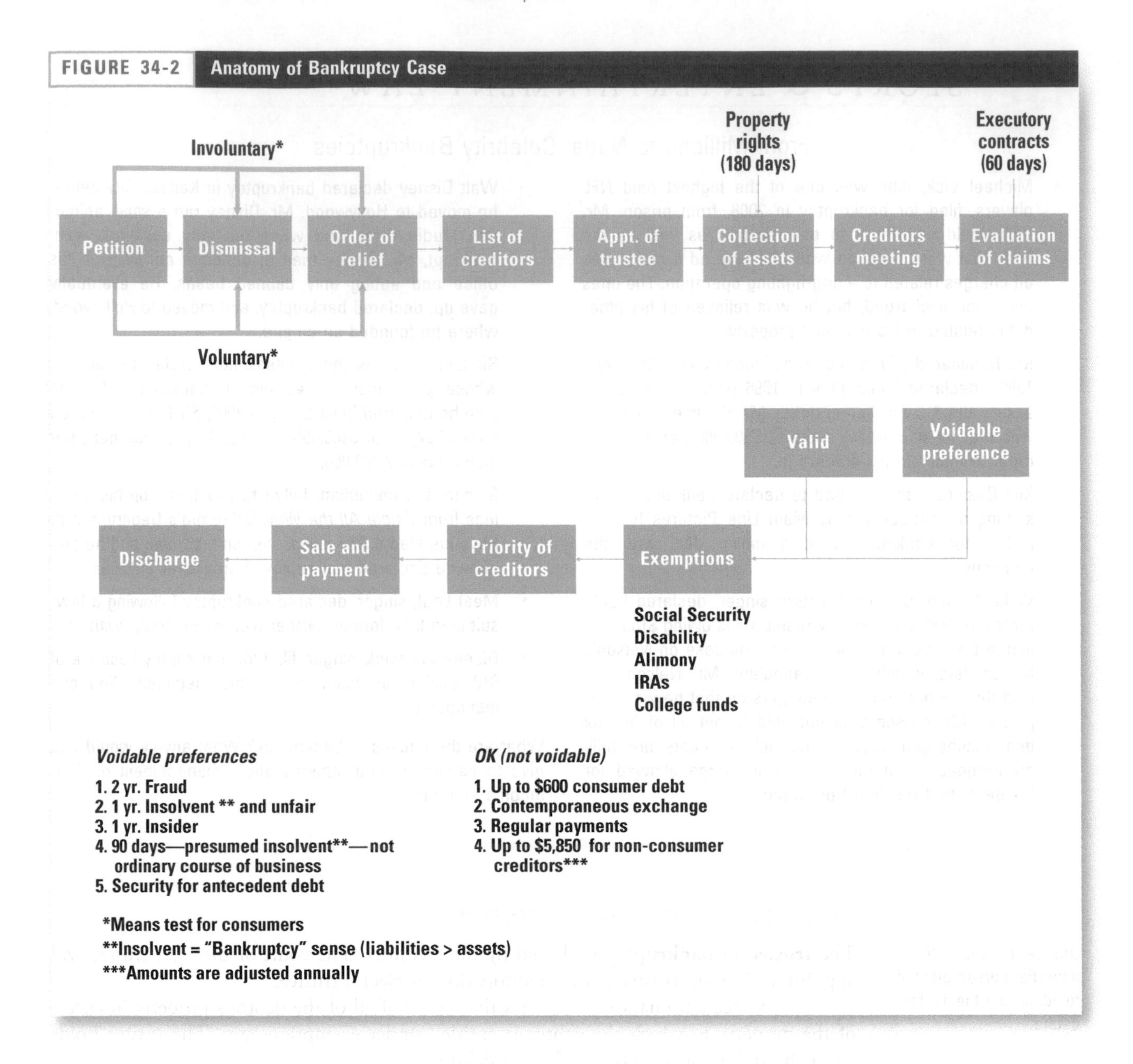

the creditor to obtain payment of a higher percentage of the creditor's claim than the creditor would have received if the debtor's assets had been liquidated in bankruptcy, and (3) statutory liens that became effective against the debtor at the commencement of the bankruptcy.

34-3e Voidable Preferences

A debtor may not transfer property to prevent creditors from satisfying their legal claims. The trustee may void any such transfer, known as *a fraudulent transfer*, made or obligation incurred by the debtor within one year of bankruptcy when the debtor's actual intent was to hinder, delay, or defraud creditors by doing so.

The trustee may also void certain transfers of property made by a debtor merely because their effect is to make the debtor insolvent or to reduce the debtor's assets to an unreasonably low amount.[16]

CPA

The Insolvent Debtor

insolvency–excess of debts and liabilities over assets, or inability to pay debts as they mature.

balance sheet test–comparison of assets to liabilities made to determine solvency.

A debtor is insolvent for purposes of determining voidable transfers when the total fair value of all of the debtor's assets does not exceed the debts owed by the debtor. This test for **insolvency** under voidable transfers is commonly called the **balance sheet test** because it is merely a comparison of assets to liabilities without considering whether the debtor will be able to meet future obligations as they become due. The debtor is presumed to be insolvent in the 90 days prior to declaration of bankruptcy.

Preferential Transfers

preferential transfers–certain transfers of money or security interests in the time frame just prior to bankruptcy that can be set aside if voidable.

A transfer of property by the debtor to a creditor may be set aside as **preferential transfers** and the property recovered by the debtor's trustee in bankruptcy if (1) the transfer was made to pay a debt incurred at some earlier time, (2) the transfer was made when the debtor was insolvent and within 90 days before the filing of the bankruptcy petition, and (3) the transfer resulted in the creditor receiving more than the creditor would have received in a liquidation of the debtor's estate. A debtor is presumed to be insolvent on and during the 90 days immediately preceding the date of the filing of the bankruptcy petition.[17]

insider–full-time corporate employee or a director or their relatives.

Transfers made to **insiders** within the 12 months prior to the filing of the petition may be set aside.[18] **For Example,** if a building contractor transferred title to one of his model homes to the company accountant just six months before declaring bankruptcy, the transfer would be a preferential one that would be set aside. However, a transfer by an insider to a noninsider is not subject to recovery by the trustee. The sale of that same model home to a good faith buyer just three days before bankruptcy would be valid. **For Example,** the trustee in the Bernie Madoff case sought to set aside several transfers made to companies and individuals just prior to the time Mr. Madoff admitted that he had an insolvent, $50 billion Ponzi scheme. The trustee used several of the voidable preferences theories to seek a return of funds.

The trustee may not set aside certain transfers by a debtor as preferences. A transaction for present consideration, such as a cash sale, is not set aside.[19] A payment by a debtor in the ordinary course of business, such as the payment of a utility bill, will not be set aside. Under the prior bankruptcy law, a payment was not a voidable preference if it was made in the ordinary course of business and it was made according to industry terms and practices. Nonconsumer debt payments that have a value of less than $6,225 are not subject to the voidable preference standards. The expectation is that the time and effort spent by bankruptcy trustees and courts will be reduced because of the minimum amount required before a challenge can be made. In nonconsumer debts, transfers of less than $6,225 within the voidable preference period are not considered voidable preferences.

[16] 11 U.S.C. §548.

[17] 11 U.S.C. §547(f).

[18] 11 U.S.C. §547(b)(4)(B). In re *First Pay, Inc.*, 773 F.3d 583 (4th Cir. 2014).

[19] Payments made 50.29 days after the invoice date were not made in the ordinary course of business. In re *Quebecor World (USA), Inc.*, 518 B.R. 757 (S.D.N.Y. 2014).

CASE SUMMARY

The Honda Pilot Preference

FACTS: On July 3, 2013, Scott and Nicole Conklin (Debtors) entered into a retail installment contract with Hannigan Auto Sales, LLC, in Emmett, Idaho, to purchase a Honda Pilot. CAC agreed to finance Debtors' purchase in the amount $12,871.20. Debtors took possession of the Honda the same day.

CAC thereafter mailed a "Report of Sale and Application for Certificate of Title" to Gem County. The Application was received by Gem County on August 2, 2013, as is evidenced by a date stamp appearing on the Application. However, while the certificate of title issued for the Honda by the State of Idaho properly listed CAC as the "lienholder," it indicated that CAC's lien was "recorded" on August 6, 2013. August 2, 2013, is 30 days after July 3, 2013, the day Debtors purchased and took possession of the Honda.

Debtors filed their Chapter 7 case on September 4, 2013. On October 21, 2013, the Trustee commenced this adversary proceeding against CAC contending that because CAC's security interest in the Honda was not perfected until August 6, as evidenced by the recording date on the title, that security interest was a voidable preference.

The discrepancy between the date the Application was received by Gem County, and the lien recording date listed in the title record for the Honda occurred when the information was transmitted by Gem County to the Department to create the certificate of title. Legal Counsel for the Conklins made a request to have the date changed and, thereafter, the date in the electronic records for the Honda title certificate was changed to reflect a recording date of August 2, instead of August 6, 2013. A certified copy of a printout of the electronic record of title for the Honda, which shows August 2, 2013, as the "recorded" date for CAC's lien, was submitted in evidence.

Both parties moved for summary judgment.

DECISION: Currently under Idaho Code, there is a twenty (20) day time frame from the date of sale in which a lender can perfect a security interest. Federal bankruptcy code was amended to allow a thirty (30) day time frame to perfect a lien.

Applying the revised Idaho statute, the Court concluded Debtors and CAC had shown that the lien on the Honda was perfected under Idaho law on August 2, 2013, the 30th day after Debtors received possession of the Honda. Therefore, under §547(c)(3), Debtors' transfer of the security interest to CAC is protected from avoidance. Summary judgment for the Debtors. **[In re *Conklin*, 511 B.R. 688 (D. Idaho 2014)]**

Self-Settled Trust

Under the Reform Act, the trustee has the ability to set aside the transfer of property into a "self-settled" (a self-created personal trust) any time within the past 10 years if the trustee can establish that the trust was created with actual intent to hinder, delay, or defraud existing or future creditors.[20] This section was added to address the problem of the many assets of individuals being in personal trusts for which those individuals serve as trustees.

34-3f Proof of Claim

claim–creditor's right to payment.

proof of claim–written statement, signed by the creditor or an authorized representative, setting forth any claim made against the debtor and the basis for it.

Bankruptcy law regulates the manner in which creditors present their claims and the way in which the debtor's assets are distributed in payment of these claims.

After the debtor has filed a list of creditors, the court then sends a notice of the bankruptcy proceedings to listed creditors. The creditors who wish to participate in the distribution of the proceeds of the liquidation of the debtor's estate must file a proof of claim. A **claim** is a right to payment, whether liquidated (certain and not disputed), unliquidated, contingent, unmatured, disputed, legal, or equitable. A **proof of claim** is a written statement, signed by the creditor or an authorized representative, setting forth any claim

[20] 11 U.S.C. §548(e).

made against the debtor and the basis for it. It must ordinarily be filed within 90 days after the first meeting of creditors.[21] A creditor must file within that time even though the trustee in bankruptcy in fact knows of the existence of the creditor's claim.

CPA 34-3g Priority of Claims

Creditors who hold security for payment, such as a lien or a mortgage on the debtor's property, are less affected by the debtor's bankruptcy. Secured creditors may enforce their security interest to obtain payment of their claims up to the value of their security, the collateral in which they hold an interest. **For Example,** suppose that First Bank holds a mortgage on a company's office building. The mortgage amount is $750,000. The building is sold for $700,000. First Bank is entitled to the $700,000 from the sale. For the remaining portion of the debt, First Bank drops down in priority to wait with the other unsecured creditors for its remaining $50,000. Unsecured creditors with unsecured debts have a statutory order of priority following the secured creditors' rights in their collateral as outlined in the list that appears next.[22] Once the bottom of the priority list is reached, any remaining unsecured creditors share on *a pro rata* basis any remaining assets of the debtor. Any balance remaining after all creditors have been paid goes to the debtor. However, in 98 to 99 percent of all bankruptcies, no unsecured creditors receive any payments, so it is highly unlikely that the debtor would ever receive anything from the bankruptcy litigation of the debtor's property and funds.

The list that follows is the statutory one for priorities of the unsecured creditors following the payment to any secured creditors from the debtors' pledged property:

1. Allowed claims for debts to a spouse, former spouse, or child of the debtor and for alimony to, maintenance for, or support of such spouse or child (that were obligations at the time of the filing of the bankruptcy petition).[23]
2. Costs and expenses of administration of the bankruptcy case, including fees to trustees, attorneys, and accountants, and the reasonable expenses of creditors in recovering property transferred or concealed by the debtor.
3. Claims arising in the ordinary course of a debtor's business or financial affairs after the commencement of the case but before the order of relief (involuntary).
4. Claims for wages, salaries, or commissions, including vacation, severance, or sick leave pay earned within 180 days before the filing of the petition or the date of cessation of the debtor's business, whichever occurred first, limited, however, to $12,475 for each person.
5. Claims arising for contributions to employee benefit plans, based on services rendered within 180 days before the filing of the petition or when the debtor ceased doing business, whichever occurred first; the maximum amount is $12,475. Payments of key-employee retention plans are not permitted unless the plans are "essential" to keeping the key employee at the company that is in bankruptcy. Proving that they are essential requires the key employee actually to have a "bona fide" offer of employment from another company. In addition, there are limits on how much can be paid under key-employee retention plans.
6. Farm producers (up to $6,150) and fishers against debtors who operate grain storage facilities or fish storage or processing facilities, up to $6,150 per claim.

[21] 11 U.S.C. §302(c).

[22] 11 U.S.C. §507(1)–(6). Secured creditors' priority is determined by the priority rules related to Article 9, liens, and mortgages. In re *Restivo Auto Body, Inc.*, 772 F.3d 168 (4th Cir. 2014).

[23] In re *Coon*, 522 B.R. 357 (M.D. Ala. 2014).

7. Claims by consumer creditors, not to exceed $2,775 for each claimant, arising from the purchase of consumer goods or services when such property or services were not delivered or provided.
8. Certain taxes and penalties due government, such as income and property taxes (there are time limits, for example, three years is the general time limit, with exceptions for fraud).
9. All other unsecured creditors.
10. Tort claims for death or personal injury resulting from operation of a vehicle or vessel while intoxicated from alcohol, drug, and other substances.
11. Remainder (if any) to debtor.

Each claim must be paid in full before any lower claim is paid anything. If a class of claims cannot be paid in full, the claims in that case are paid on *a pro rata* basis. **For Example,** suppose that following the payment of all secured creditors, $10,000 is left to be distributed. The accountants who performed work on the bankruptcy are owed $15,000, and the lawyers who worked on it are owed $10,000. Because there is not enough to pay two parties in the same priority ranking, the $10,000 is split proportionately. The accountants will receive 15/25, or 3/5, of the $10,000, or $6,000, and the lawyers will receive 10/25, or 2/5, of the $10,000, or $4,000.

34-4 Debtor's Duties and Exemptions

Bankruptcy law imposes certain duties on the debtor and provides for specific exemptions of some of the debtor's estate from the claims of creditors.

34-4a Debtor's Duties

A debtor must file with the court a list of creditors, a schedule of assets and liabilities, and a statement of her financial affairs. The debtor must also appear for examination under oath at the first meeting of creditors.

CPA 34-4b Debtor's Exemptions

A debtor is permitted to claim certain property of the estate in the trustee's possession and keep it free from claims of creditors. Exemptions are provided under federal law, but state laws also provide for exemptions. Examples of exempt property from the federal code include wedding rings, property used to earn a living, one VCR, and one car. New York exemptions include "all stoves in the home, one sewing machine, the family Bible, a pew in a public house of worship, enough food for sixty days, a wedding ring, and a watch not exceeding thirty-five dollars in value."[24] California exempts tools of the trade and the family cemetery plot.[25]

The principal exemptions provided by the Bankruptcy Code are the debtor's interest in real or personal property used as a residence.[26] The homestead exemption is now greatly limited and, in effect, preempts state law on this debtor exemption. Debtors are required to have lived in the home for two years prior to bankruptcy, and the amount

[24] N.Y. C.P.L.R. §5205 (2014).
[25] Cal. Civ. Proc. Code §704.010-704.210 (2014).
[26] A married couple gets a single homestead exemption.

of the homestead exemption would be limited to $155,675.[27] To be able to use a higher state homestead exemption, the debtor must have lived in the home for 1,215 days (40 months).[28] Labeled as the most flagrant abuse of the existing bankruptcy system, debtors have used the homestead exemption to shift their assets into expensive homes to shield everything from bankruptcy. Known as the "mansion loophole," the changes in the Reform Act related to the homestead exemption were among the most debated and the most dramatic.[29] **For Example,** prior to the reforms actor Burt Reynolds declared bankruptcy in Florida and was relieved of millions in debt, but he was able to keep his $2.5 million Valhalla estate there. Corporate raider Paul Bilzerian, who was convicted of securities fraud, also declared bankruptcy in Florida but kept his mansion, the largest home in Hillsborough County, Florida. Former WorldCom CFO Scott Sullivan (who entered a guilty plea to fraud and other charges and is serving a five-year sentence) built a multimillion-dollar home in Florida to gain homestead protections. Wendy Gramm, who sat on Enron's board, purchased 200 acres of land in Texas and constructed a large home with her husband, former senator Phil Gramm, to take advantage of homestead exemptions then available in Texas. However, the Reform Act closed this corporate executive loophole by requiring that the $155,675 exemption apply to debtors who are convicted of securities fraud or bankruptcy fraud.[30]

Other exemptions include payments under a life insurance contract, alimony and child support payments, and awards from personal injury litigation.[31] Under the Reform Act, college savings accounts and IRAs are exempt property under the federal exemptions and can be used even by those debtors who are using state exemptions. The IRA exemption is limited to $1,245,475.[32]

CASE SUMMARY

Planning for Bankruptcy: Can You Stash Cash Away in College and Retirement Accounts?

FACTS: Leonard Bronk, a retiree living in Stevens Point, Wisconsin, incurred significant debts providing for his wife's medical care before her death in 2007, and he himself suffered a stroke in early 2009. With his medical debts mounting—they exceeded $345,000 by the time he filed for bankruptcy—Bronk sought the advice of an attorney about pre-bankruptcy exemption planning. His assets included his home, which he owned free and clear, and a certificate of deposit in the amount of $42,000. On the advice of counsel, Bronk sought to protect these nonexempt assets by converting them to exempt assets.

In May 2009, a few months before filing his Chapter 7 petition, Bronk borrowed $95,000 from Citizens Bank and mortgaged his previously unencumbered home. He used these funds to establish five college savings accounts for the benefit of his grandchildren under section 529 of the Internal Revenue Code.

Account owners control the funds in these accounts (known as "Edvest" accounts) and may designate and change account beneficiaries. Beneficiaries do not control account assets.

In addition to creating the college savings accounts using the equity in his home, Bronk converted the $42,000 certificate of deposit into an annuity with CM Life Insurance Company. The annuity contract was issued on May 4, 2009, and does not begin making payments until January 3, 2035, but it also includes a death benefit.

[27] The time requirement is at 11 U.S.C. §522(b)(3)(A), and the amount limitation is at 11 U.S.C. §522(o)(1). This amount refers to those who elect state exemptions. In the absence of state exemptions, the federal maximum is $22,975.

[28] 11 U.S.C. §522(p)(2)(B).

[29] 11 U.S.C. §522(p).

[30] 11 U.S.C. §522(q).

[31] 11 U.S.C. §522(d) (including automatic adjustments).

[32] 11 U.S.C. §522(n). There are time requirements on college savings (529) accounts in order to obtain the exemption.

Planning for Bankruptcy: Can You Stash Cash Away in College and Retirement Accounts? continued

On August 5, 2009, Bronk filed for bankruptcy under Chapter 7. The trustee objected to the college-fund and annuity transactions, arguing that Bronk had transferred his property with the intent to hinder, delay, or defraud his creditors and thus should be denied a discharge.

The judge accepted Bronk's argument about the annuity, holding that it was fully exempt as a retirement benefit as were the Edvest accounts.

Both sides appealed to the district court. The district judge agreed that Bronk was entitled to a discharge because the trustee had not proven that the asset transfers were made with intent to hinder, delay, or defraud creditors. Second, the district judge agreed with the bankruptcy judge's interpretation and upheld the decision to deny the claimed exemption for Bronk's Edvest accounts (which was reversed on remand). Finally, the judge narrowed the bankruptcy court's interpretation of "retirement benefit" and remanded the case for additional fact-finding on whether the annuity qualified under the statute.

Bronk appealed, challenging the disallowance of the exemption for his college savings accounts. The trustee filed a cross-appeal challenging the court's ruling on the annuity.

DECISION: Wisconsin's exemption statute allows debtors to exempt "[a]n interest in a college savings account" from execution by creditors. The term "interest" is not specifically defined in the statute or by regulation, but an "interest" is generally defined as "[a] legal share in something; all or part of a legal or equitable claim to or a right in property." Bronk clearly has a legal interest in each of the Edvest college savings accounts. He owned the accounts and could at any time select and change beneficiaries, transfer funds between accounts, receive distributions from the accounts, and (subject to certain limitations) remove funds from the accounts.

To qualify for full exemption, the retirement plan or contract must meet one of two additional requirements: (1) it must be employer sponsored; or (2) it must comply with the Internal Revenue Code.

The statute requires that the retirement product "provid[e] benefits" by reason of age, illness, death, etc., not that it be "purchased" by reason of age. Moreover, there is no special test for annuities.

Bronk's annuity begins paying on a fixed date—January 3, 2035—and thus does not pay benefits because of age, length of service, or the onset of an illness or disability. But the annuity also contains a death benefit. That feature brings it under the umbrella of an exemption.

To qualify for full exemption as a "retirement benefit," a retirement product must be either employer sponsored or "compl[y] with the provisions of the internal revenue code." The trustee raised this issue for the first time in the district court, and even then simply asserted—without developing an argument—that Bronk's annuity was not tax qualified. The argument was held to be waived.

The court held that the exemption statute applied to the college savings accounts. However, the court held that there were still issues about the retirement plan that required the court to make some factual findings. Because the plan was not employer-sponsored, a finding that it met the Internal Revenue Code standards was still needed. **[In re *Bronk*, 775 F.3d 871 (7th Cir. 2015)]**

34-4c Debtor's Protection against Discrimination

Federal, state, and local law may not discriminate against anyone on the basis of a discharge in bankruptcy. For example, a state cannot refuse to issue a new license to an individual if the license fees on a previous one have been discharged as a debt in the individual's declaration of bankruptcy.

34-5 Discharge in Bankruptcy

discharge in bankruptcy– order of the bankruptcy court relieving the debtor from obligation to pay the unpaid balance of most claims.

The main objectives of a bankruptcy proceeding are to collect and distribute the debtor's assets and then issue a **discharge in bankruptcy** of the debtor from obligations. The decree terminating the bankruptcy proceeding is generally a discharge that releases the debtor from most debts. Under the BAPCPA, a discharge is available only once every eight years.

34-5a Denial of Discharge

The court will refuse to grant a discharge if the debtor has (1) within one year of the filing of the petition fraudulently transferred or concealed property with intent to hinder, delay,

ETHICS & THE LAW

The Skies Are Not So Friendly to Employee Pensions

As part of its Chapter 11 bankruptcy, United Airlines was relieved of its pension liabilities. Employees and unions wonder how a company can be permitted to renege on those benefits when so many protections were built into the law under ERISA. Congressional hearings revealed that there were loopholes in the accounting processes for pension fund reporting that permitted United, and many others, to report pension numbers that made the pension funds look healthy when they really were not. The loopholes were Enron-esque in nature. Companies could spin the pension obligations off the books so that the existing levels of obligations of the plan looked small and the assets very rich.

Because of United's pension bailout, Congress changed the accounting for pension plans to avoid the problem of the rosy picture when the funds really need further funding. One interesting approach to protecting pension plans is to require companies to fund the pension plans according to the numbers they have reported to the SEC in their financials. If United had funded its plans when its SEC numbers indicated it needed to (e.g., in 1998), the plan would have been sufficiently funded. Under ERISA guidelines, it was not required to kick in funds until 2002 when it was grossly underfunded.

Were companies acting ethically on their pension accounting? Were they acting legally?*

*Marry Williams Walsh, "Pension Law Loopholes Helped United Hide Its Troubles," *New York Times*, June 7, 2005, C1.

or defraud creditors, (2) failed to keep proper financial records, (3) made a false oath or account,[33] (4) failed to explain satisfactorily any loss of assets, (5) refused to obey any lawful order of the court or refused to testify after having been granted immunity, (6) obtained a discharge within the last eight years,[34] (7) filed a written waiver of discharge that is approved by the court,[35] or (8) in the case of a consumer debtor, has failed to complete a personal financial management instructional course.[36] A discharge releases the debtor from the unpaid balance of most debts except for taxes, customs duties, child support obligations, and tax penalties.[37] Student loan obligations are not discharged in bankruptcy unless the loan first became due more than seven years before bankruptcy or unless not allowing a discharge would impose undue hardship on the debtor.

CASE SUMMARY

Your Living Expenses Are Fairly Minimal in Maximum Security

FACTS: Bryan Anthony Looper (Debtor) had over $300,000 in student loans that were used to finance his education at Mercer University where he obtained an A.B., an M.B.A, and another unspecified graduate degree as well as a large number of courses toward his J.D. degree. He did not make payments on these student loans.

In 1996, he was elected assessor for Putnam County, Tennessee, a position he held for two years

[33] The debtor must actually make a false statement. Obtaining a credit card under false pretenses is fraud. In re *Levasseur*, 737 F.3d 814 (1st Cir. 2013). However, just the use of a credit card for unnecessary purchases is not fraud, In re *Quinn*, 492 B.R. 341 (N.D. Ga. 2013).

[34] 11 U.S.C. §727(a)(8).

[35] 11 U.S.C. §523.

[36] 11 U.S.C. §727(a)(11). The financial management course requirement applies to both Chapter 7 and Chapter 13 consumer bankruptcies.

[37] Child support obligations enjoy additional protections and priorities in bankruptcy. 11 U.S.C §507(a).

Your Living Expenses Are Fairly Minimal in Maximum Security continued

and four months. He was then convicted of the first-degree murder of state senator Tommy Burks. He exhausted all of his appeals and is currently serving a life sentence without the possibility of parole. Looper has one dependent, a son born in August 1998. The circuit court for Putnam County, Tennessee, ordered Looper to pay child support of $161.00 per month plus $7,254.20 in medical expenses. Looper did not make any of the court-ordered child support payments and was in arrears by more than $23,515.00.

Looper asked to have his student loans discharged on the basis of his hardship.

DECISION: The court refused to discharge the student loans. Looper had all of his living expenses covered by the Tennessee Department of Corrections. Looper had made no effort to make any payments on any of his student loans and had also not made attempts to try and work with his lenders or apply to programs set up to help with student loans. The court also noted that Looper's circumstances were the result of his choices and conduct, not the result of unforeseen and uncontrollable events. He had three degrees and the capability of earning a living but, through poor choices, produced his own difficult circumstances. **[In re *Looper*, 2007 WL 1231700 (B. E.D. Tenn. 2007)]**

In addition, the following debts are not discharged by bankruptcy: (1) loans obtained by use of a false financial statement made with intent to deceive and on which the creditor reasonably relied, (2) debts not scheduled or listed with the court in time for allowance, (3) debts arising from fraud while the debtor was acting in a fiduciary capacity or by reason of embezzlement or larceny, (4) alimony and child support, (5) a judgment for willful and malicious injury, (6) a consumer debt to a single creditor totaling more than $650 for luxury goods or services (within 90 days of the order of relief) and cash advances exceeding $925 based on consumer open-end credit, such as a credit card (within 70 days of the order of relief),[38] (7) damages arising from drunk driving or the

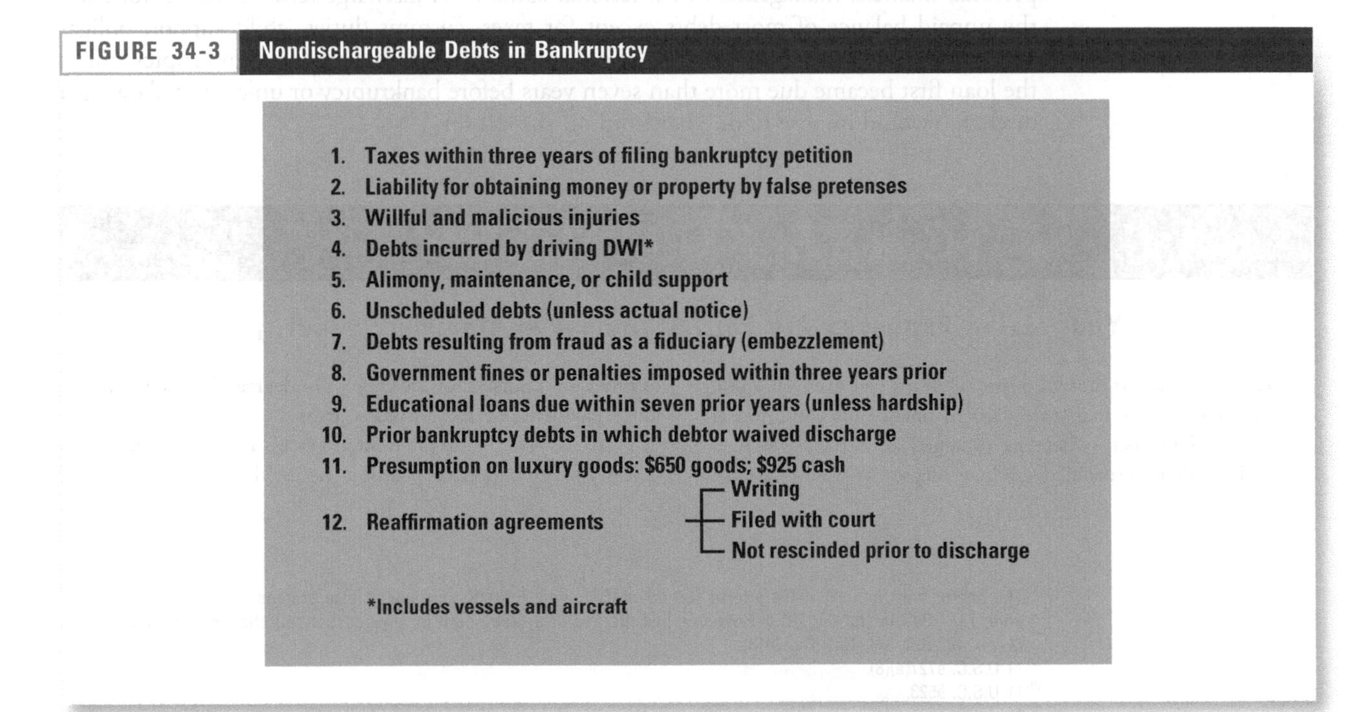
FIGURE 34-3 Nondischargeable Debts in Bankruptcy

1. Taxes within three years of filing bankruptcy petition
2. Liability for obtaining money or property by false pretenses
3. Willful and malicious injuries
4. Debts incurred by driving DWI*
5. Alimony, maintenance, or child support
6. Unscheduled debts (unless actual notice)
7. Debts resulting from fraud as a fiduciary (embezzlement)
8. Government fines or penalties imposed within three years prior
9. Educational loans due within seven prior years (unless hardship)
10. Prior bankruptcy debts in which debtor waived discharge
11. Presumption on luxury goods: $650 goods; $925 cash
12. Reaffirmation agreements — Writing; Filed with court; Not rescinded prior to discharge

*Includes vessels and aircraft

[38] 11 U.S.C. §523(a)(2)(c)(i). (Amounts are adjusted each year.)

operation of vessels and aircrafts by people who are inebriated,[39] (8) loans used to pay taxes (including credit cards),[40] (9) taxes not paid as a result of a fraudulent return, although other unpaid taxes beyond the past three years can be discharged,[41] (10) pre-bankruptcy fees and assessments owed to homeowners associations, and (11) debts owed to tax-qualified retirement plans. **For Example,** one of the financial concerns facing athlete Lance Armstrong is that the litigation against him may include findings of malice with the result being that those judgments cannot be discharged in bankruptcy, thus making all those judgments a lifetime obligation. Figure 34-3 has a listing of non-dischargeable debts.

34-6 Reorganization Plans under Chapter 11

In addition to liquidation under Chapter 7, the Bankruptcy Code permits debtors to restructure the organization and finances of their businesses so that they may continue to operate. In these rehabilitation plans, the debtor keeps all of the assets (exempt and nonexempt), continues to operate the business, and makes a settlement that is acceptable to the majority of the creditors. This settlement is binding on the minority creditors.

Individuals, partnerships, and corporations in business may all be reorganized under the Bankruptcy Code. The first step is to file a plan for the debtor's reorganization. This plan may be filed by the debtor, any party in interest, or a committee of creditors. If the debtor wishes to move from a Chapter 11 proceeding (in the case of an individual debtor), the debtor must survive the means test that is now a requirement for determining eligibility for bankruptcy.

34-6a Contents of the Plan

The plan divides ownership interests and debts into those that will be affected by the adoption of the plan and those that will not be. It then specifies what will be done to those interests and claims that are affected. **For Example,** when mortgage payments are too high for the income of a corporation, a possible plan would be to reduce the mortgage payments and give the mortgage holder preferred stock to compensate for the loss sustained.

All creditors, shareholders, and other interest holders within a particular class must be treated the same way. **For Example,** the holders of first mortgage bonds must all be treated similarly. The treatment of the bondholders in the Chrysler and GM bankruptcies was a point of contention and negotiation in those reorganizations.

A plan can also provide for the assumption, rejection, or assignment of executory contracts. The trustee or debtor can, under certain circumstances, suspend performance of a contract not yet fully performed. **For Example,** collective bargaining agreements may be rejected with the approval of the bankruptcy court.[42]

34-6b Confirmation of the Plan

After the plan is prepared, the court must approve or confirm it. A plan will be confirmed if it has been submitted in good faith and if its provisions are reasonable.[43] After the plan is confirmed, the owners and creditors of the enterprise have only the rights that are specified in the plan. They cannot go back to their original contract positions.

[39] 11 U.S.C. §523(a)(9).
[40] 11 U.S.C. §523(a)(14A), (14B).
[41] 11 U.S.C. §§1129(a)(9)(c), (D), 1129(b)(2)(B), 1141(d)(6)(B).
[42] 11 U.S.C. §1113.
[43] 11 U.S.C. §1129.

CPA 34-7 Payment Plans under Chapter 13

The Bankruptcy Code also provides for the adoption of extended-time payment plans for individual debtors who have regular income. These debtors must owe unsecured debts of less than $383,175 and secured debts of less than $1,149,525.

An individual debtor who has a regular income may submit a plan for the installment payment of outstanding debts. If the court approves it, the debtor may then pay the debts in the installments specified by the plan even if the creditors had not originally agreed to such installment payments.

34-7a Contents of the Plan

The individual debtor plan is, in effect, a budget of the debtor's future income with respect to outstanding debts. The plan must provide for the eventual payment in full of all claims entitled to priority under the Bankruptcy Code. All creditors holding the same kind or class of claim must be treated the same way.

34-7b Confirmation of the Plan

The plan has no effect until the court approves or confirms it. A plan will be confirmed if it was submitted in good faith and is in the best interests of the creditors.[44] When the plan is confirmed, debts are payable in the manner specified in the plan.

34-7c Discharge of the Debtor

After all of the payments called for by the plan have been made, the debtor is given a discharge. The discharge releases the debtor from liability for all debts except those that would not be discharged by an ordinary bankruptcy discharge.[45] Under the bankruptcy reforms, the court cannot grant a discharge until the debtor has completed an instructional course concerning personal financial management.[46] If the debtor does not perform under the plan, the creditors can move to transfer the debtor's case to a Chapter 7 proceeding, but they would still face the means test in qualifying for this move to Chapter 7.

Make the Connection

Summary

Jurisdiction over bankruptcy cases is in U.S. district courts, which may refer all cases and related proceedings to adjunct bankruptcy courts.

Three bankruptcy proceedings are available: liquidation (Chapter 7), reorganization (Chapter 11), and extended-time payment (Chapter 13). A liquidation proceeding under Chapter 7 may be either voluntary or involuntary.

A *voluntary case* is commenced by the debtor's filing a petition with the bankruptcy court. A voluntary petition is subject to the means test to determine if the debtor meets the standard for declaring bankruptcy. An involuntary case is commenced by the creditors' filing a petition with the bankruptcy court. If there are 12 or more creditors, at least 3 whose unsecured claims total $15,325 or more

[44] 11 U.S.C. §1325.
[45] 11 U.S.C. §1328.
[46] 11 U.S.C. §1328(g)(1).

must sign the involuntary petition. If there are fewer than 12 creditors, any creditor whose unsecured claim is at least $15,325 may sign the petition. If the debtor contests the bankruptcy petition, it must be shown that the debtor is not paying debts as they become due.

Eligibility for Chapters 7 and 11 bankruptcy excludes railroads, municipalities, and Small Business Administration companies. Individual debtors are restricted on Chapters 7 and 11 filings by their ability to repay. If found to have the means to pay, they go into a Chapter 13 proceeding. Chapter 13 eligibility is limited to consumers with $383,175 in unsecured debt and $1,149,525 in secured debt.

An automatic stay prevents creditors from taking legal action against the debtor after a bankruptcy petition is filed. The trustee in bankruptcy is elected by the creditors and is the successor to, and acquires the rights of, the debtor. In certain cases, the trustee can avoid transfers of property to prevent creditors from satisfying their claims. Preferential transfers may be set aside. A transfer for a present consideration, such as a cash sale, is not a preference.

Bankruptcy law regulates the way creditors present their claims and how the assets of the debtor are to be distributed in payment of the claims. Some assets of the debtor are exempt from the bankruptcy estate, such as a portion of the value of the debtor's home.

Secured claims are not affected by the debtor's bankruptcy. Unsecured claims are paid in the following order of priority:

1. Support or maintenance for a spouse, former spouse, or child.
2. Costs and expenses of administration of the bankruptcy case.
3. Claims arising in the ordinary course of a debtor's business or financial affairs after the commencement of the case but before the order of relief (involuntary).
4. Claims for wages, salaries, or commissions, including vacation, severance, or sick leave pay earned within 180 days before the filing of the petition or the date of cessation of the debtor's business, limited to $12,475 for each person.
5. Claims arising for contributions (up to $6,225) to employee benefit plans based on services rendered within 180 days before the filing of the petition or when the debtor ceased doing business.
6. Farm producers (up to $6,150) and fishers against debtors who operate grain storage facilities or fish produce storage or processing facilities, up to $6,150 per claim.
7. Claims by consumer creditors, not to exceed $2,775 for each claimant.
8. Certain taxes and penalties due government units, such as income and property taxes.
9. All other unsecured creditors.
10. Remainder (if any) to debtor.

The decree terminating bankruptcy proceedings is generally a discharge that releases the debtor from most debts. Certain debts, such as income taxes, student loans, loans obtained by use of a false financial statement, alimony, and debts not listed by the debtor, are not discharged.

Under Chapter 11 bankruptcy, individuals, partnerships, and corporations in business may be reorganized so that the business can continue to operate. A plan for reorganization must be approved by the court. Under a Chapter 13 bankruptcy proceeding, individual debtors with a regular income may adopt extended-time payment plans for the payment of debts. A plan for extended-time payment must also be confirmed by the court. Federal, state, and local law may not discriminate against anyone on the basis of a discharge in bankruptcy.

Learning Outcomes

After studying this chapter, you should be able to clearly explain:

34-1 Bankruptcy Law

34-2 How Bankruptcy Is Declared

LO.1 List the requirements for the commencement of a voluntary bankruptcy case and an involuntary bankruptcy case

See the Sports & Entertainment Law discussion of celebrity bankruptcies, page 679.

See the discussion of Chapters 7, 11, and 13 and Figure 34-1, pages 672–673, 678.

See the In re *Gomery* case for a discussion of relationships between Chapter 7 and Chapter 13, page 675.

34-3 Administration of the Bankruptcy Estate

LO.2 Explain the procedure for the administration of a debtor's estate

See the list of priorities in the section titled "Priority of Claims," pages 683–684.

See In re *Conklin* on priority positions of the creditor, page 682.

34-4 Debtor's Duties and Exemptions

LO.3 List a debtor's duties and exemptions

See the discussion of the homestead exemptions, pages 684–685.

See the In re *Bronk* case for a discussion of structuring exemptions prior to bankruptcy, pages 685–686.

34-5 Discharge in Bankruptcy

LO.4 Explain the significance of a discharge in bankruptcy

See In re *Looper* for a discussion of hardship, pages 687–688.

34-6 Reorganization Plans under Chapter 11

See Ethics & the Law, "The Skies Are Not So Friendly to Employee Pensions," page 687.

34-7 Payment Plans under Chapter 13

LO.5 Explain when a business reorganization plan or an extended-time payment plan might be used

See the Ethics & the Law discussion of United Airlines, page 687.

Key Terms

automatic stay
balance sheet test
bankruptcy courts
bona fide
Chapter 7 bankruptcy
Chapter 11 bankruptcy
Chapter 13 bankruptcy
claim
discharge in bankruptcy
insiders
insolvency
involuntary bankruptcy
liquidated
means test
order of relief
preferences
preferential transfers
proof of claim
trustee in bankruptcy
voluntary bankruptcy

Questions and Case Problems

1. Hall-Mark regularly supplied electronic parts to Peter Lee. On September 11, 1992, Lee gave Hall-Mark a $100,000 check for parts it had received. Hall-Mark continued to ship parts to Lee. On September 23, 1992, Lee's check was dishonored by the bank. On September 25, 1992, Lee delivered to Hall-Mark a cashier's check for $100,000. Hall-Mark shipped nothing more to Lee after receipt of the cashier's check. On December 24, 1992, Lee filed a voluntary petition for bankruptcy. The trustee filed a complaint to have the $100,000 payment to Hall-Mark set aside as a voidable preference. Hall-Mark said it was entitled to the payment because it gave value to Lee. The trustee said that the payment was not actually made until the cashier's check was delivered on September 25, 1992, and that Hall-Mark gave no further value to Lee after that check was paid. Who was correct? [In re *Lee*, 108 F.3d 239 (9th Cir.)]

2. Orso, who had declared bankruptcy, received a structured tort settlement in a personal injury claim he had pending. The settlement would pay him an annuity each year for 30 years because the claim was the result of an auto accident that left him permanently and severely brain damaged with an IQ of about 70. His ex-wife had a pending claim for $48,000 in arrearages on Orso's $1,000 per month child support payments. His ex-wife wanted the annuity included in the bankruptcy estate. Would this property have been included in Orso's bankruptcy estate? [In re *Orso*, 214 F.3d 637 (5th Cir.)]

3. Harold McClellan sold ice-making machinery to Bobbie Cantrell's brother for $200,000 to be paid in installment payments. McClellan took a security interest in the ice machine but did not perfect it by filing a financing statement. The brother defaulted when he owed $100,000, and McClellan brought suit. With the suit pending, the brother "sold" the ice machine to Bobbie Cantrell for $10. Bobbie then sold the machine to someone for $160,000 and refused to explain what happened to that money. McClellan added Bobbie as a defendant in his suit against her brother. Bobbie then declared bankruptcy. McClellan sought to have the various transfers set aside. The trial court refused to do so, and McClellan appealed. Should the transfers be set aside? Why or why not? [*McClellan v. Cantrell*, 217 F.3d 890 (7th Cir.)]

4. Okamoto owed money to Hornblower & Weeks-Hemphill, Noyes (a law firm and hereafter Hornblower). Hornblower filed an involuntary bankruptcy petition against Okamoto, who moved to dismiss the petition on the ground that he had more than 12 creditors and the petition could not be filed by only 1 creditor. Hornblower replied that the other creditors' claims were too small to count and,

therefore, the petition could be filed by one creditor. Decide. [In re *Okamoto*, 491 F.2d 496 (9th Cir.)]

5. Jane Leeves declared voluntary Chapter 7 bankruptcy. The trustee included the following property in her bankruptcy estate:
   - Jane's wedding ring
   - Jane's computer for her consulting business that she operated from her home
   - Jane's car payment from a client in the amount of $5,000 that was received 91 days after Jane filed bankruptcy

   After collecting all of Jane's assets, the bankruptcy trustee was trying to decide how to distribute the assets. Jane had the following creditors:
   - Mortgage company—owed $187,000 (the trustee sold Jane's house for $190,000)
   - Expenses of the bankruptcy—$3,000
   - Federal income taxes—$11,000
   - Utility bills—$1,000
   - Office supply store open account—$1,000

   The trustee had $11,500 in cash, including the $3,000 additional cash left from the sale of the house after the mortgage company was paid. How should the trustee distribute this money? What if the amount were $14,500; how should that be distributed?
6. Kentile sold goods over an extended period of time to Winham. The credit relationship began without Winham's being required to furnish a financial statement. After a time, payments were not made regularly, and Kentile requested a financial statement. Winham submitted a statement for the year just ended. Kentile requested a second statement. The second statement was false. Kentile objected to Winham's discharge in bankruptcy because of the false financial statement. Should the discharge be granted? Why or why not?
7. D. Erik Von Kiel obtained loans from the U.S. Department of Health & Human Services so that he could complete his education as an osteopathic physician. He works at the International Academy of Life (IAL) in Orem, Utah, for no salary but receives gifts from IAL that total $150,000 per year, or about $12,787 per month. He pays no taxes on these "gifts" and has received them since 2005. Dr. Von Kiel pays all but $1,000 to his ex-wife and nine children for their support. He has given up his practice, taken a vow of poverty, and works at IAL to concentrate on alternative medicine. He has signed over full authority for the management of his financial affairs to two individuals, who apparently failed to manage wisely. As a result, Dr. Von Kiel filed for bankruptcy in order to be discharged from his HHS loans. HHS says that Dr. Von Kiel should not be discharged because of bad faith. Who is correct and why? [In re *Von Kiel*, 461 B.R. 323 (E.D. Pa.)]
8. Sonia, a retailer, has the following assets: a factory worth $1 million; accounts receivable amounting to $750,000, which fall due in four to six months; and $20,000 cash in the bank. Sonia's sole liability is a $200,000 note falling due today, which she is unable to pay. Can Sonia be forced into involuntary bankruptcy under the Bankruptcy Code? [In re *35th & Morgan Development Corp*., 510 B.R. 832 (N.D. Ill.)]
9. Samson Industries ceased doing business and is in bankruptcy proceedings. Among the creditors are five employees seeking unpaid wages. Three of the employees are owed $3,500 each, and two are owed $1,500 each. These amounts became due within 90 days preceding the filing of the petition. Where, in the priority of claims, will the employees' wage claims fall?
10. Carol Cott, doing business as Carol Cott Fashions, is worried about an involuntary bankruptcy proceeding being filed by her creditors. Her net worth, using a balance sheet approach, is $8,000 ($108,000 in assets minus $100,000 in liabilities). However, her cash flow is negative, and she has been hard pressed to meet current obligations as they mature. She is in fact some $17,000 in arrears in payments to her creditors on bills submitted during the past two months. Will the fact that Cott is solvent in the balance sheet sense result in the court's dismissing the creditors' petition if Cott objects to the petition? Explain. [*Forever Green Athletic Fields, Inc. v. Dawson*, 514 B.R. 768 (E.D. Pa.)]
11. On July 1, Roger Walsh, a sole proprietor operating a grocery, was involuntarily petitioned into bankruptcy by his creditors. At that time, and for at least 90 days prior to that time, Walsh was unable to pay current obligations. On June 16, Walsh paid the May electric bill for his business. The trustee in bankruptcy claimed that this payment was a voidable preference. Was the trustee correct? Explain.
12. Steven and Teresa Hornsby are married and have three young children. On May 25, 1993, the Hornsbys filed a voluntary Chapter 7 petition. They had by that date accumulated more than $30,000 in debt, stemming almost entirely from student loans. They wanted a discharge of their student loans on grounds of undue hardship. The Hornsbys attended

a succession of small Tennessee state colleges. Both studied business and computers, but neither graduated. Although they received several deferments and forbearances on the loans, they ultimately defaulted before making any payments. Interest had accumulated on the loans to the extent that Steven was indebted to the Tennessee Student Assistance Corporation (TSAC) for $15,058.52, and Teresa was indebted to TSAC for $18,329.15.

Steven was working for AT&T in Dallas, Texas; he made $6.53 per hour, occasionally working limited overtime hours. Teresa was employed by KinderCare Learning Center. Although she had begun work in Tennessee, she had transferred to become the director of a child care facility in Dallas. Teresa was earning $17,500 per year with medical benefits at the time of the hearing. In monthly net income, Steven earned approximately $1,083.33, and Teresa earned $1,473.33, amounting to $2,556.66 of disposable income per month. The Hornsbys' reported monthly expenses came to $2,364.90. They operated with a monthly surplus of $191.76 to $280.43, depending on whether Steven earned overtime for a particular month. Under the federal bankruptcy laws, are the Hornsbys entitled to a discharge on their student loans? Explain your answer. [In re *Hornsby*, 144 F.3d 433 (6th Cir.)]

13. TLC was an Atlanta rhythm, blues, and hip-hop band that performed at clubs in 1991. The three-woman group signed a recording contract with LaFace Records. The group's first album that LaFace produced, *Ooooooohhh on the TLC Tip*, sold almost 3 million albums in 1992. The group's second album, *Crazysexycool*, also produced by LaFace, sold 5 million albums through June 1996. The two albums together had six top-of-the-chart singles.

    LaFace had the right to renew TLC's contract in 1996 following renegotiation of the contract terms. In the industry, royalty rates for unknown groups, as TLC was in 1991, are generally 7 percent of the revenues for the first 500,000 albums and 8 percent for sales on platinum albums (albums that sell over 1 million copies). The royalty rate increases to 9.5 percent for all sales on an eighth album. Established artists in the industry who renegotiate often have royalty rates of 13 percent, and artists with two platinum albums can command an even higher royalty.

    The three women in TLC—Tionne Watkins (T-Boz), Lisa Lopes (Left-Eye, who has since died), and Rozonda Thomas (Chili)—declared bankruptcy in July 1995. All three listed debts that exceeded their assets, which included sums owed to creditors for their cars and to Zale's and The Limited for credit purchases. Lopes was being sued by Lloyd's of London, which claimed she owed it $1.3 million it had paid on a policy held by her boyfriend on his home that was destroyed by fire. Lopes pleaded guilty to one count of arson in the destruction of the home but denied that she intended to destroy it. She was sentenced to five years probation and treatment at a halfway house.

    Lopes asked that the Lloyd's claim be discharged in her bankruptcy. All three members of TLC asked that their contract with LaFace be discharged in bankruptcy because being bound to their old contract could impede their fresh financial starts.

    Did the three women meet the standards for declaring bankruptcy? Evaluate whether Lopes's Lloyd's claim should be discharged. Determine whether the record contract should be discharged.

14. Place the following in order for a bankruptcy proceeding:
    a. Order of relief
    b. Collection of bankrupt's estate
    c. List of creditors
    d. Petition
    e. Evaluation of claims
    f. Voidable preferences
    g. Discharge

15. Three general unsecured creditors are owed $45,000 as follows: *A*, $15,000; *B*, $5,000; and *C*, $25,000. After all other creditors were paid, the amount left for distribution to general unsecured creditors was $9,000. How will the $9,000 be distributed?

CPA Questions

1. Which of the following statements is correct concerning the voluntary filing of a petition of bankruptcy?
    a. If the debtor has 12 or more creditors, the unsecured claims must total at least $15,325.
    b. The debtor must be solvent.
    c. If the debtor has less than 12 creditors, the unsecured claims must total at least $15,325.
    d. The petition may be filed jointly by spouses (AICPA adapted).

2. On February 28, Master, Inc., had total assets with a fair market value of $1,200,000 and total liabilities of $990,000. On January 15, Master made a monthly installment note payment to Acme Distributors Corp., a creditor holding a properly perfected security interest in equipment having a fair market value greater than the balance due on the note. On March 15, Master voluntarily filed a petition in bankruptcy under the liquidation provisions of Chapter 7 of the federal Bankruptcy Code. One year later, the equipment was sold for less than the balance due on the note to Acme.

   If a creditor challenged Master's right to file, the petition would be dismissed:

   a. If Master had less than 12 creditors at the time of filing.

   b. Unless Master can show that a reorganization under Chapter 11 of the federal Bankruptcy Code would have been unsuccessful.

   c. Unless Master can show that it is unable to pay its debts in the ordinary course of business or as they come due.

   d. If Master is an insurance company.

3. A voluntary petition filed under the liquidation provisions of Chapter 7 of the federal Bankruptcy Code:

   a. Is not available to a corporation unless it has previously filed a petition under the reorganization provisions of Chapter 11 of the federal Bankruptcy Code.

   b. Automatically stays collection actions against the debtor except by secured creditors for collateral only.

   c. Will be dismissed unless the debtor has 12 or more unsecured creditors whose claims total at least $15,325.

   d. Does not require the debtor to show that the debtor's liabilities exceed the fair market value of assets.

4. Which following conditions, if any, must a debtor meet to file a voluntary bankruptcy petition under Chapter 7 of the federal Bankruptcy Code?

	Insolvency	*Three or More Creditors*
a.	Yes	Yes
b.	Yes	No
c.	No	Yes
d.	No	No

5. On July 15, 1988, White, a sole proprietor, was involuntarily petitioned into bankruptcy under the liquidation provisions of the Bankruptcy Code. White's nonexempt property has been converted to $13,000 cash, which is available to satisfy the following claims:

Unsecured claim for 1986 state income tax	$10,000
Fee owed to Best & Co., CPAs, for services rendered from April 1, 1988, through June 30, 1988	$6,000
Unsecured claim by Stieb for wages earned as an employee of White during March 1988	$3,000

   There are no other claims.

   What is the maximum amount that will be distributed for the payment of the 1986 state income tax?

   a. $4,000
   b. $5,000
   c. $7,000
   d. $10,000

6. On May 1, 1997, two months after becoming insolvent, Quick Corp., an appliance wholesaler, filed a voluntary petition for bankruptcy under the provisions of Chapter 7 of the federal Bankruptcy Code. On October 15, 1996, Quick's board of directors had authorized and paid Erly $50,000 to repay Erly's April 1, 1996, loan to the corporation. Erly is a sibling of Quick's president. On March 15, 1996, Quick paid Kray $100,000 for inventory delivered that day. Which of the following is not relevant in determining whether the repayment of Erly's loan is a voidable preferential transfer?

   a. That Erly is an insider.

   b. That Quick's payment to Erly was made on account of an antecedent debt.

   c. Quick's solvency when the loan was made by Erly.

   d. That Quick's payment to Erly was made within one year of the filing of the bankruptcy petition.

PART 6

Agency and Employment

CHAPTER 36

Agency

Learning Outcomes <<<

After studying this chapter, you should be able to

LO.1 **Explain the difference between an agent and an independent contractor**

LO.2 **Explain three methods of creating an agency relationship**

LO.3 **Recognize that third persons who deal with an agent are required to take notice of acts contrary to the interests of the principal**

LO.4 **List and explain the duties an agent owes the principal**

LO.5 **Explain how the Uniform Durable Power of Attorney Act changes the common law rule on incapacity of the principal**

One of the most common business relationships is that of agency. By virtue of the agency device, one person can make contracts at numerous places with many different parties at the same time.

agency–relationship that exists between a person identified as a principal and another by virtue of which the latter may make contracts with third persons on behalf of the principal. (Parties—principal, agent, third person)

agent–person or firm who is authorized by the principal or by operation of law to make contracts with third persons on behalf of the principal.

36-1 Nature of the Agency Relationship

Agency is ordinarily based on the consent of the parties and for that reason is called a *consensual relationship*. However, the law sometimes imposes an agency relationship. If consideration is present, the agency relationship is contractual.

36-1a Definitions and Distinctions

Agency is a relationship based on an express or implied agreement by which one person, the **agent,** is authorized to act under the control of and for another, the **principal,** in negotiating and making contracts with third persons.[1] The acts of the agent obligate the principal to third persons and give the principal rights against third persons. (See Figure 36-1.)

The term *agency* is frequently used with other meanings. It is sometimes used to denote the fact that one has the right to sell certain products, such as when a dealer is

FIGURE 36-1 Agency Relationships

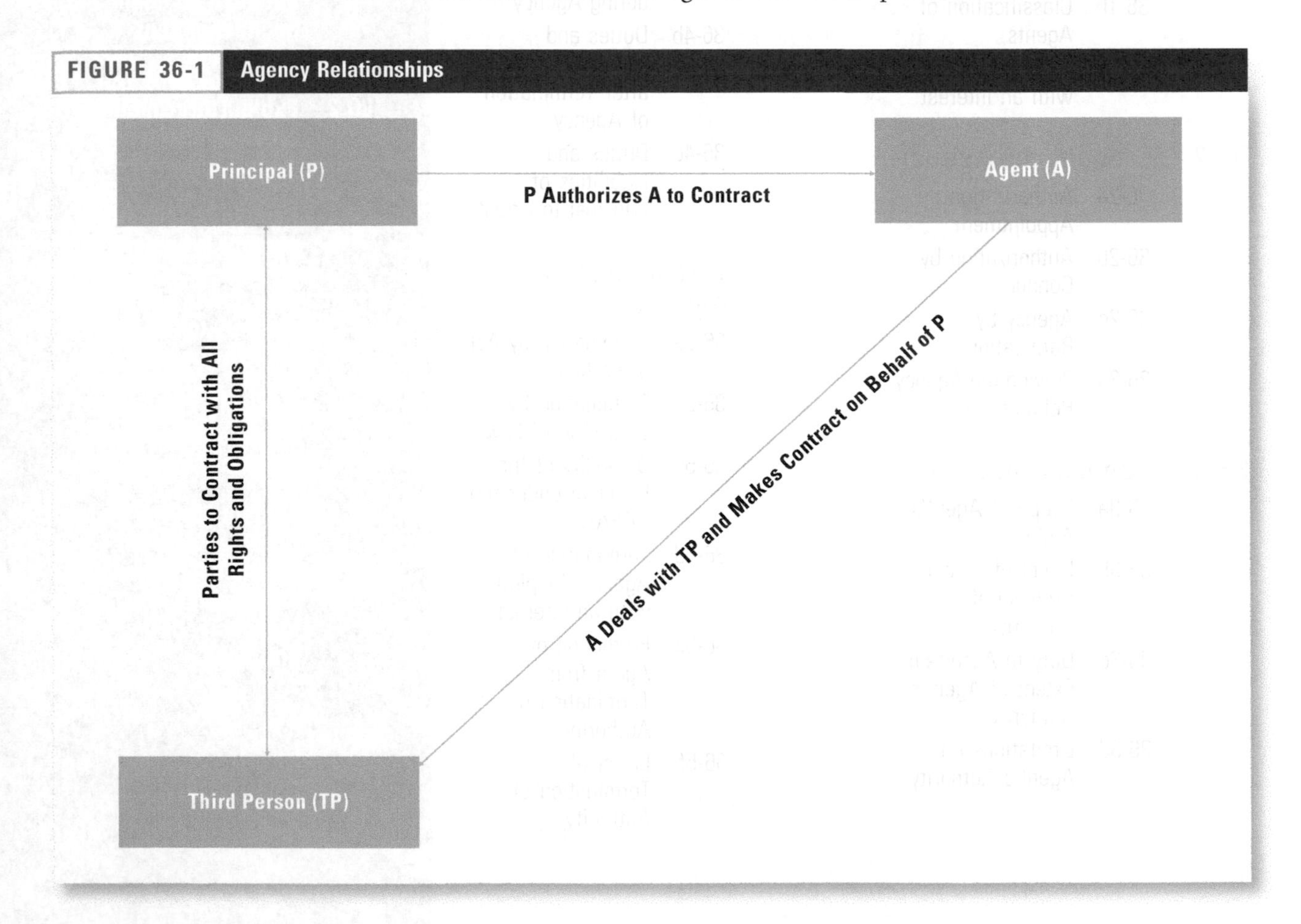

[1] Restatement (Second) of Agency §1; *Union Miniere, S.A. v. Parday Corp.*, 521 N.E.2d 700 (Ind. App. 1988).

principal–person or firm who employs an agent; person who, with respect to a surety, is primarily liable to the third person or creditor; property held in trust.

said to possess an automobile agency. In other instances, the term is used to mean an exclusive right to sell certain articles within a given territory. In these cases, however, the dealer is not an agent in the sense of representing the manufacturer.

It is important to be able to distinguish agencies from other relationships because certain rights and duties in agencies are not present in other relationships.

Employees and Independent Contractors

Control and authority are characteristics that distinguish ordinary employees and independent contractors from agents.

Employees. An agent is distinguished from an ordinary employee who is not hired to represent the employer in making contracts with third persons. It is possible, however, for the same person to be both an agent and an employee. **For Example,** the driver for a spring water delivery service is an agent in making contracts between the company and its customers but is an employee with respect to the work of delivering products.

independent contractor–contractor who undertakes to perform a specified task according to the terms of a contract but over whom the other contracting party has no control except as provided for by the contract.

Independent Contractors. An **independent contractor** is bound by a contract to produce a certain result—for example, to build a house. The actual performance of the work is controlled by the contractor, not the owner. An agent or employee differs from an independent contractor in that the principal or employer has the right to control the agent or employee, but not the contractor, in the performance of the work. **For Example,** Ned and Tracy Seizer contract with Fox Building Company to build a new home on Hilton Head Island, South Carolina, according to referenced plans and specifications. Individuals hired by Fox to work on the home are subject to the authority and control of Fox, the independent contractor, not the Seizers. However, Ned and Tracy could decide to build the home themselves, hiring two individuals from nearby Beaufort, Ted Chase and Marty Bromley, to do the work the Seizers will direct each day. Because Ted and Marty would be employees of the Seizers, the Seizers would be held responsible for any wrongs committed by these employees within the scope of their employment. As a general rule, on the other hand, the Seizers are not responsible for the torts of Fox, the independent contractor, and the contractor's employees. A "right to control" test determines whether an individual is an agent, an employee, or an independent contractor.[2]

CASE SUMMARY

Why Some Businesses Use Independent Agents Rather than Employees!

FACTS: Patricia Yelverton died from injuries sustained when an automobile owned and driven by Joseph Lamm crossed the center line of a roadway and struck the automobile driven by Yelverton. Yelverton's executor brought suit against Lamm and Lamm's alleged employer, Premier Industrial Products Inc. The relationship between Lamm and Premier was governed by a written contract entitled "Independent Agent Agreement," in which Lamm, as "Independent Agent," was given the right to sell Premier's products in a designated territory. The agreement provided that all orders were subject to acceptance by Premier and were not binding on Premier until so accepted. Lamm was paid by commission only. He was allowed to work on a self-determined schedule, retain assistants at his own expense, and sell the products of other companies not in competition with Premier. The executor claimed Lamm was an agent or

[2] *NE Ohio College of Massotherapy v. Burek,* 759 N.E.2d 869 (Ohio App. 2001).

Why Some Businesses Use Independent Agents Rather than Employees! continued

employee of Premier. Premier stated Lamm was an independent contractor.

DECISION: Judgment for Premier. Lamm had no authority to make contracts for Premier but simply took orders. Therefore, he was not an agent. Lamm was not an employee of Premier. Premier had no right to control the way he performed his work and did not in fact do so. Lamm was an independent contractor. [***Yelverton v. Lamm*, 380 S.E.2d 621 (N.C. App. 1989)**]

A person who appears to be an independent contractor may in fact be so controlled by the other party that the contractor is regarded as an agent of, or employee of, the controlling person. **For Example,** Pierce, who was under contract to Brookville Carriers, Inc., was involved in a tractor-trailer/car collision with Rich and others. Pierce owned the tractor involved in the accident on a lease from Brookville but could use it only to haul freight for Brookville; he had no authority to carry freight on his own, and all of his operating authority belonged to Brookville. The "owner/operator" was deemed an employee rather than independent contractor for purposes of assessing the liability of the employer.[3] The separate identity of an independent contractor may be concealed so that the public believes that it is dealing with the principal. When this situation occurs, the principal is liable as though the contractor were an agent or employee.

special agent–agent authorized to transact a specific transaction or to do a specific act.

general agent–agent authorized by the principal to transact all affairs in connection with a particular type of business or trade or to transact all business at a certain place.

universal agent–agent authorized by the principal to do all acts that can lawfully be delegated to a representative.

36-1b Classification of Agents

A **special agent** is authorized by the principal to handle a definite business transaction or to do a specific act. One who is authorized by another to purchase a particular house is a special agent.

A **general agent** is authorized by the principal to transact all affairs in connection with a particular type of business or trade or to transact all business at a certain place. To illustrate, a person who is appointed as manager by the owner of a store is a general agent.

A **universal agent** is authorized by the principal to do all acts that can be delegated lawfully to a representative. This form of agency arises when a person absent because of being in the military service gives another person a blanket power of attorney to do anything that must be done during such absence.

CPA

interest in the authority–form of agency in which an agent has been given or paid for the right to exercise authority.

interest in the subject matter–form of agency in which an agent is given an interest in the property with which that agent is dealing.

36-1c Agency Coupled with an Interest

An agent has an **interest in the authority** when consideration has been given or paid for the right to exercise the authority. **For Example,** when a lender, in return for making a loan of money, is given, as security, authority to collect rents due the borrower and to apply those rents to the payment of the debt, the lender becomes the borrower's agent with an interest in the authority given to collect the rents.

An agent has an **interest in the subject matter** when, for a consideration, she is given an interest in the property with which she is dealing. Hence, when the agent is authorized to sell property of the principal and is given a lien on such property as security for a debt owed to her by the principal, she has an interest in the subject matter.

36-2 Creating the Agency

An agency may arise by appointment, conduct, ratification, or operation of law.

[3] *Rich v. Brookville Carriers, Inc.*, 256 F. Supp. 2d 26 (D. Me. 2003).

36-2a Authorization by Appointment

express authorization–authorization of an agent to perform a certain act.

The usual method of creating an agency is by **express authorization;** that is, a person is appointed to act for, or on behalf of, another.

The authorization of the agent may be oral or in writing. **For Example,** Russell Jones, the owner of Westex, gave equipment operator Daniel Flores actual authority to sign an equipment rental agreement on behalf of Westex that acknowledged delivery of a loader to a job site.[4] However, some appointments must be made in a particular way. A majority of the states, by statute, require the appointment of an agent to be in writing when the agency is created to acquire or dispose of any interest in land. A written authorization of agency is called a **power of attorney.** An agent acting under a power of attorney is referred to as an **attorney in fact.**[5]

power of attorney–written authorization to an agent by the principal.

attorney in fact–agent authorized to act for another under a power of attorney.

36-2b Authorization by Conduct

Conduct consistent with the existence of an agency relationship may be sufficient to show authorization. The principal may have such dealing with third persons as to cause them to believe that the "agent" has authority. Thus, if the owner of a store places another person in charge, third persons may assume that the person in charge is the agent for the owner in that respect. The "agent" then appears to be authorized and is said to have *apparent authority*, and the principal is estopped from contradicting the appearance that has been created.[6]

CASE SUMMARY

The "Bulletproof Against Rust" Case. Oops! Now What?

FACTS: While constructing a hotel in Lincoln City, Oregon, the owner, Todd Taylor, became concerned about possible rusting in the exterior stucco system manufactured by ChemRex that was being installed at the hotel. The general contractor, Ramsay-Gerding, arranged a meeting with the owner, the installer, and ChemRex's territory manager for Oregon, Mike McDonald, to discuss Mr. Taylor's concerns. McDonald told those present that the SonoWall system was "bulletproof against rust," and stated that "you're getting a five-year warranty." He followed up with a letter confirming the five-year warranty on parts and labor. A year later rust discoloration appeared, and no one from ChemRex ever fixed the problem. Taylor sued ChemRex for breach of warranty. ChemRex defended that McDonald did not have actual or apparent authority to declare such a warranty.

DECISION: Judgment for Taylor. The evidence indicated that ChemRex clothed Mike McDonald with the title of "territory manager" and gave him the actual authority to visit job sites and resolve problems. Although it denies he had actual authority, ChemRex took sufficient steps to create apparent authority to provide the five-year warranty on the stucco system. [***Taylor v. Ramsay-Gerding Construction Co.*, 196 P.3d 532 (Or. 2008)**]

The term *apparent authority* is used when there is only the appearance of authority but no actual authority, and that appearance of authority was created by the principal. The test for the existence of apparent authority is an objective test determined by the principal's outward manifestations through words or conduct that lead a third person reasonably to believe that the "agent" has authority. A principal's express restriction on authority not made known to a third person is no defense.

[4] *Jones v. Pomroy Equipment Rental, Inc.*, 438 S.W.3d 125 (Tex. App. 2014).
[5] *Lamb v. Scott*, 643 So. 2d 972 (Ala. 1994).
[6] *Intersparex Leddin KG v. AL-Haddad*, 852 S.W.2d 245 (Tenn. App. 1992).

Apparent authority extends to all acts that a person of ordinary prudence, familiar with business usages and the particular business, would be justified in believing that the agent has authority to perform. It is essential to the concept of apparent authority that the third person reasonably believe that the agent has authority. The mere placing of property in the possession of another does not give that person either actual or apparent authority to sell the property.

CPA 36-2c Agency by Ratification

An agent may attempt, on behalf of the principal, to do an act that was not authorized, or a person who is not the agent of another may attempt to act as such an agent. Very generally, notification may be express, where the principal explicitly approves the contract, or implied, where the principal does not object to the contract and accepts the contract's benefits. **For Example,** Morang-Kelly Investments, Inc., doing business as Farmer's Best Supermarket, denied that Mike Awdish was its authorized agent regarding the purchase and installation of used supermarket refrigerators at its Wyoming Street market. Nevertheless, by accepting the goods and services as well as the invoices for those goods and services for equipment still in use at the market it ratified Mr. Awdish's actions.[7]

Intention to Ratify

Initially, ratification is a question of intention. Just as in the case of authorization, when there is a question of whether the principal authorized the agent, there is a question of whether the principal intended to approve or ratify the action of the unauthorized agent.

The intention to ratify may be expressed in words, or it may be found in conduct indicating an intention to ratify. **For Example,** James Reiner signed a five-year lease of commercial space on 320 West Main Street in Avon, Connecticut, because his father, Calvin, was away on vacation, and the owner, Robert Udolf, told James that if he did not come in and sign the lease, his father would lose the opportunity to rent the space in question. James was aware that his father had an interest in the space, and while telling Robert several times that he had no authority, James did sign his name to the lease. In fact, his father took occupancy of the space and paid rent for three years and then abandoned the space. James is not liable on the remainder of the lease because the owner knew at the time of signing that James did not have authority to act. Although he did not sign the lease, Calvin ratified the lease signed by James by his conduct of moving into the space and doing business there for three years with full knowledge of all material facts relating to the transaction. The owner, therefore, had to bring suit against Calvin, not James.[8]

CPA Conditions for Ratification

In addition to the intent to ratify, expressed in some instances with a certain formality, the following conditions must be satisfied for the intention to take effect as a ratification:

1. The agent must have purported to act on behalf of or as agent for the identified principal.
2. The principal must have been capable of authorizing the act both at the time of the act and at the time it was ratified.
3. The principal must have full knowledge of all material facts.

[7] *Bellevue Ventures, Inc. v. Morang-Kelly Investments, Inc.* 836 N.W.2d 898 (Mich. App. 2013).
[8] *Udolf v. Reiner,* 2000 WL 726953 (Conn. Super. May 19, 2000).

It is not always necessary, however, to show that the principal had actual knowledge. Knowledge will be imputed if a principal knows of other facts that would lead a prudent person to make inquiries or if that knowledge can be inferred from the knowledge of other facts or from a course of business. **For Example,** Stacey, without authorization but knowing that William needed money, contracted to sell one of William's paintings to Courtney for $298. Stacey told William about the contract that evening; William said nothing and helped her wrap the painting in a protective plastic wrap for delivery. A favorable newspaper article about William's art appeared the following morning and dramatically increased the value of all of his paintings. William cannot recover the painting from Courtney on the theory that he never authorized the sale because he ratified the unauthorized contract made by Stacey by his conduct in helping her wrap the painting with full knowledge of the terms of the sale. The effect is a legally binding contract between William and Courtney.

Effect of Ratification

When an unauthorized act is ratified, the effect is the same as though the act had been originally authorized. Ordinarily, this means that the principal and the third party are bound by the contract made by the agent.[9] When the principal ratifies the act of the unauthorized person, such ratification releases that person from the liability that would otherwise be imposed for having acted without authority.

CPA 36-2d Proving the Agency Relationship

The burden of proving the existence of an agency relationship rests on the person who seeks to benefit by such proof. The third person who desires to bind the principal because of the act of an alleged agent has the burden of proving that the latter person was in fact the authorized agent of the principal and possessed the authority to do the act in question.[10]

36-3 Agent's Authority

When there is an agent, it is necessary to determine the scope of the agent's authority.

36-3a Scope of Agent's Authority

The scope of an agent's authority may be determined from the express words of the principal to the agent or it may be implied from the principal's words or conduct or from the customs of the trade or business.

Express Authority

If the principal tells the agent to perform a certain act, the agent has express authority to do so. Express authority can be given orally or in writing.

Incidental Authority

incidental authority–authority of an agent that is reasonably necessary to execute express authority.

An agent has implied **incidental authority** to perform any act reasonably necessary to execute the express authority given to the agent. **For Example,** if the principal authorizes the agent to purchase goods without furnishing funds to the agent to pay for them, the agent has the implied incidental authority to purchase the goods on credit.[11]

[9] *McCurley Chevrolet v. Rutz*, 808 P.2d 1167 (Wash. App. 1991).
[10] *Cummings, Inc. v. Nelson*, 115 P.3d 536 (Alaska 2005).
[11] *Badger v. Paulson Investment Co.*, 803 P.2d 1178 (Or. 1991).

customary authority–authority of an agent to do any act that, according to the custom of the community, usually accompanies the transaction for which the agent is authorized to act.

Customary Authority

An agent has implied **customary authority** to do any act that, according to the custom of the community, usually accompanies the transaction for which the agent is authorized to act. An agent who has express authority to receive payments from third persons, for example, has the implied customary authority to issue receipts.

apparent authority–appearance of authority created by the principal's words or conduct.

Apparent Authority

A person has **apparent authority** as an agent when the principal's words or conduct leads a third person to reasonably believe that the person has that authority and the third person relies on that appearance.[12]

CASE SUMMARY

CSX Gets Railroaded by Albert Arillotta

FACTS: Recovery Express and Interstate Demolition (IDEC) are two separate corporations located at the same business address in Boston. On August 22, 2003, Albert Arillotta, a "partner" at IDEC, sent an e-mail to Len Whitehead, Jr., of CSX Transportation expressing an interest in buying "rail cars as scrap." Arillotta represented himself to be "from interstate demolition and recovery express" in the e-mail. The e-mail address from which he sent his inquiry was **albert@recoveryexpress.com.** Arillotta went to the CSX rail yard, disassembled the cars, and transported them away. Thereafter CSX sent invoices for the scrap rail cars totaling $115,757.36 addressed to IDEC at its Boston office shared with Recovery Express. Whitehead believed Arillotta was authorized to act for Recovery Express, based on the e-mail's domain name, recoveryexpress.com. Recovery claims that Arillotta never worked for it. Recovery's president, Thomas Trafton, allowed the "fledgling" company to use telephone, fax, and e-mail services at its offices but never shared anything—assets, funds, books of business, or financials with IDEC—CSX sued Recovery for the invoice amount on the doctrine of "apparent authority." IDEC is now defunct. Recovery claims that Arillotta never worked for it and that it is not liable.

DECISION: Judgment for Recovery. Issuance of an e-mail address with Recovery's domain name to an individual who shared office space with Recovery did not give the individual, Albert Arillotta, apparent authority to enter contracts on Recovery's behalf. No reasonable person could conclude that Arillotta had apparent authority on the basis of an e-mail domain name by itself. Given the anonymity of the Internet, the court warned businesses to take additional action to verify a purported agent's authority to make a deal. [***CSX Transportation, Inc. v. Recovery Express, Inc.*, 415 F. Supp. 2d 6 (D. Mass. 2006)**]

36-3b Effect of Proper Exercise of Authority

When an agent with authority properly makes a contract with a third person that purports to bind the principal, there is by definition a binding contract between the principal and the third person. The agent is not a party to this contract. Consequently, when the owner of goods is the principal, the owner's agent is not liable for breach of warranty with respect to the goods "sold" by the agent. The owner-principal, not the agent, was the "seller" in the sales transaction.

[12] *Alexander v. Chandler*, 179 S.W.2d 385 (Mo. App. 2005).

CPA 36-3c Duty to Ascertain Extent of Agent's Authority

A third person who deals with a person claiming to be an agent cannot rely on the statements made by the agent concerning the extent of authority.[13] If the agent is not authorized to perform the act or is not even the agent of the principal, the transaction between the alleged agent and the third person will have no legal effect between the principal and the third person. It is imperative that one who deals exclusively with an agent must recognize that it is his or her responsibility to ascertain the scope of that agent's authority. **For Example,** the Articles of Organization of limited liability company, Zions Gate R.V. Resort, provide that Zions Gate shall be managed by two managers, Jones and Sorpold, and the Articles require the consent and approval of both managers to constitute the act of the entity. Utah LLC law states that Articles of Organization filed with the state constitute notice of its content to third persons. Thus a 99-year RV lot lease to Oliphant signed only by manager Sorpold was invalid because Oliphant was deemed to have notice of the limitation on Sorpold's authority. Oliphant argued that it was unreasonable and unrealistic to expect individuals to acquire Articles of Organization to determine if the signatory to an agreement is authorized to act for the entity. The court responded that it is not its prerogative to question the statutory scheme enacted by the legislation.[14]

Third persons who deal with an agent whose authority is limited to a special purpose are bound at their peril to find out the extent of the agent's authority. An attorney is such an agent. Unless the client holds the attorney out as having greater authority than usual, the attorney has no authority to settle a claim without approval from the client.

Agent's Acts Adverse to Principal

The third person who deals with an agent is required to take notice of any acts that are clearly adverse to the interest of the principal. Thus, if the agent is obviously using funds of the principal for the agent's personal benefit, persons dealing with the agent should recognize that the agent may be acting without authority and that they are dealing with the agent at their peril.

The only certain way that third persons can protect themselves is to inquire of the principal whether the agent is in fact the agent of the principal and has the necessary authority. **For Example,** Ron Fahd negotiated the sale of a fire truck to the Edinburg Volunteer Fire Company on behalf of the manufacturer, Danko Company, at a price of $158,000. On Danko forms and letterhead Fahd drafted a "Proposal for Fire Apparatus" and it was signed by the president of the Fire Company and Fahd, as a dealer for Danko. Fahd gave a special $2,000 discount for prepayment of the cost of the chassis. Fahd directed that the prepayment check of $55,000 be made payable to "Ron Fahd Sales" in order to obtain the discount. The Fire Company's treasurer inquired of Fahd why the prepayment check was being made out to Fahd rather than Danko, and he accepted Fahd's answer without contacting Danko to confirm this unusual arrangement. Fahd absconded with the proceeds of the check. The Fire Company sued Danko, claiming Fahd had apparent authority to receive the prepayment. While there was some indicia of agency, the court found that the Fire Company had failed to make reasonable inquiry with Danko to verify Fahd's authority to receive the prepayment in Fahd's name, and it rejected the claim that Fahd had apparent authority to accept the prepayment check made out to Fahd as opposed to Danko.[15]

[13] *Breed v. Hughes Aircraft Col.*, 35 Fed. App. 864 (Fed. Cir. 2002).
[14] *Zions Gate R.V. Resort, LLC v. Oliphant*, 326 P.3d 118 (Utah App. 2014).
[15] *Edinburg Volunteer Fire Company v. Danko*, 867 N.Y.S.2d 547 (A.D. 2008).

36-3d Limitations on Agent's Authority

A person who has knowledge of a limitation on the agent's authority cannot ignore that limitation. When the third person knows that the authority of the agent depends on whether financing has been obtained, the principal is not bound by the act of the agent if the financing in fact was not obtained. If the authority of the agent is based on a writing and the third person knows that there is such a writing, the third person is charged with knowledge of limitations contained in it.

"Obvious" Limitations

In some situations, it may be obvious to third persons that they are dealing with an agent whose authority is limited. When third persons know that they are dealing with a representative of a government agency, they should recognize that such a person will ordinarily have limited authority. Third persons should recognize that a contract made with such an officer or representative may not be binding unless ratified by the principal.

The federal government places the risk on any individual making arrangements with the government to accurately ascertain that the government agent is within the bounds of his or her authority.

CASE SUMMARY

Humlen Was Had?

FACTS: The FBI approached Humlen for assistance in securing the conviction of a drug trafficker. Humlen executed an agreement with the FBI to formalize his status as an informant. The agreement he signed contained compensation figures significantly less than those he had been promised by the FBI agents with whom he was dealing. Humlen claims that five agents repeatedly assured him that he would receive the extra compensation they had discussed with him, despite the wording of the contract. It was explained that the agreement had to be "couched" in that way because it was a discoverable document in any future criminal prosecution and thus could be used to destroy his credibility. Based on the information provided by Humlen, an arrest was made, and Humlen sought the remainder of his promised monetary reward from the FBI. The FBI refused to pay him any more than the contract stipulated. When no additional payment was forthcoming, Humlen sued the U.S. government.

DECISION: Judgment for the United States. The government, unlike private parties, cannot be bound by the apparent authority of its agents. When an agent exceeds his or her authority, the government can disavow the agent's words and is not bound by an implied contract. As a general rule, FBI agents lack the requisite actual authority—either express or implied—to contractually bind the United States to remit rewards to confidential informants. Moreover, Humlen's claims directly collide with the plain language of the agreement. [***Humlen v. United States*, 49 Fed. Cl. 497 (2001)**]

Secret Limitations

If the principal has clothed an agent with authority to perform certain acts but the principal gives secret instructions that limit the agent's authority, the third person is allowed to take the authority of the agent at its face value. The third person is not bound by the secret limitations of which the third person has no knowledge.

36-4 Duties and Liabilities of Principal and Agent

The creation of the principal-agent relationship gives rise to duties and liabilities.

36-4a Duties and Liabilities of Agent during Agency

While the agency relationship exists, the agent owes certain duties to the principal.

Loyalty

An agent must be loyal or faithful to the principal.[16] The agent must not obtain any secret benefit from the agency.

CASE SUMMARY

Impermissible Practices Involving Art Dealers with Russian Clients? No Way!

FACTS: On July 23, 2008, Luba Mosionzhnik, a 25 percent shareholder and vice president of the Gallery, was summoned to a meeting by Ezra Chowaiki, a 25 percent shareholder and president of the Gallery, and financial backer David Dangoor, a 50 percent shareholder. She was accused of a myriad of improprieties and fired from her employment. Section 42 of the Shareholders Agreement provided that upon termination of an employee who owned stock, he or she would be required to sell their shares to the Gallery. Mosionzhnik admitted to committing the most egregious of the alleged improper acts. She secretly opened a Swiss bank account, which she used to divert approximately $500,000 related to the Gallery's art sales, and used over $13 million of art consigned by the Gallery's clients as collateral for loans without the clients' consent. Rather than deny these allegations, at her deposition, Mosionzhnik testified that her actions were not improper and noted that "plenty of advisors take a kickback ... that's not ethical but it happens because it's the art world." With respect to illegally using client art as collateral, her defense is that Chowaiki also did so and told her that such a thing was accepted practice in the industry. The Holtz accounting firm determined that Mosionzhnik shares were worth $170,000. The Gallery seeks to recover from Mosionzhnik for her improprieties. She seeks to keep the $500,000 in the Swiss bank account and believes her shares are worth $4,367,200 as valued by her experts "GMSL."

DECISION: While the Shareholder's Agreement permitted Mosionzknik to engage in private art transactions for her own benefit, the deals that led to the $500,000 secretly transferred to a Swiss bank account were all related to Gallery transactions with Russian clients. Taking a kickback on a finder's fee is legally impermissible, even if such a practice is pervasive in the art world. Consequently she must pay the $500,000 in kickbacks to the Gallery. Mosionzhnik's and Chowaiki's cross-accusations of improprieties are barred from consideration by the court by the doctrine of *in pari delicto*. The court will not intercede to resolve disputes between wrongdoers, especially with the Gallery itself benefitting from all sorts of shady practices regarding its Russian business. Mosionzhnik is nevertheless entitled to be paid the fair market valid of her shares, $170,000 as calculated by the Holtz accounting firm in accordance with the Shareholder's Agreement, because her equity is not compensation for services. [***Mosionzhnik v. Chowaiki*, 972 N.Y.S.2d 841 (A.D. 2013)**]

Alternatively, the principal can approve the transaction and sue the agent for any secret profit obtained by the agent.

A contract is voidable by the principal if the agent who was employed to sell the property purchases the property, either directly or indirectly, without full disclosure to the principal.

An agent cannot act as agent for both parties to a transaction unless both know of the dual capacity and agree to it. If the agent does act in this capacity without the consent of both parties, any principal who did not know of the agent's double status can avoid the transaction.

[16] *Patterson Custom Homes v. Bach,* 536 F. Supp. 2d 1026 (E.D. Ill. 2008).

An agent must not accept secret gifts or commissions from third persons in connection with the agency. If the agent does so, the principal may sue the agent for those gifts or commissions. Such practices are condemned because the judgment of the agent may be influenced by the receipt of gifts or commissions.

It is a violation of an agent's duty of loyalty to make and retain secret profits or to secretly usurp the business opportunities of the principal.

CASE SUMMARY

Was Grappolini a "Bad Boy"?

FACTS: Arthur Frigo, an adjunct professor at the Kellogg Graduate School of Management, formed Lucini Italia Co. (Lucini) to import and sell premium extra virgin olive oil and other products from Italy. Lucini's officers hired Guiseppe Grappolini as their olive oil supplier. They also hired him as their consultant. Grappolini signed an exclusivity agreement and a confidentiality agreement acknowledging the confidential nature of Lucini's product development, plans, and strategies. Grappolini was "branded" as a "master cultivator" in Lucini's literature and commercials.

In 1998, Lucini and Grappolini, as his consultant, discussed adding a line of extra virgin olive oils blended with "essential oils," for example, natural extracts such as lemon and garlic. It spent more than $800,000 developing the market information, testing flavors, designing labels and packaging, creating recipes, and generating trade secrets for the new products. Vegetal-Progress s.r.l. (Vegetal) was identified as the only company in Italy that was capable of producing the superior products Lucini sought, and Grappolini was assigned responsibility to obtain an exclusive supply contract with Vegetal.

In direct contravention of his representations to Lucini, Grappolini secretly negotiated an exclusive supply contract for the Grappolini Co., not for Lucini. Moreover, Grappolini Co. began to sell flavored olive oils in the United States, which coincided with Lucini's market research and recipe development that had been disclosed to Grappolini. When Lucini officers contacted Vegetal, they acknowledged that Grappolini was a "bad boy" in procuring the contract for his own company rather than for Lucini, but they would not renege on the contract. Lucini sued Grappolini.

DECISION: Judgment for Lucini. Grappolini was Lucini's agent and owed Lucini a duty to advance Lucini's interests, not his own. When he obtained an exclusive supply agreement with Vegetal for the Grappolini Co. instead of Lucini, he was disloyal and breached his fiduciary duties. As a result, Lucini suffered lost profits and damages of $4.17 million. In addition to these damages, Grappolini was ordered to pay $1,000,000 in punitive damages to deter similar acts in the future. Additionally, a permanent injunction was issued prohibiting Grappolini from using Lucini's trade secrets. **[*Lucini Italia Co. v. Grappolini*, 2003 WL 1989605 (N.D. Ill. 2003)]**

An agent is, of course, prohibited from aiding the competitors of a principal or disclosing to them information relating to the business of the principal. It is also a breach of duty for the agent to knowingly deceive a principal.[17]

Obedience and Performance

An agent is under a duty to obey all lawful instructions.[18] The agent is required to perform the services specified for the period and in the way specified. An agent who does not do so is liable to the principal for any harm caused. For example, if an agent is instructed to take cash payments only but accepts a check in payment, the agent is liable for the loss caused the principal if a check is dishonored by nonpayment.

[17] *Koontz v. Rosener,* 787 P.2d 192 (Colo. App. 1990).
[18] *Stanford v. Neiderer,* 341 S.E.2d 892 (Ga. App. 1986).

Reasonable Care

It is the duty of an agent to act with the care that a reasonable person would exercise under the circumstances. **For Example,** Ethel Wilson applied for fire insurance for her house with St. Paul Reinsurance Co., Ltd., through her agent Club Services Corp. She thought she was fully covered. Unbeknown to her, however, St. Paul had refused coverage and returned her premium to Club Services, which did not refund it to Ms. Wilson or inform her that coverage had been denied. Fire destroyed her garage and St. Paul denied coverage. Litigation resulted, and St. Paul ended up expending $305,406 to settle the Wilson matter. Thereafter, St. Paul successfully sued Club Services Corp. under basic agency law principles that an agent (Club Services) is liable to its principal for all damages resulting from the agent's failure to discharge its duties.[19] In addition, if the agent possesses a special skill, as in the case of a broker or an attorney, the agent must exercise that skill.

Accounting

An agent must account to the principal for all property or money belonging to the principal that comes into the agent's possession. The agent must, within a reasonable time, give notice of collections made and render an accurate account of all receipts and expenditures. The agency agreement may state at what intervals or on what dates such accountings are to be made. An agent must keep the principal's property and money separate and distinct from that of the agent.

Information

It is the duty of an agent to keep the principal informed of all facts relating to the agency that are relevant to protecting the principal's interests.[20]

36-4b Duties and Liabilities of Agent after Termination of Agency

When the agency relationship ends, the duties of the agent continue only to the extent necessary to perform prior obligations. For example, the agent must return to the former principal any property that had been entrusted to the agent for the purpose of the agency. With the exception of such "winding-up" duties, the agency relationship is terminated, and the former agent can deal with the principal as freely as with a stranger.[21]

36-4c Duties and Liabilities of Principal to Agent

The principal must perform the contract, compensate the agent for services, make reimbursement for proper expenditures, and, under certain circumstances, must indemnify the agent for loss.

Employment According to Terms of Contract

When the contract is for a specified time, the principal is obligated to permit the agent to act as agent for the term of the contract. Exceptions are made for just cause or contract provisions that permit the principal to terminate the agency sooner. If the principal gives the agent an exclusive right to act in that capacity, the principal cannot give anyone else

[19] *St. Paul Reinsurance Co., Ltd. v. Club Services Corp.*, 30 Fed. Appx. 834 (10th Cir. 2002).

[20] Restatement (Second) of Agency §381; *Lumberman's Mutual Ins. Co. v. Franey Muha Alliant Ins.*, 388 F. Supp. 2d 292 (S.D.N.Y. 2005).

[21] *Corron & Black of Illinois, Inc. v. Magner*, 494 N.E.2d 785 (Ill. App. 1986).

the authority to act as agent, nor may the principal do the act to which the exclusive agent's authority relates. **For Example,** if Jill Baker gives Brett Stamos the exclusive right for six months to sell her house, she cannot give another real estate agent the right to sell it during the six-month period or undertake to sell the house herself. If the principal or another agent sells the house, the exclusive agent is entitled to full compensation just as though the act had been performed by the exclusive agent.

Compensation

The principal must pay the agent the agreed compensation.[22] If the parties have not fixed the amount of the compensation by their agreement but intended that the agent should be paid, the agent may recover the customary compensation for such services. If there is no established compensation, the agent may recover the reasonable value of the services rendered.

Repeating Transactions. In certain industries, third persons make repeated transactions with the principal. In these cases, the agent who made the original contract with the third person commonly receives a certain compensation or percentage of commissions on all subsequent renewal or additional contracts. In the insurance business, for example, the insurance agent obtaining the policyholder for the insurer receives a substantial portion of the first year's premiums and then receives a smaller percentage of the premiums paid by the policyholder in subsequent years.

Postagency Transactions. An agent is not ordinarily entitled to compensation in connection with transactions, such as sales or renewals of insurance policies, occurring after the termination of the agency even if the postagency transactions are the result of the agent's former activities. However, if the parties' employment contract calls for such compensation, it must be paid. **For Example,** real estate agent Laura McLane's contract called for her to receive $1.50 for every square foot the Atlanta Committee for the Olympic Games, Inc. (ACOG), leased at an Atlanta building; and even though she had been terminated at the time ACOG executed a lease amendment for 164,412 additional square feet, she was contractually entitled to a $246,618 commission.[23]

36-5 Termination of Agency

An agency may be terminated by the act of one or both of the parties to the agency agreement or by operation of law. When the authority of an agent is terminated, the agent loses all right to act for the principal.

36-5a Termination by Act of Parties

The duration of the agency relationship is commonly stated in the contract creating the relationship. In most cases, either party has the power to terminate the agency relationship at any time. However, the terminating party may be liable for damages to the other if the termination is in violation of the agency contract.

When a principal terminates an agent's authority, it is not effective until the agent receives the notice. Because a known agent will have the appearance of still being an agent, notice must be given to third persons of the termination, and the agent may have the power to bind the principal and third persons until this notice is given.

[22] *American Chocolates, Inc. v. Mascot Pecan Co., Inc.*, 592 So. 2d 93 (Miss. 1992).
[23] *McLane v. Atlanta Market Center Management Co.*, 486 S.E.2d 30 (Ga. App. 1997).

36-5b Termination by Operation of Law

The agency relationship is a personal one, and anything that renders one of the parties incapable of performing will result in the termination of the relationship by operation of law. The death of either the principal or the agent ordinarily terminates the authority of an agent automatically even if the death is unknown to the other.[24]

An agency is also terminated by operation of law on the (1) insanity of the principal or agent, (2) bankruptcy of the principal or agent, (3) impossibility of performance, such as the destruction of the subject matter, or (4) when the country of the principal is at war with that of the agent.

CASE SUMMARY

Missing Out by Minutes

FACTS: William Moore, a fire chief for the city of San Francisco, suffered severe head injuries in a fall while fighting a fire. Moore sued the building owner, Lera, for negligence. The attorneys for the parties held a conference and reached a settlement at 5:15 P.M. Unknown to them, Moore had died at 4:50 P.M. on that day. Was the settlement agreement binding?

DECISION: No. The death of either the principal or the agent terminates the agency. Thus, the death of a client terminates the authority of his agent to act on his behalf. Because Moore died at 4:50 P.M., his attorney no longer had authority to act on his behalf, and the settlement was not enforceable. [***Moore v. Lera Development Inc.*, 274 Cal. Rptr. 658 (Cal. App. 1990)**]

36-5c Disability of the Principal under the UDPAA

The Uniform Durable Power of Attorney Act (UDPAA) permits the creation of an agency by specifying that "this power of attorney shall not be affected by subsequent disability or incapacity of the principal." Alternatively, the UDPAA permits the agency to come into existence upon the disability or incapacity of the principal. For this to be effective, the principal must designate the attorney in fact in writing. The writing must contain words showing the intent of the principal that the authority conferred shall continue notwithstanding the disability or incapacity of the principal. The UDPAA, which has been adopted by most states,[25] changes the common law and the general rule that insanity of the principal terminates the agent's authority to act for the principal. Society today recognizes that it may be in the best interest of a principal and good for the business environment for a principal to designate another as an attorney in fact to act for the principal when the principal becomes incapacitated.[26] It may be prudent to grant durable powers of attorney to different persons for property matters and for health care decisions.

[24] *New York Life Ins. Co. v. Estate of Haelen*, 521 N.Y.S.2d 970 (N.Y. Civ. Ct. 1987).

[25] The Uniform Durable Power of Attorney Act has been adopted in some fashion in all states except Connecticut, Florida, Georgia, Illinois, Indiana, Kansas, Louisiana, and Missouri.

[26] The Uniform Probate Code and the Uniform Durable Power of Attorney Act provide for the coexistence of durable powers and guardians or conservators. These acts allow the attorney in fact to continue to manage the principal's financial affairs while the court-appointed fiduciary takes the place of the principal in overseeing the actions of the attorney in fact. See *Rice v. Flood*, 768 S.W.2d 57 (Ky. 1989).

Durable powers of attorney grant only those powers that are specified in the instrument.[27] A durable power of attorney may be terminated by revocation by a competent principal and by the death of the principal.

CASE SUMMARY

Broad Powers ... But There Is a Limit, Lucille

FACTS: On May 31, 2000, Thomas Graham made his niece Lucille Morrison his attorney in fact by executing a durable power of attorney. It was notarized and filed at the Registry of Deeds. The power of attorney granted Lucille broad powers and discretion in Graham's affairs. However, it did not contain express authority to make gifts. On October 26, 2000, Lucille conveyed 11.92 acres of property valued at between $400,000 and $700,000 to herself based on consideration of services rendered to the principal, Thomas Graham. On June 5, 2001, Lucille, as attorney in fact for Graham, conveyed Graham's house in Charlotte to her son Ladd Morrison. On June 20, 2001, she conveyed Graham's Oakview Terrace property to her brother John Hallman for $3,000 to pay for an attorney to defend Graham in a competency proceeding. Thomas Graham died on August 7, 2001, and his estate sued to set aside the deeds, alleging Lucille's breach of fiduciary duties. After a judgment for the defendants, the estate appealed.

DECISION: Judgment for the estate regarding the 11.92-acre parcel of land Lucille conveyed to herself. When an attorney in fact conveys property to herself based on consideration of services rendered to the principal, the consideration must reflect a fair and reasonable price when compared with the market value of the property. There was no testimony regarding the value of Lucille's services compared with the value of the real property. The deed must be set aside. The conveyance of Graham's home to Ladd Morrison was a gift that was not authorized by her power of attorney and must be set aside. Lucille had authority to sell the principal's property to John Hallman to obtain funds to pay an attorney to represent the principal. The estate's claim of conversion regarding this sale was denied. **[*Estate of Graham v. Morrison*, 607 S.E.2d 295 (N.C. App. 2005)]**

36-5d Termination of Agency Coupled with an Interest

An agency coupled with an interest is an exception to the general rule as to the termination of an agency. Such an agency cannot be revoked by the principal before the expiration of the interest. It is not terminated by the death or insanity of either the principal or the agent.

36-5e Protection of Agent from Termination of Authority

The modern world of business has developed several methods of protecting an agent from the termination of authority for any reason.[28]

These methods include the use of an exclusive agency contract, a secured transaction, an escrow deposit, a standby letter of agreement, or a guarantee agreement.

[27] An attorney in fact (the holder of a power of attorney) may make decisions concerning litigation for the principal, such as deciding to settle a case, but a non-lawyer attorney in fact may not act as a lawyer to implement those decisions, nor may such an individual testify in place of an otherwise competent party in matters such as a divorce. See *Marisco v. Marisco*, 94 A.3d 947 (N.J. Super. 2013).

[28] These methods generally replace the concept of an agency coupled with an interest because of the greater protection given to the agent. Typically, the rights of the agent under these modern devices cannot be defeated by the principal, by operation of law, or by claims of other creditors.

36-5f Effect of Termination of Authority

If the principal revokes the agency, the authority to act for the principal is not terminated until the agent receives notice of revocation. As between the principal and the agent, the right of the agent to bind the principal to third persons generally ends immediately upon the termination of the agent's authority. This termination is effective without giving notice to third persons.

When the agency is terminated by the act of the principal, notice must be given to third persons. If this notice is not given, the agent may have the power to make contracts that will bind the principal and third persons. This rule is predicated on the theory that a known agent will have the appearance of still being the agent unless notice to the contrary is given to third persons.[29] **For Example,** Seltzer owns property in Boca Raton that he uses for the month of February and leases the remainder of the year. O'Neil has been Seltzer's rental agent for the past seven years, renting to individuals like Ed Tucker under a power of attorney that gives him authority to lease the property for set seasonal and off-season rates. O'Neil's right to bind Seltzer on a rental agreement ended when Seltzer faxed O'Neil a revocation of the power of attorney on March 1. A rental contract with Ed Tucker signed by O'Neil on behalf of Seltzer on March 2 will bind Seltzer, however, because O'Neil still appeared to be Seltzer's agent and Tucker had no notice to the contrary.

When the law requires giving notice in order to end the power of the agent to bind the principal, individual notice must be given or mailed to all persons who had prior dealings with the agent. In addition, notice to the general public can be given by publishing in a newspaper of general circulation in the affected geographic area a statement that the agency has been terminated.

If a notice is actually received, the power of the agent is terminated without regard to whether the method of giving notice was proper. Conversely, if proper notice is given, it is immaterial that it does not actually come to the attention of the party notified. Thus, a member of the general public cannot claim that the principal is bound on the ground that the third person did not see the newspaper notice stating that the agent's authority had been terminated.

Make the Connection

Summary

An agency relationship is created by an express or implied agreement by which one person, the agent, is authorized to make contracts with third persons on behalf of, and subject to, the control of another person, the principal. An agent differs from an independent contractor in that the principal, who controls the acts of an agent, does not have control over the details of performance of work by the independent contractor. Likewise, an independent contractor does not have authority to act on behalf of the other contracting party.

A special agent is authorized by the principal to handle a specific business transaction. A general agent is

[29] See *Stout Street Funding, LLC v. Johnson*, 2012 WL 1994800 (E.D. Pa. June 1, 2012). TRGC terminated its contract with Mabstract to serve as TRGC's closing agent on July 12, 2010, and obtained a court injunction barring Mabstract from engaging in any business on behalf of TRGC on July 15. Stout asserts that it had no actual notice of Mabstract's termination nor were there any red flags when it transmitted $480,000 into an escrow account held by Mabstract for a July 19 real estate transaction, which funds were misappropriated by Mabstract. It asserts that apparent authority lasts until a third party has actual notice of an agent's termination or until the third party has enough information to put that individual on inquiry.

authorized by the principal to transact all business affairs of the principal at a certain place. A universal agent is authorized to perform all acts that can be lawfully delegated to a representative.

The usual method of creating an agency is by express authorization. However, an agency relationship may be found to exist when the principal causes or permits a third person to reasonably believe that an agency relationship exists. In such a case, the "agent" appears to be authorized and is said to have apparent authority.

An unauthorized transaction by an agent for a principal may be ratified by the principal.

An agent acting with authority has the power to bind the principal. The scope of an agent's authority may be determined from the express words of the principal to the agent; this is called express authority. An agent has incidental authority to perform any act reasonably necessary to execute the authority given the agent. An agent's authority may be implied so as to enable the agent to perform any act in accordance with the general customs or usages in a business or an industry. This authority is often referred to as customary authority.

The effect of a proper exercise of authority by an agent is to bind the principal and third person to a contract. The agent, not being a party to the contract, is not liable in any respect under the contract. A third person dealing with a person claiming to be an agent has a duty to ascertain the extent of the agent's authority and a duty to take notice of any acts that are clearly adverse to the principal's interests. The third person cannot claim that apparent authority existed when that person has notice that the agent's conduct is adverse to the interests of the principal. A third person who has knowledge of limitations on an agent's authority is bound by those limitations. A third person is not bound by secret limitations.

While the agency relationship exists, the agent owes the principal the duties of (1) being loyal, (2) obeying all lawful instructions, (3) exercising reasonable care, (4) accounting for all property or money belonging to the principal, and (5) informing the principal of all facts relating to the agency that are relevant to the principal's interests. An agency relationship can be terminated by act of either the principal or the agent. However, the terminating party may be liable for damages to the other if the termination is in violation of the agency contract.

Because a known agent will have the appearance of still being an agent, notice must be given to third persons of the termination, and the agent may have the power to bind the principal and third persons until this notice is given.

An agency is terminated by operation of law upon (1) the death of the principal or agent, (2) insanity of the principal or agent, (3) bankruptcy of the principal or agent, (4) impossibility of performance, caused, for example, by the destruction of the subject matter, or (5) war. In states that have adopted the Uniform Durable Power of Attorney Act (UDPAA), an agency may be created that is not affected by subsequent disability or incapacity of the principal. In UDPAA states, the agency may also come into existence upon the "disability or incapacity of the principal." The designation of an attorney in fact under the UDPAA must be in writing.

Learning Outcomes

After studying this chapter, you should be able to clearly explain:

36-1 Nature of the Agency Relationship

LO.1 Explain the difference between an agent and an independent contractor

See the Ned and Tracy Seizer example and the "right to control" test, page 721.

36-2 Creating the Agency

LO.2 Explain three methods of creating an agency relationship

See the discussion on the usual method of creating an agency (which is by express authorization), page 723.

See the *Taylor* case where actual authority to perform some tasks created apparent authority to perform other related tasks, page 723.

See the agency by ratification example of James and Calvin Reiner, page 724.

36-3 Agent's Authority

LO.3 Recognize that third persons who deal with an agent are required to take notice of acts contrary to the interests of the principal

See the example of the Fire Company that failed to verify with the principal an agent's authority to receive a prepayment check of $55,000 made out in the agent's name, page 727.

36-4 Duties and Liabilities of Principal and Agent

LO.4 List and explain the duties an agent owes the principal

See the discussion concerning an agent's duty of loyalty, obedience, reasonable care, accounting, and information, pages 729–731.

See the *Mosionzhnik* case exposing an agent's breach of her duty of loyalty, page 729.

36-5 Termination of Agency

LO.5 Explain how the Uniform Durable Power of Attorney Act changes the common law rule on incapacity of the principal

See the *Estate of Graham* case on the limits of a durable power of attorney, page 734.

Key Terms

agency
agent
apparent authority
attorney in fact
customary authority
express authorization
general agent
incidental authority
independent contractor
interest in the authority
interest in the subject matter
power of attorney
principal
special agent
universal agent

Questions and Case Problems

1. How does an agent differ from an independent contractor?
2. Compare authorization of an agent by (a) appointment and (b) ratification.
3. Ernest A. Kotsch executed a durable power of attorney when he was 85 years old, giving his son, Ernie, the power to manage and sell his real estate and personal property "and to do all acts necessary for maintaining and caring for [the father] during his lifetime." Thereafter, Kotsch began "keeping company" with a widow, Margaret Gradl. Ernie believed that the widow was attempting to alienate his father from him, and he observed that she was exerting a great deal of influence over his father. Acting under the durable power of attorney and without informing his father, Ernie created the "Kotsch Family Irrevocable Trust," to which he transferred $700,000, the bulk of his father's liquid assets, with the father as grantor and initial beneficiary and Ernie's three children as additional beneficiaries. Ernie named himself trustee. His father sued to avoid the trust. Ernie defended his action on the ground that he had authority to create the trust under the durable power of attorney. Decide. [*Kotsch v. Kotsch*, 608 So. 2d 879 (Fla. App.)]
4. Ken Jones, the number-one-ranked prizefighter in his weight class, signed a two-year contract with Howard Stayword. The contract obligated Stayword to represent and promote Jones in all business and professional matters, including the arrangement of fights. For these services, Jones was to pay Stayword 10 percent of gross earnings. After a year, when Stayword proved unsuccessful in arranging a title match with the champion, Jones fired Stayword. During the following year, Jones earned $4 million. Stayword sued Jones for $400,000. Jones defended himself on the basis that a principal has the absolute power at any time to terminate an agency relationship by discharging the agent, so he was not liable to Stayword. Was Jones correct?
5. Paul Strich did business as an optician in Duluth, Minnesota. Paul used only the products of the Plymouth Optical Co., a national manufacturer of optical products and supplies with numerous retail outlets and some franchise arrangements in areas other than Duluth. To increase business, Paul renovated his office and changed the sign on it to read "Plymouth Optical Co." Paul did business this way for more than three years—advertised under that name, paid bills with checks bearing the name of Plymouth Optical Co., and listed himself in the telephone and city directories by that name. Plymouth immediately became aware of what Paul was doing. However, because Paul used only Plymouth products and Plymouth did not have a franchise in Duluth, it saw no advantage at that time in prohibiting Paul from using the name and losing him as a customer. Paul contracted with the *Duluth Tribune* for advertising, making the contract in the name of Plymouth Optical Co. When the advertising bill was not paid, the *Duluth Tribune* sued Plymouth Optical Co. for payment. Plymouth's defense was that it

never authorized Paul to do business under the name, nor authorized him to make a contract with the newspaper. Decide.

6. Record owned a farm that was managed by his agent, Berry, who lived on the farm. Berry hired Wagner to bale the hay and told him to bill Record for this work. Wagner did so and was paid by Record. By the summer of the following year, the agency had been terminated by Record, but Berry remained in possession as tenant of the farm and nothing appeared changed. Late in the summer, Berry asked Wagner to bale the hay as he had done the previous year and bill Record for the work. He did so, but Record refused to pay on the ground that Berry was not then his agent. Wagner sued him. Decide. [*Record v. Wagner*, 128 A.2d 921 (N.H.)]
7. Gilbert Church owned Church Farms, Inc., in Manteno, Illinois. Church advertised its well-bred stallion Imperial Guard for breeding rights at $50,000, directing all inquiries to "Herb Bagley, Manager." Herb Bagley lived at Church Farms and was the only person available to visitors. Vern Lundberg answered the ad, and after discussions in which Bagley stated that Imperial Guard would remain in Illinois for at least a two-year period, Lundberg and Bagley executed a two-year breeding rights contract. The contract was signed by Lundberg and by Bagley as "Church Farms, Inc., H. Bagley, Mgr." When Gil Church moved Imperial Guard to Oklahoma prior to the second year of the contract, Lundberg brought suit for breach of contract. Church testified that Bagley had no authority to sign contracts for Church Farms. Decide. [*Lundberg v. Church Farms, Inc.*, 502 N.E.2d 806 (Ill.)]
8. The Holzmans signed an exclusive listing agreement with the Blum real estate brokerage firm. The contract provided that the Holzmans had an obligation to pay a commission "if they enter into a written agreement to sell the property to any person during the term of this exclusive listing agreement." The Holzmans entered into a written agreement to sell their house for $715,000 to the Noravians. On the advice of their attorney, the Holzmans included a default provision in this contract stating that in the event of default by the Holzmans, the Noravians' only remedy would be a refund of their deposit. Subsequently, the Sterns offered $850,000 for the property and the Holzmans canceled their contract with the Noravians and returned their deposit. After the exclusive listing period expired, the Holzmans executed a contract to sell their property to the Sterns at the offered price of $850,000—with the contract calling for the Holzmans to pay half the real estate fee to Blum and half to a cooperating broker. Blum was paid this fee of $21,500. Blum brought suit against the Holzmans seeking the full commission for the Noravian contract under the exclusive listing agreement. Did Blum have a legal obligation or ethical duty to advise the Holzmans when considering the Sterns' offer that he believed they were obligated to him for the full commission under the Novarian contract? Decide. [*Holzman v. Blum*, 726 A.2d 818 (Md. App.)]
9. Tillie Flinn properly executed a durable power of attorney designating her nephew James C. Flanders and/or Martha E. Flanders, his wife, as her attorney in fact. Seven months later, Martha Flanders went to the Capitol Federal Savings and Loan Association office. She had the durable power of attorney instrument, five certificates of deposit, and a handprinted letter identifying Martha as an attorney in fact and stating that Tillie wished to cash her five CDs that Martha had with her. At approximately 10:31 A.M., five checks were given to Martha in the aggregate amount of $135,791.34, representing the funds in the five CDs less penalties for early withdrawal. Some of the checks were drawn to the order of Martha individually and some to the order of James and Martha, as individuals. Tillie was found dead of heart disease later that day. The time of death stated on her death certificate was 11:30 A.M. The Flanderses spent the money on themselves. Bank IV, as administrator of Tillie's estate, sued Capitol Federal to recover the amount of the funds paid to the Flanderses. It contended that Capitol Federal breached its duty to investigate before issuing the checks. Capitol Federal contended that it did all that it had a duty to do. Decide. [*Bank IV v. Capitol Federal Savings and Loan Ass'n*, 828 P.2d 355 (Kan.)]
10. Lew owns a store on Canal Street in New Orleans. He paid a person named Mike and other individuals commissions for customers brought into the store. Lew testified that he had known Mike for less than a week. Boulos and Durso, partners in a wholesale jewelry business, were visiting New Orleans on a business trip when Mike brought them into the store to buy a stereo. While Durso finalized the stereo transaction with the store's manager, Boulos and Mike negotiated to buy 2 cameras, 3 videos, and 20 gold Dupont lighters. Unknown to the store's manager, Mike was given $8,250 in cash and was to deliver the merchandise later that evening to the

Marriott Hotel, where Boulos and Durso were staying. Mike gave a receipt for the cash, but it showed no sales tax or indication that the goods were to be delivered. Boulos testified that he believed Mike was the store owner. Mike never delivered the merchandise and disappeared. Boulos and Durso contended that Lew is liable for the acts of his agent, Mike. Lew denied that Mike was his agent, and the testimony showed that Mike had no actual authority to make a sale, to use a cash register, or even to go behind a sales counter. What ethical principle applies to the conduct of Boulos and Durso? Decide. [*Boulos v. Morrison*, 503 So. 2d 1 (La.)]

11. Martha Christiansen owns women's apparel stores bearing her name in New Seabury, Massachusetts; Lake Placid, New York; Palm Beach, Florida; and Palm Springs, California. At a meeting with her four store managers, she discussed styles she thought appropriate for the forthcoming season, advised them as always to use their best judgment in the goods they purchased for each of their respective stores, and cautioned "but no blue jeans." Later, Jane Farley, the manager of the Lake Placid store, purchased a line of high-quality blue denim outfits (designer jeans with jacket and vest options) from Women's Wear, Inc., for the summer season. The outfits did not sell. Martha refused to pay for them, contending that she had told all of her managers "no blue jeans" and that if it came to a lawsuit, she would fly in three managers to testify that Jane Farley had absolutely no authority to purchase denim outfits and was, in fact, expressly forbidden to do so. Women's Wear sued Martha, and the three managers testified for her. Is the fact that Martha had explicitly forbidden Farley to purchase the outfits in question sufficient to protect her from liability for the purchases made by Farley?

12. Fred Schilling, the president and administrator of Florence General Hospital, made a contract, dated August 16, 1989, on behalf of the hospital with CMK Associates to transfer the capacity to utilize 25 beds from the hospital to the Faith Nursing Home. Schilling, on behalf of the hospital, had previously made a contract with CMK Associates on May 4, 1987. Schilling had been specifically authorized by the hospital board to make the 1987 contract. The hospital refused to honor the 1989 contract because the board had not authorized it. CMK contended that Schilling had apparent authority to bind the hospital because he was president and administrator of the hospital and he had been the person who negotiated and signed a contract with CMK in 1987. Thus, according to CMK, the hospital had held out Schilling as having apparent authority to make the contract. The hospital disagreed. Decide. [*Pee Dee Nursing Home v. Florence General Hospital*, 419 S.E.2d 843 (S.C. App.)]

13. Real estate broker Donald Alley Sr. had a listing contract that gave him the exclusive right to sell Wayman Ellison's farm for at least $200,000. Ellison was told that a buyer was found. The buyer, Cora Myers, who had been paid $585,000 for her small farm because the land was needed for a commercial development, agreed to pay $380,000 for the large Ellison farm. Alley told Ellison that the sale price was $200,000. The buyer paid $380,000, however, and Alley kept the difference. When Ellison later learned of these details, he sued Alley for the $180,000. From a judgment for Ellison, Alley appealed, seeking at least his commission on the sale since he procured a ready, willing, and able buyer. Decide. [*Ellison v. Alley*, 842 S.W.2d 605 (Tenn)].

14. Francis Gagnon, an elderly gentleman, signed a power of attorney authorizing his daughter, Joan, "to sell any of my real estate and to execute any document needed to carry out the sale ... and to add property to a trust of which I am grantor or beneficiary." This power was given in case Gagnon was not available to take care of matters personally because he was traveling. When Joan learned that Gagnon intended to sell his Shelburne property to Cosby for $750,000, she created an irrevocable trust naming Gagnon as beneficiary and herself as trustee. Acting then on the basis of the authority set forth in the power of attorney, she conveyed the Shelburne property to herself as trustee of the irrevocable trust, thus blocking the sale to Cosby. When Gagnon learned of this, he demanded that Joan return the Shelburne property to him, but she refused, saying she had acted within the authority set forth in the power of attorney. Did Joan violate any duty owed to Gagnon? Must she reconvey the property to Gagnon? [*Gagnon v. Coombs*, 654 N.E.2d 54 (Mass. App.)]

15. Daniels and Julian were employed by the Marriott Hotel in New Orleans and were close personal friends. One day after work, Daniels and Julian went to Werlein's music store to open a credit account. Julian, with Daniels's authorization and in her

presence, applied for credit using Daniels's name and credit history. Later, Julian went to Werlein's without Daniels and charged the purchase of a television set to Daniels's account, executing a retail installment contract by signing Daniels's name. Daniels saw the new television in Julian's home and was informed that it was charged to the Werlein's account. Daniels told Julian to continue making payments. When Werlein's credit manager first contacted Daniels to inform her that her account was delinquent, she claimed that a money order for the television was in the mail. On the second call, she asked for a "payment balance." Some four months after the purchase, she informed Werlein's that she had not authorized the purchase of the television nor ratified the purchase. Werlein's sued Daniels for the unpaid balance. Decide. [*Philip Werlein, Ltd. v. Daniels*, 536 So. 2d 722 (La. App.)]

CPA Questions

1. Generally, an agency relationship is terminated by operation of law in all of the following situations except the:
   a. Principal's death.
   b. Principal's incapacity.
   c. Agent's renunciation of the agency.
   d. Agent's failure to acquire a necessary business license.
2. Able, on behalf of Pix Corp., entered into a contract with Sky Corp., by which Sky agreed to sell computer equipment to Pix. Able disclosed to Sky that she was acting on behalf of Pix. However, Able had exceeded her actual authority by entering into the contract with Sky. If Pix wishes to ratify the contract with Sky, which of the following statements is correct?
   a. Pix must notify Sky that Pix intends to ratify the contract.
   b. Able must have acted reasonably and in Pix's best interest.
   c. Able must be a general agent of Pix.
   d. Pix must have knowledge of all material facts relating to the contract at the time it is ratified.
3. Which of the following actions requires an agent for a corporation to have a written agency agreement?
   a. Purchasing office supplies for the principal's business.
   b. Purchasing an interest in undeveloped land for the principal.
   c. Hiring an independent general contractor to renovate the principal's office building.
   d. Retaining an attorney to collect a business debt owed the principal.
4. Simmons, an agent for Jensen, has the express authority to sell Jensen's goods. Simmons also has the express authority to grant discounts of up to 5 percent of list price. Simmons sold Hemple a 10 percent discount. Hemple had not previously dealt with either Simmons or Jensen. Which of the following courses of action may Jensen properly take?
   a. Seek to void the sale to Hemple.
   b. Seek recovery of $50 from Hemple only.
   c. Seek recovery of $50 from Simmons only.
   d. Seek recovery of $50 from either Hemple or Simmons.
5. Ogden Corp. hired Thorp as a sales representative for nine months at a salary of $3,000 per month plus 4 percent of sales. Which of the following statements is correct?
   a. Thorp is obligated to act solely in Ogden's interest in matters concerning Ogden's business.
   b. The agreement between Ogden and Thorp formed an agency coupled with an interest.
   c. Ogden does not have the power to dismiss Thorp during the nine-month period without cause.
   d. The agreement between Ogden and Thorp is not enforceable unless it is in writing and signed by Thorp.
6. Frost's accountant and business manager has the authority to:
   a. Mortgage Frost's business property.
   b. Obtain bank loans for Frost.
   c. Insure Frost's property against fire loss.
   d. Sell Frost's business.

CHAPTER 41

Partnerships

Learning Outcomes

After studying this chapter, you should be able to

LO.1 Explain how partnerships are created by agreement, and understand that only when the partnership agreement does not resolve an issue does partnership law apply

LO.2 Understand that no writing is needed to form a partnership, nor a tax ID number, nor a partnership name. All that is needed is clear evidence that the partners carried on as co-owners of a business for profit

LO.3 Distinguish between express authority and customary authority of a partner to act for a partnership

LO.4 List the duties of partners to one another

LO.5 Explain the nature and extent of a partner's liability on firm contracts and torts

LO.6 Describe how a partnership may be dissolved by the acts of partners, by operation of law, and by order of the court

Partnerships may be created without the formality of even a written partnership agreement when two or more individuals simply operate a business for a profit as co-owners. **For Example,** in July 2008, Paula Balzer was recruited to work for Blue Flame, a firm specializing in the business of marketing and live promotions. As of October 1, 2008, she states she was made a partner. Two firm e-mails reference her as a partner; she was paid a monthly $15,000 draw; and the firm's 2008 and 2009 tax returns listed her as a partner of Blue Flame. In October 2010, the partners had a falling-out with Paula. She disengaged from the firm on November 12, 2010, upon completion of two events she was committed to staging. The partners never executed a written partnership agreement with Paula and as a result did not believe she had partnership rights. When the firm failed to pay her certain money and expenses, the court reverted to basic partnership law that a written contract of partnership is not necessary to the formation of a partnership and concluded that a partnership existed on the basis of the facts before the court.[1] Partnership relations are governed by the partnership agreement. Only when the partnership agreement does not resolve an issue does partnership law apply. In many instances, individuals do not obtain legal advice in choosing the partnership form of business organization. Properly informed individuals today will probably not choose the partnership form of organization because partners are open to unlimited personal liability; they may choose a limited liability company to insulate the members from personal liability.

partnership–pooling of capital resources and the business or professional talents of two or more individuals (partners) with the goal of making a profit.

general partnership–partnership in which the partners conduct as co-owners a business for profit, and each partner has a right to take part in the management of the business and has unlimited liability.

partner–one of two or more persons who jointly own and carry on a business for profit.

general partners–partners who publicly and actively engage in the transaction of firm business.

41-1 Nature and Creation

Partnerships are created by agreement. States have partnership laws that apply when there is no written agreement or to fill gaps in the partnership agreement. All states except Louisiana have adopted either the Uniform Partnership Act (UPA) or the Revised Uniform Partnership Act (RUPA), which is more detailed than the UPA.[2] Certain features of the RUPA that differ from those of the UPA are identified in the text. At common law, a partnership was considered to be an aggregate of the individual partners. Under the UPA and the RUPA, the partnership may be viewed as an entity separate from the partners for certain purposes. The RUPA enhances the entity theory of partnerships.[3] Under the aggregate theory, a partnership is characterized by the collection of its individual members. Consequently, if a partner dies or withdraws, the partnership ceases to exist. Under the entity theory, the partnership continues to exist as distinct from its partners, even if a partner dies or withdraws.[4] Even under the entity theory, however, each partner remains personally liable for the obligations of the partnership.[5] The 1994 or 1997 versions of the Revised Uniform Partnership Act apply in 38 states.[6] Limited partnerships (LPs) and limited liability partnerships (LLPs) differ significantly from general partnerships and are discussed in the next chapter.

41-1a Definition

A **partnership** (also called a **general partnership**) is a relationship created by the voluntary "association of two or more persons to carry on as co-owners a business for profit."[7] The persons so associated are called **partners** or **general partners.** A partner is the agent

[1] *Balzer v. Millward,* 2011 WL 1547211 (D. Conn. April 21, 2011).
[2] The Louisiana Civil Code has many provisions similar to those in the UPA and RUPA.
[3] See *Mission West v. Republic,* 873 A.2d 372 (Md. App. 2005).
[4] See *Robertson v. Jacobs Cattle Co.,* 830 N.W.2d 191 (Neb. 2013).
[5] The UPA or the RUPA is in effect in all states except Louisiana.
[6] The RUPA was approved in 1992 and amended in 1993, 1994, and 1997. States that have adopted the RUPA provide for a transition period after passage during which only newly created partnerships come under the new law, with all partnerships in the state eventually being governed by the RUPA (see R.U.P.A. §1206(a)).
[7] U.P.A. §6(1).

of the partnership and of each partner with respect to partnership matters. A partner is not an employee of the partnership even when doing work that would ordinarily be done by an employee.

CASE SUMMARY

A Partner Is Not an Employee

FACTS: Ford and Mitcham were partners engaged in construction. Ford was killed at work. His widow made a claim for workers' compensation against the partnership. Mitcham opposed the claim on the ground that Ford was a partner, not an employee.

DECISION: Workers' compensation denied. While a working partner does work, a partner is not an employee. The essential element of an employment relationship is the right of the employer to control the employee. Although a partner is required to act in a proper manner, a partner is not subject to the control of the partnership in the same sense as an employee and therefore is not an "employee" of the partnership for the purpose of workers' compensation. [***Ford v. Mitcham*, 298 So. 2d 34 (Ala. App. 1974)**]

41-1b Characteristics of a Partnership

A partnership has distinguishing characteristics:

1. A partnership is a voluntary, consensual relationship.
2. A partnership involves partners' contributions of capital, services, or a combination of these.
3. The partners are associated as co-owners to transact the business of the firm for profit.

unincorporated association– combination of two or more persons for the furtherance of a common nonprofit purpose.

If profit is not the object, the group will commonly be an **unincorporated association.**

Under the UPA, the partnership is not an entity separate from its partners and cannot bring suit in its own name, unless a special statute or procedural rule specifically allows. In RUPA states, however, partnerships are recognized as entities and suit may be brought against the partnership. In either case, plaintiffs must name the individual partners to have access to their individual assets.

41-1c Rights of Partners

The rights of partners are determined by the partnership agreement. If written, this agreement is interpreted by the same rules that govern the interpretation of any other written document. Any matter not covered by the partnership agreement may be covered by a provision of the UPA or RUPA, depending on which version the state has adopted.

41-1d Partnership Agreement

Partnership agreements are typically written to cover numerous, complex issues. However, there is no requirement that they be in writing unless compliance with a statute of frauds is required. **For Example,** the world's highest-paid performers in the early 1990s, the New Kids on the Block, who grossed $74.1 million in one year, were a group started by promoter Maurice Starr. He obtained $60,000 from James Martorano, who was connected with organized crime, and $50,000 from businessman Jeffrey Furst to finance the initial recording and promotion of the group. Martorano and Furst testified that, ultimately, all three agreed with a handshake that 50 percent of the profits from the group would be shared between Martorano as a silent partner and Furst, who would also provide limousine service and security. They testified that Starr would keep half of the profits. Starr denied that a partnership existed because he believed that such an alleged business arrangement would have had to be reduced to writing with great detail. However, based on the evidence, which included damaging testimony that Starr tried to buy some witnesses' silence, a jury decided that a binding oral partnership agreement existed.[8]

partnership agreement–document prepared to evidence the contract of the parties. (Parties—partners or general partners)

articles of partnership–see *partnership agreement.*

articles of copartnership–see *partnership agreement.*

To reduce or avoid disputes and litigation, partnership agreements should be in writing. Courts will enforce partnership agreements, under the standards of the law of contracts, according to the terms of the agreement.[9] **For Example,** dentist Steven Schwartz was terminated from a three-dentist practice "without cause" by vote of his two other partners. The partnership agreement allowed for termination of a partner as long as either party gave the other 90 days' notice. The appeals court held that the written terms of the agreement were determinative. The parties were sophisticated and highly educated professionals and the provision was not in violation of public policy.[10]

The formal document that is prepared to evidence the contract of the parties is termed a **partnership agreement, articles of partnership,** or **articles of copartnership.** The partnership agreement governs the partnership during its existence and may contain provisions relating to dissolution. (See Figure 41-1.)

FIGURE 41-1 Partnership Agreement

PARTNERSHIP AGREEMENT

THIS IS A PARTNERSHIP AGREEMENT EXECUTED AT CINCINNATI, OHIO, THIS 9TH DAY OF SEPTEMBER, 1998, BY AND AMONG LOUIS K. HALL, SHARON B. YOUNG, AND C. LYNN MUELLER, INDIVIDUALS RESIDING IN CINCINNATI, OHIO, HEREINAFTER SOMETIMES REFERRED TO INDIVIDUALLY AS "PARTNER" AND COLLECTIVELY AS "PARTNERS."

RECITALS

THE PARTNERS TO THIS AGREEMENT DESIRE TO ACQUIRE A CERTAIN PARCEL OF REAL ESTATE AND TO DEVELOP SUCH REAL ESTATE FOR LEASE OR SALE, ALL FOR INVESTMENT PURPOSES. THIS AGREEMENT IS BEING EXECUTED TO DELINEATE THE BASIS OF THEIR RELATIONSHIP.

PROVISIONS

1. NAME; AND PRINCIPAL OFFICES. THE NAME OF THE PARTNERSHIP SHALL BE: HALL, YOUNG AND MUELLER, ASSOCIATES. ITS PRINCIPAL PLACE OF BUSINESS SHALL BE AT: 201 RIVER ROAD, CINCINNATI, OHIO 45238.

2. PURPOSE. THE PURPOSE OF THE PARTNERSHIP SHALL BE TO PURCHASE AND OWN FOR INVESTMENT PURPOSES, A CERTAIN PARCEL OF REAL ESTATE LOCATED AT 602 SIXTH STREET, CINCINNATI, OHIO, AND TO ENGAGE IN ANY OTHER TYPE OF INVESTMENT ACTIVITIES THAT THE PARTNERSHIP MAY FROM TIME TO TIME HEREINAFTER UNANIMOUSLY AGREE UPON.

3. CAPITAL CONTRIBUTIONS. THE CAPITAL OF THE PARTNERSHIP SHALL BE THE AGGREGATE AMOUNT OF CASH AND PROPERTY CONTRIBUTED BY THE PARTNERS. A CAPITAL ACCOUNT SHALL BE MAINTAINED FOR EACH PARTNER.

A. CAPITAL CONTRIBUTIONS. ANY ADDITIONAL CAPITAL WHICH MAY BE REQUIRED BY THE PARTNERSHIP SHALL BE CONTRIBUTED TO THE PARTNERSHIP BY THE PARTNERS IN THE SAME RATIO AS THAT PARTNER'S ORIGINAL CONTRIBUTION TO CAPITAL AS TO THE TOTAL OF ALL ORIGINAL CAPITAL CONTRIBUTIONS TO THE PARTNERSHIP UNLESS OTHERWISE AGREED BY THE PARTNERS.

[8] Judy Rakowsky, "New Kids' Profits on the Block," *Boston Globe*, November 18, 1995.
[9] *Krajacich v. Great Falls Clinic*, 276 P.3d 922 (Mont. 2012).
[10] *Schwartz v. Family Dental Group*, P.C., 943 A.2d 1122 (Conn. App. 2008).

CPA 41-1e Determining the Existence of a Partnership

If the parties agree to operate a business for profit as co-owners, a partnership is created even though the parties may not have labeled their new relationship as such.[11] The law is concerned with the substance of the relationship rather than the name. Conversely, a partnership does not arise if the parties do not agree to the elements of a partnership even though they call it one.[12]

CASE SUMMARY

The Case of the Absolutely Dumbfounded Investor (Partner)

FACTS: David Byker, an accountant, and Tom Mannes, a real estate professional, agreed to engage in an ongoing business enterprise to raise investment funds for separate real estate–related ventures and to share equally in the profits, losses, and expenses. Over the years, the parties pursued various individual limited partnerships, sharing equally in commissions, financing fees, and termination costs. Byker and Mannes then created a subsequent entity, Pier 1000, Ltd., to own and manage a marina. This venture was not successful, and they took profits from a prior entity and borrowed money to continue operations. The unsuccessful marina was later returned to its previous owners in exchange for assumption of Byker's and Mannes's direct obligations to that business. The nine-year business relationship between them ceased. Later, Byker approached Mannes and requested that he share in the payments resulting from losses that were incurred from their various entities. Mannes was, in his words, "absolutely dumbfounded" by the request, and he refused payment. Byker sued, contending that a general partnership was underlying all their business affairs. Mannes asserted that he merely invested in separate business ventures with Byker and that there were no other understandings between them.

DECISION: Judgment for David Byker. Partnership law does not require that individuals be aware of their status as "partners" to have a legal partnership. The intent to create a partnership is not required if the acts and the conduct of the parties otherwise evidence that the parties carried on as co-owners of a business for profit. No writing is needed to form a partnership. No name or tax ID number is necessary to attain legal status as a partnership, nor is it required that the parties must aggregate all entities under a general partnership tax return. Mannes filed his tax returns based on his share of the income and expense from the individual legal entities that existed with the legal status of each entity controlling his tax obligations. However, additional evidence indicated that a partnership existed, including the general agreement in principle from the beginning that they would share profits and losses together in their real estate investment business. While they should have created a legal entity to address the situation that precipitated the lawsuit, because they did not, partnership law applies. **[*Byker v. Mannes*, 641 N.W.2d 210 (Mich. 2002)]**

A partnership is shown to exist when it is established that the parties have agreed to the formation of a business organization that has the characteristics of a partnership. The burden of proving the existence of a partnership is on the person who claims that one exists.[13]

When the nature of the relationship is not clear, the following rules aid in determining whether the parties have created a partnership.

CPA Control

The presence or absence of control of a business enterprise is significant in determining whether there is a partnership and whether a particular person is a partner.

[11] *Swecker v. Swecker*, 360 S.W.3d 422 (Tenn. App. 2011).
[12] See *Cleland v. Thirion*, 704 N.Y.S.2d 316 (A.D. 2000).
[13] *MacArthur v. Stein*, 934 P.2d 214 (Mont. 1997).

CPA

Sharing Profits and Losses

The fact that the parties share profits and losses is strong evidence of a partnership.[14]

CPA

Sharing Profits

An agreement that does not provide for sharing losses but does provide for sharing profits is evidence that the parties are partners. If the partners share profits, it is assumed that they will also share losses. Sharing profits is prima facie evidence of a partnership. However, a partnership is not to be inferred when profits are received in payment (1) of a debt, (2) of wages, (3) of an annuity to a deceased partner's surviving spouse or representative, (4) of interest, or (5) for the goodwill of the business.[15] **For Example,** the fact that one doctor receives one-half of the net income does not establish that doctor as a partner of another doctor when the former was guaranteed a minimum annual amount. Also, federal income tax and Social Security contributions were deducted from the payments to the doctor, thus indicating that the relationship was that of employer and employee. If there is no evidence of the reason for receiving the profits, a partnership of the parties involved exists.

CPA

Gross Returns

The sharing of gross returns is itself very slight, if any, evidence of a partnership.

CPA

Contribution of Skill or Labor

The fact that all persons have not contributed capital to an enterprise does not establish that the enterprise is not a partnership. A partnership may be formed even though some of its members furnish only skill or labor.

CPA

Fixed Payment

When a person who performs continuing services for another receives a fixed payment that does not depend on the existence of profit and is not affected by losses, that person is not a partner.

CPA

41-1f Partners as to Third Persons

In some instances, persons who are in fact not partners may be held liable to third persons as though they were partners. This liability arises when they conduct themselves in such a manner that others are reasonably led to believe that they are partners and to act in reliance on that belief to their injury.[16] A person who is held liable as a partner under such circumstances is termed a *nominal partner, a partner by estoppel,* or an *ostensible partner.*

Partnership liability may arise by estoppel when a person who in fact is not a partner represents herself as a partner or consents to another representing her as a partner. The person is liable to any such person to whom such representation is made. To prevail on a partnership by estoppel claim, the plaintiff must have reasonably relied on the representation of partnership or joint venture status. **For Example,** purchasers of condominiums at Las Vegas Cay Club sued those who represented that they were in a partnership with the developer. The purchasers claimed that they relied on marketing materials that indicated Cay Clubs was in a partnership with certain entities and that they bought the condominiums relying on the expertise and resources of these purported partners to develop the luxury resort. When the developers abandoned the project, the purchasers were left

[14] *Botsee Gates v. Houston,* 897 N.E.2d 532 (Ind. App. 2008).

[15] U.P.A. §7(4).

[16] U.P.A. §16(1); *Andrews v. Elwell,* 367 F. Supp. 2d 35 (D. Mass. 2005).

with "worthless property." The court concluded that under Nevada law partnership by estoppel applied because the purchasers reasonably relied on the representation that Cay Clubs was in a partnership with established developers.[17] Under the RUPA, an apparent partnership or partnership by estoppel is called a *purported* partnership, and a third person who relies on the partnership's representations that the purported partner had authority to bind the partnership can hold it liable as if the purported partner were an actual partner with authority.[18] Under the RUPA, a partnership can limit potential liability with a publicly recorded statement of partnership authority or limitation on partner authority.[19]

CPA 41-1g Partnership Property

In general, partnership property consists of all property contributed by the partners or acquired for the firm or with its funds.

There is usually no limitation on the type and amount of property that a partnership may acquire. The firm may own real as well as personal property unless it is prohibited from doing so by statute or by the partnership agreement.

The parties may agree that real estate owned by one of the partners should become partnership property. When this intent exists, the particular property constitutes partnership property even if it is still in the name of the original owner.

Article 2 of the RUPA recognizes that partnerships are "entities" that can acquire and own property in the partnership's name. If a partner desires to retain an interest in property contributed to the partnership in RUPA states, the partner must condition the transfer of the property to the partnership to reflect this interest or set forth the condition in the partnership agreement. Otherwise, the property becomes partnership property under the entity theory, and the contributing partner has no right to get it back, even in liquidation.[20]

41-1h Tenancy in Partnership

tenancy in partnership–ownership relationship that exists between partners under the Uniform Partnership Act.

Under the UPA, partners hold title to firm property by **tenancy in partnership.**[21] The characteristics of such a tenancy are as follows:

1. Each partner has an equal right to use firm property for partnership purposes in the absence of a contrary agreement.
2. A partner possesses no divisible interest in any specific item of partnership property that can be voluntarily sold, assigned, or mortgaged by a partner.
3. A creditor of a partner cannot proceed against any specific items of partnership property. The creditor can proceed only against the partner's interest in the partnership. This is done by applying to a court for a **charging order.** By this procedure, the share of any profits that would be paid to the debtor-partner is paid to a receiver on behalf of the creditor, or the court may direct the sale of the interest of the debtor-partner in the partnership.
4. Upon the death of a partner, the partnership property vests in the surviving partners for partnership purposes and is not subject to the rights of the surviving spouse of the deceased partner.

charging order–order by a court, after a business partner's personal assets are exhausted, requiring that the partner's share of the profits be paid to a creditor until the debt is discharged.

[17] In re *Cay Clubs*, 130 Nev. Adv. 14 (2014).
[18] R.U.P.A. §308.
[19] R.U.P.A. §303.
[20] R.U.P.A. §204.
[21] U.P.A. §25(1); *Krause v. Vollmar*, 614 N.E.2d 1136 (Ohio App. 1992).

CPA 41-1i Assignment of a Partner's Interest

Although a partner cannot transfer specific items of partnership property in the absence of authority to so act on behalf of the partnership, a partner's interest in the partnership may be voluntarily assigned by the partner. The assignee does not become a partner without the consent of the other partners. Without this consent, the assignee is entitled to receive only the assignor's share of the profits during the continuance of the partnership and the assignor's interest upon the dissolution of the firm. The assignee has no right to participate in the management of the partnership or to inspect the books of the partnership.

41-2 Authority of Partners

The scope of a partner's authority is determined by the partnership agreement and by the nature of the partnership. **For Example,** in a family farming partnership, the agreement specified that whenever there were more than two managing partners, the approval of a majority of the managing partners was required to act on behalf of the partnership. One of the managing partners entered into a series of grain contracts on behalf of the partnership, which led to substantial losses. The court found that he had no right to bind the partnership to the contracts without a majority vote of the managing partners. The consequences for the unauthorized partner were grave. Because he did not have authority and did not act in good faith, he was held personally liable for the partnership's losses.[22]

41-2a Authority of Majority of Partners

When there are more than two partners in a firm, the decision of the majority prevails in matters involving how the ordinary functions of the business will be conducted. Thus, if a majority of the partners of a firm decide to increase the firm's advertising and enter into a contract for that purpose, the transaction is valid and binds the firm and all of the partners.

Majority action is not binding if it contravenes the partnership agreement. For such matters, unanimous action is required.[23] Thus, the majority of the members cannot change the nature of the business against the protests of the minority.

When there is an even number of partners, an even division on a matter that requires majority approval is always a possibility. In such a case, the partnership is deadlocked. When the partners are evenly divided on any question, one partner has no authority to act.

If the division is over a basic issue and the partners persist in the deadlock so that it is impossible to continue the business, any one of the partners may petition the court to order the dissolution of the firm.

41-2b Express Authority of Individual Partners

express authority– authority of an agent to perform a certain act.

An individual partner may have **express authority** to perform certain acts either because the partnership agreement provides for such authority or because a sufficient number of partners have agreed to it.

A partner's authority to act for the firm is similar to that of an agent to act for a principal. Thus, in addition to express authority, a partner has the authority to do those acts that are customary for a member of a partnership conducting the particular business of that partnership.[24] As in the case of an agent, the acts of a partner in excess of authority do not ordinarily bind the partnership.

[22] *Elting v. Elting,* 849 N.W.2d 444 (Neb. 2014).
[23] U.P.A. §18(h).
[24] *Ball v. Carlson,* 641 P.2d 303 (Colo. App. 1981).

41-2c Customary Authority of Individual Partners

A partner, by virtue of being a comanager of the business, customarily has certain powers necessary and proper for carrying out that business. The scope of such powers varies with the nature of the partnership and with the business customs and usages of the area in which the partnership operates.

A partner may make any contract necessary to transact the firm's business.

CASE SUMMARY

"Jerry Should Have Run It by Me," Silvio Seethed

FACTS: Silvio Giannetti and his daughter and son-in-law, Anne Marie and Jerry Pruzinsky, are partners in a general partnership known as Giannetti Investment Company (GIC), which owns and operates Brougham Manor Apartments. Jerry entered into an access agreement with Omnicom, a provider of cable television services, giving Omnicom the right to enter Brougham Manor for purposes of installing, maintaining, and promoting cable service. Some time later, when he learned of the contract, Silvio denied Omnicom access to the property. Omnicom was unable to repair a signal leakage problem and was forced to discontinue cable service. Omnicom sued GIC for breach of contract. GIC contended that Jerry did not sign the agreement in the partnership name and thereby failed to bind GIC.

DECISION: Judgment for Omnicom. A contract executed in the name of a partner is binding on the partnership. Jerry executed the contract in the usual course of GIC's business, for it is a typical activity for an apartment complex to contract for cable television. [***Omnicom v. Giannetti Investment Co.*, 561 N.W.2d 138 (Mich. App. 1997)**]

A partner can sell the firm's goods in the regular course of business, make purchases within the scope of the business, and borrow money for firm purposes. When borrowing money, a partner may execute commercial paper in the firm's name or give security such as a mortgage.[25] A partner may purchase insurance, hire employees, and adjust claims for or against the firm. Notice given to a partner is effective notice to the partnership.[26]

41-2d Limitations on Authority

The partners may agree to limit the powers of each partner. When a partner, contrary to such an agreement, executes a contract on behalf of the firm with a third person, the firm is bound if the third person was unaware of the limitation and the partner violating the agreement is liable to the other partners for any loss caused by the breach of the limitation.[27] Under the UPA, if the third person knew of the limitation, the firm would not be bound.[28] Under the RUPA, the term *knew* is confined to actual knowledge,[29] which is cognitive awareness. Under the RUPA, a partnership may file a statement of partnership authority setting forth any restrictions on a general partner's authority.[30] **For Example,** Bernard Roeger was a general partner of RNR, with three limited partners. Restrictions were clearly set forth in the partnership agreement limiting Roeger's borrowing authority to no more than $650,000 for the construction of a building on partnership property. Roeger on behalf of RNR entered a construction loan agreement with People's Bank

[25] *U.S. Leather v. H&W Partnership*, 60 F.3d 222 (5th Cir. 1995).
[26] *Cham, Hill, Inc., v. Block & Veatch*, 557 N.W.2d 829 (Wis. App. 1996).
[27] *Blankenship v. Smalley*, 324 P.3d 573 (Or. App. 2014).
[28] U.P.A. §9(4).
[29] R.U.P.A. §102(a).
[30] R.U.P.A. §303.

FIGURE 41-2 Limitations on Authority of Individual Partner to Bind Partnership

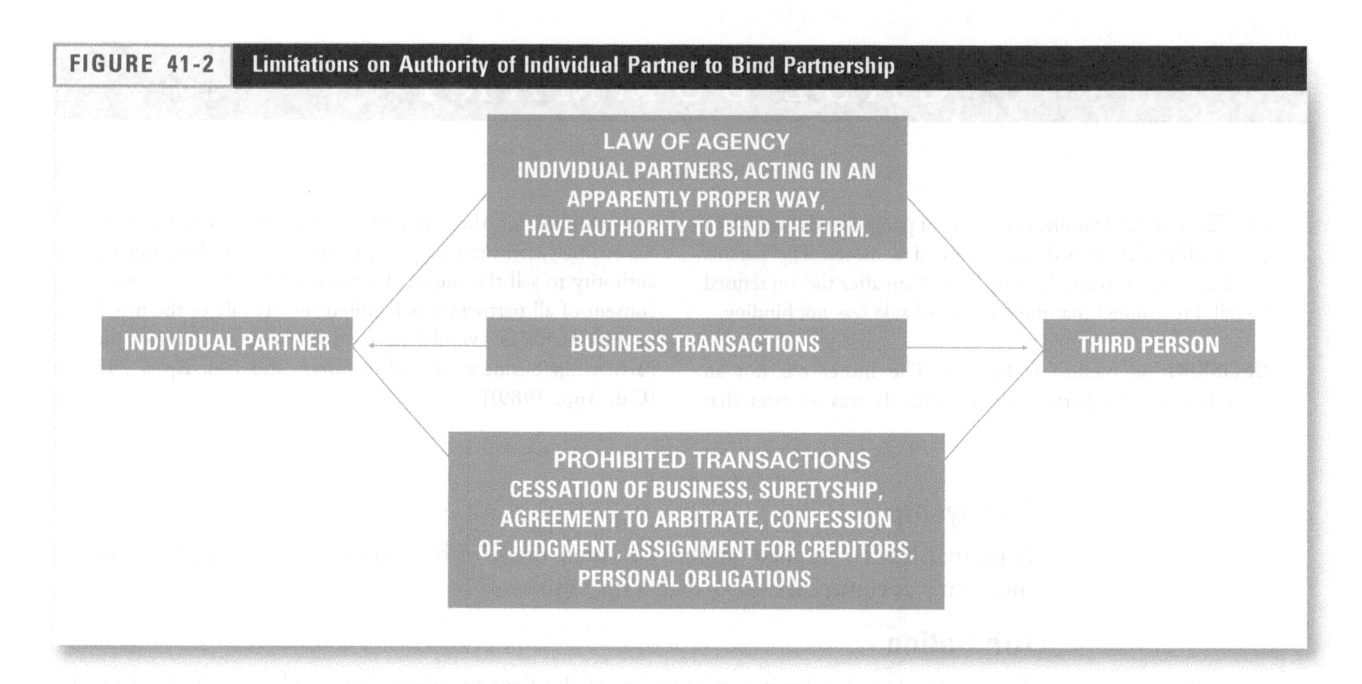

with a note and mortgage in the amount of $990,000, and over an 18-month period, the bank disbursed an aggregate sum of $952,699. The bank did not request a written consent from any of the other partners or review the partnership agreement. When the loan was not paid, the bank foreclosed on the property. RNR defended on behalf of the partnership that the bank negligently failed to investigate and discover the limitation on Roeger's authority to borrow. The case was decided for the bank because it had no actual knowledge or notice of the restriction on the general partner's authority. The court also pointed out that the partnership could have protected itself by filing a statement of partnership authority setting forth the restrictions on the general partner under RUPA section 303.[31]

A third person must not assume that a partner has all of the authority that the partner purports to have. If there is anything that would put a reasonable person on notice that the partner's powers are limited, the third person is bound by that limitation.

The third person must be on the alert for the following prohibited transactions because they warn that the partner with whom the third person deals has either restricted authority or no authority at all. (See Figure 41-2.)

41-2e Prohibited Transactions

A partner cannot enter into certain transactions on behalf of the partnership unless expressly authorized to do so. A third person entering into such a transaction does so at the risk that the partner has not been authorized. The following are prohibited transactions.

Cessation of Business

A partner cannot bind the firm by a contract that would make it impossible for the firm to conduct its usual business.[32]

[31] *RNR Investments, Ltd. v. People's First Community Bank*, 812 So. 2d 561 (Fla. App. 2002).
[32] *Wales v. Roll*, 769 P.2d 899 (Wyo. 1989).

CASE SUMMARY

Family Feud

FACTS: The Patel family, consisting of parents and a son, was a partnership that owned and operated a motel. The parents made a contract to sell the motel, but thereafter the son refused to sell. He claimed that the contract of sale was not binding.

DECISION: Judgment for the son. The motel was not an asset held by the partnership for sale. It was an asset that was essential for the running of the partnership/business. Accordingly, neither one partner nor a majority had implied authority to sell the motel. To the contrary, the unanimous consent of all partners was required for the sale of the motel because such a sale would make it impossible to continue the partnership business. **[*Patel v. Patel*, 260 Cal. Rptr. 255 (Cal. App. 1989)]**

Suretyship

A partner has no implied authority to bind the firm by contracts of surety, guarantee, or indemnity for purposes other than firm business.[33]

Arbitration

A partner cannot submit controversies of the firm to arbitration "unless authorized by the other partners or unless they have abandoned the business."[34]

Confession of Judgment

All partners should have an opportunity to defend in court. Consequently, a partner cannot confess judgment against the firm on one of its obligations. Exceptions exist when the other partners consent or when they have abandoned the business.

Assignment for Creditors

A partner cannot make a general assignment of firm property for the benefit of creditors unless authorized by the other partners or unless they have abandoned the business.

Personal Obligations

A partner cannot discharge personal obligations or claims of the firm by interchanging them in any way.

41-3 Duties, Rights, and Liabilities of Partners

The rights and duties of partners are based on their dual capacity of agent and co-owner.

41-3a Duties of Partners

In many respects, the duties of a partner are the same as those of an agent.

Loyalty and Good Faith

Each partner must act in good faith toward the partnership. One partner must not take advantage of the other(s) by the slightest misrepresentation or concealment.[35] Famous

[33] *First Interstate Bank of Oregon v. Bergendahl*, 723 P.2d 1005 (Or. App. 1986).
[34] U.P.A. §9(3)(e).
[35] *Brosseau v. Ranzau*, 81 S.W.3d 381 (Tex. App. 2002).

language from a decision authored by Justice Cardozo describes the duty of partners and joint venturers to each other, as follows: "Not honesty alone, but the punctilio of an honor the most sensitive, is then the standard of behavior."[36] Each partner also owes a duty of loyalty to the firm. This duty requires a partner's devotion to the firm's business and bars making any secret profit at the expense of the firm.[37]

Moreover, the duty of loyalty bars the use of the firm's property for personal benefit or the exploitation of a business opportunity of the partnership for personal gain. A partner cannot promote a competing business. A partner who does so is liable for damages sustained by the partnership.

Each partner also owes a fiduciary duty of good faith to all other partners. This duty extends to any transaction connected with the formation, conduct, or liquidation of the partnership.

A breach of fiduciary duty requires the complete forfeiture of all compensation during the period of the breach. **For Example,** general partners Michael Morton and Scott DeGraff breached their fiduciary duty to their partners when they did not disclose the parts of a deal they were keeping for themselves relating to a proposed relocation of the partnership's Las Vegas nightclub, Drink. Morton and DeGraff had been paid $833,190 in management fees during the period of time they were found to be in breach of their fiduciary duty to the partnership. The court ordered them to return these funds to the partnership.[38]

Obedience

Each partner is obligated to perform all duties and to obey all restrictions imposed by the partnership agreement or by the vote of the required number of partners.[39] **For Example,** when the partnership agreement required that each partner in an insurance sales firm give his "entire time" to the business and "not engage in any other business that would work to the disadvantage of the partnership," Richard Levatino's engaging in an insurance-related business outside the firm was a breach of the partnership agreement and was a proper basis for the assessment of punitive damages.[40]

Other Duties

The RUPA states that a partner must refrain from engaging in grossly negligent or intentional misconduct in transacting firm business.[41] Partners are accountable as a fiduciary and must hold as trustee for the firm any profits derived by a partner without the consent of the other partners.[42]

CPA 41-3b Rights of Partners as Owners

Each partner, in the absence of a contrary agreement, has the following rights. These rights stem from the fact that the partner is a co-owner of the partnership business.

CPA Management

Each partner has a right to take an equal part in transacting the business of the firm. It is immaterial that one partner contributed more than another or that one contributed only services.

[36] *Meinhard v. Salmon*, 164 N.E. 545, 546 (N.Y. 1928).
[37] Under R.U.P.A. 404(e), partners may pursue their own interests without automatically violating their fiduciary duties to the firm.
[38] *Caparos v. Morton*, 845 N.E.2d 773 (Ill. App. 2006).
[39] *Cobin v. Rice*, 823 F. Supp. 1419 (D. Ind. 1993).
[40] *Gates, Duncan, and VanCamp v. Levatino*, 962 S.W.2d 21 (Tenn. App. 1997).
[41] R.U.P.A. §404(c).
[42] U.P.A. §21; R.U.P.A. §404(b)(1).

Incidental to the right to manage the partnership, each partner has the right to possession of the partnership property for the purposes of the partnership.

CPA

Inspection of Books

All partners are equally entitled to inspect the books of the firm. "The partnership books shall be kept, subject to any agreement between the partners, at the principal place of business of the partnership, and every partner shall at all times have access to and may inspect and copy any of them."[43]

CPA

Share of Profits

Each partner is entitled to a share of the profits. The partners may provide, if they so wish, that profits shall be shared in unequal proportions. In the absence of such a provision in the partnership agreement, each partner is entitled to an equal share of the profits without regard to the amount of capital contributed or services performed for the partnership.

CPA

Compensation

In the absence of a contrary agreement, a partner is not entitled to compensation for services performed for the partnership. There is no right to compensation even if the services are unusual or more extensive than the services rendered by other partners. Consequently, when one partner becomes seriously ill and the other partners transact all of the firm's business, they are not entitled to compensation for those services. The sickness of a partner is considered a risk assumed in the relationship. No agreement can be inferred that the active partners are to be compensated even though the services rendered by them are such that they would ordinarily be rendered in the expectation of receiving compensation. As an exception, "a surviving partner is entitled to reasonable compensation for services performed in winding up the partnership affairs."[44]

Partners may agree that one of the partners will work full time as manager of the business and receive for such services a salary in addition to the managing partner's share of the profits.

Repayment of Loans

A partner is entitled to the return of any money advanced to or for the firm. Such amounts must be separate and distinct from original or additional contributions to the capital of the firm.

CPA

Payment of Interest

In the absence of an agreement to the contrary, contributions to capital do not draw interest. The theory is that the profits constitute sufficient compensation. Advances by a partner in the form of loans are treated as if they were made by a stranger and bear interest from the date the advance is made. When the partnership business continues after dissolution, a retiring partner is entitled to interest on the value of her interest in the partnership.[45]

CPA

Contribution and Indemnity

A partner who pays more than a proportionate share of the debts of the firm has a right to contribution from the other partners. Under this principle, if an employee of a

[43] U.P.A. §19. See *Smith v. Brown & Jones*, 633 N.Y.S.2d 436 (Sup. Ct. 1995).
[44] U.P.A. §18(f).
[45] *Lewis v. Edwards*, 554 S.E.2d 17 (N.C. App. 2001).

partnership negligently injures a third person while acting within the scope of employment and if the injured party collects damages from one partner, the latter may enforce contribution from the other partners to divide the loss proportionately among them.

The partnership must indemnify every partner for payments made and personal liabilities reasonably incurred in the ordinary and proper conduct of its business or for the preservation of its business or property. A partner has no right, however, to indemnity or reimbursement if the partner has (1) acted in bad faith, (2) negligently caused the necessity for payment, or (3) previously agreed to assume the expense alone.[46]

CPA

Distribution of Capital

After the payment of all creditors and the repayment of loans made to the firm by partners, every partner is entitled to receive a share of the firm property upon dissolution. Unless otherwise stated in the partnership agreement, all partners are entitled to the return of their capital contributions.

After such distribution is made, each partner is the sole owner of the fractional part distributed to that partner rather than a co-owner of all the property as during the existence of the partnership.

CPA

41-3c Liability of Partners and Partnership

The liability of a partnership and of the partners for the acts of individual partners and of employees is governed by the same principles that apply to the liability of an employer or a principal for the acts of an employee or agent. A partner may be vicariously liable for the acts of his partners, even if those acts are fraudulent. **For Example,** Joseph Palilla had a common law partnership in a used auto sales business with Lowell Andrews. Andrews bought used cars, purportedly to resell them, but never delivered the money to the sellers. Even though Palilla was unaware of his partner's fraud, the court held that the embezzlement was imputed to the innocent partner.[47]

joint liability–apportions partners' responsibility for partnership debt equally.

joint and several liability–disproportionate satisfaction of partnership debt rendering each partner liable for the entire debt with the right to contribution from other partners.

CPA

Nature and Extent of Partner's Liability

Partners are **jointly liable** on all firm contracts. They are **jointly and severally liable** for all torts committed by an employee or one of the partners in the scope of the partnership business.[48] When partners are liable for the wrongful injury caused a third person, the latter may sue all or any of the members of the firm.

Partners who have satisfied a claim against the partnership have the right to contribution from the other partners, whereby the liability is apportioned among all partners. Unlike the UPA, partners under the RUPA are jointly and severally liable for both tort and contract obligations of the firm.[49] However, the RUPA alters the traditional applications of "joint and several" liability by requiring that the creditors and tort victims satisfy their claims against the partnership before pursuing the personal assets of a partner.

[46] *Gramacy Equities Corp. v. DuMont*, 531 N.E.2d 629 (N.Y.A.D.1988).

[47] In re *Palilla*, 439 B.R. 248 (D. Colo. 2013).

[48] See *Wayne Smith Construction v. Wolman, Durberstein*, 604 N.E.2d 157 (Ohio 1992), where the Ohio Supreme Court described joint liability and joint and several liability as follows: Joint liability apportions responsibility for a contractual debt equally, in the absence of a partnership agreement to the contrary, among the partners and thereby limits the creditor's execution on one individual partner's personal property to a *pro rata* share of the debt. Joint and several liability, on the other hand, allows for disproportionate satisfaction of the partnership obligation by rendering each general partner responsible for the entire amount of the partnership debt.

[49] R.U.P.A. §307(d).

CASE SUMMARY

"Joint Liability" and "Joint and Several Liability": A Big Difference

FACTS: PNC Bank sued two of the eight general partners of Washington Square Enterprises, Farinacci and Gruttadauria, for the unpaid balance of their partnership's business line of credit. The trial court entered judgment in the amount of $4,190.33 plus interest against each of the two partners. The trial court determined that the eight general partners were jointly liable, not jointly and severally liable, for the debt to PNC. In addition, it issued a separate judgment against Farinacci and Gruttadauria in the amount of one-eighth each of the entire debt of $33,522. PNC appealed, contending that the trial court should have found the partners jointly and severally liable or that the trial court should have apportioned the debt according to the percentages of each partner's ownership interest in the partnership, rather than dividing the debt equally among the eight partners.

DECISION: The trial court properly decided the case, holding the two partners jointly liable. In 2007 Ohio adopted the Revised Uniform Partnership Act (RUPA) effective January 1, 2010, which provides that all partners are liable jointly and severally for all obligations of the partnership unless otherwise agreed by the claimant or provided by law. However, the new law states that the RUPA language does not apply to partnerships formed prior to January 1, 2009. The Washington Square Partnership was formed in 1978. "Joint liability" apportions responsibility for a contractual debt equally among all general partners in the absence of a partnership agreement to the contrary. PNC Bank's contention that the judgment be apportioned according to the percentage of the partners' ownership interests is without legal precedent. **[*PNC Bank N.A. v. Farinacci*, 964 N.E.2d 1124 (Ohio App. 2011)]**

CPA

Liability of New Partners

A person admitted as a partner into an existing partnership has *limited liability* for all obligations of the partnership arising before such admission. The preadmission claim may be satisfied only out of partnership property and does not extend to the individual property of the newly admitted partner.[50] **For Example,** Citizens Bank was unsuccessful in its attempt to satisfy part of a $1.2 million deficiency judgment against the Parkham-Woodman Medical partnership from the individual property of Dr. Hunley, who had joined the practice after the underlying obligation leading to the deficiency judgment was assumed.[51]

Effect of Dissolution on Partner's Liability

A partner remains liable after dissolution of the partnership unless expressly released by the creditors or unless all claims against the partnership have been satisfied. The dissolution of the partnership does not of itself discharge the existing liability of any partner. The individual property of a deceased partner may be reached to satisfy obligations of the partnership that were incurred while the deceased partner was alive. However, the individual creditors of the deceased partner have priority over the partnership creditors with respect to such property.[52]

41-3d Enforcement and Satisfaction of Creditors' Claims

A firm may be sued in the name of all individual partners doing business as the partnership, such as "*Plaintiff v. A, B, C, doing business as the Ajax Warehouse.*" The partners

[50] U.P.A. §17; see also U.P.A. §41(1), (7).
[51] *Citizens Bank v. Parkman Woodman Medical Associates*, 874 F. Supp. 705 (D. Mass. 1995).
[52] U.P.A. §36.

named are bound by the judgment against the firm if they have been properly served in the suit.

If a debt is contractual in origin, common law requires that the partnership's assets be resorted to and exhausted before partnership creditors can reach a partner's individual assets.[53]

Personal creditors of a partner must first pursue the assets of that partner for satisfaction of their claims. After a partner's personal assets are exhausted, the creditor may enforce the unpaid portion of a judgment by obtaining a charging order against the partner's interest in the partnership. Under such an order, a court requires that the partner's share of the profits be paid to the creditor until the debt is discharged.

41-4 Dissolution and Termination

The end of a partnership's existence is marked by dissolution and termination.

CPA

41-4a Effect of Dissolution

Dissolution is the "change in the relationship of the partners caused by any partner ceasing to be associated in the carrying on as distinguished from the winding-up of the business."[54] Dissolution does not necessarily mean that the business has ended. If the partnership agreement provides that the business is to be continued by the remaining partner(s), it will continue without a winding up, and the former partner's interest will be bought out according to the partnership agreement. Also, when breach of the partnership agreement causes dissolution, innocent partners may continue the business, provided they pay the breaching partner the value of his or her interest.[55]

If no legal basis exists to continue the business, dissolution ends the right of the partnership to exist as a going concern, but it does not end the existence of the partnership.[56] Dissolution is followed by a winding-up period at the conclusion of which the partnership's legal existence terminates.

Dissolution reduces the authority of the partners. From the moment of dissolution, the partners lose authority to act for the firm "except so far as may be necessary to wind up partnership affairs or to complete transactions begun but not then finished."[57] The vested rights of the partners are not extinguished by dissolving the firm, and the existing liabilities remain.

41-4b Dissolution by Act of the Parties

A partnership may be dissolved by action of the parties. However, certain acts of the parties do not cause a dissolution.

Agreement

A partnership may be dissolved in accordance with the terms of the original agreement of the parties. This may be by the expiration of the period for which the relationship was to continue or by the performance of the object for which the partnership was organized.[58] The relationship may also be dissolved by subsequent agreement. The partners may agree to dissolve the firm before the lapse of the time specified in the articles of partnership or before the attainment of the object for which the firm was created.

[53] *McCune & McCune v. Mountain Bell Tel. Co.*, 758 P.2d 914 (Utah 1988).
[54] U.P.A. §29.
[55] U.P.A. §38 (2)(b).
[56] *Sheppard v. Griffin*, 776 S.W.2d 119 (Tenn. App. 1989).
[57] U.P.A. §33.
[58] U.P.A. §31(1)(a).

Expulsion

A partnership is dissolved by the expulsion of any partner from the business, whether or not authorized by the partnership agreement.[59]

Alienation of Interest

Neither a voluntary sale of a partner's interest nor an involuntary sale for the benefit of creditors works a dissolution of the partnership.

Withdrawal

A partner has the power to withdraw from the partnership at any time. However, if the withdrawal violates the partnership agreement, the withdrawing partner becomes liable to the copartners for damages for breach of contract.[60] When the relationship is for no definite purpose or time, a partner may withdraw without liability at any time.

CASE SUMMARY

The Business School Graduate Who Should Have Taken Business Law

FACTS: Geoffrey Buehler and Antonio Gelman formed a partnership by oral agreement after they graduated from business school. They aimed to raise $600,000 to search for and acquire a business with growth potential. They planned to sell the business at a profit. When they disagreed over ownership interest in the partnership, Buehler withdrew from the partnership. Gelman sued for breach of contract, claiming that Buehler could not unilaterally terminate his obligations under the agreement.

DECISION: Judgment for Buehler. New York's version of the Uniform Partnership Act states that a partnership may be dissolved by "the express will of any partner when no definite or particular undertaking is specified" in the partnership agreement. The critical issue is whether the partnership agreement set forth a "definite term" or identified a particular objective to be achieved. The temporal framework for the partnership plan was flexible. The length of time for soliciting investors, identifying the business, and purchasing and operating the enterprise before the sale could not be determined with reasonable certainty. The plan was also too "amorphous" to meet the statutory "particular undertaking" standard. Consequently, the breach of contract claim must be dismissed. **[*Gelman v. Buehler*, 986 N.E.2d 914 (N.Y. App. 2013)]**

41-4c Dissolution by Operation of Law

operation of law–attaching of certain consequences to certain facts because of legal principles that operate automatically, as contrasted with consequences that arise because of the voluntary action of a party designed to create those consequences.

A partnership is dissolved by **operation of law** in the following instances.

Death

A partnership is dissolved immediately upon the death of any partner. Thus, when the executor of a deceased partner carries on the business with the remaining partner, there is legally a new firm.

Bankruptcy

Bankruptcy of the firm or of one of the partners causes the dissolution of the firm; insolvency alone does not.

[59] *Susman v. Cypress Venture*, 543 N.E.2d 184 (Ill. App. 1989).
[60] *BPR Group v. Bendetson*, 906 N.E.2d 956 (Mass. 2009).

Illegality

A partnership is dissolved by an event that makes it unlawful for the business of the partnership to be carried on or for the members to carry it on in partnership. For example, when a statute specifies that it is unlawful for judges to engage in the practice of law, a law firm is dissolved when one of its members becomes a judge.

41-4d Dissolution by Decree of Court

A court may decree the dissolution of a partnership for proper cause. A court will not order the dissolution for trifling causes or temporary grievances that do not involve a permanent harm or injury to the partnership.

The filing of a complaint seeking a judicial dissolution does not in itself cause a dissolution of the partnership; it is the decree of the court that has that effect.

A partner may obtain a decree of dissolution for any of the following reasons.

Insanity

A partner has been judicially declared insane or of unsound mind.

Incapacity

One of the partners has become incapable of performing the terms of the partnership agreement.

Misconduct

One of the partners has been guilty of conduct that substantially prejudices the continuance of the business. The habitual drunkenness of a partner is a sufficient cause for judicial dissolution.

Impracticability

One of the partners persistently or willfully acts in such a way that it is not reasonably practicable to carry on the partnership business. Dissolution will be granted when dissensions are so serious and persistent that continuance is impracticable or when all confidence and cooperation between the partners have been destroyed. If management of the partnership is deadlocked, a court may exercise its discretion to dissolve the partnership.[61]

CASE SUMMARY

Strategy = Squeeze Out Dyas
Ethics (Trust, Fairness, Loyalty, Doing No Harm) = None
Law = Dissociation, Dissolution

FACTS: Edward Dyas and Joseph Della Ratta were equal owners of two hotels in Ocean City, Maryland. The "old" hotel was completed in 1988 and the "new" hotel was completed in 2006, with both properties owned under their Spa Motel General Partnership (Spa). They were also developers and equal owners of the Maresol Condominium project in Ocean City, which was completed in 2004 and held under Dyas's and Della Ratta's Bay View Limited Liability Company (Bay View). Della Ratta owned the construction company that built these projects, "DRI," and he also owned

[61] *Maree et al. v. ROMAR Joint Venture*, 763 S.E.2d 899 (Ga. App. 2014).

Strategy = Squeeze Out Dyas Ethics (Trust, Fairness, Loyalty, Doing No Harm) = None Law = Dissociation, Dissolution continued

"CMC," the company that managed the two hotels. Dyas believed that Della Ratta was attempting to squeeze him out from ownership of Spa and Bay View. Under Dyas's analysis, Della Ratta's strategy in the general partnership, Spa, was to call for a very substantial capital contribution to pay claims asserted by CMC for alleged advances made by it to pay for operational expenses and to pay claims to DRI for the new hotel's construction costs. Dyas contended that those calls were unauthorized because the underlying claims could not be substantiated and the partnership agreement required that the developers first seek a commercial loan.

With respect to Bay View, Dyas's theory of Della Ratta's squeeze-out strategy involved two ploys. First, that Della Ratta sought personally to purchase the loan from Severn Bank and obtain from it an assignment of the security instrument, on which Della Ratta then would foreclose, so that he could buy in at the foreclosure sale. Severn Bank, however, would not assign the loan to Della Ratta. Dyas further alleged that, as an alternate squeeze-out strategy, Della Ratta wrongfully refused to sell condominium units in Maresol. The resulting illiquidity would deprive Bay View of the cash needed to repay Severn Bank, so that Della Ratta could buy Maresol at a foreclosure sale conducted by Severn Bank. After a 10-day trial, the circuit court concluded that Dyas had proven these allegations. The ultimate findings of the trial court were that it was "no longer reasonably practicable to carry on the business" of Spa or of Bay View and that Dyas "had proved to the court's satisfaction facts sufficient for the court to grant a dissolution" of the entities. The court further ordered dissociation of Della Ratta as a partner in Spa. The court supervised the winding up of the general partnership. Della Ratta appealed.

DECISION: Judgment for Dyas. A review of Della Ratta's activities while a partner in Spa demonstrates satisfactory grounds for the dissociation and dissolution determinations of the trial court since his conduct was such that it was "not reasonably practicable to carry on the business in partnership with him." **[*Della Ratta v. Dyas*, 961 A.2d 629 (Md. App. 2008)]**

Lack of Success

The partnership cannot continue in business except at a loss.

Equitable Circumstances

A decree of dissolution will be granted under any other circumstances that equitably call for a dissolution. Such a situation exists when one partner was induced by fraud to enter into the partnership.

CPA 41-4e Dissociation under the RUPA

Under the RUPA and its "entity" concept, a partner can leave the firm and not disrupt the partnership's legal existence. The RUPA uses the term *dissociation* for the departure of a partner[62] and reserves the term *dissolution* for those instances when a partner's departure results in the winding up and termination of the business.[63]

A partner has the absolute power to dissociate at will, just as a partner has the power to withdraw under the UPA, even if it is wrongful.[64] If wrongful, the partner is liable for damages for breach of contract.

A partner's dissociation from a firm ends the individual's right to participate in the management of the business.[65] It also ends the duty of loyalty owed the firm, and the individual may compete with the firm once dissociated.[66] If the partnership business continues after a partner dissociates from a firm, the partnership must buy out the dissociated

[62] R.U.P.A. §601 cmt 1.
[63] R.U.P.A. §801.
[64] R.U.P.A. §601(1), 602(a).
[65] In a two-person partnership, when one partner withdraws, the partnership is dissolved by operation of law because there cannot be a one-person partnership. The buyout rule of RUPA §701(b) does not apply, and the dissolution procedures take over. See *Corrales v. Corrales*, 129 Cal. Rptr. 3d 428 (Cal. App. 2011).
[66] R.U.P.A. §404(2).

partner's interest based on his share of the higher of the liquidation value of the firm or the value of the firm's business as a going concern on the date of dissociation, with interest.[67]

The RUPA created "notices" to deal with lingering authority of a dissociated partner based on apparent authority. To avoid liability, notice of lack of authority or liability should be given to customers and creditors regarding the dissociation of a partner. A filing with the Secretary of State limits liability and authority to 90 days after filing.[68] If no notice is given or filed, the partnership may be bound by the acts of a dissociated partner for up to two years after dissociation based on apparent authority.[69]

CPA 41-4f Notice of Dissolution

Under some circumstances, one partner may continue to possess the power to make a contract that binds the partnership even though the partnership has been dissolved.

Notice to Partners

When the firm is dissolved by the act of a partner, notice must be given to the other partners unless that partner's act clearly shows an intent to withdraw from or to dissolve the firm. If the withdrawing partner acts without notice to the other partners, that partner is bound by contracts created for the firm.

When the dissolution is caused by the act, death, or bankruptcy of a partner, each partner is liable to the copartners for a share of any liability created by any other partner acting for the partnership without knowledge or notice of the act, death, or bankruptcy of the partner who caused the dissolution.

CPA Notice to Third Persons

When dissolution is caused by the act of a partner or of the partners, notice must be given to third parties. A notice should expressly state that the partnership has been dissolved. Circumstances from which a termination may be inferred are generally not sufficient notice.

Thus, the fact that the partnership checks added the abbreviation *Inc.* after the partnership name was not sufficient notice that the partnership did not exist and that the business had been incorporated.

Actual notice of dissolution must be given to persons who have dealt with the firm.

CASE SUMMARY

Notice Necessary!

FACTS: Paul Babich ran a business under the name of House of Paul. The business became a partnership between Babich, Dyson, and Schnepp but continued under the same name. The partners arranged for printing advertising material with Philipp Lithographing Company, making contracts on three separate occasions for such printing. During the course of these dealings, the House of Paul became a corporation. When the printing bills were not paid in full, Philipp sued the partners as individuals. They claimed they were not liable because the corporation had made the contracts.

[67] R.U.P.A. §701(b). In *Rapport v. Gelfand*, 129 Cal. Rptr. 3d 670, 680 (Cal. App. 2011), the court interpreted the term *liquidation value* as used in R.U.P.A. §701(b) to mean the sale price of the separate assets based on their market value as determined by a willing and knowledgeable buyer and a willing and knowledgeable seller, neither of whom is under any compulsion to buy or sell. Thus, for purposes of section 701, subdivision (b), "liquidation value" does not incorporate the common definition of "liquidation," which generally implies some urgency for immediate cash.

[68] R.U.P.A. §704.

[69] R.U.P.A. §702.

Notice Necessary! continued

DECISION: Whether or not the House of Paul was a corporation with respect to a particular contract was not important because no notice had been given of its change from a partnership to a corporation. Having originally done business with the defendant as a partnership, Philipp could hold the individual persons liable as partners until notice to the contrary was given to Philipp. [***Philipp Lithographing Co. v. Babich*, 135 N.W.2d 343 (Wis. 1965)**]

For persons who have had no dealings with the firm, a publication of the fact of dissolution is sufficient. Such notice may be by newspaper publication, by posting a placard in a public place, or by any similar method. Failure to give proper notice continues the power of each partner to bind the others with respect to third persons on contracts within the scope of the business.

When dissolution has been caused by operation of law, notice to third persons is not required. As between the partners, however, the UPA requires knowledge or notice of dissolution by death and bankruptcy.

41-4g Winding Up Partnership Affairs

Most established partnerships deal with the question of how to proceed with the business upon the death of a partner in the written partnership agreement. The agreement may set forth a method for establishing the value of the deceased partner's interest as of the date of death or allow for the remaining partners to purchase the deceased partner's interest. The agreement may also allow for the continuation of the business as usual while the valuation process is completed. However, in the absence of an agreement, either express or implied, permitting the surviving partners to continue the business, the partners must wind up the business and account for the share of the deceased partner.[70]

When dissolution is obtained by court decree, the court may appoint a receiver to conduct the winding up of the partnership business. This may be done in the usual manner, or the receiver may sell the business as a going concern to those partners who wish to continue its operation.

With a few exceptions, all partners have the right to participate in the winding up of the business.[71]

CPA 41-4h Distribution of Assets

Creditors of the firm have first claim on the assets of the partnership.[72] Difficulty arises when there is a contest between the creditors of the firm and the creditors of the individual partners. The general rule is that firm creditors have first claim on assets of the firm. The individual creditors share in the remaining assets, if any.

After the firm's liabilities to nonpartners have been paid, the assets of the partnership are distributed as follows: (1) each partner is entitled to a refund of advances made to or for the firm, (2) contributions to the capital of the firm are then returned, and (3) the remaining assets, if any, are divided equally as profits among the partners unless there is some other agreement. A partner who contributes only services to the partnership is not considered to have made a capital contribution, absent an agreement to the contrary.

[70] *Chaney v. Burdett*, 560 S.E.2d 21 (Ga. 2002); *King v. Stoddard*, 104 Cal. Rptr. 903 (Cal. App. 1972).
[71] U.P.A. §37. In *Urbain v. Beierling*, 835 N.W.2d 455 (Mich. App. 2013), the court found that a partner who was excluded from the winding up should have been given the right to participate, but she could not show that she was damaged.
[72] *Holmes v. Holmes*, 849 P.2d 1140 (Or. App. 1993).

CASE SUMMARY

Are Time and Labor Capital Contributions? Fred Ott Says They Ought to Be

FACTS: Fred Ott and Charles Corley were partners doing business as "Lakewood Associates, a general partnership." Corley provided the capital to purchase the land to be sold by the partnership, called Lakewood Estates. Corley brought suit for the dissolution of the partnership, and Ott contended that his contributions of time and labor in improving Lakewood Estates should be credited to him as capital contributions in the distribution of assets.

DECISION: Judgment for Corley. There was no evidence of any agreement between the partners that Ott's services should be credited as capital contributions. Therefore, the value of the services could not be credited as capital contributions in the distribution of assets. [*Corley v. Ott*, **485 S.E.2d 97 (S.C. 1997)**]

If the partnership has sustained a loss, the partners assume it equally in the absence of a contrary agreement. Distribution of partnership assets must be made on the basis of actual value when it is clear that the book values are merely nominal or arbitrary amounts.

A provision in a partnership agreement that upon the death of a partner the interest of the partner shall pass to that partner's surviving spouse is valid. Such a provision takes effect against the contention that it is not valid because it does not satisfy the requirements applicable to wills.

41-4i Continuation of Partnership Business

As a practical matter, the business of the partnership is commonly continued after dissolution and winding up. In all cases, however, there is a technical dissolution, winding up, and termination of the life of the original partnership.

If the business continues, either with the surviving partners or with additional partners, it is a new partnership. Again, as a practical matter, the liquidation of the old partnership may in effect be merely a matter of bookkeeping entries, with all partners contributing again or relending to the new business any payment to which they would be entitled from the liquidation of the original partnership.

Make the Connection

Summary

A *partnership* is a relationship created by the voluntary association of two or more persons to carry on as co-owners a business for profit.

A partnership agreement governs the partnership during its existence and may also contain provisions relating to dissolution. The partnership agreement will generally be in writing, and this may be required by the statute of frauds. The existence of a partnership may be found from the existence of shared control in the running of the business and the fact that the parties share profits and losses. The sharing of gross returns, as opposed to profits, is slight evidence of a partnership.

Partners hold title to firm property by tenancy in partnership. A creditor of a partner cannot proceed against any specific item of partnership property but must obtain a charging order to seize the debtor-partner's share of the profits. An assignee of a partner's interest does not become a partner without the consent of the other partners and is entitled only to a share of the profits and the assignor's interest upon dissolution.

When there are more than two partners in a firm, the decisions of the majority prevail on ordinary matters relating to the firm's business unless the partnership agreement provides otherwise. A partner's authority to act for the firm is similar to that of an agent to act for a principal. A partner may not bind the firm by a contract that makes it impossible for the firm to conduct its business.

A partner's duties are the same as those of an agent. If there is no contrary agreement, each partner has the right to take an equal part in the management of the business, to inspect the books, to share in the profits, and after payment of all of the firm's debts and the return of capital, to share in the firm's property or surplus upon dissolution.

Partners have unlimited personal liability for partnership liabilities. Partners are jointly liable on all firm contracts. They are jointly and severally liable for all torts committed by one of the partners or by a firm employee within the scope of the partnership's business. A partner remains liable after dissolution unless expressly released by creditors. An incoming partner is not liable for the existing debts of the partnership unless the new partner expressly assumes those debts.

Dissolution ends the right of the partnership to exist as a going concern. Dissolution is followed by a winding-up period and the distribution of assets. A partnership may be dissolved by the parties themselves in accordance with the terms of the partnership agreement, by the expulsion of a partner, by the withdrawal of a partner, or by the bankruptcy of the firm or one of the partners. A court may order dissolution of a partnership upon the petition of a partner because of the insanity, incapacity, or major misconduct of a partner. Dissolution may be decreed because of lack of success, impracticability, or other circumstances that equitably call for dissolution. Notice of dissolution, except dissolution by operation of law, must be given. Actual notice must be given to those who have dealt with the firm as a partnership.

All partners generally have a right to participate in the winding up of the business. After the firm's liabilities to nonpartners have been paid, the assets are distributed among the partners as follows: (1) refund of advances, (2) return of contributions to capital, and (3) division of remaining assets in accordance with the partnership agreement or, if no agreement is stated, division of net assets equally among the partners.

Learning Outcomes

After studying this chapter, you should be able to clearly explain:

41-1 Nature and Creation

LO.1 Explain how partnerships are created by agreement, and understand that only when the partnership agreement does not resolve an issue does partnership law apply

See the example of the dentist who was terminated from the three-person dental partnership without cause by majority vote, where the partnership agreement allowed for such a termination, page 843.

LO.2 Understand that no writing is needed to form a partnership, nor a tax ID number, nor a partnership name. All that is needed is clear evidence that the partners carried on as co-owners of a business for profit

See the *Byker* case where one individual who carried on a business for a profit was dumbfounded to find out that he was, by law, a partner, page 844.

41-2 Authority of Partners

LO.3 Distinguish between express authority and customary authority of a partner to act for a partnership

See the discussion on the role of individual partners to act as expressly directed by a majority of partners (express authority) and to act on their own to make ordinary contracts necessary to transact the firm's business (customary authority), pages 847–848.

41-3 Duties, Rights, and Liabilities of Partners

LO.4 List the duties of partners to one another

See the discussion and examples of partners' duties of loyalty, good faith, and obedience, pages 850–851.

LO.5 Explain the nature and extent of a partner's liability on firm contracts and torts

41-4 Dissolution and Termination

LO.6 Describe how a partnership may be dissolved by the acts of partners, by operation of law, and by order of the court

See the *Della Ratta* case involving partnership dissolution by decree of court because of impracticability, pages 857–858.

See the *Gelman* case discussing unilateral termination of an oral partnership agreement, page 856.

Key Terms

articles of copartnership
articles of partnership
charging order
express authority
general partners
general partnership
jointly and severally liable
jointly liable
operation of law
partners
partnership
partnership agreement
tenancy in partnership
unincorporated association

Questions and Case Problems

1. Ray, Linda, and Nancy form a partnership. Ray and Linda contribute property and cash. Nancy contributes only services. Linda dies, and the partnership is liquidated. After all debts are paid, the surplus is not sufficient to pay back Linda's estate and Ray for the property and cash originally contributed by Linda and Ray. Nancy claims that the balance should be divided equally among Ray, Linda's estate, and Nancy. Is she correct?
2. Baxter, Bigelow, Owens, and Dailey were partners in a New York City advertising agency. Owens, who was in poor health and wanted to retire, advised the partners that she had assigned her full and complete interest in the partnership to her son, Bartholomew, a highly qualified person with 10 years of experience in the advertising business. Baxter, Bigelow, and Dailey refused to allow Bartholomew to attend management meetings and refused his request to inspect the books. Bartholomew pointed out that his mother had invested as much in the firm as any other partner. He believed, as assignee of his mother's full and complete partnership interest, that he is entitled to (a) inspect the books as he sees fit and (b) participate fully in the management of the firm. Was Bartholomew correct?
3. Amy Gargulo and Paula Frisken operated as a partnership Kiddies Korner, an infants' and children's clothing store. They operated the business very successfully for three years, with both Paula and Amy doing the buying and Paula keeping the books and paying the bills. Amy and Paula decided to expand the business when an adjoining store became vacant. At the same time, they incorporated the business. Children's Apparel, Inc., was a major supplier to the business before the expansion. After the expansion, business did not increase as anticipated, and when a nationally known manufacturer of children's apparel opened a factory outlet nearby, the business could no longer pay its bills. Children's Apparel, which had supplied most of the store's stock after expansion, sued Amy and Paula as partners for bills due for expansion stock. Children's Apparel did not know that Amy and Paula had incorporated. Amy and Paula contended that the business was incorporated and that they therefore were not liable for business debts occurring after incorporation. Were Amy and Paula correct?
4. Calvin Johnson and Rudi Basecke did business as the Stockton Cheese Co., a partnership, which owned a building and equipment. The partners agreed to dissolve the partnership but never got around to completing the winding-up process. Calvin continued to use the building and to pay insurance on it but removed Rudi's name as an insured on the policy. When the building was later destroyed by fire, Calvin claimed the proceeds of the fire insurance policy because he and his wife were the named insureds on the policy and they had paid the premiums. Rudi claimed that although the partnership was dissolved before the fire, the winding up of the partnership was not completed at the time of the fire. He therefore claimed that he was entitled to half of the net proceeds of the policy. Decide. [*State Casualty v. Johnson*, 766 S.W.2d 113 (Mo. App.)]
5. Samuel Shaw purchased a ticket through Delta Airlines to fly a "Delta Connection" flight on SkyWest Airlines to Elko, Nevada. He was seriously injured when the SkyWest plane crashed near Elko. SkyWest's relationship with Delta was a contractual business referral arrangement, whereby Delta benefits through its charges for issuing tickets to connecting passengers to and from smaller communities, and SkyWest benefits from revenue generated by passengers sent to it by Delta. Both firms make a profit from this arrangement. SkyWest and Delta are often mentioned together by Delta in national print advertisements. Shaw believed that regardless of how the airlines characterize themselves, these airlines are in fact partners because they share profits from their combined efforts. Delta contended that it had no control over SkyWest's airplane operations and that sharing profits as compensation for services does not

create a partnership. Decide. [*Shaw v. Delta Airlines, Inc.*, 798 F. Supp. 1453 (D. Nev.)]

6. After graduating from Vanderbilt University with a degree in economics, James Pettes worked for Video Magic, a video rental business. In 1987, Dr. Gordon Yukon, a pediatrician, wanted to invest in a two-store video business called Rent-a-Flick. One store was located on Quince Road and the other in Germantown. Pettes testified that Yukon paid $42,000 for the business and that he and Yukon agreed they would be partners. Pettes would manage the two stores and earn the same amount he earned at Video Magic. Pettes testified that he worked 70 to 80 hours a week and that his "sweat equity" was a capital contribution to the partnership. He also testified that Yukon frequently referred to him as a partner. According to Pettes, in 1992, the parties agreed to divide the business, with the Germantown store going to Yukon and the Quince Road store to Pettes. In December 1992, Pettes made a written demand for an accounting. On January 5, 1993, Dr. Yukon "fired" Pettes. Sutherland, an employee, testified that when she questioned Yukon about firing a partner, Yukon did not deny that there was a partnership but stated that Pettes could not prove there was a partnership because there was no written agreement. Pettes sued for breach of an oral partnership agreement and an accounting. Decide. [*Pettes v. Yukon*, 912 S.W.2d (Tenn. App.)]
7. Two brothers, Eugene and Marlowe Mehl, formed a partnership to operate the family farm. One year, Eugene Mehl withdrew $7,200 from the partnership account and bought the Dagmar Bar. The warranty deed and the liquor license to the bar were obtained in the names of Eugene Mehl and his wife, Bonnie. In a subsequent lawsuit, Marlowe claimed that the bar was a partnership asset. Decide. [*Mehl v. Mehl*, 786 P.2d 1173 (Mont.)]
8. Summers and Dooley formed a partnership to collect trash. Summers became unable to work and he hired a third man to do his work and paid him out of his personal funds. Summers suggested to Dooley that the third man be paid from the partnership funds, but Dooley refused to do so. Summers sued Dooley for reimbursement of the money he spent to pay the third man. Decide.
9. Thomas Bartomeli decided to leave his employment to join his brother Raymond full-time in a small construction company. The brothers each contributed individual assets to the company and worked together to acquire equipment with both signing notes jointly to acquire certain equipment. Thomas considered himself a partner in the company; Raymond often referred to Thomas as his partner. It was the practice of the company to garage the equipment at Thomas's house. In 1983, the company was incorporated, but Thomas never held any shares in the company. On several occasions, Thomas's careless operation of equipment resulted in loss or damage to the company. Raymond became dissatisfied with Thomas's work performance, and on January 17, 1991, Thomas was removed as secretary of the corporation.

   On April 19, 1991, Thomas went to the company office and demanded a blank check from the secretary. Raymond found out about this demand and fired him. On April 20, 1991, Thomas demanded from Raymond either 50 percent of the company or certain equipment owned by the company. On April 22, 1991, Thomas was removed as vice president of the company. Raymond attempted to reach an agreement with Thomas on a division of company assets at that point but was not successful. Thereafter, Thomas sued his brother, alleging that Raymond had breached the brothers' contract of partnership. Because the company was a corporation, is it legally inconsistent for Thomas to contend that there was a contract for partnership in the company? How would you decide this case? [*Bartomeli v. Bartomeli*, 783 A.2d 1050 (Ct. App.)]
10. Friedman, the "O" Street Carpet Shop, Inc., and Langness formed a partnership known as NFL Associates. "O" Street Carpet's net contribution to capital was $5,004; Langness contributed $14,000 in cash; and Friedman contributed his legal services, on which no value was placed by the articles of partnership. The articles stated that Friedman was entitled to 10 percent of the profits and that Langness was to receive payments of $116.66 per month. The partnership's accountant treated the payments to Langness as a return of her capital. Years later, the partnership sold the rental property owned by the partnership, and the partnership was wound up. Friedman claimed that he was entitled to 10 percent of the partnership capital upon dissolution. Langness claimed that Friedman was not entitled to a capital distribution and that the monthly payments to her should not have been treated as a return of capital. Decide. [*Langness v. "O" Street Carpet, Inc.*, 353 N.W.2d 709 (Neb.)]

11. Ross, Marcos, and Albert are partners. Ross and Marcos each contributed $60,000 to the partnership; Albert contributed $30,000. At the end of the fiscal year, distributable profits total $150,000. Ross claims $60,000 as his share of the profits. Is he entitled to this sum?
12. Leland McElmurry was one of three partners of MHS Enterprises, a Michigan partnership. Commonwealth Capital Investment Corp. sued the partnership and obtained a judgment of $1,137,285 against it, but the partnership could not pay the judgment. Commonwealth then sued McElmurry for the entire debt on the theory that, as a partner of MHS, he was liable for its debts. What, if any, is McElmurry's liability? [*Commonwealth Capital Investment Corp. v. McElmurry*, 302 N.W.2d 222 (Mich. App.)]
13. Thomas Smith and Jackie Lea were partners in the logging business. In January 1981, they joined Gordon Redd and went into business running a sawmill, calling the business Industrial Hardwood Products (IHP). Smith and Lea used their logging equipment at the mill site. Smith hauled 400 loads of gravel, worth some $26,000, from his father's land for the mill yard in the process of getting the mill operational. Smith and Lea received $300 a week compensation for their work, which was reported on federal W-2 forms. They worked up to 65 hours per week and were not paid overtime. All three discussed business decisions. Smith and Lea had the authority to write checks and to hire and fire employees. Lea left the business in 1983 and was paid $20,000 by Redd. The testimony indicated that the three individuals agreed in January 1981 that as soon as the bank was paid off and Redd was paid his investment, Lea and Smith would be given an interest in the mill. No written agreement existed. Redd invested $410,452 in the business and withdrew $500,475 from it. As of December 31, 1986, IHP had sufficient retained earnings to retire the bank debt. In April 1987, Smith petitioned the Chancery Court for dissolution of the "partnership" and an accounting. Redd denied that any partnership agreement was formed and asserted that Smith was an employee because he was paid wages. He offered to pay Smith $50,000 for the gravel and use of his equipment. Decide. [*Smith v. Redd*, 593 So. 2d 989 (Miss.)]
14. Mason and Phyllis Ledbetter operated a business in Northbrook, Illinois, as a partnership called Ledbetters' Nurseries that specialized in the sale of garden lilies. The grounds of the nurseries were planted with numerous species of garden lilies, and hundreds of people toured the Ledbetters' gardens every day. After a tour, Sheila Clark offered to buy the facilities at a "top-notch price." Mason felt he could not refuse the high offer, and he signed a contract to sell all the facilities, including all flowers and the business name. When Phyllis refused to go along with the contract, Clark sued the Ledbetters' Nurseries partnership, seeking to obtain specific performance of the sales contract. Decide.
15. St. John Transportation Co., a corporation, made a contract with the partnership of Bilyeu and Herstel, contractors, by which the latter was to construct a ferryboat. Herstel, a member of the firm of contractors, executed a contract in the firm name with Benbow for certain materials and labor in connection with the construction of the ferryboat. In an action brought by Benbow to enforce a lien against the ferryboat, the *James Johns*, it was contended that all members of the firm were bound by the contract made by Herstel. Do you agree? [*Benbow v. The Ferryboat James Johns*, 108 P. 634 (Or.)]

CPA Questions

1. Acorn and Bean were general partners in a farm machinery business. Acorn contracted, on behalf of the partnership, to purchase 10 tractors from Cobb Corp. Unknown to Cobb, Acorn was not authorized by the partnership to make such contracts. Bean refused to allow the partnership to accept delivery of the tractors, and Cobb sought to enforce the contract. Cobb will:
   a. Lose, because Acorn's action was beyond the scope of Acorn's implied authority.
   b. Prevail, because Acorn had implied authority to bind the partnership.
   c. Prevail, because Acorn had apparent authority to bind the partnership.
   d. Lose, because Acorn's express authority was restricted, in writing, by the partnership agreement.

2. Upon dissolution of a general partnership, distributions will be made on account of:
   I. Partners' capital accounts.
   II. Amounts owed partners with respect to profits.
   III. Amounts owed partners for loans to the partnership in the following order:
   a. III, I, II
   b. I, II, III
   c. II, III, I
   d. III, II, I
3. Which of the following statements is correct with respect to a limited partnership?
   a. A limited partner may *not* be an unsecured creditor of the limited partnership.
   b. A general partner may *not* also be a limited partner at the same time.
   c. A general partner may be a secured creditor of the limited partnership.
   d. A limited partnership can be formed with limited liability for all partners.
4. When a partner in a general partnership lacks actual or apparent authority to contract on behalf of the partnership, and the party contracted with is aware of this fact, the partnership will be bound by the contract if the other partners:

	Ratify the Contract	*Amend the Partnership Agreement*
a.	Yes	Yes
b.	Yes	No
c.	No	Yes
d.	No	No

CHAPTER 43

Corporation Formation

Learning Outcomes <<<

After studying this chapter, you should be able to

LO.1 Recognize that a corporation is a separate legal entity, distinct and apart from its stockholders and that individual shareholders are not liable for claims against the corporation

LO.2 Explain the wide range of power given to corporations under modern corporate codes

LO.3 Understand that the promoter is personally liable for preincorporation contracts

LO.4 Understand that after a corporate charter has been dissolved the owners and officers may be personally responsible for contracts made in the corporate name if they knew or should have known of the dissolution

LO.5 Explain a stockholder's option when he or she objects to a proposed consolidation or merger of the corporation

LO.6 Recognize that liabilities of predecessor corporations can be imposed on successor corporations when the transaction is a de facto merger or a continuation of the predecessor

The corporation is one of the most important forms of business organization.

43-1 Nature and Classes

A *corporation* is an artificial person that is created by government action.

43-1a The Corporation as a Person

corporation–artificial being created by government grant, which for many purposes is treated as a natural person.

certificate of incorporation–written approval from the state or national government for a corporation to be formed.

A **corporation** is an artificial person created by government action and granted certain powers. It exists in the eyes of the law as a person, separate and distinct from the persons who own the corporation.

The concept that the corporation is a distinct legal person means that the corporation's property is owned not by the persons who own shares in the corporation but by the corporation itself. Debts of the corporation are debts of this artificial person, not of the persons running the corporation or owning shares of stock in it.[1] The corporation can sue and be sued in its own name, but shareholders cannot be sued or held liable for corporate actions or obligations.[2] The cardinal rule is that a corporation has a legal existence separate and apart from its officers and shareholders.[3] Consequently, even a sole shareholder is not ordinarily liable for corporate acts.[4]

CASE SUMMARY

Personal Liability versus Corporate Liability

FACTS: Thomas Sauers asked a family friend, Robert Crozier, to lend him money to expand his auto glass business. Crozier loaned $180,000 pursuant to an oral agreement. The loan was to purchase an existing auto glass company and to be a down payment on two buildings for corporate purposes. Crozier gave Sauers four checks made out to T & M Corp. The buildings were never purchased but Sauers testified that the funds were used to cover operating expenses of T & M Corp. Crozier sued for repayment of the loan amount, maintaining that Thomas Sauers was personally liable for the repayment of the loan.

DECISION: Judgment for Sauers. The parties understood that the funds were for corporate purposes, were advanced to the corporation, were deposited in the corporation's account, and were used for corporate purposes. There was no evidence that Sauers agreed to be personally responsible for repaying the loan. The complaint against Sauers must be dismissed. **[*Crozier v. Sauers*, 109 A.D.3d 507 (N.Y. App. Div. 2013)]**

articles of incorporation–See *certificate of incorporation.*

charter–grant of authority from a government to exist as a corporation. Generally replaced today by a certificate of incorporation approving the articles of incorporation.

A corporation is formed by obtaining approval of a **certificate of incorporation, articles of incorporation,** or a **charter** from the state or national government.[5]

[1] *American Truck Lines, Inc. v. Albino*, 424 S.E.2d 367 (Ga. App. 1992).

[2] Also, a corporation does not have standing to pursue a claim on behalf of its sole shareholder. See *Accurate Printers, Inc. v. Stark*, 671 S.E.2d 228 (Ga. App. 2008).

[3] *Hayes v. Collins*, 538 S.E.2d 785 (Ga. App. 2000).

[4] If a court finds that a corporation is merely the alter ego of an individual shareholder, the court may "pierce the corporate veil" and hold the individual personally liable. Piercing the corporate veil is addressed in Chapter 44, Shareholders Rights in Corporations.

[5] *Charter, certificate of incorporation*, and *articles of incorporation* are all terms used to refer to the documents that serve as evidence of a government's grant of corporate existence and powers. Most state incorporation statutes now provide for a certificate of incorporation issued by the Secretary of State, but a Revised Model Business Corporation Act (RMBCA) has done away with the certificate of incorporation. Under the RMBCA, corporate existence begins when articles of incorporation are filed with the Secretary of State. An endorsed copy of the articles together with a fee, receipt, or acknowledgment replaces the certificate of incorporation. See RMBCA §§1.25 and 2.03.

43-1b Classifications of Corporations

Corporations may be classified in terms of their relationship to the public, the source of their authority, and the nature of their activities.

public corporation–corporation that has been established for governmental purposes and for the administration of public affairs.

private corporation–corporation organized for charitable and benevolent purposes or for purposes of finance, industry, and commerce.

quasi-public corporation–private corporation furnishing services on which the public is particularly dependent, for example, a gas and electric company.

authorities–corporations formed by government that perform public service.

domestic corporation–corporation that has been incorporated by the state in question as opposed to incorporation by another state.

foreign corporation–corporation incorporated under the laws of another state.

close corporation–corporation whose shares are held by a single shareholder or a small group of shareholders.

Public, Private, and Quasi-Public Corporations

A **public corporation** is one established for governmental purposes and for the administration of public affairs. A city is a public or municipal corporation acting under authority granted to it by the state.

A **private corporation** is one organized for charitable and benevolent purposes or for purposes of finance, industry, and commerce. Private corporations are often called *public* in business circles when their stock is sold to the public.

A **quasi-public corporation,** sometimes known as a public service corporation or a public utility, is a private corporation furnishing services on which the public is particularly dependent, such as a gas or electric company.

Public Authorities

The public increasingly demands that government perform services. Some of these are performed directly by government. Others are performed by separate corporations or **authorities** created by government. **For Example,** a city parking facility may be organized as a separate municipal parking authority, or a public housing project may be operated as an independent housing authority.

Domestic and Foreign Corporations

A corporation is called a **domestic corporation** with respect to the state under whose law it has been incorporated. Any other corporation going into that state is called a **foreign corporation.** Thus, a corporation holding a Texas charter is a domestic corporation in Texas but a foreign corporation in all other states.[6]

Special Service Corporations

Corporations formed for transportation, banking, insurance, and savings and loan operations and similar specialized functions are subject to separate codes or statutes with regard to their organization. In addition, federal and state laws and administrative agencies regulate in detail the way these businesses are conducted.

Close Corporations

A corporation whose shares are held by a single shareholder or a small group of shareholders is known as a **close corporation.** Its shares are not traded publicly. Many such corporations are small firms that are incorporated to obtain either the advantage of limited liability or a tax benefit, or both.

Many states have statutes that have liberalized corporation law as it applies to close corporations. **For Example,** a brother and sister inherited their parents' stock in a domestic close corporation, Hall's Mortuary, Inc., a prominent and successful funeral home in

[6] Failure of a foreign corporation to obtain a certificate of authority to do business within the state, under that state's door-closing statute, may mean that the foreign corporation cannot enforce a contract entered into in the state. For Example, TradeWinds Environmental Restoration, Inc., a New York–based company, entered into a contract with Alabama contractor BBC to do structural-drying services at a number of coastal condominiums after Hurricane Ivan in 2004. TradeWinds performed the work under the contract valued at $400,000. When TradeWinds sued for the money owed under the contract, the court determined that the "labor" performed is not an article of commerce nor is the agreement to supply it an act of commerce. The court determined that TradeWinds' business was intrastate, rather than interstate, and without a certificate of authority to perform the work, TradeWinds could not enforce the contract. *TradeWinds Environmental Restoration, Inc. v. Brown Brothers Construction, LLC,* 999 So. 2d 875 (Ala. 2008).

Louisiana. Nancy was the secretary-treasurer, a director, and the shareholder of 50 percent of the corporation's stock. Hall was president, a director, and the shareholder of the other 50 percent of the corporation's stock. The siblings had a falling out that involved Nancy demanding more participation in the management of the business. Hall maintained that he and Nancy were deadlocked in the management of corporate affairs and petitioned the court for involuntary dissolution and the appointment of a liquidator. The court applied a statute, nearly identical to the Delaware statute, "designed to obviate a deadlocked vote of two equal shareholders" of a close corporation and ordered the dissolution of the corporation.[7]

CPA

Subchapter S Corporations

Subchapter S is a subdivision of the Internal Revenue Code. If corporate shareholders meet the requirements of this subdivision, they may elect Subchapter S status, which allows the shareholders to be treated as partners for tax purposes and retain the benefit of limited liability under the corporate form. A Subchapter S corporation is limited to 100 shareholders.[8]

Professional Corporations

A corporation may be organized for the purpose of conducting a profession, such as law, medicine, accounting, architecture, or engineering. Each officer, director, and shareholder of a professional corporation must be licensed to practice the profession. Professional incorporation does not shield a practitioner from personal liability relating to the professional services rendered. State laws vary, with some states recognizing professional corporations, or P.C.s, and other states recognizing a Professional Limited Liability Company (PLLC). In addition to approval from the Secretary of State, professional corporations may need approval from the state professional licensing body.

Nonprofit Corporations

eleemosynary corporation–corporation organized for a charitable or benevolent purpose.

A *nonprofit corporation* (or an **eleemosynary corporation**), is one that is organized for charitable or benevolent purposes. Nonprofit corporations include hospitals, nursing homes, and universities.[9] Special procedures for incorporation are prescribed, and provision is made for a detailed examination of and hearing regarding the purpose, function, and methods of raising money for the enterprise. State laws vary and may require a nonprofit corporation to include a brief statement of its purpose.[10]

Benefit Corporations

benefit corporation–for-profit corporation that sets a goal to create a public benefit while still providing economic returns to its investors.

Benefit, or **B-corporations** are for-profit corporations that set a goal to create a public benefit while still providing economic returns to their investors. **For Example,** Patagonia, registered under California's benefit corporation statute, uses the benefit corporation to emphasize its commitment to the environment. State laws typically recognize that directors will take benefits to society or the environment into account when making corporate decisions and require benefit corporations to adopt independent, third-party standards to measure their success or failure. At least 26 states have benefit corporation statutes and several have legislation pending. The state of Washington recognizes a social purpose corporation, or SPC.

[7] *Judson v. Davis,* 916 So. 2d 1106 (La. App. 2005).

[8] See IRS, S Corporations, **http://www.irs.gov/Businesses/Small-Businesses-&-Self-Employed/S-Corporations.**

[9] The Committee on Corporate Laws of the American Bar Association has prepared a Model Nonprofit Corporation Act. A revised Model Nonprofit Corporation Act was approved in 1986.

[10] See *Peters Creek United Presbyterian Church v. Washington Presbytery of Penn.,* 90 A.3d 95 (2014).

43-1c Corporations and Governments

The power of governments to create and regulate corporations may involve several issues.

Power to Create

By definition a corporation is created by government. Thus, the right to be a corporation must be obtained from the proper governmental agency. The federal government may create corporations whenever appropriate to carry out the powers granted to it.

police power–power to govern; the power to adopt laws for the protection of the public health, welfare, safety, and morals.

general corporation code–state's code listing certain requirements for creation of a corporation.

Generally, a state by virtue of its **police power** may create any kind of corporation for any purpose. Most states have a **general corporation code,** which lists certain requirements, and anyone who satisfies the requirements and files the necessary papers with the government may automatically form a corporation. In 1950, the American Bar Association (ABA) published a Model Business Corporation Act (MBCA) to assist legislative bodies in the modernization of state corporation laws. An updated version was published in 1969. Statutory language similar to that contained in the 1969 version of the MBCA has been adopted in whole or in part by 35 states. A complete revision of the model act was approved in 1984 (RMBCA).[11] Jurisdictions following the model act have made numerous modifications to reflect differing views about balancing the interests of public corporations, shareholders, and management. Caution must therefore be exercised in making generalizations about model act jurisdictions. There is no *uniform* corporation act.

Power to Regulate

Subject to constitutional limitations, corporations may be regulated by statutes.

Protection of the Corporation as a Person. The Constitution of the United States prohibits the national government and state governments from depriving any person of life, liberty, or property without due process of law. Many state constitutions contain a similar limitation on their respective state governments. A corporation is regarded as a "person" within the meaning of such provisions.

The federal Constitution prohibits a state from denying to any person within its jurisdiction the equal protection of the laws. No such express limitation is placed on the federal government, although the due process clause binding the federal government is liberally interpreted so that it prohibits substantial inequality of treatment.

Recall the *Citizens United* case in Chapter 4 in which the Supreme Court held that the government may not suppress political speech on the basis of the speaker's corporate identity.[12]

Protection of the Corporation as a Citizen. For certain purposes, such as determining the right to bring a lawsuit in a federal court, a corporation is a citizen of any state in which it has been incorporated and of the state where it has its principal place of business.

43-2 Corporate Powers

Except for limitations in the federal Constitution or the state's own constitution, a state legislature may give corporations any lawful powers. The RMBCA contains a general provision on corporate powers granting a corporation "the same powers as an individual to do all things necessary or convenient to carry out its business and affairs."[13]

[11] The Revised Model Business Corporation Act (1984) was approved by the Committee on Corporate Laws Section of Business Law of the American Bar Association. Model act citations are to the 1984 Revised Model Business Corporation Act (RMBCA) unless designated otherwise.

[12] *Citizens United v. Federal Election Com'n*, 558 U.S. 310 (2010).

[13] RMBCA §3.02. State statutes generally contain similar broad catchall grants of powers.

43-2a Particular Powers

Modern corporation codes give corporations a wide range of powers.

Perpetual Life

One of the distinctive features of a corporation is its perpetual or continuous life—the power to continue as an entity forever or for a stated period of time regardless of changes in stock ownership or the death of any shareholders.

Corporate Name

A corporation must have a name to identify it. As a general rule, it may select any name for this purpose. Most states require that the corporate name contain some word indicating the corporate character[14] and that the name not be the same as, or deceptively similar to, the name of any other corporation. Some statutes prohibit the use of a name that is likely to mislead the public.

Corporate Seal

A corporation may have a distinctive seal. However, a corporation need not use a seal in the transaction of business unless it is required by statute or a natural person in transacting that business would be required to use a seal.

CPA

Bylaws

bylaws–rules and regulations enacted by a corporation to govern the affairs of the corporation and its shareholders, directors, and officers.

Bylaws are the rules and regulations enacted by a corporation to govern the affairs of the corporation and its shareholders, directors, and officers.

Bylaws are adopted by shareholders, although in some states they may be adopted by the directors of the corporation. Approval by the state or an amendment of the corporate charter is not required to make the bylaws effective.

The bylaws are subordinate to the general law of the state, the statute under which the corporation is formed, and the charter of the corporation.[15] Bylaws that conflict with such superior authority or that are in themselves unreasonable are invalid. Bylaws that are valid are binding on all shareholders regardless of whether they know of the existence of those bylaws or were among the majority that consented to their adoption. Bylaws are not binding on third persons, however, unless they have notice or knowledge of them.

Stock

A corporation may issue certificates representing corporate stock. Under the RMBCA, authorized, but unissued, shares may be issued at the price set by the board of directors. Under UCC Article 8 (1978 and 1994 versions), securities may be "uncertificated," or not represented by an instrument.

Making Contracts

Corporation codes give corporations the power to make contracts.

Borrowing Money

Corporations have the implied power to borrow money in carrying out their authorized business purposes.

[14] RMBCA §4.01(a) declares that the corporate name must contain the word *corporation, company, incorporated*, or *limited* or an abbreviation of one of these words.

[15] *Roach v. Bynum*, 403 So. 2d 187 (Ala. 1981).

Executing Negotiable Instruments

Corporations have the power to issue or indorse negotiable instruments and to accept drafts.

Issuing Bonds

A corporation may exercise its power to borrow money by issuing bonds.

Transferring Property

The corporate property may be leased, assigned for the benefit of creditors, or sold. In many states, however, a solvent corporation may not transfer all of its property without the consent of all or a substantial majority of its shareholders.

A corporation, having power to incur debts, may mortgage or pledge its property as security for those debts. This rule does not apply to public service companies, such as street transit systems and gas and electric companies.

Acquiring Property

A corporation has the power to acquire and hold such property as is reasonably necessary for carrying out its express powers.

Buying Back Stock

Generally, a corporation may purchase its own stock if it is solvent at the time and the purchase does not impair capital. Stock that is reacquired by the corporation that issued it is commonly called **treasury stock.**

treasury stock–corporate stock that the corporation has reacquired.

Although treasury stock retains the character of outstanding stock, it has an inactive status while it is held by the corporation.[16] Thus, the treasury shares cannot be voted nor can dividends be declared on them.

Doing Business in Another State

A corporation has the power to engage in business in other states. However, such power does not exempt the corporation from satisfying valid restrictions imposed by the foreign state in which it seeks to do business.

Participating in an Enterprise

Corporations may generally participate in an enterprise to the same extent as individuals. They may enter into joint ventures and partnerships. A corporation may also be a limited partner. The RMBCA authorizes a corporation "to be a promoter, partner, member, associate, or manager of any partnership, joint venture, trust, or other entity."[17]

Paying Employee Benefits

The RMBCA empowers a corporation "to pay pensions and establish pension plans, pension trusts, profit-sharing plans, share bonus plans, share option plans, and benefit or incentive plans for any or all of its current or former directors, officers, employees, and agents."[18]

[16] When a corporation reacquires its own shares, it has the choice of retiring them and thus restoring them to the status of authorized, but unissued, shares or of treating them as still issued and available for transfer. The latter are described as treasury shares.

[17] RMBCA §3.02(9).

[18] RMBCA §3.02(12).

Charitable Contributions

The RMBCA authorizes a corporation, without any limitation, "to make donations for the public welfare or for charitable, scientific, or educational purposes."[19] In some states, a limitation is imposed on the amount that can be donated for charitable purposes.

43-2b *Ultra Vires* Acts

ultra vires–act or contract that the corporation does not have authority to do or make.

When a corporation acts in excess of or beyond the scope of its powers, the corporation's act is described as ***ultra vires.*** Such an action is improper in the same way that it is improper for an agent to act beyond the scope of the authority given by the principal. It is also improper with respect to shareholders and creditors of the corporation because corporate funds have been diverted to unauthorized uses.

The modern corporation statute will state that every corporation formed under it will have certain powers unless the articles of incorporation expressly exclude some of the listed powers, and then the statute will list every possible power that is needed to run a business. In some states, the legislature makes a blanket grant of all power that a natural person running the business would possess.[20] The net result is that the modern corporation possesses such a broad scope of powers that it is difficult to find an action that is *ultra vires.* If a mining corporation should begin to manufacture television sets, that might be an *ultra vires* transaction but such an extreme departure rarely happens.

Because nonprofit corporations have a more restricted range of powers than business corporations, actions not authorized by the charters of nonprofit corporations are more likely to be found *ultra vires.*[21]

43-3 Creation and Termination of the Corporation

All states have general laws governing the creation of corporations.

CPA

43-3a Promoters

promoters–persons who plan the formation of the corporation and sell or promote the idea to others.

Corporations come into existence as the result of the activities of one or more persons known as **promoters** who bring together persons interested in the enterprise, aid in obtaining subscriptions to stock, and set in motion the machinery that leads to the formation of the corporation itself.

A corporation is not liable on a contract made by its promoter for its benefit unless the corporation takes some affirmative action to adopt the contract, such as express words of adoption or acceptance of the contract's benefits.[22] A corporation may also become bound by such contracts through assignment or novation.

The promoter is personally liable for all contracts made on behalf of the corporation before its existence unless the promoter is exempted by the terms of the agreement or by the circumstances surrounding it.[23]

[19] RMBCA §3.02(13).

[20] Note the broad powers granted under RMBCA §3.02; see also *MIC v. Battle Mountain Corp.*, 70 P.3d 1176 (Colo. 2003), where Colorado's *ultra vires* statute prohibits claims that a corporation is acting beyond the scope of its powers.

[21] *Lovering v. Seabrook Island Property Owners Ass'n*, 344 S.E.2d 862 (S.C. App. 1986). But see *St. Louis v. Institute of Med. Ed. & Res.*, 786 S.W.2d 885 (Mo. App. 1990).

[22] The *Hansen v. Fields Company, LLC* case, summarized in Chapter 42, addresses the distinction between an LLC's liability and that of the promoter.

[23] See *GS Petroleum, Inc. v. R and S Fuel, Inc.*, 2009 WL 1554680 (Del. Super. June 4, 2009), where the court found that the promoters were not liable on the preincorporation contract for the sale of a Shell gas station. The court reasoned that the terms of the contract did not intend promoter liability, and the business was incorporated by the buyer before taking possession of the business.

A promoter is liable for all torts committed in connection with the promoter's activities. The corporation is not ordinarily liable for the torts of the promoter, but it may become liable by its conduct after incorporation. If a promoter induces making a contract by fraud, the corporation is liable for the fraud if it assumes or ratifies the contract with knowledge or notice of such fraud.

A promoter stands in a fiduciary relation to the corporation and to stock subscribers and cannot make secret profits at their expense. Accordingly, if a promoter makes a secret profit on a sale of land to the corporation, the promoter must surrender the profit to the corporation.

The corporation is not liable in most states for the expenses and services of the promoter unless it subsequently promises to pay for them or the corporation's charter or a statute imposes such liability on it.

43-3b Incorporation

incorporator–one or more natural persons or corporations who sign and file appropriate incorporation forms with a designated government official.

One or more natural persons or corporations may act as **incorporators** of a corporation by signing and filing appropriate forms with a designated government official.[24] These papers are filed in duplicate, and a filing fee must be paid. The designated official (usually the Secretary of State), after being satisfied that the forms conform to statutory requirements, stamps "Filed" and the date on each copy. The official then retains one copy and returns the other copy, along with a filing fee receipt, to the corporation.[25]

Statutes may require incorporators to give some form of public notice, such as by advertising in a newspaper, of their intention to form a corporation, stating its name, address, and general purpose.

43-3c Application for Incorporation

In most states, the process of forming a corporation is begun by filing an application for a certificate of incorporation. This application contains or is accompanied by articles of incorporation. The instrument is filed with the Secretary of State and sets forth certain information about the new corporation. The articles of incorporation must contain (1) the name of the corporation, (2) the number of shares of stock the corporation is authorized to issue, (3) the street address of the corporation's initial registered office and the name of its initial registered agent, and (4) the name and address of each incorporator.[26] The articles of incorporation may also state the purpose or purposes for which the corporation is organized. If there is no "purpose clause," the corporation automatically has the purpose of engaging in any lawful business.[27] Also, if no reference is made to the duration of the corporation in the articles of incorporation, it will automatically have perpetual duration.[28]

43-3d The Certificate of Incorporation

Most state incorporation statutes now provide for a certificate of incorporation to be issued by the Secretary of State after articles of incorporation that conform to state requirements have been filed. The Revised Model Business Corporation Act (RMBCA) has eliminated the certificate of incorporation in an effort to reduce the volume of paperwork handled by the Secretary of State.

[24] RMBCA §2.01.
[25] RMBCA §1.25.
[26] RMBCA §2.02.
[27] RMBCA §3.01.
[28] RMBCA §3.02.

Under the RMBCA, corporate existence begins when the articles are filed with the Secretary of State.[29] In some states, corporate existence begins when the proper government official issues a certificate of incorporation. In other states, it does not begin until an organizational meeting is held by the new corporation.

43-3e Proper and Defective Incorporation

If the procedure for incorporation has been followed, the corporation has a legal right to exist. It is then called a **corporation de jure,** meaning that it is a corporation by virtue of law.

corporation de jure–corporation with a legal right to exist by virtue of law.

The law usually overlooks defects that are not material and holds that the corporation is a corporation de jure.

The RMBCA abolishes objections to irregularities and defects in incorporating. It provides that the

> *secretary of state's filing of the articles of incorporation is conclusive proof that the incorporators satisfied all conditions precedent to incorporation....*[30]

De Facto Corporation

The defect in the incorporation may be so substantial that it cannot be ignored, and the corporation will not be accepted as a corporation de jure, yet compliance may be sufficient for recognizing that there is a corporation. When this occurs, the association is called a **de facto** corporation.

de facto–existing in fact as distinguished from as of right, as in the case of an officer or a corporation purporting to act as such without being elected to the office or having been properly incorporated.

Although conflict exists among authorities, the traditional elements of a de facto corporation are that (1) a valid law exists under which the corporation could have been properly incorporated, (2) an attempt to organize the corporation has been made in good faith, (3) a genuine attempt to organize in compliance with statutory requirements has been made, and (4) corporate powers have been used.

Corporation by Estoppel

The defect in incorporation may be so great that by law the association cannot be accepted as a de facto corporation. In such a case, there is no corporation. If the individuals involved proceed to run the business in spite of such irregularity, they may be held personally liable as partners for the business's debts.[31] This rule is sometimes not applied when a person has dealt with the business as though it were a corporation.[32] In such instances, the party is estopped from denying that the "corporation" had legal existence. In effect, there is **corporation by estoppel** with respect to that party.

corporation by estoppel–corporation that comes about when parties estop themselves from denying that the corporation exists.

Several jurisdictions that follow the 1969 MBCA have expressly retained the doctrines of corporation by estoppel and de facto corporations.[33] Other courts interpreting the language of the 1969 MBCA, however, have held that the doctrines of de facto corporation and corporation by estoppel no longer exist.

The language of the 1984 version allows some jurisdictions sufficient room for the de facto and estoppel doctrines to operate through Section 2.04 of the MBCA.

With respect to preincorporation debts, the 1984 act imposes liability only on persons who act as, or on behalf of, a corporation while knowing that no corporation

[29] RMBCA §2.03(a).

[30] RMBCA §2.03(b).

[31] In a minority of states, a court will not hold individuals liable as partners but will hold liable the person who committed the act on behalf of the business on the theory that that person was an agent who acted without authority and is therefore liable for breach of the implied warranties of the existence of a principal possessing capacity and of proper authorization.

[32] *Am. South Bank v. Holland,* 669 So. 2d 151 (Ala. Civ. App. 1994).

[33] See Ga. Bus. Corp Code §22-5103; Minn. Bus. Corp Act §301:08. See also *H. Rich Corp. v. Feinberg,* 518 So. 2d 377 (Fla. App. 1987).

exists.[34] Courts may allow a corporation to sue to enforce a preincorporation agreement if the corporation had a "personal stake" in the agreement.[35]

43-3f Insolvency, Bankruptcy, and Reorganization

When a corporation has financial troubles so serious that it is insolvent, the best thing may be to go through bankruptcy or reorganization proceedings. The law with respect to bankruptcy and reorganizations is discussed in Chapter 34.

43-3g Forfeiture of Charter

In states that have adopted the RMBCA, the Secretary of State may commence proceedings to administratively dissolve a corporation if (1) the corporation does not pay franchise taxes within 60 days after they are due, (2) the corporation does not file its annual report within 60 days after it is due, or (3) the corporation is without a registered agent or registered office for 60 days or more.[36] After a corporate charter has been dissolved, the owners and officers of the dissolved corporation are not shielded from personal liability by using the corporate name when making contracts if they knew or should have known of the dissolution. **For Example,** on October 2, 2004, Dinky, Inc., was involuntarily dissolved for failure to file an annual report and pay an annual franchise tax. Elaine Kostopulos, the president and sole shareholder of Dinky, Inc., had incorporated her business in 1989 and regularly purchased products manufactured by Benetton USA, Inc., since that time. During the five years after Dinky was dissolved, she continued to operate as a corporation, ordering and making payments to Benetton through June 7, 2009. Between June and November 2009, Benetton sought payment of over $200,000 owed by Dinky. Ms. Kostopulos claims she was unaware of the dissolution until late 2009, when payment problems arose. Dinky applied for reinstatement at that time. With corporate status reinstated, Ms. Kostopulos contended that she was not personally liable for the debts incurred by the dissolved corporation during the time of its dissolution. The court determined that Ms. Kostopulos could not escape personal liability by reinstating her corporation, holding that "she should have known" about the dissolution of Dinky, over such a long period of time.[37]

After a corporation is dissolved, a contract made by an officer of the dissolved corporation cannot be enforced against the other party to the contract. **For Example,** a lucrative contract with Florio Entertainment, Inc., was signed "Louis Lofredo, LL Associates as company president" using a letterhead "LL Associates, Inc." In fact, the corporation "LL Associates, Inc." had been dissolved years before the contract was negotiated and signed, and Lofredo had made no effort to reinstate the corporation. LL Associates, Inc., had no legal existence and thus could not be a party to the contract and could not enforce the contract.[38]

A corporation whose powers are suspended for nonpayment of taxes cannot sue or defend a lawsuit while its taxes remain unpaid.[39] Upon payment of taxes, however, corporate powers are revived. Thus, if a corporation filed a timely appeal while its powers were suspended, it could proceed with the appeal after paying its taxes.[40]

[34] RMBCA §2.04.
[35] *De La Garza v. Clean Oil Innovations, Inc.*, 2013 WL 1222109 (S.D. Tex. March 20, 2013).
[36] RMBCA §14.20.
[37] *Benetton U.S.A. Corp. v. Dinky, Inc.*, 2011 WL 5024549 (N.D. Ill. Oct. 19, 2011). But see section 2.04 of the 1984 RMBCA, which provides that all persons purporting to act for or on behalf of a corporation "knowing that there was no incorporation" under the act are jointly and severally liable for all liabilities while so acting. There would be no liability for an individual who did not and should not have known of the dissolution.
[38] *Animazing Entertainment, Inc. v. Louis Lofredo Associates, Inc.*, 88 F. Supp. 2d 265 (S.D.N.Y. 2000).
[39] *Kaufman, Inc. v. Performance Plastering, Inc.*, 39 Cal. Rptr. 3d 33 (Cal. App. 2006).
[40] See *Bourhis v. Lord*, 295 P.3d 895 (Cal. 2013).

43-3h Judicial Dissolution

Judicial dissolution of a corporation may be decreed when its management is deadlocked and the deadlock cannot be broken by the shareholders.[41] In some states, a "custodian" may be appointed for a corporation when the shareholders are unable to break a deadlock in the board of directors and irreparable harm is threatened to, or sustained by, the corporation because of the deadlock.

43-3i Voluntary Dissolution

State laws describe the requirements for voluntary dissolution of a corporation. For example, publication in a paper of general circulation may be required. Compliance with such statutes is important to protect the company from subsequent claims. A state law may state that a claim against the corporation will be barred unless the claim is brought within two years of publication of the notice of dissolution.[42]

consolidation (of corporations)– combining of two or more corporations in which the corporate existence of each one ceases and a new corporation is created.

43-4 Consolidations, Mergers, and Conglomerates

Two or more corporations may be combined to form a new structure or enterprise.

CPA

43-4a Definitions

Enterprises may be combined by a consolidation or merger of corporations or by the formation of a conglomerate.

CPA

Consolidation

In a **consolidation** of two or more corporations, the separate existence of the two corporations ceases, and a new corporation with the property and assets of the old corporations comes into being (Figure 43-1).

FIGURE 43-1 Consolidation

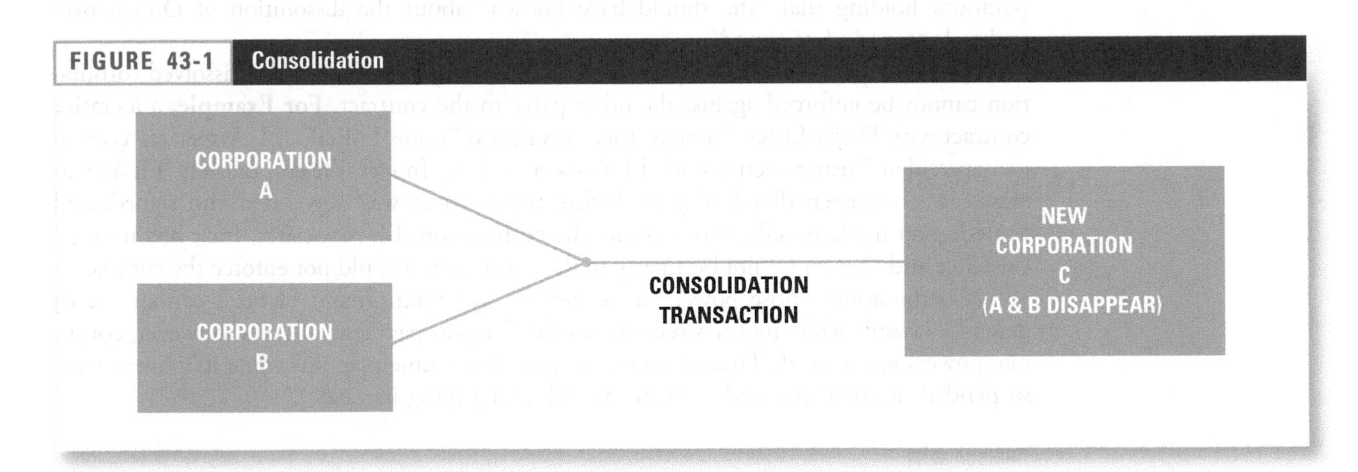

[41] After a shareholder has requested dissolution of a corporation, a state statute may offer an option to the corporation or other existing shareholders to purchase shares owned by the petitioning shareholder(s) for "fair value" in lieu of dissolution. See *Dawkins v. Hickman Family Corp.*, 2010 WL 4683472 (N.D. Miss. Nov. 10, 2010).

[42] *Lewis Oil, Inc. v. Bourbon Mini-Mart, Inc.*, 16 N.E.3d (Ind. App. 2014). Lewis Oil gave reasonable notice of voluntary dissolution in a paper of general circulation. The notice stated that claims against the corporation had to be filed within two years after publication of the notice. A suit by a liquor store claiming that Lewis Oil contributed to environmental contamination on the property was dismissed because it was time-barred by the notice of dissolution.

FIGURE 43-2 Merger

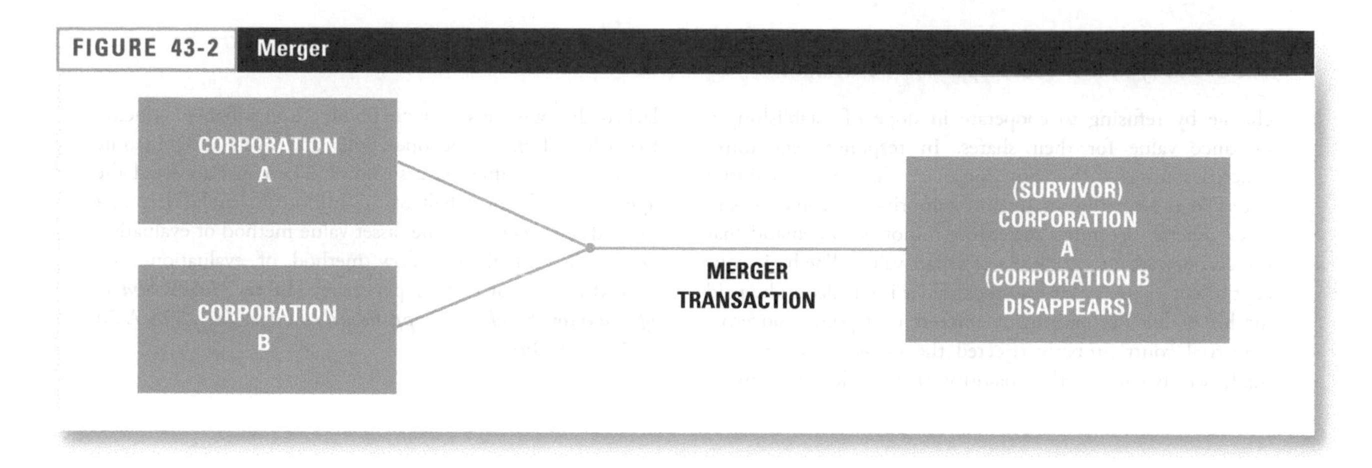

When a consolidation occurs, the new corporation ordinarily succeeds to the rights, powers, and immunities of its component parts. However, limitations may be imposed by constitution, statute, or certificate of incorporation.

CPA

Merger

merger (of corporations)–combining of corporations by which one absorbs the other and continues to exist, preserving its original charter and identity while the other corporation ceases to exist.

When two corporations **merge,** one absorbs the other. One corporation retains its original charter and identity and continues to exist; the other disappears, and its corporate existence terminates (Figure 43-2).

A stockholder who objects to a proposed consolidation or merger or who fails to convert existing shares into stock of the new or continuing corporation may apply to a court to appraise the value of the stock that she holds.[43] Should either party act arbitrarily, vexatiously, or not in good faith in the appraisal process, the courts have the right to assess court costs and attorney fees. The new or continuing corporation is then required to pay the "fair value" of the stock to the stockholder.[44]

CASE SUMMARY

The Sound of Music: $63.44 per Share

FACTS: The Trapp Family Lodge, Inc. (TFL), was incorporated in 1962 as a holding company for certain assets of the Von Trapp family, including the Trapp Family Lodge, a resort hotel complex located in Stowe, Vermont, and other assets, including certain royalty rights related to the family's story as portrayed in a Broadway musical and a movie. A majority of TFL shareholders approved a merger with a new corporation in 1994, and the merger took place on January 28, 1995. The dissenting shareholders, holding 76,529 of the corporation's 198,000 outstanding shares, were paid $33.84 per share as fair value by the TFL board of directors. The dissenting shareholders brought suit seeking a higher price as fair value. After the trial court set the fair value of $63.44, TFL appealed.

DECISION: Judgment for the dissenting shareholders. Dissenters' rights statutes were enacted in response to the common law rule that required unanimous consent from shareholders to make fundamental changes in a corporation. Under this rule minority shareholders could block corporate

[43] *Delaware Open MRI Radiology v. Kessler*, 898 A.2d 290 (Del. Ch. 2006).

[44] See *Spenlinhauer v. Spencer Press Inc.*, 959 N.E.2d 436 (Mass. App. 2011), where a minority shareholder dissented to a proposed merger, and after executing a cash-out merger, the court determined the "fair value" of the minority shares as the pro rata percentage of the net selling price.

The Sound of Music: $63.44 per Share continued

change by refusing to cooperate in hope of establishing a nuisance value for their shares. In response, legislatures enacted statutes authorizing corporate changes by majority vote. To protect the interests of minority shareholders, statutes generally permit a dissenting minority to demand that the corporation buy back shares at fair value. The basic concept of fair value is that the stockholder is entitled to be paid for his or her "proportionate interest in a going concern." The trial court properly rejected the fact-specific appraisal made on behalf of the majority shareholders because it lacked thoroughness and credibility, unjustifiably reducing the value of the lodge operations and overstating income taxes to reduce after-tax cash flows. The court accepted the appraisal made on behalf of the minority shareholders that utilized the average of a net asset value method of evaluation and a discounted cash flow method of evaluation, and yielded a value of $63.44 per share. **[In re *75,629 Shares of Common Stock of Trapp Family Lodge, Inc.*, 725 A.2d 927 (Vt. 1999)]**

Conglomerate

conglomerate–relationship of a parent corporation to subsidiary corporations engaged in diversified fields of activity unrelated to the field of activity of the parent corporation.

Conglomerate describes the relationship of a parent corporation to subsidiary corporations engaged in diversified fields of activity unrelated to the parent corporation's field of activity. **For Example,** a wire-manufacturing corporation that owns all the stock of a newspaper corporation and of a drug-manufacturing corporation would be described as a conglomerate. In contrast, if the wire-manufacturing company owned a mill that produced the metal used in making the wire and a mine that produced the ore that was used by the mill, the relationship would probably be described as an *integrated industry* rather than as a conglomerate. This term is merely a matter of usage rather than of legal definition. Likewise, when the parent company is not engaged in production or the rendering of services, it is customary to call it a *holding company.*

Without regard to whether the enterprise is a holding company or whether the group of corporations constitutes a conglomerate or an integrated industry, each part is a distinct corporation to which ordinary corporation law applies. In some instances, additional principles apply because of the nature of the relationships existing among the several corporations involved.

43-4b Legality

Consolidations, mergers, and asset acquisitions between enterprises are prohibited by federal antitrust legislation when the effect is to lessen competition in interstate commerce. A business corporation may not merge with a charitable corporation because this combination would divert the assets of the respective corporations to purposes not intended by their shareholders.

43-4c Liability of Successor Corporations

When corporations are combined in any way, the question of who is liable for the debts and obligations of the predecessor corporation arises.

Mergers and Consolidations

Generally, the enterprise engaging in or continuing the business after a merger or consolidation succeeds to all of the rights and property of the predecessor, or disappearing, corporation.[45]

[45] *Corporate Express Office Products, Inc. v. Phillips,* 847 So. 2d 406 (Fla. 2003).

CASE SUMMARY

A Marshmallow of a Case for the Plaintiff Marsh USA

FACTS: The Orleans Parish School Board ("School Board") in New Orleans, Louisiana, hired Johnson & Higgins, Inc. (J&H), in 1996, creating an ongoing insurance consulting agreement between them. The terms of the agreement provided that the School Board would pay J&H, Inc., for its consulting services and would later be reimbursed by the insurance carrier eventually selected by the School Board. Pursuant to their agreement, over the next few years, J&H's Mrs. Ippolito prepared several Requests for Proposals ("RFP") on behalf of the School Board. The School Board paid its fees for this consulting work without complaint. During this time, Johnson & Higgins merged with Marsh McLennan, a company that thereafter merged into Marsh USA, Inc. In 2001, Mrs. Ippolito prepared, at the request of the School Board, two more requests for proposals. Per the terms of the RFPs, Marsh was to receive $70,000 as its consulting fee under NO. 7656 and a $5,000 consulting fee under NO. 7657. Mrs. Ippolito and her staff spent several months working on the project for the School Board. The School Board never paid Marsh for the services and Marsh USA, Inc., sued the School Board for breach of contract, seeking payment of $75,000. The School Board asserted that Marsh USA was not a proper party to the lawsuit and that no contract had existed with it. From a judgment for Marsh USA, Inc., the School Board appealed.

DECISION: Judgment for Marsh USA, Inc. When two corporations merge or consolidate, the new successor corporation acquires all of the assets and rights of the former corporation. The minutes of a School Board meeting reflect the School Board's awareness of the merger in this case as well as its continuing contract with the firm. ***[Marsh Advantage America v. Orleans Parish School Board*, 995 So. 2d 53 (La. App. 2008)]**

The enterprise continuing the business is also subject to all of the debts and liabilities of the predecessor corporation.[46]

Liabilities of predecessor corporations can be imposed on a successor corporation when the transaction is a de facto merger[47] or the successor is a mere continuation of the predecessor. **For Example,** Steven Stepp manufactured pleasure boats through Thoroughbred Power Boats, Inc., until August 1996 at which time Thoroughbred Power Boats, Inc., ceased manufacturing and selling boats. In August 1996, Velocity Power Boats, Inc., began manufacturing and selling pleasure boats at the same location. Stephen Stepp and his wife were the only officers and board members of both corporations. Finding that Velocity was merely a "new hat" for Thoroughbred Power Boats, Inc., with the same or similar management and ownership, Velocity Power Boats, Inc., was held liable as a successor corporation for damages for a May 6, 1995, boating accident caused by a defective Thoroughbred Power Boats, Inc., manufactured boat.[48]

Asset Sales

In contrast with a merger or consolidation, a corporation may merely purchase the assets of another business. In that case, the purchaser does not become liable for the obligations of the predecessor business. **For Example,** Hull Corporation sold one of its operating divisions to SP Industries, Inc. (SPI), for $6 million under an asset purchase agreement (APA) that stated that the buyer SPI assumed no liability for preclosing claims against Hull. In fact as Hull and SPI were negotiating the APA, Hull was having difficulties regarding engineering and installation work the division had performed in China for Berg Chilling Systems, Inc. Berg Chilling sued SPI under the doctrine of successor liability for the payment of a

[46] *Beck v. Roper Whitney, Inc.*, 190 F. Supp. 2d 524 (W.D.N.Y. 2001).
[47] *Ulanet v. D'Artagnan, Inc.*, 170 F. Supp. 2d 356 (E.D.N.Y. 2001); see *Callahan & Sons, Inc. v. Dykeman Electric Co. Inc.*, 266 F. Supp. 2d 208 (D. Mass 2003).
[48] *Paten v. Thoroughbred Power Boats, Inc.*, 294 F.3d 640 (5th Cir. 2002).

$1,650,000 arbitration award because of the defective work done by Hull in China. The court held that SPI did not assume Hull's contractual liability to Berg under any exception to the traditional corporate rule of successor nonliability.[49]

Corporations may seek to avoid liability for the obligations of a predecessor corporation by attempting to disguise a consolidation or merger as being merely a sale of assets. Courts will not recognize such a transaction and will impose a successor's liability on the successor corporation.[50] In addition, even when the old corporate entity is not formally dissolved, a finding of a de facto merger resulting in successor liability may occur.

CASE SUMMARY

Corporate Shell Games Not Allowed

FACTS: Since 1976, McGhan/Cal. Inc., a manufacturer of prostheses used in breast augmentation surgery, and later McGhan/Del., received numerous complaints about its implants. It also received inquiries from the Food and Drug Administration. In April 1977, Mary Marks had surgery; two McGhan implants were used. Because of defects in the McGhan implants, Marks underwent three additional operations, eventually having the McGhan products replaced with implants manufactured by another company. In June 1977, McGhan/Cal. was acquired by a Delaware subsidiary of 3M, called McGhan/Del. Inc. McGhan/Del. removed the implants from the market in April 1979. On January 1, 1981, 3M's wholly owned subsidiary, McGhan/Del. Inc., was reorganized as a division of 3M and dissolved. In January 1982, following her fourth surgery, Marks brought a product liability suit against 3M. 3M contended that it was not liable for the actions of the predecessor corporation.

DECISION: The transaction between the 3M subsidiary McGhan/Del. Inc. and McGhan/Cal. Inc. amounted to a de facto merger of the seller and the purchaser. McGhan/Cal. changed its name, distributed 3M stock to its shareholders, and dissolved, and all key employees signed employment contracts to work for the purchaser. No cash was paid for the business. The transaction was not an assets sale. The second reorganization amounted to a continuation of the de facto merger. Public policy requires that 3M, having accepted the benefits of a going concern, should also assume the costs that all other going concerns must bear. It should not be allowed to avoid liability to an injured person by merely shuffling paper and manipulating corporate entities. [***Marks v. Minnesota Mining and Manufacturing Co.*, 232 Cal. Rptr. 594 (Cal. App. 1986)**]

Make the Connection

Summary

A *corporation* is an artificial person created by government action. It exists as a separate and distinct entity possessing certain powers. In most states, the corporation comes into existence when the Secretary of State issues a certificate of incorporation. The most common forms of corporations are private business corporations whose stock is sold to the public (publicly held) and close corporations, which are business firms whose shares are not traded publicly. Corporations may be formed for purposes other than conducting a business. For example, there are nonprofit corporations, municipal corporations, and public authorities for governmental purposes.

An *ultra vires* act occurs when a corporation acts beyond the scope of the powers given it. Because states now grant broad powers to corporations, it is unlikely that a modern corporation would act beyond the scope of its powers.

[49] *Berg Chilling Systems Inc. v. Hull Corp.*, 435 F.3d 455 (3d Cir. 2006).
[50] *State v. Westwood Squibb Pharmaceutical Co., Inc.*, 981 F. Supp. 760 (W.D.N.Y. 1997).

A *promoter* is a person who brings together the persons interested in the enterprise and sets in motion all that must be done to form a corporation. A corporation is not liable on contracts made by its promoter for the corporation unless it adopts the contracts. The promoter is personally liable for contracts made for the corporation before its existence. A promoter stands in a fiduciary relation to the corporation and stockholders.

The procedures for incorporation are set forth in the statutes of each state. In most states, the corporation comes into existence on issuance of the certificate of incorporation. When all requirements have been satisfied, the corporation is a corporation de jure. When there has not been full compliance with all requirements for incorporation, a de facto corporation may be found to exist. Or when sufficient compliance for a de facto corporation does not exist, in some jurisdictions a third person may be estopped from denying the legal existence of the "corporation" with which it did business (corporation by estoppel).

A corporation has the power to continue as an entity forever or for a stated period of time regardless of changes in the ownership of the stock or the death of a shareholder. It may make contracts, issue stocks and bonds, borrow money, execute commercial paper, transfer and acquire property, acquire its own stock if it is solvent and the purchase does not impair capital, and make charitable contributions. Subject to limitations, a corporation has the power to do business in other states. A corporation may also participate in a business enterprise to the same extent as an individual; that is, it may be a partner in a partnership, or it may enter a joint venture or other enterprise. Special service corporations, such as banks, insurance companies, and railroads, are subject to separate statutes governing their organization and powers.

Two or more corporations may be combined to form a new enterprise. This combination may be a consolidation, with a new corporation coming into existence, or a merger, in which one corporation absorbs the other.

Learning Outcomes

After studying this chapter, you should be able to clearly explain:

43-1 Nature and Classes

LO.1 Recognize that a corporation is a separate legal entity, distinct and apart from its stockholders and that individual shareholders are not liable for claims against the corporation

43-2 Corporate Powers

LO.2 Explain the wide range of power given to corporations under modern corporate codes

See the RMBCA general provision granting corporations "the same powers as an individual to do all things necessary or convenient to carry out its business and affairs," page 887.

43-3 Creation and Termination of the Corporation

LO.3 Understand that the promoter is personally liable for preincorporation contracts

LO.4 Understand that after a corporate charter has been dissolved the owners and officers may be personally responsible for contracts made in the corporate name if they knew or should have known of the dissolution

See the example where Ms. Kostopulos was personally liable for debts incurred during the time of dissolution because she should have known about the dissolution, page 893.

43-4 Consolidations, Mergers, and Conglomerates

LO.5 Explain a stockholder's option when he or she objects to a proposed consolidation or merger of the corporation

See the *Trapp Family Lodge* case, page 895.

LO.6 Recognize that liabilities of predecessor corporations can be imposed on successor corporations when the transaction is a de facto merger or a continuation of the predecessor

See the example of Velocity Power Boats, Inc., which became essentially a "new hat" for Thoroughbred Power Boats, Inc., with liability as a corporate successor for a defective Thoroughbred boat, page 897.

Key Terms

articles of incorporation
authorities
benefit corporation
bylaws
certificate of incorporation
charter
close corporation
conglomerate
consolidation
corporation
corporation by estoppel
corporation de jure
de facto
domestic corporation
eleemosynary corporation

foreign corporation
general corporation code
incorporators
merge
police power
private corporation
promoters
public corporation
quasi-public corporation
treasury stock
ultra vires

Questions and Case Problems

1. Edwin Edwards and Karen Davis owned EEE, Inc., which owned three convenience stores, all of which sold gasoline. Reid Ellis delivered to the three convenience stores $26,675.02 worth of gasoline for which he was not paid. Ellis proved that Edwards and Davis owned the business, ran it, and in fact personally ordered the gasoline. He claimed that they were personally liable for the debt owed him by EEE, Inc. Decide. [*Ellis v. Edwards*, 348 S.E.2d 764 (Ga. App.)]
2. Clinton Investors Company, as landlord, entered into a three-year lease with the Clifton Park Learning Center as tenant. The lease was executed by Bernie Watkins who represented himself as the treasurer of the Learning Center. On May 31, 1984, the day before the lease term began, Watkins signed a rider to the lease. He again signed as treasurer of the tenant, identifying the tenant as "the Clifton Park Learning Center, Inc." Watkins had not consulted an attorney regarding the formation of the corporation. He mistook the reservation of the business name with the Secretary of State for the filing of a certificate of incorporation. On February 11, 1985, a certificate of incorporation was filed. By March 1986, the Learning Center had become delinquent in rental payments and other fees in the amount of $18,103. Clinton sued Watkins and the Learning Center for the amounts due. Watkins claimed that only the corporation was liable. Decide. [*Clinton Investors Co. v. Watkins*, 536 N.Y.S. 2d 270 (A.D. 1989)]
3. Compare and contrast consolidations, mergers, and conglomerates.
4. On January 27, 1982, Joe Walker purchased a wheel-loader machine from Thompson & Green Machinery Co. (T&G). Walker signed a promissory note for $37,886.30 on behalf of "Music City Sawmill, Inc., by Joe Walker, President." When Sawmill was unable to make payments on the loader, the machine was returned to T&G. T&G brought suit against Sawmill and subsequently discovered that Sawmill had not been incorporated on January 27, 1982, when the machine was purchased but had been incorporated the next day. T&G then sued Walker individually. The lawsuit was Walker's first notice that Sawmill was not incorporated on the date of the sale. Walker's defense was that T&G dealt with Sawmill as a corporation and did not intend to bind him personally on the note and therefore was estopped to deny Sawmill's corporate existence. Decide based on the 1969 MBCA. What would be the result if the RMBCA applied? [*Thompson & Green Machinery Co. v. Music City Lumber Co., Inc., Music City Sawmill Co., Inc.*, 683 S.W.2d 340 (Tenn. App.)]
5. North Pole, Inc., approved a plan to merge with its subsidiary, Santa's Workshop, Inc. The merger plan provided that certain of Workshop's shareholders would receive $3.50 per share. The highest independent appraisal of the stock was $4.04 per share. Hirschfeld, Inc., a shareholder, claimed that the fair value was $16.80 per share. Workshop offered to make its corporate books and records available to Hirschfeld to assess the validity of the $16.80 demand. This offer was declined. Hirschfeld did not attempt to base the $16.80 demand on any recognizable method of stock valuation. Hirschfeld contended that it had a right to get the asking price. Refer to RMBCA §§13.02, 13.28, and 13.31. Could Hirschfeld have blocked the merger until Workshop paid the $16.80? Decide. [*Santa's Workshop v. Hirschfeld, Inc.*, 851 P.2d 265 (Colo. App.)]
6. Richard Ramlall was hired by CloseCall (MD) Inc. to negotiate a billing dispute with Verizon involving some $2 million in asserted overcharges. CloseCall (MD) agreed to a contingent fee "bonus" for its negotiators of 10 percent of the refund. The negotiations were successful. However, before he could collect his fee CloseCall (MD) merged with MVCC Acquisition Corp., a wholly owned subsidiary of MobilePro Corp., which was created for the express purpose of merging with CloseCall (MD). MVCC survived and CloseCall (MD) dissolved. MVCC then changed its name to CloseCall (DE). The merger agreement between CloseCall and MVCC referenced the 10 percent bonus due on the Verizon billing dispute. The surviving Delaware corporation created by the merger of CloseCall (MD) into MVCC is CloseCall (DE). Ramlall sued CloseCall (DE) for the bonus as the successor corporation of

CloseCall (MD). CloseCall (DE) contends that after the merger CloseCall (DE) did not owe any money to Ramlall. Is CloseCall (DE) a successor corporation? Is it liable to Ramlall for the "bonus fee"? [*Ramlall v. Mobile Pro Corp.*, 30 A.2d 1003 (Md. App.)]

7. The Community Youth Center (CYC) Corporation failed to pay its annual registration fee in 2000 and was automatically dissolved by the state corporation commission. CYC continued to operate and held itself out as a corporation well into 2005 when it obtained a loan from the First Community Bank to finance a swimming pool at its facility. The loan was secured by the CYC property. After the corporation defaulted on its loan payments, the bank foreclosed and subsequently purchased the property at a foreclosure sale. CYC contended that the president, vice president, and treasurer of CYC had no standing to make the 2005 loan transaction because CYC's corporate status had been terminated. The bank contended that under the doctrine of corporation by estoppel, CYC continued to exist in 2005, and, consequently, the officer-directors had authority to borrow money and grant a deed of trust, thereby giving the bank a valid lien on the property. Decide. [*First Community Bank, N.A. v. Community Youth Center*, 2010 WL 8696179 (Ca. Cir. Ct.)]

8. Emmick was a director and shareholder of Colonial Manors, Inc. (CM). He organized another corporation named Oahe Enterprises, Inc. To obtain shares of the Oahe stock, Emmick transferred CM shares arbitrarily valued by him at $19 per share to Oahe. The CM shares had a book value of $.47 per share, but Emmick believed that the stock would increase to a value of $19. The directors of Oahe approved Emmick's payment with the valuation of $19 per share. Golden sued Emmick on the ground that he had fraudulently deceived Oahe Corp. about the value of the CM shares and thus had made a secret profit when he received the Oahe shares that had a much greater value than the CM shares he gave in exchange. Emmick contended that his firm opinion was that the future potential value of CM shares would surely reach $19 per share. Decide. [*Golden v. Oahe Enterprises, Inc.*, 295 N.W.2d 160 (S.D.)]

9. Madison Associates purchased control of the majority of shares of 79 Realty Corp. from the Kimmelmans and the Zauders, who then resigned as directors. The Alpert group, which owned the remaining 26 percent of 79 Realty refused to sell their shares. Partners of Madison Associates replaced the Kimmelmans and Zauders as directors of 79 Realty Corp., and as controlling directors, they approved a plan to merge 79 Realty Corp. with the Williams Street Corp., which was owned by Madison Associates. A shareholders' meeting was called, and the merger was approved by two-thirds of the shareholders. The Alpert group's shares were then forcibly canceled, with the price paid for these shares determined at their fair market value. The Alpert group brought suit contending that the merger was unlawful because the sole purpose was to benefit the Madison Associates. Decide. [*Alpert v. 28 Williams Street Corp.*, 473 N.E.2d 19 (N.Y.)]

10. The Seabrook Island Property Owners Association, Inc., is a nonprofit corporation organized under state law to maintain streets and open spaces owned by property owners of Seabrook Island. Seabrook Island Co. is the developer of Seabrook Island and has majority control of the board of directors of the association. The association's bylaws empower the board of directors to levy an annual maintenance charge. Neither the association's charter nor its bylaws authorize the board to assess any other charges. When the board levied, in addition to the annual maintenance charge, an emergency budget assessment on all members to rebuild certain bridges and to revitalize the beach, the Loverings and other property owners challenged in court the association's power to impose the assessment. Decide. [*Lovering v. Seabrook Island Property Owners Ass'n*, 344 S.E.2d 862 (S.C. App.)]

11. Adams and two other persons were promoters for a new corporation, Aldrehn Theaters Co. The promoters retained Kridelbaugh to perform legal services in connection with the incorporation of the new business and promised to pay him $1,500. Aldrehn was incorporated through Kridelbaugh's services, and the promoters became its only directors. Kridelbaugh attended a meeting of the board of directors at which he was told that he should obtain a permit for the corporation to sell stock because the directors wished to pay him for his previous services. The promoters failed to pay Kridelbaugh, and he sued the corporation. Was the corporation liable? [*Kridelbaugh v. Aldrehn Theaters Co.*, 191 N.W. 803 (Iowa)]

12. On August 19, 1980, Joan Ioviero injured her hand when she slipped and fell while leaving the dining room at the Hotel Excelsior in Venice, Italy. This hotel was owned by an Italian corporation, Cigahotels, S.p.A. (The designation *S.p.A.* stands for *Societa per Azionean*, the Italian term for *corporation*.)

In 1973, a firm called Ciga Hotels, Inc., was incorporated in New York. Its certificate of incorporation was amended in 1979, changing the name of the firm to Landia International Services, Inc. This New York corporation was employed by the Italian corporation Cigahotels, S.p.A., to provide sales and promotional services in the United States and Canada. Ioviero sought to hold the New York corporation liable for her hand injury at the Venice hotel. She pointed to the similarity of the first corporate name used by the New York firm to the name Cigahotels, S.p.A., and the fact that the New York firm represented the interests of the Italian firm in the United States as clear evidence that the two firms were the same single legal entity. She asked that the court disregard the separate corporate entities. The New York corporation moved that the case be dismissed because it was duly incorporated in New York and did not own the Excelsior Hotel in which Ioviero was injured. Decide. [*Ioviero v. CigaHotel, Inc., aka Landia I.S., Inc.*, 475 N.Y.S.2d 880 (A.D.)]

13. William Sullivan was ousted from the presidency of the New England Patriots Football Club, Inc. Later, he borrowed $5,348,000 to buy 100 percent control of the voting shares of the corporation. A condition of the loan was that he reorganize the Patriots so that the income from the corporation could be devoted to repayment of the personal loan and the team's assets could be used as collateral. Sullivan, therefore, arranged for a cash freeze-out merger of the holders of the 120,000 shares of nonvoting stock. David Coggins, who owned 10 shares of nonvoting stock and took special pride in the fact that he was an owner of the team, refused the $15-a-share buyout and challenged the merger in court. He contended that the merger was not for a legitimate corporate purpose but to enable Sullivan to satisfy his personal loan. Sullivan contended that legitimate business purposes were given in the merger proxy statement, such as the National Football League's policy of discouraging public ownership of teams. Coggins responded that before the merger, Sullivan had 100 percent control of the voting stock and thus control of the franchise and that no legal basis existed to eliminate public ownership. Decide. [*Coggins v. New England Patriots Football Club*, 492 N.E.2d 1112 (Mass.)]

CPA Questions

1. Which of the following statements is correct concerning the similarities between a limited partnership and a corporation?

   a. Each is created under a statute and must file a copy of its certificate with the proper state authorities.

   b. All corporate stockholders and all partners in a limited partnership have limited liability.

   c. Both are recognized for federal income tax purposes as taxable entities.

   d. Both are allowed statutorily to have perpetual existence.

2. Rice is a promoter of a corporation to be known as Dex Corp. On January 1, 1985, Rice signed a nine-month contract with Roe, a CPA, which provided that Roe would perform certain accounting services for Dex. Rice did not disclose to Roe that Dex had not been formed. Prior to the incorporation of Dex on February 1, 1985, Roe rendered accounting services pursuant to the contract. After rendering accounting services for an additional period of six months pursuant to the contract, Roe was discharged without cause by the board of directors of Dex. In the absence of any agreements to the contrary, who will be liable to Roe for breach of contract?

   a. Both Rice and Dex

   b. Rice only

   c. Dex only

   d. Neither Rice nor Dex

3. In general, which of the following must be contained in articles of incorporation?

   a. The names of the states in which the corporation will be doing business

   b. The name of the state in which the corporation will maintain its principal place of business

   c. The names of the initial officers and their terms of office

   d. The classes of stock authorized for issuance

CHAPTER 50

Leases

Learning Outcomes <<<

After studying this chapter, you should be able to

LO.1 **List the ways in which a lease may be terminated**

LO.2 **List and explain the rights and duties of the parties to a lease**

LO.3 **Describe a landlord's liability for a tenant's and a third person's injuries sustained on the premises**

LO.4 **Define *sublease* and *assignment of a lease* and distinguish between them**

50-1 Creation and Termination

Leases are governed by the common law of property as modified by judicial decisions and statutes.[1]

50-1a Definition and Nature

lease–agreement between the owner of property and a tenant by which the former agrees to give possession of the property to the latter in consideration of the payment of rent. (Parties—landlord or lessor, tenant or lessee)

lessor–one who conveys real or personal property by a lease; a landlord.

landlord–one who leases real property to another.

lessee–one who has a possessory interest in real or personal property under a lease; a tenant.

tenant–one who holds or possesses real property by any kind of right or title; one who pays rent for the temporary use and occupation of another's real property under a lease.

A **lease** is the relationship in which one person is in lawful possession of real property owned by another. In common usage, *lease* also refers to the agreement that creates that relationship.

The person who owns the real property and permits the occupation of the premises is known as the **lessor,** or **landlord.** The **lessee,** or **tenant,** is the one who occupies the property. A lease establishes the relationship of landlord and tenant.

50-1b Creation of the Lease Relationship

The relationship of landlord and tenant is created by an express or implied contract. An oral lease is valid at common law, but statutes in most states require written leases for certain tenancies. Many states provide that a lease for a term exceeding one year must be in writing.

Antidiscrimination

Statutes in many states prohibit an owner who rents property for profit from discriminating against prospective tenants on the basis of race, color, religion, or national origin. Also, the federal *Fair Housing Act* prohibits such discrimination. In addition, landlords are subject to the Americans with Disabilities Act (ADA) and must make reasonable accommodations for tenants with disabilities. **For Example,** a tenant whose physician has prescribed a comfort pet must be allowed to have that pet in his or her apartment even if the complex does not allow pets.[2] However, the use of medical marijuana in leased premises is not protected under the ADA.[3]

Unconscionability

At common law, the parties to a lease had freedom to include such terms as they chose. However, that freedom has been curbed in some states that require that leases follow the pattern of UCC section 2-302 and not include terms and conditions that are unconscionable. **For Example,** a provision in a residential lease stating that the landlord cutting off heat or water will not constitute an eviction is unconscionable. Such a clause does not prevent the tenant from recovering on the grounds of unconscionability or for breach of the implied warranty of habitability when there has been no heat or water.

50-1c Classification of Tenancies

Tenancies are classified by duration as tenancies for years, from year to year, at will, and by sufferance.

[1] A uniform act, the Uniform Residential Landlord and Tenant Act (URLTA), has been adopted in some form, often just in sections, in 21 states. URLTA does not apply to dorm rooms, fraternities, homeless shelters, or halfway houses. *Picken v. Multnomah County,* 2012 WL 1151037 (D. Or. 2012).

[2] *Bhogaita v. Altamonte Heights Condominium Ass'n, Inc.,* 765 F.3d 1277 (11th Cir. 2014).

[3] *Forest City Residential Management, Inc. ex rel. Plymouth Square Ltd. Dividend Housing Ass'n v. Beasley,* 71 F. Supp. 3d 715 (E.D. Mich. 2014).

CPA

Tenancy for Years

tenancy for years–tenancy for a fixed period of time, even though the time is less than a year.

A **tenancy for years** is one under which the tenant has a lease that runs for a definite duration. The expression "for years" is used to describe such a tenancy whether the duration of the tenancy is for only six months or as long as 10 years.

Periodic Tenancy

periodic tenancy–tenancy that continues indefinitely for a specified rental period until terminated; often called a month-to-month tenancy.

A **periodic tenancy** is one under which a tenant has a lease that has an indefinite duration and under which the tenant pays annual, monthly, or weekly rent. This tenancy does not terminate at the end of a year, month, or week except with proper notice. Proper notice, in most states, means giving notice for at least one period before ending the lease.[4] **For Example,** on a month-to-month tenancy, the notice must be at least one month prior to ending the lease.

In almost all states, a periodic tenancy is implied if the tenant, with the consent of the landlord, stays in possession of property after a tenancy for years. Consent exists when there is an express statement or by conduct, such as when a landlord continues to accept rent.[5]

CPA

Tenancy at Will

tenancy at will–holding of land for an indefinite period that may be terminated at any time by the landlord or by the landlord and tenant acting together.

When a lease runs for an indefinite period, which may be terminated at any time by the landlord or the tenant, a **tenancy at will** exists. A person who possesses land for an indefinite period with the owner's permission but without any agreement as to rent is a tenant at will. Statutes in some states and decisions in others require advance notice of termination of this kind of tenancy.

CPA

Tenancy at Sufferance

tenancy at sufferance–lease arrangement in which the tenant occupies the property at the discretion of the landlord.

When a tenant remains in possession after the termination of the lease without permission of the landlord, the landlord may treat the tenant as either a trespasser or a tenant.[6] Until the landlord elects to do one or the other, a **tenancy at sufferance** exists. **For Example,** if John's one-year lease expired on January 31, 2016, and John remained in the apartment for a week, he would be a tenant at sufferance during that week. If John's landlord accepted a rental payment at the end of the first week, John would be a *periodic* or *month-to-month tenant.* In this situation, John was a tenant for years, a tenant at sufferance, and then a periodic tenant.[7]

50-1d Termination of Lease

A lease is generally not terminated by the death, insanity, or bankruptcy of either party except in the case of a tenancy at will. Leases may be terminated in the following ways.

Termination by Notice

Unless prohibited by statute, a lease may give the landlord the power to terminate it by giving notice to the tenant. In states that follow the common law on termination by notice, it is immaterial why the landlord terminates. A provision in a lease giving the landlord the right to terminate the lease by notice is strictly construed against the landlord.

Expiration of Term in a Tenancy for Years

A tenancy for years ends upon the expiration of the term. There is no requirement that one party give the other any notice of termination. However, a lease may require express

[4] *Meek v. Mallory and Evans, Inc.,* 734 S.E.2d 109 (Ga. App. 2012). URLTA §1.303.
[5] In re *2408 W. Kennedy, LLC,* 512 B.R. 708 (M.D. Fla. 2014).
[6] *Coinmach Corp. v. Aspenwood Apartment Corp.,* 417 S.W.3d 909 (Tex. 2013).
[7] *Brittany Sobery Family Ltd. Partnership v. Coinmach Corp.,* 392 S.W.3d 46 (Mo. App. 2013).

notice in this type of lease with a specified term except when a statute prohibits the landlord from imposing such a requirement.

Notice in a Periodic Tenancy

In the absence of an agreement of the parties, notice for termination of a periodic tenancy is now usually governed by statute. It is common practice for the parties to require 30 or 60 days' notice to end a tenancy from year to year.

Destruction of Property

By either an express provision in a lease or under a statutory provision, tenants are released from their liability to pay rent if the leased premises are destroyed. Alternatively, the amount of rent may be reduced in proportion to the loss. **For Example,** a tenant may only be able to use one-half of the property, so the rent would be cut in half. Such statutes do not require the landlord to repair or restore the property to its former condition. When the lease covers rooms or an apartment in a building, a destruction of the leased premises terminates the lease.

Fraud

Because a lease is based on a contract, a lease agreement is subject to the contract defense of fraud. (See Chapter 13.)

Transfer of the Tenant

Residential leases may contain a provision for termination if there is a change in the tenant's circumstances, such as the tenant's being transferred by an employer to another city or on the tenant's being called into active military service. Such provisions are strictly construed against the tenant. Tenants should be certain to request personal circumstances provisions in their leases that are broad enough to cover these types of job events and military duty.

50-1e Notice of Termination

When notice of termination is required, no particular words are necessary to constitute a sufficient notice so long as the words used clearly indicate the intention of the party. The notice, whether given by the landlord or the tenant, must be definite. Statutes sometimes require that the notice be in writing. In the absence of such a provision, however, oral notice is generally sufficient.

50-1f Renewal of Lease

When a lease terminates for any reason, the landlord and the tenant ordinarily enter into a new agreement if they wish to extend or renew the lease. The power to renew the lease may be stated in the original lease by declaring that the lease runs indefinitely, as from year to year, subject to being terminated by either party's giving written notice of a specified number of days or months before the termination date. Renewal provisions are strictly construed against the tenant.

The lease may require the tenant to give written notice of intention to renew the lease. In such a case, there is no renewal if the tenant does not give the required notice but merely remains on the premises after the expiration of the original term.[8]

[8] *Faison v. RTFX, Inc.*, 6 N.E.3d 376 (Ill. App. 2014).

50-2 Rights and Duties of Parties

The rights and duties of the landlord and tenant are based on principles of real estate law and contract law. There is an increasing tendency to treat the residential lease like any other type of consumer contract and to govern the rights and duties of the parties by general principles of contract law.

50-2a Possession

possession–exclusive dominion and control of property.

The tenant has the right to acquire **possession** of the property and to remain in possession of that property until the term of the lease has expired or he or she is removed according to legal proceedings provided to landlords for removal of tenants in breach of the lease.

Right of Possession

By making a lease, the lessor or landlord agrees to give possession of the premises to the tenant at the time specified in the lease. If the landlord rents a building that is being constructed, there is an implied promise in the contract that the leased premises will be ready for occupancy on the date specified in the lease for the beginning of the lease term.

If the landlord interferes with the tenant's possession, the landlord has breached the lease agreement, and legal remedies are available to the tenant. *Interference* is generally defined to be an eviction that occurs by judicial proceedings or when the landlord prevents access by the tenant, as when the locks are changed and the tenant does not have a key. If the landlord wrongfully deprives the tenant of the use of one room when the tenant is entitled to use an entire apartment or building, there is a partial eviction. An eviction in violation of the lease or law entitles the tenant to collect damages from the landlord for interference with possession of the leased premises.

Covenant of Quiet Enjoyment

covenant of quiet enjoyment–covenant by the grantor of an interest in land to not disturb the grantee's possession of the land.

Most written leases today contain an express promise by the landlord called a **covenant of quiet enjoyment.** Such a provision protects the tenant from interference with possession by the landlord or the landlord's agent, but it does not impose liability on the landlord for the unlawful acts of third persons.[9]

Constructive Eviction

constructive eviction–act or omission of the landlord that substantially deprives the tenant of the use and enjoyment of the premises.

A **constructive eviction** occurs when some act or omission of the landlord substantially deprives the tenant of the use and enjoyment of the premises.

To establish a constructive eviction, the tenant must show that the condition of the property is such that it is impossible for the tenant to remain in possession. In addition, constructive eviction is not established unless the tenant actually leaves the premises. If the tenant continues to occupy the premises for more than a reasonable time after what is claimed to be a constructive eviction, the tenant waives or loses the right to object to the landlord's conduct. The definition of constructive eviction requires the establishment of conditions so awful that a tenant is forced to leave. The tenant's remaining behind in the leased premises contradicts one of the elements required for establishing constructive eviction.[10] **For Example,** a condition of constructive eviction would be sewage backing up

[9] *Haslam-James v. Lawrence*, 39 A.3d 1121 (Conn. 2012).

[10] Some states prohibit a landlord of residential property from willfully turning off the utilities of a tenant for the purpose of evicting the tenant. *City and County of San Francisco v. Sainez*, 77 Cal. App. 4th 1302, 92 Cal. Rprt. 2d 418 (Cal. App. 2009) (imposing civil penalty of $663,000 for shutting off utilities for 530 days). Such conduct is also a violation of URLTA §§2.104 and 4.105. *Mik v. Federal Home Loan Mortgage Corp.*, 743 F.3d 149 (6th Cir. 2014).

through the bathtub. The tenant could claim that the sewage in the apartment constituted constructive eviction, but the tenant would also need to move out of the apartment.

50-2b Use of Premises

The lease generally specifies those uses authorized for the tenant. In the absence of express or implied restrictions, a tenant is entitled to use the premises for any lawful purpose for which they are adapted or for which they are ordinarily employed or in a manner contemplated by the parties in executing the lease. A provision specifying the use to be made of the property is strictly construed against the tenant.

Change of Use

If the tenant uses the property for any purpose other than the one specified, the landlord has the option to declare the lease terminated.

Continued Use of Property

A tenant is ordinarily required to give the landlord notice of nonuse or vacancy of the premises. This notice is a practical issue; landlords need to be aware when premises are vacant because there is an increased danger of damage to the premises by vandalism or fire. Also, there is commonly a provision in the landlord's fire insurance policy making it void if a vacancy continues for a specified time.

Rules

The modern lease generally contains a blanket agreement by the tenant to abide by the provisions of rules and regulations adopted by the landlord. These rules are generally binding on the tenant whether they exist at the time the lease was made or are adopted afterward.

Prohibition of Pets

A lease restriction prohibiting pet ownership is valid, as are cleaning fees for violations of the restriction.

50-2c Rent

The tenant is under a duty to pay rent as compensation to the landlord. The amount of rent agreed to by the parties may be subject to government regulation, as when a city or county has enacted rent control laws.

Time of Payment

The time of payment of rent is ordinarily fixed by the lease. However, statutes or custom may require rent to be paid monthly or may require a substantial deposit before the lease begins.

CPA

Assignment

sublessee–person with lease rights for a period of less than the term of the original lease (also *subtenant*).

If the lease is assigned (the tenant's entire interest is transferred to a third person), the assignee is liable to the landlord for the rent. However, the assignment does not in itself discharge the tenant from the duty to pay the rent. If the assignee of the lease does not make the lease payments, the landlord may bring an action for the rent against either the original tenant or the assignee, or both, but is entitled to payment of only what is due under the lease, not a double amount as collected from each party. A **sublessee** (a person to whom part of a tenant's interest is transferred) ordinarily is not liable to the original lessor for rent unless that liability has been expressly assumed or is imposed by statute.

Rent Escalation

When property is rented for a long term, it is common to include some provision for the automatic increase of the rent at periodic intervals. Such a provision is often tied to increases in the cost of living or in the landlord's operating costs and is called an **escalation clause.** There may, however, also be rent controls that would prohibit such rent increases.[11]

escalation clause– provision for the automatic increase of the rent at periodic intervals.

50-2d Repairs and Condition of Premises

In the absence of an agreement to the contrary, the tenant has no duty to make repairs. When the landlord makes repairs, reasonable care must be exercised to make them in a proper manner. The tenant is liable for any damage to the premises caused by his or her willful or negligent acts.

Inspection of Premises

Under the URLTA, the landlord has the right to enter the leased premises for emergency purposes or with notice to the tenant for repairs, evaluations, and estimates.

Housing Laws

Various laws protect tenants by requiring landlords to observe specified safety, health, and fire prevention standards. Some statutes require a landlord who leases a building for dwelling purposes to keep it in a condition fit for habitation. Leases commonly require the tenant to obey local ordinances and laws relating to the care and use of the premises.

Landlords must comply with the ADA. Compliance means that landlords cannot discriminate on the basis of disability in deciding whether to rent to a particular tenant.[12] Also, landlords are required to make reasonable modifications to accommodate tenants with disabilities, which can include everything from making sure that sidewalks on the property are smooth enough for operation of wheelchairs to permitting guide dogs to live with their sight-impaired owners.

THINKING THINGS THROUGH

The Rotting Balcony

Cayetano Giron stepped out onto the balcony of the apartment that he and his wife Robin leased from Jane Bailey. After taking four steps onto the balcony, Cayetano's foot sank into the soft floorboards and he fell toward the railing. He tried to grab the railing, but the railing broke off in his hand and he fell from the balcony to the street below (a two-story fall) and was injured. Robin had notified Mrs. Bailey, shortly after moving into the apartment, that the wooden balcony was "a little lopped." No repair attempts were made. Cayetano brought suit to recover for his injuries. Can he recover from Mrs. Bailey? Why or why not? **[*Giron v. Bailey*, 985 A.2d 1003 (2009)]**

In the summer of 2015, six students were killed and seven were injured when a balcony collapsed during one of the student's 21st birthday celebration. Would the landlord be liable? What if the balcony had passed inspection less than one year ago?

[11] *Fisher v. City of Berkeley, California*, 475 U.S. 260 (1986); N.Y. Comp. Codes R. & Regs. tit. 9, §2520.1 (2014).
[12] *Short v. Manhattan Apartments, Inc.*, 915 F. Supp. 2d 375 (S.D.N.Y. 2012).

One of the developing areas of landlord-tenant law involves landlords' rights with regard to leasing to convicts and those who are registered as sex offenders. About 600,000 inmates are released from prisons each year, and their housing choices generally involve leasing.[13] The federal government requires public housing authorities to screen and evict tenants for drug-related or "safety-threatening" behavior. Public housing authorities that receive federal funds must include a lease clause that requires automatic lease termination for any drug or violent criminal activity, even if the activity does not occur on the landlord's property.

CASE SUMMARY

But I'm Innocent!!!

FACTS: Several young men, grandsons of William Lee and Barbara Hill, both of whom were residents on leases of the Oakland Housing Authority (OHA), were caught in the apartment complex parking lot smoking marijuana. The daughter of Pearlie Rucker, who resided with her and was listed on the OHA lease as a resident, was found with cocaine and a crack cocaine pipe three blocks from Rucker's apartment. On three instances within a two-month period, Herman Walker's, another OHA resident, caregiver and two others were found with cocaine in Walker's apartment.

After OHA initiated the eviction proceedings in state court against the Hills, Rucker, and Walker (respondents), they commenced actions against OHA in federal district court, challenging the Department of Housing and Urban Development's (HUD's) interpretation of the federal statute requiring eviction of tenants for criminal activity or the failure to control criminal activity in their apartments. The tenants of OHA argued that the federal statute and HUD regulations result in the eviction of "innocent" tenants and are unconstitutional.

The district court issued a preliminary injunction, enjoining OHA from terminating the leases of the tenants. A panel of the court of appeals reversed, and the full court of appeals reversed the panel and reinstated the district court's injunction. HUD appealed to the U.S. Supreme Court.

DECISION: Congress, wanting to ensure the safety of public housing, allowed the eviction for criminal activity in leased property even when the tenants were not involved. There are no constitutional issues as long as the proper processes under state law for eviction are followed. [***Department of Housing and Urban Development v. Rucker***, **535 U.S. 125 (2002)**]

ETHICS & THE LAW

Screening Tenants for Criminal Records

There are several suits pending around the country against landlords who refuse to rent to tenants who have criminal records. The suits are brought by nonprofit groups that seek to help ex-cons with rehabilitation by getting them housing and jobs. However, the landlords note that once they are aware of criminal history and rent to that tenant, then they can be held liable for any crimes that individual might commit against tenants in their rental properties. San Francisco and Newark have ordinances that prohibit landlords from asking about criminal history. Many landlords have an individual review of applicants, not a blanket policy where they consider the nature of the crime, the time spent in prison, and the time since being released from prison. Discuss the ethical issues in setting policies on screening applicants with criminal records.

[13] Meghan L. Schneider, "From Criminal Confinement to Social Confinement: Helping Ex-Offenders Obtain Public Housing with a Certificate of Rehabilitation," 36 *New. Eng. J. on Crim. & Civil Confinment*, 335 (2010).

CPA

Warranty of Habitability

warranty of habitability– implied warranty that the leased property is fit for dwelling by tenants.

At common law, a landlord was not bound by any obligation that the premises be fit for use unless the lease contained an express warranty to that effect. Most jurisdictions now reject this view and have created a **warranty of habitability** to protect tenants. The warranty of habitability requires, in most states, that the premises have running water, have heat in winter, and be free from structural defects and infestation. If the landlord breaches a warranty of habitability, the tenant is entitled to damages. These damages may be offset against the rent that is due, or if no rent is due, the tenant may bring an independent lawsuit to recover damages from the landlord.[14]

CASE SUMMARY

Don't Let the Bedbugs Bite

FACTS: Geoffrey Green lived in a rent-control apartment in New York City. Bedbugs in his apartment forced him and his partner, Dana Shapiro, to sleep with the lights on, and rotate between sleeping in the bedroom, the kitchen, and the living room. They did not use the bedroom between May and August in 2005 and 2006.

Mr. Green testified that from April 2005 through July 2008, he did not have a single full night's sleep during the summer months. Lack of sleep affected Mr. Green's relationship with Ms. Shapiro and his ability to get to work on time.

Mr. Green withheld rent from October 2005 through January 2007, but only for the prime bedbug months, that is, non-winter months, during this period for a total amount of $5,665.84. His landlord (Petitioner) brought a forcible detainer action to have him evicted. Mr. Green counterclaimed for his damages from the bedbugs. Mr. Green offered into evidence two zip-loc bags containing dead bedbugs.

The exterminator for the complex had come to spray the building but said he never saw any live or dead bedbugs in the Green/Shapiro apartment except the specimens that Mr. Green had shown him, in a zip lock bag.* The exterminator believed Green and Shapiro (Respondents) may have brought the bedbugs with them from their previous apartment. Theresa Lonng, a neighbor, testified that she had bedbugs in her apartment, but that she also had them in her apartment in the building next door, where she had lived until moving next to Mr. Green and Ms. Shapiro.

DECISION: The presence of bedbugs was a breach of the warranty of habitability, regardless of where the bugs came from. As the court noted, those who travel run the risk of bedbugs and landlords must be prepared to eliminate the bugs, wherever and however they land.

The court did question the credibility of tenants who would stay in a bug-infested place for three years without some more diligent form of action. However, the court awarded the tenants a rent abatement to cover September 2005 through December 2006. The first documented notification to the landlord regarding the alleged condition was in September 2005. That was the first documented phone call to the exterminator, and the tenants withheld their rent in September and October of 2005. Based on the log of bites that was kept by the tenants for January 2007 forward, the court found that the tenants had failed to establish the presence of bedbugs from January 2007 forward, and that the bites documented were in all likelihood other insect bites.

The tenants received a 12 percent abatement in rent, for the period of September 2005 through December 2006, totaling $2724.21. **[*Bender v. Green*, 874 N.Y.S.2d 786 (N.Y. Civ. Ct. 2009)]**

*The court used the terms "zip lock" and "zip-loc" rather than the registered term, "Ziploc."

Abatement and Escrow Payment of Rent

To protect tenants from unsound living conditions, statutes sometimes provide that a tenant is not required to pay rent as long as the premises are not fit to live in. As a compromise, some statutes require the tenant to continue to pay the rent but require that it be paid into an escrow or agency account. The money in the escrow account is paid to the landlord only upon proof that the necessary repairs have been made to the premises.

[14] *Erlach v. Sierra Asset Servicing, LLC*, 173 Cal. Rptr. 3d 159 (Cal. App. 2014).

50-2e Improvements

In the absence of a special agreement, neither the tenant nor the landlord is under a duty to make improvements, as contrasted with repairs.[15] Either party may, as a term of the original lease, agree to make improvements, in which case a failure to perform will result in liability in an action for damages for breach of contract brought by the other party. In the absence of an agreement to the contrary, improvements become part of the realty and belong to the landlord.

50-2f Taxes and Assessments

In the absence of an agreement to the contrary, the landlord, not the tenant, is usually under a duty to pay taxes and/or assessments. The lease may provide for an increase in rent if taxes on the rented property are increased.[16]

If taxes or assessments are increased because of improvements made by the tenant, the landlord is liable for such increases if the improvements remain with the property. If the improvements can be removed by the tenant, the amount of the increase must be paid by the tenant.

50-2g Tenant's Deposit

A landlord may require a tenant to make a deposit to protect the landlord from any default on the part of the tenant.[17] There may be statutory limits on the amount of the deposit. Some states provide tenants with protections on these deposits. For example, the landlord may have to hold the deposits in a trust fund or be responsible for paying interest for the period the deposit is held. The landlord may be subject to a penalty if the money is used before the lease would allow for its use.

50-2h Protection from Retaliation

The URLTA and most state laws protect tenants from retaliation by the landlord for the tenants' exercise of their lawful rights or reporting the landlord for violations of housing and sanitation codes. The types of retaliation from which reporting tenants are protected include refusing to renew a lease and evicting the tenant.

50-2i Remedies of Landlord

If a tenant fails to pay rent, the landlord may bring an ordinary lawsuit to collect the amount due and in some states may seize and hold the property of the tenant.

Landlord's Lien

In the absence of an agreement or a statute, the landlord does not have a lien on the personal property or crops of the tenant for money due for rent. The parties may create, by express or implied contract, a lien in favor of the landlord for rent and also for advances, taxes, or damages for failure to make repairs. In the absence of a statutory provision, the lien of the landlord is superior to the claims of all other persons except prior lienors and good-faith purchasers.

[15] The Americans with Disabilities Act requires commercial landlords and tenants to comply with legal requirements for access by the disabled. Shopping centers, medical offices, banks, and professional buildings must be in compliance. *Brooks Shopping Centers, LLC v. DCHWWC Restaurants, Inc.*, 929 N.Y.S.2d 354 (N.Y. App. 2012). *Anderson v. Little League Baseball, Inc.*, 794 F. Supp. 342 (D. Ariz. 1992).

[16] *Reach Community Development v. Stanley*, 274 P.3d 211 (Or. App. 2012).

[17] URLTA §2.101.

Suit for Rent

Whether or not the landlord has a lien for unpaid rent, the landlord may collect rent from the tenant as specified in the lease. In some states, the landlord is permitted to bring a combined action against the tenant to recover the possession of the premises and the overdue rent at the same time.

Recovery of Possession

A lease commonly provides that on the breach of any of its provisions by the tenant, such as the failure to pay rent, the lease terminates or the landlord may exercise the option to declare the lease terminated. When the lease is terminated for any reason, the landlord then has the right to evict the tenant and retake possession of the property.

A landlord cannot lock out a tenant for overdue rent. The landlord must employ legal process to regain possession even if the lease expressly gives the landlord the right to self-help.

The landlord may resort to legal process to evict the tenant to enforce the right to possession of the premises. Statutes in many states provide a summary remedy to recover possession that is much more efficient than the slow common law remedies. Often referred to as a **forcible entry and detainer,** this action restores the property to the landlord's possession unless the tenant complies with payment requirements.

forcible entry and detainer–action by the landlord to have the tenant removed for nonpayment of rent.

Landlord's Duty to Mitigate Damages

If the tenant leaves the premises before the expiration of the lease, is the landlord under any duty to rent the premises again to reduce the rent or damages for which the departing tenant will be liable? By common law and majority rule, a tenant holds a possessory estate in land, and if the tenant abandons it, there is no duty on the landlord to find a new tenant for the premises. But a growing minority view places greater emphasis on the contractual aspects of a lease. Under this view, when the tenant abandons the property, thereby defaulting on the contract, the landlord has a duty to seek to mitigate the damages caused by the tenant's breach and make a reasonable effort to rent the abandoned property.

50-3 Liability for Injury on Premises

When the tenant, a member of the tenant's family, or a third person is injured because of the condition of the premises, the question of who is liable for the damages sustained by the injured person arises.

50-3a Landlord's Liability to Tenant

At common law, in the absence of a covenant to keep the premises in repair, the landlord was not liable for the tenant's personal injuries caused by the defective condition of the premises that, by the lease, are placed under the control of the tenant. However, recent cases have imposed liability on landlords for their failure to keep leased premises in repair, even when there is no covenant of repair. Tenants must still take reasonable precautions when they are aware of a defect. Giving the landlord notice, avoiding the broken step, and even stepping carefully are required when the tenant becomes aware of a dangerous condition and the landlord has not had an opportunity to make repairs.[18]

[18] *Mauskopf v. 1528 Owners Corp.*, 958 N.Y.S.2d 759 (N.Y.A.D. 2013).

Crimes of Third Persons

Ordinarily, the landlord is not liable to the tenant for crimes committed on the premises by third persons, such as when a third person enters the premises and commits larceny or murder.[19] The landlord is not required to establish a security system to protect the tenant from crimes of third persons.

In contrast, when the criminal acts of third persons are reasonably foreseeable, the landlord may be held liable for the harm caused a tenant. **For Example,** when a tenant has repeatedly reported that the deadbolt on the apartment door is broken, the landlord is liable for the tenant's loss when a thief enters through the door because such criminal conduct was foreseeable. Likewise, when the landlord of a large apartment complex does not take reasonable steps to prevent repeated criminal acts, the landlord is liable to the tenant for the harm caused by the foreseeable criminal act of a third person.

CASE SUMMARY

Parking Outside the Gate and Living in a Gated Community: High Risk

FACTS: Arnel Management Company manages the Pheasant Ridge Apartments. Pheasant Ridge is a 620-unit, multibuilding apartment complex with over 1,000 residents, situated on 20.59 acres in Rowland Heights, California. Before the gated entrance to the complex are two parking lots; one is a visitor lot, and the other is the parking lot for the leasing office, located on the other side of the road. There are two security gates just past the parking lot. The gates are remote-control operated. Most of the property's parking spaces lie behind these gates by the apartments.

Yu Fang Tan and his wife, Chun Kuei Chang, and their child moved into Pheasant Ridge in July 2002 and received one assigned parking space. Tenants could pay an additional fee for a garage, but Tan chose not to rent one. Tenants with a second car could park in unassigned parking spaces located throughout the complex, or in one of the two lots—as long as the car was removed from the leasing office lot before 7:00 A.M.

At around 11:30 P.M. on December 28, 2002, Tan returned home and tried to find an unassigned open parking space because his wife had parked the family's other car in their assigned space. Unable to locate an available space, he parked in the leasing office parking lot outside the gated area. As Tan was parking his car, an unidentified man approached him and asked for help. When Tan opened his window, the man pointed a gun and told him to get out of the car because the man wanted it. Tan responded, "Okay. Let me park my car first." But then the car rolled a little, and at that point, the assailant shot Tan in the neck. The incident rendered Tan a quadriplegic. Tan and Chang filed suit against Arnel for their negligent management of the complex as well as its policy of not providing sufficient parking inside the gated area and of charging more for such additional spaces. The trial court granted judgment on the pleadings for Arnel, and Tan and Chang appealed.

DECISION: Judgment for Tan. There had been a chain of events at the apartment complex and, particularly, in the parking lots that put the landlord on notice that there was a need for additional precautions. An expert had recommended various solutions that did not require a great deal of expense such as (1) moving the existing security gates from the back of the access road, and (2) installing "very similar" gates before the visitor and leasing office parking lots. The expert also noted that you don't get much more foreseeability in a property situation than was present in this situation. Reversed. **[*Yu Fang Tan v. Arnel Management Co.*, 170 Cal. App. 4th 1087, 88 Cal. Rprt. 3d 754 (2009)]**

Limitation of Liability

A number of courts, however, have restricted the landlord's power to limit liability in the case of residential, as distinguished from commercial, leasing. A provision in a residential lease excusing a landlord from liability for damage caused by water, snow, or ice is void.

[19] *Galanis v. CMA Management Co.*, ____ So. 3d ____, 2014 WL 5556196 (Miss. App. 2014). A co-tenant's application revealing credit-card fraud criminal history does not result in liability of landlord for tenant's murder.

Indemnification of Landlord

The modern lease commonly contains a provision declaring that the tenant will indemnify the landlord for any liability of the landlord to a third person that arises from the tenant's use of the rented premises.

50-3b Landlord's Liability to Third Persons

A landlord is ordinarily not liable to third persons injured because of the condition of any part of the rented premises that is in the possession of a tenant by virtue of a lease. If the landlord retains control over a portion of the premises, such as hallways or stairways, however, a landlord's liability exists for injuries to third persons caused by failure to exercise proper care in connection with that part of the premises. Most courts impose liability on the landlord for harm caused to a third person when the landlord was obligated, under a contract with the tenant, to correct the condition that caused the harm or to keep the premises in repair.

CPA

50-3c Tenant's Liability to Third Persons

A tenant in possession has control of the property and is liable when his or her failure to use due care under the circumstances causes harm to (1) licensees, such as a person allowed to use a telephone, and (2) invitees, such as customers entering a store. For both classes, the liability is the same as that of an owner in possession of property. It is likewise immaterial whether the property is used for residential or business purposes.

The liability of the tenant to third persons is not affected by the fact that the landlord may have contracted in the lease to make repairs that, if made, would have avoided the injury. The tenant can be protected, however, in the same manner that the landlord can be protected: by procuring liability insurance for indemnity against loss from claims of third persons.

SPORTS & ENTERTAINMENT LAW

The Quarter Pipe 360 Liability Issue

Timothy Lucier, two days shy of his thirteenth birthday, went with his father and several of his friends to Impact (a commercial skate park located in East Providence, Rhode Island) to skateboard to celebrate his birthday. At the skate park, Timothy's father signed the waiver that was required of all who used the park. Timothy donned a helmet, kneepads, and elbow pads, and then he and his friends used the skate park half pipes and quarter pipes. At one point, Timothy climbed on top of the quarter pipe, and as he pushed forward to go down the ramp, the front wheel of his skateboard caught inside a "nub" or "little tiny hole" in the ramp, causing the tail of his skateboard to swing around in a clockwise direction. Timothy twisted off the skateboard and fell on his right leg, causing a spiral fracture in his right leg. Timothy said that after he fell, he looked back at the ramp and saw that there was a split in the wood covering the ramp.

Timothy's parents filed suit against Impact Recreation, Ltd., the operator of the skateboard facility, and Eugene Voll, Impact's landlord. They alleged that there had been a failure by the landlord to ensure that the commercial tenant was not engaging in an activity that was inherently dangerous to the public at large.

Voll required Impact to have insurance, obtain signed waivers from all participants, and obtain his approval prior to the installation of any equipment. Do you believe the landlord is liable to the Luciers? Why or why not?

[*Lucier v. Impact Recreation, LTD.*, 864 A.2d 635 (R.I. 2005)]

50-4 Transfer of Rights

Both the landlord and the tenant have property and contract rights with respect to the lease. Can they be transferred or assigned? A landlord who sells his property transfers the rights in the leased premises to the buyer. The tenant also has transfer rights that are covered next.

CPA

50-4a Tenant's Assignment of Lease and Sublease

assignment–transfer of a right. Generally used in connection with personal property rights, as rights under a contract, commercial paper, an insurance policy, a mortgage, or a lease. (Parties—assignor, assignee)

sublease–a transfer of the premises by the lessee to a third person, the sublessee or subtenant, for a period of less than the term of the original lease.

An **assignment** of a lease is a transfer by the tenant of the tenant's entire interest in the premises to a third person. A tenancy for years may be assigned by the tenant unless the tenant is restricted from making such an assignment by the terms of the lease or by a statute. A **sublease** is a transfer to a third person, the *sublessee*, of less than the tenant's entire interest, or full lease term.

Limitations on Rights

The lease may contain provisions denying or limiting the right to assign or sublet. Such restrictions protect the landlord from new tenants who might damage the property or be financially irresponsible.

Restrictions in the lease are construed liberally in favor of the tenant. No violation of a provision prohibiting assignment or subleasing occurs when the tenant merely permits someone else to use the premises.

Effect of Assignment or Sublease

An assignee or a sublessee has no greater rights than the original lessee.[20] An assignee becomes bound by the obligations of the lease by the act of taking possession of the premises.

Neither the act of subletting nor the landlord's agreement to it releases the original tenant from liability under the terms of the original lease. When a lease is assigned, the original tenant remains liable for the rent that becomes due thereafter.

The tenant should require the sublessee to perform all obligations under the original lease and to indemnify the tenant for any loss caused if the sublessee defaults. Such liability on the part of the sublessee requires an express covenant. The fact that the sublease is made "subject to" the terms of the original lease merely recognizes the superiority of the original lease but does not impose any duty on the sublessee to perform the tenant's obligation under the original lease. If the sublessee promises to assume the obligations of the original lease, the landlord, as a third-party beneficiary, may recover from the sublessee for breach of the provisions of the original lease.

Make the Connection

Summary

The agreement between a lessor and a lessee by which the latter holds possession of real property owned by the former is a lease. Statutes in many states prohibit discrimination by an owner who rents property. Statutes in some states require that the lease not be unconscionable. Tenancies are classified according to duration as tenancies for years, from year to year, at will, and at sufferance.

A lease is generally not terminated by the death, insanity, or bankruptcy of either party except for a tenancy at will. Leases are usually terminated by the expiration of the

[20] *First Hudson Capital LLC v. Seaborn*, 862 N.Y.S.2d 501 (N.Y.A.D. 2008).

specified term, notice, surrender, forfeiture, or destruction of the property or because of fraud. A tenant has the right to acquire possession at the beginning of the lease and has the right to retain possession until the lease is ended. Evictions may be either actual or constructive. The tenant is under a duty to pay rent as compensation to the landlord.

An assignment of a lease by the tenant is a transfer of the tenant's entire interest in the property to a third person; a sublease is a transfer of less than an entire interest—in either space or time. A lease may prohibit both an assignment and a sublease. If the lease is assigned, the assignee is liable to the landlord for the rent. Such an assignment, however, does not discharge the tenant from the duty to pay rent. In a sublease, the sublessee is not liable to the original lessor for rent unless that liability has been assumed or is imposed by statute.

The tenant need not make repairs to the premises, absent an agreement to the contrary. A warranty of habitability was not implied at common law, but most states now reject this view and imply in residential leases a warranty that the premises are fit for habitation.

A landlord is usually liable to the tenant only for injuries caused by latent defects or by defects that are not apparent but of which the landlord had knowledge. The landlord is not liable to the tenant for crimes of third persons unless they are reasonably foreseeable.

Learning Outcomes

After studying this chapter, you should be able to clearly explain:

50-1 Creation and Termination

LO.1 List the ways in which a lease may be terminated

See the discussion of the types of tenancies, page 1047.

See the Ethics & the Law feature on screening tenants for criminal records, page 1052.

See *Department of Housing and Urban Development v. Rucker* for a discussion of federal housing policy on eviction for drug use, page 1052.

50-2 Rights and Duties of Parties

LO.2 List and explain the rights and duties of the parties to a lease

See the *Bender v. Green* case, page 1053.

See the Thinking Things Through feature about the rotting balcony, page 1051.

50-3 Liability for Injury on Premises

LO.3 Describe a landlord's liability for a tenant's and a third person's injuries sustained on the premises

See the *Yu Fang Tan v. Arnel Management Co.* case, page 1056.

See the Sports & Entertainment Law discussion of the quarter pipe, page 1057.

50-4 Transfer of Rights

LO.4 Define *sublease* and *assignment of a lease* and distinguish between them

See the discussion of transfer of rights, pages 1057–1058.

Key Terms

assignment
constructive eviction
covenant of quiet enjoyment
escalation clause
forcible entry and detainer
landlord
lease
lessee
lessor
periodic tenancy
possession
sublease
sublessee
tenancy at sufferance
tenancy at will
tenancy for years
tenant
warranty of habitability

Questions and Case Problems

1. Johnny C. Carpenter and Harvey E. Hill died of asphyxiation when a fire broke out in their Hattiesburg, Mississippi, apartment on the morning of February 20, 1983. There were no smoke detectors in the apartment at the time of the fire, as required under Hattiesburg City Ordinance 2021. The administrators of the estates of Carpenter and Hill filed suit against London, Stetelman, and Kirkwood, the owners and managers of the apartment complex. Who is liable? [*Hill v. London,*

Stetelman, and Kirkwood, Inc., 906 F.2d 204 (5th Cir.)]

2. Petra Valoma and her three roommates rented an apartment in New York City with a security deposit of $2,850, two months of rent for $5,700, and a property loss payment of $800. Less than a month after the group of four took possession of the property, they found bedbugs. The manager sent an exterminator each week for six weeks, with no effective results. The four had to move out and lost most of their furniture because it was infected with bedbugs. The four sought to recover the rent that they had paid as well as damages for their lost furniture. What can they recover? [*Valoma v. G-Way Management, LLC*, 918 N.Y.S.2d 401 (N.Y. Cir. Ct.)]

3. Rod had a five-year lease in a building owned by Darwood and had agreed to pay $800 a month rent. After two years, Rod assigned his rights under the lease to Kelly. Kelly moved in and paid the rent for a year and then, owing two months' rent, moved out without Darwood's knowledge or consent. Darwood demanded that Rod pay him the past-due rent. Must Rod do so? Why or why not?

4. Sue A. Merrill injured her right shoulder when she fell as she was ascending the front steps leading to the porch and front door of the mobile home that her daughter, Sherri Pritchard, rented from Alvina Jansma. The step became loose during the time Ms. Pritchard rented the home. Prior to the fall, Ms. Pritchard had attempted to repair the step by securing it with nails. When that failed, she informed the manager of the property that the step was loose. The manager suggested that Ms. Pritchard try using screws to secure the step. Ms. Pritchard told the manager that she did not have a screw gun. The manager had one and said she would screw the step into place. Subsequently, and without Ms. Pritchard's knowledge, the manager attempted to repair the step. Apparently, that effort was unsuccessful and Ms. Merrill fell when the step separated from the porch as she stepped on it. Ms. Merrill filed a negligence claim against Ms. Jansma to recover for her medical expenses, lost wages, and damages for emotional distress and pain and suffering. Could Ms. Merrill recover? [*Merrill v. Jansma*, 86 P.3d 270 (Wyo.)]

5. Jennifer Sanchez and her three children lived in a two-story townhome operated by CAA (the Cincinnati Community Action Agency). CAA is a nonprofit entity that provides housing for single mothers in financial need. Sanchez requested maintenance on an area behind her toilet on the second floor of the townhome. Josh Hill, a maintenance employee for CAA, came to fix the area. Hill's plan was to simply plaster over the moist area. However, Ms. Sanchez's boyfriend and the father of her children, Ruben, was present and offered his expertise as someone who earned a living doing drywall work. He loaned Hill a box cutter to cut out the moist portion of the wall and Ruben walked Hill through the repair. As Hill finished the work, Ms. Sanchez called Ruben downstairs and Hill left.

   The two- and four-year-olds ended up in the bathroom near the repair area and found the box cutter. In a fight over the box cutter, the four-year-old (V.R.) sliced her finger trying to seize it from the two-year-old. V.R. had to have several surgeries for nerve and tendon damage. Ms. Sanchez, Ruben, and V.R. sued CAA alleging that it had breached its duty as a landowner and caused the injury for their failure to maintain the premises. Can they recover? [In re *V.R.*, 2014 WL 6090396 (Ohio App.)]

6. On June 21, 1997, Julio Ramos was helping his cousin move out of a second-floor apartment. He positioned himself on the outer side of the second-floor balcony railing, his feet between its spindles, to pass furniture to a friend on the ground below. While perched in this precarious position, Ramos held onto the railing with one hand and used his other hand to move the furniture. The reason for this method of removing the furniture was that many pieces were too large to be taken down the stairs. After approximately an hour of moving furniture in this manner, Ramos heard some cracking and felt the railing giving way. He released the furniture and attempted to grab onto the railing with both hands, but the spindles broke, and Ramos fell to the ground.

   Ramos brought suit against the landlord to recover for his injuries. How does this case compare to the *Tan* case? Should the landlord in this case be held liable? [*Ramos v. Granajo*, 822 A.2d 936 (R.I.)]

7. A tenant leased an apartment in which so much noise emanated from surrounding apartments late at night and in the wee hours of the morning that he could not get much sleep. The tenant brought suit against the landlord, alleging that the landlord had breached the implied warranty of habitability. Is the tenant correct? Can noise be a breach of the warranty

of habitability? [*Nostrand Gardens Co-op v. Howard*, 634 N.Y.S.2d 505]

8. James Santelli was staying at a motel owned by Abu Rahmatullah for several months as he worked at a nearby construction project.

   Joseph Pryor had been previously employed at the motel as a general maintenance man. There was no criminal background check done on Pryor. Pryor had a prior conviction and was wanted at the time he was hired for probation violations. When he left his job at the motel, Pryor kept his master keycard. Pryor used the keycard to enter Santelli's room and later confessed to robbing and killing him, with a resulting sentence of 85 years. Mr. Santelli's widow brought suit against Rahmatullah for his negligence in hiring Pryor. Can Rahmatullah be held liable for Mr. Santelli's death? [*Santelli v. Rahmatullah*, 966 N.E.2d 661 (Ind. App.)]

9. During the remodeling of an apartment building, tenants had so much dust from the construction settle in their apartment that they experienced damage to their expensive sound and recording equipment. They had rented the very specialized and large apartment because it was suitable to use as a recording studio. Would the presence of the dust be grounds for constructive eviction? Would it be a breach of the warranty of habitability? [*Minjak Co. v. Rudolph*, 528 N.Y.S.2d 554]

10. Cantanese leased a building for the operation of his drugstore from Saputa. He moved his drugstore from Saputa's building to another location but continued to pay rent to Saputa. Saputa, fearing that he was losing his tenant, entered the premises without Cantanese's permission and made extensive alterations to the premises to suit two physicians who had agreed to rent the premises from Saputa. Cantanese informed Saputa that he regarded the making of the unauthorized repairs as grounds for canceling the lease. Saputa then claimed that Cantanese was liable for the difference between the rent that Cantanese had agreed to pay and the rent that the doctors would pay for the remainder of the term of the Cantanese lease. Was Cantanese liable for such rent? [*Saputa v. Cantanese*, 182 So. 2d 826 (La. App.)]

11. Sargent rented a second-floor apartment in a building owned by Ross. Anna, Sargent's four-year-old daughter, fell from an outdoor stairway and was killed. Sargent brought suit against Ross for her daughter's death. Ross contended that she did not have control over the stairway and therefore was not liable for its condition. Was this defense valid? [*Sargent v. Ross*, 308 A.2d 528 (N.H.)]

12. Charles leased a house from Donald for four years. The rent agreed on was $850 per month. After two years, Charles assigned his rights under the lease to Smith, who moved in and paid rent regularly for a year. Owing rent, Smith moved out sometime later without Donald's knowledge or consent. Donald demanded that Charles pay the rent. Is Charles liable?

13. Green rented an apartment from Stockton Realty. The three-story building had a washroom and clothesline on the roof for use by the tenants. The clothesline ran very near the skylight, and there was no guard rail between the clothesline and the skylight. Green's friend, who was 14 years old, was helping Green remove clothes from the line when she tripped on an object and fell against the skylight. The glass was too weak to support her weight, and she fell to the floor below, sustaining serious injuries. Is the landlord responsible for damages for the injury sustained? Decide. [*Reiman v. Moore*, 180 P.2d 452 (Cal.)]

14. Suzanne Andres was injured when she fell from the balcony of her second-floor apartment in the Roswell-Windsor Village Apartments. Andres was leaning against the railing on the balcony when it gave out, and she and the railing fell to the ground. Andres filed suit against Roswell-Windsor for its failure to maintain the railing. Roswell-Windsor maintains that the railing was not in a common area and was in Andres's exclusive possession and that she was responsible for its maintenance or at least letting the manager know the railing needed repairs. Should Andres recover from the landlord for her injuries? [*Andres v. Roswell-Windsor Village Apartments*, 777 F.2d 671 (11th Cir.)]

15. Williams, an elderly man who was sensitive to heat, rented an apartment in the Parker House. His apartment was fully air-conditioned, which enabled him to stand the otherwise unbearable heat of the summer. The landlord was dissatisfied with the current rent, and although the lease had a year to run, insisted that Williams agree to an increase. Williams refused. The landlord attempted to force Williams to pay the increase by turning off the electricity and thereby stopping the apartment's air conditioners. He also sent up heat on the hot days. After one week of such treatment, Williams, claiming that he had been evicted, moved out. Has there been an eviction? Explain.

CPA Questions

1. Which of the following provisions must be included to have an enforceable written residential lease?

	A Description of the Leased Premises	*A Due Date for the Payment of Rent*
a.	Yes	Yes
b.	Yes	No
c.	No	Yes
d.	No	No

2. Bronson is a residential tenant with a 10-year written lease. In the absence of specific provisions in the lease to the contrary, which of the following statements is correct?
   a. The premises may not be sublet for less than the full remaining term.
   b. Bronson may not assign the lease.
   c. The landlord's death will automatically terminate the lease.
   d. Bronson's purchase of the property will terminate the lease.

3. Which of the following provisions must be included in a residential lease agreement?
   a. A description of the leased premises.
   b. The due date for payment of rent.
   c. A requirement that the tenant have public liability insurance.
   d. A requirement that the landlord will perform all structural repairs to the property.

Appendix 1

How to Find the Law

In order to determine what the law on a particular question or issue is, it may be necessary to examine (1) compilations of constitutions, treaties, statutes, executive orders, proclamations, and administrative regulations; (2) reports of state and federal court decisions; (3) digests of opinions; (4) treatises on the law; and (5) loose-leaf services. These sources can be either researched traditionally or using fee and/or non-fee-based computerized legal research, accessed through the World Wide Web.

Compilations

In the consideration of a legal problem in business it is necessary to determine whether the matter is affected or controlled by a constitution, national or state; by a national treaty; by an Act of Congress, a state legislature, or a city ordinance; by a decree or proclamation of the President of the United States, a governor, or a mayor; or by a regulation of a federal, state, or local administrative agency.

Each body or person that makes laws, regulations, or ordinances usually compiles and publishes at the end of each year or session all of the matter that it has adopted. In addition to the periodical or annual volumes, it is common to compile all the treaties, statutes, regulations, or ordinances in separate volumes. To illustrate, the federal Anti-Injunction Act may be cited as the Act of March 23, 1932, 47 Stat. 70, 29 U.S.C. § 101 et seq. This means that this law was enacted on March 23, 1932, and that it can be found at page 70 in Volume 47 of the reports that contain all of the statutes adopted by the Congress.

The second part of the citation, 29 U.S.C. § 101 et seq., means that in the collection of all of the federal statutes, which is known as the United States Code, the full text of the statute can be found in the sections of the 29th title beginning with Section 101.

Court Decisions

For complicated or important legal cases or when an appeal is to be taken, a court will generally write an opinion, which explains why the court made the decision. Appellate courts as a rule write opinions. The great majority of these decisions, particularly in the case of the appellate courts, are collected and printed. In order to avoid confusion, the opinions of each court are ordinarily printed in a separate set of reports, either by official reporters or private publishers.

In the reference "*Pennoyer v. Neff*, 95 U.S. 714, 24 L.Ed. 565," the first part states the names of the parties. It does not necessarily tell who was the plaintiff and who was the defendant. When an action is begun in a lower court, the first name is that of the plaintiff and the second name that of the defendant. When the case is appealed, generally the name of the person taking the appeal appears on the records of the higher court as the first one and that of the adverse party as the second. Sometimes, therefore, the original order of the names of the parties is reversed.

The balance of the reference consists of two citations. The first citation, 95 U.S. 714, means that the opinion which the court filed in the case of *Pennoyer v. Neff* may be found on page 714 of the 95th volume of a series of books in which are printed officially the opinions of the United States Supreme Court. Sometimes the same opinion is printed in two different sets of volumes. In the example, 24 L.Ed. 565 means that in the 24th volume of another set of books, called Lawyer's Edition, of the United States Supreme Court Reports, the same opinion begins on page 565.

In opinions by a state court there may also be two citations, as in the case of *Morrow v. Corbin*, 122 Tex. 553, 62 S.W.2d 641. This means that the opinion in the lawsuit between Morrow and Corbin may be found in the 122nd volume of the reports of the highest court of Texas, beginning on page 553; and also in Volume 62 of the Southwestern Reporter, Second Series, at page 641.

The West Publishing Company publishes a set of sectional reporters covering the entire United States. They are called "sectional" because each reporter, instead of being limited to a particular court or a particular state, covers the decisions of the courts of a particular section of the country. Thus the decisions of the courts of Arkansas, Kentucky, Missouri, Tennessee, and Texas are printed by the West Publishing company as a group in a sectional reporter called the Southwestern Reporter.[1] Because of the large number of decisions involved, generally only the opinions of the state appellate courts are printed. A number of states[2] have discontinued publication of the opinions of their courts, and those opinions are now found only in the West reporters.

The reason for the "Second Series" in the Southwestern citation is that when there were 300 volumes in the original series, instead of calling the next volume 301, the publisher called it Volume 1, Second Series. Thus 62 S.W.2d Series really means the 362nd volume of the Southwestern Reporter. Six to eight volumes appear in a year for each geographic section.

In addition to these state reporters, the West Publishing Company publishes a Federal Supplement, which primarily reports the opinions of the Federal District Courts; the Federal Reporter, which primarily reports the decisions of the United States Courts of Appeals; and the Supreme Court Reporter, which reports the decisions of the United States Supreme Court. The Supreme Court decisions are also reported in a separate set called the Lawyers' Edition, published by the Lawyers Cooperative Publishing Company.

The reports published by the West Publishing Company and Lawyers Cooperative Publishing Company are unofficial reports, while those bearing the name or abbreviation of the United States or of a state, such as "95 U.S. 714" or "122 Tex. 553" are official reports. This means that in the case of the latter, the particular court, such as the United States Supreme Court, has officially authorized that its decisions be printed and that by federal statute such official printing is made. In the case of the unofficial reporters, the publisher prints the decisions of a court on its own initiative. Such opinions are part of the public domain and not subject to any copyright or similar restriction.

Digests of Opinions

The reports of court decisions are useful only if one has the citation, that is, the name and volume number of the book and the page number of the opinion one is seeking. For this reason, digests of the decisions have been prepared. These digests organize the entire field of law under major headings, which are then arranged in alphabetical order. Under each heading, such as "Contracts," the subject is divided into the different questions that can arise with respect to that field. A master outline is thus created on the subject. This outline includes short paragraphs describing what each case holds and giving its citation.

Treatises and Restatements

Very helpful in finding a case or a statute are the treatises on the law. These may be special books, each written by an author on a particular subject, such as Williston on Contracts, Bogert on Trusts, Fletcher on Corporations, or they may be general encyclopedias, as in the case of *American Jurisprudence, American Jurisprudence, Second,* and *Corpus Juris Secundum.*

Another type of treatise is found in the restatements of the law prepared by the American Law Institute. Each restatement consists of one or more volumes devoted to a particular phase of the law, such as the Restatement of the Law of Contracts, Restatement of the Law of Agency, and Restatement of the Law of Property. In each restatement, the American Law Institute, acting through special committees of judges, lawyers, and professors of law, has set forth what the law is; and in many areas where there is no law or the present rule is regarded as unsatisfactory, the restatement specifies what the Institute deems to be the desirable rule.

Loose-Leaf Services

A number of private publishers, notably Commerce Clearing House and Prentice-Hall, publish loose-leaf books devoted to particular branches of the law. Periodically, the publisher sends to the purchaser a number of pages that set forth any decision, regulation, or statute made or adopted since the prior set of pages was prepared. Such services are unofficial.

[1] The sectional reporters are: Atlantic—A. (Connecticut, Delaware, District of Columbia, Maine, Maryland, New Hampshire, New Jersey, Pennsylvania, Rhode Island, Vermont); Northeastern—N.E. (Illinois, Indiana, Massachusetts, New York, Ohio); Northwestern—N.W. (Iowa, Michigan, Minnesota, Nebraska, North Dakota, South Dakota, Wisconsin); Pacific—P. (Alaska, Arizona, California, Colorado, Hawaii, Idaho, Kansas, Montana, Nevada, New Mexico, Oklahoma, Oregon, Utah, Washington, Wyoming); Southeastern—S.E. (Georgia, North Carolina, South Carolina, Virginia, West Virginia); Southwestern—S.W. (Arkansas, Kentucky, Missouri, Tennessee, Texas); and Southern—So. (Alabama, Florida, Louisiana, Mississippi). There is also a special New York State reporter known as the New York Supplement and a special California State reporter known as the California Reporter.

[2] See, for example, Alaska, Florida, Iowa, Kentucky, Louisiana, Maine, Mississippi, Missouri, North Dakota, Oklahoma, Texas, and Wyoming.

Computerized Legal Research

National and local computer services are providing constantly widening assistance for legal research. The database in such a system may be opinions, statutes, or administrative regulations stored word for word; or the later history of a particular case giving its full citation and showing whether the case has been followed by other courts; or the text of forms and documents. By means of a terminal connected to the system, the user can retrieve the legal information at a great saving of time and with the assurance that it is up-to-date.

There are two leading, fee-based systems for computer-aided research. Listed alphabetically, they are LEXIS and WESTLAW.

A specialized service of legal forms for business is provided by Shepard's BUSINESS LAW CASE MANAGEMENT SYSTEM. A monthly fee is required for usage.

Numerous free, private sites offer a lot of legal resources. The federal government offers a variety of case law, regulations, and code enactments, either pending or newly promulgated. To find the most comprehensive source of government-maintained legal information, go to **http://www.house.gov**. The United States Supreme Court has information about both its current term and past terms at **www.supremecourt.gov**. Another website that provides excellent information about current controversies that reach the United States Supreme Court is **www.scotusblog.com**.

State governments provide access to regulations and codes online. As an example, go to the State of California's site, **http://www.leginfo.ca.gov**. You can access an array of information about both state and federal government through links at **www.USA.gov**.

Appendix 2

The Constitution of the United States

We the people of the United States of America, in order to form a more perfect union, establish justice, insure domestic tranquility, provide for the common defense, promote the general welfare, and secure the blessings of liberty to ourselves and our posterity, do ordain and establish this Constitution for the United States of America.

Article I

SECTION 1

All legislative powers herein granted shall be vested in a Congress of the United States, which shall consist of a Senate and House of Representatives.

SECTION 2

1. The House of Representatives shall be composed of members chosen every second year by the people of the several States, and the electors in each State shall have the qualifications requisite for electors of the most numerous branch of the State legislature.

2. No person shall be a representative who shall not have attained to the age of twenty-five years, and been seven years a citizen of the United States, and who shall not, when elected, be an inhabitant of that State in which he shall be chosen.

3. Representatives and direct taxes shall be apportioned among the several States which may be included within this Union, according to their respective numbers, which shall be determined by adding to the whole number of free persons, including those bound to service for a term of years, and excluding Indians not taxed, three fifths of all other persons.[1] The actual enumeration shall be made within three years after the first meeting of the Congress of the United States, and within every subsequent term of ten years, in such manner as they shall by law direct. The number of representatives shall not exceed one for every thirty thousand, but each State shall have at least one representative; and until such enumeration shall be made, the State of New Hampshire shall be entitled to choose three, Massachusetts eight, Rhode Island and Providence Plantations one, Connecticut five, New York six, New Jersey four, Pennsylvania eight, Delaware one, Maryland six, Virginia ten, North Carolina five, South Carolina five, and Georgia three.

4. When vacancies happen in the representation from any State, the executive authority thereof shall issue writs of election to fill such vacancies.

5. The House of Representatives shall choose their speaker and other officers; and shall have the sole power of impeachment.

SECTION 3

1. The Senate of the United States shall be composed of two senators from each State, chosen by the legislature thereof, for six years; and each senator shall have one vote.

2. Immediately after they shall be assembled in consequence of the first election, they shall be divided as equally as may be into three classes. The seats of the senators of the first class shall be vacated at the expiration of the second year, of the second class at the expiration of the fourth year, and of the third class at the expiration of the sixth year, so that one third may be chosen every second year; and if vacancies happen by resignation, or otherwise, during the recess of the legislature of any State, the executive thereof may make temporary appointments until the next meeting of the legislature, which shall then fill such vacancies.[2]

3. No person shall be a senator who shall not have attained to the age of thirty years, and been nine years a citizen of the United States, and who shall not, when elected, be an inhabitant of that State for which he shall be chosen.

4. The Vice President of the United States shall be President of the Senate, but shall have no vote, unless they be equally divided.

[1] See the 14th Amendment.

[2] See the 17th Amendment.

5. The Senate shall choose their other officers, and also a president pro tempore, in the absence of the Vice President, or when he shall exercise the office of the President of the United States.

6. The Senate shall have the sole power to try all impeachments. When sitting for that purpose, they shall be on oath or affirmation. When the President of the United States is tried, the chief justice shall preside: and no person shall be convicted without the concurrence of two thirds of the members present.

7. Judgment in cases of impeachment shall not extend further than to removal from office, and disqualification to hold and enjoy any office of honor, trust or profit under the United States: but the party convicted shall nevertheless be liable and subject to indictment, trial, judgment and punishment, according to law.

SECTION 4

1. The times, places, and manner of holding elections for senators and representatives, shall be prescribed in each State by the legislature thereof; but the Congress may at any time by law make or alter such regulations, except as to the places of choosing senators.

2. The Congress shall assemble at least once in every year, and such meeting shall be on the first Monday in December, unless they shall by law appoint a different day.

SECTION 5

1. Each House shall be the judge of the elections, returns and qualifications of its own members, and a majority of each shall constitute a quorum to do business; but a smaller number may adjourn from day to day, and may be authorized to compel the attendance of absent members, in such manner, and under such penalties as each House may provide.

2. Each House may determine the rules of its proceedings, punish its members for disorderly behavior, and, with the concurrence of two thirds, expel a member.

3. Each House shall keep a journal of its proceedings, and from time to time publish the same, excepting such parts as may in their judgment require secrecy; and the yeas and nays of the members of either House on any question shall, at the desire of one fifth of those present, be entered on the journal.

4. Neither House, during the session of Congress, shall, without the consent of the other, adjourn for more than three days, nor to any other place than that in which the two Houses shall be sitting.

SECTION 6

1. The senators and representatives shall receive a compensation for their services, to be ascertained by law, and paid out of the Treasury of the United States. They shall in all cases, except treason, felony, and breach of the peace, be privileged from arrest during their attendance at the session of their respective Houses, and in going to and returning from the same; and for any speech or debate in either House, they shall not be questioned in any other place.

2. No senator or representative shall, during the time for which he was elected, be appointed to any civil office under the authority of the United States, which shall have been created, or the emoluments whereof shall have been increased during such time; and no person holding any office under the United States shall be a member of either House during his continuance in office.

SECTION 7

1. All bills for raising revenue shall originate in the House of Representatives; but the Senate may propose or concur with amendments as on other bills.

2. Every bill which shall have passed the House of Representatives and the Senate, shall, before it becomes a law, be presented to the President of the United States; if he approves he shall sign it, but if not he shall return it, with his objections to that House in which it shall have originated, who shall enter the objections at large on their journal, and proceed to reconsider it. If after such reconsideration two thirds of that House shall agree to pass the bill, it shall be sent, together with the objections, to the other House, by which it shall likewise be reconsidered, and if approved by two thirds of that House, it shall become a law. But in all such cases the votes of both Houses shall be determined by yeas and nays, and the names of the persons voting for and against the bill shall be entered on the journal of each House respectively. If any bill shall not be returned by the President within ten days (Sundays excepted) after it shall have been presented to him, the same shall be a law, in like manner as if he had signed it, unless the Congress by their adjournment prevent its return, in which case it shall not be a law.

3. Every order, resolution, or vote to which the concurrence of the Senate and the House of Representatives may be necessary (except on a question of adjournment) shall be presented to the President of the United States; and before the same shall take effect, shall be approved

by him, or being disapproved by him, shall be repassed by two thirds of the Senate and House of Representatives, according to the rules and limitations prescribed in the case of a bill.

SECTION 8

The Congress shall have the power

1. To lay and collect taxes, duties, imposts, and excises, to pay the debts and provide for the common defense and general welfare of the United States; but all duties, imposts, and excises shall be uniform throughout the United States;

2. To borrow money on the credit of the United States;

3. To regulate commerce with foreign nations, and among the several States, and with the Indian tribes;

4. To establish a uniform rule of naturalization, and uniform laws on the subject of bankruptcies throughout the United States;

5. To coin money, regulate the value thereof, and of foreign coin, and fix the standard of weights and measures;

6. To provide for the punishment of counterfeiting the securities and current coin of the United States;

7. To establish post offices and post roads;

8. To promote the progress of science and useful arts, by securing for limited times to authors and inventors the exclusive rights to their respective writings and discoveries;

9. To constitute tribunals inferior to the Supreme Court;

10. To define and punish piracies and felonies committed on the high seas, and offenses against the law of nations;

11. To declare war, grant letters of marque and reprisal, and make rules concerning captures on land and water;

12. To raise and support armies, but no appropriation of money to that use shall be for a longer term than two years;

13. To provide and maintain a navy;

14. To make rules for the government and regulation of the land and naval forces;

15. To provide for calling forth the militia to execute the laws of the Union, suppress insurrections and repel invasions;

16. To provide for organizing, arming, and disciplining the militia, and for governing such part of them as may be employed in the service of the United States, reserving to the States respectively, the appointment of the officers, and the authority of training the militia according to the discipline prescribed by Congress;

17. To exercise exclusive legislation in all cases whatsoever, over such district (not exceeding ten miles square) as may, by cession of particular States, and the acceptance of Congress, become the seat of the government of the United States, and to exercise like authority over all places purchased by the consent of the legislature of the State in which the same shall be, for the erection of forts, magazines, arsenals, dockyards, and other needful buildings; and

18. To make all laws which shall be necessary and proper for carrying into execution the foregoing powers, and all other powers vested by this Constitution in the government of the United States, or in any department or officer thereof.

SECTION 9

1. The migration or importation of such persons as any of the States now existing shall think proper to admit, shall not be prohibited by the Congress prior to the year one thousand eight hundred and eight, but a tax or duty may be imposed on such importation, not exceeding ten dollars for each person.

2. The privilege of the writ of habeas corpus shall not be suspended, unless when in cases of rebellion or invasion the public safety may require it.

3. No bill of attainder or ex post facto law shall be passed.

4. No capitation, or other direct, tax shall be laid, unless in proportion to the census or enumeration hereinbefore directed to be taken.[3]

5. No tax or duty shall be laid on articles exported from any State.

6. No preference shall be given by any regulation of commerce or revenue to the ports of one State over those of another: nor shall vessels bound to, or from, one State be obliged to enter, clear, or pay duties in another.

7. No money shall be drawn from the treasury, but in consequence of appropriations made by law; and a regular statement and account of the receipts and expenditures of all public money shall be published from time to time.

[3] See the 16th Amendment.

8. No title of nobility shall be granted by the United States: and no person holding any office of profit or trust under them, shall, without the consent of the Congress, accept of any present, emolument, office, or title, of any kind whatever, from any king, prince, or foreign State.

SECTION 10

1. No State shall enter into any treaty, alliance, or confederation; grant letters of marque and reprisal; coin money; emit bills of credit; make anything but gold and silver coin a tender in payment of debts; pass any bill of attainder, ex post facto law, or law impairing the obligation of contracts, or grant any title of nobility.

2. No State shall, without the consent of the Congress, lay any imposts or duties on imports or exports, except what may be absolutely necessary for executing its inspection laws: and the net produce of all duties and imposts laid by any State on imports or exports, shall be for the use of the treasury of the United States; and all such laws shall be subject to the revision and control of the Congress.

3. No State shall, without the consent of the Congress, lay any duty of tonnage, keep troops, or ships of war in time of peace, enter into any agreement or compact with another State, or with a foreign power, or engage in war, unless actually invaded, or in such imminent danger as will not admit of delay.

Article II

SECTION 1

1. The executive power shall be vested in a President of the United States of America. He shall hold his office during the term of four years, and, together with the Vice President, chosen for the same term, be elected as follows:

2. Each State shall appoint, in such manner as the legislature thereof may direct, a number of electors, equal to the whole number of senators and representatives to which the State may be entitled in the Congress: but no senator or representative, or person holding an office of trust or profit under the United States, shall be appointed an elector.

The electors shall meet in their respective States, and vote by ballot for two persons, of whom one at least shall not be an inhabitant of the same State with themselves. And they shall make a list of all the persons voted for, and of the number of votes for each; which list they shall sign and certify, and transmit sealed to the seat of the government of the United States, directed to the president of the Senate. The president of the Senate shall, in the presence of the Senate and House of Representatives, open all the certificates, and the votes shall then be counted. The person having the greatest number of votes shall be the President, if such number be a majority of the whole number of electors appointed; and if there be more than one who have such majority, and have an equal number of votes, then the House of Representatives shall immediately choose by ballot one of them for President; and if no person have a majority, then from the five highest on the list the said House shall in like manner choose the President. But in choosing the President, the votes shall be taken by States, the representation from each State having one vote; a quorum for this purpose shall consist of a member or members from two thirds of the States, and a majority of all the States shall be necessary to a choice. In every case, after the choice of the President, the person having the greatest number of votes of the electors shall be the Vice President. But if there should remain two or more who have equal votes, the Senate shall choose from them by ballot the Vice President.[4]

3. The Congress may determine the time of choosing the electors, and the day on which they shall give their votes; which day shall be the same throughout the United States.

4. No person except a natural born citizen, or a citizen of the United States, at the time of the adoption of this Constitution, shall be eligible to the office of President; neither shall any person be eligible to that office who shall not have attained to the age of thirty-five years, and been fourteen years a resident within the United States.

5. In the case of removal of the President from office, or of his death, resignation, or inability to discharge the powers and duties of the said office, the same shall devolve on the Vice President, and the Congress may by law provide for the case of removal, death, resignation, or inability, both of the President and Vice President, declaring what officer shall then act as President, and such officer shall act accordingly, until the disability be removed, or a President shall be elected.

6. The President shall, at stated times, receive for his services a compensation, which shall neither be

[4] Superseded by the 12th Amendment.

increased nor diminished during the period for which he shall have been elected, and he shall not receive within that period any other emolument from the United States, or any of them.

7. Before he enter on the execution of his office, he shall take the following oath or affirmation:—"I do solemnly swear (or affirm) that I will faithfully execute the office of President of the United States, and will to the best of my ability, preserve, protect and defend the Constitution of the United States."

SECTION 2

1. The President shall be commander in chief of the army and navy of the United States, and of the militia of the several States, when called into the actual service of the United States; he may require the opinion, in writing, of the principal officer in each of the executive departments, upon any subject relating to the duties of their respective office, and he shall have power to grant reprieves and pardons for offenses against the United States, except in cases of impeachment.

2. He shall have power, by and with the advice and consent of the Senate, to make treaties, provided two thirds of the senators present concur; and he shall nominate, and by and with the advice and consent of the Senate, shall appoint ambassadors, other public ministers and consuls, judges of the Supreme Court, and all other officers of the United States, whose appointments are not herein otherwise provided for, and which shall be established by law: but the Congress may by law vest the appointment of such inferior officers, as they think proper, in the President alone, in the courts of law, or in the heads of departments.

3. The President shall have power to fill up all vacancies that may happen during the recess of the Senate, by granting commissions which shall expire at the end of their next session.

SECTION 3

He shall from time to time give to the Congress information of the state of the Union, and recommend to their consideration such measures as he shall judge necessary and expedient; he may, on extraordinary occasions, convene both Houses, or either of them, and in case of disagreement between them with respect to the time of adjournment, he may adjourn them to such time as he shall think proper; he shall receive ambassadors and other public ministers; he shall take care that the laws be faithfully executed, and shall commission all the officers of the United States.

SECTION 4

The President, Vice President, and all civil officers of the United States, shall be removed from office on impeachment for, and conviction of, treason, bribery, or other high crimes and misdemeanors.

Article III

SECTION 1

The judicial power of the United States shall be vested in one Supreme Court, and in such inferior courts as the Congress may from time to time ordain and establish. The judges, both of the Supreme and inferior courts, shall hold their offices during good behavior, and shall, at stated times, receive for their services, a compensation, which shall not be diminished during their continuance in office.

SECTION 2

1. The judicial power shall extend to all cases, in law and equity, arising under this Constitution, the laws of the United States, and treaties made, or which shall be made, under their authority;—to all cases affecting ambassadors, other public ministers and consuls;—to all cases of admiralty and maritime jurisdiction;—to controversies to which the United States shall be a party;—to controversies between two or more States; between a State and citizens of another State;[5]—between citizens of different States;—between citizens of the same State claiming lands under grants of different States, and between a State, or the citizens thereof, and foreign States, citizens or subjects.

2. In all cases affecting ambassadors, other public ministers and consuls, and those in which a State shall be party, the Supreme Court shall have original jurisdiction. In all the other cases before mentioned, the Supreme Court shall have appellate jurisdiction, both as to law and to fact, with such exceptions, and under such regulations as the Congress shall make.

3. The trial of all crimes, except in cases of impeachment, shall be by jury; and such trial shall be held in the State where the said crimes shall have been committed; but when not committed within any State, the trial shall be at such place or places as the Congress may by law have directed.

[5] See the 11th Amendment.

SECTION 3

1. Treason against the United States shall consist only in levying war against them, or in adhering to their enemies, giving them aid and comfort. No person shall be convicted of treason unless on the testimony of two witnesses to the same overt act, or on confession in open court.

2. The Congress shall have power to declare the punishment of treason, but no attainder of treason shall work corruption of blood, or forfeiture except during the life of the person attainted.

Article IV

SECTION 1

Full faith and credit shall be given in each State to the public acts, records, and judicial proceedings of every other State. And the Congress may by general laws prescribe the manner in which such acts, records and proceedings shall be proved, and the effect thereof.

SECTION 2

1. The citizens of each State shall be entitled to all privileges and immunities of citizens in the several States.[6]

2. A person charged in any State with treason, felony, or other crime, who shall flee from justice, and be found in another State, shall on demand of the executive authority of the State from which he fled, be delivered up to be removed to the State having jurisdiction of the crime.

3. No person held to service or labor in one State under the laws thereof, escaping into another, shall in consequence of any law or regulation therein, be discharged from such service or labor, but shall be delivered up on claim of the party to whom such service or labor may be due.[7]

SECTION 3

1. New States may be admitted by the Congress into this Union; but no new State shall be formed or erected within the jurisdiction of any other State, nor any State be formed by the junction of two or more States, or parts of States, without the consent of the legislatures of the States concerned as well as of the Congress.

2. The Congress shall have power to dispose of and make all needful rules and regulations respecting the territory or other property belonging to the United States; and nothing in this Constitution shall be so construed as to prejudice any claims of the United States, or of any particular State.

SECTION 4

The United States shall guarantee to every State in this Union a republican form of government, and shall protect each of them against invasion; and on application of the legislature, or of the executive (when the legislature cannot be convened) against domestic violence.

Article V

The Congress, whenever two thirds of both Houses shall deem it necessary, shall propose amendments to this Constitution, or, on the application of the legislature of two thirds of the several States, shall call a convention for proposing amendments, which in either case, shall be valid to all intents and purposes, as part of this Constitution when ratified by the legislatures of three fourths of the several States, or by conventions in three fourths thereof, as the one or the other mode of ratification may be proposed by the Congress; provided that no amendment which may be made prior to the year one thousand eight hundred and eight shall in any manner affect the first and fourth clauses in the ninth section of the first article; and that no State, without its consent, shall be deprived of its equal suffrage in the Senate.

Article VI

1. All debts contracted and engagements entered into, before the adoption of this Constitution, shall be as valid against the United States under this Constitution, as under the Confederation.[8]

2. This Constitution, and the laws of the United States which shall be made in pursuance thereof; and all treaties made, or which shall be made, under the authority of the United States, shall be the supreme law of the land; and the judges in every State shall be bound thereby, anything in the Constitution or laws of any State to the contrary notwithstanding.

3. The senators and representatives before mentioned, and the members of the several State legislatures, and all executive and judicial officers, both of the United States and of the several States, shall be bound by oath or affirmation to support this Constitution; but no

[6] See the 14th Amendment, Sec. 1.

[7] See the 13th Amendment.

[8] See the 14th Amendment, Sec. 4.

religious test shall ever be required as a qualification to any office or public trust under the United States.

Article VII

The ratification of the conventions of nine States shall be sufficient for the establishment of this Constitution between the States so ratifying the same.

Done in Convention by the unanimous consent of the States present the seventeenth day of September in the year of our Lord one thousand seven hundred and eighty-seven, and of the independence of the United States of America the twelfth. In witness whereof we have hereunto subscribed our names.

Amendments

First Ten Amendments passed by Congress Sept. 25, 1789.

Ratified by three-fourths of the States December 15, 1791.

Amendment I

Congress shall make no law respecting an establishment of religion, or prohibiting the free exercise thereof; or abridging the freedom of speech, or of the press; or the right of the people peaceably to assemble, and to petition the government for a redress of grievances.

Amendment II

A well regulated militia, being necessary to the security of a free State, the right of the people to keep and bear arms, shall not be infringed.

Amendment III

No soldier shall, in time of peace be quartered in any house, without the consent of the owner, nor in time of war, but in a manner to be prescribed by law.

Amendment IV

The right of the people to be secure in their persons, houses, papers, and effects, against unreasonable searches and seizures, shall not be violated, and no warrants shall issue, but upon probable cause, supported by oath or affirmation, and particularly describing the place to be searched, and the person or things to be seized.

Amendment V

No person shall be held to answer for a capital, or otherwise infamous crime, unless on a presentment or indictment of a grand jury, except in cases arising in the land or naval forces, or in the militia, when in actual service in time of war or public danger; nor shall any person be subject for the same offense to be twice put in jeopardy of life or limb; nor shall be compelled in any criminal case to be a witness against himself, nor be deprived of life, liberty, or property, without due process of law; nor shall private property be taken for public use without just compensation.

Amendment VI

In all criminal prosecutions, the accused shall enjoy the right to a speedy and public trial, by an impartial jury of the State and district wherein the crime shall have been committed, which district shall have been previously ascertained by law, and to be informed of the nature and cause of the accusation; to be confronted with the witnesses against him; to have compulsory process for obtaining witnesses in his favor, and to have the assistance of counsel for his defense.

Amendment VII

In suits at common law, where the value in controversy shall exceed twenty dollars, the right of trial by jury shall be preserved, and no fact tried by a jury shall be otherwise reexamined in any court of the United States, then according to the rules of the common law.

Amendment VIII

Excessive bail shall not be required, nor excessive fines imposed, nor cruel and unusual punishments inflicted.

Amendment IX

The enumeration in the Constitution of certain rights shall not be construed to deny or disparage others retained by the people.

Amendment X

The powers not delegated to the United States by the Constitution, nor prohibited by it to the States, are reserved to the States respectively, or to the people.

Amendment XI

Passed by Congress March 5, 1794. Ratified January 8, 1798.

The judicial power of the United States shall not be construed to extend to any suit in law or equity, commenced or prosecuted against one of the United States by citizens of another State, or by citizens or subjects of any foreign State.

Amendment XII

Passed by Congress December 12, 1803. Ratified September 25, 1804.

The electors shall meet in their respective States, and vote by ballot for President and Vice President, one of whom, at least, shall not be an inhabitant of the same State with themselves; they shall name in their ballots the person voted for as President, and in distinct ballots, the person voted for as Vice President, and they shall make distinct lists of all persons voted for as President and of all persons voted for as Vice President, and of the number of votes for each, which lists they shall sign and certify, and transmit sealed to the seat of the government of the United States, directed to the President of the Senate;—The President of the Senate shall, in the presence of the Senate and House of Representatives, open all the certificates and the votes shall then be counted;—The person having the greatest number of votes for President, shall be the President, if such number be a majority of the whole number of electors appointed; and if no person have such majority, then from the persons having the highest numbers not exceeding three on the list of those voted for as President, the House of Representatives shall choose immediately, by ballot, the President. But in choosing the President, the votes shall be taken by States, the representation from each State having one vote; a quorum for this purpose shall consist of a member or members from two thirds of the States, and a majority of all the States shall be necessary to a choice. And if the House of Representatives shall not choose a President whenever the right of choice shall devolve upon them, before the fourth day of March next following, then the Vice President shall act as President, as in the case of the death or other constitutional disability of the President. The person having the greatest number of votes as Vice President shall be the Vice President, if such number be a majority of the whole number of electors appointed, and if no person have a majority, then from the two highest numbers on the list, the Senate shall choose the Vice President; a quorum for the purpose shall consist of two thirds of the whole number of Senators, and a majority of the whole number shall be necessary to a choice. But no person constitutionally ineligible to the office of President shall be eligible to that of Vice President of the United States.

Amendment XIII

Passed by Congress February 1, 1865. Ratified December 18, 1865.

SECTION 1

Neither slavery nor involuntary servitude, except as punishment for crime whereof the party shall have been duly convicted, shall exist within the United States, or any place subject to their jurisdiction.

SECTION 2

Congress shall have power to enforce this article by appropriate legislation.

Amendment XIV

Passed by Congress June 16, 1866. Ratified July 23, 1868.

SECTION 1

All persons born or naturalized in the United States, and subject to the jurisdiction thereof, are citizens of the United States and of the State wherein they reside. No State shall make or enforce any law which shall abridge the privileges or immunities of citizens of the United States; nor shall any State deprive any person of life, liberty, or property, without due process of law; nor deny to any person within its jurisdiction the equal protection of the laws.

SECTION 2

Representatives shall be apportioned among the several States according to their respective numbers, counting the whole number of persons in each State, excluding Indians not taxed. But when the right to vote at any election for the choice of electors for President and Vice President of the United States, representatives in Congress, the executive and judicial officers of a State, or the members of the legislature thereof, is denied to any of the male inhabitants of such State, being twenty-one years of age, and citizens of the United States, or in any way abridged, except for participation in rebellion, or other crime, the basis of representation therein shall be reduced in the proportion which the number of such male citizens shall bear to the whole number of male citizens twenty-one years of age in such State.

SECTION 3

No person shall be a senator or representative in Congress, or elector of President and Vice President, or hold any office, civil or military, under the United States, or under any State, who having previously taken an oath, as a member of Congress, or as an officer of the United States, or as a member of any State legislature, or as an executive or judicial officer of any State, to support the Constitution of the United States, shall have engaged in insurrection or rebellion against the same, or given aid or comfort to the enemies thereof. But Congress may by a vote of two thirds of each House, remove such disability.

SECTION 4

The validity of the public debt of the United States, authorized by law, including debts incurred for payment of pensions and bounties for services in suppressing insurrection or rebellion, shall not be questioned. But neither the United States nor any State shall assume or pay any debt or obligation incurred in aid of insurrection or rebellion against the United States, or any claim for the loss or emancipation of any slave; but all such debts, obligations, and claims shall be held illegal and void.

SECTION 5

The Congress shall have power to enforce, by appropriate legislation, the provisions of this article.

Amendment XV

Passed by Congress February 27, 1869. Ratified March 30, 1870.

SECTION 1

The right of citizens of the United States to vote shall not be denied or abridged by the United States or by any State on account of race, color, or previous condition of servitude.

SECTION 2

The Congress shall have power to enforce this article by appropriate legislation.

Amendment XVI

Passed by Congress July 12, 1909. Ratified February 25, 1913.

The Congress shall have power to lay and collect taxes on incomes, from whatever source derived, without apportionment among the several States, and without regard to any census or enumeration.

Amendment XVII

Passed by Congress May 16, 1912. Ratified May 31, 1913.

The Senate of the United States shall be composed of two senators from each State, elected by the people thereof, for six years; and each senator shall have one vote. The electors in each State shall have the qualifications requisite for electors of the most numerous branch of the State legislature.

When vacancies happen in the representation of any State in the Senate, the executive authority of such State shall issue writs of election to fill such vacancies: Provided, That the legislature of any State may empower the executive thereof to make temporary appointments until the people fill the vacancies by election as the legislature may direct.

This amendment shall not be so construed as to affect the election or term of any senator chosen before it becomes valid as part of the Constitution.

Amendment XVIII

Passed by Congress December 17, 1917. Ratified January 29, 1919.

After one year from the ratification of this article, the manufacture, sale, or transportation of intoxicating liquors within, the importation thereof into, or the exportation thereof from the United States and all territory subject to the jurisdiction thereof for beverage purposes is hereby prohibited.

The Congress and the several States shall have concurrent power to enforce this article by appropriate legislation.

This article shall be inoperative unless it shall have been ratified as an amendment to the Constitution by the legislatures of the several States, as provided in the Constitution, within seven years from the date of the submission hereof to the States by Congress.

Amendment XIX

Passed by Congress June 5, 1919. Ratified August 26, 1920.

The right of citizens of the United States to vote shall not be denied or abridged by the United States or by any State on account of sex.

The Congress shall have power by appropriate legislation to enforce the provisions of this article.

Amendment XX

Passed by Congress March 3, 1932. Ratified January 23, 1933.

SECTION 1

The terms of the President and Vice President shall end at noon on the 20th day of January, and the terms of Senators and Representatives at noon on the 3d day of January, of the years in which such terms would have ended if this article had not been ratified; and the terms of their successors shall then begin.

SECTION 2

The Congress shall assemble at least once in every year, and such meeting shall begin at noon on the 3d day of January, unless they shall by law appoint a different day.

SECTION 3

If, at the time fixed for the beginning of the term of the President, the President-elect shall have died, the Vice President-elect shall become President. If a President shall not have been chosen before the time fixed for the beginning of his term, or if the President-elect shall have failed to qualify, then the Vice President-elect shall act as President until a President shall have qualified; and the Congress may by law provide for the case wherein neither a President-elect nor a Vice President-elect shall have qualified, declaring who shall then act as President, or the manner in which one who is to act shall be selected, and such person shall act accordingly until a President or Vice President shall have qualified.

SECTION 4

The Congress may by law provide for the case of the death of any of the persons from whom the House of Representatives may choose a President whenever the right of choice shall have devolved upon them, and for the case of the death of any of the persons from whom the Senate may choose a Vice President whenever the right of choice shall have devolved upon them.

SECTION 5

Sections 1 and 2 shall take effect on the 15th day of October following the ratification of this article.

SECTION 6

This article shall be inoperative unless it shall have been ratified as an amendment to the Constitution by the legislatures of three-fourths of the several States within seven years from the date of its submission.

Amendment XXI

Passed by Congress February 20, 1933. Ratified December 5, 1933.

SECTION 1

The eighteenth article of amendment to the Constitution of the United States is hereby repealed.

SECTION 2

The transportation or importation into any State, Territory, or possession of the United States for delivery or use therein of intoxicating liquors in violation of the laws thereof, is hereby prohibited.

SECTION 3

This article shall be inoperative unless it shall have been ratified as an amendment to the Constitution by conventions in the several States, as provided in the Constitution, within seven years from the date of the submission thereof to the States by the Congress.

Amendment XXII

Passed by Congress March 24, 1947. Ratified February 26, 1951.

SECTION 1

No person shall be elected to the office of the President more than twice, and no person who has held the office of President, or acted as President, for more than two years of a term to which some other person was elected President shall be elected to the office of the President more than once. But this article shall not apply to any person holding the office of President when this article was proposed by the Congress, and shall not prevent any person who may be holding the office of President, or acting as President, during the term within which this article becomes operative from holding the office of President or acting as President during the remainder of such term.

SECTION 2

This article shall be inoperative unless it shall have been ratified as an amendment to the Constitution by the legislatures of three-fourths of the several States within seven years from the date of its submission to the States by the Congress.

Amendment XXIII

Passed by Congress June 16, 1960. Ratified April 3, 1961.

SECTION 1

The District constituting the seat of Government of the United States shall appoint in such manner as the Congress may direct:

A number of electors of President and Vice President equal to the whole number of Senators and

Representatives in Congress to which the District would be entitled if it were a State, but in no event more than the least populous State; they shall be in addition to those appointed by the States, but they shall be considered, for the purposes of the election of President and Vice President, to be electors appointed by a State; and they shall meet in the District and perform such duties as provided by the twelfth article of amendment.

SECTION 2

The Congress shall have power to enforce this article by appropriate legislation.

Amendment XXIV

Passed by Congress August 27, 1962. Ratified February 4, 1964.

SECTION 1

The right of citizens of the United States to vote in any primary or other election for President or Vice President, for electors for President or Vice President, or for Senator or Representative in Congress, shall not be denied or abridged by the United States or any State by reason of failure to pay any poll tax or other tax.

SECTION 2

The Congress shall have power to enforce this article by appropriate legislation.

Amendment XXV

Passed by Congress July 6, 1965. Ratified February 23, 1967.

SECTION 1

In case of the removal of the President from office or of his death or resignation, the Vice President shall become President.

SECTION 2

Whenever there is a vacancy in the office of the Vice President, the President shall nominate a Vice President who shall take office upon confirmation by a majority vote of both Houses of Congress.

SECTION 3

Whenever the President transmits to the President pro tempore of the Senate and the Speaker of the House of Representatives his written declaration that he is unable to discharge the powers and duties of his office, and until he transmits to them a written declaration to the contrary, such powers and duties shall be discharged by the Vice President as Acting President.

SECTION 4

Whenever the Vice President and a majority of either the principal officers of the executive departments or of such other body as Congress may by law provide, transmit to the President pro tempore of the Senate and the Speaker of the House of Representatives their written declaration that the President is unable to discharge the powers and duties of his office, the Vice President shall immediately assume the powers and duties of the office as Acting President.

Thereafter, when the President transmits to the President pro tempore of the Senate and the Speaker of the House of Representatives his written declaration that no inability exists, he shall resume the powers and duties of his office unless the Vice President and a majority of either the principal officers of the executive department or of such other body as Congress may by law provide, transmit within four days to the President pro tempore of the Senate and the Speaker of the House of Representatives their written declaration that the President is unable to discharge the powers and duties of his office. Thereupon Congress shall decide the issue, assembling within forty-eight hours for that purpose if not in session. If the Congress, within twenty-one days after receipt of the latter written declaration, or, if Congress is not in session, within twenty-one days after Congress is required to assemble, determines by two-thirds vote of both Houses that the President is unable to discharge the powers and duties of his office, the Vice President shall continue to discharge the same as Acting President; otherwise, the President shall resume the powers and duties of his office.

Amendment XXVI

Passed by Congress March 23, 1971. Ratified July 5, 1971.

SECTION 1

The right of citizens of the United States, who are eighteen years of age or older, to vote shall not be denied or abridged by the United States or by any State on account of age.

Amendment XXVII

Passed by Congress September 25, 1789. Ratified May 18, 1992.

No law, varying the compensation for the services of the Senators and Representatives, shall take effect, until an election of Representatives shall have intervened.

Appendix 3

Uniform Commercial Code (Selected Sections)

(Adopted in fifty-two jurisdictions; all fifty States, although Louisiana has adopted only Articles 1, 3, 4, 7, 8, and 9; the District of Columbia; and the Virgin Islands.)

Articles

1. General Provisions
2. Sales

   2A. Leases

3. Negotiable Instruments
4. Bank Deposits and Collections

   4A. Funds Transfers

5. Letters of Credit
6. Repealer of Article 6—Bulk Transfers and [Revised] Article 6—Bulk Sales
7. Warehouse Receipts, Bills of Lading and Other Documents of Title
8. Investment Securities
9. Secured Transactions

Article 1 General Provisions

Part 1 Short Title, Construction, Application and Subject Matter of the Act

* * * *

§1—103. SUPPLEMENTARY GENERAL PRINCIPLES OF LAW APPLICABLE

Unless displaced by the particular provisions of this Act, the principles of law and equity, including the law merchant and the law relative to capacity to contract, principal and agent, estoppel, fraud, misrepresentation, duress, coercion, mistake, bankruptcy, or other validating or invalidating cause shall supplement its provisions.

* * * *

§1—201. GENERAL DEFINITIONS

* * * *

(3) "Agreement" means the bargain of the parties in fact as found in their language or by implication from other circumstances including course of dealing or usage of trade or course of performance as provided in this Act (Sections 1—205 and 2—208). Whether an agreement has legal consequences is determined by the provisions of this Act, if applicable; otherwise by the law of contracts (Section 1—103). (Compare "Contract".)

(4) "Bank" means any person engaged in the business of banking.

(5) "Bearer" means the person in possession of an instrument, document of title, or certificated security payable to bearer or indorsed in blank.

(6) "Bill of lading" means a document evidencing the receipt of goods for shipment issued by a person engaged in the business of transporting or forwarding goods, and includes an airbill. "Airbill" means a document serving for air transportation as a bill of lading does for marine or rail transportation, and includes an air consignment note or air waybill.

* * * *

(9) "Buyer in ordinary course of business" means a person that buys goods in good faith, without knowledge that the sale violates the rights of another person in the goods, and in the ordinary course from a person, other than a pawnbroker, in the business of selling goods of that kind. A person buys goods in the ordinary course if the sale to the person comports with the usual or customary practices in the kind of business in which the seller is engaged or with the seller's own usual or customary practices. A person that sells oil, gas, or other minerals at the wellhead or minehead is a person in the business of selling goods of that kind. A buyer in ordinary course of business may buy for cash, by exchange of other property, or on secured or unsecured credit, and may acquire goods or documents of title under a pre-existing contract for sale. Only a buyer that takes

possession of the goods or has a right to recover the goods from the seller under Article 2 may be a buyer in ordinary course of business. A person that acquires goods in a transfer in bulk or as security for or in total or partial satisfaction of a money debt is not a buyer in ordinary course of business.

(10) "Conspicuous": A term or clause is conspicuous when it is so written that a reasonable person against whom it is to operate ought to have noticed it. A printed heading in capitals (as: NON-NEGOTIABLE BILL OF LADING) is conspicuous. Language in the body of a form is "conspicuous" if it is in larger or other contrasting type or color. But in a telegram any stated term is "conspicuous". Whether a term or clause is "conspicuous" or not is for decision by the court.

(11) "Contract" means the total legal obligation which results from the parties' agreement as affected by this Act and any other applicable rules of law. (Compare "Agreement".)

* * * *

(15) "Document of title" includes bill of lading, dock warrant, dock receipt, warehouse receipt or order for the delivery of goods, and also any other document which in the regular course of business or financing is treated as adequately evidencing that the person in possession of it is entitled to receive, hold and dispose of the document and the goods it covers. To be a document of title a document must purport to be issued by or addressed to a bailee and purport to cover goods in the bailee's possession which are either identified or are fungible portions of an identified mass.

* * * *

(17) "Fungible" with respect to goods or securities means goods or securities of which any unit is, by nature or usage of trade, the equivalent of any other like unit. Goods which are not fungible shall be deemed fungible for the purposes of this Act to the extent that under a particular agreement or document unlike units are treated as equivalents.

* * * *

(19) "Good faith" means honesty in fact in the conduct or transaction concerned.

(20) "Holder" with respect to a negotiable instrument, means the person in possession if the instrument is payable to bearer or, in the cases of an instrument payable to an identified person, if the identified person is in possession. "Holder" with respect to a document of title means the person in possession if the goods are deliverable to bearer or to the order of the person in possession.

* * * *

(23) A person is "insolvent" who either has ceased to pay his debts in the ordinary course of business or cannot pay his debts as they become due or is insolvent within the meaning of the federal bankruptcy law.

(24) "Money" means a medium of exchange authorized or adopted by a domestic or foreign government and includes a monetary unit of account established by an intergovernmental organization or by agreement between two or more nations.

(25) A person has "notice" of a fact when

(a) he has actual knowledge of it; or

(b) he has received a notice or notification of it; or

(c) from all the facts and circumstances known to him at the time in question he has reason to know that it exists.

* * * *

(37) "Security interest" means an interest in personal property or fixtures which secures payment or performance of an obligation. The term also includes any interest of a consignor and a buyer of accounts, chattel paper, a payment intangible, or a promissory note in a transaction that is subject to Article 9. The special property interest of a buyer of goods on identification of those goods to a contract for sale under Section 2—401 is not a "security interest", but a buyer may also acquire a "security interest" by complying with Article 9. Except as otherwise provided in Section 2—505, the right of a seller or lessor of goods under Article 2 or 2A to retain or acquire possession of the goods is not a "security interest", but a seller or lessor may also acquire a "security interest" by complying with Article 9. The retention or reservation of title by a seller of goods notwithstanding shipment or delivery to the buyer (Section 2—401) is limited in effect to a reservation of a "security interest".

Whether a transaction creates a lease or security interest is determined by the facts of each case; however, a transaction creates a security interest if the consideration the lessee is to pay the lessor for the right to possession and use of the goods is an obligation for the term of the lease not subject to termination by the lessee, and

(a) the original term of the lease is equal to or greater than the remaining economic life of the goods,

(b) the lessee is bound to renew the lease for the remaining economic life of the goods or is bound to become the owner of the goods,

(c) the lessee has an option to renew the lease for the remaining economic life of the goods for no additional consideration or nominal additional consideration upon compliance with the lease agreement, or

(d) the lessee has an option to become the owner of the goods for no additional consideration or nominal additional consideration upon compliance with the lease agreement.

A transaction does not create a security interest merely because it provides that

(a) the present value of the consideration the lessee is obligated to pay the lessor for the right to possession and use of the goods is substantially equal to or is greater than the fair market value of the goods at the time the lease is entered into,

(b) the lessee assumes risk of loss of the goods, or agrees to pay taxes, insurance, filing, recording, or registration fees, or service or maintenance costs with respect to the goods,

(c) the lessee has an option to renew the lease or to become the owner of the goods,

(d) the lessee has an option to renew the lease for a fixed rent that is equal to or greater than the reasonably predictable fair market rent for the use of the goods for the term of the renewal at the time the option is to be performed, or

(e) the lessee has an option to become the owner of the goods for a fixed price that is equal to or greater than the reasonably predictable fair market value of the goods at the time the option is to be performed.

* * * *

(39) "Signed" includes any symbol executed or adopted by a party with present intention to authenticate a writing.

(40) "Surety" includes guarantor.

* * * *

(43) "Unauthorized" signature means one made without actual, implied or apparent authority and includes a forgery.

(44) "Value". Except as otherwise provided with respect to negotiable instruments and bank collections (Sections 3—303, 4—210 and 4—211) a person gives "value" for rights if he acquires them

(a) in return for a binding commitment to extend credit or for the extension of immediately available credit whether or not drawn upon and whether or not a chargeback is provided for in the event of difficulties in collection; or

(b) as security for or in total or partial satisfaction of a pre-existing claim; or

(c) by accepting delivery pursuant to a preexisting contract for purchase; or

(d) generally, in return for any consideration sufficient to support a simple contract.

(45) "Warehouse receipt" means a receipt issued by a person engaged in the business of storing goods for hire.

(46) "Written" or "writing" includes printing, typewriting or any other intentional reduction to tangible form.

* * * *

§1—203. OBLIGATION OF GOOD FAITH

Every contract or duty within this Act imposes an obligation of good faith in its performance or enforcement.

§1—204. TIME; REASONABLE TIME; "SEASONABLY"

(1) Whenever this Act requires any action to be taken within a reasonable time, any time which is not manifestly unreasonable may be fixed by agreement.

(2) What is a reasonable time for taking any action depends on the nature, purpose and circumstances of such action.

(3) An action is taken "seasonably" when it is taken at or within the time agreed or if no time is agreed at or within a reasonable time.

§1—205. COURSE OF DEALING AND USAGE OF TRADE

(1) A course of dealing is a sequence of previous conduct between the parties to a particular transaction which is fairly to be regarded as establishing a common basis of understanding for interpreting their expressions and other conduct.

(2) A usage of trade is any practice or method of dealing having such regularity of observance in a place, vocation or trade as to justify an expectation that it will be observed with respect to the transaction in question. The existence and scope of such a usage are to be proved as facts. If it is established that such a usage is embodied in a written trade code or similar writing the interpretation of the writing is for the court.

(3) A course of dealing between parties and any usage of trade in the vocation or trade in which they are engaged or of which they are or should be aware give particular meaning to and supplement or qualify terms of an agreement.

(4) The express terms of an agreement and an applicable course of dealing or usage of trade shall be construed wherever reasonable as consistent with each other; but

when such construction is unreasonable express terms control both course of dealing and usage of trade and course of dealing controls usage trade.

(5) An applicable usage of trade in the place where any part of performance is to occur shall be used in interpreting the agreement as to that part of the performance.

(6) Evidence of a relevant usage of trade offered by one party is not admissible unless and until he has given the other party such notice as the court finds sufficient to prevent unfair surprise to the latter.

* * * *

Article 2 Sales

§2—102. SCOPE; CERTAIN SECURITY AND OTHER TRANSACTIONS EXCLUDED FROM THIS ARTICLE

Unless the context otherwise requires, this Article applies to transactions in goods; it does not apply to any transaction which although in the form of an unconditional contract to sell or present sale is intended to operate only as a security transaction nor does this Article impair or repeal any statute regulating sales to consumers, farmers or other specified classes of buyers.

§2—103. DEFINITIONS AND INDEX OF DEFINITIONS

(1) In this Article unless the context otherwise requires

(a) "Buyer" means a person who buys or contracts to buy goods.

(b) "Good faith" in the case of a merchant means honesty in fact and the observance of reasonable commercial standards of fair dealing in the trade.

(c) "Receipt" of goods means taking physical possession of them.

(d) "Seller" means a person who sells or contracts to sell goods.

§2—104. DEFINITIONS: "MERCHANT"; "BETWEEN MERCHANTS"; "FINANCING AGENCY"

(1) "Merchant" means a person who deals in goods of the kind or otherwise by his occupation holds himself out as having knowledge or skill peculiar to the practices or goods involved in the transaction or to whom such knowledge or skill may be attributed by his employment of an agent or broker or other intermediary who by his occupation holds himself out as having such knowledge or skill.

§2—105. DEFINITIONS: TRANSFERABILITY; "GOODS"; "FUTURE" GOODS; "LOT"; "COMMERCIAL UNIT"

(1) "Goods" means all things (including specially manufactured goods) which are movable at the time of identification to the contract for sale other than the money in which the price is to be paid, investment securities (Article 8) and things in action. "Goods" also includes the unborn young of animals and growing crops and other identified things attached to realty as described in the section on goods to be severed from realty (Section 2—107).

(2) Goods must be both existing and identified before any interest in them can pass. Goods which are not both existing and identified are "future" goods. A purported present sale of future goods or of any interest therein operates as a contract to sell.

(3) There may be a sale of a part interest in existing identified goods.

(4) An undivided share in an identified bulk of fungible goods is sufficiently identified to be sold although the quantity of the bulk is not determined. Any agreed proportion of such a bulk or any quantity thereof agreed upon by number, weight or other measure may to the extent of the seller's interest in the bulk be sold to the buyer who then becomes an owner in common.

(5) "Lot" means a parcel or a single article which is the subject matter of a separate sale or delivery, whether or not it is sufficient to perform the contract.

(6) "Commercial unit" means such a unit of goods as by commercial usage is a single whole for purposes of sale and division of which materially impairs its character or value on the market or in use. A commercial unit may be a single article (as a machine) or a set of articles (as a suite of furniture or an assortment of sizes) or a quantity (as a bale, gross, or carload) or any other unit treated in use or in the relevant market as a single whole.

* * * *

§2—107. GOODS TO BE SEVERED FROM REALTY: RECORDING

(1) A contract for the sale of minerals or the like (including oil and gas) or a structure or its materials to be removed from realty is a contract for the sale of goods within this Article if they are to be severed by the seller but until severance a purported present sale thereof which is not effective as a transfer of an interest in land is effective only as a contract to sell.

(2) A contract for the sale apart from the land of growing crops or other things attached to realty and capable of severance without material harm thereto but not described in subsection (1) or of timber to be cut is a contract for the sale of goods within this Article whether the subject matter is to be severed by the buyer or by the seller even though it forms part of the realty at the time of contracting, and the parties can by identification effect a present sale before severance.

(3) The provisions of this section are subject to any third party rights provided by the law relating to realty records, and the contract for sale may be executed and recorded as a document transferring an interest in land and shall then constitute notice to third parties of the buyer's rights under the contract for sale.

§2—201. FORMAL REQUIREMENTS; STATUTE OF FRAUDS

(1) Except as otherwise provided in this section a contract for the sale of goods for the price of $500 [some states have increased this amount to $5,000] or more is not enforceable by way of action or defense unless there is some writing sufficient to indicate that a contract for sale has been made between the parties and signed by the party against whom enforcement is sought or by his authorized agent or broker. A writing is not insufficient because it omits or incorrectly states a term agreed upon but the contract is not enforceable under this paragraph beyond the quantity of goods shown in such writing.

(2) Between merchants if within a reasonable time a writing in confirmation of the contract and sufficient against the sender is received and the party receiving it has reason to know its contents, it satisfies the requirements of subsection (1) against such party unless written notice of objection to its contents is given within ten days after it is received.

(3) A contract which does not satisfy the requirements of subsection (1) but which is valid in other respects is enforceable

(a) if the goods are to be specially manufactured for the buyer and are not suitable for sale to others in the ordinary course of the seller's business and the seller, before notice of repudiation is received and under circumstances which reasonably indicate that the goods are for the buyer, has made either a substantial beginning of their manufacture or commitments for their procurement; or

(b) if the party against whom enforcement is sought admits in his pleading, testimony or otherwise in court that a contract for sale was made, but the contract is not enforceable under this provision beyond the quantity of goods admitted; or

(c) with respect to goods for which payment has been made and accepted or which have been received and accepted (Sec. 2—606).

§2—202. FINAL WRITTEN EXPRESSION: PAROL OR EXTRINSIC EVIDENCE

Terms with respect to which the confirmatory memoranda of the parties agree or which are otherwise set forth in a writing intended by the parties as a final expression of their agreement with respect to such terms as are included therein may not be contradicted by evidence of any prior agreement or of a contemporaneous oral agreement but may be explained or supplemented

(a) by course of dealing or usage of trade (Section 1—205) or by course of performance (Section 2—208); and

(b) by evidence of consistent additional terms unless the court finds the writing to have been intended also as a complete and exclusive statement of the terms of the agreement.

* * * *

§2—204. FORMATION IN GENERAL

(1) A contract for sale of goods may be made in any manner sufficient to show agreement, including conduct by both parties which recognizes the existence of such a contract.

(2) An agreement sufficient to constitute a contract for sale may be found even though the moment of its making is undetermined.

(3) Even though one or more terms are left open a contract for sale does not fail for indefiniteness if the parties have intended to make a contract and there is a reasonably certain basis for giving an appropriate remedy.

§2—205. FIRM OFFERS

An offer by a merchant to buy or sell goods in a signed writing which by its terms gives assurance that it will be held open is not revocable, for lack of consideration, during the time stated or if no time is stated for a reasonable time, but in no event may such period of irrevocability exceed three months; but any such term of assurance on a form supplied by the offeree must be separately signed by the offeror.

§2—206. OFFER AND ACCEPTANCE IN FORMATION OF CONTRACT

(1) Unless other unambiguously indicated by the language or circumstances

(a) an offer to make a contract shall be construed as inviting acceptance in any manner and by any medium reasonable in the circumstances;

(b) an order or other offer to buy goods for prompt or current shipment shall be construed as inviting acceptance either by a prompt promise to ship or by the prompt or current shipment of conforming or non-conforming goods, but such a shipment of non-conforming goods does not constitute an acceptance if the seller seasonably notifies the buyer that the shipment is offered only as an accommodation to the buyer.

(2) Where the beginning of a requested performance is a reasonable mode of acceptance an offeror who is not notified of acceptance within a reasonable time may treat the offer as having lapsed before acceptance.

§2—207. ADDITIONAL TERMS IN ACCEPTANCE OR CONFIRMATION

(1) A definite and seasonable expression of acceptance or a written confirmation which is sent within a reasonable time operates as an acceptance even though it states terms additional to or different from those offered or agreed upon, unless acceptance is expressly made conditional on assent to the additional or different terms.

(2) The additional terms are to be construed as proposals for addition to the contract. Between merchants such terms become part of the contract unless:

(a) the offer expressly limits acceptance to the terms of the offer;

(b) they materially alter it; or

(c) notification of objection to them has already been given or is given within a reasonable time after notice of them is received.

(3) Conduct by both parties which recognizes the existence of a contract is sufficient to establish a contract for sale although the writings of the parties do not otherwise establish a contract. In such case the terms of the particular contract consist of those terms on which the writings of the parties agree, together with any supplementary terms incorporated under any other provisions of this Act.

§2—208. COURSE OF PERFORMANCE OR PRACTICAL CONSTRUCTION

(1) Where the contract for sale involves repeated occasions for performance by either party with knowledge of the nature of the performance and opportunity for objection to it by the other, any course of performance accepted or acquiesced in without objection shall be relevant to determine the meaning of the agreement.

(2) The express terms of the agreement and any such course of performance, as well as any course of dealing and usage of trade, shall be construed whenever reasonable as consistent with each other; but when such construction is unreasonable, express terms shall control course of performance and course of performance shall control both course of dealing and usage of trade (Section 1—205).

(3) Subject to the provisions of the next section on modification and waiver, such course of performance shall be relevant to show a waiver or modification of any term inconsistent with such course of performance.

§2—209. MODIFICATION, RESCISSION AND WAIVER

(1) An agreement modifying a contract within this Article needs no consideration to be binding.

(2) A signed agreement which excludes modification or rescission except by a signed writing cannot be otherwise modified or rescinded, but except as between merchants such a requirement on a form supplied by the merchant must be separately signed by the other party.

(3) The requirements of the statute of frauds section of this Article (Section 2—201) must be satisfied if the contract as modified is within its provisions.

(4) Although an attempt at modification or rescission does not satisfy the requirements of subsection (2) or (3) it can operate as a waiver.

(5) A party who has made a waiver affecting an executory portion of the contract may retract the waiver by reasonable notification received by the other party that strict performance will be required of any term waived, unless the retraction would be unjust in view of a material change of position in reliance on the waiver.

§2—210. DELEGATION OF PERFORMANCE; ASSIGNMENT OF RIGHTS

* * * *

(5) An assignment of "the contract" or of "all my rights under the contract" or an assignment in similar general terms is an assignment of rights and unless the language or the circumstances (as in an assignment for security) indicate the contrary, it is a delegation of performance of the duties of the assignor and its acceptance by the assignee constitutes a promise by him to perform those duties. This promise is enforceable by either the assignor or the other party to the original contract.

§2—301. GENERAL OBLIGATIONS OF PARTIES

The obligation of the seller is to transfer and deliver and that of the buyer is to accept and pay in accordance with the contract.

§2—302. UNCONSCIONABLE CONTRACT OR CLAUSE

(1) If the court as a matter of law finds the contract or any clause of the contract to have been unconscionable at the time it was made the court may refuse to enforce the contract, or it may enforce the remainder of the contract without the unconscionable clause, or it may so limit the application of any unconscionable clause as to avoid any unconscionable result.

(2) When it is claimed or appears to the court that the contract or any clause thereof may be unconscionable the parties shall be afforded a reasonable opportunity to present evidence as to its commercial setting, purpose and effect to aid the court in making the determination.

§2—303. ALLOCATIONS OR DIVISION OF RISKS

Where this Article allocates a risk or a burden as between the parties "unless otherwise agreed", the agreement may not only shift the allocation but may also divide the risk or burden.

§2—304. PRICE PAYABLE IN MONEY, GOODS, REALTY, OR OTHERWISE

(1) The price can be made payable in money or otherwise. If it is payable in whole or in part in goods each party is a seller of the goods which he is to transfer.

(2) Even though all or part of the price is payable in an interest in realty the transfer of the goods and the seller's obligations with reference to them are subject to this Article, but not the transfer of the interest in realty or the transferor's obligations in connection therewith.

§2—305. OPEN PRICE TERM

(1) The parties if they so intend can conclude a contract for sale even though the price is not settled. In such a case the price is a reasonable price at the time for delivery if

(a) nothing is said as to price; or

(b) the price is left to be agreed by the parties and they fail to agree; or

(c) the price is to be fixed in terms of some agreed market or other standard as set or recorded by a third person or agency and it is not so set or recorded.

(2) A price to be fixed by the seller or by the buyer means a price for him to fix in good faith.

(3) When a price left to be fixed otherwise than by agreement of the parties fails to be fixed through fault of one party the other may at his option treat the contract as cancelled or himself fix a reasonable price.

(4) Where, however, the parties intend not to be bound unless the price be fixed or agreed and it is not fixed or agreed there is no contract. In such a case the buyer must return any goods already received or if unable so to do must pay their reasonable value at the time of delivery and the seller must return any portion of the price paid on account.

§2—306. OUTPUT, REQUIREMENTS AND EXCLUSIVE DEALINGS

(1) A term which measures the quantity by the output of the seller or the requirements of the buyer means such actual output or requirements as may occur in good faith, except that no quantity unreasonably disproportionate to any stated estimate or in the absence of a stated estimate to any normal or otherwise comparable prior output or requirements may be tendered or demanded.

(2) A lawful agreement by either the seller or the buyer for exclusive dealing in the kind of goods concerned imposes unless otherwise agreed an obligation by the seller to use best efforts to supply the goods and by the buyer to use best efforts to promote their sale.

§2—307. DELIVERY IN SINGLE LOT OR SEVERAL LOTS

Unless otherwise agreed all goods called for by a con tract for sale must be tendered in a single delivery and payment is due only on such tender but where the circumstances give either party the right to make or demand delivery in lots the price if it can be apportioned may be demanded for each lot.

§2—308. ABSENCE OF SPECIFIED PLACE FOR DELIVERY

Unless otherwise agreed

(a) the place for delivery of goods is the seller's place of business or if he has none his residence; but

(b) in a contract for sale of identified goods which to the knowledge of the parties at the time of contracting are in some other place, that place is the place for their delivery; and

(c) documents of title may be delivered through customary banking channels.

§2—309. ABSENCE OF SPECIFIC TIME PROVISIONS; NOTICE OF TERMINATION

(1) The time for shipment or delivery or any other action under a contract if not provided in this Article or agreed upon shall be a reasonable time.

§2—310. OPEN TIME FOR PAYMENT OR RUNNING OF CREDIT; AUTHORITY TO SHIP UNDER RESERVATION

Unless otherwise agreed

(a) payment is due at the time and place at which the buyer is to receive the goods even though the place of shipment is the place of delivery; and

(b) if the seller is authorized to send the goods he may ship them under reservation, and may tender the documents of title, but the buyer may inspect the goods after their arrival before payment is due unless such inspection is inconsistent with the terms of the contract (Section 2—513).

* * * *

§2—312. WARRANTY OF TITLE AND AGAINST INFRINGEMENT; BUYER'S OBLIGATION AGAINST INFRINGEMENT

(1) Subject to subsection (2) there is in a contract for sale a warranty by the seller that

(a) the title conveyed shall be good, and its transfer rightful; and

(b) the goods shall be delivered free from any security interest or other lien or encumbrance of which the buyer at the time of contracting has no knowledge.

(2) A warranty under subsection (1) will be excluded or modified only by specific language or by circumstances which give the buyer reason to know that the person selling does not claim title in himself or that he is purporting to sell only such right or title as he or a third person may have.

(3) Unless otherwise agreed a seller who is a merchant regularly dealing in goods of the kind warrants that the goods shall be delivered free of the rightful claim of any third person by way of infringement or the like but a buyer who furnishes specifications to the seller must hold the seller harmless against any such claim which arises out of compliance with the specifications.

§2—313. EXPRESS WARRANTIES BY AFFIRMATION, PROMISE, DESCRIPTION, SAMPLE

(1) Express warranties by the seller are created as follows:

(a) Any affirmation of fact or promise made by the seller to the buyer which relates to the goods and becomes part of the basis of the bargain creates an express warranty that the goods shall conform to the affirmation or promise.

(b) Any description of the goods which is made part of the basis of the bargain creates an express warranty that the goods shall conform to the description.

(c) Any sample or model which is made part of the basis of the bargain creates an express warranty that the whole of the goods shall conform to the sample or model.

(2) It is not necessary to the creation of an express warranty that the seller use formal words such as "warrant" or "guarantee" or that he have a specific intention to make a warranty, but an affirmation merely of the value of the goods or a statement purporting to be merely the seller's opinion or commendation of the goods does not create a warranty.

§2—314. IMPLIED WARRANTY: MERCHANTABILITY; USAGE OF TRADE

(1) Unless excluded or modified (Section 2—316), a warranty that the goods shall be merchantable is implied in a contract for their sale if the seller is a merchant with respect to goods of that kind. Under this section the serving for value of food or drink to be consumed either on the premises or elsewhere is a sale.

(2) Goods to be merchantable must be at least such as

(a) pass without objection in the trade under the contract description; and

(b) in the case of fungible goods, are of fair average quality within the description; and

(c) are fit for the ordinary purposes for which such goods are used; and

(d) run, within the variations permitted by the agreement, of even kind, quality and quantity within each unit and among all units involved; and

(e) are adequately contained, packaged, and labeled as the agreement may require; and

(f) conform to the promises or affirmations of fact made on the container or label if any.

(3) Unless excluded or modified (Section 2—316) other implied warranties may arise from course of dealing or usage of trade.

§2—315. IMPLIED WARRANTY: FITNESS FOR PARTICULAR PURPOSE

Where the seller at the time of contracting has reason to know any particular purpose for which the goods are required and that the buyer is relying on the seller's skill or judgment to select or furnish suitable goods, there is unless excluded or modified under the next section an implied warranty that the goods shall be fit for such purpose.

§2—316. EXCLUSION OR MODIFICATION OF WARRANTIES

(1) Words or conduct relevant to the creation of an express warranty and words or conduct tending to negate or limit warranty shall be construed wherever reasonable as consistent with each other; but subject to the provisions of this Article on parol or extrinsic evidence (Section 2—202) negation or limitation is inoperative to the extent that such construction is unreasonable.

(2) Subject to subsection (3), to exclude or modify the implied warranty of merchantability or any part of it the language must mention merchantability and in case of a writing must be conspicuous, and to exclude or modify any implied warranty of fitness the exclusion must be by a writing and conspicuous. Language to exclude all implied warranties of fitness is sufficient if it states, for example, that "There are no warranties which extend beyond the description on the face hereof."

(3) Notwithstanding subsection (2)

(a) unless the circumstances indicate otherwise, all implied warranties are excluded by expressions like "as is", "with all faults" or other language which in common understanding calls the buyer's attention to the exclusion of warranties and makes plain that there is no implied warranty; and

(b) when the buyer before entering into the contract has examined the goods or the sample or model as fully as he desired or has refused to examine the goods there is no implied warranty with regard to defects which an examination ought in the circumstances to have revealed to him; and

(c) an implied warranty can also be excluded or modified by course of dealing or course of performance or usage of trade.

(4) Remedies for breach of warranty can be limited in accordance with the provisions of this Article on liquidation or limitation of damages and on contractual modification of remedy (Sections 2—718 and 2—719).

§2—317. CUMULATION AND CONFLICT OF WARRANTIES EXPRESS OR IMPLIED

Warranties whether express or implied shall be construed as consistent with each other and as cumulative, but if such construction is unreasonable the intention of the parties shall determine which warranty is dominant. In ascertaining that intention the following rules apply:

(a) Exact or technical specifications displace an inconsistent sample or model or general language of description.

(b) A sample from an existing bulk displaces inconsistent general language of description.

(c) Express warranties displace inconsistent implied warranties other than an implied warranty of fitness for a particular purpose.

§2—318. THIRD PARTY BENEFICIARIES OF WARRANTIES EXPRESS OR IMPLIED

Note: If this Act is introduced in the Congress of the United States this section should be omitted. (States to select one alternative.)

Alternative A

A seller's warranty whether express or implied extends to any natural person who is in the family or household of his buyer or who is a guest in his home if it is reasonable to expect that such person may use, consume or be affected by the goods and who is injured in person by breach of the warranty. A seller may not exclude or limit the operation of this section.

Alternative B

A seller's warranty whether express or implied extends to any natural person who may reasonably be expected to use, consume or be affected by the goods and who is injured in person by breach of the warranty. A seller may not exclude or limit the operation of this section.

Alternative C

A seller's warranty whether express or implied extends to any person who may reasonably be expected to use, consume or be affected by the goods and who is injured by breach of the warranty. A seller may not exclude or limit the operation of this section with respect to injury to the person of an individual to whom the warranty extends.

§2—319. F.O.B. AND F.A.S. TERMS

(1) Unless otherwise agreed the term F.O.B. (which means "free on board") at a named place, even though used only in connection with the stated price, is a delivery term under which

(a) when the term is F.O.B. the place of shipment, the seller must at that place ship the goods in the manner provided in this Article (Section 2—504) and bear the expense and risk of putting them into the possession of the carrier; or

(b) when the term is F.O.B. the place of destination, the seller must at his own expense and risk transport the goods to that place and there tender delivery of them in the manner provided in this Article (Section 2—503);

(c) when under either (a) or (b) the term is also F.O. B. vessel, car or other vehicle, the seller must in addition at his own expense and risk load the goods on board. If the term is F.O.B. vessel the buyer must name the vessel and in an appropriate case the seller must comply with the provisions of this Article on the form of bill of lading (Section 2—323).

(2) Unless otherwise agreed the term F.A.S. vessel (which means "free alongside") at a named port, even though used only in connection with the stated price, is a delivery term under which the seller must

(a) at his own expense and risk deliver the goods alongside the vessel in the manner usual in that port or on a dock designated and provided by the buyer; and

(b) obtain and tender a receipt for the goods in exchange for which the carrier is under a duty to issue a bill of lading.

(3) Unless otherwise agreed in any case falling within subsection (1)(a) or (c) or subsection (2) the buyer must seasonably give any needed instructions for making delivery, including when the term is F.A.S. or F.O.B. the loading berth of the vessel and in an appropriate case its name and sailing date. The seller may treat the failure of needed instructions as a failure of cooperation under this Article (Section 2—311). He may also at his option move the goods in any reasonable manner preparatory to delivery or shipment.

(4) Under the term F.O.B. vessel or F.A.S. unless otherwise agreed the buyer must make payment against tender of the required documents and the seller may not tender nor the buyer demand delivery of the goods in substitution for the documents.

§2—320. C.I.F. AND C. & F. TERMS

(1) The term C.I.F. means that the price includes in a lump sum the cost of the goods and the insurance and freight to the named destination. The term C. & F. or C.F. means that the price so includes cost and freight to the named destination.

(2) Unless otherwise agreed and even though used only in connection with the stated price and destination, the term C.I.F. destination or its equivalent requires the seller at his own expense and risk to

(a) put the goods into the possession of a carrier at the port for shipment and obtain a negotiable bill or bills of lading covering the entire transportation to the named destination; and

(b) load the goods and obtain a receipt from the carrier (which may be contained in the bill of lading) showing that the freight has been paid or provided for; and

(c) obtain a policy or certificate of insurance, including any war risk insurance, of a kind and on terms then current at the port of shipment in the usual amount, in the currency of the contract, shown to cover the same goods covered by the bill of lading and providing for payment of loss to the order of the buyer or for the account of whom it may concern; but the seller may add to the price the amount of the premium for any such war risk insurance; and

(d) prepare an invoice of the goods and procure any other documents required to effect shipment or to comply with the contract; and

(e) forward and tender with commercial promptness all the documents in due form and with any indorsement necessary to perfect the buyer's rights.

(3) Unless otherwise agreed the term C. & F. or its equivalent has the same effect and imposes upon the seller the same obligations and risks as a C.I.F. term except the obligation as to insurance.

(4) Under the term C.I.F. or C. & F. unless otherwise agreed the buyer must make payment against tender of the required documents and the seller may not tender nor the buyer demand delivery of the goods in substitution for the documents.

* * * *

§2—322. DELIVERY "EX-SHIP"

(1) Unless otherwise agreed a term for delivery of goods "ex-ship" (which means from the carrying vessel) or in equivalent language is not restricted to a particular ship and requires delivery from a ship which has reached a place at the named port of destination where goods of the kind are usually discharged.

(2) Under such a term unless otherwise agreed

(a) the seller must discharge all liens arising out of the carriage and furnish the buyer with a direction which puts the carrier under a duty to deliver the goods; and

(b) the risk of loss does not pass to the buyer until the goods leave the ship's tackle or are otherwise properly unloaded.

* * * *

§2—324. "NO ARRIVAL, NO SALE" TERM

Under a term "no arrival, no sale" or terms of like meaning, unless otherwise agreed,

(a) the seller must properly ship conforming goods and if they arrive by any means he must tender them on arrival but he assumes no obligation that the goods will arrive unless he has caused the non-arrival; and

(b) where without fault of the seller the goods are in part lost or have so deteriorated as no longer to conform to the contract or arrive after the contract time, the buyer may proceed as if there had been casualty to identified goods (Section 2—613).

* * * *

§2—326. SALE ON APPROVAL AND SALE OR RETURN; RIGHTS OF CREDITORS

(1) Unless otherwise agreed, if delivered goods may be returned by the buyer even though they conform to the contract, the transaction is

(a) a "sale on approval" if the goods are delivered primarily for use, and

(b) a "sale or return" if the goods are delivered primarily for resale.

(2) Goods held on approval are not subject to the claims of the buyer's creditors until acceptance; goods held on sale or return are subject to such claims while in the buyer's possession.

(3) Any "or return" term of a contract for sale is to be treated as a separate contract for sale within the statute of frauds section of this Article (Section 2—201) and as contradicting the sale aspect of the contract within the provisions of this Article or on parol or extrinsic evidence (Section 2—202).

§2—327. SPECIAL INCIDENTS OF SALE ON APPROVAL AND SALE OR RETURN

(1) Under a sale on approval unless otherwise agreed

(a) although the goods are identified to the contract the risk of loss and the title do not pass to the buyer until acceptance; and

(b) use of the goods consistent with the purpose of trial is not acceptance but failure seasonably to notify the seller of election to return the goods is acceptance, and if the goods conform to the contract acceptance of any part is acceptance of the whole; and

(c) after due notification of election to return, the return is at the seller's risk and expense but a merchant buyer must follow any reasonable instructions.

(2) Under a sale or return unless otherwise agreed

(a) the option to return extends to the whole or any commercial unit of the goods while in substantially their original condition, but must be exercised seasonably; and

(b) the return is at the buyer's risk and expense.

§2—328. SALE BY AUCTION

(1) In a sale by auction if goods are put up in lots each lot is the subject of a separate sale.

(2) A sale by auction is complete when the auctioneer so announces by the fall of the hammer or in other customary manner. Where a bid is made while the hammer is falling in acceptance of a prior bid the auctioneer may in his discretion reopen the bidding or declare the goods sold under the bid on which the hammer was falling.

(3) Such a sale is with reserve unless the goods are in explicit terms put up without reserve. In an auction with reserve the auctioneer may withdraw the goods at any time until he announces completion of the sale. In an auction without reserve, after the auctioneer calls for bids on an article or lot, that article or lot cannot be withdrawn unless no bid is made within a reasonable time. In either case a bidder may retract his bid until the auctioneer's announcement of completion of the sale, but a bidder's retraction does not revive any previous bid.

(4) If the auctioneer knowingly receives a bid on the seller's behalf or the seller makes or procures such a bid, and notice has not been given that liberty for such bidding is reserved, the buyer may at his option avoid the sale or take the goods at the price of the last good faith bid prior to the completion of the sale. This subsection shall not apply to any bid at a forced sale.

§2—401. PASSING OF TITLE; RESERVATION FOR SECURITY; LIMITED APPLICATION OF THIS SECTION

Each provision of this Article with regard to the rights, obligations and remedies of the seller, the buyer, purchasers or other third parties applies irrespective of title to the goods except where the provision refers to such title. Insofar as situations are not covered by the other provisions of this Article and matters concerning title became material the following rules apply:

(1) Title to goods cannot pass under a contract for sale prior to their identification to the contract

(Section 2—501), and unless otherwise explicitly agreed the buyer acquires by their identification a special property as limited by this Act. Any retention or reservation by the seller of the title (property) in goods shipped or delivered to the buyer is limited in effect to a reservation of a security interest. Subject to these provisions and to the provisions of the Article on Secured Transactions (Article 9), title to goods passes from the seller to the buyer in any manner and on any conditions explicitly agreed on by the parties.

(2) Unless otherwise explicitly agreed title passes to the buyer at the time and place at which the seller completes his performance with reference to the physical delivery of the goods, despite any reservation of a security interest and even though a document of title is to be delivered at a different time or place; and in particular and despite any reservation of a security interest by the bill of lading

(a) if the contract requires or authorizes the seller to send the goods to the buyer but does not require him to deliver them at destination, title passes to the buyer at the time and place of shipment; but

(b) if the contract requires delivery at destination, title passes on tender there.

(3) Unless otherwise explicitly agreed where delivery is to be made without moving the goods,

(a) if the seller is to deliver a document of title, title passes at the time when and the place where he delivers such documents; or

(b) if the goods are at the time of contracting already identified and no documents are to be delivered, title passes at the time and place of contracting.

(4) A rejection or other refusal by the buyer to receive or retain the goods, whether or not justified, or a justified revocation of acceptance revests title to the goods in the seller. Such revesting occurs by operation of law and is not a "sale".

* * * *

§2—403. POWER TO TRANSFER; GOOD FAITH PURCHASE OF GOODS; "ENTRUSTING"

(1) A purchaser of goods acquires all title which his transferor had or had power to transfer except that a purchaser of a limited interest acquires rights only to the extent of the interest purchased. A person with voidable title has power to transfer a good title to a good faith purchaser for value. When goods have been delivered under a transaction of purchase the purchaser has such power even though

(a) the transferor was deceived as to the identity of the purchaser, or

(b) the delivery was in exchange for a check which is later dishonored, or

(c) it was agreed that the transaction was to be a "cash sale", or

(d) the delivery was procured through fraud punishable as larcenous under the criminal law.

(2) Any entrusting of possession of goods to a merchant who deals in goods of that kind gives him power to transfer all rights of the entruster to a buyer in ordinary course of business.

(3) "Entrusting" includes any delivery and any acquiescence in retention of possession regardless of any condition expressed between the parties to the delivery or acquiescence and regardless of whether the procurement of the entrusting or the possessor's disposition of the goods have been such as to be larcenous under the criminal law.

(4) The rights of other purchasers of goods and of lien creditors are governed by the Articles on Secured Transactions (Article 9), Bulk Transfers (Article 6) and Documents of Title (Article 7).

§2—501. INSURABLE INTEREST IN GOODS; MANNER OF IDENTIFICATION OF GOODS

(1) The buyer obtains a special property and an insurable interest in goods by identification of existing goods as goods to which the contract refers even though the goods so identified are non-conforming and he has an option to return or reject them. Such identification can be made at any time and in any manner explicitly agreed to by the parties. In the absence of explicit agreement identification occurs

(a) when the contract is made if it is for the sale of goods already existing and identified;

(b) if the contract is for the sale of future goods other than those described in paragraph (c), when goods are shipped, marked or otherwise designated by the seller as goods to which the contract refers;

(c) when the crops are planted or otherwise become growing crops or the young are conceived if the contract is for the sale of unborn young to be born within twelve months after contracting or for the sale of crops to be harvested within twelve months or the next normal harvest season after contracting whichever is longer.

(2) The seller retains an insurable interest in goods so long as title to or any security interest in the goods

remains in him and where the identification is by the seller alone he may until default or insolvency or notification to the buyer that the identification is final substitute other goods for those identified.

(3) Nothing in this section impairs any insurable interest recognized under any other statute or rule of law.

§2—502. BUYER'S RIGHT TO GOODS ON SELLER'S INSOLVENCY

(1) Subject to subsections (2) and (3) and even though the goods have not been shipped a buyer who has paid a part or all of the price of goods in which he has a special property under the provisions of the immediately preceding section may on making and keeping good a tender of any unpaid portion of their price recover them from the seller if:

(a) in the case of goods bought for personal, family, or household purposes, the seller repudiates or fails to deliver as required by the contract; or

(b) in all cases, the seller becomes insolvent within ten days after receipt of the first installment on their price.

(2) The buyer's right to recover the goods under subsection (1)(a) vests upon acquisition of a special property, even if the seller had not then repudiated or failed to deliver.

(3) If the identification creating his special property has been made by the buyer he acquires the right to recover the goods only if they conform to the contract for sale.

As amended in 1999.

§2—503. MANNER OF SELLER'S TENDER OF DELIVERY

(1) Tender of delivery requires that the seller put and hold conforming goods at the buyer's disposition and give the buyer any notification reasonably necessary to enable him to take delivery. The manner, time and place for tender are determined by the agreement and this Article, and in particular

(a) tender must be at a reasonable hour, and if it is of goods they must be kept available for the period reasonably necessary to enable the buyer to take possession; but

(b) unless otherwise agreed the buyer must furnish facilities reasonably suited to the receipt of the goods.

(2) Where the case is within the next section respecting shipment tender requires that the seller comply with its provisions.

(3) Where the seller is required to deliver at a particular destination tender requires that he comply with subsection (1) and also in any appropriate case tender documents as described in subsections (4) and (5) of this section.

(4) Where goods are in the possession of a bailee and are to be delivered without being moved

(a) tender requires that the seller either tender a negotiable document of title covering such goods or procure acknowledgment by the bailee of the buyer's right to possession of the goods; but

(b) tender to the buyer of a non-negotiable document of title or of a written direction to the bailee to deliver is sufficient tender unless the buyer seasonably objects, and receipt by the bailee of notification of the buyer's rights fixes those rights as against the bailee and all third persons; but risk of loss of the goods and of any failure by the bailee to honor the non-negotiable document of title or to obey the direction remains on the seller until the buyer has had a reasonable time to present the document or direction, and a refusal by the bailee to honor the document or to obey the direction defeats the tender.

(5) Where the contract requires the seller to deliver documents

(a) he must tender all such documents in correct form, except as provided in this Article with respect to bills of lading in a set (subsection (2) of Section 2—323); and

(b) tender through customary banking channels is sufficient and dishonor of a draft accompanying the documents constitutes non-acceptance or rejection.

§2—504. SHIPMENT BY SELLER

Where the seller is required or authorized to send the goods to the buyer and the contract does not require him to deliver them at a particular destination, then unless otherwise agreed he must

(a) put the goods in the possession of such a carrier and make such a contract for their transportation as may be reasonable having regard to the nature of the goods and other circumstances of the case; and

(b) obtain and promptly deliver or tender in due form any document necessary to enable the buyer to obtain possession of the goods or otherwise required by the agreement or by usage of trade; and

(c) promptly notify the buyer of the shipment. Failure to notify the buyer under paragraph (c) or to make a proper contract under paragraph (a) is a ground for rejection only if material delay or loss ensues.

* * * *

§2—506. RIGHTS OF FINANCING AGENCY

(1) A financing agency by paying or purchasing for value a draft which relates to a shipment of goods acquires to the extent of the payment or purchase and in addition to its own rights under the draft and any document of title securing it any rights of the shipper in the goods including the right to stop delivery and the shipper's right to have the draft honored by the buyer.

(2) The right to reimbursement of a financing agency which has in good faith honored or purchased the draft under commitment to or authority from the buyer is not impaired by subsequent discovery of defects with reference to any relevant document which was apparently regular on its face.

§2—507. EFFECT OF SELLER'S TENDER; DELIVERY ON CONDITION

(1) Tender of delivery is a condition to the buyer's duty to accept the goods and, unless otherwise agreed, to his duty to pay for them. Tender entitles the seller to acceptance of the goods and to payment according to the contract.

(2) Where payment is due and demanded on the delivery to the buyer of goods or documents of title, his right as against the seller to retain or dispose of them is conditional upon his making the payment due.

§2—508. CURE BY SELLER OF IMPROPER TENDER OR DELIVERY; REPLACEMENT

(1) Where any tender or delivery by the seller is rejected because non-conforming and the time for performance has not yet expired, the seller may seasonably notify the buyer of his intention to cure and may then within the contract time make a conforming delivery.

(2) Where the buyer rejects a non-conforming tender which the seller had reasonable grounds to believe would be acceptable with or without money allowance the seller may if he seasonably notifies the buyer have a further reasonable time to substitute a conforming tender.

§2—509. RISK OF LOSS IN THE ABSENCE OF BREACH

(1) Where the contract requires or authorizes the seller to ship the goods by carrier

(a) if it does not require him to deliver them at a particular destination, the risk of loss passes to the buyer when the goods are duly delivered to the carrier even though the shipment is under reservation (Section 2—505); but

(b) if it does require him to deliver them at a particular destination and the goods are there duly tendered while in the possession of the carrier, the risk of loss passes to the buyer when the goods are there duly so tendered as to enable the buyer to take delivery.

(2) Where the goods are held by a bailee to be delivered without being moved, the risk of loss passes to the buyer

(a) on his receipt of a negotiable document of title covering the goods; or

(b) on acknowledgment by the bailee of the buyer's right to possession of the goods; or

(c) after his receipt of a non-negotiable document of title or other written direction to deliver, as provided in subsection (4)(b) of Section 2—503.

(3) In any case not within subsection (1) or (2), the risk of loss passes to the buyer on his receipt of the goods if the seller is a merchant; otherwise the risk passes to the buyer on tender of delivery.

(4) The provisions of this section are subject to contrary agreement of the parties and to the provisions of this Article on sale on approval (Section 2—327) and on effect of breach on risk of loss (Section 2—510).

§2—510. EFFECT OF BREACH ON RISK OF LOSS

(1) Where a tender or delivery of goods so fails to conform to the contract as to give a right of rejection the risk of their loss remains on the seller until cure or acceptance.

(2) Where the buyer rightfully revokes acceptance he may to the extent of any deficiency in his effective insurance coverage treat the risk of loss as having rested on the seller from the beginning.

(3) Where the buyer as to conforming goods already identified to the contract for sale repudiates or is otherwise in breach before risk of their loss has passed to him, the seller may to the extent of any deficiency in his effective insurance coverage treat the risk of loss as resting on the buyer for a commercially reasonable time.

§2—511. TENDER OF PAYMENT BY BUYER; PAYMENT BY CHECK

(1) Unless otherwise agreed tender of payment is a condition to the seller's duty to tender and complete any delivery.

(2) Tender of payment is sufficient when made by any means or in any manner current in the ordinary course of business unless the seller demands payment in legal tender and gives any extension of time reasonably necessary to procure it.

(3) Subject to the provisions of this Act on the effect of an instrument on an obligation (Section 3—310), payment by check is conditional and is defeated as between the parties by dishonor of the check on due presentment.

As amended in 1994.

§2—512. PAYMENT BY BUYER BEFORE INSPECTION

(1) Where the contract requires payment before inspection non-conformity of the goods does not excuse the buyer from so making payment unless

(a) the non-conformity appears without inspection; or

(b) despite tender of the required documents the circumstances would justify injunction against honor under this Act (Section 5—109(b)).

(2) Payment pursuant to subsection (1) does not constitute an acceptance of goods or impair the buyer's right to inspect or any of his remedies.

§2—513. BUYER'S RIGHT TO INSPECTION OF GOODS

(1) Unless otherwise agreed and subject to subsection (3), where goods are tendered or delivered or identified to the contract for sale, the buyer has a right before payment or acceptance to inspect them at any reasonable place and time and in any reasonable manner. When the seller is required or authorized to send the goods to the buyer, the inspection may be after their arrival.

(2) Expenses of inspection must be borne by the buyer but may be recovered from the seller if the goods do not conform and are rejected.

(3) Unless otherwise agreed and subject to the provisions of this Article on C.I.F. contracts (subsection (3) of Section 2—321), the buyer is not entitled to inspect the goods before payment of the price when the contract provides

(a) for delivery "C.O.D." or on other like terms; or

(b) for payment against documents of title, except where such payment is due only after the goods are to become available for inspection.

(4) A place or method of inspection fixed by the parties is presumed to be exclusive but unless otherwise expressly agreed it does not postpone identification or shift the place for delivery or for passing the risk of loss. If compliance becomes impossible, inspection shall be as provided in this section unless the place or method fixed was clearly intended as an indispensable condition failure of which avoids the contract.

* * * *

§2—601. BUYER'S RIGHTS ON IMPROPER DELIVERY

Subject to the provisions of this Article on breach in installment contracts (Section 2—612) and unless otherwise agreed under the sections on contractual limitations of remedy (Sections 2—718 and 2—719), if the goods or the tender of delivery fail in any respect to conform to the contract, the buyer may

(a) reject the whole; or

(b) accept the whole; or

(c) accept any commercial unit or units and reject the rest.

§2—602. MANNER AND EFFECT OF RIGHTFUL REJECTION

(1) Rejection of goods must be within a reasonable time after their delivery or tender. It is ineffective unless the buyer seasonably notifies the seller.

(2) Subject to the provisions of the two following sections on rejected goods (Sections 2—603 and 2—604),

(a) after rejection any exercise of ownership by the buyer with respect to any commercial unit is wrongful as against the seller; and

(b) if the buyer has before rejection taken physical possession of goods in which he does not have a security interest under the provisions of this Article (subsection (3) of Section 2—711), he is under a duty after rejection to hold them with reasonable care at the seller's disposition for a time sufficient to permit the seller to remove them; but

(c) the buyer has no further obligations with regard to goods rightfully rejected.

(3) The seller's rights with respect to goods wrongfully rejected are governed by the provisions of this Article on Seller's remedies in general (Section 2—703).

§2—603. MERCHANT BUYER'S DUTIES AS TO RIGHTFULLY REJECTED GOODS

(1) Subject to any security interest in the buyer (subsection (3) of Section 2—711), when the seller has no agent or place of business at the market of rejection a merchant buyer is under a duty after rejection of goods in his possession or control to follow any reasonable instructions received from the seller with respect to the goods and in the absence of such instructions to make reasonable efforts to sell them for the seller's account if they are perishable or threaten to decline in value speedily. Instructions are not reasonable if on demand indemnity for expenses is not forthcoming.

(2) When the buyer sells goods under subsection (1), he is entitled to reimbursement from the seller or out of the proceeds for reasonable expenses of caring for and selling them, and if the expenses include no selling commission then to such commission as is usual in the trade or if there is none to a reasonable sum not exceeding ten per cent on the gross proceeds.

(3) In complying with this section the buyer is held only to good faith and good faith conduct hereunder is neither acceptance nor conversion nor the basis of an action for damages.

§2—604. BUYER'S OPTIONS AS TO SALVAGE OF RIGHTFULLY REJECTED GOODS

Subject to the provisions of the immediately preceding section on perishables if the seller gives no instructions within a reasonable time after notification of rejection the buyer may store the rejected goods for the seller's account or reship them to him or resell them for the seller's account with reimbursement as provided in the preceding section. Such action is not acceptance or conversion.

§2—605. WAIVER OF BUYER'S OBJECTIONS BY FAILURE TO PARTICULARIZE

(1) The buyer's failure to state in connection with rejection a particular defect which is ascertainable by reasonable inspection precludes him from relying on the unstated defect to justify rejection or to establish breach

(a) where the seller could have cured it if stated seasonably; or

(b) between merchants when the seller has after rejection made a request in writing for a full and final written statement of all defects on which the buyer proposes to rely.

(2) Payment against documents made without reservation of rights precludes recovery of the payment for defects apparent on the face of the documents.

§2—606. WHAT CONSTITUTES ACCEPTANCE OF GOODS

(1) Acceptance of goods occurs when the buyer

(a) after a reasonable opportunity to inspect the goods signifies to the seller that the goods are conforming or that he will take or retain them in spite of their non-conformity; or

(b) fails to make an effective rejection (subsection (1) of Section 2—602), but such acceptance does not occur until the buyer has had a reasonable opportunity to inspect them; or

(c) does any act inconsistent with the seller's ownership; but if such act is wrongful as against the seller it is an acceptance only if ratified by him.

(2) Acceptance of a part of any commercial unit is acceptance of that entire unit.

§2—607. EFFECT OF ACCEPTANCE; NOTICE OF BREACH; BURDEN OF ESTABLISHING BREACH AFTER ACCEPTANCE; NOTICE OF CLAIM OR LITIGATION TO PERSON ANSWERABLE OVER

(1) The buyer must pay at the contract rate for any goods accepted.

(2) Acceptance of goods by the buyer precludes rejection of the goods accepted and if made with knowledge of a non-conformity cannot be revoked because of it unless the acceptance was on the reasonable assumption that the non-conformity would be seasonably cured but acceptance does not of itself impair any other remedy provided by this Article for non-conformity.

(3) Where a tender has been accepted

(a) the buyer must within a reasonable time after he discovers or should have discovered any breach notify the seller of breach or be barred from any remedy; and

(b) if the claim is one for infringement or the like (subsection (3) of Section 2—312) and the buyer is sued as a result of such a breach he must so notify the seller within a reasonable time after he receives notice of the litigation or be barred from any remedy over for liability established by the litigation.

(4) The burden is on the buyer to establish any breach with respect to the goods accepted.

(5) Where the buyer is sued for breach of a warranty or other obligation for which his seller is answerable over

(a) he may give his seller written notice of the litigation. If the notice states that the seller may come in and defend and that if the seller does not do so he will be bound in any action against him by his buyer by any determination of fact common to the two litigations, then unless the seller after seasonable receipt of the notice does come in and defend he is so bound.

(b) if the claim is one for infringement or the like (subsection (3) of Section 2—312) the original seller may demand in writing that his buyer turn over to him control of the litigation including settlement or else be barred from any remedy over and if he also agrees to bear all expense and to satisfy any adverse judgment, then unless the buyer after seasonable receipt of the demand does turn over control the buyer is so barred.

(6) The provisions of subsections (3), (4) and (5) apply to any obligation of a buyer to hold the seller harmless against infringement or the like (subsection (3) of Section 2—312).

§2—608. REVOCATION OF ACCEPTANCE IN WHOLE OR IN PART

(1) The buyer may revoke his acceptance of a lot or commercial unit whose non-conformity substantially impairs its value to him if he has accepted it

(a) on the reasonable assumption that its non-conformity would be cured and it has not been seasonably cured; or

(b) without discovery of such non-conformity if his acceptance was reasonably induced either by the difficulty of discovery before acceptance or by the seller's assurances.

(2) Revocation of acceptance must occur within a reasonable time after the buyer discovers or should have discovered the ground for it and before any substantial change in condition of the goods which is not caused by their own defects. It is not effective until the buyer notifies the seller of it.

(3) A buyer who so revokes has the same rights and duties with regard to the goods involved as if he had rejected them.

§2—609. RIGHT TO ADEQUATE ASSURANCE OF PERFORMANCE

(1) A contract for sale imposes an obligation on each party that the other's expectation of receiving due performance will not be impaired. When reasonable grounds for insecurity arise with respect to the performance of either party the other may in writing demand adequate assurance of due performance and until he receives such assurance may if commercially reasonable suspend any performance for which he has not already received the agreed return.

(2) Between merchants the reasonableness of grounds for insecurity and the adequacy of any assurance offered shall be determined according to commercial standards.

(3) Acceptance of any improper delivery or payment does not prejudice the party's right to demand adequate assurance of future performance.

(4) After receipt of a justified demand failure to provide within a reasonable time not exceeding thirty days such assurance of due performance as is adequate under the circumstances of the particular case is a repudiation of the contract.

§2—610. ANTICIPATORY REPUDIATION

When either party repudiates the contract with respect to a performance not yet due the loss of which will substantially impair the value of the contract to the other, the aggrieved party may

(a) for a commercially reasonable time await performance by the repudiating party; or

(b) resort to any remedy for breach (Section 2—703 or Section 2—711), even though he has notified the repudiating party that he would await the latter's performance and has urged retraction; and

(c) in either case suspend his own performance or proceed in accordance with the provisions of this Article on the seller's right to identify goods to the contract notwithstanding breach or to salvage unfinished goods (Section 2—704).

§2—611. RETRACTION OF ANTICIPATORY REPUDIATION

(1) Until the repudiating party's next performance is due he can retract his repudiation unless the aggrieved party has since the repudiation cancelled or materially changed his position or otherwise indicated that he considers the repudiation final.

(2) Retraction may be by any method which clearly indicates to the aggrieved party that the repudiating party intends to perform, but must include any assurance justifiably demanded under the provisions of this Article (Section 2—609).

(3) Retraction reinstates the repudiating party's rights under the contract with due excuse and allowance to the aggrieved party for any delay occasioned by the repudiation.

§2—612. "INSTALLMENT CONTRACT"; BREACH

(1) An "installment contract" is one which requires or authorizes the delivery of goods in separate lots to be separately accepted, even though the contract contains a clause "each delivery is a separate contract" or its equivalent.

(2) The buyer may reject any installment which is non-conforming if the non-conformity substantially impairs the value of that installment and cannot be cured or if the non-conformity is a defect in the required documents; but if the non-conformity does not fall within subsection (3) and the seller gives adequate assurance of its cure the buyer must accept that installment.

(3) Whenever non-conformity or default with respect to one or more installments substantially impairs the value of the whole contract there is a breach of the whole. But the aggrieved party reinstates the contract if he accepts a non-conforming installment without seasonably notifying of cancellation or if he brings an action with respect only to past installments or demands performance as to future installments.

§2—613. CASUALTY TO IDENTIFIED GOODS

Where the contract requires for its performance goods identified when the contract is made, and the goods suffer casualty without fault of either party before the risk of loss passes to the buyer, or in a proper case under a "no arrival, no sale" term (Section 2—324) then

(a) if the loss is total the contract is avoided; and

(b) if the loss is partial or the goods have so deteriorated as no longer to conform to the contract the buyer may nevertheless demand inspection and at his option either treat the contract as voided or accept the goods with due allowance from the contract price for the deterioration or the deficiency in quantity but without further right against the seller.

§2—614. SUBSTITUTED PERFORMANCE

(1) Where without fault of either party the agreed berthing, loading, or unloading facilities fail or an agreed type of carrier becomes unavailable or the agreed manner of delivery otherwise becomes commercially impracticable but a commercially reasonable substitute is available, such substitute performance must be tendered and accepted.

(2) If the agreed means or manner of payment fails because of domestic or foreign governmental regulation, the seller may withhold or stop delivery unless the buyer provides a means or manner of payment which is commercially a substantial equivalent. If delivery has already been taken, payment by the means or in the manner provided by the regulation discharges the buyer's obligation unless the regulation is discriminatory, oppressive or predatory.

§2—615. EXCUSE BY FAILURE OF PRESUPPOSED CONDITIONS

Except so far as a seller may have assumed a greater obligation and subject to the preceding section on substituted performance:

(a) Delay in delivery or non-delivery in whole or in part by a seller who complies with paragraphs (b) and (c) is not a breach of his duty under a contract for sale if performance as agreed has been made impracticable by the occurrence of a contingency the nonoccurrence of which was a basic assumption on which the contract was made or by compliance in good faith with any applicable foreign or domestic governmental regulation or order whether or not it later proves to be invalid.

(b) Where the causes mentioned in paragraph (a) affect only a part of the seller's capacity to perform, he must allocate production and deliveries among his customers but may at his option include regular customers not then under contract as well as his own requirements for further manufacture. He may so allocate in any manner which is fair and reasonable.

(c) The seller must notify the buyer seasonably that there will be delay or non-delivery and, when allocation is required under paragraph (b), of the estimated quota thus made available for the buyer.

* * * *

§2—702. SELLER'S REMEDIES ON DISCOVERY OF BUYER'S INSOLVENCY

(1) Where the seller discovers the buyer to be insolvent he may refuse delivery except for cash including payment for all goods theretofore delivered under the contract, and stop delivery under this Article (Section 2—705).

(2) Where the seller discovers that the buyer has received goods on credit while insolvent he may reclaim the goods upon demand made within ten days after the receipt, but if misrepresentation of solvency has been made to the particular seller in writing within three months before delivery the ten day limitation does not apply. Except as provided in this subsection the seller may not base a right to reclaim goods on the buyer's fraudulent or innocent misrepresentation of solvency or of intent to pay.

(3) The seller's right to reclaim under subsection (2) is subject to the rights of a buyer in ordinary course or other good faith purchaser under this Article (Section 2—403). Successful reclamation of goods excludes all other remedies with respect to them.

§2—703. SELLER'S REMEDIES IN GENERAL

Where the buyer wrongfully rejects or revokes acceptance of goods or fails to make a payment due on or before delivery or repudiates with respect to a part or the whole, then with respect to any goods directly affected and, if the breach is of the whole contract

(Section 2—612), then also with respect to the whole undelivered balance, the aggrieved seller may

(a) withhold delivery of such goods;

(b) stop delivery by any bailee as hereafter provided (Section 2—705);

(c) proceed under the next section respecting goods still unidentified to the contract;

(d) resell and recover damages as hereafter provided (Section 2—706);

(e) recover damages for non-acceptance (Section 2—708) or in a proper case the price (Section 2—709);

(f) cancel.

§2—704. SELLER'S RIGHT TO IDENTIFY GOODS TO THE CONTRACT NOTWITHSTANDING BREACH OR TO SALVAGE UNFINISHED GOODS

(1) An aggrieved seller under the preceding section may

(a) identify to the contract conforming goods not already identified if at the time he learned of the breach they are in his possession or control;

(b) treat as the subject of resale goods which have demonstrably been intended for the particular contract even though those goods are unfinished.

(2) Where the goods are unfinished an aggrieved seller may in the exercise of reasonable commercial judgment for the purposes of avoiding loss and of effective realization either complete the manufacture and wholly identify the goods to the contract or cease manufacture and resell for scrap or salvage value or proceed in any other reasonable manner.

§2—705. SELLER'S STOPPAGE OF DELIVERY IN TRANSIT OR OTHERWISE

(1) The seller may stop delivery of goods in the possession of a carrier or other bailee when he discovers the buyer to be insolvent (Section 2—702) and may stop delivery of carload, truckload, planeload or larger shipments of express or freight when the buyer repudiates or fails to make a payment due before delivery or if for any other reason the seller has a right to withhold or reclaim the goods.

(2) As against such buyer the seller may stop delivery until

(a) receipt of the goods by the buyer; or

(b) acknowledgment to the buyer by any bailee of the goods except a carrier that the bailee holds the goods for the buyer; or

(c) such acknowledgment to the buyer by a carrier by reshipment or as warehouseman; or

(d) negotiation to the buyer of any negotiable document of title covering the goods.

(3) ****

(a) To stop delivery the seller must so notify as to enable the bailee by reasonable diligence to prevent delivery of the goods.

(b) After such notification the bailee must hold and deliver the goods according to the directions of the seller but the seller is liable to the bailee for any ensuing charges or damages.

(c) If a negotiable document of title has been issued for goods the bailee is not obliged to obey a notification to stop until surrender of the document.

(d) A carrier who has issued a non-negotiable bill of lading is not obliged to obey a notification to stop received from a person other than the consignor.

§2—706. SELLER'S RESALE INCLUDING CONTRACT FOR RESALE

(1) Under the conditions stated in Section 2—703 on seller's remedies, the seller may resell the goods concerned or the undelivered balance thereof. Where the resale is made in good faith and in a commercially reasonable manner the seller may recover the difference between the resale price and the contract price together with any incidental damages allowed under the provisions of this Article (Section 2—710), but less expenses saved in consequence of the buyer's breach.

(2) Except as otherwise provided in subsection (3) or unless otherwise agreed resale may be at public or private sale including sale by way of one or more contracts to sell or of identification to an existing contract of the seller. Sale may be as a unit or in parcels and at any time and place and on any terms but every aspect of the sale including the method, manner, time, place and terms must be commercially reasonable. The resale must be reasonably identified as referring to the broken contract, but it is not necessary that the goods be in existence or that any or all of them have been identified to the contract before the breach.

(3) Where the resale is at private sale the seller must give the buyer reasonable notification of his intention to resell.

(4) Where the resale is at public sale

(a) only identified goods can be sold except where there is a recognized market for a public sale of futures in goods of the kind; and

(b) it must be made at a usual place or market for public sale if one is reasonably available and except in the case of goods which are perishable or threaten to decline in value speedily the seller must give the buyer reasonable notice of the time and place of the resale; and

(c) if the goods are not to be within the view of those attending the sale the notification of sale must state the place where the goods are located and provide for their reasonable inspection by prospective bidders; and

(d) the seller may buy.

(5) A purchaser who buys in good faith at a resale takes the goods free of any rights of the original buyer even though the seller fails to comply with one or more of the requirements of this section.

(6) The seller is not accountable to the buyer for any profit made on any resale. A person in the position of a seller (Section 2—707) or a buyer who has rightfully rejected or justifiably revoked acceptance must account for any excess over the amount of his security interest, as hereinafter defined (subsection (3) of Section 2—711).

* * * *

§2—708. SELLER'S DAMAGES FOR NON-ACCEPTANCE OR REPUDIATION

(1) Subject to subsection (2) and to the provisions of this Article with respect to proof of market price (Section 2—723), the measure of damages for non-acceptance or repudiation by the buyer is the difference between the market price at the time and place for tender and the unpaid contract price together with any incidental damages provided in this Article (Section 2—710), but less expenses saved in consequence of the buyer's breach.

(2) If the measure of damages provided in subsection (1) is inadequate to put the seller in as good a position as performance would have done then the measure of damages is the profit (including reasonable overhead) which the seller would have made from full performance by the buyer, together with any incidental damages provided in this Article (Section 2—710), due allowance for costs reasonably incurred and due credit for payments or proceeds of resale.

§2—709. ACTION FOR THE PRICE

(1) When the buyer fails to pay the price as it becomes due the seller may recover, together with any incidental damages under the next section, the price

(a) of goods accepted or of conforming goods lost or damaged within a commercially reasonable time after risk of their loss has passed to the buyer; and

(b) of goods identified to the contract if the seller is unable after reasonable effort to resell them at a reasonable price or the circumstances reasonably indicate that such effort will be unavailing.

(2) Where the seller sues for the price he must hold for the buyer any goods which have been identified to the contract and are still in his control except that if resale becomes possible he may resell them at any time prior to the collection of the judgment. The net proceeds of any such resale must be credited to the buyer and payment of the judgment entitles him to any goods not resold.

(3) After the buyer has wrongfully rejected or revoked acceptance of the goods or has failed to make a payment due or has repudiated (Section 2—610), a seller who is held not entitled to the price under this section shall nevertheless be awarded damages for non-acceptance under the preceding section.

§2—710. SELLER'S INCIDENTAL DAMAGES

Incidental damages to an aggrieved seller include any commercially reasonable charges, expenses or commissions incurred in stopping delivery, in the transportation, care and custody of goods after the buyer's breach, in connection with return or resale of the goods or otherwise resulting from the breach.

§2—711. BUYER'S REMEDIES IN GENERAL; BUYER'S SECURITY INTEREST IN REJECTED GOODS

(1) Where the seller fails to make delivery or repudiates or the buyer rightfully rejects or justifiably revokes acceptance then with respect to any goods involved, and with respect to the whole if the breach goes to the whole contract (Section 2—612), the buyer may cancel and whether or not he has done so may in addition to recovering so much of the price as has been paid

(a) "cover" and have damages under the next section as to all the goods affected whether or not they have been identified to the contract; or

(b) recover damages for non-delivery as provided in this Article (Section 2—713).

(2) Where the seller fails to deliver or repudiates the buyer may also

(a) if the goods have been identified recover them as provided in this Article (Section 2—502); or

(b) in a proper case obtain specific performance or replevy the goods as provided in this Article (Section 2—716).

(3) On rightful rejection or justifiable revocation of acceptance a buyer has a security interest in goods in his possession or control for any payments made on their price and any expenses reasonably incurred in their inspection, receipt, transportation, care and custody and may hold such goods and resell them in like manner as an aggrieved seller (Section 2—706).

§2—712. "COVER"; BUYER'S PROCUREMENT OF SUBSTITUTE GOODS

(1) After a breach within the preceding section the buyer may "cover" by making in good faith and without unreasonable delay any reasonable purchase of or contract to purchase goods in substitution for those due from the seller.

(2) The buyer may recover from the seller as damages the difference between the cost of cover and the contract price together with any incidental or consequential damages as hereinafter defined (Section 2—715), but less expenses saved in consequence of the seller's breach.

(3) Failure of the buyer to effect cover within this section does not bar him from any other remedy.

§2—713. BUYER'S DAMAGES FOR NON-DELIVERY OR REPUDIATION

(1) Subject to the provisions of this Article with respect to proof of market price (Section 2—723), the measure of damages for non-delivery or repudiation by the seller is the difference between the market price at the time when the buyer learned of the breach and the contract price together with any incidental and consequential damages provided in this Article (Section 2—715), but less expenses saved in consequence of the seller's breach.

(2) Market price is to be determined as of the place for tender or, in cases of rejection after arrival or revocation of acceptance, as of the place of arrival.

§2—714. BUYER'S DAMAGES FOR BREACH IN REGARD TO ACCEPTED GOODS

(1) Where the buyer has accepted goods and given notification (subsection (3) of Section 2—607) he may recover as damages for any non-conformity of tender the loss resulting in the ordinary course of events from the seller's breach as determined in any manner which is reasonable.

(2) The measure of damages for breach of warranty is the difference at the time and place of acceptance between the value of the goods accepted and the value they would have had if they had been as warranted, unless special circumstances show proximate damages of a different amount.

(3) In a proper case any incidental and consequential damages under the next section may also be recovered.

§2—715. BUYER'S INCIDENTAL AND CONSEQUENTIAL DAMAGES

(1) Incidental damages resulting from the seller's breach include expenses reasonably incurred in inspection, receipt, transportation and care and custody of goods rightfully rejected, any commercially reasonable charges, expenses or commissions in connection with effecting cover and any other reasonable expense incident to the delay or other breach.

(2) Consequential damages resulting from the seller's breach include

(a) any loss resulting from general or particular requirements and needs of which the seller at the time of contracting had reason to know and which could not reasonably be prevented by cover or otherwise; and

(b) injury to person or property proximately resulting from any breach of warranty.

§2—716. BUYER'S RIGHT TO SPECIFIC PERFORMANCE OR REPLEVIN

(1) Specific performance may be decreed where the goods are unique or in other proper circumstances.

(2) The decree for specific performance may include such terms and conditions as to payment of the price, damages, or other relief as the court may deem just.

(3) The buyer has a right of replevin for goods identified to the contract if after reasonable effort he is unable to effect cover for such goods or the circumstances reasonably indicate that such effort will be unavailing or if the goods have been shipped under reservation and satisfaction of the security interest in them has been made or tendered. In the case of goods bought for personal, family, or household purposes, the buyer's right of replevin vests upon acquisition of a special property, even if the seller had not then repudiated or failed to deliver.

§2—717. DEDUCTION OF DAMAGES FROM THE PRICE

The buyer on notifying the seller of his intention to do so may deduct all or any part of the damages resulting from any breach of the contract from any part of the price still due under the same contract.

§2—718. LIQUIDATION OR LIMITATION OF DAMAGES; DEPOSITS

(1) Damages for breach by either party may be liquidated in the agreement but only at an amount which is reasonable in the light of the anticipated or actual harm caused by the breach, the difficulties of proof of loss, and the inconvenience or nonfeasibility of otherwise obtaining an adequate remedy. A term fixing unreasonably large liquidated damages is void as a penalty.

(2) Where the seller justifiably withholds delivery of goods because of the buyer's breach, the buyer is entitled to restitution of any amount by which the sum of his payments exceeds

(a) the amount to which the seller is entitled by virtue of terms liquidating the seller's damages in accordance with subsection (1), or

(b) in the absence of such terms, twenty per cent of the value of the total performance for which the buyer is obligated under the contract or $500, whichever is smaller.

(3) The buyer's right to restitution under subsection (2) is subject to offset to the extent that the seller establishes

(a) a right to recover damages under the provisions of this Article other than subsection (1), and

(b) the amount or value of any benefits received by the buyer directly or indirectly by reason of the contract.

(4) Where a seller has received payment in goods their reasonable value or the proceeds of their resale shall be treated as payments for the purposes of subsection (2); but if the seller has notice of the buyer's breach before reselling goods received in part performance, his resale is subject to the conditions laid down in this Article on resale by an aggrieved seller (Section 2—706).

§2—719. CONTRACTUAL MODIFICATION OR LIMITATION OF REMEDY

(1) Subject to the provisions of subsections (2) and (3) of this section and of the preceding section on liquidation and limitation of damages,

(a) the agreement may provide for remedies in addition to or in substitution for those provided in this Article and may limit or alter the measure of damages recoverable under this Article, as by limiting the buyer's remedies to return of the goods and repayment of the price or to repair and replacement of non-conforming goods or parts; and

(b) resort to a remedy as provided is optional unless the remedy is expressly agreed to be exclusive, in which case it is the sole remedy.

(2) Where circumstances cause an exclusive or limited remedy to fail of its essential purpose, remedy may be had as provided in this Act.

(3) Consequential damages may be limited or excluded unless the limitation or exclusion is unconscionable. Limitation of consequential damages for injury to the person in the case of consumer goods is prima facie unconscionable but limitation of damages where the loss is commercial is not.

§2—720. EFFECT OF "CANCELLATION" OR "RESCISSION" ON CLAIMS FOR ANTECEDENT BREACH

Unless the contrary intention clearly appears, expressions of "cancellation" or "rescission" of the contract or the like shall not be construed as a renunciation or discharge of any claim in damages for an antecedent breach.

§2—721. REMEDIES FOR FRAUD

Remedies for material misrepresentation or fraud include all remedies available under this Article for non-fraudulent breach. Neither rescission or a claim for rescission of the contract for sale nor rejection or return of the goods shall bar or be deemed inconsistent with a claim for damages or other remedy.

§2—722. WHO CAN SUE THIRD PARTIES FOR INJURY TO GOODS

Where a third party so deals with goods which have been identified to a contract for sale as to cause actionable injury to a party to that contract

(a) a right of action against the third party is in either party to the contract for sale who has title to or a security interest or a special property or an insurable interest in the goods; and if the goods have been destroyed or converted a right of action is also in the party who either bore the risk of loss under the contract for sale or has since the injury assumed that risk as against the other;

(b) if at the time of the injury the party plaintiff did not bear the risk of loss as against the other party to the contract for sale and there is no arrangement between them for disposition of the recovery, his suit or settlement is, subject to his own interest, as a fiduciary for the other party to the contract;

(c) either party may with the consent of the other sue for the benefit of whom it may concern.

§2—723. PROOF OF MARKET PRICE: TIME AND PLACE

(1) If an action based on anticipatory repudiation comes to trial before the time for performance with respect to some or all of the goods, any damages based on market price (Section 2—708 or Section 2—713) shall be determined according to the price of such goods prevailing at the time when the aggrieved party learned of the repudiation.

(2) If evidence of a price prevailing at the times or places described in this Article is not readily available the price prevailing within any reasonable time before or after the time described or at any other place which in commercial judgment or under usage of trade would serve as a reasonable substitute for the one described may be used, making any proper allowance for the cost of transporting the goods to or from such other place.

(3) Evidence of a relevant price prevailing at a time or place other than the one described in this Article offered by one party is not admissible unless and until he has given the other party such notice as the court finds sufficient to prevent unfair surprise.

§2—724. ADMISSIBILITY OF MARKET QUOTATIONS

Whenever the prevailing price or value of any goods regularly bought and sold in any established commodity market is in issue, reports in official publications or trade journals or in newspapers or periodicals of general circulation published as the reports of such market shall be admissible in evidence. The circumstances of the preparation of such a report may be shown to affect its weight but not its admissibility.

§2—725. STATUTE OF LIMITATIONS IN CONTRACTS FOR SALE

(1) An action for breach of any contract for sale must be commenced within four years after the cause of action has accrued. By the original agreement the parties may reduce the period of limitation to not less than one year but may not extend it.

(2) A cause of action accrues when the breach occurs, regardless of the aggrieved party's lack of knowledge of the breach. A breach of warranty occurs when tender of delivery is made, except that where a warranty explicitly extends to future performance of the goods and discovery of the breach must await the time of such performance the cause of action accrues when the breach is or should have been discovered.

(3) Where an action commenced within the time limited by subsection (1) is so terminated as to leave available a remedy by another action for the same breach such other action may be commenced after the expiration of the time limited and within six months after the termination of the first action unless the termination resulted from voluntary discontinuance or from dismissal for failure or neglect to prosecute.

(4) This section does not alter the law on tolling of the statute of limitations nor does it apply to causes of action which have accrued before this Act becomes effective.

Article 2 Amendments (Excerpts)

Part 1 Short Title, General Construction and Subject Matter

* * * *

§2—103. DEFINITIONS AND INDEX OF DEFINITIONS

(1) In this article unless the context otherwise requires

* * * *

(b) "Conspicuous", with reference to a term, means so written, displayed, or presented that a reasonable person against which it is to operate ought to have noticed it. A term in an electronic record intended to evoke a response by an electronic agent is conspicuous if it is presented in a form that would enable a reasonably configured electronic agent to take it into account or react to it without review of the record by an individual. Whether a term is "conspicuous" or not is a decision for the court. Conspicuous terms include the following:

(i) for a person:

(A) a heading in capitals equal to or greater in size than the surrounding text, or in contrasting type, font, or color to the surrounding text of the same or lesser size;

(B) language in the body of a record or display in larger type than the surrounding text, or in contrasting type, font, or color to the surrounding text of the same size, or set off from surrounding text of the same size by symbols or other marks that call attention to the language; and

(ii) for a person or an electronic agent, a term that is so placed in a record or display that the person or electronic agent cannot proceed without taking action with respect to the particular term.

(c) "Consumer" means an individual who buys or contracts to buy goods that, at the time of contracting, are intended by the individual to be used primarily for personal, family, or household purposes.

(d) "Consumer contract" means a contract between a merchant seller and a consumer.

* * * *

(j) "Good faith" means honesty in fact and the observance of reasonable commercial standards of fair dealing.

(k) "Goods" means all things that are movable at the time of identification to a contract for sale. The term includes future goods, specially manufactured goods, the unborn young of animals, growing crops, and other identified things attached to realty as described in Section 2—107. The term does not include information, the money in which the price is to be paid, investment securities under Article 8, the subject matter of foreign exchange transactions, and choses in action.

* * * *

(m) "Record" means information that is inscribed on a tangible medium or that is stored in an electronic or other medium and is retrievable in perceivable form.

(n) "Remedial promise" means a promise by the seller to repair or replace the goods or to refund all or part of the price upon the happening of a specified event.

* * * *

(p) "Sign" means, with present intent to authenticate or adopt a record,

(i) to execute or adopt a tangible symbol; or

(ii) to attach to or logically associate with the record an electronic sound, symbol, or process.

* * * *

Part 2 Form, Formation, Terms and Readjustment of Contract; Electronic Contracting

§2—201. FORMAL REQUIREMENTS; STATUTE OF FRAUDS

(1) A contract for the sale of goods for the price of $5,000 or more is not enforceable by way of action or defense unless there is some record sufficient to indicate that a contract for sale has been made between the parties and signed by the party against whom which enforcement is sought or by the party's authorized agent or broker. A record is not insufficient because it omits or incorrectly states a term agreed upon but the contract is not enforceable under this subsection beyond the quantity of goods shown in the record.

(2) Between merchants if within a reasonable time a record in confirmation of the contract and sufficient against the sender is received and the party receiving it has reason to know its contents, it satisfies the requirements of subsection (1) against such party the recipient unless notice of objection to its contents is given in a record within 10 days after it is received.

(3) A contract which does not satisfy the requirements of subsection (1) but which is valid in other respects is enforceable

(a) if the goods are to be specially manufactured for the buyer and are not suitable for sale to others in the ordinary course of the seller's business and the seller, before notice of repudiation is received and under circumstances which reasonably indicate that the goods are for the buyer, has made either a substantial beginning of their manufacture or commitments for their procurement; or

(b) if the party against whom which enforcement is sought admits in the party's pleading, or in the party's testimony or otherwise under oath that a contract for sale was made, but the contract is not enforceable under this paragraph beyond the quantity of goods admitted; or

(c) with respect to goods for which payment has been made and accepted or which have been received and accepted (Sec. 2—606).

(4) A contract that is enforceable under this section is not rendered unenforceable merely because it is not capable of being performed within one year or any other applicable period after its making.

* * * *

§2—207. TERMS OF CONTRACT; EFFECT OF CONFIRMATION

If (i) conduct by both parties recognizes the existence of a contract although their records do not otherwise establish a contract, (ii) a contract is formed by an offer and acceptance, or (iii) a contract formed in any manner is confirmed by a record that contains terms additional to or different from those in the contract being confirmed, the terms of the contract, subject to Section 2—202, are:

(a) terms that appear in the records of both parties;

(b) terms, whether in a record or not, to which both parties agree; and

(c) terms supplied or incorporated under any provision of this Act.

* * * *

Part 3 General Obligation and Construction of Contract

* * * *

§2—312. WARRANTY OF TITLE AND AGAINST INFRINGEMENT; BUYER'S OBLIGATION AGAINST INFRINGEMENT

(1) Subject to subsection (2) there is in a contract for sale a warranty by the seller that

(a) the title conveyed shall be good, good and its transfer rightful and shall not, because of any colorable claim to or interest in the goods, unreasonably expose the buyer to litigation; and

(b) the goods shall be delivered free from any security interest or other lien or encumbrance of which the buyer at the time of contracting has no knowledge.

(2) Unless otherwise agreed a seller that is a merchant regularly dealing in goods of the kind warrants that the goods shall be delivered free of the rightful claim of any third person by way of infringement or the like but a buyer that furnishes specifications to the seller must hold the seller harmless against any such claim that arises out of compliance with the specifications.

(3) A warranty under this section may be disclaimed or modified only by specific language or by circumstances that give the buyer reason to know that the seller does not claim title, that the seller is purporting to sell only the right or title as the seller or a third person may have, or that the seller is selling subject to any claims of infringement or the like.

§2—313. EXPRESS WARRANTIES BY AFFIRMATION, PROMISE, DESCRIPTION, SAMPLE; REMEDIAL PROMISE

(1) In this section, "immediate buyer" means a buyer that enters into a contract with the seller.

* * * *

(4) Any remedial promise made by the seller to the immediate buyer creates an obligation that the promise will be performed upon the happening of the specified event.

§2—313A. OBLIGATION TO REMOTE PURCHASER CREATED BY RECORD PACKAGED WITH OR ACCOMPANYING GOODS

(1) This section applies only to new goods and goods sold or leased as new goods in a transaction of purchase in the normal chain of distribution. In this section:

(a) "Immediate buyer" means a buyer that enters into a contract with the seller.

(b) "Remote purchaser" means a person that buys or leases goods from an immediate buyer or other person in the normal chain of distribution.

(2) If a seller in a record packaged with or accompanying the goods makes an affirmation of fact or promise that relates to the goods, provides a description that relates to the goods, or makes a remedial promise, and the seller reasonably expects the record to be, and the record is, furnished to the remote purchaser, the seller has an obligation to the remote purchaser that:

(a) the goods will conform to the affirmation of fact, promise or description unless a reasonable person in the position of the remote purchaser would not believe that the affirmation of fact, promise or description created an obligation; and

(b) the seller will perform the remedial promise.

(3) It is not necessary to the creation of an obligation under this section that the seller use formal words such as "warrant" or "guarantee" or that the seller have a specific intention to undertake an obligation, but an affirmation merely of the value of the goods or a statement purporting to be merely the seller's opinion or commendation of the goods does not create an obligation.

(4) The following rules apply to the remedies for breach of an obligation created under this section:

(a) The seller may modify or limit the remedies available to the remote purchaser if the modification or limitation is furnished to the remote purchaser no later than the time of purchase or if the modification or limitation is contained in the record that contains the affirmation of fact, promise or description.

(b) Subject to a modification or limitation of remedy, a seller in breach is liable for incidental or consequential damages under Section 2—715, but the seller is not liable for lost profits.

(c) The remote purchaser may recover as damages for breach of a seller's obligation arising under subsection (2) the loss resulting in the ordinary course of events as determined in any manner that is reasonable.

(5) An obligation that is not a remedial promise is breached if the goods did not conform to the affirmation of fact, promise or description creating the obligation when the goods left the seller's control.

§2—313B. OBLIGATION TO REMOTE PURCHASER CREATED BY COMMUNICATION TO THE PUBLIC

(1) This section applies only to new goods and goods sold or leased as new goods in a transaction of purchase in the normal chain of distribution. In this section:

(a) "Immediate buyer" means a buyer that enters into a contract with the seller.

(b) "Remote purchaser" means a person that buys or leases goods from an immediate buyer or other person in the normal chain of distribution.

(2) If a seller in advertising or a similar communication to the public makes an affirmation of fact or promise that relates to the goods, provides a description that relates to the goods, or makes a remedial promise, and the remote purchaser enters into a transaction of purchase with knowledge of and with the expectation that the goods will conform to the affirmation of fact, promise, or description, or that the seller will perform the remedial promise, the seller has an obligation to the remote purchaser that:

(a) the goods will conform to the affirmation of fact, promise or description unless a reasonable person in the position of the remote purchaser would not believe that the affirmation of fact, promise or description created an obligation; and

(b) the seller will perform the remedial promise.

(3) It is not necessary to the creation of an obligation under this section that the seller use formal words such as "warrant" or "guarantee" or that the seller have a specific intention to undertake an obligation, but an affirmation merely of the value of the goods or a statement purporting to be merely the seller's opinion or commendation of the goods does not create an obligation.

(4) The following rules apply to the remedies for breach of an obligation created under this section:

(a) The seller may modify or limit the remedies available to the remote purchaser if the modification or limitation is furnished to the remote purchaser no later than the time of purchase. The modification or limitation may be furnished as part of the communication that contains the affirmation of fact, promise or description.

(b) Subject to a modification or limitation of remedy, a seller in breach is liable for incidental or consequential damages under Section 2—715, but the seller is not liable for lost profits.

(c) The remote purchaser may recover as damages for breach of a seller's obligation arising under subsection (2) the loss resulting in the ordinary course of events as determined in any manner that is reasonable.

(5) An obligation that is not a remedial promise is breached if the goods did not conform to the affirmation of fact, promise or description creating the obligation when the goods left the seller's control.

* * * *

§2—316. EXCLUSION OR MODIFICATION OF WARRANTIES.

* * * *

(2) Subject to subsection (3), to exclude or modify the implied warranty of merchantability or any part of it in a consumer contract the language must be in a record, be conspicuous and state "The seller undertakes no responsibility for the quality of the goods except as otherwise provided in this contract," and in any other contract the language must mention merchantability and in case of a record must be conspicuous. Subject to subsection (3), to exclude or modify the implied warranty of fitness the exclusion must be in a record and be conspicuous. Language to exclude all implied warranties of fitness in a consumer contract must state "The seller assumes no responsibility that the goods will be fit for any particular purpose for which you may be buying these goods, except as otherwise provided in the contract," and in any other contract the language is sufficient if it states, for example, that "There are no warranties which extend beyond the description on the face hereof." Language that satisfies the requirements of this subsection for the exclusion and modification of a warranty in a consumer contract also satisfies the requirements for any other contract.

(3) Notwithstanding subsection (2):

(a) unless the circumstances indicate otherwise, all implied warranties are excluded by expressions like "as is", "with all faults" or other language which in common understanding calls the buyer's attention to the exclusion of warranties, makes plain that there is no implied warranty, and in a consumer contract evidenced by a record is set forth conspicuously in the record; and

(b) when the buyer before entering into the contract has examined the goods or the sample or model as fully as desired or has refused to examine the goods after a demand by the seller there is no implied warranty with regard to defects which an examination ought in the circumstances to have revealed to the buyer; and

(c) an implied warranty can also be excluded or modified by course of dealing or course of performance or usage of trade.

* * * *

§2—318. THIRD PARTY BENEFICIARIES OF WARRANTIES EXPRESS OR IMPLIED

(1) In this section:

(a) "Immediate buyer" means a buyer that enters into a contract with the seller.

(b) "Remote purchaser" means a person that buys or leases goods from an immediate buyer or other person in the normal chain of distribution.

Alternative A to subsection (2)

(2) A seller's warranty whether express or implied to an immediate buyer, a seller's remedial promise to an immediate buyer, or a seller's obligation to a remote purchaser under Section 2—313A or 2—313B extends to any natural person who is in the family or household of the immediate buyer or the remote purchaser or who is a guest in the home of either if it is reasonable to expect that the person may use, consume or be affected by the goods and who is injured in person by breach of the warranty, remedial promise or obligation. A seller may not exclude or limit the operation of this section.

Alternative B to subsection (2)

(2) A seller's warranty whether express or implied to an immediate buyer, a seller's remedial promise to an immediate buyer, or a seller's obligation to a remote purchaser under Section 2—313A or 2—313B extends to any natural person who may reasonably be expected to use, consume or be affected by the goods and who is injured in person by breach of the warranty, remedial promise or obligation. A seller may not exclude or limit the operation of this section.

Alternative C to subsection (2)

(2) A seller's warranty whether express or implied to an immediate buyer, a seller's remedial promise to an immediate buyer, or a seller's obligation to a remote purchaser under Section 2—313A or 2—313B extends to any person that may reasonably be expected to use, consume or be affected by the goods and that is injured by breach of the warranty, remedial promise or obligation. A seller may not exclude or limit the operation of this section with respect to injury to the person of an individual to whom the warranty, remedial promise or obligation extends.

* * * *

Part 5 Performance

* * * *

§2—502. BUYER'S RIGHT TO GOODS ON SELLER'S INSOLVENCY

(1) Subject to subsections (2) and (3) and even though the goods have not been shipped a buyer who that has paid a part or all of the price of goods in which the buyer has a special property under the provisions of the immediately preceding section may on making and keeping good a tender of any unpaid portion of their price recover them from the seller if:

(a) in the case of goods bought by a consumer, the seller repudiates or fails to deliver as required by the contract; or

(b) in all cases, the seller becomes insolvent within ten days after receipt of the first installment on their price.

(2) The buyer's right to recover the goods under subsection (1) vests upon acquisition of a special property, even if the seller had not then repudiated or failed to deliver.

(3) If the identification creating the special property has been made by the buyer, the buyer acquires the right to recover the goods only if they conform to the contract for sale.

* * * *

§2—508. CURE BY SELLER OF IMPROPER TENDER OR DELIVERY; REPLACEMENT

(1) Where the buyer rejects goods or a tender of delivery under Section 2—601 or 2—612 or except in a consumer contract justifiably revokes acceptance under Section 2—608(1)(b) and the agreed time for performance has not expired, a seller that has performed in good faith, upon seasonable notice to the buyer and at the seller's own expense, may cure the breach of contract by making a conforming tender of delivery within the agreed time. The seller shall compensate the buyer for all of the buyer's reasonable expenses caused by the seller's breach of contract and subsequent cure.

(2) Where the buyer rejects goods or a tender of delivery under Section 2—601 or 2—612 or except in a consumer contract justifiably revokes acceptance under Section 2—608(1)(b) and the agreed time for performance has expired, a seller that has performed in good faith, upon seasonable notice to the buyer and at the seller's own expense, may cure the breach of contract, if the cure is appropriate and timely under the

circumstances, by making a tender of conforming goods. The seller shall compensate the buyer for all of the buyer's reasonable expenses caused by the seller's breach of contract and subsequent cure.

§2—509. RISK OF LOSS IN THE ABSENCE OF BREACH

(1) Where the contract requires or authorizes the seller to ship the goods by carrier

(a) if it does not require the seller to deliver them at a particular destination, the risk of loss passes to the buyer when the goods are delivered to the carrier even though the shipment is under reservation (Section 2—505); but

(b) if it does require the seller to deliver them at a particular destination and the goods are there tendered while in the possession of the carrier, the risk of loss passes to the buyer when the goods are there so tendered as to enable the buyer to take delivery.

(2) Where the goods are held by a bailee to be delivered without being moved, the risk of loss passes to the buyer

(a) on the buyer's receipt of a negotiable document of title covering the goods; or

(b) on acknowledgment by the bailee to the buyer of the buyer's right to possession of the goods; or

(c) after the buyer's receipt of a non-negotiable document of title or other direction to deliver in a record, as provided in subsection (4)(b) of Section 2—503.

(3) In any case not within subsection (1) or (2), the risk of loss passes to the buyer on the buyer's receipt of the goods.

* * * *

§2—513. BUYER'S RIGHT TO INSPECTION OF GOODS

* * * *

(3) Unless otherwise agreed, the buyer is not entitled to inspect the goods before payment of the price when the contract provides

(a) for delivery on terms that under applicable course of performance, course of dealing, or usage of trade are interpreted to preclude inspection before payment; or

(b) for payment against documents of title, except where such payment is due only after the goods are to become available for inspection.

* * * *

Part 6 Breach, Repudiation and Excuse

* * * *

§2—605. WAIVER OF BUYER'S OBJECTIONS BY FAILURE TO PARTICULARIZE

(1) The buyer's failure to state in connection with rejection a particular defect or in connection with revocation of acceptance a defect that justifies revocation precludes the buyer from relying on the unstated defect to justify rejection or revocation of acceptance if the defect is ascertainable by reasonable inspection

(a) where the seller had a right to cure the defect and could have cured it if stated seasonably; or

(b) between merchants when the seller has after rejection made a request in a record for a full and final statement in record form of all defects on which the buyer proposes to rely.

(2) A buyer's payment against documents tendered to the buyer made without reservation of rights precludes recovery of the payment for defects apparent on the face of the documents.

* * * *

§2—607. EFFECT OF ACCEPTANCE; NOTICE OF BREACH; BURDEN OF ESTABLISHING BREACH AFTER ACCEPTANCE; NOTICE OF CLAIM OR LITIGATION TO PERSON ANSWERABLE OVER

* * * *

(3) Where a tender has been accepted

(a) the buyer must within a reasonable time after the buyer discovers or should have discovered any breach notify the seller; however, failure to give timely notice bars the buyer from a remedy only to the extent that the seller is prejudiced by the failure and

(b) if the claim is one for infringement or the like (subsection (3) of Section 2—312) and the buyer is sued as a result of such a breach the buyer must so notify the seller within a reasonable time after the buyer receives notice of the litigation or be barred from any remedy over for liability established by the litigation.

* * * *

§2—608. REVOCATION OF ACCEPTANCE IN WHOLE OR IN PART

* * * *

(4) If a buyer uses the goods after a rightful rejection or justifiable revocation of acceptance, the following rules apply:

(a) Any use by the buyer that is unreasonable under the circumstances is wrongful as against the seller and is an acceptance only if ratified by the seller.

(b) Any use of the goods that is reasonable under the circumstances is not wrongful as against the seller and is not an acceptance, but in an appropriate case the buyer shall be obligated to the seller for the value of the use to the buyer.

* * * *

§2—612. "INSTALLMENT CONTRACT"; BREACH

* * * *

(2) The buyer may reject any installment which is non-conforming if the non-conformity substantially impairs the value of that installment to the buyer or if the non-conformity is a defect in the required documents; but if the non-conformity does not fall within subsection (3) and the seller gives adequate assurance of its cure the buyer must accept that installment.

(3) Whenever non-conformity or default with respect to one or more installments substantially impairs the value of the whole contract there is a breach of the whole. But the aggrieved party reinstates the contract if the party accepts a non-conforming installment without seasonably notifying of cancellation or if the party brings an action with respect only to past installments or demands performance as to future installments.

* * * *

Part 7 Remedies

§2—702. SELLER'S REMEDIES ON DISCOVERY OF BUYER'S INSOLVENCY

* * * *

(2) Where the seller discovers that the buyer has received goods on credit while insolvent the seller may reclaim the goods upon demand made within a reasonable time after the buyer's receipt of the goods. Except as provided in this subsection the seller may not base a right to reclaim goods on the buyer's fraudulent or innocent misrepresentation of solvency or of intent to pay.

* * * *

§2—705. SELLER'S STOPPAGE OF DELIVERY IN TRANSIT OR OTHERWISE

(1) The seller may stop delivery of goods in the possession of a carrier or other bailee when the seller discovers the buyer to be insolvent (Section 2—702) or when the buyer repudiates or fails to make a payment due before delivery or if for any other reason the seller has a right to withhold or reclaim the goods.

* * * *

§2—706. SELLER'S RESALE INCLUDING CONTRACT FOR RESALE

In an appropriate case involving breach by the buyer, the seller may resell the goods concerned or the undelivered balance thereof. Where the resale is made in good faith and in a commercially reasonable manner the seller may recover the difference between the contract price and the resale price together with any incidental or consequential damages allowed under the provisions of this Article (Section 2—710), but less expenses saved in consequence of the buyer's breach.

* * * *

§2—708. SELLER'S DAMAGES FOR NON-ACCEPTANCE OR REPUDIATION

(1) Subject to subsection (2) and to the provisions of this Article with respect to proof of market price (Section 2—723)

(a) the measure of damages for non-acceptance by the buyer is the difference between the contract price and the market price at the time and place for tender together with any incidental or consequential damages provided in this Article (Section 2—710), but less expenses saved in consequence of the buyer's breach; and

(b) the measure of damages for repudiation by the buyer is the difference between the contract price and the market price at the place for tender at the expiration of a commercially reasonable time after the seller learned of the repudiation, but no later than the time stated in paragraph (a), together with any incidental or consequential damages provided in this Article (Section 2—710), but less expenses saved in consequence of the buyer's breach.

(2) If the measure of damages provided in subsection (1) or in Section 2—706 is inadequate to put the seller in as good a position as performance would have done then the measure of damages is the profit (including reasonable overhead) which the seller would have made from full performance by the buyer, together with any incidental or consequential damages provided in this Article (Section 2—710).

§2—709. ACTION FOR THE PRICE

(1) When the buyer fails to pay the price as it becomes due the seller may recover, together with any incidental or consequential damages under the next section, the price

(a) of goods accepted or of conforming goods lost or damaged within a commercially reasonable time after risk of their loss has passed to the buyer; and

(b) of goods identified to the contract if the seller is unable after reasonable effort to resell them at a reasonable price or the circumstances reasonably indicate that such effort will be unavailing.

* * * *

§2—710. SELLER'S INCIDENTAL AND CONSEQUENTIAL DAMAGES

(1) Incidental damages to an aggrieved seller include any commercially reasonable charges, expenses or commissions incurred in stopping delivery, in the transportation, care and custody of goods after the buyer's breach, in connection with return or resale of the goods or otherwise resulting from the breach.

(2) Consequential damages resulting from the buyer's breach include any loss resulting from general or particular requirements and needs of which the buyer at the time of contracting had reason to know and which could not reasonably be prevented by resale or otherwise.

(3) In a consumer contract, a seller may not recover consequential damages from a consumer.

* * * *

§2—713. BUYER'S DAMAGES FOR NON-DELIVERY OR REPUDIATION

(1) Subject to the provisions of this Article with respect to proof of market price (Section 2—723), if the seller wrongfully fails to deliver or repudiates or the buyer rightfully rejects or justifiably revokes acceptance

(a) the measure of damages in the case of wrongful failure to deliver by the seller or rightful rejection or justifiable revocation of acceptance by the buyer is the difference between the market price at the time for tender under the contract and the contract price together with any incidental or consequential damages provided in this Article (Section 2—715), but less expenses saved in consequence of the seller's breach; and

(b) the measure of damages for repudiation by the seller is the difference between the market price at the expiration of a commercially reasonable time after the buyer learned of the repudiation, but no later than the time stated in paragraph (a), and the contract price together with any incidental or consequential damages provided in this Article (Section 2—715), but less expenses saved in consequence of the seller's breach.

* * * *

§2—725. STATUTE OF LIMITATIONS IN CONTRACTS FOR SALE

(1) Except as otherwise provided in this section, an action for breach of any contract for sale must be commenced within the later of four years after the right of action has accrued under subsection (2) or (3) or one year after the breach was or should have been discovered, but no longer than five years after the right of action accrued. By the original agreement the parties may reduce the period of limitation to not less than one year but may not extend it; however, in a consumer contract, the period of limitation may not be reduced.

(2) Except as otherwise provided in subsection (3), the following rules apply:

(a) Except as otherwise provided in this subsection, a right of action for breach of a contract accrues when the breach occurs, even if the aggrieved party did not have knowledge of the breach.

(b) For breach of a contract by repudiation, a right of action accrues at the earlier of when the aggrieved party elects to treat the repudiation as a breach or when a commercially reasonable time for awaiting performance has expired.

* * * *

Article 2A Leases

§2A—102. SCOPE

This Article applies to any transaction, regardless of form, that creates a lease.

§2A—103. DEFINITIONS AND INDEX OF DEFINITIONS

* * * *

(e) "Consumer lease" means a lease that a lessor regularly engaged in the business of leasing or selling makes to a lessee who is an individual and who takes under the lease primarily for a personal, family, or household purpose [, if the total payments to be made under the lease contract, excluding payments for options to renew or buy, do not exceed $___].

* * * *

(g) "Finance lease" means a lease with respect to which:

(i) the lessor does not select, manufacture or supply the goods;

(ii) the lessor acquires the goods or the right to possession and use of the goods in connection with the lease; and

(iii) one of the following occurs:

(A) the lessee receives a copy of the contract by which the lessor acquired the goods or the right to possession and use of the goods before signing the lease contract;

(B) the lessee's approval of the contract by which the lessor acquired the goods or the right to possession and use of the goods is a condition to effectiveness of the lease contract;

(C) the lessee, before signing the lease contract, receives an accurate and complete statement designating the promises and warranties, and any disclaimers of warranties, limitations or modifications of remedies, or liquidated damages, including those of a third party, such as the manufacturer of the goods, provided to the lessor by the person supplying the goods in connection with or as part of the contract by which the lessor acquired the goods or the right to possession and use of the goods; or

(D) if the lease is not a consumer lease, the lessor, before the lessee signs the lease contract, informs the lessee in writing (a) of the identity of the person supplying the goods to the lessor, unless the lessee has selected that person and directed the lessor to acquire the goods or the right to possession and use of the goods from that person, (b) that the lessee is entitled under this Article to any promises and warranties, including those of any third party, provided to the lessor by the person supplying the goods in connection with or as part of the contract by which the lessor acquired the goods or the right to possession and use of the goods, and (c) that the lessee may communicate with the person supplying the goods to the lessor and receive an accurate and complete statement of those promises and warranties, including any disclaimers and limitations of them or of remedies.

* * * *

(h) "Goods" means all things that are movable at the time of identification to the lease contract, or are fixtures (Section 2A—309), but the term does not include money, documents, instruments, accounts, chattel paper, general intangibles, or minerals or the like, including oil and gas, before extraction. The term also includes the unborn young of animals.

(i) "Installment lease contract" means a lease contract that authorizes or requires the delivery of goods in separate lots to be separately accepted, even though the lease contract contains a clause "each delivery is a separate lease" or its equivalent.

(j) "Lease" means a transfer of the right to possession and use of goods for a term in return for consideration, but a sale, including a sale on approval or a sale or return, or retention or creation of a security interest is not a lease. Unless the context clearly indicates otherwise, the term includes a sublease.

(k) "Lease agreement" means the bargain, with respect to the lease, of the lessor and the lessee in fact as found in their language or by implication from other circumstances including course of dealing or usage of trade or course of performance as provided in this Article. Unless the context clearly indicates otherwise, the term includes a sublease agreement.

(l) "Lease contract" means the total legal obligation that results from the lease agreement as affected by this Article and any other applicable rules of law. Unless the context clearly indicates otherwise, the term includes a sublease contract.

* * * *

(o) "Lessee in ordinary course of business" means a person who in good faith and without knowledge that the lease to him [or her] is in violation of the ownership rights or security interest or leasehold interest of a third party in the goods, leases in ordinary course from a person in the business of selling or leasing goods of that kind but does not include a pawnbroker. "Leasing" may be for cash or by exchange of other property or on secured or unsecured credit and includes receiving goods or documents of title under a pre-existing lease contract but does not include a transfer in bulk or as security for or in total or partial satisfaction of a money debt.

(p) "Lessor" means a person who transfers the right to possession and use of goods under a lease. Unless the context clearly indicates otherwise, the term includes a sublessor.

(q) "Lessor's residual interest" means the lessor's interest in the goods after expiration, termination, or cancellation of the lease contract.

* * * *

§2A—104. LEASES SUBJECT TO OTHER LAW

(1) A lease, although subject to this Article, is also subject to any applicable:

(a) certificate of title statute of this State: (list any certificate of title statutes covering automobiles, trailers, mobile homes, boats, farm tractors, and the like);

(b) certificate of title statute of another jurisdiction (Section 2A—105); or

(c) consumer protection statute of this State, or final consumer protection decision of a court of this State existing on the effective date of this Article.

§2A—105. TERRITORIAL APPLICATION OF ARTICLE TO GOODS COVERED BY CERTIFICATE OF TITLE

Subject to the provisions of Sections 2A—304(3) and 2A—305(3), with respect to goods covered by a certificate of title issued under a statute of this State or of another jurisdiction, compliance and the effect of compliance or noncompliance with a certificate of title statute are governed by the law (including the conflict of laws rules) of the jurisdiction issuing the certificate until the earlier of (a) surrender of the certificate, or (b) four months after the goods are removed from that jurisdiction and thereafter until a new certificate of title is issued by another jurisdiction.

* * * *

§2A—108. UNCONSCIONABILITY

(1) If the court as a matter of law finds a lease contract or any clause of a lease contract to have been unconscionable at the time it was made the court may refuse to enforce the lease contract, or it may enforce the remainder of the lease contract without the unconscionable clause, or it may so limit the application of any unconscionable clause as to avoid any unconscionable result.

(2) With respect to a consumer lease, if the court as a matter of law finds that a lease contract or any clause of a lease contract has been induced by unconscionable conduct or that unconscionable conduct has occurred in the collection of a claim arising from a lease contract, the court may grant appropriate relief.

(3) Before making a finding of unconscionability under subsection (1) or (2), the court, on its own motion or that of a party, shall afford the parties a reasonable opportunity to present evidence as to the setting, purpose, and effect of the lease contract or clause thereof, or of the conduct.

(4) In an action in which the lessee claims unconscionability with respect to a consumer lease:

(a) If the court finds unconscionability under subsection (1) or (2), the court shall award reasonable attorney's fees to the lessee.

(b) If the court does not find unconscionability and the lessee claiming unconscionability has brought or maintained an action he [or she] knew to be groundless, the court shall award reasonable attorney's fees to the party against whom the claim is made.

(c) In determining attorney's fees, the amount of the recovery on behalf of the claimant under subsections (1) and (2) is not controlling.

§2A—109. OPTION TO ACCELERATE AT WILL

(1) A term providing that one party or his [or her] successor in interest may accelerate payment or performance or require collateral or additional collateral "at will" or "when he [or she] deems himself [or herself] insecure" or in words of similar import must be construed to mean that he [or she] has power to do so only if he [or she] in good faith believes that the prospect of payment or performance is impaired.

(2) With respect to a consumer lease, the burden of establishing good faith under subsection (1) is on the party who exercised the power; otherwise the burden of establishing lack of good faith is on the party against whom the power has been exercised.

Part 2 Formation and Construction of Lease Contract

§2A—201. STATUTE OF FRAUDS

(1) A lease contract is not enforceable by way of action or defense unless:

(a) the total payments to be made under the lease contract, excluding payments for options to renew or buy, are less than $1,000; or

(b) there is a writing, signed by the party against whom enforcement is sought or by that party's authorized agent, sufficient to indicate that a lease contract has been made between the parties and to describe the goods leased and the lease term.

(2) Any description of leased goods or of the lease term is sufficient and satisfies subsection (1)(b), whether or not it is specific, if it reasonably identifies what is described.

(3) A writing is not insufficient because it omits or incorrectly states a term agreed upon, but the lease

contract is not enforceable under subsection (1)(b) beyond the lease term and the quantity of goods shown in the writing.

(4) A lease contract that does not satisfy the requirements of subsection (1), but which is valid in other respects, is enforceable:

(a) if the goods are to be specially manufactured or obtained for the lessee and are not suitable for lease or sale to others in the ordinary course of the lessor's business, and the lessor, before notice of repudiation is received and under circumstances that reasonably indicate that the goods are for the lessee, has made either a substantial beginning of their manufacture or commitments for their procurement;

(b) if the party against whom enforcement is sought admits in that party's pleading, testimony or otherwise in court that a lease contract was made, but the lease contract is not enforceable under this provision beyond the quantity of goods admitted; or

(c) with respect to goods that have been received and accepted by the lessee.

(5) The lease term under a lease contract referred to in subsection (4) is:

(a) if there is a writing signed by the party against whom enforcement is sought or by that party's authorized agent specifying the lease term, the term so specified;

(b) if the party against whom enforcement is sought admits in that party's pleading, testimony, or otherwise in court a lease term, the term so admitted; or

(c) a reasonable lease term.

§2A—202. FINAL WRITTEN EXPRESSION: PAROL OR EXTRINSIC EVIDENCE

Terms with respect to which the confirmatory memoranda of the parties agree or which are otherwise set forth in a writing intended by the parties as a final expression of their agreement with respect to such terms as are included therein may not be contradicted by evidence of any prior agreement or of a contemporaneous oral agreement but may be explained or supplemented:

(a) by course of dealing or usage of trade or by course of performance; and

(b) by evidence of consistent additional terms unless the court finds the writing to have been intended also as a complete and exclusive statement of the terms of the agreement.

* * * *

§2A—205. FIRM OFFERS

An offer by a merchant to lease goods to or from another person in a signed writing that by its terms gives assurance it will be held open is not revocable, for lack of consideration, during the time stated or, if no time is stated, for a reasonable time, but in no event may the period of irrevocability exceed 3 months. Any such term of assurance on a form supplied by the offeree must be separately signed by the offeror.

§2A—206. OFFER AND ACCEPTANCE IN FORMATION OF LEASE CONTRACT

(1) Unless otherwise unambiguously indicated by the language or circumstances, an offer to make a lease contract must be construed as inviting acceptance in any manner and by any medium reasonable in the circumstances.

(2) If the beginning of a requested performance is a reasonable mode of acceptance, an offeror who is not notified of acceptance within a reasonable time may treat the offer as having lapsed before acceptance.

§2A—207. COURSE OF PERFORMANCE OR PRACTICAL CONSTRUCTION

(1) If a lease contract involves repeated occasions for performance by either party with knowledge of the nature of the performance and opportunity for objection to it by the other, any course of performance accepted or acquiesced in without objection is relevant to determine the meaning of the lease agreement.

(2) The express terms of a lease agreement and any course of performance, as well as any course of dealing and usage of trade, must be construed whenever reasonable as consistent with each other; but if that construction is unreasonable, express terms control course of performance, course of performance controls both course of dealing and usage of trade, and course of dealing controls usage of trade.

(3) Subject to the provisions of Section 2A—208 on modification and waiver, course of performance is relevant to show a waiver or modification of any term inconsistent with the course of performance.

§2A—208. MODIFICATION, RESCISSION AND WAIVER

(1) An agreement modifying a lease contract needs no consideration to be binding.

(2) A signed lease agreement that excludes modification or rescission except by a signed writing may not be otherwise modified or rescinded, but, except as between merchants, such a requirement on a form supplied by a merchant must be separately signed by the other party.

(3) Although an attempt at modification or rescission does not satisfy the requirements of subsection (2), it may operate as a waiver.

(4) A party who has made a waiver affecting an executory portion of a lease contract may retract the waiver by reasonable notification received by the other party that strict performance will be required of any term waived, unless the retraction would be unjust in view of a material change of position in reliance on the waiver.

* * * *

§2A—216. THIRD-PARTY BENEFICIARIES OF EXPRESS AND IMPLIED WARRANTIES

Alternative A

A warranty to or for the benefit of a lessee under this Article, whether express or implied, extends to any natural person who is in the family or household of the lessee or who is a guest in the lessee's home if it is reasonable to expect that such person may use, consume, or be affected by the goods and who is injured in person by breach of the warranty. This section does not displace principles of law and equity that extend a warranty to or for the benefit of a lessee to other persons. The operation of this section may not be excluded, modified, or limited, but an exclusion, modification, or limitation of the warranty, including any with respect to rights and remedies, effective against the lessee is also effective against any beneficiary designated under this section.

Alternative B

A warranty to or for the benefit of a lessee under this Article, whether express or implied, extends to any natural person who may reasonably be expected to use, consume, or be affected by the goods and who is injured in person by breach of the warranty. This section does not displace principles of law and equity that extend a warranty to or for the benefit of a lessee to other persons. The operation of this section may not be excluded, modified, or limited, but an exclusion, modification, or limitation of the warranty, including any with respect to rights and remedies, effective against the lessee is also effective against the beneficiary designated under this section.

Alternative C

A warranty to or for the benefit of a lessee under this Article, whether express or implied, extends to any person who may reasonably be expected to use, consume, or be affected by the goods and who is injured by breach of the warranty. The operation of this section may not be excluded, modified, or limited with respect to injury to the person of an individual to whom the warranty extends, but an exclusion, modification, or limitation of the warranty, including any with respect to rights and remedies, effective against the lessee is also effective against the beneficiary designated under this section.

* * * *

§2A—219. RISK OF LOSS

(1) Except in the case of a finance lease, risk of loss is retained by the lessor and does not pass to the lessee. In the case of a finance lease, risk of loss passes to the lessee.

(2) Subject to the provisions of this Article on the effect of default on risk of loss (Section 2A—220), if risk of loss is to pass to the lessee and the time of passage is not stated, the following rules apply:

(a) If the lease contract requires or authorizes the goods to be shipped by carrier

(i) and it does not require delivery at a particular destination, the risk of loss passes to the lessee when the goods are duly delivered to the carrier; but

(ii) if it does require delivery at a particular destination and the goods are there duly tendered while in the possession of the carrier, the risk of loss passes to the lessee when the goods are there duly so tendered as to enable the lessee to take delivery.

(b) If the goods are held by a bailee to be delivered without being moved, the risk of loss passes to the lessee on acknowledgment by the bailee of the lessee's right to possession of the goods.

(c) In any case not within subsection (a) or (b), the risk of loss passes to the lessee on the lessee's receipt of the goods if the lessor, or, in the case of a finance lease, the supplier, is a merchant; otherwise the risk passes to the lessee on tender of delivery.

§2A—220. EFFECT OF DEFAULT ON RISK OF LOSS

(1) Where risk of loss is to pass to the lessee and the time of passage is not stated:

(a) If a tender or delivery of goods so fails to conform to the lease contract as to give a right of rejection, the risk of their loss remains with the lessor, or, in the case of a finance lease, the supplier, until cure or acceptance.

(b) If the lessee rightfully revokes acceptance, he [or she], to the extent of any deficiency in his [or her] effective insurance coverage, may treat the risk of loss as having remained with the lessor from the beginning.

(2) Whether or not risk of loss is to pass to the lessee, if the lessee as to conforming goods already identified to a lease contract repudiates or is otherwise in default under the lease contract, the lessor, or, in the case of a finance lease, the supplier, to the extent of any deficiency in his [or her] effective insurance coverage may treat the risk of loss as resting on the lessee for a commercially reasonable time.

* * * *

§2A—304. SUBSEQUENT LEASE OF GOODS BY LESSOR

(1) Subject to Section 2A—303, a subsequent lessee from a lessor of goods under an existing lease contract obtains, to the extent of the leasehold interest transferred, the leasehold interest in the goods that the lessor had or had power to transfer, and except as provided in subsection (2) and Section 2A—527(4), takes subject to the existing lease contract. A lessor with voidable title has power to transfer a good leasehold interest to a good faith subsequent lessee for value, but only to the extent set forth in the preceding sentence. If goods have been delivered under a transaction of purchase the lessor has that power even though:

(a) the lessor's transferor was deceived as to the identity of the lessor;

(b) the delivery was in exchange for a check which is later dishonored;

(c) it was agreed that the transaction was to be a "cash sale"; or

(d) the delivery was procured through fraud punishable as larcenous under the criminal law.

(2) A subsequent lessee in the ordinary course of business from a lessor who is a merchant dealing in goods of that kind to whom the goods were entrusted by the existing lessee of that lessor before the interest of the subsequent lessee became enforceable against that lessor obtains, to the extent of the leasehold interest transferred, all of that lessor's and the existing lessee's rights to the goods, and takes free of the existing lease contract.

(3) A subsequent lessee from the lessor of goods that are subject to an existing lease contract and are covered by a certificate of title issued under a statute of this State or of another jurisdiction takes no greater rights than those provided both by this section and by the certificate of title statute.

§2A—305. SALE OR SUBLEASE OF GOODS BY LESSEE

(1) Subject to the provisions of Section 2A—303, a buyer or sublessee from the lessee of goods under an existing lease contract obtains, to the extent of the interest transferred, the leasehold interest in the goods that the lessee had or had power to transfer, and except as provided in subsection (2) and Section 2A—511(4), takes subject to the existing lease contract. A lessee with a voidable leasehold interest has power to transfer a good leasehold interest to a good faith buyer for value or a good faith sublessee for value, but only to the extent set forth in the preceding sentence. When goods have been delivered under a transaction of lease the lessee has that power even though:

(a) the lessor was deceived as to the identity of the lessee;

(b) the delivery was in exchange for a check which is later dishonored; or

(c) the delivery was procured through fraud punishable as larcenous under the criminal law.

(2) A buyer in the ordinary course of business or a sublessee in the ordinary course of business from a lessee who is a merchant dealing in goods of that kind to whom the goods were entrusted by the lessor obtains, to the extent of the interest transferred, all of the lessor's and lessee's rights to the goods, and takes free of the existing lease contract.

(3) A buyer or sublessee from the lessee of goods that are subject to an existing lease contract and are covered by a certificate of title issued under a statute of this State or of another jurisdiction takes no greater rights than those provided both by this section and by the certificate of title statute.

* * * *

§2A—501. DEFAULT: PROCEDURE

(1) Whether the lessor or the lessee is in default under a lease contract is determined by the lease agreement and this Article.

(2) If the lessor or the lessee is in default under the lease contract, the party seeking enforcement has rights and remedies as provided in this Article and, except as limited by this Article, as provided in the lease agreement.

(3) If the lessor or the lessee is in default under the lease contract, the party seeking enforcement may reduce the party's claim to judgment, or otherwise enforce the lease contract by self-help or any available judicial procedure or nonjudicial procedure, including administrative proceeding, arbitration, or the like, in accordance with this Article.

(4) Except as otherwise provided in Section 1—106 (1) or this Article or the lease agreement, the rights and remedies referred to in subsections (2) and (3) are cumulative.

(5) If the lease agreement covers both real property and goods, the party seeking enforcement may proceed under this Part as to the goods, or under other applicable law as to both the real property and the goods in accordance with that party's rights and remedies in respect of the real property, in which case this Part does not apply.

§2A—502. NOTICE AFTER DEFAULT

Except as otherwise provided in this Article or the lease agreement, the lessor or lessee in default under the lease contract is not entitled to notice of default or notice of enforcement from the other party to the lease agreement.

§2A—503. MODIFICATION OR IMPAIRMENT OF RIGHTS AND REMEDIES

(1) Except as otherwise provided in this Article, the lease agreement may include rights and remedies for default in addition to or in substitution for those provided in this Article and may limit or alter the measure of damages recoverable under this Article.

(2) Resort to a remedy provided under this Article or in the lease agreement is optional unless the remedy is expressly agreed to be exclusive. If circumstances cause an exclusive or limited remedy to fail of its essential purpose, or provision for an exclusive remedy is unconscionable, remedy may be had as provided in this Article.

(3) Consequential damages may be liquidated under Section 2A—504, or may otherwise be limited, altered, or excluded unless the limitation, alteration, or exclusion is unconscionable. Limitation, alteration, or exclusion of consequential damages for injury to the person in the case of consumer goods is prima facie unconscionable but limitation, alteration, or exclusion of damages where the loss is commercial is not prima facie unconscionable.

(4) Rights and remedies on default by the lessor or the lessee with respect to any obligation or promise collateral or ancillary to the lease contract are not impaired by this Article.

As amended in 1990.

§2A—504. LIQUIDATION OF DAMAGES

(1) Damages payable by either party for default, or any other act or omission, including indemnity for loss or diminution of anticipated tax benefits or loss or damage to lessor's residual interest, may be liquidated in the lease agreement but only at an amount or by a formula that is reasonable in light of the then anticipated harm caused by the default or other act or omission.

(2) If the lease agreement provides for liquidation of damages, and such provision does not comply with subsection (1), or such provision is an exclusive or limited remedy that circumstances cause to fail of its essential purpose, remedy may be had as provided in this Article.

(3) If the lessor justifiably withholds or stops delivery of goods because of the lessee's default or insolvency (Section 2A—525 or 2A—526), the lessee is entitled to restitution of any amount by which the sum of his [or her] payments exceeds:

(a) the amount to which the lessor is entitled by virtue of terms liquidating the lessor's damages in accordance with subsection (1); or

(b) in the absence of those terms, 20 percent of the then present value of the total rent the lessee was obligated to pay for the balance of the lease term, or, in the case of a consumer lease, the lesser of such amount or $500.

(4) A lessee's right to restitution under subsection (3) is subject to offset to the extent the lessor establishes:

(a) a right to recover damages under the provisions of this Article other than subsection (1); and

(b) the amount or value of any benefits received by the lessee directly or indirectly by reason of the lease contract.

§2A—505. CANCELLATION AND TERMINATION AND EFFECT OF CANCELLATION, TERMINATION, RESCISSION, OR FRAUD ON RIGHTS AND REMEDIES

(1) On cancellation of the lease contract, all obligations that are still executory on both sides are discharged, but any right based on prior default or performance

survives, and the cancelling party also retains any remedy for default of the whole lease contract or any unperformed balance.

(2) On termination of the lease contract, all obligations that are still executory on both sides are discharged but any right based on prior default or performance survives.

(3) Unless the contrary intention clearly appears, expressions of "cancellation," "rescission," or the like of the lease contract may not be construed as a renunciation or discharge of any claim in damages for an antecedent default.

(4) Rights and remedies for material misrepresentation or fraud include all rights and remedies available under this Article for default.

(5) Neither rescission nor a claim for rescission of the lease contract nor rejection or return of the goods may bar or be deemed inconsistent with a claim for damages or other right or remedy.

§2A—506. STATUTE OF LIMITATIONS

(1) An action for default under a lease contract, including breach of warranty or indemnity, must be commenced within 4 years after the cause of action accrued. By the original lease contract the parties may reduce the period of limitation to not less than one year.

(2) A cause of action for default accrues when the act or omission on which the default or breach of warranty is based is or should have been discovered by the aggrieved party, or when the default occurs, whichever is later. A cause of action for indemnity accrues when the act or omission on which the claim for indemnity is based is or should have been discovered by the indemnified party, whichever is later.

(3) If an action commenced within the time limited by subsection (1) is so terminated as to leave available a remedy by another action for the same default or breach of warranty or indemnity, the other action may be commenced after the expiration of the time limited and within 6 months after the termination of the first action unless the termination resulted from voluntary discontinuance or from dismissal for failure or neglect to prosecute.

(4) This section does not alter the law on tolling of the statute of limitations nor does it apply to causes of action that have accrued before this Article becomes effective.

* * * *

§2A—508. LESSEE'S REMEDIES

(1) If a lessor fails to deliver the goods in conformity to the lease contract (Section 2A—509) or repudiates the lease contract (Section 2A—402), or a lessee rightfully rejects the goods (Section 2A—509) or justifiably revokes acceptance of the goods (Section 2A—517), then with respect to any goods involved, and with respect to all of the goods if under an installment lease contract the value of the whole lease contract is substantially impaired (Section 2A—510), the lessor is in default under the lease contract and the lessee may:

(a) cancel the lease contract (Section 2A—505(1));

(b) recover so much of the rent and security as has been paid and is just under the circumstances;

(c) cover and recover damages as to all goods affected whether or not they have been identified to the lease contract (Sections 2A—518 and 2A—520), or recover damages for nondelivery (Sections 2A—519 and 2A—520);

(d) exercise any other rights or pursue any other remedies provided in the lease contract.

(2) If a lessor fails to deliver the goods in conformity to the lease contract or repudiates the lease contract, the lessee may also:

(a) if the goods have been identified, recover them (Section 2A—522); or

(b) in a proper case, obtain specific performance or replevy the goods (Section 2A—521).

(3) If a lessor is otherwise in default under a lease contract, the lessee may exercise the rights and pursue the remedies provided in the lease contract, which may include a right to cancel the lease, and in Section 2A—519(3).

(4) If a lessor has breached a warranty, whether express or implied, the lessee may recover damages (Section 2A—519(4)).

(5) On rightful rejection or justifiable revocation of acceptance, a lessee has a security interest in goods in the lessee's possession or control for any rent and security that has been paid and any expenses reasonably incurred in their inspection, receipt, transportation, and care and custody and may hold those goods and dispose of them in good faith and in a commercially reasonable manner, subject to Section 2A—527(5).

(6) Subject to the provisions of Section 2A—407, a lessee, on notifying the lessor of the lessee's intention to do so, may deduct all or any part of the damages resulting from any default under the lease contract

from any part of the rent still due under the same lease contract.

§2A—509. LESSEE'S RIGHTS ON IMPROPER DELIVERY; RIGHTFUL REJECTION

(1) Subject to the provisions of Section 2A—510 on default in installment lease contracts, if the goods or the tender or delivery fail in any respect to conform to the lease contract, the lessee may reject or accept the goods or accept any commercial unit or units and reject the rest of the goods.

(2) Rejection of goods is ineffective unless it is within a reasonable time after tender or delivery of the goods and the lessee seasonably notifies the lessor.

* * * *

§2A—512. LESSEE'S DUTIES AS TO RIGHTFULLY REJECTED GOODS

(1) Except as otherwise provided with respect to goods that threaten to decline in value speedily (Section 2A—511) and subject to any security interest of a lessee (Section 2A—508(5)):

(a) the lessee, after rejection of goods in the lessee's possession, shall hold them with reasonable care at the lessor's or the supplier's disposition for a reasonable time after the lessee's seasonable notification of rejection;

(b) if the lessor or the supplier gives no instructions within a reasonable time after notification of rejection, the lessee may store the rejected goods for the lessor's or the supplier's account or ship them to the lessor or the supplier or dispose of them for the lessor's or the supplier's account with reimbursement in the manner provided in Section 2A—511; but

(c) the lessee has no further obligations with regard to goods rightfully rejected.

(2) Action by the lessee pursuant to subsection (1) is not acceptance or conversion.

§2A—513. CURE BY LESSOR OF IMPROPER TENDER OR DELIVERY; REPLACEMENT

(1) If any tender or delivery by the lessor or the supplier is rejected because non-conforming and the time for performance has not yet expired, the lessor or the supplier may seasonably notify the lessee of the lessor's or the supplier's intention to cure and may then make a conforming delivery within the time provided in the lease contract.

(2) If the lessee rejects a non-conforming tender that the lessor or the supplier had reasonable grounds to believe would be acceptable with or without money allowance, the lessor or the supplier may have a further reasonable time to substitute a conforming tender if he [or she] seasonably notifies the lessee.

* * * *

Revised Article 3 Negotiable Instruments

Part 1 General Provisions and Definitions

§3—102. SUBJECT MATTER

(a) This Article applies to negotiable instruments. It does not apply to money, to payment orders governed by Article 4A, or to securities governed by Article 8.

(b) If there is conflict between this Article and Article 4 or 9, Articles 4 and 9 govern.

(c) Regulations of the Board of Governors of the Federal Reserve System and operating circulars of the Federal Reserve Banks supersede any inconsistent provision of this Article to the extent of the inconsistency.

§3—103. DEFINITIONS

(a) In this Article:

(1) "Acceptor" means a drawee who has accepted a draft.

(2) "Drawee" means a person ordered in a draft to make payment.

(3) "Drawer" means a person who signs or is identified in a draft as a person ordering payment.

(4) "Good faith" means honesty in fact and the observance of reasonable commercial standards of fair dealing.

(5) "Maker" means a person who signs or is identified in a note as a person undertaking to pay.

(6) "Order" means a written instruction to pay money signed by the person giving the instruction. The instruction may be addressed to any person, including the person giving the instruction, or to one or more persons jointly or in the alternative but not in succession. An authorization to pay is not an order unless the person authorized to pay is also instructed to pay.

(7) "Ordinary care" in the case of a person engaged in business means observance of reasonable

commercial standards, prevailing in the area in which the person is located, with respect to the business in which the person is engaged. In the case of a bank that takes an instrument for processing for collection or payment by automated means, reasonable commercial standards do not require the bank to examine the instrument if the failure to examine does not violate the bank's prescribed procedures and the bank's procedures do not vary unreasonably from general banking usage not disapproved by this Article or Article 4.

(8) "Party" means a party to an instrument.

§3—104. NEGOTIABLE INSTRUMENT

(a) Except as provided in subsections (c) and (d), "negotiable instrument" means an unconditional promise or order to pay a fixed amount of money, with or without interest or other charges described in the promise or order, if it:

(1) is payable to bearer or to order at the time it is issued or first comes into possession of a holder;

(2) is payable on demand or at a definite time; and

(3) does not state any other undertaking or instruction by the person promising or ordering payment to do any act in addition to the payment of money, but the promise or order may contain (i) an undertaking or power to give, maintain, or protect collateral to secure payment, (ii) an authorization or power to the holder to confess judgment or realize on or dispose of collateral, or (iii) a waiver of the benefit of any law intended for the advantage or protection of an obligor.

(b) "Instrument" means a negotiable instrument.

(c) An order that meets all of the requirements of subsection (a), except paragraph (1), and otherwise falls within the definition of "check" in subsection (f) is a negotiable instrument and a check.

(d) A promise or order other than a check is not an instrument if, at the time it is issued or first comes into possession of a holder, it contains a conspicuous statement, however expressed, to the effect that the promise or order is not negotiable or is not an instrument governed by this Article.

(e) An instrument is a "note" if it is a promise and is a "draft" if it is an order. If an instrument falls within the definition of both "note" and "draft," a person entitled to enforce the instrument may treat it as either.

(f) "Check" means (i) a draft, other than a documentary draft, payable on demand and drawn on a bank or (ii) a cashier's check or teller's check. An instrument may be a check even though it is described on its face by another term, such as "money order."

(g) "Cashier's check" means a draft with respect to which the drawer and drawee are the same bank or branches of the same bank.

(h) "Teller's check" means a draft drawn by a bank (i) on another bank, or (ii) payable at or through a bank.

(i) "Traveler's check" means an instrument that (i) is payable on demand, (ii) is drawn on or payable at or through a bank, (iii) is designated by the term "traveler's check" or by a substantially similar term, and (iv) requires, as a condition to payment, a countersignature by a person whose specimen signature appears on the instrument.

(j) "Certificate of deposit" means an instrument containing an acknowledgment by a bank that a sum of money has been received by the bank and a promise by the bank to repay the sum of money. A certificate of deposit is a note of the bank.

* * * *

§3—106. UNCONDITIONAL PROMISE OR ORDER

(a) Except as provided in this section, for the purposes of Section 3—104(a), a promise or order is unconditional unless it states (i) an express condition to payment, (ii) that the promise or order is subject to or governed by another writing, or (iii) that rights or obligations with respect to the promise or order are stated in another writing. A reference to another writing does not of itself make the promise or order conditional.

(b) A promise or order is not made conditional (i) by a reference to another writing for a statement of rights with respect to collateral, prepayment, or acceleration, or (ii) because payment is limited to resort to a particular fund or source.

(c) If a promise or order requires, as a condition to payment, a countersignature by a person whose specimen signature appears on the promise or order, the condition does not make the promise or order conditional for the purposes of Section 3—104(a). If the person whose specimen signature appears on an instrument fails to countersign the instrument, the failure to countersign is a defense to the obligation of the issuer, but the failure does not prevent a transferee of the instrument from becoming a holder of the instrument.

(d) If a promise or order at the time it is issued or first comes into possession of a holder contains a statement, required by applicable statutory or administrative law, to the effect that the rights of a holder or transferee are subject to claims or defenses that the issuer could assert against the original payee, the promise or order is not thereby made conditional for the purposes of Section 3—104(a); but if the promise or order is an instrument, there cannot be a holder in due course of the instrument.

§3—107. INSTRUMENT PAYABLE IN FOREIGN MONEY

Unless the instrument otherwise provides, an instrument that states the amount payable in foreign money may be paid in the foreign money or in an equivalent amount in dollars calculated by using the current bank-offered spot rate at the place of payment for the purchase of dollars on the day on which the instrument is paid.

§3—108. PAYABLE ON DEMAND OR AT DEFINITE TIME

(a) A promise or order is "payable on demand" if it (i) states that it is payable on demand or at sight, or otherwise indicates that it is payable at the will of the holder, or (ii) does not state any time of payment.

(b) A promise or order is "payable at a definite time" if it is payable on elapse of a definite period of time after sight or acceptance or at a fixed date or dates or at a time or times readily ascertainable at the time the promise or order is issued, subject to rights of (i) prepayment, (ii) acceleration, (iii) extension at the option of the holder, or (iv) extension to a further definite time at the option of the maker or acceptor or automatically upon or after a specified act or event.

(c) If an instrument, payable at a fixed date, is also payable upon demand made before the fixed date, the instrument is payable on demand until the fixed date and, if demand for payment is not made before that date, becomes payable at a definite time on the fixed date.

§3—109. PAYABLE TO BEARER OR TO ORDER

(a) A promise or order is payable to bearer if it:

(1) states that it is payable to bearer or to the order of bearer or otherwise indicates that the person in possession of the promise or order is entitled to payment;

(2) does not state a payee; or

(3) states that it is payable to or to the order of cash or otherwise indicates that it is not payable to an identified person.

(b) A promise or order that is not payable to bearer is payable to order if it is payable (i) to the order of an identified person or (ii) to an identified person or order. A promise or order that is payable to order is payable to the identified person.

(c) An instrument payable to bearer may become payable to an identified person if it is specially indorsed pursuant to Section 3—205(a). An instrument payable to an identified person may become payable to bearer if it is indorsed in blank pursuant to Section 3—205(b).

§3—110. IDENTIFICATION OF PERSON TO WHOM INSTRUMENT IS PAYABLE

(a) The person to whom an instrument is initially payable is determined by the intent of the person, whether or not authorized, signing as, or in the name or behalf of, the issuer of the instrument. The instrument is payable to the person intended by the signer even if that person is identified in the instrument by a name or other identification that is not that of the intended person. If more than one person signs in the name or behalf of the issuer of an instrument and all the signers do not intend the same person as payee, the instrument is payable to any person intended by one or more of the signers.

(b) If the signature of the issuer of an instrument is made by automated means, such as a check-writing machine, the payee of the instrument is determined by the intent of the person who supplied the name or identification of the payee, whether or not authorized to do so.

(c) A person to whom an instrument is payable may be identified in any way, including by name, identifying number, office, or account number.

§3—111. PLACE OF PAYMENT

Except as otherwise provided for items in Article 4, an instrument is payable at the place of payment stated in the instrument. If no place of payment is stated, an instrument is payable at the address of the drawee or maker stated in the instrument. If no address is stated, the place of payment is the place of business of the drawee or maker. If a drawee or maker has more than one place of business, the place of payment is any place of business of the drawee or maker chosen by the person entitled to enforce the instrument. If the drawee or maker has no place of business, the place of payment is the residence of the drawee or maker.

§3—112. INTEREST

(a) Unless otherwise provided in the instrument, (i) an instrument is not payable with interest, and (ii) interest on an interest-bearing instrument is payable from the date of the instrument.

(b) Interest may be stated in an instrument as a fixed or variable amount of money or it may be expressed as a fixed or variable rate or rates. The amount or rate of interest may be stated or described in the instrument in any manner and may require reference to information not contained in the instrument. If an instrument provides for interest, but the amount of interest payable cannot be ascertained from the description, interest is payable at the judgment rate in effect at the place of payment of the instrument and at the time interest first accrues.

§3—113. DATE OF INSTRUMENT

(a) An instrument may be antedated or postdated. The date stated determines the time of payment if the instrument is payable at a fixed period after date. Except as provided in Section 4—401(c), an instrument payable on demand is not payable before the date of the instrument.

(b) If an instrument is undated, its date is the date of its issue or, in the case of an unissued instrument, the date it first comes into possession of a holder.

§3—114. CONTRADICTORY TERMS OF INSTRUMENT

If an instrument contains contradictory terms, typewritten terms prevail over printed terms, handwritten terms prevail over both, and words prevail over numbers.

§3—115. INCOMPLETE INSTRUMENT

(a) "Incomplete instrument" means a signed writing, whether or not issued by the signer, the contents of which show at the time of signing that it is incomplete but that the signer intended it to be completed by the addition of words or numbers.

(b) Subject to subsection (c), if an incomplete instrument is an instrument under Section 3—104, it may be enforced according to its terms if it is not completed, or according to its terms as augmented by completion. If an incomplete instrument is not an instrument under Section 3—104, but, after completion, the requirements of Section 3—104 are met, the instrument may be enforced according to its terms as augmented by completion.

(c) If words or numbers are added to an incomplete instrument without authority of the signer, there is an alteration of the incomplete instrument under Section 3—407.

(d) The burden of establishing that words or numbers were added to an incomplete instrument without authority of the signer is on the person asserting the lack of authority.

§3—116. JOINT AND SEVERAL LIABILITY; CONTRIBUTION

(a) Except as otherwise provided in the instrument, two or more persons who have the same liability on an instrument as makers, drawers, acceptors, indorsers who indorse as joint payees, or anomalous indorsers are jointly and severally liable in the capacity in which they sign.

(b) Except as provided in Section 3—419(e) or by agreement of the affected parties, a party having joint and several liability who pays the instrument is entitled to receive from any party having the same joint and several liability contribution in accordance with applicable law.

(c) Discharge of one party having joint and several liability by a person entitled to enforce the instrument does not affect the right under subsection (b) of a party having the same joint and several liability to receive contribution from the party discharged.

* * * *

§3—118. STATUTE OF LIMITATIONS

(a) Except as provided in subsection (e), an action to enforce the obligation of a party to pay a note payable at a definite time must be commenced within six years after the due date or dates stated in the note or, if a due date is accelerated, within six years after the accelerated due date.

(b) Except as provided in subsection (d) or (e), if demand for payment is made to the maker of a note payable on demand, an action to enforce the obligation of a party to pay the note must be commenced within six years after the demand. If no demand for payment is made to the maker, an action to enforce the note is barred if neither principal nor interest on the note has been paid for a continuous period of 10 years.

(c) Except as provided in subsection (d), an action to enforce the obligation of a party to an unaccepted draft to pay the draft must be commenced within three years after dishonor of the draft or 10 years after the date of the draft, whichever period expires first.

(d) An action to enforce the obligation of the acceptor of a certified check or the issuer of a teller's check, cashier's check, or traveler's check must be commenced within three years after demand for payment is made to the acceptor or issuer, as the case may be.

(e) An action to enforce the obligation of a party to a certificate of deposit to pay the instrument must be commenced within six years after demand for payment is made to the maker, but if the instrument states a due date and the maker is not required to pay before that date, the six-year period begins when a demand for payment is in effect and the due date has passed.

(f) An action to enforce the obligation of a party to pay an accepted draft, other than a certified check, must be commenced (i) within six years after the due date or dates stated in the draft or acceptance if the obligation of the acceptor is payable at a definite time, or (ii) within six years after the date of the acceptance if the obligation of the acceptor is payable on demand.

(g) Unless governed by other law regarding claims for indemnity or contribution, an action (i) for conversion of an instrument, for money had and received, or like action based on conversion, (ii) for breach of warranty, or (iii) to enforce an obligation, duty, or right arising under this Article and not governed by this section must be commenced within three years after the [cause of action] accrues.

* * * *

Part 2 Negotiation, Transfer, and Indorsement

§3—201. NEGOTIATION

(a) "Negotiation" means a transfer of possession, whether voluntary or involuntary, of an instrument by a person other than the issuer to a person who thereby becomes its holder.

(b) Except for negotiation by a remitter, if an instrument is payable to an identified person, negotiation requires transfer of possession of the instrument and its indorsement by the holder. If an instrument is payable to bearer, it may be negotiated by transfer of possession alone.

* * * *

§3—203. TRANSFER OF INSTRUMENT; RIGHTS ACQUIRED BY TRANSFER

(a) An instrument is transferred when it is delivered by a person other than its issuer for the purpose of giving to the person receiving delivery the right to enforce the instrument.

(b) Transfer of an instrument, whether or not the transfer is a negotiation, vests in the transferee any right of the transferor to enforce the instrument, including any right as a holder in due course, but the transferee cannot acquire rights of a holder in due course by a transfer, directly or indirectly, from a holder in due course if the transferee engaged in fraud or illegality affecting the instrument.

(c) Unless otherwise agreed, if an instrument is transferred for value and the transferee does not become a holder because of lack of indorsement by the transferor, the transferee has a specifically enforceable right to the unqualified indorsement of the transferor, but negotiation of the instrument does not occur until the indorsement is made.

(d) If a transferor purports to transfer less than the entire instrument, negotiation of the instrument does not occur. The transferee obtains no rights under this Article and has only the rights of a partial assignee.

§3—204. INDORSEMENT

(a) "Indorsement" means a signature, other than that of a signer as maker, drawer, or acceptor, that alone or accompanied by other words is made on an instrument for the purpose of (i) negotiating the instrument, (ii) restricting payment of the instrument, or (iii) incurring indorser's liability on the instrument, but regardless of the intent of the signer, a signature and its accompanying words is an indorsement unless the accompanying words, terms of the instrument, place of the signature, or other circumstances unambiguously indicate that the signature was made for a purpose other than indorsement. For the purpose of determining whether a signature is made on an instrument, a paper affixed to the instrument is a part of the instrument.

(b) "Indorser" means a person who makes an indorsement.

(c) For the purpose of determining whether the transferee of an instrument is a holder, an indorsement that transfers a security interest in the instrument is effective as an unqualified indorsement of the instrument.

(d) If an instrument is payable to a holder under a name that is not the name of the holder, indorsement may be made by the holder in the name stated in the instrument or in the holder's name or both, but signature in both names may be required by a person paying or taking the instrument for value or collection.

§3—205. SPECIAL INDORSEMENT; BLANK INDORSEMENT; ANOMALOUS INDORSEMENT

(a) If an indorsement is made by the holder of an instrument, whether payable to an identified person or payable to bearer, and the indorsement identifies a person to whom it makes the instrument payable, it is a "special indorsement." When specially indorsed, an instrument becomes payable to the identified person and may be negotiated only by the indorsement of that person. The principles stated in Section 3—110 apply to special indorsements.

(b) If an indorsement is made by the holder of an instrument and it is not a special indorsement, it is a "blank indorsement." When indorsed in blank, an instrument becomes payable to bearer and may be negotiated by transfer of possession alone until specially indorsed.

(c) The holder may convert a blank indorsement that consists only of a signature into a special indorsement by writing, above the signature of the indorser, words identifying the person to whom the instrument is made payable.

(d) "Anomalous indorsement" means an indorsement made by a person who is not the holder of the instrument. An anomalous indorsement does not affect the manner in which the instrument may be negotiated.

§3—206. RESTRICTIVE INDORSEMENT

(a) An indorsement limiting payment to a particular person or otherwise prohibiting further transfer or negotiation of the instrument is not effective to prevent further transfer or negotiation of the instrument.

(b) An indorsement stating a condition to the right of the indorsee to receive payment does not affect the right of the indorsee to enforce the instrument. A person paying the instrument or taking it for value or collection may disregard the condition, and the rights and liabilities of that person are not affected by whether the condition has been fulfilled.

(c) If an instrument bears an indorsement (i) described in Section 4—201(b), or (ii) in blank or to a particular bank using the words "for deposit," "for collection," or other words indicating a purpose of having the instrument collected by a bank for the indorser or for a particular account, the following rules apply:

(1) A person, other than a bank, who purchases the instrument when so indorsed converts the instrument unless the amount paid for the instrument is received by the indorser or applied consistently with the indorsement.

(2) A depositary bank that purchases the instrument or takes it for collection when so indorsed converts the instrument unless the amount paid by the bank with respect to the instrument is received by the indorser or applied consistently with the indorsement.

(3) A payor bank that is also the depositary bank or that takes the instrument for immediate payment over the counter from a person other than a collecting bank converts the instrument unless the proceeds of the instrument are received by the indorser or applied consistently with the indorsement.

(4) Except as otherwise provided in paragraph (3), a payor bank or intermediary bank may disregard the indorsement and is not liable if the proceeds of the instrument are not received by the indorser or applied consistently with the indorsement.

(d) Except for an indorsement covered by subsection (c), if an instrument bears an indorsement using words to the effect that payment is to be made to the indorsee as agent, trustee, or other fiduciary for the benefit of the indorser or another person, the following rules apply:

(1) Unless there is notice of breach of fiduciary duty as provided in Section 3—307, a person who purchases the instrument from the indorsee or takes the instrument from the indorsee for collection or payment may pay the proceeds of payment or the value given for the instrument to the indorsee without regard to whether the indorsee violates a fiduciary duty to the indorser.

(2) A subsequent transferee of the instrument or person who pays the instrument is neither given notice nor otherwise affected by the restriction in the indorsement unless the transferee or payor knows that the fiduciary dealt with the instrument or its proceeds in breach of fiduciary duty.

(e) The presence on an instrument of an indorsement to which this section applies does not prevent a purchaser of the instrument from becoming a holder in due course of the instrument unless the purchaser is a converter under subsection (c) or has notice or knowledge of breach of fiduciary duty as stated in subsection (d).

(f) In an action to enforce the obligation of a party to pay the instrument, the obligor has a defense if payment would violate an indorsement to which this section applies and the payment is not permitted by this section.

§3—207. REACQUISITION

Reacquisition of an instrument occurs if it is transferred to a former holder, by negotiation or otherwise. A former holder who reacquires the instrument may cancel indorsements made after the reacquirer first became a holder of the instrument. If the cancellation causes the instrument to be payable to the reacquirer or to bearer, the reacquirer may negotiate the instrument. An indorser whose indorsement is canceled is discharged, and the discharge is effective against any subsequent holder.

Part 3 Enforcement of Instruments

§3—301. PERSON ENTITLED TO ENFORCE INSTRUMENT

"Person entitled to enforce" an instrument means (i) the holder of the instrument, (ii) a nonholder in possession of the instrument who has the rights of a holder, or (iii) a person not in possession of the instrument who is entitled to enforce the instrument pursuant to Section 3—309 or 3—418(d). A person may be a person entitled to enforce the instrument even though the person is not the owner of the instrument or is in wrongful possession of the instrument.

§3—302. HOLDER IN DUE COURSE

(a) Subject to subsection (c) and Section 3—106(d), "holder in due course" means the holder of an instrument if:

(1) the instrument when issued or negotiated to the holder does not bear such apparent evidence of forgery or alteration or is not otherwise so irregular or incomplete as to call into question its authenticity; and

(2) the holder took the instrument (i) for value, (ii) in good faith, (iii) without notice that the instrument is overdue or has been dishonored or that there is an uncured default with respect to payment of another instrument issued as part of the same series, (iv) without notice that the instrument contains an unauthorized signature or has been altered, (v) without notice of any claim to the instrument described in Section 3—306, and (vi) without notice that any party has a defense or claim in recoupment described in Section 3—305(a).

(b) Notice of discharge of a party, other than discharge in an insolvency proceeding, is not notice of a defense under subsection (a), but discharge is effective against a person who became a holder in due course with notice of the discharge. Public filing or recording of a document does not of itself constitute notice of a defense, claim in recoupment, or claim to the instrument.

(c) Except to the extent a transferor or predecessor in interest has rights as a holder in due course, a person does not acquire rights of a holder in due course of an instrument taken (i) by legal process or by purchase in an execution, bankruptcy, or creditor's sale or similar proceeding, (ii) by purchase as part of a bulk transaction not in ordinary course of business of the transferor, or (iii) as the successor in interest to an estate or other organization.

(d) If, under Section 3—303(a)(1), the promise of performance that is the consideration for an instrument has been partially performed, the holder may assert rights as a holder in due course of the instrument only to the fraction of the amount payable under the instrument equal to the value of the partial performance divided by the value of the promised performance.

(e) If (i) the person entitled to enforce an instrument has only a security interest in the instrument and (ii) the person obliged to pay the instrument has a defense, claim in recoupment, or claim to the instrument that may be asserted against the person who granted the security interest, the person entitled to enforce the instrument may assert rights as a holder in due course only to an amount payable under the instrument which, at the time of enforcement of the instrument, does not exceed the amount of the unpaid obligation secured.

(f) To be effective, notice must be received at a time and in a manner that gives a reasonable opportunity to act on it.

(g) This section is subject to any law limiting status as a holder in due course in particular classes of transactions.

§3—303. VALUE AND CONSIDERATION

(a) An instrument is issued or transferred for value if:

(1) the instrument is issued or transferred for a promise of performance, to the extent the promise has been performed;

(2) the transferee acquires a security interest or other lien in the instrument other than a lien obtained by judicial proceeding;

(3) the instrument is issued or transferred as payment of, or as security for, an antecedent claim against any person, whether or not the claim is due;

(4) the instrument is issued or transferred in exchange for a negotiable instrument; or

(5) the instrument is issued or transferred in exchange for the incurring of an irrevocable obligation to a third party by the person taking the instrument.

(b) "Consideration" means any consideration sufficient to support a simple contract. The drawer or maker of an instrument has a defense if the instrument is issued without consideration. If an instrument is issued for a promise of performance, the issuer has a defense to the extent performance of the promise is due and the promise has not been performed. If an instrument is issued for value as stated in subsection (a), the instrument is also issued for consideration.

§3—304. OVERDUE INSTRUMENT

(a) An instrument payable on demand becomes overdue at the earliest of the following times:

(1) on the day after the day demand for payment is duly made;

(2) if the instrument is a check, 90 days after its date; or

(3) if the instrument is not a check, when the instrument has been outstanding for a period of time after its date which is unreasonably long under the circumstances of the particular case in light of the nature of the instrument and usage of the trade.

(b) With respect to an instrument payable at a definite time the following rules apply:

(1) If the principal is payable in installments and a due date has not been accelerated, the instrument becomes overdue upon default under the instrument for nonpayment of an installment, and the instrument remains overdue until the default is cured.

(2) If the principal is not payable in installments and the due date has not been accelerated, the instrument becomes overdue on the day after the due date.

(3) If a due date with respect to principal has been accelerated, the instrument becomes overdue on the day after the accelerated due date.

(c) Unless the due date of principal has been accelerated, an instrument does not become overdue if there is default in payment of interest but no default in payment of principal.

§3—305. DEFENSES AND CLAIMS IN RECOUPMENT

(a) Except as stated in subsection (b), the right to enforce the obligation of a party to pay an instrument is subject to the following:

(1) a defense of the obligor based on (i) infancy of the obligor to the extent it is a defense to a simple contract, (ii) duress, lack of legal capacity, or illegality of the transaction which, under other law, nullifies the obligation of the obligor, (iii) fraud that induced the obligor to sign the instrument with neither knowledge nor reasonable opportunity to learn of its character or its essential terms, or (iv) discharge of the obligor in insolvency proceedings;

(2) a defense of the obligor stated in another section of this Article or a defense of the obligor that would be available if the person entitled to enforce the instrument were enforcing a right to payment under a simple contract; and

(3) a claim in recoupment of the obligor against the original payee of the instrument if the claim arose from the transaction that gave rise to the instrument; but the claim of the obligor may be asserted against a transferee of the instrument only to reduce the amount owing on the instrument at the time the action is brought.

(b) The right of a holder in due course to enforce the obligation of a party to pay the instrument is subject to defenses of the obligor stated in subsection (a)(1), but is not subject to defenses of the obligor stated in subsection (a)(2) or claims in recoupment stated in subsection (a)(3) against a person other than the holder.

(c) Except as stated in subsection (d), in an action to enforce the obligation of a party to pay the instrument, the obligor may not assert against the person entitled to enforce the instrument a defense, claim in recoupment, or claim to the instrument (Section 3—306) of another person, but the other person's claim to the instrument may be asserted by the obligor if the other person is joined in the action and personally asserts the claim against the person entitled to enforce the instrument. An obligor is not obliged to pay the instrument if the person seeking enforcement of the instrument does not have rights of a holder in due course and the obligor proves that the instrument is a lost or stolen instrument.

(d) In an action to enforce the obligation of an accommodation party to pay an instrument, the accommodation party may assert against the person entitled to enforce the instrument any defense or claim in recoupment under subsection (a) that the accommodated party could assert against the person entitled to enforce the instrument, except the defenses of discharge in insolvency proceedings, infancy, and lack of legal capacity.

§3—306. CLAIMS TO AN INSTRUMENT

A person taking an instrument, other than a person having rights of a holder in due course, is subject to a claim of a property or possessory right in the instrument or its proceeds, including a claim to rescind a negotiation and to recover the instrument or its proceeds. A person having rights of a holder in due course takes free of the claim to the instrument.

§3—307. NOTICE OF BREACH OF FIDUCIARY DUTY

(a) In this section:

(1) "Fiduciary" means an agent, trustee, partner, corporate officer or director, or other representative owing a fiduciary duty with respect to an instrument.

(2) "Represented person" means the principal, beneficiary, partnership, corporation, or other person to whom the duty stated in paragraph (1) is owed.

(b) If (i) an instrument is taken from a fiduciary for payment or collection or for value, (ii) the taker has knowledge of the fiduciary status of the fiduciary, and (iii) the represented person makes a claim to the instrument or its proceeds on the basis that the transaction of the fiduciary is a breach of fiduciary duty, the following rules apply:

(1) Notice of breach of fiduciary duty by the fiduciary is notice of the claim of the represented person.

(2) In the case of an instrument payable to the represented person or the fiduciary as such, the taker has notice of the breach of fiduciary duty if the instrument is (i) taken in payment of or as security for a debt known by the taker to be the personal debt of the fiduciary, (ii) taken in a transaction known by the taker to be for the personal benefit of the fiduciary, or (iii) deposited to an account other than an account of the fiduciary, as such, or an account of the represented person.

(3) If an instrument is issued by the represented person or the fiduciary as such, and made payable to the fiduciary personally, the taker does not have notice of the breach of fiduciary duty unless the taker knows of the breach of fiduciary duty.

(4) If an instrument is issued by the represented person or the fiduciary as such, to the taker as payee, the taker has notice of the breach of fiduciary duty if the instrument is (i) taken in payment of or as security for a debt known by the taker to be the personal debt of the fiduciary, (ii) taken in a transaction known by the taker to be for the personal benefit of the fiduciary, or (iii) deposited to an account other than an account of the fiduciary, as such, or an account of the represented person.

§3—308. PROOF OF SIGNATURES AND STATUS AS HOLDER IN DUE COURSE

(a) In an action with respect to an instrument, the authenticity of, and authority to make, each signature on the instrument is admitted unless specifically denied in the pleadings. If the validity of a signature is denied in the pleadings, the burden of establishing validity is on the person claiming validity, but the signature is presumed to be authentic and authorized unless the action is to enforce the liability of the purported signer and the signer is dead or incompetent at the time of trial of the issue of validity of the signature. If an action to enforce the instrument is brought against a person as the undisclosed principal of a person who signed the instrument as a party to the instrument, the plaintiff has the burden of establishing that the defendant is liable on the instrument as a represented person under Section 3—402(a).

(b) If the validity of signatures is admitted or proved and there is compliance with subsection (a), a plaintiff producing the instrument is entitled to payment if the plaintiff proves entitlement to enforce the instrument under Section 3—301, unless the defendant proves a defense or claim in recoupment. If a defense or claim in recoupment is proved, the right to payment of the plaintiff is subject to the defense or claim, except to the extent the plaintiff proves that the plaintiff has rights of a holder in due course which are not subject to the defense or claim.

§3—309. ENFORCEMENT OF LOST, DESTROYED, OR STOLEN INSTRUMENT

(a) A person not in possession of an instrument is entitled to enforce the instrument if (i) the person was in possession of the instrument and entitled to enforce it when loss of possession occurred, (ii) the loss of possession was not the result of a transfer by the person or a lawful seizure, and (iii) the person cannot reasonably obtain possession of the instrument because the instrument was destroyed, its whereabouts cannot be determined, or it is in the wrongful possession of an unknown person or a person that cannot be found or is not amenable to service of process.

(b) A person seeking enforcement of an instrument under subsection (a) must prove the terms of the instrument and the person's right to enforce the instrument. If that proof is made, Section 3—308 applies to the case as if the person seeking enforcement had produced the instrument. The court may not enter judgment in favor of the person seeking enforcement unless it finds that the person required to pay the instrument is adequately protected against loss that might occur by reason of a claim by another person to enforce the instrument. Adequate protection may be provided by any reasonable means.

§3—310. EFFECT OF INSTRUMENT ON OBLIGATION FOR WHICH TAKEN

(a) Unless otherwise agreed, if a certified check, cashier's check, or teller's check is taken for an obligation, the obligation is discharged to the same extent discharge would result if an amount of money equal to the amount of the instrument were taken in payment of the obligation. Discharge of the obligation does not affect any liability that the obligor may have as an indorser of the instrument.

(b) Unless otherwise agreed and except as provided in subsection (a), if a note or an uncertified check is taken for an obligation, the obligation is suspended to the same extent the obligation would be discharged if an amount of money equal to the amount of the instrument were taken, and the following rules apply:

(1) In the case of an uncertified check, suspension of the obligation continues until dishonor of the check or until it is paid or certified. Payment or certification of the check results in discharge of the obligation to the extent of the amount of the check.

(2) In the case of a note, suspension of the obligation continues until dishonor of the note or until it is paid. Payment of the note results in discharge of the obligation to the extent of the payment.

(3) Except as provided in paragraph (4), if the check or note is dishonored and the obligee of the obligation for which the instrument was taken is the person entitled to enforce the instrument, the obligee may enforce either the instrument or the obligation. In the case of an instrument of a third person which is negotiated to the obligee by the obligor, discharge of the obligor on the instrument also discharges the obligation.

(4) If the person entitled to enforce the instrument taken for an obligation is a person other than the obligee, the obligee may not enforce the obligation to the extent the obligation is suspended. If the obligee is the person entitled to enforce the instrument but no longer has possession of it because it was lost, stolen, or destroyed, the obligation may not be enforced to the extent of the amount payable on the instrument, and to that extent the obligee's rights against the obligor are limited to enforcement of the instrument.

(c) If an instrument other than one described in subsection (a) or (b) is taken for an obligation, the effect is (i) that stated in subsection (a) if the instrument is one on which a bank is liable as maker or acceptor, or (ii) that stated in subsection (b) in any other case.

* * * *

§3—312. LOST, DESTROYED, OR STOLEN CASHIER'S CHECK, TELLER'S CHECK, OR CERTIFIED CHECK.

(1) "Check" means a cashier's check, teller's check, or certified check.

(2) "Claimant" means a person who claims the right to receive the amount of a cashier's check, teller's check, or certified check that was lost, destroyed, or stolen.

(3) "Declaration of loss" means a written statement, made under penalty of perjury, to the effect that (i) the declarer lost possession of a check, (ii) the declarer is the drawer or payee of the check, in the case of a certified check, or the remitter or payee of the check, in the case of a cashier's check or teller's check, (iii) the loss of possession was not the result of a transfer by the declarer or a lawful seizure, and (iv) the declarer cannot reasonably obtain possession of the check because the check was destroyed, its whereabouts cannot be determined, or it is in the wrongful possession of an unknown person or a person that cannot be found or is not amenable to service of process.

(4) "Obligated bank" means the issuer of a cashier's check or teller's check or the acceptor of a certified check.

* * * *

Part 4 Liability of Parties

§3—401. SIGNATURE

(a) A person is not liable on an instrument unless (i) the person signed the instrument, or (ii) the person is represented by an agent or representative who signed the instrument and the signature is binding on the represented person under Section 3—402.

(b) A signature may be made (i) manually or by means of a device or machine, and (ii) by the use of any name, including a trade or assumed name, or by a word, mark, or symbol executed or adopted by a person with present intention to authenticate a writing.

§3—402. SIGNATURE BY REPRESENTATIVE

(a) If a person acting, or purporting to act, as a representative signs an instrument by signing either the name of the represented person or the name of the signer, the represented person is bound by the signature to the same extent the represented person would be bound if the signature were on a simple contract. If the represented person is bound, the signature of the representative is the "authorized signature of the represented person" and the represented person is liable on the instrument, whether or not identified in the instrument.

(b) If a representative signs the name of the representative to an instrument and the signature is an authorized signature of the represented person, the following rules apply:

(1) If the form of the signature shows unambiguously that the signature is made on behalf of the represented person who is identified in the instrument, the representative is not liable on the instrument.

(2) Subject to subsection (c), if (i) the form of the signature does not show unambiguously that the signature is made in a representative capacity or (ii) the represented person is not identified in the instrument, the representative is liable on the instrument to a holder in due course that took the instrument without notice that the representative was not intended to be liable on the instrument. With respect to any other person, the representative is liable on the instrument unless the representative proves that the original parties did not intend the representative to be liable on the instrument.

(c) If a representative signs the name of the representative as drawer of a check without indication of the representative status and the check is payable from an account of the represented person who is identified on the check, the signer is not liable on the check if the signature is an authorized signature of the represented person.

§3—403. UNAUTHORIZED SIGNATURE

(a) Unless otherwise provided in this Article or Article 4, an unauthorized signature is ineffective except as the signature of the unauthorized signer in favor of a person who in good faith pays the instrument or takes it for value. An unauthorized signature may be ratified for all purposes of this Article.

(b) If the signature of more than one person is required to constitute the authorized signature of an organization, the signature of the organization is unauthorized if one of the required signatures is lacking.

(c) The civil or criminal liability of a person who makes an unauthorized signature is not affected by any provision of this Article which makes the unauthorized signature effective for the purposes of this Article.

§3—404. IMPOSTORS; FICTITIOUS PAYEES

(a) If an impostor, by use of the mails or otherwise, induces the issuer of an instrument to issue the instrument to the impostor, or to a person acting in concert with the impostor, by impersonating the payee of the instrument or a person authorized to act for the payee, an indorsement of the instrument by any person in the name of the payee is effective as the indorsement of the payee in favor of a person who, in good faith, pays the instrument or takes it for value or for collection.

(b) If (i) a person whose intent determines to whom an instrument is payable (Section 3—110(a) or (b)) does not intend the person identified as payee to have any interest in the instrument, or (ii) the person identified as payee of an instrument is a fictitious person, the following rules apply until the instrument is negotiated by special indorsement:

(1) Any person in possession of the instrument is its holder.

(2) An indorsement by any person in the name of the payee stated in the instrument is effective as the indorsement of the payee in favor of a person who, in good faith, pays the instrument or takes it for value or for collection.

(c) Under subsection (a) or (b), an indorsement is made in the name of a payee if (i) it is made in a name substantially similar to that of the payee or (ii) the instrument, whether or not indorsed, is deposited in a depositary bank to an account in a name substantially similar to that of the payee.

(d) With respect to an instrument to which subsection (a) or (b) applies, if a person paying the instrument or taking it for value or for collection fails to exercise ordinary care in paying or taking the instrument and that failure substantially contributes to loss resulting from payment of the instrument, the person bearing the loss may recover from the person failing to exercise ordinary care to the extent the failure to exercise ordinary care contributed to the loss.

§3—405. EMPLOYER'S RESPONSIBILITY FOR FRAUDULENT INDORSEMENT BY EMPLOYEE

(a) In this section:

(1) "Employee" includes an independent contractor and employee of an independent contractor retained by the employer.

(2) "Fraudulent indorsement" means (i) in the case of an instrument payable to the employer, a forged indorsement purporting to be that of the employer, or (ii) in the case of an instrument with respect to which the employer is the issuer, a forged indorsement purporting to be that of the person identified as payee.

(3) "Responsibility" with respect to instruments means authority (i) to sign or indorse instruments on behalf of the employer, (ii) to process instruments received by the employer for book-keeping purposes, for deposit to an account, or for other disposition, (iii) to prepare or process instruments for issue in the name of the employer, (iv) to supply information determining the names or addresses of payees of instruments to be issued in the name of the employer, (v) to control the disposition of instruments to be issued in the name of the employer, or (vi) to act otherwise with respect to instruments in a responsible capacity. "Responsibility" does not include authority that merely allows an employee to have access to instruments or blank or incomplete instrument forms that are being stored or transported or are part of incoming or outgoing mail, or similar access.

(b) For the purpose of determining the rights and liabilities of a person who, in good faith, pays an instrument or takes it for value or for collection, if an employer entrusted an employee with responsibility with respect to the instrument and the employee or a person acting in concert with the employee makes a fraudulent indorsement of the instrument, the indorsement is effective as the indorsement of the person to whom the instrument is payable if it is made in the name of that person. If the person paying the instrument or taking it for value or for collection fails to exercise ordinary care in paying or taking the instrument and that failure substantially contributes to loss resulting from the fraud, the person bearing the loss may recover from the person failing to exercise ordinary care to the extent the failure to exercise ordinary care contributed to the loss.

(c) Under subsection (b), an indorsement is made in the name of the person to whom an instrument is payable if (i) it is made in a name substantially similar to the name of that person or (ii) the instrument, whether or not indorsed, is deposited in a depositary bank to an account in a name substantially similar to the name of that person.

§3—406. NEGLIGENCE CONTRIBUTING TO FORGED SIGNATURE OR ALTERATION OF INSTRUMENT

(a) A person whose failure to exercise ordinary care substantially contributes to an alteration of an instrument or to the making of a forged signature on an instrument is precluded from asserting the alteration or the forgery against a person who, in good faith, pays the instrument or takes it for value or for collection.

(b) Under subsection (a), if the person asserting the preclusion fails to exercise ordinary care in paying or taking the instrument and that failure substantially contributes to loss, the loss is allocated between the person precluded and the person asserting the preclusion according to the extent to which the failure of each to exercise ordinary care contributed to the loss.

(c) Under subsection (a), the burden of proving failure to exercise ordinary care is on the person asserting the preclusion. Under subsection (b), the burden of proving failure to exercise ordinary care is on the person precluded.

§3—407. ALTERATION

(a) "Alteration" means (i) an unauthorized change in an instrument that purports to modify in any respect the obligation of a party, or (ii) an unauthorized addition of words or numbers or other change to an incomplete instrument relating to the obligation of a party.

(b) Except as provided in subsection (c), an alteration fraudulently made discharges a party whose obligation is affected by the alteration unless that party assents or is precluded from asserting the alteration. No other alteration discharges a party, and the instrument may be enforced according to its original terms.

(c) A payor bank or drawee paying a fraudulently altered instrument or a person taking it for value, in good faith and without notice of the alteration, may enforce rights with respect to the instrument (i) according to its original terms, or (ii) in the case of an incomplete instrument altered by unauthorized completion, according to its terms as completed.

§3—408. DRAWEE NOT LIABLE ON UNACCEPTED DRAFT

A check or other draft does not of itself operate as an assignment of funds in the hands of the drawee available for its payment, and the drawee is not liable on the instrument until the drawee accepts it.

§3—409. ACCEPTANCE OF DRAFT; CERTIFIED CHECK

(a) "Acceptance" means the drawee's signed agreement to pay a draft as presented. It must be written on the draft and may consist of the drawee's signature alone. Acceptance may be made at any time and becomes effective when notification pursuant to instructions is given or the accepted draft is delivered for the purpose of giving rights on the acceptance to any person.

(b) A draft may be accepted although it has not been signed by the drawer, is otherwise incomplete, is overdue, or has been dishonored.

(c) If a draft is payable at a fixed period after sight and the acceptor fails to date the acceptance, the holder may complete the acceptance by supplying a date in good faith.

(d) "Certified check" means a check accepted by the bank on which it is drawn. Acceptance may be made as stated in subsection (a) or by a writing on the check which indicates that the check is certified. The drawee of a check has no obligation to certify the check, and refusal to certify is not dishonor of the check.

§3—410. ACCEPTANCE VARYING DRAFT

(a) If the terms of a drawee's acceptance vary from the terms of the draft as presented, the holder may refuse the acceptance and treat the draft as dishonored. In that case, the drawee may cancel the acceptance.

(b) The terms of a draft are not varied by an acceptance to pay at a particular bank or place in the United States, unless the acceptance states that the draft is to be paid only at that bank or place.

(c) If the holder assents to an acceptance varying the terms of a draft, the obligation of each drawer and indorser that does not expressly assent to the acceptance is discharged.

§3—411. REFUSAL TO PAY CASHIER'S CHECKS, TELLER'S CHECKS, AND CERTIFIED CHECKS

(a) In this section, "obligated bank" means the acceptor of a certified check or the issuer of a cashier's check or teller's check bought from the issuer.

(b) If the obligated bank wrongfully (i) refuses to pay a cashier's check or certified check, (ii) stops payment of a teller's check, or (iii) refuses to pay a dishonored teller's check, the person asserting the right to enforce the check is entitled to compensation for expenses and loss of interest resulting from the nonpayment and may recover consequential damages if the obligated bank refuses to pay after receiving notice of particular circumstances giving rise to the damages.

(c) Expenses or consequential damages under subsection (b) are not recoverable if the refusal of the obligated bank to pay occurs because (i) the bank suspends payments, (ii) the obligated bank asserts a claim or defense of the bank that it has reasonable grounds to believe is available against the person entitled to enforce the instrument, (iii) the obligated bank has a reasonable doubt whether the person demanding payment is the person entitled to enforce the instrument, or (iv) payment is prohibited by law.

§3—412. OBLIGATION OF ISSUER OF NOTE OR CASHIER'S CHECK

The issuer of a note or cashier's check or other draft drawn on the drawer is obliged to pay the instrument (i) according to its terms at the time it was issued or, if not issued, at the time it first came into possession of a holder, or (ii) if the issuer signed an incomplete instrument, according to its terms when completed, to the extent stated in Sections 3—115 and 3—407. The obligation is owed to a person entitled to enforce the instrument or to an indorser who paid the instrument under Section 3—415.

§3—413. OBLIGATION OF ACCEPTOR

(a) The acceptor of a draft is obliged to pay the draft (i) according to its terms at the time it was accepted, even though the acceptance states that the draft is payable "as originally drawn" or equivalent terms, (ii) if the acceptance varies the terms of the draft, according to the terms of the draft as varied, or (iii) if the acceptance is of a draft that is an incomplete instrument, according to its terms when completed, to the extent stated in Sections 3—115 and 3—407. The obligation is owed to a person entitled to enforce the draft or to the drawer or an indorser who paid the draft under Section 3—414 or 3—415.

(b) If the certification of a check or other acceptance of a draft states the amount certified or accepted, the obligation of the acceptor is that amount. If (i) the certification or acceptance does not state an amount, (ii) the amount of the instrument is subsequently raised, and (iii) the instrument is then negotiated to a holder in due course, the obligation of the acceptor is the amount of the instrument at the time it was taken by the holder in due course.

§3—414. OBLIGATION OF DRAWER

(a) This section does not apply to cashier's checks or other drafts drawn on the drawer.

(b) If an unaccepted draft is dishonored, the drawer is obliged to pay the draft (i) according to its terms at the time it was issued or, if not issued, at the time it first came into possession of a holder, or (ii) if the drawer signed an incomplete instrument, according to its terms when completed, to the extent stated in Sections 3—115 and 3—407. The obligation is owed to a person entitled to enforce the draft or to an indorser who paid the draft under Section 3—415.

(c) If a draft is accepted by a bank, the drawer is discharged, regardless of when or by whom acceptance was obtained.

(d) If a draft is accepted and the acceptor is not a bank, the obligation of the drawer to pay the draft if the draft is dishonored by the acceptor is the same as the obligation of an indorser under Section 3—415(a) and (c).

(e) If a draft states that it is drawn "without recourse" or otherwise disclaims liability of the drawer to pay the draft, the drawer is not liable under subsection (b) to pay the draft if the draft is not a check. A disclaimer of the liability stated in subsection (b) is not effective if the draft is a check.

(f) If (i) a check is not presented for payment or given to a depositary bank for collection within 30 days after its date, (ii) the drawee suspends payments after expiration of the 30-day period without paying the check, and (iii) because of the suspension of payments, the drawer is deprived of funds maintained with the drawee to cover payment of the check, the drawer to the extent deprived of funds may discharge its obligation to pay the check by assigning to the person entitled to enforce the check the rights of the drawer against the drawee with respect to the funds.

§3—415. OBLIGATION OF INDORSER

(a) Subject to subsections (b), (c), and (d) and to Section 3—419(d), if an instrument is dishonored, an indorser is obliged to pay the amount due on the instrument (i) according to the terms of the instrument at the time it was indorsed, or (ii) if the indorser indorsed an incomplete instrument, according to its terms when completed, to the extent stated in Sections 3—115 and 3—407. The obligation of the indorser is owed to a person entitled to enforce the instrument or to a subsequent indorser who paid the instrument under this section.

(b) If an indorsement states that it is made "without recourse" or otherwise disclaims liability of the indorser, the indorser is not liable under subsection (a) to pay the instrument.

(c) If notice of dishonor of an instrument is required by Section 3—503 and notice of dishonor complying with that section is not given to an indorser, the liability of the indorser under subsection (a) is discharged.

(d) If a draft is accepted by a bank after an indorsement is made, the liability of the indorser under subsection (a) is discharged.

(e) If an indorser of a check is liable under subsection (a) and the check is not presented for payment, or given to a depositary bank for collection, within 30 days after the day the indorsement was made, the liability of the indorser under subsection (a) is discharged.

As amended in 1993.

§3—416. TRANSFER WARRANTIES

(a) A person who transfers an instrument for consideration warrants to the transferee and, if the transfer is by indorsement, to any subsequent transferee that:

(1) the warrantor is a person entitled to enforce the instrument;

(2) all signatures on the instrument are authentic and authorized;

(3) the instrument has not been altered;

(4) the instrument is not subject to a defense or claim in recoupment of any party which can be asserted against the warrantor; and

(5) the warrantor has no knowledge of any insolvency proceeding commenced with respect to the maker or acceptor or, in the case of an unaccepted draft, the drawer.

(b) A person to whom the warranties under subsection (a) are made and who took the instrument in good faith may recover from the warrantor as damages for breach of warranty an amount equal to the loss suffered as a result of the breach, but not more than the amount of the instrument plus expenses and loss of interest incurred as a result of the breach.

(c) The warranties stated in subsection (a) cannot be disclaimed with respect to checks. Unless notice of a claim for breach of warranty is given to the warrantor within 30 days after the claimant has reason to know of the breach and the identity of the warrantor, the liability of the warrantor under subsection (b) is discharged to the extent of any loss caused by the delay in giving notice of the claim.

(d) A [cause of action] for breach of warranty under this section accrues when the claimant has reason to know of the breach.

§3—417. PRESENTMENT WARRANTIES

(a) If an unaccepted draft is presented to the drawee for payment or acceptance and the drawee pays or accepts the draft, (i) the person obtaining payment or acceptance, at the time of presentment, and (ii) a previous transferor of the draft, at the time of transfer, warrant to the drawee making payment or accepting the draft in good faith that:

(1) the warrantor is, or was, at the time the warrantor transferred the draft, a person entitled to enforce the draft or authorized to obtain payment or acceptance of the draft on behalf of a person entitled to enforce the draft;

(2) the draft has not been altered; and

(3) the warrantor has no knowledge that the signature of the drawer of the draft is unauthorized.

(b) A drawee making payment may recover from any warrantor damages for breach of warranty equal to the amount paid by the drawee less the amount the drawee received or is entitled to receive from the drawer because of the payment. In addition, the drawee is entitled to compensation for expenses and loss of interest resulting from the breach. The right of the drawee to recover damages under this subsection is not affected by any failure of the drawee to exercise ordinary care in making payment. If the drawee accepts the draft, breach of warranty is a defense to the obligation of the acceptor. If the acceptor makes payment with respect to the draft, the acceptor is entitled to recover from any warrantor for breach of warranty the amounts stated in this subsection.

(c) If a drawee asserts a claim for breach of warranty under subsection (a) based on an unauthorized indorsement of the draft or an alteration of the draft, the warrantor may defend by proving that the indorsement is effective under Section 3—404 or 3—405 or the drawer is precluded under Section 3—406 or 4—406 from asserting against the drawee the unauthorized indorsement or alteration.

(d) If (i) a dishonored draft is presented for payment to the drawer or an indorser or (ii) any other instrument is presented for payment to a party obliged to pay the instrument, and (iii) payment is received, the following rules apply:

(1) The person obtaining payment and a prior transferor of the instrument warrant to the person making payment in good faith that the warrantor is, or was, at the time the warrantor transferred the instrument, a person entitled to enforce the instrument or authorized to obtain payment on behalf of a person entitled to enforce the instrument.

(2) The person making payment may recover from any warrantor for breach of warranty an amount equal to the amount paid plus expenses and loss of interest resulting from the breach.

(e) The warranties stated in subsections (a) and (d) cannot be disclaimed with respect to checks. Unless notice of a claim for breach of warranty is given to the warrantor within 30 days after the claimant has reason to know of the breach and the identity of the warrantor, the liability of the warrantor under subsection (b) or (d) is discharged to the extent of any loss caused by the delay in giving notice of the claim.

(f) A [cause of action] for breach of warranty under this section accrues when the claimant has reason to know of the breach.

§3—418. PAYMENT OR ACCEPTANCE BY MISTAKE

(a) Except as provided in subsection (c), if the drawee of a draft pays or accepts the draft and the drawee acted on the mistaken belief that (i) payment of the draft had not been stopped pursuant to Section 4—403 or (ii) the signature of the drawer of the draft was authorized, the drawee may recover the amount of the draft from the person to whom or for whose benefit payment was made or, in the case of acceptance, may revoke the acceptance. Rights of the drawee under this subsection are not affected by failure of the drawee to exercise ordinary care in paying or accepting the draft.

(b) Except as provided in subsection (c), if an instrument has been paid or accepted by mistake and the case is not covered by subsection (a), the person paying or accepting may, to the extent permitted by the law governing mistake and restitution, (i) recover the payment from the person to whom or for whose benefit payment was made or (ii) in the case of acceptance, may revoke the acceptance.

(c) The remedies provided by subsection (a) or (b) may not be asserted against a person who took the instrument in good faith and for value or who in good faith changed position in reliance on the payment or acceptance. This subsection does not limit remedies provided by Section 3—417 or 4—407.

(d) Notwithstanding Section 4—215, if an instrument is paid or accepted by mistake and the payor or acceptor recovers payment or revokes acceptance under subsection (a) or (b), the instrument is deemed not to have been paid or accepted and is treated as dishonored, and the person from whom payment is recovered has rights as a person entitled to enforce the dishonored instrument.

§3—419. INSTRUMENTS SIGNED FOR ACCOMMODATION

(a) If an instrument is issued for value given for the benefit of a party to the instrument ("accommodated party") and another party to the instrument ("accommodation party") signs the instrument for the purpose of incurring liability on the instrument without being a direct beneficiary of the value given for the instrument, the instrument is signed by the accommodation party "for accommodation."

(b) An accommodation party may sign the instrument as maker, drawer, acceptor, or indorser and, subject to subsection (d), is obliged to pay the instrument in the capacity in which the accommodation party signs. The obligation of an accommodation party may be enforced notwithstanding any statute of frauds and whether or not the accommodation party receives consideration for the accommodation.

* * * *

(e) An accommodation party who pays the instrument is entitled to reimbursement from the accommodated party and is entitled to enforce the instrument against the accommodated party. An accommodated party who pays the instrument has no right of recourse against, and is not entitled to contribution from, an accommodation party.

§3—420. CONVERSION OF INSTRUMENT

(a) The law applicable to conversion of personal property applies to instruments. An instrument is also converted if it is taken by transfer, other than a negotiation, from a person not entitled to enforce the instrument or a bank makes or obtains payment with respect to the instrument for a person not entitled to enforce the instrument or receive payment. An action for conversion of an instrument may not be brought by (i) the issuer or acceptor of the instrument or (ii) a payee or indorsee who did not receive delivery of the instrument either directly or through delivery to an agent or a co-payee.

(b) In an action under subsection (a), the measure of liability is presumed to be the amount payable on the instrument, but recovery may not exceed the amount of the plaintiff's interest in the instrument.

(c) A representative, other than a depositary bank, who has in good faith dealt with an instrument or its proceeds on behalf of one who was not the person entitled to enforce the instrument is not liable in conversion to that person beyond the amount of any proceeds that it has not paid out.

§3—501. PRESENTMENT

(a) "Presentment" means a demand made by or on behalf of a person entitled to enforce an instrument (i) to pay the instrument made to the drawee or a party obliged to pay the instrument or, in the case of a note or accepted draft payable at a bank, to the bank, or (ii) to accept a draft made to the drawee.

(b) The following rules are subject to Article 4, agreement of the parties, and clearing-house rules and the like:

(1) Presentment may be made at the place of payment of the instrument and must be made at the place of payment if the instrument is payable at a bank in the United States; may be made by any commercially reasonable means, including an oral, written, or electronic communication; is effective when the demand for payment or acceptance is received by the person to whom presentment is made; and is effective if made to any one of two or more makers, acceptors, drawees, or other payors.

(2) Upon demand of the person to whom presentment is made, the person making presentment must (i) exhibit the instrument, (ii) give reasonable identification and, if presentment is made on behalf of another person, reasonable evidence of authority to do so, and (…) sign a receipt on the instrument for any payment made or surrender the instrument if full payment is made.

(3) Without dishonoring the instrument, the party to whom presentment is made may (i) return the instrument for lack of a necessary indorsement, or (ii) refuse payment or acceptance for failure of the presentment to comply with the terms of the instrument, an agreement of the parties, or other applicable law or rule.

(4) The party to whom presentment is made may treat presentment as occurring on the next business day after the day of presentment if the party to whom presentment is made has established a

cut-off hour not earlier than 2 P.M. for the receipt and processing of instruments presented for payment or acceptance and presentment is made after the cut-off hour.

§3—502. DISHONOR

(a) Dishonor of a note is governed by the following rules:

(1) If the note is payable on demand, the note is dishonored if presentment is duly made to the maker and the note is not paid on the day of presentment.

(2) If the note is not payable on demand and is payable at or through a bank or the terms of the note require presentment, the note is dishonored if presentment is duly made and the note is not paid on the day it becomes payable or the day of presentment, whichever is later.

(3) If the note is not payable on demand and paragraph (2) does not apply, the note is dishonored if it is not paid on the day it becomes payable.

(b) Dishonor of an unaccepted draft other than a documentary draft is governed by the following rules:

(1) If a check is duly presented for payment to the payor bank otherwise than for immediate payment over the counter, the check is dishonored if the payor bank makes timely return of the check or sends timely notice of dishonor or nonpayment under Section 4—301 or 4—302, or becomes accountable for the amount of the check under Section 4—302.

(2) If a draft is payable on demand and paragraph (1) does not apply, the draft is dishonored if presentment for payment is duly made to the drawee and the draft is not paid on the day of presentment.

(3) If a draft is payable on a date stated in the draft, the draft is dishonored if (i) presentment for payment is duly made to the drawee and payment is not made on the day the draft becomes payable or the day of presentment, whichever is later, or (ii) presentment for acceptance is duly made before the day the draft becomes payable and the draft is not accepted on the day of presentment.

(4) If a draft is payable on elapse of a period of time after sight or acceptance, the draft is dishonored if presentment for acceptance is duly made and the draft is not accepted on the day of presentment.

(c) Dishonor of an unaccepted documentary draft occurs according to the rules stated in subsection (b)(2), (3), and (4), except that payment or acceptance may be delayed without dishonor until no later than the close of the third business day of the drawee following the day on which payment or acceptance is required by those paragraphs.

(d) Dishonor of an accepted draft is governed by the following rules:

(1) If the draft is payable on demand, the draft is dishonored if presentment for payment is duly made to the acceptor and the draft is not paid on the day of presentment.

(2) If the draft is not payable on demand, the draft is dishonored if presentment for payment is duly made to the acceptor and payment is not made on the day it becomes payable or the day of presentment, whichever is later.

(e) In any case in which presentment is otherwise required for dishonor under this section and presentment is excused under Section 3—504, dishonor occurs without presentment if the instrument is not duly accepted or paid.

(f) If a draft is dishonored because timely acceptance of the draft was not made and the person entitled to demand acceptance consents to a late acceptance, from the time of acceptance the draft is treated as never having been dishonored.

§3—503. NOTICE OF DISHONOR

(a) The obligation of an indorser stated in Section 3—415 (a) and the obligation of a drawer stated in Section 3—414 (d) may not be enforced unless (i) the indorser or drawer is given notice of dishonor of the instrument complying with this section or (ii) notice of dishonor is excused under Section 3—504(b).

(b) Notice of dishonor may be given by any person; may be given by any commercially reasonable means, including an oral, written, or electronic communication; and is sufficient if it reasonably identifies the instrument and indicates that the instrument has been dishonored or has not been paid or accepted. Return of an instrument given to a bank for collection is sufficient notice of dishonor.

(c) Subject to Section 3—504(c), with respect to an instrument taken for collection by a collecting bank, notice of dishonor must be given (i) by the bank before midnight of the next banking day following the banking day on which the bank receives notice of dishonor of the instrument, or (ii) by any other person within 30 days following the day on which the person receives notice of dishonor. With respect to any other instrument, notice of dishonor must be given within 30 days following the day on which dishonor occurs.

* * * *

§3—601. DISCHARGE AND EFFECT OF DISCHARGE

(a) The obligation of a party to pay the instrument is discharged as stated in this Article or by an act or agreement with the party which would discharge an obligation to pay money under a simple contract.

(b) Discharge of the obligation of a party is not effective against a person acquiring rights of a holder in due course of the instrument without notice of the discharge.

§3—602. PAYMENT

(a) Subject to subsection (b), an instrument is paid to the extent payment is made (i) by or on behalf of a party obliged to pay the instrument, and (ii) to a person entitled to enforce the instrument. To the extent of the payment, the obligation of the party obliged to pay the instrument is discharged even though payment is made with knowledge of a claim to the instrument under Section 3—306 by another person.

(b) The obligation of a party to pay the instrument is not discharged under subsection (a) if:

(1) a claim to the instrument under Section 3—306 is enforceable against the party receiving payment and (i) payment is made with knowledge by the payor that payment is prohibited by injunction or similar process of a court of competent jurisdiction, or (ii) in the case of an instrument other than a cashier's check, teller's check, or certified check, the party making payment accepted, from the person having a claim to the instrument, indemnity against loss resulting from refusal to pay the person entitled to enforce the instrument; or

(2) the person making payment knows that the instrument is a stolen instrument and pays a person it knows is in wrongful possession of the instrument.

§3—603. TENDER OF PAYMENT

(a) If tender of payment of an obligation to pay an instrument is made to a person entitled to enforce the instrument, the effect of tender is governed by principles of law applicable to tender of payment under a simple contract.

(b) If tender of payment of an obligation to pay an instrument is made to a person entitled to enforce the instrument and the tender is refused, there is discharge, to the extent of the amount of the tender, of the obligation of an indorser or accommodation party having a right of recourse with respect to the obligation to which the tender relates.

(c) If tender of payment of an amount due on an instrument is made to a person entitled to enforce the instrument, the obligation of the obligor to pay interest after the due date on the amount tendered is discharged. If presentment is required with respect to an instrument and the obligor is able and ready to pay on the due date at every place of payment stated in the instrument, the obligor is deemed to have made tender of payment on the due date to the person entitled to enforce the instrument.

§3—604. DISCHARGE BY CANCELLATION OR RENUNCIATION

(a) A person entitled to enforce an instrument, with or without consideration, may discharge the obligation of a party to pay the instrument (i) by an intentional voluntary act, such as surrender of the instrument to the party, destruction, mutilation, or cancellation of the instrument, cancellation or striking out of the party's signature, or the addition of words to the instrument indicating discharge, or (ii) by agreeing not to sue or otherwise renouncing rights against the party by a signed writing.

(b) Cancellation or striking out of an indorsement pursuant to subsection (a) does not affect the status and rights of a party derived from the indorsement.

§3—605. DISCHARGE OF INDORSERS AND ACCOMMODATION PARTIES

(a) In this section, the term "indorser" includes a drawer having the obligation described in Section 3—414(d).

(b) Discharge, under Section 3—604, of the obligation of a party to pay an instrument does not discharge the obligation of an indorser or accommodation party having a right of recourse against the discharged party.

(c) If a person entitled to enforce an instrument agrees, with or without consideration, to an extension of the due date of the obligation of a party to pay the instrument, the extension discharges an indorser or accommodation party having a right of recourse against the party whose obligation is extended to the extent the indorser or accommodation party proves that the extension caused loss to the indorser or accommodation party with respect to the right of recourse.

(d) If a person entitled to enforce an instrument agrees, with or without consideration, to a material modification of the obligation of a party other than an extension of the due date, the modification discharges the obligation of an indorser or accommodation party having a right of recourse against the person whose obligation is modified to the extent the modification causes loss to the indorser or accommodation party with respect to the right of recourse. The loss suffered by the indorser or accommodation party as a result of the modification is equal to the amount of the right of recourse unless the person enforcing the instrument proves that no loss was caused by the modification or that the loss caused by the modification was an amount less than the amount of the right of recourse.

(e) If the obligation of a party to pay an instrument is secured by an interest in collateral and a person entitled to enforce the instrument impairs the value of the interest in collateral, the obligation of an indorser or accommodation party having a right of recourse against the obligor is discharged to the extent of the impairment. The value of an interest in collateral is impaired to the extent (i) the value of the interest is reduced to an amount less than the amount of the right of recourse of the party asserting discharge, or (ii) the reduction in value of the interest causes an increase in the amount by which the amount of the right of recourse exceeds the value of the interest. The burden of proving impairment is on the party asserting discharge.

(f) If the obligation of a party is secured by an interest in collateral not provided by an accommodation party and a person entitled to enforce the instrument impairs the value of the interest in collateral, the obligation of any party who is jointly and severally liable with respect to the secured obligation is discharged to the extent the impairment causes the party asserting discharge to pay more than that party would have been obliged to pay, taking into account rights of contribution, if impairment had not occurred. If the party asserting discharge is an accommodation party not entitled to discharge under subsection (e), the party is deemed to have a right to contribution based on joint and several liability rather than a right to reimbursement. The burden of proving impairment is on the party asserting discharge.

* * * *

(h) An accommodation party is not discharged under subsection (c), (d), or (e) unless the person entitled to enforce the instrument knows of the accommodation or has notice under Section 3—419(c) that the instrument was signed for accommodation.

(i) A party is not discharged under this section if (i) the party asserting discharge consents to the event or conduct that is the basis of the discharge, or (ii) the instrument or a separate agreement of the party provides for waiver of discharge under this section either specifically or by general language indicating that parties waive defenses based on suretyship or impairment of collateral.

* * * *

Revised Article 4 Bank Deposits and Collections

Part 1 General Provisions and Definitions

§4—103. VARIATION BY AGREEMENT; MEASURE OF DAMAGES; ACTION CONSTITUTING ORDINARY CARE

(a) The effect of the provisions of this Article may be varied by agreement, but the parties to the agreement cannot disclaim a bank's responsibility for its lack of good faith or failure to exercise ordinary care or limit the measure of damages for the lack or failure. However, the parties may determine by agreement the standards by which the bank's responsibility is to be measured if those standards are not manifestly unreasonable.

(b) Federal Reserve regulations and operating circulars, clearing-house rules, and the like have the effect of agreements under subsection (a), whether or not specifically assented to by all parties interested in items handled.

* * * *

§4—104. DEFINITIONS AND INDEX OF DEFINITIONS

(1) "Account" means any deposit or credit account with a bank, including a demand, time, savings, passbook, share draft, or like account, other than an account evidenced by a certificate of deposit;

* * * *

(3) "Banking day" means the part of a day on which a bank is open to the public for carrying on substantially all of its banking functions;

(4) "Clearing house" means an association of banks or other payors regularly clearing items;

* * * *

(7) "Draft" means a draft as defined in Section 3—104 or an item, other than an instrument, that is an order;

(8) "Drawee" means a person ordered in a draft to make payment;

* * * *

(10) "Midnight deadline" with respect to a bank is midnight on its next banking day following the banking day on which it receives the relevant item or notice or from which the time for taking action commences to run, whichever is later;

* * * *

§4—105. "BANK"; "DEPOSITARY BANK"; "PAYOR BANK"; "INTERMEDIARY BANK"; "COLLECTING BANK"; "PRESENTING BANK"

In this Article:

(1) "Bank" means a person engaged in the business of banking, including a savings bank, savings and loan association, credit union, or trust company;

(2) "Depositary bank" means the first bank to take an item even though it is also the payor bank, unless the item is presented for immediate payment over the counter;

(3) "Payor bank" means a bank that is the drawee of a draft;

(4) "Intermediary bank" means a bank to which an item is transferred in course of collection except the depositary or payor bank;

(5) "Collecting bank" means a bank handling an item for collection except the payor bank;

(6) "Presenting bank" means a bank presenting an item except a payor bank.

§4—106. PAYABLE THROUGH OR PAYABLE AT BANK: COLLECTING BANK

(a) If an item states that it is "payable through" a bank identified in the item, (i) the item designates the bank as a collecting bank and does not by itself authorize the bank to pay the item, and (ii) the item may be presented for payment only by or through the bank.

Alternative A

(b) If an item states that it is "payable at" a bank identified in the item, the item is equivalent to a draft drawn on the bank.

Alternative B

(b) If an item states that it is "payable at" a bank identified in the item, (i) the item designates the bank as a collecting bank and does not by itself authorize the bank to pay the item, and (ii) the item may be presented for payment only by or through the bank.

(c) If a draft names a nonbank drawee and it is unclear whether a bank named in the draft is a co-drawee or a collecting bank, the bank is a collecting bank.

§4—107. SEPARATE OFFICE OF BANK

A branch or separate office of a bank is a separate bank for the purpose of computing the time within which and determining the place at or to which action may be taken or notices or orders shall be given under this Article and under Article 3.

§4—108. TIME OF RECEIPT OF ITEMS

(a) For the purpose of allowing time to process items, prove balances, and make the necessary entries on its books to determine its position for the day, a bank may fix an afternoon hour of 2 P.M. or later as a cutoff hour for the handling of money and items and the making of entries on its books.

(b) An item or deposit of money received on any day after a cutoff hour so fixed or after the close of the banking day may be treated as being received at the opening of the next banking day.

§4—109. DELAYS

(a) Unless otherwise instructed, a collecting bank in a good faith effort to secure payment of a specific item drawn on a payor other than a bank, and with or without the approval of any person involved, may waive, modify, or extend time limits imposed or permitted by this [act] for a period not exceeding two additional banking days without discharge of drawers or indorsers or liability to its transferor or a prior party.

(b) Delay by a collecting bank or payor bank beyond time limits prescribed or permitted by this [act] or by instructions is excused if (i) the delay is caused by interruption of communication or computer facilities, suspension of payments by another bank, war, emergency conditions, failure of equipment, or other circumstances beyond the control of the bank, and (ii) the bank exercises such diligence as the circumstances require.

§4—110. ELECTRONIC PRESENTMENT

(a) "Agreement for electronic presentment" means an agreement, clearing-house rule, or Federal Reserve regulation or operating circular, providing that presentment of an item may be made by transmission of an image of an item or information describing the item ("presentment notice") rather than delivery of the item itself. The agreement may provide for procedures governing retention, presentment, payment, dishonor, and other matters concerning items subject to the agreement.

* * * *

§4—111. STATUTE OF LIMITATIONS

An action to enforce an obligation, duty, or right arising under this Article must be commenced within three years after the [cause of action] accrues.

§4—201. STATUS OF COLLECTING BANK AS AGENT AND PROVISIONAL STATUS OF CREDITS; APPLICABILITY OF ARTICLE; ITEM INDORSED "PAY ANY BANK"

(a) Unless a contrary intent clearly appears and before the time that a settlement given by a collecting bank for an item is or becomes final, the bank, with respect to an item, is an agent or sub-agent of the owner of the item and any settlement given for the item is provisional. This provision applies regardless of the form of indorsement or lack of indorsement and even though credit given for the item is subject to immediate withdrawal as of right or is in fact withdrawn; but the continuance of ownership of an item by its owner and any rights of the owner to proceeds of the item are subject to rights of a collecting bank, such as those resulting from outstanding advances on the item and rights of recoupment or setoff. If an item is handled by banks for purposes of presentment, payment, collection, or return, the relevant provisions of this Article apply even though action of the parties clearly establishes that a particular bank has purchased the item and is the owner of it.

(b) After an item has been indorsed with the words "pay any bank" or the like, only a bank may acquire the rights of a holder until the item has been:

(1) returned to the customer initiating collection; or

(2) specially indorsed by a bank to a person who is not a bank.

§4—202. RESPONSIBILITY FOR COLLECTION OR RETURN; WHEN ACTION TIMELY

(a) A collecting bank must exercise ordinary care in:

(1) presenting an item or sending it for presentment;

(2) sending notice of dishonor or nonpayment or returning an item other than a documentary draft to the bank's transferor after learning that the item has not been paid or accepted, as the case may be;

(3) settling for an item when the bank receives final settlement; and

(4) notifying its transferor of any loss or delay in transit within a reasonable time after discovery thereof.

(b) A collecting bank exercises ordinary care under subsection (a) by taking proper action before its midnight deadline following receipt of an item, notice, or settlement. Taking proper action within a reasonably longer time may constitute the exercise of ordinary care, but the bank has the burden of establishing timeliness.

(c) Subject to subsection (a)(1), a bank is not liable for the insolvency, neglect, misconduct, mistake, or default of another bank or person or for loss or destruction of an item in the possession of others or in transit.

* * * *

§4—205. DEPOSITARY BANK HOLDER OF UNINDORSED ITEM

If a customer delivers an item to a depositary bank for collection:

(1) the depositary bank becomes a holder of the item at the time it receives the item for collection if the customer at the time of delivery was a holder of the item, whether or not the customer indorses the item, and, if the bank satisfies the other requirements of Section 3—302, it is a holder in due course; and

(2) the depositary bank warrants to collecting banks, the payor bank or other payor, and the drawer that the amount of the item was paid to the customer or deposited to the customer's account.

* * * *

§4—207. TRANSFER WARRANTIES

(a) A customer or collecting bank that transfers an item and receives a settlement or other consideration warrants to the transferee and to any subsequent collecting bank that:

(1) the warrantor is a person entitled to enforce the item;

(2) all signatures on the item are authentic and authorized;

(3) the item has not been altered;

(4) the item is not subject to a defense or claim in recoupment (Section 3—305(a)) of any party that can be asserted against the warrantor; and

(5) the warrantor has no knowledge of any insolvency proceeding commenced with respect to the

maker or acceptor or, in the case of an unaccepted draft, the drawer.

(b) If an item is dishonored, a customer or collecting bank transferring the item and receiving settlement or other consideration is obliged to pay the amount due on the item (i) according to the terms of the item at the time it was transferred, or (ii) if the transfer was of an incomplete item, according to its terms when completed as stated in Sections 3—115 and 3—407. The obligation of a transferor is owed to the transferee and to any subsequent collecting bank that takes the item in good faith. A transferor cannot disclaim its obligation under this subsection by an indorsement stating that it is made "without recourse" or otherwise disclaiming liability.

(c) A person to whom the warranties under subsection (a) are made and who took the item in good faith may recover from the warrantor as damages for breach of warranty an amount equal to the loss suffered as a result of the breach, but not more than the amount of the item plus expenses and loss of interest incurred as a result of the breach.

(d) The warranties stated in subsection (a) cannot be disclaimed with respect to checks. Unless notice of a claim for breach of warranty is given to the warrantor within 30 days after the claimant has reason to know of the breach and the identity of the warrantor, the warrantor is discharged to the extent of any loss caused by the delay in giving notice of the claim.

(e) A cause of action for breach of warranty under this section accrues when the claimant has reason to know of the breach.

§4—208. PRESENTMENT WARRANTIES

(a) If an unaccepted draft is presented to the drawee for payment or acceptance and the drawee pays or accepts the draft, (i) the person obtaining payment or acceptance, at the time of presentment, and (ii) a previous transferor of the draft, at the time of transfer, warrant to the drawee that pays or accepts the draft in good faith that:

(1) the warrantor is, or was, at the time the warrantor transferred the draft, a person entitled to enforce the draft or authorized to obtain payment or acceptance of the draft on behalf of a person entitled to enforce the draft;

(2) the draft has not been altered; and

(3) the warrantor has no knowledge that the signature of the purported drawer of the draft is unauthorized.

(b) A drawee making payment may recover from a warrantor damages for breach of warranty equal to the amount paid by the drawee less the amount the drawee received or is entitled to receive from the drawer because of the payment. In addition, the drawee is entitled to compensation for expenses and loss of interest resulting from the breach. The right of the drawee to recover damages under this subsection is not affected by any failure of the drawee to exercise ordinary care in making payment. If the drawee accepts the draft (i) breach of warranty is a defense to the obligation of the acceptor, and (ii) if the acceptor makes payment with respect to the draft, the acceptor is entitled to recover from a warrantor for breach of warranty the amounts stated in this subsection.

(c) If a drawee asserts a claim for breach of warranty under subsection (a) based on an unauthorized indorsement of the draft or an alteration of the draft, the warrantor may defend by proving that the indorsement is effective under Section 3—404 or 3—405 or the drawer is precluded under Section 3—406 or 4—406 from asserting against the drawee the unauthorized indorsement or alteration.

(d) If (i) a dishonored draft is presented for payment to the drawer or an indorser or (ii) any other item is presented for payment to a party obliged to pay the item, and the item is paid, the person obtaining payment and a prior transferor of the item warrant to the person making payment in good faith that the warrantor is, or was, at the time the warrantor transferred the item, a person entitled to enforce the item or authorized to obtain payment on behalf of a person entitled to enforce the item. The person making payment may recover from any warrantor for breach of warranty an amount equal to the amount paid plus expenses and loss of interest resulting from the breach.

(e) The warranties stated in subsections (a) and (d) cannot be disclaimed with respect to checks. Unless notice of a claim for breach of warranty is given to the warrantor within 30 days after the claimant has reason to know of the breach and the identity of the warrantor, the warrantor is discharged to the extent of any loss caused by the delay in giving notice of the claim.

(f) A cause of action for breach of warranty under this section accrues when the claimant has reason to know of the breach.

* * * *

§4—211. WHEN BANK GIVES VALUE FOR PURPOSES OF HOLDER IN DUE COURSE

For purposes of determining its status as a holder in due course, a bank has given value to the extent it has a security interest in an item, if the bank otherwise complies with the requirements of Section 3—302 on what constitutes a holder in due course.

As amended in 1990.

§4—212. PRESENTMENT BY NOTICE OF ITEM NOT PAYABLE BY, THROUGH, OR AT BANK; LIABILITY OF DRAWER OR INDORSER

(a) Unless otherwise instructed, a collecting bank may present an item not payable by, through, or at a bank by sending to the party to accept or pay a written notice that the bank holds the item for acceptance or payment. The notice must be sent in time to be received on or before the day when presentment is due and the bank must meet any requirement of the party to accept or pay under Section 3—501 by the close of the bank's next banking day after it knows of the requirement.

(b) If presentment is made by notice and payment, acceptance, or request for compliance with a requirement under Section 3—501 is not received by the close of business on the day after maturity or, in the case of demand items, by the close of business on the third banking day after notice was sent, the presenting bank may treat the item as dishonored and charge any drawer or indorser by sending it notice of the facts.

* * * *

§4—214. RIGHT OF CHARGE-BACK OR REFUND; LIABILITY OF COLLECTING BANK: RETURN OF ITEM

(a) If a collecting bank has made provisional settlement with its customer for an item and fails by reason of dishonor, suspension of payments by a bank, or otherwise to receive settlement for the item which is or becomes final, the bank may revoke the settlement given by it, charge back the amount of any credit given for the item to its customer's account, or obtain refund from its customer, whether or not it is able to return the item, if by its midnight deadline or within a longer reasonable time after it learns the facts it returns the item or sends notification of the facts. If the return or notice is delayed beyond the bank's midnight deadline or a longer reasonable time after it learns the facts, the bank may revoke the settlement, charge back the credit, or obtain refund from its customer, but it is liable for any loss resulting from the delay. These rights to revoke, charge back, and obtain refund terminate if and when a settlement for the item received by the bank is or becomes final.

(b) A collecting bank returns an item when it is sent or delivered to the bank's customer or transferor or pursuant to its instructions.

(c) A depositary bank that is also the payor may charge back the amount of an item to its customer's account or obtain refund in accordance with the section governing return of an item received by a payor bank for credit on its books (Section 4—301).

(d) The right to charge back is not affected by:

(1) previous use of a credit given for the item; or

(2) failure by any bank to exercise ordinary care with respect to the item, but a bank so failing remains liable.

(e) A failure to charge back or claim refund does not affect other rights of the bank against the customer or any other party.

(f) If credit is given in dollars as the equivalent of the value of an item payable in foreign money, the dollar amount of any charge-back or refund must be calculated on the basis of the bank-offered spot rate for the foreign money prevailing on the day when the person entitled to the charge-back or refund learns that it will not receive payment in ordinary course.

§4—215. FINAL PAYMENT OF ITEM BY PAYOR BANK; WHEN PROVISIONAL DEBITS AND CREDITS BECOME FINAL; WHEN CERTAIN CREDITS BECOME AVAILABLE FOR WITHDRAWAL

(a) An item is finally paid by a payor bank when the bank has first done any of the following:

(1) paid the item in cash;

(2) settled for the item without having a right to revoke the settlement under statute, clearing- house rule, or agreement; or

(3) made a provisional settlement for the item and failed to revoke the settlement in the time and manner permitted by statute, clearing-house rule, or agreement.

(b) If provisional settlement for an item does not become final, the item is not finally paid.

* * * *

§4—216. INSOLVENCY AND PREFERENCE

(a) If an item is in or comes into the possession of a payor or collecting bank that suspends payment and the item has not been finally paid, the item must be returned by the receiver, trustee, or agent in charge of the closed bank to the presenting bank or the closed bank's customer.

(b) If a payor bank finally pays an item and suspends payments without making a settlement for the item with its customer or the presenting bank which settlement is or becomes final, the owner of the item has a preferred claim against the payor bank.

(c) If a payor bank gives or a collecting bank gives or receives a provisional settlement for an item and thereafter suspends payments, the suspension does not prevent or interfere with the settlement's becoming final if the finality occurs automatically upon the lapse of certain time or the happening of certain events.

(d) If a collecting bank receives from subsequent parties settlement for an item, which settlement is or becomes final and the bank suspends payments without making a settlement for the item with its customer which settlement is or becomes final, the owner of the item has a preferred claim against the collecting bank.

§4—301. DEFERRED POSTING; RECOVERY OF PAYMENT BY RETURN OF ITEMS; TIME OF DISHONOR; RETURN OF ITEMS BY PAYOR BANK

(a) If a payor bank settles for a demand item other than a documentary draft presented otherwise than for immediate payment over the counter before midnight of the banking day of receipt, the payor bank may revoke the settlement and recover the settlement if, before it has made final payment and before its midnight deadline, it

(1) returns the item; or

(2) sends written notice of dishonor or nonpayment if the item is unavailable for return.

(b) If a demand item is received by a payor bank for credit on its books, it may return the item or send notice of dishonor and may revoke any credit given or recover the amount thereof withdrawn by its customer, if it acts within the time limit and in the manner specified in subsection (a).

(c) Unless previous notice of dishonor has been sent, an item is dishonored at the time when for purposes of dishonor it is returned or notice sent in accordance with this section.

(d) An item is returned:

(1) as to an item presented through a clearing house, when it is delivered to the presenting or last collecting bank or to the clearing house or is sent or delivered in accordance with clearing-house rules; or

(2) in all other cases, when it is sent or delivered to the bank's customer or transferor or pursuant to instructions.

§4—302. PAYOR BANK'S RESPONSIBILITY FOR LATE RETURN OF ITEM

(a) If an item is presented to and received by a payor bank, the bank is accountable for the amount of:

(1) a demand item, other than a documentary draft, whether properly payable or not, if the bank, in any case in which it is not also the depositary bank, retains the item beyond midnight of the banking day of receipt without settling for it or, whether or not it is also the depositary bank, does not pay or return the item or send notice of dishonor until after its midnight deadline; or

(2) any other properly payable item unless, within the time allowed for acceptance or payment of that item, the bank either accepts or pays the item or returns it and accompanying documents.

(b) The liability of a payor bank to pay an item pursuant to subsection (a) is subject to defenses based on breach of a presentment warranty (Section 4—208) or proof that the person seeking enforcement of the liability presented or transferred the item for the purpose of defrauding the payor bank.

§4—303. WHEN ITEMS SUBJECT TO NOTICE, STOP-PAYMENT ORDER, LEGAL PROCESS, OR SETOFF; ORDER IN WHICH ITEMS MAY BE CHARGED OR CERTIFIED

(a) Any knowledge, notice, or stop-payment order received by, legal process served upon, or setoff exercised by a payor bank comes too late to terminate, suspend, or modify the bank's right or duty to pay an item or to charge its customer's account for the item if the knowledge, notice, stop-payment order, or legal process is received or served and a reasonable time for the bank to act thereon expires or the setoff is exercised after the earliest of the following:

(1) the bank accepts or certifies the item;

(2) the bank pays the item in cash;

(3) the bank settles for the item without having a right to revoke the settlement under statute, clearing-house rule, or agreement;

(4) the bank becomes accountable for the amount of the item under Section 4—302 dealing with the payor bank's responsibility for late return of items; or

(5) with respect to checks, a cutoff hour no earlier than one hour after the opening of the next banking day after the banking day on which the bank received the check and no later than the close of that next banking day or, if no cutoff hour is fixed,

the close of the next banking day after the banking day on which the bank received the check.

(b) Subject to subsection (a), items may be accepted, paid, certified, or charged to the indicated account of its customer in any order.

§4—401. WHEN BANK MAY CHARGE CUSTOMER'S ACCOUNT

(a) A bank may charge against the account of a customer an item that is properly payable from the account even though the charge creates an overdraft. An item is properly payable if it is authorized by the customer and is in accordance with any agreement between the customer and bank.

(b) A customer is not liable for the amount of an overdraft if the customer neither signed the item nor benefited from the proceeds of the item.

(c) A bank may charge against the account of a customer a check that is otherwise properly payable from the account, even though payment was made before the date of the check, unless the customer has given notice to the bank of the postdating describing the check with reasonable certainty. The notice is effective for the period stated in Section 4—403(b) for stop-payment orders, and must be received at such time and in such manner as to afford the bank a reasonable opportunity to act on it before the bank takes any action with respect to the check described in Section 4—303. If a bank charges against the account of a customer a check before the date stated in the notice of postdating, the bank is liable for damages for the loss resulting from its act. The loss may include damages for dishonor of subsequent items under Section 4—402.

(d) A bank that in good faith makes payment to a holder may charge the indicated account of its customer according to:

(1) the original terms of the altered item; or

(2) the terms of the completed item, even though the bank knows the item has been completed unless the bank has notice that the completion was improper.

§4—402. BANK'S LIABILITY TO CUSTOMER FOR WRONGFUL DISHONOR; TIME OF DETERMINING INSUFFICIENCY OF ACCOUNT

(a) Except as otherwise provided in this Article, a payor bank wrongfully dishonors an item if it dishonors an item that is properly payable, but a bank may dishonor an item that would create an overdraft unless it has agreed to pay the overdraft.

(b) A payor bank is liable to its customer for damages proximately caused by the wrongful dishonor of an item. Liability is limited to actual damages proved and may include damages for an arrest or prosecution of the customer or other consequential damages. Whether any consequential damages are proximately caused by the wrongful dishonor is a question of fact to be determined in each case.

(c) A payor bank's determination of the customer's account balance on which a decision to dishonor for insufficiency of available funds is based may be made at any time between the time the item is received by the payor bank and the time that the payor bank returns the item or gives notice in lieu of return, and no more than one determination need be made. If, at the election of the payor bank, a subsequent balance determination is made for the purpose of reevaluating the bank's decision to dishonor the item, the account balance at that time is determinative of whether a dishonor for insufficiency of available funds is wrongful.

§4—403. CUSTOMER'S RIGHT TO STOP PAYMENT; BURDEN OF PROOF OF LOSS

(a) A customer or any person authorized to draw on the account if there is more than one person may stop payment of any item drawn on the customer's account or close the account by an order to the bank describing the item or account with reasonable certainty received at a time and in a manner that affords the bank a reasonable opportunity to act on it before any action by the bank with respect to the item described in Section 4—303. If the signature of more than one person is required to draw on an account, any of these persons may stop payment or close the account.

(b) A stop-payment order is effective for six months, but it lapses after 14 calendar days if the original order was oral and was not confirmed in writing within that period. A stop-payment order may be renewed for additional six-month periods by a writing given to the bank within a period during which the stop-payment order is effective.

(c) The burden of establishing the fact and amount of loss resulting from the payment of an item contrary to a stop-payment order or order to close an account is on the customer. The loss from payment of an item contrary to a stop-payment order may include damages for dishonor of subsequent items under Section 4—402.

§4—404. BANK NOT OBLIGED TO PAY CHECK MORE THAN SIX MONTHS OLD

A bank is under no obligation to a customer having a checking account to pay a check, other than a certified check, which is presented more than six months after its date, but it may charge its customer's account for a payment made thereafter in good faith.

§4—405. DEATH OR INCOMPETENCE OF CUSTOMER

(a) A payor or collecting bank's authority to accept, pay, or collect an item or to account for proceeds of its collection, if otherwise effective, is not rendered ineffective by incompetence of a customer of either bank existing at the time the item is issued or its collection is undertaken if the bank does not know of an adjudication of incompetence. Neither death nor incompetence of a customer revokes the authority to accept, pay, collect, or account until the bank knows of the fact of death or of an adjudication of incompetence and has reasonable opportunity to act on it.

(b) Even with knowledge, a bank may for 10 days after the date of death pay or certify checks drawn on or before the date unless ordered to stop payment by a person claiming an interest in the account.

§4—406. CUSTOMER'S DUTY TO DISCOVER AND REPORT UNAUTHORIZED SIGNATURE OR ALTERATION

(a) A bank that sends or makes available to a customer a statement of account showing payment of items for the account shall either return or make available to the customer the items paid or provide information in the statement of account sufficient to allow the customer reasonably to identify the items paid. The statement of account provides sufficient information if the item is described by item number, amount, and date of payment.

(b) If the items are not returned to the customer, the person retaining the items shall either retain the items or, if the items are destroyed, maintain the capacity to furnish legible copies of the items until the expiration of seven years after receipt of the items. A customer may request an item from the bank that paid the item, and that bank must provide in a reasonable time either the item or, if the item has been destroyed or is not otherwise obtainable, a legible copy of the item.

(c) If a bank sends or makes available a statement of account or items pursuant to subsection (a), the customer must exercise reasonable promptness in examining the statement or the items to determine whether any payment was not authorized because of an alteration of an item or because a purported signature by or on behalf of the customer was not authorized. If, based on the statement or items provided, the customer should reasonably have discovered the unauthorized payment, the customer must promptly notify the bank of the relevant facts.

(d) If the bank proves that the customer failed, with respect to an item, to comply with the duties imposed on the customer by subsection (c), the customer is precluded from asserting against the bank:

(1) the customer's unauthorized signature or any alteration on the item, if the bank also proves that it suffered a loss by reason of the failure; and

(2) the customer's unauthorized signature or alteration by the same wrongdoer on any other item paid in good faith by the bank if the payment was made before the bank received notice from the customer of the unauthorized signature or alteration and after the customer had been afforded a reasonable period of time, not exceeding 30 days, in which to examine the item or statement of account and notify the bank.

(e) If subsection (d) applies and the customer proves that the bank failed to exercise ordinary care in paying the item and that the failure substantially contributed to loss, the loss is allocated between the customer precluded and the bank asserting the preclusion according to the extent to which the failure of the customer to comply with subsection (c) and the failure of the bank to exercise ordinary care contributed to the loss. If the customer proves that the bank did not pay the item in good faith, the preclusion under subsection (d) does not apply.

(f) Without regard to care or lack of care of either the customer or the bank, a customer who does not within one year after the statement or items are made available to the customer (subsection (a)) discover and report the customer's unauthorized signature on or any alteration on the item is precluded from asserting against the bank the unauthorized signature or alteration. If there is a preclusion under this subsection, the payor bank may not recover for breach or warranty under Section 4—208 with respect to the unauthorized signature or alteration to which the preclusion applies.

§4—407. PAYOR BANK'S RIGHT TO SUBROGATION ON IMPROPER PAYMENT

If a payor has paid an item over the order of the drawer or maker to stop payment, or after an account has been closed, or otherwise under circumstances giving a basis for objection by the drawer or maker, to prevent unjust enrichment and only to the extent necessary to prevent loss to the bank by reason of its payment of the item, the payor bank is subrogated to the rights

(1) of any holder in due course on the item against the drawer or maker;

(2) of the payee or any other holder of the item against the drawer or maker either on the item or under the transaction out of which the item arose; and

(3) of the drawer or maker against the payee or any other holder of the item with respect to the transaction out of which the item arose.

* * * *

Article 4A Funds Transfers

Part 1 Subject Matter and Definitions

§4A—104. FUNDS TRANSFER—DEFINITIONS

(a) "Funds transfer" means the series of transactions, beginning with the originator's payment order, made for the purpose of making payment to the beneficiary of the order. The term includes any payment order issued by the originator's bank or an intermediary bank intended to carry out the originator's payment order. A funds transfer is completed by acceptance by the beneficiary's bank of a payment order for the benefit of the beneficiary of the originator's payment order.

(b) "Intermediary bank" means a receiving bank other than the originator's bank or the beneficiary's bank.

(c) "Originator" means the sender of the first payment order in a funds transfer.

(d) "Originator's bank" means (i) the receiving bank to which the payment order of the originator is issued if the originator is not a bank, or (ii) the originator if the originator is a bank.

§4A—105. OTHER DEFINITIONS

(1) "Authorized account" means a deposit account of a customer in a bank designated by the customer as a source of payment of payment orders issued by the customer to the bank. If a customer does not so designate an account, any account of the customer is an authorized account if payment of a payment order from that account is not inconsistent with a restriction on the use of that account.

(2) "Bank" means a person engaged in the business of banking and includes a savings bank, savings and loan association, credit union, and trust company. A branch or separate office of a bank is a separate bank for purposes of this Article.

(3) "Customer" means a person, including a bank, having an account with a bank or from whom a bank has agreed to receive payment orders.

(4) "Funds-transfer business day" of a receiving bank means the part of a day during which the receiving bank is open for the receipt, processing, and transmittal of payment orders and cancellations and amendments of payment orders.

(5) "Funds-transfer system" means a wire transfer network, automated clearing house, or other communication system of a clearing house or other association of banks through which a payment order by a bank may be transmitted to the bank to which the order is addressed.

(6) "Good faith" means honesty in fact and the observance of reasonable commercial standards of fair dealing.

(7) "Prove" with respect to a fact means to meet the burden of establishing the fact (Section 1—201(8)).

* * * *

§4A—106. TIME PAYMENT ORDER IS RECEIVED

(a) The time of receipt of a payment order or communication cancelling or amending a payment order is determined by the rules applicable to receipt of a notice stated in Section 1—201(27). A receiving bank may fix a cut-off time or times on a funds-transfer business day for the receipt and processing of payment orders and communications cancelling or amending payment orders. Different cut-off times may apply to payment orders, cancellations, or amendments, or to different categories of payment orders, cancellations, or amendments. A cut-off time may apply to senders generally or different cut-off times may apply to different senders or categories of payment orders. If a payment order or communication cancelling or amending a payment order is received after the close of a funds-transfer business day or after the appropriate cut-off time on a funds-transfer business day, the receiving bank may treat the payment order or communication as received at the opening of the next funds-transfer business day.

(b) If this Article refers to an execution date or payment date or states a day on which a receiving bank is required to take action, and the date or day does not fall on a funds-transfer business day, the next day that is a funds- transfer business day is treated as the date or day stated, unless the contrary is stated in this Article.

* * * *

§4A—108. EXCLUSION OF CONSUMER TRANSACTIONS GOVERNED BY FEDERAL LAW

This Article does not apply to a funds transfer any part of which is governed by the Electronic Fund Transfer Act of 1978 (Title XX, Public Law 95—630, 92 Stat. 3728, 15 U.S.C. §1693 et seq.) as amended from time to time.

* * * *

Revised Article 9 Secured Transactions

§9—102. DEFINITIONS AND INDEX OF DEFINITIONS

(1) "Accession" means goods that are physically united with other goods in such a manner that the identity of the original goods is not lost.

(2) "Account", except as used in "account for", means a right to payment of a monetary obligation, whether or not earned by performance, (i) for property that has been or is to be sold, leased, licensed, assigned, or otherwise disposed of, (ii) for services rendered or to be rendered, (iii) for a policy of insurance issued or to be issued, (iv) for a secondary obligation incurred or to be incurred, (v) for energy provided or to be provided, (vi) for the use or hire of a vessel under a charter or other contract, (vii) arising out of the use of a credit or charge card or information contained on or for use with the card, or (viii) as winnings in a lottery or other game of chance operated or sponsored by a State, governmental unit of a State, or person licensed or authorized to operate the game by a State or governmental unit of a State. The term includes health-care insurance receivables. The term does not include (i) rights to payment evidenced by chattel paper or an instrument, (ii) commercial tort claims, (iii) deposit accounts, (iv) investment property, (v) letter-of-credit rights or letters of credit, or (vi) rights to payment for money or funds advanced or sold, other than rights arising out of the use of a credit or charge card or information contained on or for use with the card.

* * * *

(5) "Agricultural lien" means an interest, other than a security interest, in farm products:

(A) which secures payment or performance of an obligation for:

(i) goods or services furnished in connection with a debtor's farming operation; or

(ii) rent on real property leased by a debtor in connection with its farming operation;

(B) which is created by statute in favor of a person that:

(i) in the ordinary course of its business furnished goods or services to a debtor in connection with a debtor's farming operation; or

(ii) leased real property to a debtor in connection with the debtor's farming operation; and

(C) whose effectiveness does not depend on the person's possession of the personal property.

(6) "As-extracted collateral" means:

(A) oil, gas, or other minerals that are subject to a security interest that:

(i) is created by a debtor having an interest in the minerals before extraction; and

(ii) attaches to the minerals as extracted; or

(B) accounts arising out of the sale at the wellhead or minehead of oil, gas, or other minerals in which the debtor had an interest before extraction.

(7) "Authenticate" means:

(A) to sign; or

(B) to execute or otherwise adopt a symbol, or encrypt or similarly process a record in whole or in part, with the present intent of the authenticating person to identify the person and adopt or accept a record.

* * * *

(11) "Chattel paper" means a record or records that evidence both a monetary obligation and a security interest in specific goods, a security interest in specific goods and software used in the goods, a security interest in specific goods and license of software used in the goods, a lease of specific goods, or a lease of specific goods and license of software used in the goods. In this paragraph, "monetary obligation" means a monetary obligation secured by the goods or owed under a lease of the goods and includes a monetary obligation with respect to software used in the goods. The term does not include (i) charters or other contracts involving the use or hire of a vessel or (ii) records that evidence a right to payment arising out of the use of a credit or charge card or information contained on or for use with the card. If a transaction is evidenced by records that include an instrument or

series of instruments, the group of records taken together constitutes chattel paper.

(12) "Collateral" means the property subject to a security interest or agricultural lien. The term includes:

(A) proceeds to which a security interest attaches;

(B) accounts, chattel paper, payment intangibles, and promissory notes that have been sold; and

(C) goods that are the subject of a consignment.

(13) "Commercial tort claim" means a claim arising in tort with respect to which:

(A) the claimant is an organization; or

(B) the claimant is an individual and the claim:

(i) arose in the course of the claimant's business or profession; and

(ii) does not include damages arising out of personal injury to or the death of an individual.

* * * *

(19) "Consignee" means a merchant to which goods are delivered in a consignment.

(20) "Consignment" means a transaction, regardless of its form, in which a person delivers goods to a merchant for the purpose of sale and:

(A) the merchant:

(i) deals in goods of that kind under a name other than the name of the person making delivery;

(ii) is not an auctioneer; and

(iii) is not generally known by its creditors to be substantially engaged in selling the goods of others;

(B) with respect to each delivery, the aggregate value of the goods is $1,000 or more at the time of delivery;

(C) the goods are not consumer goods immediately before delivery; and

(D) the transaction does not create a security interest that secures an obligation.

(21) "Consignor" means a person that delivers goods to a consignee in a consignment.

(22) "Consumer debtor" means a debtor in a consumer transaction.

(23) "Consumer goods" means goods that are used or bought for use primarily for personal, family, or household purposes.

(24) "Consumer-goods transaction" means a consumer transaction in which:

(A) an individual incurs an obligation primarily for personal, family, or household purposes; and

(B) a security interest in consumer goods secures the obligation.

(25) "Consumer obligor" means an obligor who is an individual and who incurred the obligation as part of a transaction entered into primarily for personal, family, or household purposes.

(26) "Consumer transaction" means a transaction in which (i) an individual incurs an obligation primarily for personal, family, or household purposes, (ii) a security interest secures the obligation, and (iii) the collateral is held or acquired primarily for personal, family, or household purposes. The term includes consumer-goods transactions.

(27) "Continuation statement" means an amendment of a financing statement which:

(A) identifies, by its file number, the initial financing statement to which it relates; and

(B) indicates that it is a continuation statement for, or that it is filed to continue the effectiveness of, the identified financing statement.

(28) "Debtor" means:

(A) a person having an interest, other than a security interest or other lien, in the collateral, whether or not the person is an obligor;

(B) a seller of accounts, chattel paper, payment intangibles, or promissory notes; or

(C) a consignee.

(29) "Deposit account" means a demand, time, savings, passbook, or similar account maintained with a bank. The term does not include investment property or accounts evidenced by an instrument.

(30) "Document" means a document of title or a receipt of the type described in Section 7—201(2).

(31) "Electronic chattel paper" means chattel paper evidenced by a record or records consisting of information stored in an electronic medium.

(32) "Encumbrance" means a right, other than an ownership interest, in real property. The term includes mortgages and other liens on real property.

(33) "Equipment" means goods other than inventory, farm products, or consumer goods.

(34) "Farm products" means goods, other than standing timber, with respect to which the debtor is engaged in a farming operation and which are:

(A) crops grown, growing, or to be grown, including:

(i) crops produced on trees, vines, and bushes; and

(ii) aquatic goods produced in aquacultural operations;

(B) livestock, born or unborn, including aquatic goods produced in aquacultural operations;

(C) supplies used or produced in a farming operation; or

(D) products of crops or livestock in their unmanufactured states.

(35) "Farming operation" means raising, cultivating, propagating, fattening, grazing, or any other farming, livestock, or aquacultural operation.

* * * *

(39) "Financing statement" means a record or records composed of an initial financing statement and any filed record relating to the initial financing statement.

(40) "Fixture filing" means the filing of a financing statement covering goods that are or are to become fixtures and satisfying Section 9—502(a) and (b). The term includes the filing of a financing statement covering goods of a transmitting utility which are or are to become fixtures.

(41) "Fixtures" means goods that have become so related to particular real property that an interest in them arises under real property law.

(42) "General intangible" means any personal property, including things in action, other than accounts, chattel paper, commercial tort claims, deposit accounts, documents, goods, instruments, investment property, letter-of-credit rights, letters of credit, money, and oil, gas, or other minerals before extraction. The term includes payment intangibles and software.

* * * *

(44) "Goods" means all things that are movable when a security interest attaches. The term includes (i) fixtures, (ii) standing timber that is to be cut and removed under a conveyance or contract for sale, (iii) the unborn young of animals, (iv) crops grown, growing, or to be grown, even if the crops are produced on trees, vines, or bushes, and (v) manufactured homes.

The term also includes a computer program embedded in goods and any supporting information provided in connection with a transaction relating to the program if (i) the program is associated with the goods in such a manner that it customarily is considered part of the goods, or (ii) by becoming the owner of the goods, a person acquires a right to use the program in connection with the goods. The term does not include a computer program embedded in goods that consist solely of the medium in which the program is embedded. The term also does not include accounts, chattel paper, commercial tort claims, deposit accounts, documents, general intangibles, instruments, investment property, letter-of-credit rights, letters of credit, money, or oil, gas, or other minerals before extraction.

* * * *

(46) "Health-care-insurance receivable" means an interest in or claim under a policy of insurance which is a right to payment of a monetary obligation for health-care goods or services provided.

(47) "Instrument" means a negotiable instrument or any other writing that evidences a right to the payment of a monetary obligation, is not itself a security agreement or lease, and is of a type that in ordinary course of business is transferred by delivery with any necessary indorsement or assignment. The term does not include (i) investment property, (ii) letters of credit, or (iii) writings that evidence a right to payment arising out of the use of a credit or charge card or information contained on or for use with the card.

(48) "Inventory" means goods, other than farm products, which:

(A) are leased by a person as lessor;

(B) are held by a person for sale or lease or to be furnished under a contract of service;

(C) are furnished by a person under a contract of service; or

(D) consist of raw materials, work in process, or materials used or consumed in a business.

(49) "Investment property" means a security, whether certificated or uncertificated, security entitlement, securities account, commodity contract, or commodity account.

* * * *

(51) "Letter-of-credit right" means a right to payment or performance under a letter of credit, whether or not the beneficiary has demanded or is at the time entitled to demand payment or performance. The term does not include the right of a beneficiary to demand payment or performance under a letter of credit.

(52) "Lien creditor" means:

(A) a creditor that has acquired a lien on the property involved by attachment, levy, or the like;

(B) an assignee for benefit of creditors from the time of assignment;

(C) a trustee in bankruptcy from the date of the filing of the petition; or

(D) a receiver in equity from the time of appointment.

* * * *

(55) "Mortgage" means a consensual interest in real property, including fixtures, which secures payment or performance of an obligation.

(56) "New debtor" means a person that becomes bound as debtor under Section 9—203(d) by a security agreement previously entered into by another person.

(57) "New value" means (i) money, (ii) money's worth in property, services, or new credit, or (iii) release by a transferee of an interest in property previously transferred to the transferee. The term does not include an obligation substituted for another obligation.

* * * *

(61) "Payment intangible" means a general intangible under which the account debtor's principal obligation is a monetary obligation.

* * * *

(64) "Proceeds", except as used in Section 9—609 (b), means the following property:

(A) whatever is acquired upon the sale, lease, license, exchange, or other disposition of collateral;

(B) whatever is collected on, or distributed on account of, collateral;

(C) rights arising out of collateral;

(D) to the extent of the value of collateral, claims arising out of the loss, non-conformity, or interference with the use of, defects or infringement of rights in, or damage to, the collateral; or

(E) to the extent of the value of collateral and to the extent payable to the debtor or the secured party, insurance payable by reason of the loss or non-conformity of, defects or infringement of rights in, or damage to, the collateral.

* * * *

(69) "Record", except as used in "for record", "of record", "record or legal title", and "record owner", means information that is inscribed on a tangible medium or which is stored in an electronic or other medium and is retrievable in perceivable form.

* * * *

(72) "Secured party" means:

(A) a person in whose favor a security interest is created or provided for under a security agreement, whether or not any obligation to be secured is outstanding;

(B) a person that holds an agricultural lien;

(C) a consignor;

(D) a person to which accounts, chattel paper, payment intangibles, or promissory notes have been sold;

(E) a trustee, indenture trustee, agent, collateral agent, or other representative in whose favor a security interest or agricultural lien is created or provided for; or

(F) a person that holds a security interest arising under Section 2—401, 2—505, 2—711(3), 2A—508(5), 4—210, or 5—118.

(73) "Security agreement" means an agreement that creates or provides for a security interest.

* * * *

(78) "Tangible chattel paper" means chattel paper evidenced by a record or records consisting of information that is inscribed on a tangible medium.

(79) "Termination statement" means an amendment of a financing statement which:

(A) identifies, by its file number, the initial financing statement to which it relates; and

(B) indicates either that it is a termination statement or that the identified financing statement is no longer effective.

* * * *

§9—103. PURCHASE-MONEY SECURITY INTEREST; APPLICATION OF PAYMENTS; BURDEN OF ESTABLISHING

(a) In this section:

(1) "purchase-money collateral" means goods or software that secures a purchase-money obligation incurred with respect to that collateral; and

(2) "purchase-money obligation" means an obligation of an obligor incurred as all or part of the price of the collateral or for value given to enable the debtor to acquire rights in or the use of the collateral if the value is in fact so used.

(b) A security interest in goods is a purchase-money security interest:

(1) to the extent that the goods are purchase-money collateral with respect to that security interest;

(2) if the security interest is in inventory that is or was purchase-money collateral, also to the extent that the security interest secures a purchase-money obligation incurred with respect to other inventory in which the secured party holds or held a purchase-money security interest; and

(3) also to the extent that the security interest secures a purchase-money obligation incurred with respect to software in which the secured party holds or held a purchase-money security interest.

(c) A security interest in software is a purchase-money security interest to the extent that the security interest also secures a purchase-money obligation incurred with respect to goods in which the secured party holds or held a purchase-money security interest if:

(1) the debtor acquired its interest in the software in an integrated transaction in which it acquired an interest in the goods; and

(2) the debtor acquired its interest in the software for the principal purpose of using the software in the goods.

(d) The security interest of a consignor in goods that are the subject of a consignment is a purchase-money security interest in inventory.

(e) In a transaction other than a consumer-goods transaction, if the extent to which a security interest is a purchase-money security interest depends on the application of a payment to a particular obligation, the payment must be applied:

(1) in accordance with any reasonable method of application to which the parties agree;

(2) in the absence of the parties' agreement to a reasonable method, in accordance with any intention of the obligor manifested at or before the time of payment; or

(3) in the absence of an agreement to a reasonable method and a timely manifestation of the obligor's intention, in the following order:

(A) to obligations that are not secured; and

(B) if more than one obligation is secured, to obligations secured by purchase-money security interests in the order in which those obligations were incurred.

(f) In a transaction other than a consumer-goods transaction, a purchase-money security interest does not lose its status as such, even if:

(1) the purchase-money collateral also secures an obligation that is not a purchase-money obligation;

(2) collateral that is not purchase-money collateral also secures the purchase-money obligation; or

(3) the purchase-money obligation has been renewed, refinanced, consolidated, or restructured.

(g) In a transaction other than a consumer-goods transaction, a secured party claiming a purchase-money security interest has the burden of establishing the extent to which the security interest is a purchase-money security interest.

(h) The limitation of the rules in subsections (e), (f), and (g) to transactions other than consumer-goods transactions is intended to leave to the court the determination of the proper rules in consumer-goods transactions. The court may not infer from that limitation the nature of the proper rule in consumer-goods transactions and may continue to apply established approaches.

§9—104. CONTROL OF DEPOSIT ACCOUNT

(a) A secured party has control of a deposit account if:

(1) the secured party is the bank with which the deposit account is maintained;

(2) the debtor, secured party, and bank have agreed in an authenticated record that the bank will comply with instructions originated by the secured party directing disposition of the funds in the deposit account without further consent by the debtor; or

(3) the secured party becomes the bank's customer with respect to the deposit account.

(b) A secured party that has satisfied subsection (a) has control, even if the debtor retains the right to direct the disposition of funds from the deposit account.

§9—105. CONTROL OF ELECTRONIC CHATTEL PAPER

A secured party has control of electronic chattel paper if the record or records comprising the chattel paper are created, stored, and assigned in such a manner that:

(1) a single authoritative copy of the record or records exists which is unique, identifiable and, except as otherwise provided in paragraphs (4), (5), and (6), unalterable;

(2) the authoritative copy identifies the secured party as the assignee of the record or records;

(3) the authoritative copy is communicated to and maintained by the secured party or its designated custodian;

(4) copies or revisions that add or change an identified assignee of the authoritative copy can be made only with the participation of the secured party;

(5) each copy of the authoritative copy and any copy of a copy is readily identifiable as a copy that is not the authoritative copy; and

(6) any revision of the authoritative copy is readily identifiable as an authorized or unauthorized revision.

§9—106. CONTROL OF INVESTMENT PROPERTY

(a) A person has control of a certificated security, uncertificated security, or security entitlement as provided in Section 8—106.

(b) A secured party has control of a commodity contract if:

(1) the secured party is the commodity intermediary with which the commodity contract is carried; or

(2) the commodity customer, secured party, and commodity intermediary have agreed that the commodity intermediary will apply any value distributed on account of the commodity contract as directed by the secured party without further consent by the commodity customer.

(c) A secured party having control of all security entitlements or commodity contracts carried in a securities account or commodity account has control over the securities account or commodity account.

§9—107. CONTROL OF LETTER-OF-CREDIT RIGHT

A secured party has control of a letter-of-credit right to the extent of any right to payment or performance by the issuer or any nominated person if the issuer or nominated person has consented to an assignment of proceeds of the letter of credit under Section 5—114(c) or otherwise applicable law or practice.

§9—108. SUFFICIENCY OF DESCRIPTION

(a) Except as otherwise provided in subsections (c), (d), and (e), a description of personal or real property is sufficient, whether or not it is specific, if it reasonably identifies what is described.

(b) Except as otherwise provided in subsection (d), a description of collateral reasonably identifies the collateral if it identifies the collateral by:

(1) specific listing;

(2) category;

(3) except as otherwise provided in subsection (e), a type of collateral defined in [the Uniform Commercial Code];

(4) quantity;

(5) computational or allocational formula or procedure; or

(6) except as otherwise provided in subsection (c), any other method, if the identity of the collateral is objectively determinable.

(c) A description of collateral as "all the debtor's assets" or "all the debtor's personal property" or using words of similar import does not reasonably identify the collateral.

(d) Except as otherwise provided in subsection (e), a description of a security entitlement, securities account, or commodity account is sufficient if it describes:

(1) the collateral by those terms or as investment property; or

(2) the underlying financial asset or commodity contract.

(e) A description only by type of collateral defined in [the Uniform Commercial Code] is an insufficient description of:

(1) a commercial tort claim; or

(2) in a consumer transaction, consumer goods, a security entitlement, a securities account, or a commodity account.

§9-109 SCOPE

* * * *

This article does not apply to:

(1) a landlord's lien, other than an agricultural lien;

(2) a lien, other than an agricultural lien, given by statute or other rule of law for services or materials, but Section 9—333 applies with respect to priority of the lien;

(3) an assignment of a claim for wages, salary, or other compensation of an employee;

(4) a sale of accounts, chattel paper, payment intangibles, or promissory notes as part of a sale of the business out of which they arose;

(5) an assignment of accounts, chattel paper, payment intangibles, or promissory notes which is for the purpose of collection only;

(6) an assignment of a right to payment under a contract to an assignee that is also obligated to perform under the contract;

(7) an assignment of a single account, payment intangible, or promissory note to an assignee in full or partial satisfaction of a preexisting indebtedness;

(8) a transfer of an interest in or an assignment of a claim under a policy of insurance, other than an

assignment by or to a health-care provider of a health-care-insurance receivable and any subsequent assignment of the right to payment, but Sections 9—315 and 9—322 apply with respect to proceeds and priorities in proceeds;

(9) an assignment of a right represented by a judgment, other than a judgment taken on a right to payment that was collateral;

(10) a right of recoupment or set-off, but:

(A) Section 9—340 applies with respect to the effectiveness of rights of recoupment or set-off against deposit accounts; and

(B) Section 9—404 applies with respect to defenses or claims of an account debtor;

(11) the creation or transfer of an interest in or lien on real property, including a lease or rents thereunder, except to the extent that provision is made for:

(A) liens on real property in Sections 9—203 and 9—308;

(B) fixtures in Section 9—334;

(C) fixture filings in Sections 9—501, 9—502, 9—512, 9—516, and 9—519; and

(D) security agreements covering personal and real property in Section 9—604;

(12) an assignment of a claim arising in tort, other than a commercial tort claim, but Sections 9—315 and 9—322 apply with respect to proceeds and priorities in proceeds; or

(13) an assignment of a deposit account in a consumer transaction, but Sections 9—315 and 9—322 apply with respect to proceeds and priorities in proceeds.

* * * *

§9—201. GENERAL EFFECTIVENESS OF SECURITY AGREEMENT

(a) Except as otherwise provided in [the Uniform Commercial Code], a security agreement is effective according to its terms between the parties, against purchasers of the collateral, and against creditors.

(b) A transaction subject to this article is subject to any applicable rule of law which establishes a different rule for consumers and [insert reference to (i) any other statute or regulation that regulates the rates, charges, agreements, and practices for loans, credit sales, or other extensions of credit and (ii) any consumer-protection statute or regulation].

(c) In case of conflict between this article and a rule of law, statute, or regulation described in subsection (b), the rule of law, statute, or regulation controls. Failure to comply with a statute or regulation described in subsection (b) has only the effect the statute or regulation specifies.

(d) This article does not:

(1) validate any rate, charge, agreement, or practice that violates a rule of law, statute, or regulation described in subsection (b); or

(2) extend the application of the rule of law, statute, or regulation to a transaction not otherwise subject to it.

§9—202. TITLE TO COLLATERAL IMMATERIAL

Except as otherwise provided with respect to consignments or sales of accounts, chattel paper, payment intangibles, or promissory notes, the provisions of this article with regard to rights and obligations apply whether title to collateral is in the secured party or the debtor.

§9—203. ATTACHMENT AND ENFORCEABILITY OF SECURITY INTEREST; PROCEEDS; SUPPORTING OBLIGATIONS; FORMAL REQUISITES

(a) A security interest attaches to collateral when it becomes enforceable against the debtor with respect to the collateral, unless an agreement expressly postpones the time of attachment.

(b) Except as otherwise provided in subsections (c) through (i), a security interest is enforceable against the debtor and third parties with respect to the collateral only if:

(1) value has been given;

(2) the debtor has rights in the collateral or the power to transfer rights in the collateral to a secured party; and

(3) one of the following conditions is met:

(A) the debtor has authenticated a security agreement that provides a description of the collateral and, if the security interest covers timber to be cut, a description of the land concerned;

(B) the collateral is not a certificated security and is in the possession of the secured party under Section 9—313 pursuant to the debtor's security agreement;

(C) the collateral is a certificated security in registered form and the security certificate has been delivered to the secured party under Section 8—301 pursuant to the debtor's security agreement; or

(D) the collateral is deposit accounts, electronic chattel paper, investment property, or letter-of-credit rights, and the secured party has control under Section 9—104, 9—105, 9—106, or 9—107 pursuant to the debtor's security agreement.

(c) Subsection (b) is subject to Section 4—210 on the security interest of a collecting bank, Section 5—118 on the security interest of a letter-of-credit issuer or nominated person, Section 9—110 on a security interest arising under Article 2 or 2A, and Section 9—206 on security interests in investment property.

(d) A person becomes bound as debtor by a security agreement entered into by another person if, by operation of law other than this article or by contract:

(1) the security agreement becomes effective to create a security interest in the person's property; or

(2) the person becomes generally obligated for the obligations of the other person, including the obligation secured under the security agreement, and acquires or succeeds to all or substantially all of the assets of the other person.

(e) If a new debtor becomes bound as debtor by a security agreement entered into by another person:

(1) the agreement satisfies subsection (b)(3) with respect to existing or after-acquired property of the new debtor to the extent the property is described in the agreement; and

(2) another agreement is not necessary to make a security interest in the property enforceable.

(f) The attachment of a security interest in collateral gives the secured party the rights to proceeds provided by Section 9—315 and is also attachment of a security interest in a supporting obligation for the collateral.

(g) The attachment of a security interest in a right to payment or performance secured by a security interest or other lien on personal or real property is also attachment of a security interest in the security interest, mortgage, or other lien.

(h) The attachment of a security interest in a securities account is also attachment of a security interest in the security entitlements carried in the securities account.

(i) The attachment of a security interest in a commodity account is also attachment of a security interest in the commodity contracts carried in the commodity account.

§9—204. AFTER-ACQUIRED PROPERTY; FUTURE ADVANCES

(a) Except as otherwise provided in subsection (b), a security agreement may create or provide for a security interest in after-acquired collateral.

(b) A security interest does not attach under a term constituting an after-acquired property clause to:

(1) consumer goods, other than an accession when given as additional security, unless the debtor acquires rights in them within 10 days after the secured party gives value; or

(2) a commercial tort claim.

(c) A security agreement may provide that collateral secures, or that accounts, chattel paper, payment intangibles, or promissory notes are sold in connection with, future advances or other value, whether or not the advances or value are given pursuant to commitment.

§9—205. USE OR DISPOSITION OF COLLATERAL PERMISSIBLE

(a) A security interest is not invalid or fraudulent against creditors solely because:

(1) the debtor has the right or ability to:

(A) use, commingle, or dispose of all or part of the collateral, including returned or repossessed goods;

(B) collect, compromise, enforce, or otherwise deal with collateral;

(C) accept the return of collateral or make repossessions; or

(D) use, commingle, or dispose of proceeds; or

(2) the secured party fails to require the debtor to account for proceeds or replace collateral.

(b) This section does not relax the requirements of possession if attachment, perfection, or enforcement of a security interest depends upon possession of the collateral by the secured party.

§9—206. SECURITY INTEREST ARISING IN PURCHASE OR DELIVERY OF FINANCIAL ASSET

(a) A security interest in favor of a securities intermediary attaches to a person's security entitlement if:

(1) the person buys a financial asset through the securities intermediary in a transaction in which the person is obligated to pay the purchase price to the securities intermediary at the time of the purchase; and

(2) the securities intermediary credits the financial asset to the buyer's securities account before the buyer pays the securities intermediary.

(b) The security interest described in subsection (a) secures the person's obligation to pay for the financial asset.

* * * *

§9—207. RIGHTS AND DUTIES OF SECURED PARTY HAVING POSSESSION OR CONTROL OF COLLATERAL

(a) Except as otherwise provided in subsection (d), a secured party shall use reasonable care in the custody and preservation of collateral in the secured party's possession. In the case of chattel paper or an instrument, reasonable care includes taking necessary steps to preserve rights against prior parties unless otherwise agreed.

(b) Except as otherwise provided in subsection (d), if a secured party has possession of collateral:

(1) reasonable expenses, including the cost of insurance and payment of taxes or other charges, incurred in the custody, preservation, use, or operation of the collateral are chargeable to the debtor and are secured by the collateral;

(2) the risk of accidental loss or damage is on the debtor to the extent of a deficiency in any effective insurance coverage;

(3) the secured party shall keep the collateral identifiable, but fungible collateral may be commingled; and

(4) the secured party may use or operate the collateral:

(A) for the purpose of preserving the collateral or its value;

(B) as permitted by an order of a court having competent jurisdiction; or

(C) except in the case of consumer goods, in the manner and to the extent agreed by the debtor.

(c) Except as otherwise provided in subsection (d), a secured party having possession of collateral or control of collateral under Section 9—104, 9—105, 9—106, or 9—107:

(1) may hold as additional security any proceeds, except money or funds, received from the collateral;

(2) shall apply money or funds received from the collateral to reduce the secured obligation, unless remitted to the debtor; and

(3) may create a security interest in the collateral.

(d) If the secured party is a buyer of accounts, chattel paper, payment intangibles, or promissory notes or a consignor:

(1) subsection (a) does not apply unless the secured party is entitled under an agreement:

(A) to charge back uncollected collateral; or

(B) otherwise to full or limited recourse against the debtor or a secondary obligor based on the nonpayment or other default of an account debtor or other obligor on the collateral; and

(2) subsections (b) and (c) do not apply.

§9—208. ADDITIONAL DUTIES OF SECURED PARTY HAVING CONTROL OF COLLATERAL

(a) This section applies to cases in which there is no outstanding secured obligation and the secured party is not committed to make advances, incur obligations, or otherwise give value.

(b) Within 10 days after receiving an authenticated demand by the debtor:

(1) a secured party having control of a deposit account under Section 9—104(a)(2) shall send to the bank with which the deposit account is maintained an authenticated statement that releases the bank from any further obligation to comply with instructions originated by the secured party;

(2) a secured party having control of a deposit account under Section 9—104(a)(3) shall:

(A) pay the debtor the balance on deposit in the deposit account; or

(B) transfer the balance on deposit into a deposit account in the debtor's name;

(3) a secured party, other than a buyer, having control of electronic chattel paper under Section 9—105 shall:

(A) communicate the authoritative copy of the electronic chattel paper to the debtor or its designated custodian;

(B) if the debtor designates a custodian that is the designated custodian with which the authoritative copy of the electronic chattel paper is maintained for the secured party, communicate to the custodian an authenticated record releasing the designated custodian from any further obligation to comply with instructions originated by the secured party and instructing the custodian to comply with instructions originated by the debtor; and

(C) take appropriate action to enable the debtor or its designated custodian to make copies of or revisions to the authoritative copy which add or change an identified assignee of the authoritative copy without the consent of the secured party;

(4) a secured party having control of investment property under Section 8—106(d)(2) or 9—106 (b) shall send to the securities intermediary or commodity intermediary with which the security entitlement or commodity contract is maintained an authenticated record that releases the securities intermediary or commodity intermediary from any further obligation to comply with entitlement orders or directions originated by the secured party; and

(5) a secured party having control of a letter-of-credit right under Section 9—107 shall send to each person having an unfulfilled obligation to pay or deliver proceeds of the letter of credit to the secured party an authenticated release from any further obligation to pay or deliver proceeds of the letter of credit to the secured party.

§9—209. DUTIES OF SECURED PARTY IF ACCOUNT DEBTOR HAS BEEN NOTIFIED OF ASSIGNMENT

(a) Except as otherwise provided in subsection (c), this section applies if:

(1) there is no outstanding secured obligation; and

(2) the secured party is not committed to make advances, incur obligations, or otherwise give value.

(b) Within 10 days after receiving an authenticated demand by the debtor, a secured party shall send to an account debtor that has received notification of an assignment to the secured party as assignee under Section 9—406(a) an authenticated record that releases the account debtor from any further obligation to the secured party.

* * * *

§9—301. LAW GOVERNING PERFECTION AND PRIORITY OF SECURITY INTERESTS

Except as otherwise provided in Sections 9—303 through 9—306, the following rules determine the law governing perfection, the effect of perfection or nonperfection, and the priority of a security interest in collateral:

(1) Except as otherwise provided in this section, while a debtor is located in a jurisdiction, the local law of that jurisdiction governs perfection, the effect of perfection or nonperfection, and the priority of a security interest in collateral.

(2) While collateral is located in a jurisdiction, the local law of that jurisdiction governs perfection, the effect of perfection or nonperfection, and the priority of a possessory security interest in that collateral.

(3) Except as otherwise provided in paragraph (4), while negotiable documents, goods, instruments, money, or tangible chattel paper is located in a jurisdiction, the local law of that jurisdiction governs:

(A) perfection of a security interest in the goods by filing a fixture filing;

(B) perfection of a security interest in timber to be cut; and

(C) the effect of perfection or nonperfection and the priority of a nonpossessory security interest in the collateral.

(4) The local law of the jurisdiction in which the wellhead or minehead is located governs perfection, the effect of perfection or nonperfection, and the priority of a security interest in as-extracted collateral.

* * * *

§9—309. SECURITY INTEREST PERFECTED UPON ATTACHMENT

The following security interests are perfected when they attach:

(1) a purchase-money security interest in consumer goods, except as otherwise provided in Section 9—311(b) with respect to consumer goods that are subject to a statute or treaty described in Section 9—311(a);

(2) an assignment of accounts or payment intangibles which does not by itself or in conjunction with other assignments to the same assignee transfer a significant part of the assignor's outstanding accounts or payment intangibles;

(3) a sale of a payment intangible;

(4) a sale of a promissory note;

(5) a security interest created by the assignment of a health-care-insurance receivable to the provider of the health-care goods or services;

(6) a security interest arising under Section 2—401, 2—505, 2—711(3), or 2A—508(5), until the debtor obtains possession of the collateral;

(7) a security interest of a collecting bank arising under Section 4—210;

(8) a security interest of an issuer or nominated person arising under Section 5—118;

(9) a security interest arising in the delivery of a financial asset under Section 9—206(c);

(10) a security interest in investment property created by a broker or securities intermediary;

(11) a security interest in a commodity contract or a commodity account created by a commodity intermediary;

(12) an assignment for the benefit of all creditors of the transferor and subsequent transfers by the assignee thereunder; and

(13) a security interest created by an assignment of a beneficial interest in a decedent's estate; and

(14) a sale by an individual of an account that is a right to payment of winnings in a lottery or other game of chance.

§9—310. WHEN FILING REQUIRED TO PERFECT SECURITY INTEREST OR AGRICULTURAL LIEN; SECURITY INTERESTS AND AGRICULTURAL LIENS TO WHICH FILING PROVISIONS DO NOT APPLY

(a) Except as otherwise provided in subsection (b) and Section 9—312(b), a financing statement must be filed to perfect all security interests and agricultural liens.

(b) The filing of a financing statement is not necessary to perfect a security interest:

(1) that is perfected under Section 9—308(d), (e), (f), or (g);

(2) that is perfected under Section 9—309 when it attaches;

(3) in property subject to a statute, regulation, or treaty described in Section 9—311(a);

(4) in goods in possession of a bailee which is perfected under Section 9—312(d)(1) or (2);

(5) in certificated securities, documents, goods, or instruments which is perfected without filing or possession under Section 9—312(e), (f), or (g);

(6) in collateral in the secured party's possession under Section 9—313;

(7) in a certificated security which is perfected by delivery of the security certificate to the secured party under Section 9—313;

(8) in deposit accounts, electronic chattel paper, investment property, or letter-of-credit rights which is perfected by control under Section 9—314;

(9) in proceeds which is perfected under Section 9—315; or

(10) that is perfected under Section 9—316.

(c) If a secured party assigns a perfected security interest or agricultural lien, a filing under this article is not required to continue the perfected status of the security interest against creditors of and transferees from the original debtor.

§9—311. PERFECTION OF SECURITY INTERESTS IN PROPERTY SUBJECT TO CERTAIN STATUTES, REGULATIONS, AND TREATIES

(a) Except as otherwise provided in subsection (d), the filing of a financing statement is not necessary or effective to perfect a security interest in property subject to:

(1) a statute, regulation, or treaty of the United States whose requirements for a security interest's obtaining priority over the rights of a lien creditor with respect to the property preempt Section 9—310(a);

(2) [list any certificate-of-title statute covering automobiles, trailers, mobile homes, boats, farm tractors, or the like, which provides for a security interest to be indicated on the certificate as a condition or result of perfection, and any non Uniform Commercial Code central filing statute]; or

(3) a certificate-of-title statute of another jurisdiction which provides for a security interest to be indicated on the certificate as a condition or result of the security interest's obtaining priority over the rights of a lien creditor with respect to the property.

* * * *

§9—312. PERFECTION OF SECURITY INTERESTS IN CHATTEL PAPER, DEPOSIT ACCOUNTS, DOCUMENTS, GOODS COVERED BY DOCUMENTS, INSTRUMENTS, INVESTMENT PROPERTY, LETTER-OF-CREDIT RIGHTS, AND MONEY; PERFECTION BY PERMISSIVE FILING; TEMPORARY PERFECTION WITHOUT FILING OR TRANSFER OF POSSESSION

(a) A security interest in chattel paper, negotiable documents, instruments, or investment property may be perfected by filing.

(b) Except as otherwise provided in Section 9—315 (c) and (d) for proceeds:

(1) a security interest in a deposit account may be perfected only by control under Section 9—314;

(2) and except as otherwise provided in Section 9—308(d), a security interest in a letter-of-credit

right may be perfected only by control under Section 9—314; and

(3) a security interest in money may be perfected only by the secured party's taking possession under Section 9—313.

(c) While goods are in the possession of a bailee that has issued a negotiable document covering the goods:

(1) a security interest in the goods may be perfected by perfecting a security interest in the document; and

(2) a security interest perfected in the document has priority over any security interest that becomes perfected in the goods by another method during that time.

(d) While goods are in the possession of a bailee that has issued a nonnegotiable document covering the goods, a security interest in the goods may be perfected by:

(1) issuance of a document in the name of the secured party;

(2) the bailee's receipt of notification of the secured party's interest; or

(3) filing as to the goods.

(e) A security interest in certificated securities, negotiable documents, or instruments is perfected without filing or the taking of possession for a period of 20 days from the time it attaches to the extent that it arises for new value given under an authenticated security agreement.

(f) A perfected security interest in a negotiable document or goods in possession of a bailee, other than one that has issued a negotiable document for the goods, remains perfected for 20 days without filing if the secured party makes available to the debtor the goods or documents representing the goods for the purpose of:

(1) ultimate sale or exchange; or

(2) loading, unloading, storing, shipping, transshipping, manufacturing, processing, or otherwise dealing with them in a manner preliminary to their sale or exchange.

(g) A perfected security interest in a certificated security or instrument remains perfected for 20 days without filing if the secured party delivers the security certificate or instrument to the debtor for the purpose of:

(1) ultimate sale or exchange; or

(2) presentation, collection, enforcement, renewal, or registration of transfer.

(h) After the 20-day period specified in subsection (e), (f), or (g) expires, perfection depends upon compliance with this article.

§9—313. WHEN POSSESSION BY OR DELIVERY TO SECURED PARTY PERFECTS SECURITY INTEREST WITHOUT FILING

(a) Except as otherwise provided in subsection (b), a secured party may perfect a security interest in negotiable documents, goods, instruments, money, or tangible chattel paper by taking possession of the collateral. A secured party may perfect a security interest in certificated securities by taking delivery of the certificated securities under Section 8—301.

(b) With respect to goods covered by a certificate of title issued by this State, a secured party may perfect a security interest in the goods by taking possession of the goods only in the circumstances described in Section 9—316(d).

(c) With respect to collateral other than certificated securities and goods covered by a document, a secured party takes possession of collateral in the possession of a person other than the debtor, the secured party, or a lessee of the collateral from the debtor in the ordinary course of the debtor's business, when:

(1) the person in possession authenticates a record acknowledging that it holds possession of the collateral for the secured party's benefit; or

(2) the person takes possession of the collateral after having authenticated a record acknowledging that it will hold possession of collateral for the secured party's benefit.

(d) If perfection of a security interest depends upon possession of the collateral by a secured party, perfection occurs no earlier than the time the secured party takes possession and continues only while the secured party retains possession.

(e) A security interest in a certificated security in registered form is perfected by delivery when delivery of the certificated security occurs under Section 8—301 and remains perfected by delivery until the debtor obtains possession of the security certificate.

(f) A person in possession of collateral is not required to acknowledge that it holds possession for a secured party's benefit.

(g) If a person acknowledges that it holds possession for the secured party's benefit:

(1) the acknowledgment is effective under subsection (c) or Section 8—301(a), even if the

acknowledgment violates the rights of a debtor; and

(2) unless the person otherwise agrees or law other than this article otherwise provides, the person does not owe any duty to the secured party and is not required to confirm the acknowledgment to another person.

(h) A secured party having possession of collateral does not relinquish possession by delivering the collateral to a person other than the debtor or a lessee of the collateral from the debtor in the ordinary course of the debtor's business if the person was instructed before the delivery or is instructed contemporaneously with the delivery:

(1) to hold possession of the collateral for the secured party's benefit; or

(2) to redeliver the collateral to the secured party.

(i) A secured party does not relinquish possession, even if a delivery under subsection (h) violates the rights of a debtor. A person to which collateral is delivered under subsection (h) does not owe any duty to the secured party and is not required to confirm the delivery to another person unless the person otherwise agrees or law other than this article otherwise provides.

§9—314. PERFECTION BY CONTROL

(a) A security interest in investment property, deposit accounts, letter-of-credit rights, or electronic chattel paper may be perfected by control of the collateral under Section 9—104, 9—105, 9—106, or 9—107.

(b) A security interest in deposit accounts, electronic chattel paper, or letter-of-credit rights is perfected by control under Section 9—104, 9—105, or 9—107 when the secured party obtains control and remains perfected by control only while the secured party retains control.

(c) A security interest in investment property is perfected by control under Section 9—106 from the time the secured party obtains control and remains perfected by control until:

(1) the secured party does not have control; and

(2) one of the following occurs:

(A) if the collateral is a certificated security, the debtor has or acquires possession of the security certificate;

(B) if the collateral is an uncertificated security, the issuer has registered or registers the debtor as the registered owner; or

(C) if the collateral is a security entitlement, the debtor is or becomes the entitlement holder.

§9—315. SECURED PARTY'S RIGHTS ON DISPOSITION OF COLLATERAL AND IN PROCEEDS

(a) Except as otherwise provided in this article and in Section 2—403(2):

(1) a security interest or agricultural lien continues in collateral notwithstanding sale, lease, license, exchange, or other disposition thereof unless the secured party authorized the disposition free of the security interest or agricultural lien; and

(2) a security interest attaches to any identifiable proceeds of collateral.

(b) Proceeds that are commingled with other property are identifiable proceeds:

(1) if the proceeds are goods, to the extent provided by Section 9—336; and

(2) if the proceeds are not goods, to the extent that the secured party identifies the proceeds by a method of tracing, including application of equitable principles, that is permitted under law other than this article with respect to commingled property of the type involved.

(c) A security interest in proceeds is a perfected security interest if the security interest in the original collateral was perfected.

(d) A perfected security interest in proceeds becomes unperfected on the 21st day after the security interest attaches to the proceeds unless:

(1) the following conditions are satisfied:

(A) a filed financing statement covers the original collateral;

(B) the proceeds are collateral in which a security interest may be perfected by filing in the office in which the financing statement has been filed; and

(C) the proceeds are not acquired with cash proceeds;

(2) the proceeds are identifiable cash proceeds; or

(3) the security interest in the proceeds is perfected other than under subsection (c) when the security interest attaches to the proceeds or within 20 days thereafter.

(e) If a filed financing statement covers the original collateral, a security interest in proceeds which remains perfected under subsection (d)(1) becomes unperfected at the later of:

(1) when the effectiveness of the filed financing statement lapses under Section 9—515 or is terminated under Section 9—513; or

(2) the 21st day after the security interest attaches to the proceeds.

§9—316. CONTINUED PERFECTION OF SECURITY INTEREST FOLLOWING CHANGE IN GOVERNING LAW

(a) A security interest perfected pursuant to the law of the jurisdiction designated in Section 9—301(1) or 9—305(c) remains perfected until the earliest of:

(1) the time perfection would have ceased under the law of that jurisdiction;

(2) the expiration of four months after a change of the debtor's location to another jurisdiction; or

(3) the expiration of one year after a transfer of collateral to a person that thereby becomes a debtor and is located in another jurisdiction.

(b) If a security interest described in subsection (a) becomes perfected under the law of the other jurisdiction before the earliest time or event described in that subsection, it remains perfected thereafter. If the security interest does not become perfected under the law of the other jurisdiction before the earliest time or event, it becomes unperfected and is deemed never to have been perfected as against a purchaser of the collateral for value.

(c) A possessory security interest in collateral, other than goods covered by a certificate of title and as-extracted collateral consisting of goods, remains continuously perfected if:

(1) the collateral is located in one jurisdiction and subject to a security interest perfected under the law of that jurisdiction;

(2) thereafter the collateral is brought into another jurisdiction; and

(3) upon entry into the other jurisdiction, the security interest is perfected under the law of the other jurisdiction.

(d) Except as otherwise provided in subsection (e), a security interest in goods covered by a certificate of title which is perfected by any method under the law of another jurisdiction when the goods become covered by a certificate of title from this State remains perfected until the security interest would have become unperfected under the law of the other jurisdiction had the goods not become so covered.

(e) A security interest described in subsection (d) becomes unperfected as against a purchaser of the goods for value and is deemed never to have been perfected as against a purchaser of the goods for value if the applicable requirements for perfection under Section 9—311(b) or 9—313 are not satisfied before the earlier of:

(1) the time the security interest would have become unperfected under the law of the other jurisdiction had the goods not become covered by a certificate of title from this State; or

(2) the expiration of four months after the goods had become so covered.

(f) A security interest in deposit accounts, letter-of-credit rights, or investment property which is perfected under the law of the bank's jurisdiction, the issuer's jurisdiction, a nominated person's jurisdiction, the securities intermediary's jurisdiction, or the commodity intermediary's jurisdiction, as applicable, remains perfected until the earlier of:

(1) the time the security interest would have become unperfected under the law of that jurisdiction; or

(2) the expiration of four months after a change of the applicable jurisdiction to another jurisdiction.

(g) If a security interest described in subsection (f) becomes perfected under the law of the other jurisdiction before the earlier of the time or the end of the period described in that subsection, it remains perfected thereafter. If the security interest does not become perfected under the law of the other jurisdiction before the earlier of that time or the end of that period, it becomes unperfected and is deemed never to have been perfected as against a purchaser of the collateral for value.

§9—317. INTERESTS THAT TAKE PRIORITY OVER OR TAKE FREE OF SECURITY INTEREST OR AGRICULTURAL LIEN

(a) A security interest or agricultural lien is subordinate to the rights of:

(1) a person entitled to priority under Section 9—322; and

(2) except as otherwise provided in subsection (e), a person that becomes a lien creditor before the earlier of the time:

(A) the security interest or agricultural lien is perfected; or

(B) one of the conditions specified in Section 9—203(b)(3) is met and a financing statement covering the collateral is filed.

(b) Except as otherwise provided in subsection (e), a buyer, other than a secured party, of tangible chattel paper, documents, goods, instruments, or a security certificate takes free of a security interest or agricultural lien if the buyer gives value and receives delivery of the collateral without knowledge of the security interest or agricultural lien and before it is perfected.

(c) Except as otherwise provided in subsection (e), a lessee of goods takes free of a security interest or agricultural lien if the lessee gives value and receives delivery of the collateral without knowledge of the security interest or agricultural lien and before it is perfected.

(d) A licensee of a general intangible or a buyer, other than a secured party, of accounts, electronic chattel paper, general intangibles, or investment property other than a certificated security takes free of a security interest if the licensee or buyer gives value without knowledge of the security interest and before it is perfected.

(e) Except as otherwise provided in Sections 9—320 and 9—321, if a person files a financing statement with respect to a purchase-money security interest before or within 20 days after the debtor receives delivery of the collateral, the security interest takes priority over the rights of a buyer, lessee, or lien creditor which arise between the time the security interest attaches and the time of filing.

§9—318. NO INTEREST RETAINED IN RIGHT TO PAYMENT THAT IS SOLD; RIGHTS AND TITLE OF SELLER OF ACCOUNT OR CHATTEL PAPER WITH RESPECT TO CREDITORS AND PURCHASERS

(a) A debtor that has sold an account, chattel paper, payment intangible, or promissory note does not retain a legal or equitable interest in the collateral sold.

(b) For purposes of determining the rights of creditors of, and purchasers for value of an account or chattel paper from, a debtor that has sold an account or chattel paper, while the buyer's security interest is unperfected, the debtor is deemed to have rights and title to the account or chattel paper identical to those the debtor sold.

§9—319. RIGHTS AND TITLE OF CONSIGNEE WITH RESPECT TO CREDITORS AND PURCHASERS

(a) Except as otherwise provided in subsection (b), for purposes of determining the rights of creditors of, and purchasers for value of goods from, a consignee, while the goods are in the possession of the consignee, the consignee is deemed to have rights and title to the goods identical to those the consignor had or had power to transfer.

(b) For purposes of determining the rights of a creditor of a consignee, law other than this article determines the rights and title of a consignee while goods are in the consignee's possession if, under this part, a perfected security interest held by the consignor would have priority over the rights of the creditor.

§9—320. BUYER OF GOODS

(a) Except as otherwise provided in subsection (e), a buyer in ordinary course of business, other than a person buying farm products from a person engaged in farming operations, takes free of a security interest created by the buyer's seller, even if the security interest is perfected and the buyer knows of its existence.

(b) Except as otherwise provided in subsection (e), a buyer of goods from a person who used or bought the goods for use primarily for personal, family, or household purposes takes free of a security interest, even if perfected, if the buyer buys:

(1) without knowledge of the security interest;

(2) for value;

(3) primarily for the buyer's personal, family, or household purposes; and

(4) before the filing of a financing statement covering the goods.

(c) To the extent that it affects the priority of a security interest over a buyer of goods under subsection (b), the period of effectiveness of a filing made in the jurisdiction in which the seller is located is governed by Section 9—316(a) and (b).

(d) A buyer in ordinary course of business buying oil, gas, or other minerals at the wellhead or minehead or after extraction takes free of an interest arising out of an encumbrance.

(e) Subsections (a) and (b) do not affect a security interest in goods in the possession of the secured party under Section 9—313.

* * * *

§9—322. PRIORITIES AMONG CONFLICTING SECURITY INTERESTS IN AND AGRICULTURAL LIENS ON SAME COLLATERAL

(a) Except as otherwise provided in this section, priority among conflicting security interests and agricultural liens in the same collateral is determined according to the following rules:

(1) Conflicting perfected security interests and agricultural liens rank according to priority in time of filing or perfection. Priority dates from the earlier of the time a filing covering the collateral is first made or the security interest or agricultural lien is first perfected, if there is no period thereafter when there is neither filing nor perfection.

(2) A perfected security interest or agricultural lien has priority over a conflicting unperfected security interest or agricultural lien.

(3) The first security interest or agricultural lien to attach or become effective has priority if conflicting security interests and agricultural liens are unperfected.

(b) For the purposes of subsection (a)(1):

(1) the time of filing or perfection as to a security interest in collateral is also the time of filing or perfection as to a security interest in proceeds; and

(2) the time of filing or perfection as to a security interest in collateral supported by a supporting obligation is also the time of filing or perfection as to a security interest in the supporting obligation.

(c) Except as otherwise provided in subsection (f), a security interest in collateral which qualifies for priority over a conflicting security interest under Section 9—327, 9—328, 9—329, 9—330, or 9—331 also has priority over a conflicting security interest in:

(1) any supporting obligation for the collateral; and

(2) proceeds of the collateral if:

(A) the security interest in proceeds is perfected;

(B) the proceeds are cash proceeds or of the same type as the collateral; and

(C) in the case of proceeds that are proceeds of proceeds, all intervening proceeds are cash proceeds, proceeds of the same type as the collateral, or an account relating to the collateral.

(d) Subject to subsection (e) and except as otherwise provided in subsection (f), if a security interest in chattel paper, deposit accounts, negotiable documents, instruments, investment property, or letter-of-credit rights is perfected by a method other than filing, conflicting perfected security interests in proceeds of the collateral rank according to priority in time of filing.

(e) Subsection (d) applies only if the proceeds of the collateral are not cash proceeds, chattel paper, negotiable documents, instruments, investment property, or letter-of-credit rights.

(f) Subsections (a) through (e) are subject to:

(1) subsection (g) and the other provisions of this part;

(2) Section 4—210 with respect to a security interest of a collecting bank;

(3) Section 5—118 with respect to a security interest of an issuer or nominated person; and

(4) Section 9—110 with respect to a security interest arising under Article 2 or 2A.

(g) A perfected agricultural lien on collateral has priority over a conflicting security interest in or agricultural lien on the same collateral if the statute creating the agricultural lien so provides.

§9—323. FUTURE ADVANCES

(a) Except as otherwise provided in subsection (c), for purposes of determining the priority of a perfected security interest under Section 9—322(a)(1), perfection of the security interest dates from the time an advance is made to the extent that the security interest secures an advance that:

(1) is made while the security interest is perfected only:

(A) under Section 9—309 when it attaches; or

(B) temporarily under Section 9—312(e), (f), or (g); and

(2) is not made pursuant to a commitment entered into before or while the security interest is perfected by a method other than under Section 9—309 or 9—312(e), (f), or (g).

(b) Except as otherwise provided in subsection (c), a security interest is subordinate to the rights of a person that becomes a lien creditor to the extent that the security interest secures an advance made more than 45 days after the person becomes a lien creditor unless the advance is made:

(1) without knowledge of the lien; or

(2) pursuant to a commitment entered into without knowledge of the lien.

(c) Subsections (a) and (b) do not apply to a security interest held by a secured party that is a buyer of accounts, chattel paper, payment intangibles, or promissory notes or a consignor.

(d) Except as otherwise provided in subsection (e), a buyer of goods other than a buyer in ordinary course of business takes free of a security interest to the extent that it secures advances made after the earlier of:

(1) the time the secured party acquires knowledge of the buyer's purchase; or

(2) 45 days after the purchase.

(e) Subsection (d) does not apply if the advance is made pursuant to a commitment entered into without knowledge of the buyer's purchase and before the expiration of the 45-day period.

(f) Except as otherwise provided in subsection (g), a lessee of goods, other than a lessee in ordinary course of business, takes the leasehold interest free of a security interest to the extent that it secures advances made after the earlier of:

(1) the time the secured party acquires knowledge of the lease; or

(2) 45 days after the lease contract becomes enforceable.

(g) Subsection (f) does not apply if the advance is made pursuant to a commitment entered into without knowledge of the lease and before the expiration of the 45 day period.

§9—324. PRIORITY OF PURCHASE-MONEY SECURITY INTERESTS

(a) Except as otherwise provided in subsection (g), a perfected purchase-money security interest in goods other than inventory or livestock has priority over a conflicting security interest in the same goods, and, except as otherwise provided in Section 9—327, a perfected security interest in its identifiable proceeds also has priority, if the purchase-money security interest is perfected when the debtor receives possession of the collateral or within 20 days thereafter.

(b) Subject to subsection (c) and except as otherwise provided in subsection (g), a perfected purchase-money security interest in inventory has priority over a conflicting security interest in the same inventory, has priority over a conflicting security interest in chattel paper or an instrument constituting proceeds of the inventory and in proceeds of the chattel paper, if so provided in Section 9—330, and, except as otherwise provided in Section 9—327, also has priority in identifiable cash proceeds of the inventory to the extent the identifiable cash proceeds are received on or before the delivery of the inventory to a buyer, if:

(1) the purchase-money security interest is perfected when the debtor receives possession of the inventory;

(2) the purchase-money secured party sends an authenticated notification to the holder of the conflicting security interest;

(3) the holder of the conflicting security interest receives the notification within five years before the debtor receives possession of the inventory; and

(4) the notification states that the person sending the notification has or expects to acquire a purchase-money security interest in inventory of the debtor and describes the inventory.

(c) Subsections (b)(2) through (4) apply only if the holder of the conflicting security interest had filed a financing statement covering the same types of inventory:

(1) if the purchase-money security interest is perfected by filing, before the date of the filing; or

(2) if the purchase-money security interest is temporarily perfected without filing or possession under Section 9—312(f), before the beginning of the 20-day period thereunder.

(d) Subject to subsection (e) and except as otherwise provided in subsection (g), a perfected purchase-money security interest in livestock that are farm products has priority over a conflicting security interest in the same livestock, and, except as otherwise provided in Section 9—327, a perfected security interest in their identifiable proceeds and identifiable products in their unmanufactured states also has priority, if:

(1) the purchase-money security interest is perfected when the debtor receives possession of the livestock;

(2) the purchase-money secured party sends an authenticated notification to the holder of the conflicting security interest;

(3) the holder of the conflicting security interest receives the notification within six months before the debtor receives possession of the livestock; and

(4) the notification states that the person sending the notification has or expects to acquire a purchase-money security interest in livestock of the debtor and describes the livestock.

(e) Subsections (d)(2) through (4) apply only if the holder of the conflicting security interest had filed a financing statement covering the same types of livestock:

(1) if the purchase-money security interest is perfected by filing, before the date of the filing; or

(2) if the purchase-money security interest is temporarily perfected without filing or possession under Section 9—312(f), before the beginning of the 20-day period thereunder.

(f) Except as otherwise provided in subsection (g), a perfected purchase-money security interest in software has priority over a conflicting security interest in the same collateral, and, except as otherwise provided in Section 9—327, a perfected security interest in its identifiable proceeds also has priority, to the extent that the purchase-money security interest in the goods in which the software was acquired for use has priority in the goods and proceeds of the goods under this section.

(g) If more than one security interest qualifies for priority in the same collateral under subsection (a), (b), (d), or (f):

(1) a security interest securing an obligation incurred as all or part of the price of the collateral has priority over a security interest securing an obligation incurred for value given to enable the debtor to acquire rights in or the use of collateral; and

(2) in all other cases, Section 9—322(a) applies to the qualifying security interests.

§9—325. PRIORITY OF SECURITY INTERESTS IN TRANSFERRED COLLATERAL

(a) Except as otherwise provided in subsection (b), a security interest created by a debtor is subordinate to a security interest in the same collateral created by another person if:

(1) the debtor acquired the collateral subject to the security interest created by the other person;

(2) the security interest created by the other person was perfected when the debtor acquired the collateral; and

(3) there is no period thereafter when the security interest is unperfected.

(b) Subsection (a) subordinates a security interest only if the security interest:

(1) otherwise would have priority solely under Section 9—322(a) or 9—324; or

(2) arose solely under Section 2—711(3) or 2A—508(5).

§9—326. PRIORITY OF SECURITY INTERESTS CREATED BY NEW DEBTOR

(a) Subject to subsection (b), a security interest created by a new debtor which is perfected by a filed financing statement that is effective solely under Section 9—508 in collateral in which a new debtor has or acquires rights is subordinate to a security interest in the same collateral which is perfected other than by a filed financing statement that is effective solely under Section 9—508.

(b) The other provisions of this part determine the priority among conflicting security interests in the same collateral perfected by filed financing statements that are effective solely under Section 9—508. However, if the security agreements to which a new debtor became bound as debtor were not entered into by the same original debtor, the conflicting security interests rank according to priority in time of the new debtor's having become bound.

* * * *

§9—330. PRIORITY OF PURCHASER OF CHATTEL PAPER OR INSTRUMENT

(a) A purchaser of chattel paper has priority over a security interest in the chattel paper which is claimed merely as proceeds of inventory subject to a security interest if:

(1) in good faith and in the ordinary course of the purchaser's business, the purchaser gives new value and takes possession of the chattel paper or obtains control of the chattel paper under Section 9—105; and

(2) the chattel paper does not indicate that it has been assigned to an identified assignee other than the purchaser.

(b) A purchaser of chattel paper has priority over a security interest in the chattel paper which is claimed other than merely as proceeds of inventory subject to a security interest if the purchaser gives new value and takes possession of the chattel paper or obtains control of the chattel paper under Section 9—105 in good faith, in the ordinary course of the purchaser's business, and without knowledge that the purchase violates the rights of the secured party.

(c) Except as otherwise provided in Section 9—327, a purchaser having priority in chattel paper under subsection (a) or (b) also has priority in proceeds of the chattel paper to the extent that:

(1) Section 9—322 provides for priority in the proceeds; or

(2) the proceeds consist of the specific goods covered by the chattel paper or cash proceeds of the specific goods, even if the purchaser's security interest in the proceeds is unperfected.

(d) Except as otherwise provided in Section 9—331 (a), a purchaser of an instrument has priority over a security interest in the instrument perfected by a method other than possession if the purchaser gives value and takes possession of the instrument in good faith and without knowledge that the purchase violates the rights of the secured party.

(e) For purposes of subsections (a) and (b), the holder of a purchase-money security interest in inventory gives new value for chattel paper constituting proceeds of the inventory.

(f) For purposes of subsections (b) and (d), if chattel paper or an instrument indicates that it has been assigned to an identified secured party other than the purchaser, a purchaser of the chattel paper or instrument has knowledge that the purchase violates the rights of the secured party.

* * * *

§9—333. PRIORITY OF CERTAIN LIENS ARISING BY OPERATION OF LAW

(a) In this section, "possessory lien" means an interest, other than a security interest or an agricultural lien:

(1) which secures payment or performance of an obligation for services or materials furnished with respect to goods by a person in the ordinary course of the person's business;

(2) which is created by statute or rule of law in favor of the person; and

(3) whose effectiveness depends on the person's possession of the goods.

(b) A possessory lien on goods has priority over a security interest in the goods unless the lien is created by a statute that expressly provides otherwise.

§9—334. PRIORITY OF SECURITY INTERESTS IN FIXTURES AND CROPS

(a) A security interest under this article may be created in goods that are fixtures or may continue in goods that become fixtures. A security interest does not exist under this article in ordinary building materials incorporated into an improvement on land.

(b) This article does not prevent creation of an encumbrance upon fixtures under real property law.

(c) In cases not governed by subsections (d) through (h), a security interest in fixtures is subordinate to a conflicting interest of an encumbrancer or owner of the related real property other than the debtor.

(d) Except as otherwise provided in subsection (h), a perfected security interest in fixtures has priority over a conflicting interest of an encumbrancer or owner of the real property if the debtor has an interest of record in or is in possession of the real property and:

(1) the security interest is a purchase-money security interest;

(2) the interest of the encumbrancer or owner arises before the goods become fixtures; and

(3) the security interest is perfected by a fixture filing before the goods become fixtures or within 20 days thereafter.

(e) A perfected security interest in fixtures has priority over a conflicting interest of an encumbrancer or owner of the real property if:

(1) the debtor has an interest of record in the real property or is in possession of the real property and the security interest:

(A) is perfected by a fixture filing before the interest of the encumbrancer or owner is of record; and

(B) has priority over any conflicting interest of a predecessor in title of the encumbrancer or owner;

(2) before the goods become fixtures, the security interest is perfected by any method permitted by this article and the fixtures are readily removable:

(A) factory or office machines;

(B) equipment that is not primarily used or leased for use in the operation of the real property; or

(C) replacements of domestic appliances that are consumer goods;

(3) the conflicting interest is a lien on the real property obtained by legal or equitable proceedings after the security interest was perfected by any method permitted by this article; or

(4) the security interest is:

(A) created in a manufactured home in a manufactured-home transaction; and

(B) perfected pursuant to a statute described in Section 9—311(a)(2).

(f) A security interest in fixtures, whether or not perfected, has priority over a conflicting interest of an encumbrancer or owner of the real property if:

(1) the encumbrancer or owner has, in an authenticated record, consented to the security interest or disclaimed an interest in the goods as fixtures; or

(2) the debtor has a right to remove the goods as against the encumbrancer or owner.

(g) The priority of the security interest under paragraph (f)(2) continues for a reasonable time if the debtor's right to remove the goods as against the encumbrancer or owner terminates.

(h) A mortgage is a construction mortgage to the extent that it secures an obligation incurred for the construction of an improvement on land, including the acquisition cost of the land, if a recorded record of the mortgage so indicates. Except as otherwise provided in subsections (e) and (f), a security interest in fixtures is subordinate to a construction mortgage if a record of the mortgage is recorded before the goods become fixtures and the goods become fixtures before the completion of the construction. A mortgage has this priority to the same extent as a construction mortgage to the extent that it is given to refinance a construction mortgage.

(i) A perfected security interest in crops growing on real property has priority over a conflicting interest of an encumbrancer or owner of the real property if the debtor has an interest of record in or is in possession of the real property.

* * * *

§9—336. COMMINGLED GOODS

(a) In this section, "commingled goods" means goods that are physically united with other goods in such a manner that their identity is lost in a product or mass.

(b) A security interest does not exist in commingled goods as such. However, a security interest may attach to a product or mass that results when goods become commingled goods.

(c) If collateral becomes commingled goods, a security interest attaches to the product or mass.

(d) If a security interest in collateral is perfected before the collateral becomes commingled goods, the security interest that attaches to the product or mass under subsection (c) is perfected.

(e) Except as otherwise provided in subsection (f), the other provisions of this part determine the priority of a security interest that attaches to the product or mass under subsection (c).

(f) If more than one security interest attaches to the product or mass under subsection (c), the following rules determine priority:

(1) A security interest that is perfected under subsection (d) has priority over a security interest that is unperfected at the time the collateral becomes commingled goods.

(2) If more than one security interest is perfected under subsection (d), the security interests rank equally in proportion to the value of the collateral at the time it became commingled goods.

* * * *

§9—501. FILING OFFICE

(a) Except as otherwise provided in subsection (b), if the local law of this State governs perfection of a security interest or agricultural lien, the office in which to file a financing statement to perfect the security interest or agricultural lien is:

(1) the office designated for the filing or recording of a record of a mortgage on the related real property, if:

(A) the collateral is as-extracted collateral or timber to be cut; or

(B) the financing statement is filed as a fixture filing and the collateral is goods that are or are to become fixtures; or

(2) the office of [ ] [or any office duly authorized by [ ]], in all other cases, including a case in which the collateral is goods that are or are to become fixtures and the financing statement is not filed as a fixture filing.

(b) The office in which to file a financing statement to perfect a security interest in collateral, including fixtures, of a transmitting utility is the office of [ ]. The financing statement also constitutes a fixture filing as to the collateral indicated in the financing statement which is or is to become fixtures.

Legislative Note: The State should designate the filing office where the brackets appear. The filing office may be that of a governmental official (e.g., the Secretary of State) or a private party that maintains the State's filing system.

§9—502. CONTENTS OF FINANCING STATEMENT; RECORD OF MORTGAGE AS FINANCING STATEMENT; TIME OF FILING FINANCING STATEMENT

(a) Subject to subsection (b), a financing statement is sufficient only if it:

(1) provides the name of the debtor;

(2) provides the name of the secured party or a representative of the secured party; and

(3) indicates the collateral covered by the financing statement.

(b) Except as otherwise provided in Section 9—501 (b), to be sufficient, a financing statement that covers as-extracted collateral or timber to be cut, or which is filed as a fixture filing and covers goods that are or are to become fixtures, must satisfy subsection (a) and also:

(1) indicate that it covers this type of collateral;

(2) indicate that it is to be filed [for record] in the real property records;

(3) provide a description of the real property to which the collateral is related [sufficient to give constructive notice of a mortgage under the law of this State if the description were contained in a record of the mortgage of the real property]; and

(4) if the debtor does not have an interest of record in the real property, provide the name of a record owner.

(c) A record of a mortgage is effective, from the date of recording, as a financing statement filed as a fixture filing or as a financing statement covering as-extracted collateral or timber to be cut only if:

(1) the record indicates the goods or accounts that it covers;

(2) the goods are or are to become fixtures related to the real property described in the record or the collateral is related to the real property described in the record and is as-extracted collateral or timber to be cut;

(3) the record satisfies the requirements for a financing statement in this section other than an indication that it is to be filed in the real property records; and

(4) the record is [duly] recorded.

(d) A financing statement may be filed before a security agreement is made or a security interest otherwise attaches.

Legislative Note: Language in brackets is optional. Where the State has any special recording system for real property other than the usual grantor-grantee index (as, for instance, a tract system or a title registration or Torrens system) local adaptations of subsection (b) and Section 9—519(d) and (e) may be necessary. See, e.g., Mass. Gen. Laws Chapter 106, Section 9—410.

§9—503. NAME OF DEBTOR AND SECURED PARTY

(a) A financing statement sufficiently provides the name of the debtor:

(1) if the debtor is a registered organization, only if the financing statement provides the name of the debtor indicated on the public record of the debtor's jurisdiction of organization which shows the debtor to have been organized;

(2) if the debtor is a decedent's estate, only if the financing statement provides the name of the decedent and indicates that the debtor is an estate;

(3) if the debtor is a trust or a trustee acting with respect to property held in trust, only if the financing statement:

(A) provides the name specified for the trust in its organic documents or, if no name is specified, provides the name of the settlor and additional information sufficient to distinguish the debtor from other trusts having one or more of the same settlors; and

(B) indicates, in the debtor's name or otherwise, that the debtor is a trust or is a trustee acting with respect to property held in trust; and

(4) in other cases:

(A) if the debtor has a name, only if it provides the individual or organizational name of the debtor; and

(B) if the debtor does not have a name, only if it provides the names of the partners, members, associates, or other persons comprising the debtor.

(b) A financing statement that provides the name of the debtor in accordance with subsection (a) is not rendered ineffective by the absence of:

(1) a trade name or other name of the debtor; or

(2) unless required under subsection (a)(4)(B), names of partners, members, associates, or other persons comprising the debtor.

(c) A financing statement that provides only the debtor's trade name does not sufficiently provide the name of the debtor.

(d) Failure to indicate the representative capacity of a secured party or representative of a secured party does not affect the sufficiency of a financing statement.

(e) A financing statement may provide the name of more than one debtor and the name of more than one secured party.

§9—504. INDICATION OF COLLATERAL

A financing statement sufficiently indicates the collateral that it covers if the financing statement provides:

(1) a description of the collateral pursuant to Section 9—108; or

(2) an indication that the financing statement covers all assets or all personal property.

As amended in 1999.

* * * *

§9—506. EFFECT OF ERRORS OR OMISSIONS

(a) A financing statement substantially satisfying the requirements of this part is effective, even if it has minor errors or omissions, unless the errors or omissions make the financing statement seriously misleading.

(b) Except as otherwise provided in subsection (c), a financing statement that fails sufficiently to provide the name of the debtor in accordance with Section 9—503(a) is seriously misleading.

(c) If a search of the records of the filing office under the debtor's correct name, using the filing office's standard search logic, if any, would disclose a financing statement that fails sufficiently to provide the name of the debtor in accordance with Section 9—503(a), the name provided does not make the financing statement seriously misleading.

(d) For purposes of Section 9—508(b), the "debtor's correct name" in subsection (c) means the correct name of the new debtor.

* * * *

§9—509. PERSONS ENTITLED TO FILE A RECORD

(a) A person may file an initial financing statement, amendment that adds collateral covered by a financing statement, or amendment that adds a debtor to a financing statement only if:

(1) the debtor authorizes the filing in an authenticated record or pursuant to subsection (b) or (c); or

(2) the person holds an agricultural lien that has become effective at the time of filing and the financing statement covers only collateral in which the person holds an agricultural lien.

(b) By authenticating or becoming bound as debtor by a security agreement, a debtor or new debtor authorizes the filing of an initial financing statement, and an amendment, covering:

(1) the collateral described in the security agreement; and

(2) property that becomes collateral under Section 9—315(a)(2), whether or not the security agreement expressly covers proceeds.

(c) By acquiring collateral in which a security interest or agricultural lien continues under Section 9—315(a)(1), a debtor authorizes the filing of an initial financing statement, and an amendment, covering the collateral and property that becomes collateral under Section 9—315(a)(2).

(d) A person may file an amendment other than an amendment that adds collateral covered by a financing statement or an amendment that adds a debtor to a financing statement only if:

(1) the secured party of record authorizes the filing; or

(2) the amendment is a termination statement for a financing statement as to which the secured party of record has failed to file or send a termination statement as required by Section 9—513(a) or (c), the debtor authorizes the filing, and the termination statement indicates that the debtor authorized it to be filed.

(e) If there is more than one secured party of record for a financing statement, each secured party of record may authorize the filing of an amendment under subsection (d).

§9—510. EFFECTIVENESS OF FILED RECORD

(a) A filed record is effective only to the extent that it was filed by a person that may file it under Section 9—509.

(b) A record authorized by one secured party of record does not affect the financing statement with respect to another secured party of record.

(c) A continuation statement that is not filed within the six-month period prescribed by Section 9—515(d) is ineffective.

* * * *

§9—513. TERMINATION STATEMENT

(a) A secured party shall cause the secured party of record for a financing statement to file a termination statement for the financing statement if the financing statement covers consumer goods and:

(1) there is no obligation secured by the collateral covered by the financing statement and no commitment to make an advance, incur an obligation, or otherwise give value; or

(2) the debtor did not authorize the filing of the initial financing statement.

(b) To comply with subsection (a), a secured party shall cause the secured party of record to file the termination statement:

(1) within one month after there is no obligation secured by the collateral covered by the financing statement and no commitment to make an advance, incur an obligation, or otherwise give value; or

(2) if earlier, within 20 days after the secured party receives an authenticated demand from a debtor.

(c) In cases not governed by subsection (a), within 20 days after a secured party receives an authenticated demand from a debtor, the secured party shall cause the secured party of record for a financing statement to send to the debtor a termination statement for the financing statement or file the termination statement in the filing office if:

(1) except in the case of a financing statement covering accounts or chattel paper that has been sold or goods that are the subject of a consignment, there is no obligation secured by the collateral covered by the financing statement and no commitment to make an advance, incur an obligation, or otherwise give value;

(2) the financing statement covers accounts or chattel paper that has been sold but as to which the account debtor or other person obligated has discharged its obligation;

(3) the financing statement covers goods that were the subject of a consignment to the debtor but are not in the debtor's possession; or

(4) the debtor did not authorize the filing of the initial financing statement.

(d) Except as otherwise provided in Section 9—510, upon the filing of a termination statement with the filing office, the financing statement to which the termination statement relates ceases to be effective. Except as otherwise provided in Section 9—510, for purposes of Sections 9—519(g), 9—522(a), and 9—523(c), the filing with the filing office of a termination statement relating to a financing statement that indicates that the debtor is a transmitting utility also causes the effectiveness of the financing statement to lapse.

* * * *

§9—515. DURATION AND EFFECTIVENESS OF FINANCING STATEMENT; EFFECT OF LAPSED FINANCING STATEMENT

(a) Except as otherwise provided in subsections (b), (e), (f), and (g), a filed financing statement is effective for a period of five years after the date of filing.

(b) Except as otherwise provided in subsections (e), (f), and (g), an initial financing statement filed in connection with a public-finance transaction or manufactured-home transaction is effective for a period of 30 years after the date of filing if it indicates that it is filed in connection with a public-finance transaction or manufactured-home transaction.

(c) The effectiveness of a filed financing statement lapses on the expiration of the period of its effectiveness unless before the lapse a continuation statement is filed pursuant to subsection (d). Upon lapse, a financing statement ceases to be effective and any security interest or agricultural lien that was perfected by the financing statement becomes unperfected, unless the security interest is perfected otherwise. If the security interest or agricultural lien becomes unperfected upon lapse, it is deemed never to have been perfected as against a purchaser of the collateral for value.

(d) A continuation statement may be filed only within six months before the expiration of the five-year period specified in subsection (a) or the 30-year period specified in subsection (b), whichever is applicable.

(e) Except as otherwise provided in Section 9—510, upon timely filing of a continuation statement, the effectiveness of the initial financing statement continues for a period of five years commencing on the day on which the financing statement would have become ineffective in the absence of the filing. Upon the expiration of the five-year period, the financing statement lapses in the same manner as provided in subsection (c), unless, before the lapse, another continuation statement is filed pursuant to subsection (d). Succeeding continuation statements may be filed in the same manner to continue the effectiveness of the initial financing statement.

(f) If a debtor is a transmitting utility and a filed financing statement so indicates, the financing statement is effective until a termination statement is filed.

(g) A record of a mortgage that is effective as a financing statement filed as a fixture filing under Section 9—502(c) remains effective as a financing statement filed as a fixture filing until the mortgage is released or satisfied of record or its effectiveness otherwise terminates as to the real property.

* * * *

§9—601. RIGHTS AFTER DEFAULT; JUDICIAL ENFORCEMENT; CONSIGNOR OR BUYER OF ACCOUNTS, CHATTEL PAPER, PAYMENT INTANGIBLES, OR PROMISSORY NOTES

(a) After default, a secured party has the rights provided in this part and, except as otherwise provided in Section 9—602, those provided by agreement of the parties.

A secured party:

(1) may reduce a claim to judgment, foreclose, or otherwise enforce the claim, security interest, or agricultural lien by any available judicial procedure; and

(2) if the collateral is documents, may proceed either as to the documents or as to the goods they cover.

(b) A secured party in possession of collateral or control of collateral under Section 9—104, 9—105, 9—106, or 9—107 has the rights and duties provided in Section 9—207.

(c) The rights under subsections (a) and (b) are cumulative and may be exercised simultaneously.

(d) Except as otherwise provided in subsection (g) and Section 9—605, after default, a debtor and an obligor have the rights provided in this part and by agreement of the parties.

(e) If a secured party has reduced its claim to judgment, the lien of any levy that may be made upon the collateral by virtue of an execution based upon the judgment relates back to the earliest of:

(1) the date of perfection of the security interest or agricultural lien in the collateral;

(2) the date of filing a financing statement covering the collateral; or

(3) any date specified in a statute under which the agricultural lien was created.

(f) A sale pursuant to an execution is a foreclosure of the security interest or agricultural lien by judicial procedure within the meaning of this section. A secured party may purchase at the sale and thereafter hold the collateral free of any other requirements of this article.

(g) Except as otherwise provided in Section 9—607 (c), this part imposes no duties upon a secured party that is a consignor or is a buyer of accounts, chattel paper, payment intangibles, or promissory notes.

* * * *

§9—604. PROCEDURE IF SECURITY AGREEMENT COVERS REAL PROPERTY OR FIXTURES

(a) If a security agreement covers both personal and real property, a secured party may proceed:

(1) under this part as to the personal property without prejudicing any rights with respect to the real property; or

(2) as to both the personal property and the real property in accordance with the rights with respect to the real property, in which case the other provisions of this part do not apply.

(b) Subject to subsection (c), if a security agreement covers goods that are or become fixtures, a secured party may proceed:

(1) under this part; or

(2) in accordance with the rights with respect to real property, in which case the other provisions of this part do not apply.

(c) Subject to the other provisions of this part, if a secured party holding a security interest in fixtures has priority over all owners and encumbrancers of the real property, the secured party, after default, may remove the collateral from the real property.

(d) A secured party that removes collateral shall promptly reimburse any encumbrancer or owner of the real property, other than the debtor, for the cost of repair of any physical injury caused by the removal. The secured party need not reimburse the encumbrancer or owner for any diminution in value of the real property caused by the absence of the goods removed or by any necessity of replacing them. A person entitled to reimbursement may refuse permission to remove until the secured party gives adequate assurance for the performance of the obligation to reimburse.

* * * *

§9—607. COLLECTION AND ENFORCEMENT BY SECURED PARTY

(a) If so agreed, and in any event after default, a secured party:

(1) may notify an account debtor or other person obligated on collateral to make payment or otherwise render performance to or for the benefit of the secured party;

(2) may take any proceeds to which the secured party is entitled under Section 9—315;

(3) may enforce the obligations of an account debtor or other person obligated on collateral and exercise the rights of the debtor with respect to the obligation of the account debtor or other person obligated on collateral to make payment or otherwise render performance to the debtor, and with respect to any property that secures the obligations of the account debtor or other person obligated on the collateral;

(4) if it holds a security interest in a deposit account perfected by control under Section 9—104(a)(1), may apply the balance of the deposit

account to the obligation secured by the deposit account; and

(5) if it holds a security interest in a deposit account perfected by control under Section 9—104(a)(2) or (3), may instruct the bank to pay the balance of the deposit account to or for the benefit of the secured party.

(b) If necessary to enable a secured party to exercise under subsection (a)(3) the right of a debtor to enforce a mortgage nonjudicially, the secured party may record in the office in which a record of the mortgage is recorded:

(1) a copy of the security agreement that creates or provides for a security interest in the obligation secured by the mortgage; and

(2) the secured party's sworn affidavit in recordable form stating that:

(A) a default has occurred; and

(B) the secured party is entitled to enforce the mortgage nonjudicially.

(c) A secured party shall proceed in a commercially reasonable manner if the secured party:

(1) undertakes to collect from or enforce an obligation of an account debtor or other person obligated on collateral; and

(2) is entitled to charge back uncollected collateral or otherwise to full or limited recourse against the debtor or a secondary obligor.

(d) A secured party may deduct from the collections made pursuant to subsection (c) reasonable expenses of collection and enforcement, including reasonable attorney's fees and legal expenses incurred by the secured party.

(e) This section does not determine whether an account debtor, bank, or other person obligated on collateral owes a duty to a secured party.

§9—608. APPLICATION OF PROCEEDS OF COLLECTION OR ENFORCEMENT; LIABILITY FOR DEFICIENCY AND RIGHT TO SURPLUS

(a) If a security interest or agricultural lien secures payment or performance of an obligation, the following rules apply:

(1) A secured party shall apply or pay over for application the cash proceeds of collection or enforcement under Section 9—607 in the following order to:

(A) the reasonable expenses of collection and enforcement and, to the extent provided for by agreement and not prohibited by law, reasonable attorney's fees and legal expenses incurred by the secured party;

(B) the satisfaction of obligations secured by the security interest or agricultural lien under which the collection or enforcement is made; and

(C) the satisfaction of obligations secured by any subordinate security interest in or other lien on the collateral subject to the security interest or agricultural lien under which the collection or enforcement is made if the secured party receives an authenticated demand for proceeds before distribution of the proceeds is completed.

(2) If requested by a secured party, a holder of a subordinate security interest or other lien shall furnish reasonable proof of the interest or lien within a reasonable time. Unless the holder complies, the secured party need not comply with the holder's demand under paragraph (1)(C).

(3) A secured party need not apply or pay over for application noncash proceeds of collection and enforcement under Section 9—607 unless the failure to do so would be commercially unreasonable. A secured party that applies or pays over for application noncash proceeds shall do so in a commercially reasonable manner.

(4) A secured party shall account to and pay a debtor for any surplus, and the obligor is liable for any deficiency.

(b) If the underlying transaction is a sale of accounts, chattel paper, payment intangibles, or promissory notes, the debtor is not entitled to any surplus, and the obligor is not liable for any deficiency.

§9—609. SECURED PARTY'S RIGHT TO TAKE POSSESSION AFTER DEFAULT

(a) After default, a secured party:

(1) may take possession of the collateral; and

(2) without removal, may render equipment unusable and dispose of collateral on a debtor's premises under Section 9—610.

(b) A secured party may proceed under subsection (a):

(1) pursuant to judicial process; or

(2) without judicial process, if it proceeds without breach of the peace.

(c) If so agreed, and in any event after default, a secured party may require the debtor to assemble the collateral and make it available to the secured party at a place to be designated by the secured party which is reasonably convenient to both parties.

§9—610. DISPOSITION OF COLLATERAL AFTER DEFAULT

(a) After default, a secured party may sell, lease, license, or otherwise dispose of any or all of the collateral in its present condition or following any commercially reasonable preparation or processing.

(b) Every aspect of a disposition of collateral, including the method, manner, time, place, and other terms, must be commercially reasonable. If commercially reasonable, a secured party may dispose of collateral by public or private proceedings, by one or more contracts, as a unit or in parcels, and at any time and place and on any terms.

(c) A secured party may purchase collateral:

(1) at a public disposition; or

(2) at a private disposition only if the collateral is of a kind that is customarily sold on a recognized market or the subject of widely distributed standard price quotations.

(d) A contract for sale, lease, license, or other disposition includes the warranties relating to title, possession, quiet enjoyment, and the like which by operation of law accompany a voluntary disposition of property of the kind subject to the contract.

(e) A secured party may disclaim or modify warranties under subsection (d):

(1) in a manner that would be effective to disclaim or modify the warranties in a voluntary disposition of property of the kind subject to the contract of disposition; or

(2) by communicating to the purchaser a record evidencing the contract for disposition and including an express disclaimer or modification of the warranties.

(f) A record is sufficient to disclaim warranties under subsection (e) if it indicates "There is no warranty relating to title, possession, quiet enjoyment, or the like in this disposition" or uses words of similar import.

§9—611. NOTIFICATION BEFORE DISPOSITION OF COLLATERAL

(a) In this section, "notification date" means the earlier of the date on which:

(1) a secured party sends to the debtor and any secondary obligor an authenticated notification of disposition; or

(2) the debtor and any secondary obligor waive the right to notification.

(b) Except as otherwise provided in subsection (d), a secured party that disposes of collateral under Section 9—610 shall send to the persons specified in subsection (c) a reasonable authenticated notification of disposition.

(c) To comply with subsection (b), the secured party shall send an authenticated notification of disposition to:

(1) the debtor;

(2) any secondary obligor; and

(3) if the collateral is other than consumer goods:

(A) any other person from which the secured party has received, before the notification date, an authenticated notification of a claim of an interest in the collateral;

(B) any other secured party or lienholder that, 10 days before the notification date, held a security interest in or other lien on the collateral perfected by the filing of a financing statement that:

(i) identified the collateral;

(ii) was indexed under the debtor's name as of that date; and

(iii) was filed in the office in which to file a financing statement against the debtor covering the collateral as of that date; and

(C) any other secured party that, 10 days before the notification date, held a security interest in the collateral perfected by compliance with a statute, regulation, or treaty described in Section 9—311(a).

(d) Subsection (b) does not apply if the collateral is perishable or threatens to decline speedily in value or is of a type customarily sold on a recognized market.

(e) A secured party complies with the requirement for notification prescribed by subsection (c)(3)(B) if:

(1) not later than 20 days or earlier than 30 days before the notification date, the secured party requests, in a commercially reasonable manner, information concerning financing statements indexed under the debtor's name in the office indicated in subsection (c)(3)(B); and

(2) before the notification date, the secured party:

(A) did not receive a response to the request for information; or

(B) received a response to the request for information and sent an authenticated notification of disposition to each secured party or other lienholder named in that response whose financing statement covered the collateral.

§9—612. TIMELINESS OF NOTIFICATION BEFORE DISPOSITION OF COLLATERAL

(a) Except as otherwise provided in subsection (b), whether a notification is sent within a reasonable time is a question of fact.

(b) In a transaction other than a consumer transaction, a notification of disposition sent after default and 10 days or more before the earliest time of disposition set forth in the notification is sent within a reasonable time before the disposition.

* * * *

§9—615. APPLICATION OF PROCEEDS OF DISPOSITION; LIABILITY FOR DEFICIENCY AND RIGHT TO SURPLUS

(a) A secured party shall apply or pay over for application the cash proceeds of disposition under Section 9—610 in the following order to:

(1) the reasonable expenses of retaking, holding, preparing for disposition, processing, and disposing, and, to the extent provided for by agreement and not prohibited by law, reasonable attorney's fees and legal expenses incurred by the secured party;

(2) the satisfaction of obligations secured by the security interest or agricultural lien under which the disposition is made;

(3) the satisfaction of obligations secured by any subordinate security interest in or other subordinate lien on the collateral if:

(A) the secured party receives from the holder of the subordinate security interest or other lien an authenticated demand for proceeds before distribution of the proceeds is completed; and

(B) in a case in which a consignor has an interest in the collateral, the subordinate security interest or other lien is senior to the interest of the consignor; and

(4) a secured party that is a consignor of the collateral if the secured party receives from the consignor an authenticated demand for proceeds before distribution of the proceeds is completed.

(b) If requested by a secured party, a holder of a subordinate security interest or other lien shall furnish reasonable proof of the interest or lien within a reasonable time. Unless the holder does so, the secured party need not comply with the holder's demand under subsection (a)(3).

(c) A secured party need not apply or pay over for application noncash proceeds of disposition under Section 9—610 unless the failure to do so would be commercially unreasonable. A secured party that applies or pays over for application noncash proceeds shall do so in a commercially reasonable manner.

(d) If the security interest under which a disposition is made secures payment or performance of an obligation, after making the payments and applications required by subsection (a) and permitted by subsection (c):

(1) unless subsection (a)(4) requires the secured party to apply or pay over cash proceeds to a consignor, the secured party shall account to and pay a debtor for any surplus; and

(2) the obligor is liable for any deficiency.

(e) If the underlying transaction is a sale of accounts, chattel paper, payment intangibles, or promissory notes:

(1) the debtor is not entitled to any surplus; and

(2) the obligor is not liable for any deficiency.

(f) The surplus or deficiency following a disposition is calculated based on the amount of proceeds that would have been realized in a disposition complying with this part to a transferee other than the secured party, a person related to the secured party, or a secondary obligor if:

(1) the transferee in the disposition is the secured party, a person related to the secured party, or a secondary obligor; and

(2) the amount of proceeds of the disposition is significantly below the range of proceeds that a complying disposition to a person other than the secured party, a person related to the secured party, or a secondary obligor would have brought.

(g) A secured party that receives cash proceeds of a disposition in good faith and without knowledge that the receipt violates the rights of the holder of a security interest or other lien that is not subordinate to the security interest or agricultural lien under which the disposition is made:

(1) takes the cash proceeds free of the security interest or other lien;

(2) is not obligated to apply the proceeds of the disposition to the satisfaction of obligations secured by the security interest or other lien; and

(3) is not obligated to account to or pay the holder of the security interest or other lien for any surplus.

* * * *

§9—617. RIGHTS OF TRANSFEREE OF COLLATERAL

(a) A secured party's disposition of collateral after default:

1) transfers to a transferee for value all of the debtor's rights in the collateral;

2) discharges the security interest under which the disposition is made; and

3) discharges any subordinate security interest or other subordinate lien [other than liens created under [cite acts or statutes providing for liens, if any, that are not to be discharged]].

(b) A transferee that acts in good faith takes free of the rights and interests described in subsection (a), even if the secured party fails to comply with this article or the requirements of any judicial proceeding.

(c) If a transferee does not take free of the rights and interests described in subsection (a), the transferee takes the collateral subject to:

(1) the debtor's rights in the collateral;

(2) the security interest or agricultural lien under which the disposition is made; and

(3) any other security interest or other lien.

* * * *

§9—620. ACCEPTANCE OF COLLATERAL IN FULL OR PARTIAL SATISFACTION OF OBLIGATION; COMPULSORY DISPOSITION OF COLLATERAL

(a) Except as otherwise provided in subsection (g), a secured party may accept collateral in full or partial satisfaction of the obligation it secures only if:

(1) the debtor consents to the acceptance under subsection (c);

(2) the secured party does not receive, within the time set forth in subsection (d), a notification of objection to the proposal authenticated by:

(A) a person to which the secured party was required to send a proposal under Section 9—621; or

(B) any other person, other than the debtor, holding an interest in the collateral subordinate to the security interest that is the subject of the proposal;

(3) if the collateral is consumer goods, the collateral is not in the possession of the debtor when the debtor consents to the acceptance; and

(4) subsection (e) does not require the secured party to dispose of the collateral or the debtor waives the requirement pursuant to Section 9—624.

(b) A purported or apparent acceptance of collateral under this section is ineffective unless:

(1) the secured party consents to the acceptance in an authenticated record or sends a proposal to the debtor; and

(2) the conditions of subsection (a) are met.

(c) For purposes of this section:

(1) a debtor consents to an acceptance of collateral in partial satisfaction of the obligation it secures only if the debtor agrees to the terms of the acceptance in a record authenticated after default; and

(2) a debtor consents to an acceptance of collateral in full satisfaction of the obligation it secures only if the debtor agrees to the terms of the acceptance in a record authenticated after default or the secured party:

(A) sends to the debtor after default a proposal that is unconditional or subject only to a condition that collateral not in the possession of the secured party be preserved or maintained;

(B) in the proposal, proposes to accept collateral in full satisfaction of the obligation it secures; and

(C) does not receive a notification of objection authenticated by the debtor within 20 days after the proposal is sent.

(d) To be effective under subsection (a)(2), a notification of objection must be received by the secured party:

(1) in the case of a person to which the proposal was sent pursuant to Section 9—621, within 20 days after notification was sent to that person; and

(2) in other cases:

(A) within 20 days after the last notification was sent pursuant to Section 9—621; or

(B) if a notification was not sent, before the debtor consents to the acceptance under subsection (c).

(e) A secured party that has taken possession of collateral shall dispose of the collateral pursuant to Section 9—610 within the time specified in subsection (f) if:

(1) 60 percent of the cash price has been paid in the case of a purchase-money security interest in consumer goods; or

(2) 60 percent of the principal amount of the obligation secured has been paid in the case of a non-purchase-money security interest in consumer goods.

(f) To comply with subsection (e), the secured party shall dispose of the collateral:

(1) within 90 days after taking possession; or

(2) within any longer period to which the debtor and all secondary obligors have agreed in an agreement to that effect entered into and authenticated after default.

(g) In a consumer transaction, a secured party may not accept collateral in partial satisfaction of the obligation it secures.

* * * *

§9—623. RIGHT TO REDEEM COLLATERAL

(a) A debtor, any secondary obligor, or any other secured party or lienholder may redeem collateral.

(b) To redeem collateral, a person shall tender:

(1) fulfillment of all obligations secured by the collateral; and

(2) the reasonable expenses and attorney's fees described in Section 9—615(a)(1).

(c) A redemption may occur at any time before a secured party:

(1) has collected collateral under Section 9—607;

(2) has disposed of collateral or entered into a contract for its disposition under Section 9—610; or

(3) has accepted collateral in full or partial satisfaction of the obligation it secures under Section 9—622.

* * * *

§9—625. REMEDIES FOR SECURED PARTY'S FAILURE TO COMPLY WITH ARTICLE

(a) If it is established that a secured party is not proceeding in accordance with this article, a court may order or restrain collection, enforcement, or disposition of collateral on appropriate terms and conditions.

(b) Subject to subsections (c), (d), and (f), a person is liable for damages in the amount of any loss caused by a failure to comply with this article. Loss caused by a failure to comply may include loss resulting from the debtor's inability to obtain, or increased costs of, alternative financing.

(c) Except as otherwise provided in Section 9—628:

(1) a person that, at the time of the failure, was a debtor, was an obligor, or held a security interest in or other lien on the collateral may recover damages under subsection (b) for its loss; and

(2) if the collateral is consumer goods, a person that was a debtor or a secondary obligor at the time a secured party failed to comply with this part may recover for that failure in any event an amount not less than the credit service charge plus 10 percent of the principal amount of the obligation or the time-price differential plus 10 percent of the cash price.

(d) A debtor whose deficiency is eliminated under Section 9—626 may recover damages for the loss of any surplus. However, a debtor or secondary obligor whose deficiency is eliminated or reduced under Section 9—626 may not otherwise recover under subsection (b) for noncompliance with the provisions of this part relating to collection, enforcement, disposition, or acceptance.

(e) In addition to any damages recoverable under subsection (b), the debtor, consumer obligor, or person named as a debtor in a filed record, as applicable, may recover $500 in each case from a person that:

(1) fails to comply with Section 9—208;

(2) fails to comply with Section 9—209;

(3) files a record that the person is not entitled to file under Section 9—509(a);

(4) fails to cause the secured party of record to file or send a termination statement as required by Section 9—513(a) or (c);

(5) fails to comply with Section 9—616(b)(1) and whose failure is part of a pattern, or consistent with a practice, of noncompliance; or

(6) fails to comply with Section 9—616(b)(2).

(f) A debtor or consumer obligor may recover damages under subsection (b) and, in addition, $500 in each case from a person that, without reasonable cause, fails to comply with a request under Section 9—210. A recipient of a request under Section 9—210 which never claimed an interest in the collateral or obligations that are the subject of a request under that section has a reasonable excuse for failure to comply with the request within the meaning of this subsection.

(g) If a secured party fails to comply with a request regarding a list of collateral or a statement of account under Section 9—210, the secured party may claim a security interest only as shown in the list or statement included in the request as against a person that is reasonably misled by the failure.

* * * *

§9—627. DETERMINATION OF WHETHER CONDUCT WAS COMMERCIALLY REASONABLE

(a) The fact that a greater amount could have been obtained by a collection, enforcement, disposition, or acceptance at a different time or in a different method from that selected by the secured party is not of itself sufficient to preclude the secured party from establishing that the collection, enforcement, disposition, or acceptance was made in a commercially reasonable manner.

(b) A disposition of collateral is made in a commercially reasonable manner if the disposition is made:

(1) in the usual manner on any recognized market;

(2) at the price current in any recognized market at the time of the disposition; or

(3) otherwise in conformity with reasonable commercial practices among dealers in the type of property that was the subject of the disposition.

(c) A collection, enforcement, disposition, or acceptance is commercially reasonable if it has been approved:

(1) in a judicial proceeding;

(2) by a bona fide creditors' committee;

(3) by a representative of creditors; or

(4) by an assignee for the benefit of creditors.

(d) Approval under subsection (c) need not be obtained, and lack of approval does not mean that the collection, enforcement, disposition, or acceptance is not commercially reasonable.

Glossary

A

abate—put a stop to a nuisance; reduce or cancel a legacy because the estate of the decedent is insufficient to make payment in full.

absolute guaranty—agreement that creates the same obligation for the guarantor as a suretyship does for the surety; a guaranty of payment creates an absolute guaranty.

absolute privilege—complete defense against the tort of defamation, as in the speeches of members of Congress on the floor and witnesses in a trial.

abstract of title—history of the transfers of title to a given piece of land, briefly stating the parties to and the effect of all deeds, wills, and judicial proceedings relating to the land.

acceptance—unqualified assent to the act or proposal of another, such as the acceptance of an offer to make a contract; the acceptance of a draft (bill of exchange); the acceptance of goods delivered by a seller, or a gift of a deed.

acceptor—drawee who has accepted the liability of paying the amount of money specified in a draft.

accommodation party—person who signs an instrument to lend credit to another party to the paper.

accord and satisfaction—agreement to substitute for an existing debt some alternative form of discharging that debt, coupled with the actual discharge of the debt by the substituted performance.

acknowledgment—admission or confirmation, generally of an instrument and usually made before a person authorized to administer oaths, such as a notary public.

acquired distinctiveness—through advertising, use and association, over time, an ordinary descriptive word or phrase has taken on a new source-identifying meaning and functions as a mark in the eyes of the public.

act-of-state doctrine—doctrine whereby every sovereign state is bound to respect the independence of every other sovereign state, and the courts of one country will not sit in judgment of another government's acts done within its own territory.

adeemed—canceled; as in a specifically bequeathed property being sold or given away by the testator prior to death, thus canceling the bequest.

adjustable rate mortgage (ARM)—mortgage with variable financing charges over the life of the loan.

administrative agency—government body charged with administering and implementing legislation.

administrative law—law governing administrative agencies.

administrative law judge—judicial figure who hears administrative agency actions.

Administrative Procedure Act—federal law that establishes the operating rules for administrative agencies.

administrative regulations—rules made by state and federal administrative agencies.

administrator, administratrix—person (man, woman) appointed to wind up and settle the estate of a person who has died without a will.

admissibility—the quality of the evidence in a case that allows it to be presented to the jury.

adverse possession—hostile possession of real estate, which when actual, visible, notorious, exclusive, and continued for the required time, will vest the title to the land in the person in such adverse possession.

advising bank—bank that tells beneficiary that letter of credit has been issued.

affidavit—statement of facts under oath; executed before a notary public or anyone authorized to administer oaths.

affirm—action taken by an appellate court that approves the decision of the court below.

affirmative action plan (AAP)—plan to have a diverse and representative workforce.

after-acquired goods—goods acquired after a security interest has attached.

agency—the relationship that exists between a person identified as a principal and another by virtue of which the latter may make contracts with third persons on behalf of the principal. (Parties–principal, agent, third person)

agent—person or firm who is authorized by the principal or by operation of law to make contracts with third persons on behalf of the principal.

airbill—document of title issued to a shipper whose goods are being sent via air.

alteration—unauthorized change or completion of a negotiable instrument designed to modify the obligation of a party to the instrument.

alternative payees—those persons to whom a negotiable instrument is made payable, any one of whom may indorse and take delivery of it.

ambiguous—having more than one reasonable interpretation.

answer—what a defendant must file to admit or deny facts asserted by the plaintiff.

anticipatory breach—promisor's repudiation of the contract prior to the time that performance is required when such repudiation is accepted by the promisee as a breach of the contract.

anticipatory repudiation—repudiation made in advance of the time for performance of the contract obligations.

antilapse statutes—statutes providing that the children or heirs of a deceased beneficiary may take the legacy in the place of the deceased beneficiary.

apparent authority—appearance of authority created by the principal's words or conduct.

appeal—taking a case to a reviewing court to determine whether the judgment of the lower court or administrative agency was correct. (Parties—appellant, appellee)

appellate jurisdiction—the power of a court to hear and decide a given class of cases on appeal from another court or administrative agency.

arbitration—the settlement of disputed questions, whether of law or fact, by one or more arbitrators by whose decision the parties agree to be bound.

Article 2—section of the Uniform Commercial Code that governs contracts for the sale of goods.

articles of copartnership—see *partnership agreement.*

articles of incorporation—see *certificate of incorporation.*

articles of partnership—see *partnership agreement.*

assignee—third party to whom contract benefits are transferred.

assignment—transfer of a right. Generally used in connection with personal property rights, as rights under a contract, commercial paper, an insurance policy, a mortgage, or a lease. (Parties—assignor, assignee)

assignor—party who assigns contract rights to a third party.

association tribunal—a court created by a trade association or group for the resolution of disputes among its members.

assumption—mortgage transfers in which the transferee and mortgagor are liable and the property is subject to foreclosure by the mortgagee if payments are not made.

attestation clause—clause that indicates a witness has observed either the execution of the will or the testator's acknowledgment of the writing as the testator's will.

attorney in fact—agent authorized to act for another under a power of attorney.

attorney-client privilege—right of individual to have discussions with his/her attorney kept private and confidential.

attractive nuisance doctrine—a rule imposing liability upon a landowner for injuries sustained by small children playing on the land when the landowner permits a condition to exist or maintains equipment that a reasonable person should realize would attract small children who could not realize the danger. The rule does not apply if an unreasonable burden would be imposed upon the landowner in taking steps to protect the children.

authorities—corporations formed by government that perform public service.

automatic perfection—perfection given by statute without specific filing or possession requirements on the part of the creditor.

automatic stay—order to prevent creditors from taking action such as filing suits or seeking foreclosure against the debtor.

B

bad check laws—laws making it a criminal offense to issue a bad check with intent to defraud.

bailee—person who accepts possession of a property.

bailee's lien—specific, possessory lien of the bailee upon the goods for work done to them. Commonly extended by statute to any bailee's claim for compensation, eliminating the necessity of retention of possession.

bailment—relationship that exists when personal property is delivered into the possession of another under an agreement, express or implied, that the identical property will be returned or will be delivered in accordance with the agreement. (Parties—bailor, bailee)

bailment for mutual benefit—bailment in which the bailor and bailee derive a benefit from the bailment.

bailor—person who turns over the possession of a property.

balance sheet test—comparison of assets to liabilities made to determine solvency.

bankruptcy—procedure by which one unable to pay debts may surrender all assets in excess of any exemption claim to the court for administration and distribution to creditors, and the debtor is given a discharge that releases him from the unpaid balance due on most debts.

bankruptcy courts—court of special jurisdiction to determine bankruptcy issues.

battle of the forms—merchants' exchanges of invoices and purchase orders with differing boilerplate terms.

bearer—person in physical possession of commercial paper payable to bearer, a document of title directing delivery to bearer, or an investment security in bearer form.

bearer paper—instrument with no payee, payable to cash or payable to bearer.

bedrock view—a strict constructionist interpretation of a constitution.

beneficiary—person to whom the proceeds of a life insurance policy are payable, a person for whose benefit property is held in trust, or a person given property by a will; the ultimate recipient of the benefit of a funds transfer.

benefit corporation—for-profit corporation that sets a goal to create a public benefit while still providing economic returns to its investors.

beneficiary's bank—the final bank, which carries out the payment order, in the chain of a transfer of funds.

bequest—gift of personal property by will.

best available treatment—a water treatment that is the most current and best available through research, even though it may not be the treatment used most frequently.

best conventional treatment—a water treatment that is generally used among industries; not always the best treatment available.

bicameral—a two-house form of the legislative branch of government.

bilateral contract—agreement under which one promise is given in exchange for another.

bill of lading—document issued by a carrier acknowledging the receipt of goods and the terms of the contract of transportation.

bill of sale—writing signed by the seller reciting that the personal property therein described has been sold to the buyer.

blackmail—extortion demands made by a nonpublic official.

blank indorsement—an indorsement that does not name the person to whom the paper, document of title, or investment security is negotiated.

blocking laws—laws that prohibit the disclosure, copying, inspection, or removal of documents located in the enacting country in compliance with orders from foreign authorities.

blue sky laws—state statutes designed to protect the public from the sale of worthless stocks and bonds.

bona fide—in good faith; without any fraud or deceit.

bond—a debt investment; a loan to a corporation or government entity usually for a defined period of time at a fixed interest rate.

bond indenture—agreement setting forth the contractual terms of a particular bond issue.

book value—value found by dividing the value of the corporate assets by the number of shares outstanding.

breach—failure to act or perform in the manner called for in a contract.

breach of the peace—violation of the law in the repossession of the collateral.

brownfields—land that is a designated Superfund cleanup site but which lies fallow because no one is willing to risk liability by buying the property, even when the hazardous waste has been removed, or property no one is willing to spend the money to remove the hazardous waste.

bubble concept—method for determining total emissions in one area; all sources are considered in an area.

business ethics—balancing the goal of profits with values of individuals and society.

business judgment rule (BJR)—rule that allows management immunity from liability for corporate acts where there is a reasonable indication that the acts were made in good faith with due care.

bylaws—rules and regulations enacted by a corporation to govern the affairs of the corporation and its shareholders, directors, and officers.

C

cancellation provision—crossing out of a part of an instrument or a destruction of all legal effect of the instrument, whether by act of party, upon breach by the other party, or pursuant to agreement or decree of court.

capital stock—declared money value of the outstanding stock of the corporation.

cargo insurance—insurance that protects a cargo owner against financial loss if goods being shipped are lost or damaged at sea.

carrier—individual or organization undertaking the transportation of goods.

case law—law that includes principles that are expressed for the first time in court decisions.

cash surrender value—sum paid the insured upon the surrender of a policy to the insurer.

cash tender offer—general offer to all shareholders of a target corporation to purchase their shares for cash at a specified price.

cashier's check—draft drawn by a bank on itself.

cause of action—right to damages or other judicial relief when a legally protected right of the plaintiff is violated by an unlawful act of the defendant.

cease-and-desist order—order issued by a court or administrative agency to stop a practice that it decides is improper.

certificate of deposit (CD)—promise-to-pay instrument issued by a bank.

certificate of incorporation—written approval from the state or national government for a corporation to be formed.

certificate of stock—document evidencing a shareholder's ownership of stock issued by a corporation.

certified check—check for which the bank has set aside in a special account sufficient funds to pay it; payment is made when check is presented regardless of amount in drawer's account at that time; discharges all parties except certifying bank when holder requests certification.

cestui que trust—beneficiary of the trust.

CF—cost and freight.

Chapter 7 bankruptcy—liquidation form of bankruptcy under federal law.

Chapter 11 bankruptcy—reorganization form of bankruptcy under federal law.

Chapter 13 bankruptcy—proceeding of consumer debt readjustment plan bankruptcy.

charging order—order by a court, after a business partner's personal assets are exhausted, requiring that the partner's share of the profits be paid to a creditor until the debt is discharged.

charter—grant of authority from a government to exist as a corporation. Generally replaced today by a certificate of incorporation approving the articles of incorporation.

check—order by a depositor on a bank to pay a sum of money to a payee; a bill of exchange drawn on a bank and payable on demand.

choice-of-law clause—clause in an agreement that specifies which law will govern should a dispute arise.

chose in action—intangible personal property in the nature of claims against another, such as a claim for accounts receivable or wages.

CIF—cost, insurance, and freight.

civil disobedience—the term used when natural law proponents violate positive law.

civil laws—the laws that define the rights of one person against another.

claim—creditor's right to payment.

Clayton Act—a federal law that prohibits price discrimination.

Clean Air Act—federal legislation that establishes standards for air pollution levels and prevents further deterioration of air quality.

Clean Water Act—federal legislation that regulates water pollution through a control system.

close corporation—corporation whose shares are held by a single shareholder or a small group of shareholders.

close-connection doctrine—circumstantial evidence, such as an ongoing or a close relationship, that can serve as notice of a problem with an instrument.

COD—cash on delivery.

coinsurance clause—clause requiring the insured to maintain insurance on property up to a stated amount and providing that to the extent that this is not done, the insured is to be deemed a coinsurer with the insurer, so that the latter is liable only for its proportionate share of the amount of insurance required to be carried.

collateral—property pledged by a borrower as security for a debt.

comity—principle of international and national law that the laws of all nations and states deserve the respect legitimately demanded by equal participants.

commerce clause—that section of the U.S. Constitution allocating business regulation between federal and state governments.

commercial impracticability—situation that occurs when costs of performance rise suddenly and performance of a contract will result in a substantial loss.

commercial lease—any nonconsumer lease.

commercial paper—written, transferable, signed promise or order to pay a specified sum of money; a negotiable instrument.

commercial unit—standard of the trade for shipment or packaging of a good.

commission merchant—bailee to whom goods are consigned for sale.

commission or factorage—consignee's compensation.

common carrier—carrier that holds out its facilities to serve the general public for compensation without discrimination.

common law—the body of unwritten principles originally based upon the usages and customs of the community that were recognized and enforced by the courts.

common stock—stock that has no right or priority over any other stock of the corporation as to dividends or distribution of assets upon dissolution.

community property—cotenancy held by husband and wife in property acquired during their marriage under the law of some of the states, principally in the southwestern United States.

comparative negligence—defense to negligence that allows plaintiff to recover reduced damages based on his level of fault.

compensatory damages—sum of money that will compensate an injured plaintiff for actual loss.

complaint—the initial pleading filed by the plaintiff in many actions, which in many states may be served as original process to acquire jurisdiction over the defendant.

composition of creditors—agreement among creditors that each shall accept a part payment as full payment in consideration of the other creditors doing the same.

Comprehensive Environmental Response, Compensation, and Liability Act (CERCLA)—federal law that assigns liability for cleanup of hazardous sites.

computer crimes—wrongs committed using a computer or with knowledge of computers.

concealment—failure to volunteer information not requested.

condition—stipulation or prerequisite in a contract, will, or other instrument.

condition precedent—event that if unsatisfied would mean that no rights would arise under a contract.

condition subsequent—event whose occurrence or lack thereof terminates a contract.

condominium—combination of co-ownership and individual ownership.

confidential relationship—relationship in which, because of the legal status of the parties or their respective physical or mental conditions or knowledge, one party places full confidence and trust in the other.

conflict of interest—conduct that compromises an employee's allegiance to that company.

conglomerate—relationship of a parent corporation to subsidiary corporations engaged in diversified fields of activity unrelated to the field of activity of the parent corporation.

consent decrees—informal settlements of enforcement actions brought by agencies.

consequential damages—damages the buyer experiences as a result of the seller's breach with respect to a third party; also called *special damages.*

consideration—promise or performance that the promisor demands as the price of the promise.

consignee—(1) person to whom goods are shipped; (2) dealer who sells goods for others.

consignment—bailment made for the purpose of sale by the bailee. (Parties—consignor, consignee)

consignor—(1) person who delivers goods to the carrier for shipment; (2) party with title who turns goods over to another for sale.

consolidation (of corporations)—combining of two or more corporations in which the corporate existence of each one ceases and a new corporation is created.

conspiracy—agreement between two or more persons to commit an unlawful act.

constitution—a body of principles that establishes the structure of a government and the relationship of the government to the people who are governed.

constructive bailment—bailment imposed by law as opposed to one created by contract, whereby the bailee must preserve the property and redeliver it to the owner.

constructive delivery—See "*symbolic delivery.*"

constructive eviction—act or omission of the landlord that substantially deprives the tenant of the use and enjoyment of the premises.

consumer—any buyer afforded special protections by statute or regulation.

consumer credit—credit for personal, family, and household use.

Consumer Financial Protection Bureau—consumer protection bureau located within the Federal Reserve that now has jurisdiction over all consumer credit issues and statutes.

consumer goods—goods used or bought primarily for personal, family, or household use.

consumer lease—lease of goods by a natural person for personal, family, or household use.

Consumer Product Safety Improvement Act (CPSIA)—federal law that sets standards for the types of paints used in toys, a response to the lead paint found in toys made in China; requires tracking for international production; increases penalties.

contract—a binding agreement based on the genuine assent of the parties, made for a lawful object, between competent parties, in the form required by law, and generally supported by consideration.

contract carrier—carrier that transports on the basis of individual contracts that it makes with each shipper.

contract interference—tort in which a third party interferes with others' freedom to contract.

contract of adhesion—contract offered by a dominant party to a party with inferior bargaining power on a take-it-or-leave-it basis.

contract under seal—contract executed by affixing a seal or making an impression on the paper or on some adhering substance such as wax attached to the document.

contracting agent—agent with authority to make contracts; person with whom the buyer deals.

Contracts for the International Sale of Goods (CISG)—uniform international contract code contracts for international sale of goods.

contractual capacity—ability to understand that a contract is being made and to understand its general meaning.

contribution—right of a co-obligor who has paid more than a proportionate share to demand that other obligors pay their *pro rata* share.

contributory negligence—negligence of the plaintiff that contributes to injury and at common law bars recovery from the defendant although the defendant may have been more negligent than the plaintiff.

Controlling the Assault of Non-Solicited Pornography and Marketing (CAN-SPAM) Act—allows private companies to bring suit against spammers for their unauthorized use of Internet Service Providers (ISPs).

conversion—act of taking personal property by a person not entitled to it and keeping it from its true owner or prior possessor without consent.

cooperative—group of two or more persons or enterprises that acts through a common agent with respect to a common objective, such as buying or selling.

copyright—exclusive right given by federal statute to the creator of a literary or an artistic work to use, reproduce, and display the work.

corporation—artificial being created by government grant, which for many purposes is treated as a natural person.

corporation by estoppel—corporation that comes about when parties estop themselves from denying that the corporation exists.

corporation de jure—corporation with a legal right to exist by virtue of law.

correspondent bank—will honor the letter of credit from the domestic bank of the buyer.

cost plus—method of determining the purchase price or contract price equal to the seller's or contractor's costs plus a stated percentage as the profit.

co-sureties—sureties for the same debt.

cotenancy—when two or more persons hold concurrent rights and interests in the same property.

Council on Environmental Quality (CEQ)—federal agency that establishes national policies on environmental quality and then recommends legislation to implement these policies.

counterclaim—a claim that the defendant in an action may make against the plaintiff.

counteroffer—proposal by an offeree to the offeror that changes the terms of, and thus rejects, the original offer.

course of dealing—pattern of performance between two parties to a contract.

court—a tribunal established by government to hear and decide matters properly brought to it.

covenant against encumbrances—guarantee that conveyed land is not subject to any right or interest of a third person.

covenant of further assurances—promise that the grantor of an interest in land will execute any additional documents required to perfect the title of the grantee.

covenant of quiet enjoyment—covenant by the grantor of an interest in land to not disturb the grantee's possession of the land.

covenant of right to convey—guarantee that the grantor of an interest in land, if not the owner, has the right or authority to make the conveyance to a new owner.

covenant of seisin—guarantee that the grantor of an interest in land owns the estate conveyed to a new owner.

covenants (or warranties) of title—grantor's covenants of a deed that guarantee such matters as the right to make the conveyance, to ownership of the property, to freedom of the property from encumbrances, or that the grantee will not be disturbed in the quiet enjoyment of the land.

credit transfer—transaction in which a person making payment, such as a buyer, requests payment be made to the beneficiary's bank.

creditor—person (seller or lender) who is owed money; also may be a secured party.

crime—violation of the law that is punished as an offense against the state or government.

criminal laws—the laws that define wrongs against society.

cross-examination—the examination made of a witness by the attorney for the adverse party.

cumulative voting—system of voting for directors in which each shareholder has as many votes as the number of voting shares owned multiplied by the number of directors to be elected, and such votes can be distributed for the various candidates as desired.

customary authority—authority of an agent to do any act that, according to the custom of the community, usually accompanies the transaction for which the agent is authorized to act.

cybersquatters—term for those who register and set up domain names on the Internet for resale to the famous users of the names in question.

D

de facto—existing in fact as distinguished from as of right, as in the case of an officer or a corporation purporting to act as such without being elected to the office or having been properly incorporated.

debenture—unsecured bond of a corporation, with no specific corporate assets pledged as security for payment.

debit transfer—transaction in which a beneficiary entitled to money requests payment from a bank according to a prior agreement.

debtor—buyer on credit (i.e., a borrower).

decedent—person whose estate is being administered.

deed—instrument by which the grantor (owner of land) conveys or transfers the title to a grantee.

defamation—untrue statement by one party about another to a third party.

defendant—party charged with a violation of civil or criminal law in a proceeding.

defined benefit plan—an employer established pension fund obligating the employer to make specified future payments to participants upon retirement.

defined contribution plan—a plan providing individual accounts for each employee participant with benefits defined solely on the amounts contributed by each employee with matching contributions by the employer.

definite time—time of payment computable from the face of the instrument.

delegated powers—powers expressly granted the national government by the Constitution.

delegation—transfer to another of the right and power to do an act.

delegation of duties—transfer of duties by a contracting party to another person who is to perform them.

delivery—constructive or actual possession.

demand draft—draft that is payable upon presentment.

demurrer—a pleading to dismiss the adverse party's pleading for not stating a cause of action or a defense.

deposition—the testimony of a witness taken out of court before a person authorized to administer oaths.

depositor—person, or bailor, who gives property for storage.

derivative (secondary) action—secondary action for damages or breach of contract brought by one or more corporate shareholders against directors, officers, or third persons.

development statement—statement that sets forth significant details of a real estate or property development as required by the federal Land Sales Act.

devise—gift of real estate made by will.

devisee—beneficiary of a devise.

direct damages—losses that are caused by breach of a contract.

direct examination—examination of a witness by his or her attorney.

directed verdict—a direction by the trial judge to the jury to return a verdict in favor of a specified party to the action.

disability—any incapacity resulting from bodily injury or disease to engage in any occupation for remuneration or profit.

discharge in bankruptcy—order of the bankruptcy court relieving the debtor from obligation to pay the unpaid balance of most claims.

disclosed principal—principal whose identity is made known by the agent as well as the fact that the agent is acting on the principal's behalf.

discovery—procedures for ascertaining facts prior to the time of trial in order to eliminate the element of surprise in litigation.

dishonor—status when the primary party refuses to pay the instrument according to its terms.

disinherited—excluded from sharing in the estate of a decedent.

Dispute Settlement Body (DSB)—means provided by the World Trade Organization for member nations to resolve trade disputes rather than engage in unilateral trade sanctions or a trade war.

distinctiveness—capable of serving the source-identifying function of a mark.

distribution *per stirpes*—distribution of an estate made in as many equal parts as there are family lines represented in the nearest generation; also known as *stirpital distribution.*

distributor—entity that takes title to goods and bears the financial and commercial risks for the subsequent sale of the goods.

divestiture order—a court order to dispose of interests that could lead to a monopoly.

divisible contract—agreement consisting of two or more parts, each calling for corresponding performances of each part by the parties.

document of title—document treated as evidence that a person is entitled to receive, hold, and dispose of the document and the goods it covers.

Dodd-Frank Wall Street Reform and Consumer Protection Act—federal legislation passed following the financial markets collapse that includes consumer protections as well as market and mortgage lending reforms.

domestic corporation—corporation that has been incorporated by the state in question as opposed to incorporation by another state.

dominant tenement—land that is benefited by an easement.

donee—recipient of a gift.

donor—person making a gift.

double indemnity—provision for payment of double the amount specified by the insurance contract if death is caused by an accident and occurs under specified circumstances.

draft, or bill of exchange—an unconditional order in writing by one person upon another, signed by the person giving it, and ordering the person to whom it is directed to pay upon demand or at a definite time a sum certain in money to order or to bearer.

drawee—person to whom the draft is addressed and who is ordered to pay the amount of money specified in the draft.

drawer—person who writes out and creates a draft or bill of exchange, including a check.

due diligence—process of checking the environmental history and nature of land prior to purchase.

due process—the constitutional right to be heard, question witnesses, and present evidence.

due process clause—a guarantee of protection against the loss of property or rights without the chance to be heard.

dumping—selling goods in another country at less than fair value.

duress—conduct that deprives the victim of free will and that generally gives the victim the right to set aside any transaction entered into under such circumstances.

duty—obligation of law imposed on a person to perform or refrain from performing a certain act.

E

easement—permanent right that one has in the land of another, as the right to cross another's land or an easement of way.

easement by implication—easement not specifically created by deed that arises from the circumstances of the parties and the land location and access.

economic duress—threat of financial loss.

Economic Espionage Act (EEA)—federal law that makes it a felony to copy, download, transmit, or in any way transfer proprietary files, documents, and information from a computer to an unauthorized person.

economic strikers—union strikers trying to enforce bargaining demands when an impasse has been reached in the negotiation process for a collective bargaining agreement.

effects doctrine—doctrine stating that U.S. courts will assume jurisdiction and will apply antitrust laws to conduct outside of the United States when the activity of business firms has a direct and substantial effect on U.S. commerce; the rule has been modified to require that the effect on U.S. commerce also be direct and foreseeable.

effluent guidelines—EPA standards for maximum ranges of discharge into water.

electronic funds transfer (EFT)—any transfer of funds (other than a transaction originated by a check, draft, or similar paper instrument) that is initiated through an electronic terminal, a telephone, a computer, or a magnetic tape so as to authorize a financial institution to debit or credit an account.

Electronic Funds Transfer Act (EFTA)—federal law that provides consumers with rights and protections in electronic funds transfers.

eleemosynary corporation—corporation organized for a charitable or benevolent purpose.

embezzlement—statutory offense consisting of the unlawful conversion of property entrusted to the wrongdoer.

eminent domain—power of government and certain kinds of corporations to take private property against the objection of the owner, provided the taking is for a public purpose and just compensation is made for it.

emissions offset policy—controls whether new factories can be built in a nonattainment area.

employment-at-will doctrine—doctrine in which the employer has historically been allowed to terminate the employment contract at any time for any reason or for no reason.

en banc—the term used when the full panel of judges on the appellate court hears a case.

encoding warranty—warranty made by any party who encodes electronic information on an instrument; a warranty of accuracy.

Endangered Species Act (ESA)—federal law that identifies and protects species that are endangered from development or other acts that threaten their existence.

endowment insurance—insurance that pays the face amount of the policy if the insured dies within the policy period.

entitlement theory—another name for Nozick's theory that we all have certain rights that must be honored and protected by government.

environmental impact statement (EIS)—formal report prepared under NEPA to document findings on the impact of a federal project on the environment.

equitable title—beneficial interest in a trust.

equity—the body of principles that originally developed because of the inadequacy of the rules then applied by the common law courts of England.

escalation clause—provision for the automatic increase of the rent at periodic intervals.

escheat—transfer to the state of the title to a decedent's property when the owner of the property dies intestate and is not survived by anyone capable of taking the property as heir.

estate in fee—largest estate possible in which the owner has absolute and entire interest in the land.

estoppel—principle by which a person is barred from pursuing a certain course of action or of disputing the truth of certain matters.

ethical egoism—theory of ethics that we should all act in our own self-interest; the Ayn Rand theory that separates guilt from acting in our own self-interest.

ethics—a branch of philosophy dealing with values that relate to the nature of human conduct and values associated with that conduct.

***ex post facto* law**—a law making criminal an act that was lawful when done or that increases the penalty when done. Such laws are generally prohibited by constitutional provisions.

exculpatory clause—provision in a contract stating that one of the parties is not liable for damages in case of breach; also called *limitation-of-liability clause.*

executed contract—agreement that has been completely performed.

execution—the carrying out of a judgment of a court, generally directing that property owned by the defendant be sold and the proceeds first be used to pay the execution or judgment creditor.

executive branch—the branch of government (e.g., the president) formed to execute the laws.

executor, executrix—person (man, woman) named in a will to administer the estate of the decedent.

executory contract—agreement by which something remains to be done by one or both parties.

exhaustion of administrative remedies—requirement that an agency make its final decision before the parties can go to court.

existing goods—goods that physically exist and are owned by the seller at the time of a transaction.

exoneration—agreement or provision in an agreement that one party shall not be held liable for loss; the right of the surety to demand that those primarily liable pay the claim for which the surety is secondarily liable.

expert witness—one who has acquired special knowledge in a particular field as through practical experience or study, or both, whose opinion is admissible as an aid to the trier of fact.

export sale—direct sale to customers in a foreign country.

express authority—authority of an agent to perform a certain act.

express authorization—authorization of an agent to perform a certain act.

express contract—agreement of the parties manifested by their words, whether spoken or written.

express warranty—statement by the defendant relating to the goods, which statement is part of the basis of the bargain.

extortion—illegal demand by a public officer acting with apparent authority.

F

factor—bailee to whom goods are consigned for sale.

false imprisonment—intentional detention of a person without that person's consent; called the *shopkeeper's tort* when shoplifters are unlawfully detained.

FAS—free alongside the named vessel.

federal district court—a general trial court of the federal system.

Federal Register—government publication issued five days a week that lists all administrative regulations, all presidential proclamations and executive orders, and other documents and classes of documents that the president or Congress direct to be published.

Federal Register Act—federal law requiring agencies to make public disclosure of proposed rules, passed rules, and activities.

Federal Sentencing Guidelines—federal standards used by judges in determining mandatory sentence terms for those convicted of federal crimes.

federal system—the system of government in which a central government is given power to administer to national concerns while individual states retain the power to administer to local concerns.

fee simple defeasibles—fee simple interest that can be lost if restrictions on its use are violated.

fee simple estate—highest level of land ownership; full interest of unlimited duration.

felony—criminal offense that is punishable by confinement in prison for more than one year or by death, or that is expressly stated by statute to be a felony.

field warehousing—stored goods under the exclusive control of a warehouse but kept on the owner's premises rather than in a warehouse.

Fifth Amendment—constitutional protection against self-incrimination; also guarantees due process.

finance lease—three-party lease agreement in which there is a lessor, a lessee, and a financier.

financing statement—brief statement (record) that gives sufficient information to alert third persons that a particular creditor may have a security interest in the collateral described.

fire insurance policy—a contract that indemnifies the insured for property destruction or damage caused by fire.

firm offer—offer stated to be held open for a specified time, under the UCC, with respect to merchants.

first-in-time provision—creditor whose interest attached first has priority in the collateral when two creditors have a secured interest.

first-to-perfect basis—rule of priorities that holds that first in time in perfecting a security interest, mortgage, judgment, lien, or other property attachment right should have priority.

fixture—personal property attached to or adapted to real estate.

floating lien—claim in a changing or shifting stock of goods of the buyer.

FOB place of destination—shipping contract that requires the seller to deliver goods to the buyer.

FOB place of shipment—contract that requires the seller to arrange for shipment only.

forbearance—refraining from doing an act.

forcible entry and detainer—action by the landlord to have the tenant removed for nonpayment of rent.

foreclosure—procedure for enforcing a mortgage resulting in the public sale of the mortgaged property and, less commonly, in merely barring the right of the mortgagor to redeem the property from the mortgage.

foreign corporation—corporation incorporated under the laws of another state.

Foreign Corrupt Practices Act (FCPA)—federal law that makes it a felony to influence decision makers in other countries for the purpose of obtaining business, such as contracts for sales and services; also imposes financial reporting requirements on certain U.S. corporations.

Foreign Trade Antitrust Improvements Act—the act that requires that the defendant's conduct have a "direct, substantial, and reasonably foreseeable effect" on domestic commerce.

forged or unauthorized indorsement—instrument indorsed by an agent for a principal without authorization or authority.

forgery—fraudulently making or altering an instrument that apparently creates or alters a legal liability of another.

formal contracts—written contracts or agreements whose formality signifies the parties' intention to abide by the terms.

Fourth Amendment—privacy protection in the U.S. Constitution; prohibits unauthorized searches and seizures.

franchise—privilege or authorization, generally exclusive, to engage in a particular activity within a particular geographic area, such as a government franchise to operate a taxi company within a specified city, or a private franchise as the grant by a manufacturer of a right to sell products within a particular territory or for a particular number of years.

franchise agreement—sets forth rights of franchisee to use trademarks, etc., of franchisor.

Franchise Rule—FTC rule requiring detailed disclosures and prohibiting certain practices.

franchisee—person to whom franchise is granted.

franchising—granting of permission to use a trademark, trade name, or copyright under specified conditions; a form of licensing.

franchisor—party granting the franchise.

fraud—intentional making a false statement of fact, with knowledge or reckless indifference that it is false with resulting reliance by another.

fraud in the inducement—fraud that occurs when a person is persuaded or induced to execute an instrument because of fraudulent statements.

fraud-on-the-market—a theory that in an open and developed securities market, the price of a stock is determined by the information on the company available to the public, and misleading statements will defraud purchasers of stock even if they do not directly rely on these statements.

Freedom of Information Act—federal law permitting citizens to request documents and records from administrative agencies.

freight insurance—insures that shipowner will receive payment for transportation charges.

full warranty—obligation of a seller to fix or replace a defective product within a reasonable time without cost to the buyer.

funds transfer—communication of instructions or requests to pay a specific sum of money to the credit of a specified account or person without an actual physical passing of money.

fungible goods—homogeneous goods of which any unit is the equivalent of any other unit.

future goods—goods that exist physically but are not owned by the seller and goods that have not yet been produced.

G

garnishment—the name given in some states to attachment proceedings.

general agent—agent authorized by the principal to transact all affairs in connection with a particular type of business or trade or to transact all business at a certain place.

general corporation code—state's code listing certain requirements for creation of a corporation.

general jurisdiction—the power to hear and decide most controversies involving legal rights and duties.

general legacies—certain sums of money bequeathed to named persons by the testator; to be paid out of the decedent's assets generally without specifying any particular fund or source from which the payment is to be made.

general partner—partnership in which the partners conduct as co-owners a business for profit, and each partner has a right to take part in the management of the business and has unlimited liability; general partners publicly and actively engage in the transaction of firm business.

general partners—managers of a partnership who have personal liability for the partnership debts.

gift—title to an owner's personal property voluntarily transferred by a party not receiving anything in exchange.

gift causa mortis—gift, made by the donor in the belief that death was immediate and impending, that is revoked or is revocable under certain circumstances.

good faith—absence of knowledge of any defects or problems; "pure heart and an empty head."

goods—anything movable at the time it is identified as the subject of a transaction.

grantee—new owner of a land conveyance.

grantor—owner who transfers or conveys an interest in land to a new owner.

gratuitous bailment—bailment in which the bailee does not receive any compensation or advantage.

guarantor—one who undertakes the obligation of guaranty.

guaranty—agreement or promise to answer for a debt; an undertaking to pay the debt of another if the creditor first sues the debtor.

guaranty of collection—form of guaranty in which creditor cannot proceed against guarantor until after proceeding against debtor.

guaranty of payment—absolute promise to pay when a debtor defaults.

guest—transient who contracts for a room or site at a hotel.

H

hearing officer (or examiner)—another name for an administrative law judge.

hearsay evidence—statements made out of court that are offered in court as proof of the information contained in the statements and that, subject to many exceptions, are not admissible in evidence.

holder—someone in possession of an instrument that runs to that person (i.e., is made payable to that person, is indorsed to that person, or is bearer paper).

holder in due course—a holder who has given value, taken in good faith without notice of dishonor, defenses, or that instrument is overdue, and who is afforded special rights or status.

holder through a holder in due course—holder of an instrument who attains holder-in-due-course status because a holder in due course has held it previous to him or her.

holographic will—unwitnessed will written by hand.

homeowners insurance policy—combination of standard fire insurance and comprehensive personal liability insurance.

hotelkeeper—one regularly engaged in the business of offering living accommodations to all transient persons.

hull insurance—insurance that covers physical damage on a freight-moving vessel.

I

identification—point in the transaction when the buyer acquires an interest in the goods subject to the contract.

identified—term applied to particular goods selected by either the buyer or the seller as the goods called for by the sales contract.

illusory promise—promise that in fact does not impose any obligation on the promisor.

impeach—using prior inconsistent evidence to challenge the credibility of a witness.

implied contract—contract expressed by conduct or implied or deduced from the facts.

implied warranty—warranty that was not made but is implied by law.

implied warranty of the merchantability—group of promises made by the seller, the most important of which is that the goods are fit for the ordinary purposes for which they are sold.

impostor rule—an exception to the rules on liability for forgery that covers situations such as the embezzling payroll clerk.

in pari delicto—equally guilty; used in reference to a transaction as to which relief will not be granted to either party because both are equally guilty of wrongdoing.

incidental authority—authority of an agent that is reasonably necessary to execute express authority.

incidental damages—incurred by the nonbreaching party as part of the process of trying to cover (buy substitute goods) or sell (selling subject matter of contract to another); includes storage fees, commissions, and the like.

income—money earned by the principal, or property in trust, and distributed by the trustee.

incontestability clause—provision that after the lapse of a specified time the insurer cannot dispute the policy on the ground of misrepresentation or fraud of the insured or similar wrongful conduct.

incorporation by reference—contract consisting of both the original or skeleton document and the detailed statement that is incorporated in it.

incorporator—one or more natural persons or corporations who sign and file appropriate incorporation forms with a designated government official.

indemnity—right of a person secondarily liable to require that a person primarily liable pay for loss sustained when the secondary party discharges the obligation that the primary party should have discharged; an undertaking to pay another a sum of money to indemnify when loss is incurred.

indemnity contract—agreement by one person, for consideration, to pay another person a sum of money in the event that the other person sustains a specified loss.

indenture trustee—usually a commercial banking institution, to represent the interests of the bondholders and ensure that the terms and covenants of the bond issue are met by the corporation.

independent contractor—contractor who undertakes to perform a specified task according to the terms of a contract but over whom the other contracting party has no control except as provided for by the contract.

indorsee—party to whom special indorsement is made.

indorsement—signature of the payee on an instrument.

indorser—secondary party (or obligor) on a note.

informal contract—simple oral or written contract.

informal settlements—negotiated disposition of a matter before an administrative agency, generally without public sanctions.

injunction—order of a court of equity to refrain from doing (negative injunction) or to do (affirmative or mandatory injunction) a specified act.

inland marine—insurance that covers domestic shipments of goods over land and inland waterways.

insider—full-time corporate employee or a director or their relatives.

insider information—privileged information on company business known only to employees.

insolvency—excess of debts and liabilities over assets, or inability to pay debts as they mature.

instruction—summary of the law given to jurors by the judge before deliberation begins.

insurable interest—the right to hold a valid insurance policy on a person or property.

insurance—a plan of security against risks by charging the loss against a fund created by the payments made by policyholders.

insurance agent—agent of an insurance company.

insurance broker—independent contractor who is not employed by any one insurance company.

insured—person to whom the promise in an insurance contract is made.

insurer—promisor in an insurance contract.

integrity—the adherence to one's values and principles despite the costs and consequences.

intentional infliction of emotional distress—tort that produces mental anguish caused by conduct that exceeds all bounds of decency.

intentional tort—civil wrong that results from intentional conduct.

inter vivos gift—any transaction that takes place between living persons and creates rights prior to the death of any of them.

interest in the authority—form of agency in which an agent has been given or paid for the right to exercise authority.

interest in the subject matter—form of agency in which an agent is given an interest in the property with which that agent is dealing.

interlineation—writing between the lines or adding to the provisions of a document, the effect thereof depending upon the nature of the document.

intermediary bank—bank between the originator and the beneficiary bank in the transfer of funds.

interrogatories—written questions used as a discovery tool that must be answered under oath.

intervenors—in administrative actions, third parties who have an interest in the issues being determined by an ALJ.

intestate—condition of dying without a will as to any property.

intestate succession—distribution, made as directed by statute, of a decedent's property not effectively disposed of by will.

invasion of privacy—tort of intentional intrusion into the private affairs of another.

invitee—person who enters another's land by invitation.

involuntary bankruptcy—proceeding in which a creditor or creditors file the petition for relief with the bankruptcy court.

issuer—party who issues a document such as a letter of credit or a document of title such as a warehouse receipt or bill of lading.

J

joint and several liability—disproportionate satisfaction of partnership debt rendering each partner liable for the entire debt with the right to contribution from other partners.

joint liability—apportions partners' responsibility for partnership debt equally.

joint tenancy—estate held jointly by two or more with the right of survivorship as between them unless modified by statute.

joint venture—relationship in which two or more persons or firms combine their labor or property for a single undertaking and share profits and losses equally unless otherwise agreed.

judge—primary officer of the court.

judgment lien—lien obtained through the courts.

judgment n.o.v. (or *non obstante veredicto*, "notwithstanding the verdict")—a judgment entered after verdict upon the motion of the losing party on the ground that the verdict is so wrong that a judgment should be entered the opposite of the verdict.

judicial branch—the branch of government (e.g., the courts) formed to interpret the laws.

jurisdiction—the power of a court to hear and determine a given class of cases; the power to act over a particular defendant.

jurisdictional rule of reason—rule that balances the vital interests, including laws and policies, of the United States with those of a foreign country.

jury—a body of citizens sworn by a court to determine by verdict the issues of fact submitted to them.

K

Kant's categorical imperative—a standard of ethics that requires that we avoid one-sided benefit for us as a result of the conduct or decision.

L

land—earth, including all things embedded in or attached thereto, whether naturally or by the act of humans.

landlord—one who leases real property to another.

law—the order or pattern of rules that society establishes to govern the conduct of individuals and the relationships among them.

lease—agreement between the owner of property and a tenant by which the former agrees to give possession of the property to the latter for payment of rent. (Parties—landlord or lessor, tenant or lessee)

leasehold estate—interest of a tenant in rented land.

legacy—gift of money made by will.

legal title—title held by the trustee in a trust situation.

legatee—beneficiary who receives a gift of personal property by will.

legislative branch—the branch of government (e.g., Congress) formed to make the laws.

lessee—one who has a possessory interest in real or personal property under a lease; a tenant.

lessor—one who conveys real or personal property by a lease; a landlord.

letter of credit—commercial device used to guarantee payment to a seller, primarily in an international business transaction.

letters of administration—written authorization given to an administrator of an estate as evidence of appointment and authority.

letters testamentary—written authorization given to an executor of an estate as evidence of appointment and authority.

liability insurance—covers the shipowner's liability if the ship causes damage to another ship or its cargo.

libel—written or visual defamation without legal justification.

license—personal privilege to do some act or series of acts upon the land of another, as the placing of a sign thereon, not amounting to an easement or a right of possession.

licensee—someone on another's premises with the permission of the occupier, whose duty is to warn the licensee of nonobvious dangers.

licensing—transfer of technology rights to a product so that it may be produced by a different business organization in a foreign country in exchange for royalties and other payments as agreed.

lien—claim or right, against through judgment or levy.

life estate—an estate for the duration of a life.

limitation-of-liability clause—provision in a contract stating that one of the parties is not liable for damages in case of breach; also called *exculpatory clause.*

limited covenant—any covenant that does not provide the complete protection of a full covenant.

limited defenses—defenses available to secondary parties if the presenting party is a holder in due course.

limited liability company (LLC)—a partnership for federal tax treatment and the limited liability feature of the corporate form of business organization.

limited liability partnership (LLP)—partnership in which at least one partner has a liability limited to the loss of the capital contribution made to the partnership.

limited partner—partner who neither takes part in the management of the partnership nor appears to the public to be a general partner.

limited partnership—partnership that can be formed by "one or more general partners and one or more limited partners."

limited (special) jurisdiction—the authority to hear only particular kinds of cases.

limited warranty—any warranty that does not provide the complete protection of a full warranty.

lineals—relationship that exists when one person is a direct descendant of the other; also called *lineal descendants.*

liquidated damages—provision stipulating the amount of damages to be paid in the event of default or breach of contract.

liquidated damages clause—specification of exact compensation in case of a breach of contract.

liquidation—process of converting property into money whether of particular items of property or of all the assets of a business or an estate.

living trust—trust created to take effect within the lifetime of the settlor; also called *inter vivos* trust.

living will—document by which individuals may indicate that if they become unable to express their wishes and are in an irreversible, incurable condition, they do not want life-sustaining medical treatments.

living-document view—the term used when a constitution is interpreted according to changes in conditions.

lottery—any plan by which a consideration is given for a chance to win a prize; it consists of three elements: (1) there must be a payment of money or something of value for an opportunity to win, (2) a prize must be available, and (3) the prize must be offered by lot or chance.

M

mailbox rule—timing for acceptance tied to proper acceptance.

maker—party who writes or creates a promissory note.

malpractice—when services are not properly rendered in accordance with commonly accepted standards; negligence by a professional in performing his or her skill.

marine insurance—policies that cover perils relating to the transportation of goods.

market power—the ability to control price and exclude competitors.

market value—price at which a share of stock can be voluntarily bought or sold in the open market.

mask work—specific form of expression embodied in a chip design, including the stencils used in manufacturing semiconductor chip products.

mass picketing—illegal tactic of employees massing together in great numbers to effectively shut down entrances of the employer's facility.

maturity date—date that a corporation is required to repay a loan to a bondholder.

means test—new standard under the Reform Act that requires the court to find that the debtor does not have the means to repay creditors; goes beyond the past requirement of petitions being granted on the simple assertion of the debtor saying, "I have debts."

mechanic's lien—claim by laborers or materials suppliers for property improvements.

mediation—the settlement of a dispute through the use of a messenger who carries to each side of the dispute the issues and offers in the case.

merchant—seller who deals in specific goods classified by the UCC.

merger (of corporations)—combining of corporations by which one absorbs the other and continues to exist, preserving its original charter and identity while the other corporation ceases to exist.

minitrial—a trial held on portions of the case or certain issues in the case.

Miranda warnings—warnings required to prevent self-incrimination in a criminal matter.

mirror image rule—common law contract rule on acceptance that requires language to be absolutely the same as the offer, unequivocal and unconditional.

misdemeanor—criminal offense with a sentence of less than one year that is neither treason nor a felony.

misrepresentation—false statement of fact made innocently without any intent to deceive.

mistrial—a court's declaration that terminates a trial and postpones it to a later date; commonly entered when evidence has been of a highly prejudicial character or when a juror has been guilty of misconduct.

money—medium of exchange.

money order—draft issued by a bank or a nonbank.

moral relativists—those who make decisions based on circumstances and not on the basis of any predefined standards.

mortgage—interest in land given by the owner to a creditor as security for the payment of the creditor for a debt, the nature of the interest depending upon the law of the state where the land is located. (Parties— mortgagor, mortgagee)

most-favored-nation—clause in treaties between countries whereby any privilege granted to one member is extended to all members of the treaty.

motion for summary judgment—request that the court decide a case on basis of law only because there are no material issues disputed by the parties.

motion to dismiss—a pleading that may be filed to attack the adverse party's pleading as not stating a cause of action or a defense.

N

National Environmental Policy Act (NEPA)—federal law that mandates study of a project's impact on the environment before it can be undertaken by any federal agency.

National Pollutant Discharge Elimination System (NPDES)—EPA system for regulating point source emissions into water.

national treatment—a WTO requirement in which a country may not discriminate between its own products and foreign products or services.

natural law—a system of principles to guide human conduct independent of, and sometimes contrary to, enacted law and discovered by man's rational intelligence.

necessaries—things indispensable or absolutely necessary for the sustenance of human life.

negligence—failure to exercise due care under the circumstances that results in harm proximately caused to one owed a duty to exercise due care.

negotiability—quality of an instrument that affords special rights and standing.

negotiable bill of lading—document of title that by its terms calls for goods to be delivered "to the bearer" or "to the order of" a named person.

negotiable instrument—drafts, promissory notes, checks, and certificates of deposit that, in proper form, give special rights as "negotiable commercial paper."

negotiable warehouse receipt—receipt that states the covered goods will be delivered "to the bearer" or "to the order of."

negotiation—the transfer of commercial paper by indorsement and delivery by the person to whom it is then payable in the case of order paper and by physical transfer in the case of bearer paper.

Noise Control Act—federal law that controls noise emissions from low-flying aircraft.

nominal damages—nominal sum awarded the plaintiff in order to establish that legal rights have been violated although the plaintiff in fact has not sustained any actual loss or damages.

nonattainment areas—"dirty" areas that do not meet federal standards under the Clean Air Act.

nonconforming use—use of land that conflicts with a zoning ordinance at the time the ordinance goes into effect.

nonconsumer lease—lease that does not satisfy the definition of a consumer lease; also known as a *commercial lease.*

nonnegotiable bill of lading—See *straight bill of lading.*

nonnegotiable instrument—contract, note, or draft that does not meet negotiability requirements of Article 3.

nonnegotiable warehouse receipt—receipt that states the covered goods received will be delivered to a specific person.

notice of dishonor—notice that an instrument has been dishonored; such notice can be oral, written, or electronic but is subject to time limitations.

notice statute—statute under which the last good-faith or bona fide purchaser holds the title.

notice-race statute—statute under which the first bona fide purchaser to record the deed holds the title.

novation—substitution for an old contract with a new one that either replaces an existing obligation with a new obligation or replaces an original party with a new party.

nuisance—conduct that harms or prejudices another in the use of land or that harms or prejudices the public.

O

obligee—promisee who can claim the benefit of the obligation.

obligor—promisor.

ocean marine—policies that cover transportation of goods in vessels in international and coastal trade.

offer—expression of an offeror's willingness to enter into a contractual agreement.

offeree—person to whom an offer is made.

offeror—person who makes an offer.

Oil Pollution Act—federal law that assigns cleanup liability for oil spills in U.S. waters.

open meeting law—law that requires advance notice of agency meeting and public access.

opening statements—statements by opposing attorneys that tell the jury what their cases will prove.

operation of law—attaching of certain consequences to certain facts because of legal principles that operate automatically as contrasted with consequences that arise because of the voluntary action of a party designed to create those consequences.

option contract—contract to hold an offer to make a contract open for a fixed period of time.

order of relief—the order from the bankruptcy judge that starts the protection for the debtor; when the order of relief is entered by the court, the debtor's creditors must stop all proceedings and work through the bankruptcy court to recover debts (if possible). Court finding that creditors have met the standards for bankruptcy petitions.

order paper—instrument payable to the order of a party.

original jurisdiction—the authority to hear a controversy when it is first brought to court.

originator—party who originates the funds transfer.

output contract—contract of a producer to sell its entire production or output to a given buyer.

outstanding—name for shares of a company that have been issued to stockholders.

overdraft—negative balance in a drawer's account.

P

par value—specified monetary amount assigned by an issuing corporation for each share of its stock.

parol evidence rule—rule that prohibits the introduction in evidence of oral or written statements made prior to or contemporaneously with the execution of a complete written contract, deed, or instrument, in the absence of fraud, accident, or mistake.

partially disclosed principal—principal whose existence is made known but whose identity is not.

partner—one of two or more persons who jointly own and carry on a business for profit.

partnership—pooling of capital resources and the business or professional talents of two or more individuals (partners) with the goal of making a profit.

partnership agreement—document prepared to evidence the contract of the parties. (Parties—partners or general partners)

party—person involved in a legal transaction; may be a natural person, an artificial person (e.g., a corporation), or an unincorporated enterprise (e.g., a governmental agency).

past consideration—something that has been performed in the past and which, therefore, cannot be consideration for a promise made in the present.

payable to order—term stating that a negotiable instrument is payable to the order of any person described in it or to a person or order.

payee—party to whom payment is to be made.

payment order—direction given by an originator to his or her bank or by any bank to a subsequent bank to make a specified funds transfer.

Pension Benefit Guaranty Corporation (PBGC)—an insurance plan to protect employees covered by defined benefit plans in case an employer is unable to meet its payment obligations from the employer's pension fund.

per capita—method of distributing estate assets on an equal-per-person basis.

perfected security interest—security interest with priority because of filing, possession, automatic, or temporary priority status.

periodic tenancy—tenancy that continues indefinitely for a specified rental period until terminated; often called a month-to-month tenancy.

personal property—property that is movable or intangible, or rights in such things.

personal representative—administrator or executor who represents decedents under UPC.

per stirpes—method for distribution of an estate that divides property equally down family lines.

physical duress—threat of physical harm to person or property.

plaintiff—party who initiates a lawsuit.

pleadings—the papers filed by the parties in an action in order to set forth the facts and frame the issues to be tried, although, under some systems, the pleadings merely give notice or a general indication of the nature of the issues.

pledge—bailment given as security for the payment of a debt or the performance of an obligation owed to the pledgee. (Parties–pledgor, pledgee)

point sources—direct discharges into bodies of water.

police power—the power to govern; the power to adopt laws for the protection of the public health, welfare, safety, and morals.

policy—paper evidencing the contract of insurance.

positive law—law enacted and codified by governmental authority.

possession—exclusive dominion and control of property.

possibility of reverter—nature of the interest held by the grantor after conveying land outright but subject to a condition or provision that may cause the grantee's interest to become forfeited and the interest to revert to the grantor or heirs.

postdate—to insert or place on an instrument a later date than the actual date on which it was executed.

postdating—inserting or placing on an instrument a later date than the actual date on which it was executed.

potentially responsible parties (PRPs)—those beyond actual polluters who could be responsible for cleanup costs.

power of attorney—written authorization to an agent by the principal.

precedent—a decision of a court that stands as the law for a particular problem in the future.

predatory lending—a practice on the part of the subprime lending market whereby lenders take advantage of less sophisticated consumers or those who are desperate for funds by using the lenders' superior bargaining positions to obtain credit terms that go well beyond compensating them for their risk.

predicate act—qualifying underlying offense for RICO liability.

preemption—the federal government's superior regulatory position over state laws on the same subject area.

preemptive right—shareholder's right upon the increase of a corporation's capital stock to be allowed to subscribe to such a percentage of the new shares as the shareholder's old shares bore to the former total capital stock.

preferences—transfers of property by a debtor to one or more specific creditors to enable these creditors to obtain payment for debts owed.

preferential transfers—certain transfers of money or security interests in the time frame just prior to bankruptcy that can be set aside if voidable.

preferred stock—stock that has a priority or preference as to payment of dividends or upon liquidation, or both.

prescription—acquisition of a right to use the land of another, as an easement, by making hostile, visible, and notorious use of the land, continuing for the period specified by the local law.

presentment—formal request for payment on an instrument.

price discrimination—the charging practice by a seller of different prices to different buyers for commodities of similar grade and quality, resulting in reduced competition or a tendency to create a monopoly.

prima facie—evidence that, if believed, is sufficient by itself to lead to a particular conclusion.

primary offerings—the original distribution of securities by the issuing corporations.

primary party—party to whom the holder or holder in due course must turn first to obtain payment.

primary picketing—legal presentations in front of a business notifying the public of a labor dispute.

primum non nocere—above all, do no harm.

principal—person or firm who employs an agent; the person who, with respect to a surety, is primarily liable to the third person or creditor; property held in trust.

principal debtor—original borrower or debtor.

prior art—a showing that an invention as a whole would have been obvious to a person of ordinary skill in the art when the invention was patented.

private carrier—carrier owned by the shipper, such as a company's own fleet of trucks.

private corporation—corporation organized for charitable and benevolent purposes or for purposes of finance, industry, and commerce.

private law—the rules and regulations parties agree to as part of their contractual relationships.

private nuisance—nuisance that affects only one or a few individuals.

privileges and immunities clause—a clause that entitles a person going into another state to make contracts, own property, and engage in business to the same extent as citizens of that state.

privity—succession or chain of relationship to the same thing or right, such as privity of contract, privity of estate, privity of possession.

privity of contract—relationship between a promisor and the promisee.

privity rule—succession or chain of relationship to the same thing or right, such as privity of contract, privity of estate, privity of possession.

pro rata—proportionately, or divided according to a rate or standard.

probate—procedure for formally establishing or proving that a given writing is the last will and testament of the person who purportedly signed it.

procedural law—the law that must be followed in enforcing rights and liabilities.

process—paperwork served personally on a defendant in a civil case.

product disparagement—false statements made about a product or business.

profit—right to take a part of the soil or produce of another's land, such as timber or water.

promisee—person to whom a promise is made.

promisor—person who makes a promise.

promissory estoppels—doctrine that a promise will be enforced although it is not supported by consideration when the promisor should have reasonably expected that the promise would induce action or forbearance of a definite and substantial character on the part of the promised and injustice can be avoided only by enforcement of the promise.

promissory note—unconditional promise in writing made by one person to another, signed by the maker engaging to pay on demand, or at a definite time, a sum certain in money to order or to bearer. (Parties—maker, payee)

promoters—persons who plan the formation of the corporation and sell or promote the idea to others.

proof of claim—written statement, signed by the creditor or an authorized representative, setting forth any claim made against the debtor and the basis for it.

property report—condensed version of a property development statement filed with the secretary of HUD and given to a prospective customer at least 48 hours before signing a contract to buy or lease property.

prosecutor—party who originates a criminal proceeding.

prospectus—information provided to each potential purchaser of securities setting forth the key information contained in the registration statement.

proxy—written authorization by a shareholder to another person to vote the stock owned by the shareholder; the person who is the holder of such a written authorization.

public corporation—corporation that has been established for governmental purposes and for the administration of public affairs.

public nuisance—nuisance that affects the community or public at large.

public policy—certain objectives relating to health, morals, and integrity of government that the law seeks to advance by declaring invalid any contract that conflicts with those objectives even though there is no statute expressly declaring such a contract illegal.

public warehouses—entities that serve the public generally without discrimination.

punitive damages—damages, in excess of those required to compensate the plaintiff for the wrong done, that are imposed in order to punish the defendant because of the particularly wanton or willful character of wrongdoing; also called *exemplary damages.*

purchase money security interest (PMSI)—the security interest in the goods a seller sells on credit that become the collateral for the creditor/seller.

Q

qualified indorsement—an indorsement that includes words such as "without recourse" that disclaims certain liability of the indorser to a maker or a drawee.

qualified privilege—media privilege to print inaccurate information without liability for defamation, so long as a retraction is printed and there was no malice.

quantum meruit—as much as deserved; an action brought for the value of the services rendered the defendant when there was no express contract as to the purchase price.

quasi contract—court-imposed obligation to prevent unjust enrichment in the absence of a contract.

quasi-judicial proceedings—forms of hearings in which the rules of evidence and procedure are more relaxed but each side still has a chance to be heard.

quasi-public corporation—private corporation furnishing services on which the public is particularly dependent, for example, a gas and electric company.

quitclaim deed—deed by which the grantor purports to give up only whatever right or title the grantor may have in the property without specifying or warranting transfer of any particular interest.

quorum—minimum number of persons, shares represented, or directors who must be present at a meeting in order to lawfully transact business.

R

race statute—statute under which the first party to record the deed holds the title.

race-notice statute—see *notice-race statute.*

Racketeer Influenced and Corrupt Organizations (RICO) Act—federal law, initially targeting organized crime that has expanded in scope and provides penalties and civil recovery for multiple criminal offenses, or a pattern of racketeering.

real property—land and all rights in land.

recognizance—obligation entered into before a court to do some act, such as to appear at a later date for a hearing. Also called a *contract of record.*

recorder—public official in charge of deeds.

recross-examination—an examination by the other side's attorney that follows the redirect examination.

redemption—buying back of one's property, which has been sold because of a default, upon paying the amount that had been originally due together with interest and costs.

redirect examination—questioning after cross-examination, in which the attorney for the witness testifying may ask the same witness other questions to overcome effects of the cross-examination.

reference to a third person—settlement that allows a nonparty to resolve the dispute.

reformation—remedy by which a written instrument is corrected when it fails to express the actual intent of both parties because of fraud, accident, or mistake.

registered bonds—bonds held by owners whose names and addresses are registered on the books of the corporation to ensure proper payment.

registration requirements—provisions of the Securities Act of 1933 requiring advance disclosure to the public of a new securities issue through filing a statement with the SEC and sending a prospectus to each potential purchaser.

registration statement—document disclosing specific financial information regarding the security, the issuer, and the underwriter.

release—an instrument by which the signing party (releasor) relinquishes claims or potential claims against one or more persons (releasees) who might otherwise be subject to liability to the releasor.

remainder interest—land interest that follows a life estate.

remand—term used when an appellate court sends a case back to trial court for additional hearings or a new trial.

remedy—action or procedure that is followed in order to enforce a right or to obtain damages for injury to a right.

rent-a-judge plan—dispute resolution through private courts with judges paid to be referees for the cases.

representative capacity—action taken by one on behalf of another, as the act of a personal representative on behalf of a decedent's estate, or action taken both on one's behalf and on behalf of others, as a shareholder bringing a representative action.

repudiation—result of a buyer or seller refusing to perform the contract as stated.

request for production of documents—discovery tool for uncovering paper evidence in a case.

requirements contract—contract to buy all requirements of the buyer from the seller.

rescission—action of one party to a contract to set the contract aside when the other party is guilty of a breach of the contract.

reservation of rights—assertion by a party to a contract that even though a tendered performance (e.g., a defective product) is accepted, the right to damages for nonconformity to the contract is reserved.

Resource Conservation and Recovery Act (RCRA)—federal law that regulates the disposal of potentially harmful substances and encourages resource conservation and recovery.

Resource Recovery Act—early federal solid waste disposal legislation that provided funding for states and local governments with recycling programs.

respondeat superior—doctrine that the principal or employer is vicariously liable for the unauthorized torts committed by an agent or employee while acting within the scope of the agency or the course of the employment, respectively.

restrictive covenants—covenants in a deed by which the grantee agrees to refrain from doing specified acts.

restrictive indorsement—an indorsement that restricts further transfer, such as in trust for or to the use of some other person, is conditional, or for collection or deposit.

reverse—the term used when the appellate court sets aside the verdict or judgment of a lower court.

reverse mortgage—mortgage in which the owners get their equity out of their home over a period of time and return the house to the lender upon their deaths.

reversible error—an error or defect in court proceedings of so serious a nature that on appeal the appellate court will set aside the proceedings of the lower court.

revoke—testator's act of taking back his or her will and its provisions.

right—legal capacity to require another person to perform or refrain from an action.

right of escheat—right of the state to take the property of a decedent that has not been distributed.

right of first refusal—right of a party to meet the terms of a proposed contract before it is executed, such as a real estate purchase agreement.

right of privacy—the right to be free from unreasonable intrusion by others.

right to cure—second chance for a seller to make a proper tender of conforming goods.

right-to-work laws—laws restricting unions and employees from negotiating clauses in their collective bargaining agreements that make union membership compulsory.

rights theory—Nozick's theory of ethics that we all have a set of rights that must be honored and protected by government.

risk—peril or contingency against which the insured is protected by the contract of insurance.

risk of loss—in contract performance, the cost of damage or injury to the goods contracted for.

Robinson-Patman Act—a federal statute designed to eliminate price discrimination in interstate commerce.

S

Safe Drinking Water Act—a federal law that establishes national standards for contaminants in drinking water.

sale on approval—term indicating that no sale takes place until the buyer approves or accepts the goods.

sale or return—sale in which the title to the property passes to the buyer at the time of the transaction but the buyer is given the option of returning the property and restoring the title to the seller.

search warrant—judicial authorization for a search of property where there is the expectation of privacy.

seasonable—timely.

secondary meaning—a legal term signifying the words in question have taken on a new meaning with the public, capable of serving a source-identifying function of a mark.

secondary parties—called secondary obligors under Revised Article 3; parties to an instrument to whom holders turn when the primary party, for whatever reason, fails to pay the instrument.

secondary picketing—picketing an employer with which a union has no dispute to persuade the employer to stop doing business with a party to the dispute; generally illegal under the NLRA.

secrecy laws—confidentiality laws applied to home-country banks.

secured party—person owed the money, whether as a seller or a lender, in a secured transaction in personal property.

secured transaction—credit sale of goods or a secured loan that provides special protection for the creditor.

securities—stocks and bonds issued by a corporation. Under some investor protection laws, the term includes any interest in an enterprise that provides unearned income to its owner.

security agreement—agreement of the creditor and the debtor that the creditor will have a security interest.

security interest—property right that enables the creditor to take possession of the property if the debtor does not pay the amount owed.

self-help repossession—creditor's right to repossess the collateral without judicial proceedings.

self-proved wills—wills that eliminate some formalities of proof by being executed according to statutory requirements.

selling on consignment—entrusting a person with possession of property for the purpose of sale.

semiconductor chip product—product placed on a piece of semiconductor material in accordance with a predetermined pattern that is intended to perform electronic circuitry functions.

service mark—mark that identifies a service.

servient tenement—land that is subject to an easement.

settlor—one who settles property in trust or creates a trust.

severalty—ownership of property by one person.

shared powers—powers that are held by both state and national governments.

Sherman Antitrust Act—a federal statute prohibiting combinations and contracts in restraint of interstate trade, now generally inapplicable to labor union activity.

shop right—right of an employer to use in business without charge an invention discovered by an employee during working hours and with the employer's material and equipment.

shopkeeper's privilege—right of a store owner to detain a suspected shoplifter based on reasonable cause and for a reasonable time without resulting liability for false imprisonment.

short-swing profit—profit realized by a corporate insider from selling securities less than six months after purchase.

sinking fund—fixed amount of money set aside each year by the borrowing corporation toward the ultimate payment of bonds.

Sixth Amendment—the U.S. constitutional amendment that guarantees a speedy trial.

slander—defamation of character by spoken words or gestures.

slander of title—malicious making of false statements as to a seller's title.

small claims courts—courts that resolve disputes between parties when those disputes do not exceed a minimal level; no lawyers are permitted; the parties represent themselves.

social contract—the agreement under Locke and Rawls as to what our ethical standards will be.

sole or individual proprietorship—form of business ownership in which one individual owns the business.

soliciting agent—salesperson.

sovereign compliance doctrine—doctrine that allows a defendant to raise as an affirmative defense to an antitrust action the fact that the defendant's actions were compelled by a foreign state.

sovereign immunity doctrine—a doctrine that states that a foreign sovereign generally cannot be sued without its consent.

special agent—agent authorized to transact a specific transaction or to do a specific act.

special indorsement—an indorsement that specifies the person to whom the instrument is indorsed.

specific legacies—identified property bequeathed by a testator; also called *specific devises.*

specific lien—right of a creditor to hold a particular property or assert a lien on the particular property of the debtor because of the creditor's having done work on or having some other association with the property, as distinguished from having a lien generally against the assets of the debtor merely because the debtor is indebted to the lien holder.

specific performance—action brought to compel the adverse party to perform a contract on the theory that merely suing for damages for its breach will not be an adequate remedy.

spendthrift trust—a trust that, prevents creditors of the beneficiary from reaching the principal or income held by the trustee and precludes beneficiary assignments.

spot zoning—allowing individual variation in zoning.

stakeholder analysis—the term used when a decision maker views a problem from different perspectives and measures the impact of a decision on various groups.

stakeholders—those who have a stake, or interest, in the activities of a corporation; stakeholders include employees, members of the community in which the corporation operates, vendors, customers, and any others who are affected by the actions and decisions of the corporation.

stale check—a check whose date is longer than six months ago.

standby letter—letter of credit for a contractor ensuring he will complete the project as contracted.

stare decisis—"let the decision stand"; the principle that the decision of a court should serve as a guide or precedent and control the decision of a similar case in the future.

status quo ante—original positions of the parties.

statute of frauds—statute that, in order to prevent fraud through the use of perjured testimony, requires that certain kinds of transactions be evidenced in writing in order to be binding or enforceable.

statute of limitations—statute that restricts the period of time within which an action may be brought.

statutory law—legislative acts declaring, commanding, or prohibiting something.

stay (or delay) of foreclosure—delay of foreclosure obtained by the mortgagor to prevent undue hardship.

stock subscription—contract or agreement to buy a specific number and kind of shares when they are issued by the corporation.

stop payment order—order by a depositor to the bank to refuse to make payment of a check when presented for payment.

straight (or nonnegotiable) bill of lading—document of title that consigns transported goods to a named person.

strict liability—civil wrong for which there is absolute liability because of the inherent danger in the underlying activity, for example, the use of explosives.

strict tort liability—product liability theory that imposes absolute liability upon the manufacturer, seller, or distributor of goods for harm caused by defective goods.

subject matter jurisdiction—judicial authority to hear a particular type of case.

sublease—a transfer of the premises by the lessee to a third person, the sublessee or subtenant, for a period of less than the term of the original lease.

sublessee—person with lease rights for a period of less than the term of the original lease (also *subtenant*).

subprime lending market—a credit market that makes loans to high-risk consumers (those who have bankruptcies, no credit history, or a poor credit history), often loaning money to pay off other debts the consumer has due.

subrogation—right of a party secondarily liable to stand in the place of the creditor after making payment to the creditor and to enforce the creditor's right against the party primarily liable in order to obtain indemnity from such primary party.

substantial impairment—material defect in a good.

substantial performance—equitable rule that if a good-faith attempt to perform does not precisely meet the terms of the agreement, the agreement will still be considered complete if the essential purpose of the contract is accomplished.

substantive law—the law that defines rights and liabilities.

substitute check—electronic image of a paper check that a bank can create and that has the same legal effect as the original instrument.

substitution—substitution of a new contract between the same parties.

sum certain—amount due under an instrument that can be computed from its face with only reference to interest rates.

summary jury trial—a mock or dry-run trial for parties to get a feel for how their cases will play to a jury.

summation—the attorney address that follows all the evidence presented in court and sums up a case and recommends a particular verdict be returned by the jury.

Superfund Amendment and Reauthorization Act—federal law that expands scope and operation of CERCLA.

Superfund sites—areas designated by the EPA for cleanup.

surety—obligor of a suretyship; primarily liable for the debt or obligation of the principal debtor.

suretyship—undertaking to pay the debt or be liable for the default of another.

symbolic delivery—delivery of goods by delivery of the means of control, such as a key or a relevant document of title, such as a negotiable bill of lading; also called constructive delivery.

T

tariff—(1) domestically—government-approved schedule of charges that may be made by a regulated business, such as a common carrier or warehouser; (2) internationally—tax imposed by a country on goods crossing its borders, without regard to whether the purpose is to raise revenue or to discourage the traffic in the taxed goods.

tax lien—lien on property for nonpayment of taxes.

teller's check—draft drawn by a bank on another bank in which it has an account.

temporary insider—someone retained by a corporation for professional services on an as-needed basis, such as an attorney, accountant, or investment banker.

temporary perfection—perfection given for a limited period of time to creditors.

tenancy at sufferance—lease arrangement in which the tenant occupies the property at the discretion of the landlord.

tenancy at will—holding of land for an indefinite period that may be terminated at any time by the landlord or by the landlord and tenant acting together.

tenancy by entirety or tenancy by the entireties—transfer of property to both husband and wife.

tenancy for years—tenancy for a fixed period of time, even though the time is less than a year.

tenancy in common—relationship that exists when two or more persons own undivided interests in property.

tenancy in partnership—ownership relationship that exists between partners under the Uniform Partnership Act.

tenant—one who holds or possesses real property by any kind of right or title; one who pays rent for the temporary use and occupation of another's real property under a lease.

tender—goods have arrived, are available for pickup, and the buyer is notified.

term insurance—policy written for a specified number of years that terminates at the end of that period.

termination statement—document (record), which may be requested by a paid-up debtor, stating that a security interest is no longer claimed under the specified financing statement.

testamentary capacity—sufficient mental capacity to understand that a writing being executed is a will and what that entails.

testamentary intent—designed to take effect at death, as by disposing of property or appointing a personal representative.

testamentary trust—trust that takes effect upon the settlor's death.

testate—condition of leaving a will upon death.

testate distribution—distribution of an estate in accordance with the will of the decedent.

testator, testatrix—man, woman who makes a will.

theory of justice—the Locke and Rawlsian standard for ethics that requires that we all agree on certain universal principles in advance.

third-party beneficiary—third person whom the parties to a contract intend to benefit by the making of the contract and to confer upon such person the right to sue for breach of contract.

time draft—bill of exchange payable at a stated time after sight or at a definite time.

tippee—individual who receives information about a corporation from an insider or temporary insider.

tort—civil wrong that interferes with one's property or person.

Toxic Substances Control Act (TOSCA)—first federal law to control the manufacture, use, and disposal of toxic substances.

trade dress—product's total image including its overall packaging look.

trade libel—written defamation about a product or service.

trade name—name under which a business is carried on and, if fictitious, must be registered.

trade secret—formula, device, or compilation of information that is used in one's business and is of such a nature that it provides an advantage over competitors who do not have the information.

trademark—mark that identifies a product.

transferee—buyer or vendee.

Transport Rule—the rule promulgated to address downwind pollution from coal and gas-fired power plants.

traveler's check—check that is payable on demand provided it is countersigned by the person whose specimen signature appears on the check.

treasury stock—corporate stock that the corporation has reacquired.

treble damages—three times the damages actually sustained.

trespass—unauthorized action with respect to person or property.

trespasser—person who is on the land of another without permission or authorization.

tripartite—three-part division (of government).

trust—transfer of property by one person to another with the understanding or declaration that such property be held for the benefit of another; the holding of property by the owner in trust for another, upon a declaration of trust, without a transfer to another person. (Parties—settlor, trustee, beneficiary)

trust agreement—instrument creating a trust; also called *deed of trust.*

trust corpus—fund or property that is transferred to the trustee also called *trust fund, trust estate*, and *trust res.*

trustee—party who has legal title to estate and manages it.

trustee in bankruptcy—impartial person elected to administer the debtor's estate.

trustor—donor or settlor who is the owner of property.

tying—the anticompetitive practice of requiring buyers to purchase one product in order to get another.

U

ultra vires—act or contract that the corporation does not have authority to do or make.

unconscionable—unreasonable, not guided or restrained by conscience and often referring to a contract grossly unfair to one party because of the superior bargaining powers of the other party.

underwriter—insurer.

undisclosed principal—principal on whose behalf an agent acts without disclosing to the third person the fact of agency or the identity of the principal.

undue influence—influence that is asserted upon another person by one who dominates that person.

Uniform Probate Code (UPC)—uniform statute on wills and administration of estates.

Uniform Simultaneous Death Act—law providing that when survivorship cannot be established, the property of each person shall be disposed of as though he or she had survived the other.

unilateral contract—contract under which only one party makes a promise.

unincorporated association—combination of two or more persons for the furtherance of a common nonprofit purpose.

universal agent—agent authorized by the principal to do all acts that can lawfully be delegated to a representative.

universal defenses—defenses that are regarded as so basic that the social interest in preserving them outweighs the social interest of giving negotiable instruments the freely transferable qualities of money; accordingly, such defenses are given universal effect and may be raised against all holders.

USA Patriot Act—federal law that, among other things, imposes reporting requirements on banks.

usage of trade—language and customs of an industry.

usury—lending money at an interest rate that is higher than the maximum rate allowed by law.

utilitarians—theory of ethics based on doing the most good for the most people in making decisions.

uttering—crime of issuing or delivering a forged instrument to another person.

V

valid contract—agreement that is binding and enforceable.

value—consideration or antecedent debt or security given in exchange for the transfer of a negotiable instrument or creation of a security interest.

variance—permission of a landowner to use the land in a specified manner that is inconsistent with the zoning ordinance.

vicarious liability—imposing liability for the fault of another.

void agreement—agreement that cannot be enforced.

voidable contract—agreement that is otherwise binding and enforceable but may be rejected at the option of one of the parties as the result of specific circumstances.

voidable title—title of goods that carries with it the contingency of an underlying problem.

***voir dire* examination**—the preliminary examination of a juror or a witness to ascertain fitness to act as such.

voluntary bankruptcy—proceeding in which the debtor files the petition for relief.

voting by proxy—authorizing someone else to vote the shares owned by the shareholder.

voting trust—transfer by two or more persons of their shares of stock of a corporation to a trustee who is to vote the shares and act for such shareholders.

W

waiver—release or relinquishment of a known right or objection.

warehouse—entity engaged in the business of storing the goods of others for compensation.

warehouse receipt—receipt issued by the warehouser for stored goods; regulated by the UCC, which clothes the receipt with some degree of negotiability.

warranty—promise, either express or implied, about the nature, quality, or performance of the goods.

warranty against encumbrances—warranty that there are no liens or other encumbrances to goods except those noted by the seller.

warranty deed—deed by which the grantor conveys a specific estate or interest to the grantee and makes one or more of the covenants of title.

warranty of habitability—implied warranty that the leased property is fit for dwelling by tenants.

warranty of title—implied warranty that title to the goods is good and transfer is proper.

wasting assets corporation—corporation designed to exhaust or use up the assets of the corporation, such as by extracting oil, coal, iron, and other ores.

way of necessity—grantee's right to use land retained by the grantor for going to and from the conveyed land.

well-known mark—in international law a mark that both the Paris Convention and TRIPS recognize as deserving protection even if it is not registered in the foreign country; national law determines what "well-known" means but the WIPO offers a list suggesting that the value of the mark, the extent of its use and promotion, and its recognition in the relevant sector of the public are key factors.

White-Collar Crime Penalty Enhancement Act of 2002—federal reforms passed as a result of the collapses of companies such as Enron; provides for longer sentences and higher fines for both executives and companies.

white-collar crimes—crimes that do not use nor threaten to use force or violence or do not cause injury to persons or property.

whole life insurance—ordinary life insurance providing lifetime insurance protection.

will—instrument executed with the formality required by law by which a person makes a disposition of his or her property to take effect upon death.

writ of *certiorari*—the U.S. Supreme Court granting a right of review by the court of a lower court decision.

wrongfully dishonored—error by a bank in refusing to pay a check.

Z

zoning—restrictions imposed by government on the use of designated land to ensure an orderly physical development of the regulated area.

Case Index

Summarized cases are shown in boldface italic; cited cases are shown in nonbold italic.

B

C

D

E

G

H

I

J

K

L

M

N

O

P

Q

R

S

T

U

V

W

X

Y

Z

Subject Index

B

C

D

E

F

G

H

I

J

K

L

M

N

O

P

S

T

U

V

W

Z